Sally Barnhart

Understanding Reading Problems

EIGHTH EDITION

Assessment and Instruction

Jean Wallace Gillet
Fluvanna County (VA) Public Schools (Retired)

Charles Temple
Hobart and William Smith Colleges

Codruţa Temple
State University of New York at Cortland

Alan Crawford
California State University - Los Angeles (Emeritus)

Boston ▪ Columbus ▪ Indianapolis ▪ New York ▪ San Francisco ▪ Upper Saddle River
Amsterdam ▪ Cape Town ▪ Dubai ▪ London ▪ Madrid ▪ Milan ▪ Munich ▪ Paris ▪ Montreal ▪ Toronto
Delhi ▪ Mexico City ▪ Sao Paulo ▪ Sydney ▪ Hong Kong ▪ Seoul ▪ Singapore ▪ Taipei ▪ Tokyo

Vice President and Editor-in-Chief: *Aurora Martínez Ramos*
Editor: *Erin K. L. Grelak*
Editorial Assistant: *Michelle Hochberg*
Executive Marketing Manager: *Krista Clark*
Production Editor: *Janet Domingo*
Editorial Production Service: *Nesbitt Graphics, Inc.*
Manufacturing Buyer: *Megan Cochran*
Electronic Composition: *Nesbitt Graphics, Inc.*
Interior Design: *Nesbitt Graphics, Inc.*
Cover Administrator: *Linda Knowles*

Credits and acknowledgments borrowed from other sources and reproduced, with permission, in this textbook appear on the appropriate page of the text.

Library of Congress Cataloging-in-Publication Data

Gillet, Jean Wallace.
Understanding reading problems : assessment and instruction / Jean Wallace Gillet, Charles Temple. -- 8th ed.
p. cm.
Includes bibliographical references and index.
ISBN 978-0-13-261749-9
1. Reading--Ability testing. 2. Reading--Remedial teaching. I. Temple, Charles. II. Title.
LB1050.46.G55 2011
372.4'076--dc22

2011009868

10 9 8 7 6 5 4 3 2 1 EDW 15 14 13 12 11

www.pearsonhighered.com

ISBN-10: 0-13-261749-8
ISBN-13: 978-0-13-261749-9

About the Authors

Jean Gillet, now retired, has been a classroom teacher, staff development specialist, university educator, and reading specialist. Her professional interests include the diagnosis and correction of reading difficulties, children's developmental spelling, and children's writing. She has published extensively on these topics, including contributing to classroom instructional materials on writing and spelling. She is coauthor of several textbooks for teachers on language arts, reading, writing, and spelling. She holds a master's degree in reading from Oakland University, Rochester, Michigan, and a doctorate from the University of Virginia.

Charles Temple stays busy teaching education courses at Hobart and William Smith Colleges in Geneva, New York; and writing books for children. Dr. Temple studied with the late Edmund Henderson at the University of Virginia, where he explored reading instruction, reading disabilities, invented spelling, and what was to become emergent literacy with many others who have gone on to do good work in the literacy field. A former English teacher and country reading programs coordinator, he has written books on emergent literacy, invented spelling, writing instruction, language arts, diagnosis and remediation of reading disabilities, and children's literature. He is a director of Critical Thinking International, Inc. (www.criticathinkinginternational.org), a non-profit corporation that develops materials and fields mid-career professionals for teacher training projects around the world. He has most recently offered literacy workshops in Liberia, El Salvador, Argentina, Romania, and the Republic of Georgia.

Codruţa Temple taught English as a foreign language and was principal of a lyceum (advanced high school) in Cluj, Romania. She taught French as a Fulbright Scholar in California before moving permanently to the United States, where she earned a PhD in Literacy and English Education at Syracuse University. She now teaches ESL methods and linguistics at State University of New York at Cortland and Hobart and William Smith Colleges in Geneva, New York.

Alan Crawford is Emeritus Professor of Education at California State University, Los Angeles. He is Past President of the California Reading Association and has done extensive teaching, consulting, and writing on teaching reading in the elementary school, especially for English language learners. Alan has written curriculum for teaching reading in Spanish and serves on the Editorial Review Board of Lectura y Vida. He served as IRA's representative to UNESCO for many years, and was a Senior Literacy Specialist at UNESCO in Paris during International Literacy Year (1989–90). He is a director of Critical Thinking International. He frequently presents workshops on a volunteer basis for international development projects in Latin America, Europe, Asia, and Africa.

Contents

Preface

Teaching reading and writing seems to grow in importance every year. At the federal, state, and local levels, increased demand for accountability and student achievement require today's classroom teachers and literacy specialists to be able to:

- Monitor and document the instructional progress, strengths, and needs of all students
- Select, administer, and interpret diagnostic measures in reading and reading-related areas
- Plan, implement, and evaluate the effectiveness of corrective and remedial instruction
- Use a wide variety of instructional methods, materials, and strategies to teach literacy, and
- Prevent literacy problems before they develop.

Teachers need tools, strategies, and well-informed diagnostic judgment to monitor students' literacy development and implement corrective instruction when appropriate. They must be able to use continuous developmental assessment devices, teach literacy using real literature and informational text with a wide variety of teaching methods, integrate reading and writing across all subject areas, and help every student become an effective, strategic reader who meets or exceeds required benchmarks. The assessment and instructional means to do so are the heart of this edition, as they have been since the first edition appeared some 30 years ago.

The concepts and principles that guided the development of the first seven editions have been strengthened and expanded in this eighth edition.

New to This Edition

- Many of the chapters have been reordered into a developmental sequence, with chapters on emergent, beginning and fledgling, developing, and mature readers coming in order in the first half of the book.
- An entirely new chapter has been added on Response to Intervention (RTI).
- The chapter on teaching culturally and linguistically diverse students has been completely rewritten to reflect the fact that classroom teachers in virtually all

parts of the United States are teaching students who were, or whose parents were, born outside of the United States.

- Many new strategies for assessment and teaching have been added.

As with previous editions,

- Each chapter features vignettes and case studies of real teachers and learners, with clear, vivid writing that engages readers.
- Every topic and reference has been scrutinized and the most current research and practices have been cited.
- Recent legislation affecting all classrooms, students, and teachers is discussed and interpreted.

The eighth edition examines both traditional and contemporary means of assessing literacy strengths and needs, as well as developmental and corrective instruction for students in kindergarten through high school, combining the best of time-tested methods with cutting-edge strategies for diagnosing and teaching. Preventing reading problems, as well as diagnosing and correcting those already occurring, is emphasized throughout the book.

Chapter 1 presents a surprising evidence-based argument for the importance of literacy in our lives, and explains the four important "moments" of literacy assessment: assessment for screening and placement, diagnostic assessment, monitoring assessment, and outcomes-based assessment. It surveys the most important aspects of reading ability, and lays out a scheme of typical reading development from emergent to mature reading.

Chapter 2 is a new chapter that addresses Response to Intervention (RTI) in depth and relates it to assessment and instructional procedures presented in subsequent chapters. Response to Intervention is an amplification of regulations from federal laws regarding special education—-the IDEA (the Individuals with Disabilities Education Act of 1997) and the IDEIA (the Individuals with Disabilities Education Improvement Act of 2004). Response to Intervention is a model of services that guides teachers to respond quickly to results from periodic assessment processes that teachers employ. A major advance is that there is no longer a two-year lag between noting that a child is falling behind in reading and intervention to address it; intervention begins immediately.

Chapter 3 offers a comprehensive look at emergent literacy development, including aspects of language development, phonological awareness, print awareness, and book and print concepts. It lays out detailed assessment techniques for emergent readers, and includes a discussion of evidence-based emergent literacy assessment. Teaching strategies to foster emergent literacy are keyed to assessment findings. This chapter has been much enhanced with assessments of children's storybook comprehension, and several more devices for examining children's phonological awareness.

Chapter 4 continues where the previous chapter left off, and lays out strategies for assessing and teaching beginning and fledgling readers. Running Records are explained in this chapter, along with an assessment instrument that looks at invented spelling for signs of children's word knowledge.

Chapter 5 focuses on what we call "developing readers," and what others might call "transitional" and "independent" readers. Here we present a great many strategies for teaching word recognition, reading fluency, and comprehension.

Chapter 6, on informal assessments, might be considered in tandem with Chapter 5, on teaching developing readers. Learning how to administer an informal reading inventory deserves a chapter of its own—well, one shared with a few other informal assessments, including instruments to test comprehension and also students' attitudes toward reading. We are pleased to have published *The Developmental Literacy Inventory*, our own informal reading inventory, since the last edition of this book came out, and we have used samples from it to illustrate points made in this chapter.

Chapter 7 addresses the needs of older readers, those in grades four through high school, in reading, writing, and study skills. It also addresses motivational issues that often involve older students with a history of educational underachievement.

Chapter 8 is devoted to the assessment of spelling and writing development. The developmental nature of learning to spell, predictable spelling stages and strategies, and assessment devices that help place students on a developmental continuum are discussed. Monitoring and documenting progress in writing using sampling procedures, skills checklists, Six Traits writing evaluation, and writing rubrics are detailed with lively examples of student writing.

Chapter 9 is a new chapter that focuses on the literacy development of culturally and linguistically diverse students in the mainstream classroom. This chapter is for all of you: One out of four children born in the United States this year will have parents who were born somewhere else. These children will go to school not just in Texas, California, and New York City, but in North Carolina, Indiana, Arkansas, and virtually every other state. The chapter begins with a discussion of cultural differences that are particularly relevant to the teaching and learning process, and continues with an explanation of key aspects of linguistic diversity among students who speak another dialect or language other than Standard English at home. After focusing on some critical issues related to the assessment of culturally and linguistically diverse students, the chapter lays out many instructional ideas for adapting classroom instruction to meet these students' needs.

Chapter 10 deals with the nature and uses of formal assessments, including fundamental concepts of measurement, characteristics of norm-referenced and criterion-referenced tests, benchmarks and rubrics, and federal- and state-mandated standards and assessments.

Chapter 11 deals with philosophical, legal, and instructional issues related to the assessment and instruction of students with special educational needs and disabilities. Recent changes in relevant legislation are discussed and ways of identifying and assessing students with special needs are outlined. The responsibilities of regular education and special education teachers are discussed. The chapter includes an updated review of research on dyslexia.

New! CourseSmart eTextbook Available

CourseSmart is an exciting new choice for students looking to save money. As an alternative to purchasing the printed textbook, students can purchase an electronic version of the same content. With a CourseSmart eTextbook, students can search the text, make notes online, print out reading assignments that incorporate lecture notes, and bookmark important passages for later review. For more information, or to purchase access to the CourseSmart eTextbook, visit www.coursesmart.com.

The Power of Classroom Practice

In *Preparing Teachers for a Changing World*, Linda Darling-Hammond and her colleagues point out that grounding teacher education in real classrooms—among real teachers and students and among actual examples of students' and teachers' work—is an important, and perhaps even an essential, part of training teachers for the complexities of teaching in today's classrooms. MyEducationLab is an online learning solution that provides contextualized interactive exercises, simulations, and other resources designed to help develop the knowledge and skills teachers need. All of the activities and exercises in MyEducationLab are built around essential learning outcomes for teachers and are mapped to professional teaching standards. Utilizing classroom video, authentic student and teacher artifacts, case studies, and other resources and assessments, the scaffolded learning experiences in MyEducationLab offer pre-service teachers and those who teach them a unique and valuable education tool.

For each topic covered in the course you will find most or all of the following features and resources:

Connection to National Standards

Now it is easier than ever to see how coursework is connected to national standards. Each topic on MyEducationLab lists intended learning outcomes connected to the appropriate national standards. All of the activities and exercises in MyEducation Lab are mapped to the appropriate national standards and learning outcomes as well.

Assignments and Activities

Designed to enhance student understanding of concepts covered in class and save instructors preparation and grading time, these assignable exercises show concepts in action (through video, cases, and/or student and teacher artifacts). They help students deepen content knowledge and synthesize and apply concepts and strategies they read about in the book. (Correct answers for these assignments are available to the instructor only under the Instructor Resource tab.)

Building Teaching Skills and Dispositions

These learning units help students practice and strengthen skills that are essential to quality teaching. After presenting the steps involved in a core teaching process, students are given an opportunity to practice applying this skill via videos, student and teacher artifacts, and/or case studies of authentic classrooms. Providing multiple opportunities to practice a single teaching concept, each activity encourages a deeper understanding and application of concepts, as well as the use of critical thinking skills.

A+RISE As part of your access to MyEducationLab

A+RISE®, developed by three-time Teacher of the Year and administrator, Evelyn Arroyo, gives new teachers in grades K-12 quick, research-based strategies that get to the "how" of targeting their instruction and making content accessible for all students, including English language learners.

A+RISE® Standards2Strategy™ is an innovative and interactive online resource that offers new teachers in grades K-12 just in time, research-based instructional strategies that:

- Meet the linguistic needs of ELLs as they learn content
- Differentiate instruction for all grades and abilities
- Offer reading and writing techniques, cooperative learning, use of linguistic and nonlinguistic representations, scaffolding, teacher modeling, higher order thinking, and alternative classroom ELL assessment
- Provide support to help teachers be effective through the integration of listening, speaking, reading, and writing along with the content curriculum
- Improve student achievement
- Are aligned to Common Core Elementary Language Arts standards (for the literacy strategies) and to English language proficiency standards in WIDA, Texas, California, and Florida.

IRIS Center Resources

The IRIS Center at Vanderbilt University (http://iris.peabody.vanderbilt.edu) funded by the U.S. Department of Education's Office of Special Education Programs (OSEP) develops training enhancement materials for pre-service and in-service teachers. The Center works with experts from across the country to create challenge-based interactive modules, case study units, and podcasts that provide research-validated information about working with students in inclusive settings. In your MyEducationLab course we have integrated this content where appropriate.

Study Plan Specific to Your Text

A MyEducationLab Study Plan is a multiple choice assessment tied to chapter objectives, supported by study material. A well-designed Study Plan offers multiple opportunities to fully master required course content as identified by the objectives in each chapter:

- *Chapter Objectives* identify the learning outcomes for the chapter and give students targets to shoot for as you read and study.
- *Multiple Choice Assessments* assess mastery of the content. These assessments are mapped to chapter objectives, and students can take the multiple choice quiz as many times as they want. Not only do these quizzes provide overall scores for each objective, but they also explain why responses to particular items are correct or incorrect.
- *Study Material: Review, Practice and Enrichment* give students a deeper understanding of what they do and do not know related to chapter content. This material includes text excerpts, activities that include hints and feedback, and interactive multi-media exercises built around videos, simulations, cases, or classroom artifacts.

Course Resources

The Course Resources section on MyEducationLab is designed to help students put together an effective lesson plan, prepare for and begin their career, navigate their first year of teaching, and understand key educational standards, policies, and laws. The Course Resources Tab includes the following:

- The **Lesson Plan Builder** is an effective and easy-to-use tool that students can use to create, update, and share quality lesson plans. The software also makes it easy to integrate state content standards into any lesson plan.
- The **Preparing a Portfolio** module provides guidelines for creating a high-quality teaching portfolio.

- **Beginning Your Career** offers tips, advice, and other valuable information on:
  - Resume Writing *and Interviewing*: Includes expert advice on how to write impressive resumes and prepare for job interviews.
  - *Your First Year of Teaching*: Provides practical tips to set up a first classroom, manage student behavior, and more easily organize for instruction and assessment.
  - *Law and Public Policies*: Details specific directives and requirements teachers need to understand under the No Child Left Behind Act and the Individuals with Disabilities Education Improvement Act of 2004.

Certification and Licensure

The Certification and Licensure section is designed to help students pass their licensure exam by giving them access to state test requirements, overviews of what tests cover, and sample test items.

The Certification and Licensure tab includes the following:

- **State Certification Test Requirements:** Here students can click on a state and will then be taken to a list of state certification tests.
- Students can click on the **Licensure Exams** they need to take to find:
  - Basic information about each test
  - Descriptions of what is covered on each test
  - Sample test questions with explanations of correct answers
- **National Evaluation Series™** by Pearson: Here students can see the tests in the NES, learn what is covered on each exam, and access sample test items with descriptions and rationales of correct answers. They can also purchase interactive online tutorials developed by Pearson Evaluation Systems and the Pearson Teacher Education and Development group.
- **ETS Online Praxis Tutorials:** Here students can purchase interactive online tutorials developed by ETS and by the Pearson Teacher Education and Development group. Tutorials are available for the Praxis I exams and for select Praxis II exams.

Visit www.myeducationlab.com for a demonstration of this exciting new online teaching resource.

Acknowledgments

We would like to thank the reviewers of the eighth edition: Ioney James, North Carolina A&T State University; Patricia J. Pollifrone, Gannon University; and Elizabeth Yanoff, The College of Saint Rose.

As in previous editions, we express our gratitude to all of the many friends, colleagues, students, and users of this book who have, over the years, guided our thinking, challenged our biases, and opened our eyes. We are the teachers we are, and this book is what it is, because of you.

Jean Gillet
Charles Temple
Codruţa Temple
Alan Crawford

Reading and Its Assessment

CHAPTER 1

Chapter Outline

Imagine a world in which all children entered kindergarten with exactly the same preparation for reading. They all had listened to someone read to them for the same thousands of hours and gained the same familiarity with books; had amassed the same number of words in their vocabularies; and had lived with families who supported their learning in the same ways and to the same degree, and had the same expectations of success in school. Imagine that all children came from the same cultural background, too, and all the significant folk in their lives spoke the same language and used that language the same way to express the same ideas. Imagine the children carried out every task with the same ability and the same amount of energy, and every child finished every learning task at exactly the same time. As the years went by, these children learned exactly the same way from teachers who taught the same lessons with the same success. The children learned to read the same number of words, were equally interested in the same topics, had the same background knowledge that enabled them to understand the same texts, and read all the same books at the same rate.

What a nightmare! One thing you can say about such a scenario, though, is that you wouldn't be reading this book about assessing children's literacy and differentiating instruction. Here in the real world, children are delightfully different in all the ways that make us humans interesting to each other, even though these differences complicate the work of teachers. Because children and older students differ in all of the ways just mentioned and then some, the job of assessment is to help the teacher figure out as closely as possible what aspects of literacy the students have developed and to what degree—so that we can build on students' strengths to make them successful readers.

Framing the Issues

In terms of the language they bring to school, their fluency in reading, the amount of reading they do, and their ability to use reading to understand, children in the United States differ more than you may realize—and in the following sections we will show just how much. Our point here is not to suggest that our goal is to make all children the same. And we are aware that putting a strong emphasis on reading and writing standard English runs the risk of stigmatizing those who fail to do these things well (Stuckey, 1990). But there is a lot of evidence that the better people read, the better off they are.

Large-scale assessments such as the National Adult Literacy Survey (NALS, 1992) and the National Assessment of Adult Literacy (NAAL, 2002) have shown for decades that the average adult's likelihood of having a job, earning a good income, staying out of jail, and participating in civic affairs marches in close step with his or her reading ability. In addition, the United Nations Educational, Scientific, and Cultural Organization (UNESCO [2006]) has found that in society after society, people who can read are healthier and less prone to violence than those who cannot read.

Keith Stanovich (1992) demonstrated that children and adults who read more were "smarter" than those who didn't. By "smarter," he meant that they had bigger vocabularies and more knowledge of the world. He demonstrated this in a clever way, by developing a "Title Recognition Test" that mixed real book titles with fake ones. Those who could correctly recognize many books were deemed "avid readers," and they came out ahead on measures of world knowledge, vocabulary, spelling, and verbal intelligence.

In an amazing study done in rural Uzbekistan in the 1930s, when adult education was just bringing literacy and learning to traditionally illiterate peasants, the Russian psychologist, A. R. Luria (1976), found that those adults who had recently learned to read were better able than their illiterate counterparts to reason logically, ask questions about things they didn't know about, and even reflect on their emotions. Being able to read, in other words, affected people's consciousness.

This book isn't aimed at teaching adults—although much of what follows in these pages will apply to adults—so why are we talking about literacy and your quality of life as an adult? Because the foundations of adult literacy begin in the primary grades. In an often-cited study, Connie Juel (1988) found that the students who were substandard readers at the end of first grade faced an 88 percent chance of being substandard readers at the end of fourth grade; and Anne Cunningham and Keith Stanovich (1997) found that first-grade reading achievement strongly predicted reading achievement ten years later, even when intelligence was controlled for.

It is hard to avoid the conclusion that we are doing children and older students a great favor by teaching them to read well—and that we seriously fail them when we do not.

The task of teaching reading is easier in some cases than in others, though. Consider the differences in children's development of aspects of reading.

Hart and Risley's important study (1995) showed enormous differences in the language exposure of preschool children as young as four who came from different socioeconomic groups. Children from English-speaking professional families had three times as many words addressed to them as children from English-speaking families receiving welfare (see Figure 1.1).

The result, as Beck, McKeown, and Kucan (2002) reported, is that some children in first grade have at least twice as many words in their vocabularies as other children.

Why does vocabulary matter? Knowing word meanings is a major part of verbal intelligence because word knowledge is a measure of how much a student has already learned. But knowing words also makes future learning more likely because words serve us as receptors for experience: We tend to notice and remember what we already have names for (Brown, 1955).

	Professional Families	*Working Class Families*	*Families Receiving Public Assistance*
Words per hour	3,000	1,400	750
Total words in first 4 years	50,000,000	30,000,000	15,000,000

FIGURE 1.1 *Language Exposure of Preschool Children*

Source: From Hart and Risley, 1995.

Children differ tremendously in the amount of reading they do, as well. Anderson, Wilson, and Fielding's famous study (1988) found that the 20 percent of fifth-grade children who read the most read 50 times as much as the 20 percent who read the least (see Figure 1.2). The point is that far too many of our students don't read as well as we would like them to.

According to the National Assessment of Educational Progress (2005), one out of every four fourth graders could not read at a *basic level*. At fourth grade, that means they could not "locate relevant information, make simple inferences, and use their understanding of the text to identify details that support a given interpretation or

Percentile rank	*Minutes of book reading per day*	*Words read in books per year*
98	65.0	4,358,000
90	21.1	1,823,000
80	14.2	1,146,000
70	9.6	622,000
60	6.5	432,000
50	4.6	282,000
40	3.2	200,000
30	1.3	106,000
20	0.7	21,000
10	0.1	8,000
2	0.0	0

FIGURE 1.2 *Differences in Amounts of Independent Reading by Fifth Graders*

Source: Anderson, Wilson, and Fielding (1988).

conclusion, [or] interpret the meaning of a word as it is used in the text" (NAEP, 2010, p. 1).

When black and Hispanic students were singled out, three out of five could not read at this level. A *proficient* fourth grade level of performance on the NAEP reading test meant "integrate and interpret texts and apply their understanding of the text to draw conclusions and make evaluations" (NAEP, 2010, p. 1). Two out of five students tested could read at this level, and when black and Hispanic students were singled out, only one in eight could perform at that level of proficiency. The results were essentially the same at the eighth-grade level.

And they matter. In previous generations, U.S. schools were tacitly expected to reproduce a working class, a professional class, and an elite class, as sociologist Jean Anyon (1981) demonstrated years ago. The industrial jobs held by the majority of the workers—and agricultural work before that—required low levels of literacy. But in the past three decades the United States has lost huge numbers of such jobs. The modern workplace requires employees who can read, write, think, solve problems, and work cooperatively in teams. The Carnegie Corporation's *Writing Next* report (Graham & Perin, 2007) points out that the academic demands of today's workplace are no less rigorous than those of college. But the reading profile of U.S. students that emerges from the National Assessment of Educational Progress seems well adapted to the industrial era of the 1950s, and woefully ill suited to our current constantly changing, information-oriented job market.

Our responsibility as teachers of reading is not to prepare students for any particular job, but rather to help them develop the communicative and intellectual skills they will need to make the most of their schooling and have a satisfactory range of life choices. A good many of the students we teach now do not read as well as they need to in order to learn their school subjects and eventually enjoy those life choices. We will need to work with students at all levels to determine what skills they need, and we must teach in such a way that they develop these skills.

One more thing: When the late Edmund Henderson was first told about the (then) new practice of Drop Everything and Read, in which everything in the school day stopped—janitor's work included—so everyone could read for twenty minutes, he remarked: "Goodness. What a commentary on the poverty of the school curriculum!" As a nation, we recently completed a decade of devoting intense attention to developing our elementary school students' basic skills in reading, and, except for some welcome improvements in the reading ability of students from minority groups, we don't have much to show for the effort. Our hunch is that Professor Henderson was right. Focusing exclusively on building reading skills—without enriching children's minds with lively stories and interesting facts, nurturing their imaginations with the arts, encouraging them to celebrate their bodies' capabilities with exercise and sports, and cultivating their growing social sense with opportunities to work and play together and to serve others—is not likely to achieve the results we want. The school day should be rich from bell to bell with activities and knowledge that help children and young people grow in all their dimensions. And we can pay attention to helping them learn to read and write at the same time.

Reading Assessment

Assessment means gathering, analyzing, and interpreting information to tell how well a student reads. Assessment covers everything from making informal observations of a student's reading to using commercial tests. Assessment practices include

- Deciding what we need to know about a child's or group of children's reading.
- Deciding what measures will tell us what we want to know.
- Gathering information.
- Interpreting the information.
- Making decisions on what to do next, based on the new information.

There are different purposes for assessment and different audiences for the information that assessment brings to light.

1. **We assess to guide our instruction.** We assess to
   - **Determine students' reading levels** (independent, instructional, and frustration) so we can provide them with materials at the right level.
   - **Locate children's strengths and areas of need** to aim our instruction. Children need encouragement in all aspects of literacy development, and if there are a few or several aspects in which they are not progressing adequately, we need to locate those so we can offer specially tailored help. For example, a child may have learned many sight words, but have low reading fluency. We need to monitor her reading so we can identify the need to work on her fluency.
   - **Identify children's literacy strategies** so we can strengthen them. For example, we know that good readers preview texts and set purposes for reading to help them understand better. Does each child know how to do this?

2. **We assess to monitor the success of instructional approaches.** Approaches vary in their success with individual children, or with whole classrooms of children. We assess to
   - **Find out if a teaching approach or set of materials is working for a child.** For example, to build reading fluency, teachers may use "buddy reading" or a computer program. But does the child know how to take advantage of these activities? Or in teaching word study, the teacher wants each child to study words that are right at his level of development of word knowledge. Is this the case? In guided reading, we want children to read some texts that are moderately challenging, and some texts that are easier. Is this taking place for each child?
   - **Find out what strategies seem best suited to whole groups of students.** Research shows that schools that are most effective in helping all children learn to read and write are those in which teachers monitor how well instruction is working, and use this information as they work with other teachers to find ways to improve instruction (Cunningham & Allington, 2006; Taylor et. al., 1999).

Teachers may monitor a host of factors, from classroom routines and management strategies to teaching methods, to materials, to ways of working with instructional aides and parent volunteers, to ways of assessing children.

3. **We assess to give feedback to children and their parents.** Findings from assessment should be communicated to children and their parents, so both can work toward the children's success. We assess to

- **Show children what they are doing well and what they can do better.** We communicate information in a way that helps children understand, that purposefully reinforces those strategies they are using successfully, and that points the way toward improvements.
- **Help the children set goals for better performance** and to monitor their progress toward meeting those goals.
- **Help parents understand how children are performing in learning to read** and to determine what parents can do to help.

4. **We assess to make decisions on the placement of children in special instructional services.** All children in the United States are entitled by law to special education services if they need them, and they are also entitled to special support to learn the English language, if necessary. Parents may request that their children be screened for such services, but teachers may also identify students who need more support than what is likely to be available to them in the regular classroom. In either case, special screening is called for, including specialized tests that are normally administered by school psychologists. But the teacher's own observational records and assessment results also play a useful role in these decisions.

5. **We assess to make sure all students are meeting state standards for learning.** The federal No Child Left Behind Act that passed in 2002 mandated that every child in the United States be tested in reading from grades 3 through 8. The tests are developed by the individual states. Core standards for reading and writing achievement may soon be enforced on a national level. Because the tests have considerable consequences, many teachers are using more frequent assessments given throughout the year that show their students' progress toward meeting the standards on which their state tests are based.

6. **We assess ourselves as teachers or as teachers-to-be,** in order to make sure our professional knowledge is up to date and that our practices are serving our students as best they can. We assess our professional knowledge, both in order to keep ourselves up to date and to meet teaching licensing requirements.

Different Assessments for Different Phases of Instruction

Teachers use different kinds of assessments for different purposes at different points in the year. Many schools use four phases of assessment. The four are *screening assessments, diagnostic assessments, monitoring assessments,* and *outcomes-based assessments.*

Screening Assessments. Before instruction begins at the beginning of the year, teachers may administer screening measures to determine which children are at risk for reading difficulty and may need more support during the year. The screening instruments they use are as economical as possible because they may be given to an entire class or an entire grade. So they typically examine only a few key aspects of literacy, just enough to identify the children who need extra attention.

Diagnostic Assessments. Another kind of assessment is used to identify more precisely a student's needs, so that the teacher can develop a teaching plan that is right for that child. If children have been identified by the screening tests as needing special help, the diagnostic instruments take up where the screening instruments left off. They tell not just that the child needs to know more letters of the alphabet, but detail which ones; and not just that she is a struggling reader, but that she is weak in comprehension, especially in making inferences. Individual diagnostic instruments may test specific skills, such as a test of phonemic segmentation or a test of reading fluency. Others, like an Informal Reading Inventory, are more comprehensive and test many areas of reading ability.

Monitoring Assessments. Monitoring assessments, sometimes called *formative assessments*, are done to see if a child's instruction is "on track." They range from informal observations to formal probes.

Monitoring assessments may be done at regular intervals—every month or every quarter for most students, but more often for students who seem to have greater difficulty learning. It is advisable that monitoring assessments be designed with the end-of-year assessments in mind. Because of No Child Left Behind, nearly all children in U.S. public schools are now tested at the end of their third through their eighth grades. Given the impact of end-of-year state tests in reading, it is advisable that monitoring assessments be designed with end-of-year assessments in mind, to make sure all students are learning what they will be expected to know.

Outcomes-Based Assessments. Outcomes-based assessments are also referred to as grade-level reading *standards-based assessments,* because the desired outcomes of a year's teaching are reflected in each state's learning standards. Standards-based assessments are used to test the skills that are named in the state's standards for learning in literacy. In most states, those skills include phonemic awareness, phonics, fluency, vocabulary, and comprehension, since these areas were named for emphasis by the National Reading Panel (1999) and were written into the No Child Left Behind Act.

Approaches to Assessment

Below we will look further at these and other kinds of assessment approaches that are used to measure and investigate children's reading and writing abilities.

Norm-Referenced Tests. Standardized or norm-referenced tests of reading compare each child's performance with that of large numbers of other students. For example, tests such as the Stanford Achievement Test and the California Achievement Test report children's reading performance in comparison with that of other students at their grade level. The tests are given under rigorously controlled conditions, so the results will be comparable. Norm-referenced tests are typically used, along with other information, to inform decisions about placing a child for special reading services. But these tests traditionally have lacked an obvious connection with any school curriculum, so it is difficult to tell what aspect of a school's instruction has contributed or failed to contribute to a child's performance.

Standards-Based Tests. Standards-based tests have come about in recent years as individual states have set standards for achievement in reading and other subject areas at each grade level, as they have been required to do by the federal No Child Left Behind law (http://www.ed.gov/admins/lead/account/saa.html#peerreview). Standards vary from state to state, but in most states they are specific enough to guide teaching. In California, for example, first graders are expected to meet English Language Content standards, of which the following is a small sample (see Figure 1.3).

Reading

1.0 Word Analysis, Fluency, and Systematic Vocabulary Development

Students understand the basic features of reading. They select letter patterns and know how to translate them into spoken language by using phonics, syllabication, and word parts. They apply this knowledge to achieve fluent oral and silent reading.

Concepts About Print

1.1 Match oral words to printed words.
1.2 Identify the title and author of a reading selection.
1.3 Identify letters, words, and sentences.

Phonemic Awareness

1.4 Distinguish initial, medial, and final sounds in single-syllable words.
1.5 Distinguish long- and short-vowel sounds in orally stated single-syllable words (e.g., *bit/bite*).
1.6 Create and state a series of rhyming words, including consonant blends.
1.7 Add, delete, or change target sounds to change words (e.g., change *cow* to *how; pan* to *an*).
1.8 Blend two to four phonemes into recognizable words (e.g., */c/ /a/ /t/* = cat; */f/ /l/ /a/ /t/* = flat).
1.9 Segment single-syllable words into their components (e.g., */c/ /a/ /t/* = cat; */s/ /p/ /l/ /a/ /t/* = splat; */r/ /i/ /ch/* = rich). . . .

FIGURE 1.3 *English Language Content Standards*

Source: Reprinted by permission, California Department of Education, CDE Press, 1430 N. Street, Suite 3207, Sacramento, CA 95814. The reprinting of California Department of Education standards in this document is not intended to imply that this document constitutes an instructional material that has been adopted by the State Board of Education, nor does it imply that this document is aligned in any way with state standards.

Standards-based tests are meant to assess each student's performance on the standards set by the states. Students may be promoted to another grade or held back, depending on their performance, and schools may suffer sanctions if they do not make "adequate yearly progress." Standards-based tests are sometimes called *high-stakes testing* since a child's performance on such a test can determine whether she is promoted to the next grade, and the performance of many children can decide if a school is achieving or underachieving.

Informal Reading Inventories. Informal Reading Inventories or IRIs (Betts, 1946) are comprehensive measures of students' reading abilities. IRIs, which are treated in detail in Chapter 2, are administered to individual children to examine their word recognition, fluency, comprehension, and overall reading levels. They are called "informal" because in contrast to standardized reading tests, IRIs have usually not been normed by elaborate field testing with large numbers of children. Rather, they are created from samples of grade-level texts, usually written by the test authors and matched to grade levels according to readability formulas. In addition to written passages, IRIs consist of lists of words and text passages of graduated levels of difficulty—and the passages and word lists are usually from early first grade or "pre-primer" through grade 8 or higher.

Teachers may create their own IRIs, but many good ones are commercially available, including the *Qualitative Reading Inventory* (Leslie & Caldwell, 2005) and the *Classroom Reading Inventory* (Silvaroli & Wheelock, 2000). *The Developmental Literacy Inventory,* written by your present authors (Temple, Crawford, & Gillet, 2008), combines an Informal Reading Inventory with assessments of emergent literacy and phonics.

Running Records. Developed by Marie Clay (1993) to support her Reading Recovery program, running records are teacher-made assessment devices administered to individual students to monitor their fluency, word recognition accuracy, and reading levels. Running records are usually carried out with younger readers in the first two or three grades, with whom they may be used every month or more frequently, both for diagnostic testing and for monitoring.

Authentic Assessment. Sheila Valencia and her colleagues (Valencia, Hiebert, & Afflerbach, 1993) popularized the idea of the "authentic assessment" of literacy. Authentic assessment addresses the problem that most kinds of assessment have students carry out contrived tasks that are not always representative of what they do in purposeful reading and writing. Contrived tasks may not yield the full picture that includes what students have achieved and also how they think about literacy, or what their interests and motivations, preferences, strategies, and likes and dislikes are. Authentic assessment thus involves both *informal* and *structured observations* (sometimes called *kidwatching*) and *work-sampling,* including *portfolios.* Authentic assessment also includes the use of *rubrics.*

Portfolios. A type of authentic assessment, portfolios are collections of children's works. They may be maintained by the teacher as a way of keeping a diverse collection of artifacts related to a child's progress in learning to read and write. But usually they are maintained in collaboration with each child. The teacher (and the child) should decide in advance the sorts of items that should be kept in the portfolio. These might include

- Lists of books read.
- A reading journal.
- Repeated reading score sheets.
- Written works chosen as indicative of the child's best work and range of work during a particular time period.
- A list of topics for the child's writing.
- Learning logs.
- Running records.

Periodically—at least once a month or once each marking period—the teacher schedules a *conference* or *interview* with the child. Ahead of the conversation, both the child and the teacher should look through the portfolio to find signs of progress and areas that need work. During their conversation, the child describes what he has learned during this period and sets goals for improvement during the next period. The teacher may ask questions to find out what things the child likes and doesn't like to read, what strategies he is using in reading, and aspects of the reading instruction that might be changed for his benefit. The teacher makes suggestions to help the child learn.

Rubrics. According to Andrade (2000):

> A rubric is a scoring tool that lists the criteria for a piece of work, or "what counts" (for example, purpose, organization, details, voice, and mechanics are often what count in a piece of writing); it also articulates gradations of quality for each criterion, from excellent to poor.

Rubrics have the advantage of allowing teachers to observe and evaluate an authentic performance, such as a child's oral reading or a piece of writing produced for a real purpose other than testing. They also have the advantage of teaching. Especially when they are shared with a student before he or she carries out a task, the rubrics tell the child how to do a task well.

Rubrics may be already designed by educational experts. Rubrics may also be developed by teachers, or even by the students themselves. When students participate in designing a rubric, they may become more strategic in reading—that is, they have a better idea how they should try to perform.

It helps to think of a rubric like a chart. Each row names an important aspect of performance on a task, and in the boxes under each column are descriptions that range from unsatisfactory to satisfactory to excellent performance on that factor.

The Process of Learning to Read at Different Stages

The reading stages that follow are not written on stone tablets; they are, for us, a convenient way to organize our thinking about reading and our discussions about children. The stages into which we divide the process of learning to read are as follows:

- **Emergent Literacy.** Children in this stage are discovering basic concepts about print and the language that print represents, and they are learning to associate pleasure with reading, books, and being read to. Usually, these children are found in preschool, kindergarten, and first grade.
- **Beginning Reading.** Children in this stage know enough, at least on a tacit or nonverbal level, about reading and print to begin to learn individual words, or acquire a sight vocabulary, from their encounters with them. These children are often first graders, but both younger and older students may be beginning readers.
- **Fledgling Reading.** Children who are building their fluency, typically from late first into third grade, are sometimes called *fledgling readers.* They can recognize many words automatically and are reading passages that are several sentences long without too much stumbling over words. They are comprehending what they read, for the most part, so their reading has become fairly rapid and accurate and their oral reading is fairly expressive. Children at this stage are no longer beginners, but they are not yet fluent independent readers. At this stage, the amount of reading that children do and their degree of success with it have a tremendous impact on their progress to the next stage.
- **Developing Reading.** Developing readers, usually from grade 3 on up, may be reading chapter books for pleasure and homework assignments for learning. By this stage, good readers are pulling dramatically farther ahead of struggling readers in their ease of reading, the amount of time they spend reading outside of school, and the number of pages they read each week.
- **Mature Reading.** Mature readers, found (we hope) from later elementary grades and up, are those who read and compare many sources of information on a topic. They can read "against the grain" of a text and use the reading experience as a way of generating original ideas of their own. They can also recognize and appreciate an author's style and techniques. Although many readers do these things in the lower grades, this kind of adult-like reading is more common in middle school and above; high school or college students who don't have these advanced reading skills have an increasingly difficult time with literacy tasks.

Of course, individual students will go through stages of reading at different rates, but if they vary too much from the norm, difficulties can occur. As you can see from these descriptions, in each stage students develop new reading abilities, and new challenges are placed on those abilities by the curriculum.

Emergent Literacy

The stage that once was called *reading readiness* or *prereading* is now most widely known as *emergent literacy* (Teale & Sulzby, 1986). *Emergent literacy* refers to a process that represents the child's growing discoveries about print: that writing corresponds to spoken words; that the print, not the pictures, tells the story; that print is composed of a certain set of letters arranged just so on a page; and that those letters stand for spoken words in a certain way.

As Neuman and Dickinson put it:

> Emergent literacy refers to the developmental precursors of formal reading that have their origins early in the life of a child. This conceptualization departs from an older perspective on reading-acquisition that sees the process of learning to read as beginning with formal school-based instruction in reading or with reading-readiness skills taught in kindergarten. (2000, p. 12)

We should note that some use the term *emergent literacy* in a much more expansive way. Patrick Groff (n.d.), for instance, claims that *emergent literacy* carries within it the assumption that reading ability develops without being taught (a position he vigorously opposes), and he warns his followers to be suspicious of anyone who uses the term.

But the term *emergent literacy* was introduced by researchers with very different intentions. When Hermine Sinclair, Charles Read, Emilia Ferreiro, Marie Clay, Bill Teale, Elizabeth Sulzby, and Jana Mason began to instruct our field about emergent literacy more than 30 years ago, they were showing us that many literacy-related concepts can be developed early in childhood and without direct teaching. But because that was true, they worried that teachers would take it for granted that all children had these concepts established and thus would not teach the children who lacked them the important things they needed to know (see the discussion of "Teaching Print Orientation Concepts" in Chapter 3). Understanding emergent literacy puts teachers in a position to support children's literacy in concert with the ways they learn and also to help fill in gaps in children's store of literacy-related concepts.

Emergent literacy is fascinating for adults to observe, and many of the things young children say and do with writing, spelling, reading, and books are delightful and amusing. But for children, moving toward literacy is serious business. Children who successfully explore concepts about print during this period lay down a foundation that helps them to profit from reading and writing instruction later on. Children who do not acquire foundational concepts about print will very likely struggle with beginning reading and subsequently fall farther and farther behind their peers unless extraordinary steps are taken to help them. For this reason, intensive early intervention programs such as Reading Recovery (Clay, 1985; Pinnell, 1989), Success for All (Slavin et al., 1991), Book Buddies (Johnston, Invernizzi, & Juel, 1998), and Early Steps and Howard Street programs (Morris, 2005) are widely used with children in the early grades.

Beginning Reading

Children reach the stage of beginning reading when they learn to recognize words appearing in different contexts. For example, a child who recognizes the word *Coca-Cola* only when it appears on the soft drink bottle but not when it is written in plain type is recognizing the word as a meaningful symbol, but not as a word. When the same child suddenly realizes that *Coca-Cola* is the same word when it appears on signs, newspaper coupons, and Mom's shopping list, then the child has acquired it as a sight word, a word that is immediately recognizable without analysis. This stage marks the beginning of true reading, but it comes only after much prior learning. As we saw in the discussion of emergent literacy, before children can begin to acquire a sight vocabulary, or a corpus of words that they recognize immediately at sight, they must

- Be able to pay attention to spoken language and its parts.
- Understand something about the way reading is done.
- Know a good deal about the nature of print.

An additional challenge in the period of beginning reading is to learn to recognize words and attend to their meaning at the same time. If all we do is teach children to recognize words, we will give them a distorted idea of what reading is, for reading is much more than identifying the words on a page. On the other hand, we can't get around the fact that children must learn to recognize words with increasing accuracy and automaticity if they are to progress in reading.

Fledgling Reading

Children in the fledgling stage of development have moved beyond the highly predictable books that beginners enjoy. These post-beginners enjoy what are often called *easy readers*. Examples of these books are Arnold Lobel's *Frog and Toad* stories (*Days with Frog and Toad, Frog and Toad Are Friends,* and so forth), James Marshall's *Fox* books (*Fox on Wheels, Fox in Love, Fox at School,* and so forth), Cynthia Rylant's *Henry and Mudge* books, Else Holmelund Minarik's *Little Bear* books, and many of Dr. Seuss's books.

Easy readers often consist of either a single story or three or four short, catchy episodes per title, in books of about 40 to 60 pages each. They feature relatively short words that are often repeated, with one to three sentences on each page accompanied by supportive pictures. The Bank Street *Ready-to-Read* series, Scholastic's *Hello Reader!* series, Random House's *Step into Reading* books, and Harper Trophy's *I Can Read* books are typical. Since they are widely available in inexpensive paperback versions, every first-, second-, and third-grade classroom should have a good supply of these books. Any school librarian will be able to advise on their selection.

Children in the fledgling stage can also enjoy picture-story books, especially if the books have been read to them once or twice already. Books such as Mercer Mayer's *Just Me and My Dad* or Normal Bridwell's *Clifford the Big Red Dog* contain vocabulary that is challenging to some children, so the children should be familiar with them before trying to read them on their own.

If children haven't learned to recognize many words automatically by early second grade, they will not fully experience the spurt in reading rate and fluency that we associate with this period. The gap between these lagging readers and their classmates will be growing. Unfortunately, they often begin to feel like failures, and that attitude itself may compound the problem. We must keep working to build these children's abilities to recognize words, and we'll want to provide lots of easy books so that they can practice reading. We can't neglect reading to them, either. They need to keep up their intake of written language for the information, vocabulary, and text structure that it yields. Otherwise, their future hurdles will loom even higher.

Developing Reading

The stage of developing reading may begin in late second grade or early third grade and last from then on, though most students will diversify their reading with what we call *mature reading* by the time they reach middle school or even sooner. Children at this stage are reading to get somewhere. The operations of reading have become mostly automatic for them, and their full attention can be focused on reading for meaning. Reading has truly become the vehicle for learning. After students have built fluency in their reading, they enter a long period in which their reading ability is put to use, when we hope that they will read a great deal, because they find reading both an enjoyable pastime and a source of information that they wouldn't get otherwise.

At this point, reading becomes its own best teacher. Students who have the habit of reading are consuming dozens of books, hundreds of pages, and thousands of words a year. This reading practice equips them with an expanded vocabulary, familiarity with varied sentence structures, a broad knowledge of the forms of written language, and acquaintance with most of the topics they are likely to come across in print. Until recently, few would have considered any of these to be components of reading ability, but now we realize that these achievements—all of them gained through practice in reading—probably make as much difference to a person's ability to read as any of the traditional skills of reading do.

Good readers are gaining an abundance of information about the world and a wealth of vocabulary. This knowledge and this vocabulary are the tools readers use to comprehend: As the schema theory of comprehension predicts, we need to know a little bit about the topic before we can learn something new about it. Readers who read a lot are going to know a little bit about a lot more topics and will be better readers because of it.

Often after second grade and certainly after third grade, students are expected to use their reading to learn content. Learning from reading raises a new set of problems. How are questions posed in texts? How are they answered? How are arguments set up in texts? How are they resolved? For those who up to now have thought of reading as pronouncing words aloud or following a story line, these new tasks are real challenges. How will children learn to meet them? Clearly, many children will not learn how to learn from text without guided practice. That is, teachers need to show them how to do it.

When we speak of comprehension in reading, the literary critic Louise Rosenblatt (1978) suggests that we should make a distinction between what readers do with fiction and what they do with nonfiction. There is a difference between reading in which we gain information, such as reading a history text or a bus schedule, and reading for more indirect enlightenment and vicarious pleasure, such as reading a novel. She calls the first kind *efferent reading*; the second kind, she calls *aesthetic reading*.

In the moments when we are reading aesthetically, Rosenblatt believes, we are summoning up our own experiences and fantasies in response to the words in a book. The meaning of the text resides in just this event: It is a real-time experience of orchestrated thinking and reverie, jointly created by the text and our minds.

Rosenblatt's position is referred to as *reader response criticism*, and it raises interesting questions about the ways in which we should understand and teach reading comprehension. If a sizable part of the meaning of a text comes from the reader, not just from the book, then teaching reading for meaning means thinking about texts and bringing associations from personal experiences to the reading. It means that we should consider readers to be authorities on their own understanding. It means that we cannot ever fully measure reading comprehension. It also means that the potential for human misunderstanding is very great because the meaning of anything resides ultimately in what each individual makes of it.

Mature Reading

This last developmental reading stage is hard to locate in terms of grade levels, for as children progress through school, the span of reading levels in any classroom widens geometrically. The best readers in an elementary school are probably mature readers while only in fourth or fifth grade, whereas the poorest readers in those grades are likely beginning readers. The same is true for middle schoolers and high school students; the best readers in middle or high school typically can read college texts and adult best sellers comfortably. They are mature readers, regardless of their grade. Likewise, millions of adults are not mature readers, largely because they don't read enough to get very good at it.

Mature readers have arrived, through instruction and years of sustained practice, at the apex of reading development; they can read almost anything they choose to, comfortably and successfully. That is not to say that they won't ever struggle with reading; one could find college textbooks, toy assembly directions, or government documents to challenge the reading abilities of even the best adult readers. But most of what they want to read will be accessible. Because they don't struggle with it, mature readers generally read a great deal; they are the ones at the top end of the scale who read 4 or 5 million words a year (Wilson, Anderson, & Fielding, 1988).

Mature reading includes what is sometimes called *critical reading*, or mentally arguing with texts. It also includes *aesthetic reading*, reading for an appreciation of the craft of good writing. Let's look at each of these in turn.

Critical Reading. Some years ago, parent watchdog groups asked the U.S. government to place restrictions on the amount of violence and commercialism in children's television programming. The government backed away, in effect giving an old response: *caveat emptor* ("Let the buyer beware"). Since the "buyers" in this case were young children, the government's response raised the question: Should we teach our children to be critical of what they hear and read so that they can defend themselves against the manipulation of those who want their money or their loyalty for cynical purposes? Many educators believe that we should; therefore, the term *critical reading* is heard more and more these days. *Critical reading* means arguing with books or authors, in particular analyzing books for hidden biases or subtle suggestions, for example, that one group is superior to another. Box 1.1 contains an example of critical reading, in which a group of 7- and 8-year-olds discuss gender bias in fairy tales.

BOX 1.1

An Example of Critical Reading

A mixed group of second- and third-graders are discussing the story *Beauty and the Beast*.

"Suppose," says the teacher, "Beauty had been a boy in this story, and the Beast had been a girl."

A howl goes up from the class.

Alice looks troubled. "But then Beauty, the boy, would be *younger* than Beast, the girl . . ."

"So? Why would that matter? Besides, they don't tell you how old they are," says Alexander.

"But then, I mean, it's not right for a girl to ask a boy to go to the prom or something . . ." Alice still looks troubled.

"I've heard—this is what my Mom says—there's not a law against it or anything, but it's not right for a girl to ask a boy to marry her. This is what my Mom says. I don't know if it's true," says Charlotte.

"So why should that matter?" says Julian. "But I have another problem. The boys in the story are always the worse ones. I mean, the boys in the fairy tales just run up to a girl they don't even know and say 'Will you marry me?'"

"I know," adds Sarah. "I wish they'd say, 'Why no! How can I marry you? I don't even know you. I don't know what your *attitude is!*'"

"Boys in the fairy tales want to marry somebody they don't know anything about. I mean, they might not even *change their underwear!*" says Charlotte.

Allison takes a different tack. "I'm going to be a person who's the exact opposite of Beauty. Pretend there's fire in here. You go up to that person and he says, 'So! Why'd you ask me? You help 'em!'; But Beauty . . . You wouldn't have to tell her anything. She'd just go!"

"What does that have to do with how boys are and girls are?" asks the teacher.

"Well, I'm not saying boys are *always* selfish . . ." Allison doesn't want to go further.

"What bugs me is that in the fairy tales, the guys are always doing things outside, and the girls are just basking around in their beautiful dresses," says Joanne. Several children nod.

Source: Used by permission of Charles Temple.

Aesthetic Reading. Another dimension of mature reading is aesthetic reading, savoring the artistry (or examining the shortcomings) of well-crafted or slapdash prose. An illustration of aesthetic reading is found in David Bleich's (1975) approach to reader response. Bleich first asks his students to retell a work that they have all read, and he notes the variety in what students choose to include in their summaries. Then he asks students to name the most important parts of a work, and again he notes the effect of each reader's individual experiences and tastes in making such seemingly straightforward judgments because there is invariably much variety in what readers choose. Next, he asks students to comment on the most important devices in the work; he hears the students commenting on such things as voice, characterization, description, plot, and irony long before he has introduced the technical terms for these things.

A kind of aesthetic reading that teachers and students sometimes do, often without realizing it as such, is to connect reading and writing. For example, some time after they have read and discussed *Maniac Magee* by Jerry Spinelli, a teacher asks a fifth-grade class to reread the first chapter and lays out this challenge: Find as many tricks as you can that the author used to make the story of Maniac Magee seem like a legend. The students work in groups and come up with the jump-rope rhyme, the way the author introduced characters as if they were already famous, and the way the author mentioned several exaggerated versions of Maniac's background. After discussing those, the teacher then invites the students to use some of these devices in writing original legends of their own.

Now that we have described these two aspects of mature reading, it should be clear that these kinds of reading need not wait until high school or college. Indeed, the example of critical reading in Box 1.1 came from a mixed group of second and third graders. Children just as young are capable of making aesthetic responses to written works. We chose to call these activities *mature reading* only because they strike us as the most mature kinds of reading we do, even though in many cases we begin doing them at an early age.

The practices of mature reading, that is, critical reading and aesthetic reading, can be applied to any sort of text. Of course, as students grow in their reading maturity, they will seek out more challenging books. Our question is not so much what they read at this point but how much they think about what they read.

Few students will be referred to a remedial reading teacher for failing to read or write in the mature ways that we have just described. We have included this discussion, though, because it is important for reading teachers to know where reading development is headed. The ultimate goal is not just that students understand what somebody else has written, but that they know where they stand on the author's claims or are able to find an interesting interpretation of the work and can state their positions clearly. Aspects of these goals, of course, might be included in our instruction at any level.

Differentiated Instruction

Differentiated instruction begins with good assessment. *Screening assessment* indicates which students are where they are expected to be, which are above grade level, and which need additional support. *Diagnostic assessment* indicates how strong each student is in different aspects of reading and writing development. Based on diagnostic assessment, students will have different kinds of instruction designed for them. They will be placed in different levels of books for guided reading. They will be given different groups of words for word study, and possibly placed in different points in the sequence of phonics instruction. The teacher will construct focused lessons on aspects of comprehension—on setting purposes for reading, summarizing, visualizing, making inferences, understanding vocabulary from context, learning new information, and interpreting the text. The students will be placed in different levels of text for fluency practice. They will be placed at their instructional level of spelling words to learn, even if that falls a year above or below their grade placement level. The assessment picture will be rounded out by other information gained from interviews with the students to determine the topics they are interested in, the kind of reading they most prefer, and the conditions they need to help them learn.

Once a course of instruction has been established for students, they will be given *monitoring assessments*. Unlike the daily observations, these may be more formalized and done on a schedule. The results may be shared with other teachers or with the reading specialist, and will serve as an occasion to decide whether the present plan of instruction should be followed or if different strategies should be tried to improve each student's learning. In addition, though, the teacher will practice close observation by making a habit of asking a small number of children every day how they are working, what exactly they are doing when they read and write, what they appear to be interested in, what kinds of tasks they are succeeding in, when they work best, and when they get off task—in sum, how the teacher can help each one be successful in this class.

Late in the year will come the outcomes-based assessments, which are based on the state learning standards for each grade level. This is a serious accountability event. While the daily informal assessment and the periodic monitoring assessments will be focused on children's development as readers, writers, and learners in general, these monitoring assessments will also have one eye on these outcomes-based assessments.

Response to Intervention (RTI)

Response to Intervention (RTI) is a further refinement of IDEA and IDEIA, national education initiatives to address the needs of students with learning disabilities. Earlier iterations of such programs were based on a discrepancy model in which educators waited for a two-year discrepancy between the expected learning of students, based on ability measures, and their actual learning. This earlier practice resulted in most students being neglected for two years when intervention might have made a difference for them. RTI enables identification and assessment as soon as a child is observed to struggle with learning in the classroom. In this book, we are focused on literacy, but RTI addresses all areas of student disability, including emotional and related factors.

The National Center on Response to Intervention (2010) identifies four essential components of RTI: a school-wide multilevel instructional and behavioral system for the prevention of school failure; screening; progress monitoring; and data-based decision making. Students in need are identified early, and interventions to address their needs are evidence based.

The multilevel structure of RTI usually consists of three levels: Tier One, which is the general education program in the regular classroom; Tier Two, which provides small-group intervention to students identified as not making satisfactory progress in Tier One; and Tier Three, in which students not making progress in Tier Two have intensive interventions, sometimes within the structure of special education.

In this book you will find a chapter devoted to more specific aspects of RTI (Chapter 2). The rest of the book provides assessment and evidence-based instructional interventions that fit into the RTI structure.

Summary

After imagining what schools would be like if all young readers were the same, we offer a list of ways that literacy matters in people's lives: It makes people more employable and gives them access to higher income, better health, bigger vocabularies, and a different sort of consciousness.

We then catalog some of the reasons why we assess readers—to find appropriate levels for teaching, to find skills that are in greater or lesser supply, to decide if a course of instruction is having success, to place a child in special services. Then we survey the approaches to assessment that are available: Informal Reading Inventories, running records, curriculum-based assessments, observations, portfolios, rubrics, and, of course, standardized assessments.

It helps to look at literacy in different stages. In this book we consider the phases of reading to be *emergent literacy, beginning reading, fledgling reading, developing reading,* and *mature reading*. Ways of assessing and teaching reading and writing in these different phases are presented in the chapters that follow.

References

Anderson, R. C., Wilson, P. T., & Fielding, L. G. (1988). Growth in reading and how children spend their time outside school. *Reading Research Quarterly, 23,* 285–303.

Andrade, H. (2000). Using rubrics to promote thinking and learning. *Educational Leadership, 57*(5), 13–18.

Anyon, J. (1981). Social class and school knowledge. *Curriculum Inquiry, 11*(1), 3–42.

Baer, J., Kutner, M., Sabatini, J., & White, S. (2003). *Basic reading skills and the literacy of America's least literate adults: Results from the 2003 National Assessment of Adult Literacy (NAAL).* National Center for Educational Statistics. Washington, DC: U.S. Department of Education.

Beck, I. L., McKeown, M. G., & Kucan, L. (2002). *Bringing words to life*. New York, NY: Guilford.

Betts, A. E. (1946). *Foundations of reading instruction, with emphasis on differentiated guidance.* Chicago, IL: American Book.

Bleich, D. (1975). *Readings and feelings: An introduction to subjective criticism*. Champaign, IL: National Council of Teachers of English.

Brown, R. (1955). *Words and things*. Garden City, NY: Basic Books.

Clay, M. M. (1985). *The early detection of reading difficulties*. (3rd ed.). Portsmouth, NH: Heinemann.

Clay, M. M. (1986). *The early detection of reading difficulties*. Portsmouth, NH: Heinemann.

Clay, M. M. (1993). *An observational survey of early literacy achievement*. Portsmouth, NH: Heinemann.

Cunningham, A. E., & Stanovich, K. E. (1997). Early reading acquisition and its relation to reading experience and ability 10 years later. *Developmental Psychology, 33*(6), 934–945.

Cunningham, P., & Allington, R. (2006). *Classrooms that work: They can all read and write* (4th ed.). Boston, MA: Allyn & Bacon.

Graham, S., & Perin, D. (2007). *Writing next: Effective strategies to improve writing of adolescents in middle and high schools—A report to Carnegie Corporation of New York.* Washington, DC: Alliance for Excellent Education.

Groff, P. (n.d.). *Emergent literacy: A code word for whole language*. Strasburg, VA: National Right to Read Foundation. http://www.nrrf.org/031_emergent_literacy.html

Hart, B., & Risley, T. (1995). *Meaningful differences in the everyday experiences of young American children*. Baltimore, MD: Brookes Publishing.

Hayes, D. P., & Ahrens, M. (1988). "Vocabulary simplification for children" A special case of "motherse." *Journal of Child Language, 15*, 395–410.

Henderson, E. H. (1995). *Teaching spelling.* Boston, MA: Houghton Mifflin.

Johnston, F. R., Invernizzi, M., & Juel, C. (1998). *Book Buddies: Guidelines for volunteer tutors of emergent and early readers.* New York, NY: Guilford.

Juel, C. (1988). Learning to read and write: A longitudinal study of fifty-four children from first through fourth grades. *Journal of Educational Psychology, 80*, 437–447.

Kirsch, I. S., Jungeblut, A., Jenkins, L., & Kolstad, A. (1993). *Adult literacy in America: A first look at the findings of the National Adult Literacy Survey*, (NCES 93275). Washington, DC: U.S. Department of Education.

Leslie, L., & Caldwell, J. (2005). *Qualitative reading inventory* (4th ed.). Boston, MA: Allyn & Bacon.

Luria, A. (1976). *Cognitive development*. Cambridge, MA: MIT Press.

Morris, R. D. (1993). The relationship between children's concept of word in text and phoneme awareness in learning to read: A longitudinal study. *Research in the Teaching of English, 27*, 2, 133–154.

Morris, R. D. (2005). *The Howard Street tutoring manual*. New York, NY: Guilford Publishing.

National Center for Educational Statistics. (1992). *National of Adult Literacy Survey.* http://nces.ed.gov/nals

National Center for Educational Statistics. (2002). *National Assessment of Adult Literacy.* http://nces.ed.gov/naal/

National Center for Educational Statistics. (2005). *National Assessment of Educational Progress.* Washington, DC: U.S. Department of Education.

National Center for Educational Statistics. (2010). *The nation's report card: Reading 2009.* Washington, DC: U.S. Department of Education. http://nces.ed.gov/pubsearch/pubsinfo.asp?pubid=2010458

National Center for Educational Statistics. (2010). The NAEP reading achievement levels by grade: 2009 achievement-level descriptions. In *The nation's report card: Reading 2009.* Washington, DC: U.S. Department of Education. http://nces.ed.gov/nationsreportcard/reading/achieveall.asp#2009ald

National Center on Response to Intervention. (2010). *Essential components of RTI—A closer look at Response to Intervention*. Washington, DC: National Center on Response to Intervention.

National Institute of Child Health and Human Development. (2000). *Report of the National Reading Panel. Teaching children to read: An evidence-based assessment of the scientific research literature on reading and its implications for reading instruction* (NIH Publication No. 00-4769). Washington, DC: U.S. Government Printing Office.

Neuman, S. B., & Dickinson, D. K. (2000). *Handbook of emergent literacy*. New York, NY: Guilford.

Pinnell, G. S. (1989). Reading Recovery: Helping at-risk children learn to read. *Elementary School Journal, 90*(2), 161–183.

Rosenblatt, L. (1978). *The reader, the text, and the poem.* Carbondale, IL: Southern Illinois University Press.

Silvaroli, N., & Wheelock, W. (2000). *Classroom reading inventory*. Columbus, OH: Merrill.

Slavin, R. E. (1991). Synthesis of research of cooperative learning. *Educational Leadership, 48*(5), 71–82.

Slavin, R. E., Madden, N. A., Karweit, N. L., Dolan, L., Wasik, B. A., Shaw, A., Mainzer, K. L., & Haxby, B. (1991). Neverstreaming: Prevention and early intervention as alternatives to special education. *Journal of Learning Disabilities, 24*, 373–378.

Stanovich, K. (1992). Are we overselling literacy? In C. Temple & P. Collins (Eds.), *Stories and readers.* Norwood, MA: Christopher-Gordon.

Stuckey, J. E. (1990). *The violence of literacy.* Portsmouth, NH: Boynton/Cook.

Taylor, B., Person, P. D., Clark, K. F., & Walpole, S. (1999). *Beating the odds in teaching all children to read.* Ann Arbor, MI: Center for the Improvement of Early Reading Achievement. http://www.ciera.org/

Teale, W., & Sulzby, E. (1986). *Emergent literacy.* Norwood, NJ: Ablex.

Temple, C., Crawford, A., & Gillet, J. (2008). *Developmental literacy inventory: From emergent to mature levels.* Boston, MA: Allyn & Bacon.

UNESCO. (2006). Education for all. http://www.unesco.org/education.

Valencia, S., Hiebert, E., & Afflerbach, P. (1993). *Authentic reading assessment: Practices and possibilities.* Newark, DE: International Reading Association.

Wilson, P. T., Anderson, R. C., & Fielding, L. G. (1986). Children's book-reading habits: A new criterion for literacy. *Book Research Quarterly, 2*(3), 72–84.

Response to Intervention (RTI) and Struggling Readers

CHAPTER 2

Chapter Outline

From a Discrepancy Model to Response to Intervention: The Origins of RTI

It has been common practice to delay intervention in addressing struggling readers' problems and wait for a two-year discrepancy between their measured reading achievement and their expected reading achievement. A child who exhibits characteristics of a struggling reader in kindergarten, for example, would not receive intervention until second grade, which Vaughn and Fuchs (2003) identify as "waiting to fail." Juel (1988) found that students who failed to learn to read before the end of the first grade tended to be unsuccessful in reading throughout the elementary grades, the implication being that waiting for two years virtually ensures that this child will fail in reading. Response to Intervention (RTI) is a set of regulations under the Individuals with Disabilities Education Improvement Act of 2004 (IDEIA) that provides for new procedures in the identification and teaching of children with learning disabilities. The effective application of RTI can constitute a welcome change from the previous discrepancy model, permitting intervention based on identification of a struggling reader's needs as soon as a problem is recognized. A series of federal initiatives has led to this current law.

Response to Intervention (RTI) programs generally consist of three components:

- Universal screening for the early identification of students at risk of struggling in reading
- Provision of tiers of instruction ranging from the general education program to intensive intervention, sometimes in special education
- Continuous monitoring of student progress

Individuals with Disabilities Education Act of 1997 (IDEA)

Since 1997, the Individuals with Disabilities Education Act (IDEA) has governed the education of children with disabilities (Individuals with Disabilities Education Act of 1997, 1997). Under provisions of the act, students were identified as requiring assessment when they have intellectual disabilities; a hearing impairment, including deafness; a speech or language impairment; a visual impairment, including blindness; a serious emotional disturbance; an orthopedic impairment; autism; traumatic brain injury; a specific learning disability; deaf-blindness; or multiple disabilities. Their needs were assessed, and an Individual Education Plan (IEP) was developed for each identified student. The plan included the following elements:

- Current levels of educational performance
- Annual goals and short-term objectives
- Explanation of the need for special education and related services
- Explanation if the child cannot be mainstreamed in the general education classroom
- Description and schedule of special education services provided
- Description of transition services provided
- Assessment of student progress, including needed accommodations

Support services from experienced special education teachers have often been provided to the general education classroom teacher who is working with these children, but they have frequently been insufficient or not timely.

Individuals with Disabilities Education Improvement Act of 2004 (IDEIA)

IDEA was reauthorized by the Individuals with Disabilities Education Improvement Act of 2004 (IDEIA), which was carefully aligned with provisions of NCLB (NEA, 2004). It provided alternative ways for identifying a disability. Students with disabilities are assessed annually in NCLB-required assessments, with some accommodations. Identified students must meet the same state standards as all other students, including English language learners, with some exceptions for students with severe cognitive disability. Under IDEIA, special education teachers are now required to be "highly qualified."

Response to Intervention (RTI)

RTI refers to recent changes in how the two special education laws, the Individuals with Disabilities Acts of 1997 and 2004 (IDEA, IDEIA), are applied. RTI is a process that further refines IDEA with an assessment of the effectiveness of a scientific, research-based intervention in improving an identified child's academic performance. This assumes that a continuing problem is not related to a visual, hearing, or motor disability, intellectual disability, emotional disturbance, cultural factors, economic disadvantage, or limited English proficiency.

RTI regulations identify eight areas of low achievement to be used as the basis for identifying specific learning disabilities, of which six are in the language arts: oral expression, listening comprehension, written expression, basic reading skill, reading fluency skills, and reading comprehension (International Reading Association, 2009). In *Understanding Reading Problems,* we will focus on these six areas, rather than on other academic or learning problems that might be identified under RTI.

K–3 students are screened in accordance with Reading First literacy screening instruments and procedures to determine if they are at risk of not meeting prescribed benchmarks. If students do not meet benchmarks after scientifically valid interventions are applied, the RTI models provide for interventions in small groups to provide additional assistance. The children's progress is monitored using measures that are brief, but targeted at skills the children need to attain. If difficulties continue, individualized interventions are provided. If these are not effective, then each child's case is reviewed by a team of professionals to determine if he or she is eligible for special education. According to Mesmer and Mesmer (2008/2009), the RTI process is a useful alternative to a discrepancy model.

In addition, an IQ measure is no longer required as a means of assessing a discrepancy between expected and actual learning outcomes. This is especially welcome when one considers the difficulties of using an IQ test with many children, especially those who do not speak English or who speak limited English.

No Child Left Behind (NCLB) and Reading First

The interaction between IDEA and the successive effects of NCLB and Reading First created additional difficulties for the struggling reader. Despite assurances to the contrary, NCLB evolved as a one-size-fits-all approach to instruction. All children are typically provided instruction from the same materials using the same methodology and at the same level. Two third graders, one reading at a first-grade level and one reading at a sixth-grade level, will ordinarily receive the same program of instruction; this approach has effectively eliminated differentiated instruction in many schools, with the former student frustrated and continuing to fail, and the latter student bored to insensibility studying something learned years before. RTI has the potential to undo this situation with increased flexibility, providing children with appropriate reading instruction, regardless of their strengths, needs, and characteristics.

Characteristics of RTI: What It Is, What It Isn't

Educators in general and reading educators in particular have become accustomed to highly prescriptive government mandates such as No Child Left Behind (NCLB) and Reading First. RTI is an alternative process that provides considerable discretion to schools and school districts in designing their programs to meet the needs of students with reading difficulties, among other learning problems.

RTI is not based on the earlier deficit model that required a discrepancy between the student's IQ and his or her level of achievement (Johnston, 2010). It is instead designed to identify learning disabilities and ensure that identified students receive appropriate instruction. RTI provides for the early identification of reading difficulties, which results in early intervention instead of waiting for students to fail. It also serves to reduce the incidence of overidentification of English language learners and other diverse groups of students and resulting referrals to special education.

Johnston (2010) describes an instructional frame for RTI that calls for identifying students with learning disabilities, which gives RTI a measurement focus. He also describes RTI as a means for preventing learning disabilities, which gives RTI an instructional focus.

Recommended Principles of RTI from the International Reading Association

A commission of the International Reading Association prepared a set of principles for improving the language and literacy learning of all students through the implementation of RTI (International Reading Association, 2009). These principles are summarized below.

- Preventing problems by optimizing language and literacy instruction
  - Increasing differentiated assessment and instruction to reduce the incidence of learning disabilities among minority youth and English language learners

- Emphasizing assessment and instruction conducted by classroom teachers
- Providing a coherent, comprehensive, and developmentally appropriate language and literacy curriculum that is supplied by a competent classroom teacher
- Using research-based instructional practices
- Tailoring research-based practices to the needs of particular groups of children
- Planning instruction based on individual student needs, not on average student needs
- Modifying instruction when evidence indicates that it is not effective for particular students

▪ Emphasizing increasingly differentiated and intensified instruction or intervention in language and literacy

- Providing differentiated instruction based on instructionally relevant assessment, followed by small-group and individualized instruction
- Using instruction and materials based on teaching experiences with individual students, not on packaged programs
- Providing flexibility in instructional responses to intervention that do not focus on uniformity

▪ Informing literacy instruction meaningfully through assessment

- Assessing the multidimensional nature of language and literacy learning and the diversity of students being assessed
- Informing about progress relating to authentic language and literacy goals
- Selecting assessments appropriate for English language learners and children who speak a non-standard dialect of English
- Providing a central role for classroom teachers and reading/literacy specialists in assessing language and literacy and in using outcomes to plan instruction
- Ensuring that assessment is consistent with Standards for the Assessment of Reading and Writing, jointly developed by the International Reading Association and the National Council of Teachers of English (2009)

▪ Ensuring strong collaboration among literacy professionals and cooperation among professionals, parents, and students

- Providing for school-level decision-making teams that include members with expertise in language, literacy, and second-language learning
- Providing leadership from reading/literacy specialists and coaches who meet IRA Standards for Reading Professionals (IRA, 2010)
- Increasing congruence between core language and literacy instruction and RTI interventions
- Involving parents and students, especially in urban and rural areas

▪ Providing for a comprehensive, systemic approach to language and literacy assessment and instruction for all pre-K–12 students and teachers

- Improving core instruction (regular classroom) to mitigate the need for specialized interventions
- Selecting approaches that best match school needs and resources

- Ensuring active participation and collaboration of classroom teachers, reading specialists, literacy coaches, special educators, and school psychologists
- Providing instruction sensitive to language and literacy needs for students of different ages and at different grade levels
- Ensuring that administrators provide adequate resources and appropriate scheduling for collaboration of all professionals
- Providing ongoing and job-embedded professional development for all involved in the RTI process

■ Providing instruction from professionals who are well prepared and current in their own development to teach language and literacy (IRA, 2010)

- Ensuring teacher expertise in literacy teaching and learning
- Ensuring that teachers are knowledgeable about language and literacy development and the use of powerful assessment tools and techniques, and that they have the ability to translate information about student performance into relevant instructional techniques
- Providing exemplary core instruction in the regular classroom
- Ensuring that professionals who provide supplemental instruction have a high level of expertise in all aspects of language and literacy instruction and assessment, and that they are capable of accelerating language and literacy learning
- Ensuring that teachers and support personnel who work with linguistically diverse students are well prepared to teach in a variety of settings and that they have a deep knowledge of cultural and linguistic differences
- Ensuring expertise in language and literacy at pre-service, induction, and in-service educational levels, including opportunities for extended practice with knowledgeable and experienced mentors

The Multi-Tiered Structure of RTI

Most RTI programs are organized around a multi-tier system designed to prevent reading failure. It usually consists of three tiers, although this structure is not mandated by government regulation. Within this three-tier structure (see Figure 2.1), Tier One is the general education program, including the core curriculum. Tier Two provides additional intervention that is targeted to address needs identified through assessment; it usually consists of a small-group tutoring experience for identified students. Tier Three consists of intensive intervention that is often individualized or provided in small groups, sometimes by a special education teacher, sometimes by a reading specialist, and sometimes by a team.

Tier One: General Education Program

Tier One encompasses the general education program that is usually conducted by a well-trained classroom teacher in the regular classroom. According to Taylor (2008), effective core reading instruction in grades K–5 includes phonemic awareness and phonics instruction,

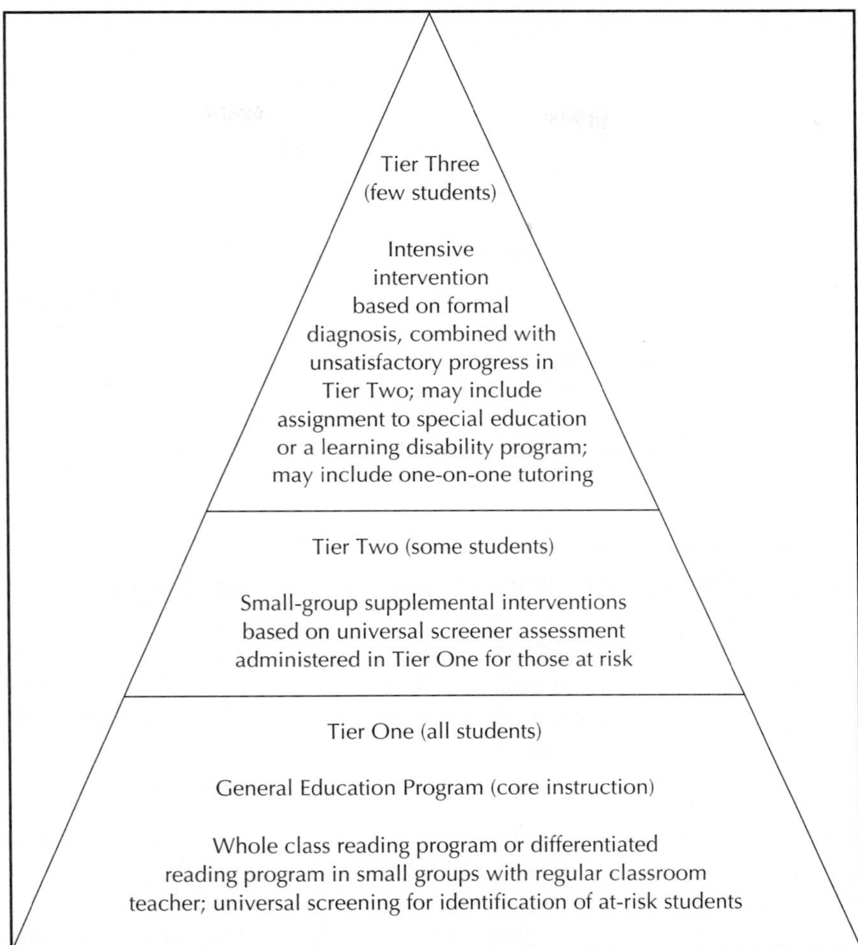

FIGURE 2.1 *RTI Tiers*

fluency instruction, vocabulary instruction, and comprehension instruction. Fuchs and Fuchs (2008) describe a benchmark assessment mode within Tier One in which a subset of the school population that may be at risk for reading failure is identified with a brief screening measure. A cut score for the measure is established, with children scoring below the cut score identified as at-risk. Some districts establish the cut score at about 20 percent of students, who will have further diagnosis. Tier One includes all students.

Tier Two: Small-Group Intervention

Tier Two is designed to meet the needs of students who have not made satisfactory progress with supplemental intervention through targeted support in Tier One. Standard treatment protocols in Tier Two call for tutoring in small groups using an evidence-based approach. The focus is on accelerating reading growth so that students can catch up. Progress monitoring indicating growth leads to students being returned to the general program in Tier One (Fuchs & Fuchs, 2008). A six- to eight-week period of progress monitoring is recommended for students within Tier Two to provide more precision to the identification process.

Tier Three: Intensive Intervention

Students who do not make satisfactory progress in Tier Two may be referred to Tier Three, which usually involves intensive intervention services, often provided by special education resources. Longer individualized sessions or in small groups include validated treatment protocols (Fuchs & Fuchs, 2008). Progress monitoring and diagnostic assessment continue in Tier Three, with the possibility that successful students may be returned to Tier Two or Tier One. The number of students in Tier Three programs is much smaller than in Tiers One and Two.

Approaches and Models for Implementing RTI

As we have indicated above, there is no prescribed approach to RTI. Two approaches have been described in the literature, along with evidence of the outcomes of each. They are the *interactive strategies approach* and the *comprehensive intervention model.*

Interactive Strategies Approach (ISA)

Scanlon and Anderson (2010) describe ISA as an approach, not a program. No particular set of materials or strategies is employed. As they point out, there is much variability among outcomes for children when instruction is centered on a single program or set of materials, and so there is no reason to focus on a single program. They take the position that reading problems can be prevented if "literacy instruction is comprehensive, responsive to individual students' needs, and fosters student independence" (Scanlon & Anderson, 2010, p. 24). They do not employ assessment instruments such as DIBELS because they do not yield information useful in guiding instructional planning. Instead, they use more comprehensive measures and administer them less often to protect valuable instructional time. Their model addresses mainly children at reading levels from kindergarten to grade two.

The ISA model is based on five major principles:

1. Providing a Vygotskian perspective on teaching and learning in which teachers help children become effective problem solvers, that is, strategic readers
2. Providing for all children opportunities that don't permit disengagement or that hide a lack of participation, as can occur in choral reading
3. Setting high expectations for all students

4. Ensuring an interface between classroom instruction and support services in such a way that they are not isolated from each other
5. Planning for success, not providing opportunities for failure

The ISA model has several goals:

1. Motivation to read and write in the sense that they are enjoyable and achievable for children
2. Alphabetics, that is, the relationship between print and speech
   - Phoneme awareness—that words are made up of sounds that can be separated out and blended to form new words
   - Letter identification
   - Letter-sound associations, that is, phonics
   - The alphabetic principle—using letters and the sounds they represent to read and spell words
   - Using single letters and spelling patterns to decode and spell words
3. Word learning, the development of sight vocabulary
   - Strategic word learning using code-based and meaning-based strategies; this includes the use of context clues (does the word you think it is make sense here?), which is discouraged in some approaches to beginning reading
   - High-frequency words read quickly and accurately
4. Vocabulary and development of oral language
5. Comprehension

In the ISA, Scanlon and Anderson (2010) recommend that the following components be included in most small-group intervention lessons: reading/rereading; phonological analysis; alphabetics; reading; high-frequency word practice; and writing. A very positive aspect of the ISA is the focus on children using both alphabetic information and the meaning of the text to effectively decode a word. In her case study of the implementation of the ISA, Anderson (2010) reinforces the importance of incorporating the interaction of code-based and meaning-based strategies.

Comprehensive Intervention Model (CIM)

Dorn and Henderson (2010) describe CIM as a systems approach to RTI. Their framework places the teacher in a key role, with differentiated classroom instruction, research-based interventions, assessment systems at individual and system levels, and extensive professional development focused on problem solving.

There are four tiers in the CIM model. Tier 1 is described as the core classroom program, but with differentiated instruction (grouped). Tier 2 includes small-group instruction, with the duration of the intervention dependent on student needs. Tier 3 consists of Reading Recovery in the first grade, and a research-based intervention with a portfolio of paired instruction or small-group strategies beyond first grade into the middle grades. Tier 4 refers students to intensive, specialized intervention after services provided in Tiers 1–3. Dorn and Henderson describe CIM as a layered approach in which assessment and intervention are followed by adjustments in teaching if progress is not made. This could include multiple interventions for a student, rather than assignment to an intervention for a period of time.

The CIM portfolio includes these evidence-based interventions (Dorn & Henderson, 2010):

- Reading Recovery
- Emergent language and literacy
- Guided Reading Plus
- Assisted writing/interactive writing
- Assisted writing/writing aloud
- Writing process group
- Comprehension focus/genre units of study
- Comprehension focus/strategy units of study
- Comprehension focus/content units of study

The CIM calls for administering a universal screener to begin the diagnostic progress in a CIM school (Dorn & Henderson, 2010). There is no specific instrument or procedure recommended, but the universal screener should accurately classify at-risk students, should predict later reading outcomes, should be sensitive to different levels of development in reading, should be easy and efficient to administer, and should permit timely and effective intervention. Strategies include classroom observation, testing, and interviews. The purpose of the universal screener is to identify about 20 percent of students who require further diagnosis.

The lowest 20 percent are then diagnosed in more depth with literacy diagnostic measures that include running records, writing samples, observation checklists and rubrics, word-identification tests, reading logs, formal test results, and selected class work (Meyer & Reindl, 2010). Progress monitoring in the CIM is a fairly complicated process that examines the trajectory of students as they hopefully progress as a result of Tier 2 interventions. An assessment wall using color-coded dots is used to help teachers analyze individual student outcomes and to see patterns in their system that need to be addressed (Dorn & Henderson, 2010).

The Role of Assessment in RTI

Assessment is a key component of RTI. Rather than including a high-stakes assessment test that informs teachers and school districts about how they are doing in their literacy program, RTI assessment is designed to provide information to help teachers and school districts meet the needs of individual students at risk of failure in literacy. It is conducted in several different modes at different stages and for different purposes.

Curriculum-Based Measurement (CBM) or Benchmark Assessment

CBM, or *benchmark assessment*, is often used as the term for the universal screening that takes place in the regular classroom Tier 1 general education program. An assessment such as PALS or DIBELS is frequently used (see Chapter 3).

Diagnostic Assessment

Diagnostic assessment is a very thorough process that is used with students who fail to reach the cut score in Tier 1 assessment. It is individualized according to the apparent needs of each student, and more formal diagnostic instruments might be used (see Chapter 6).

Progress Monitoring

According to Moore and Whitfield (2009), progress monitoring is an important component of RTI. It consists of regular and systematic assessment of the trajectory of student gains in all tiers. Mazes (modified cloze tests) are often used to check progress in reading comprehension (see Chapter 6).

False Positives

Gersten and Dimino (2006) alert us to a problem that occurs when assessment begins very early, for example, in kindergarten, and when measures have limited precision because of the children's young age. They report that many children who are identified early as at risk of having problems learning to read are, in fact, reading well two or three years later. But delaying the identification of children then runs the risk of not meeting an emerging need when it most should be addressed. Dorn and Henderson (2010) point out that the literacy diagnostic measures of the CIM help diminish the number of false positives that place students in interventions they do not need and also false negatives that result in not placing students in interventions they do need.

Evidence-Based Literacy Programs

Many evidence-based literacy curriculum packages, or validated treatment protocols, are in common use as interventions to meet instructional needs in Tier Two and Tier Three RTI programs. The following are examples of programs frequently used:

- Leveled Reader's Theater (Benchmark)
- Peer-Assisted Literacy Strategies (PALS) Series
- Read Naturally
- Reading Recovery

Evidence-based strategies also meet criteria for RTI. They are widely used strategies for specific purposes that have a strong research base. While IDEA, IDEIA, NCLB, and

RTI require the use of evidence-based literacy programs, they should not be used as scripted one-size-fits-all programs. As Johnston (2010) reminds us, an intervention that is effective for most children may not be effective for all. He points out that teacher expertise is called for in the regulations, with the implication of a strong decision-making role for the classroom teacher. He also indicates the importance of school context in making these instructional decisions.

Walmsley and Allington (2007) offer important principles that serve to strengthen programs of intervention for such struggling readers:

- All staff, classroom teachers, special education teachers, and specialists are responsible for the education of all students, with emphasis on the classroom teacher.
- All children should be provided with the same literacy experiences, materials, and expectations. Poor readers are often placed in programs that limit access to literacy because their primary focus is on low-level skill development, oral reading, and word recognition—a fragmented program.
- All children should be educated with their peers, an approach characterized by inclusion, not segregation into special classes.
- The literacy curriculum for identified students and struggling readers should contain all of the elements that successful readers encounter in their lessons, including silent reading, reading full-length material, and reading for a variety of purposes, including pleasure. Joint planning between general education classroom teachers and those who provide instructional support outside the general education classroom is needed.
- Expert teachers should provide high-quality instruction. These are usually general education classroom teachers with excellent preparation for teaching reading and writing.
- Instructional support programs for struggling readers should function as integrated wholes, rather than as a series of separately funded programs that address different issues: a single, unified instructional support program that involves all of the players in meeting children's literacy needs in an integration of remedial and special education services.

Allington (2008) adds other important elements:

- Levels of texts used should be matched to readers' reading levels.
- Reading activity should be dramatically expanded—that is, actual reading, rather than studying about reading.
- Interventions should be coordinated with the classroom curriculum.
- The focus of instruction is on meaning and metacognition.
- Expert teachers do not include paraprofessionals using workbook materials and low-level ditto sheets, a common intervention for struggling readers.

California has taken steps that reflect some of Allington's concerns about RTI. The California State Department of Education (2009) has renamed the process as *Response to Instruction and Intervention Squared (RTI²).* This reflects the alignment of their curriculum, instruction, and assessment into a system that provides periodic data about student progress in core subjects. It is designed to provide high-quality instruction and to ensure early intervention for students who are struggling. Schools using RTI² anticipate the need for extra and early support for some students.

Members of the RTI Team and Their Roles

The successful implementation of RTI requires a collaborative team effort. It includes classroom teachers, reading specialists/coaches, special education teachers, school psychologists, building principals, district level administrators, and parents. There must be mutual respect among team members for the different kinds of expertise they bring to the RTI process. RTI provides a newly recognized important role for classroom teachers in that they often have more academic preparation and literacy teaching experience than other team members, although they are often new to the processes of assessment and planning for students with reading disabilities.

Classroom Teacher

Mesmer and Mesmer (2008/2009) point out that reading teachers, including reading specialists and literacy coaches, have a major role in RTI because 80 percent of students referred to special education have difficulties with literacy. "Reading teachers" are named as qualified participants in RTI (Lyon, 1995). As Johnston (2010) concludes above, classroom teachers are included in statutes and regulations because of their expertise. Classroom teachers are now an important part of meeting the needs of students with learning disabilities, especially those with literacy problems. As indicated earlier, expert teachers do not include unsupervised paraprofessionals using workbook materials and low-level ditto sheets, a common intervention for struggling readers (Allington, 2008).

Special Education Teacher

The Council for Exceptional Children (2007) takes the position that special educators have a key role in the problem-solving RTI teams at the levels of Tier One and Tier Two. They are responsible for the implementation of most intensive interventions in Tier Three, which are based on Individualized Education Plans (IEPs) under IDEA and IDEIA.

School Psychologist

The role of the psychologist in RTI is an important one (NASP, 2006). They are charged with:

- Providing leadership in developing, implementing, and evaluating new models of service delivery.

- Providing leadership for collaborative teams, or, if not leading the team, providing leadership in dealing with issues of assessment, mental health, home-school collaboration, and school agency collaboration.
- Serving individual students and their parents, including intervention activities at school and at home, demonstrating progress-monitoring activities, observing students in the classroom, evaluating students' cognitive functioning, making referrals, and helping team members and service providers set realistic goals for students.

Building Principal

Costello, Lipson, Marinak, and Zolman (2010) conclude that, to lead an RTI team, the building principal or other designated leader must have the following characteristics:

- A vision shared with all stakeholders
- A personalized approach that focuses on students' needs, not just on data
- Concreteness in addressing needs, problems, and issues, with opportunities for feedback
- Credibility exemplified by analyzing problems to find a solution when a change is required
- Inspiring team members to act on behalf of students
- Sharing stories and student artifacts when discussing how to approach the problems of students; going beyond just the numbers from assessment procedures

Parents

Parents will continue to have a strong role in RTI when they are notified about their children's problems, as they must provide informed consent before any diagnostic assessment or intervention (Fuchs & Mellard, 2007). They are consulted about how long interventions are applied before moving on to other interventions in the event that they are not effective. Parents always have the right to request a comprehensive evaluation for their child.

RTI in Middle Schools and High Schools

Middle Schools

According to Gelzheiser, Scanlon, and Hallgren-Flynn (2010), there are several characteristics of RTI programs that are especially important for middle school students.

- As with other students with disabilities, responsive instruction is critical for middle school students.

- Helping students toward independence in their own learning, as contrasted with strong teacher-controlled interaction, is important at this level.
- Reading in the content areas of the curriculum is also of great importance in RTI at the middle school level.
- Students at the middle school level should be focused on comprehension and the importance of all of the words included in a text.
- Struggling students will benefit from reading at a variety of reading levels for different purposes and from different genres.
- Motivation and attitudes toward reading are especially important at a level where many students have given up.

High Schools

Goetze, Laster, and Ehren (2010) point out three elements of secondary schools that make them particularly challenging for implementing RTI:

- The departmentalized schedule prescribes use of time that may need to be adjusted for students in Tier Two and Tier Three programs. Common conflicts include after-school sports and lack of late bus transportation.
- Some students need homogeneous grouping for a limited amount of time to address specific problems. A school-within-a-school or a designated classroom may resolve this issue.
- School organization must be based on student needs demonstrated by data. This indicates that flexibility is important in finding a way to meet those needs, which is not an easy task in the culture of the typical secondary school.

English Language Learners and RTI

There has been great concern about the overrepresentation of children from linguistic and ethnic minorities in special education classes (Hill, Carjuzaa, Aramburo, & Baca, 1993). Historically, too often, children were assigned to special education classes because of supposed language disorders and/or intellectual disabilities that might have been nothing more than limited English proficiency. According to *Diana v. State Board of Education of California* (1970) and subsequent special education legislation, such as P.L. 94-142, this is no longer permitted. Damico (1991) suggests that referral to special education, and by extension to RTI Tier Three, should not be based on the following:

- Other factors that might explain the child's learning and language difficulties, including lack of opportunity to learn, cultural dissonance, and stressful life events, for example, among refugee children
- Language difficulties that the student has at school, but not at home or in the community

- Ordinary needs of children to acquire English as a second language or the standard American English dialect
- Cross-cultural interference
- Bias in the assessment process, including data analysis that does not take into account the child's culture, language, and life experiences

Many strategies can be used very effectively in teaching children with these needs. According to Gersten and Baker (2000), the following strategies can be used to alleviate the factors listed above:

- Build children's vocabulary and use it as a curricular anchor.
- Use visual representations to reinforce major concepts and vocabulary.
- Use the children's mother tongue as a support system.
- Adapt cognitive and language demands of instruction to the children by using sheltered English (SIOP) strategies.

A related problem has been how to measure IQ in order to identify the discrepancy between the expected and actual achievement of English language learners. Although RTI has largely eliminated the use of this discrepancy model, the need for testing IQ may remain in some circumstances. Two nonverbal IQ tests provide a way to meet this need: the Leiter-R and the Universal Nonverbal Intelligence Test (UNIT) (Farrell & Phelps, 2000). A school psychologist can help with this. (Teachers can't administer these tests anyway—they can use this information to ask a school psychologist to use the appropriate test—one of these two.)

Klingner and Edwards (2006) have proposed a four-tier model for culturally and linguistically diverse students. The first tier includes evidence-based instruction, as do other first tiers, but this instruction should be validated with the population being served. They add a second component in which teachers develop culturally responsive attributes appropriate for those populations. Teachers of English language learners should also be knowledgeable about bilingual education, teaching ESL, and second language acquisition. The second tier for students whose progress monitoring shows them needing additional intervention should supplement the core curriculum, and it should also incorporate interventions appropriate for English language learners, not just interventions validated for native English speakers. The third tier can be conducted simultaneously with the second tier in their proposed model. An additional team with a bilingual or ESL specialist should be involved, and their assessment should include classroom observation. Their fourth proposed tier is special education.

The most problematical issue with respect to English language learners is their proficiency in English, which can range from speaking no English to being quite competent in their second language, even within the same classroom. It is almost a certainty that many English language learners, if not most, will be identified as needing interventions in English reading. But their interventions in most cases will be quite different from those of English-proficient students with reading problems. Teachers and RTI team members should ask themselves if English language learners would have literacy problems if they were taught to read and write in their mother tongue, instead of English. If they would not, then their intervention should be a strong and formal ESL program. Klingner, Soltero-González, and Lesaux (2010) accordingly recommend that teachers should be knowledgeable about second language acquisition and also how to teach reading in English with children for whom English is their second language. This is also reflected in the IRA Guiding Principles on RTI cited earlier in this chapter.

Klingner, Soltero-González, and Lesaux (2010) also make valuable recommendations about important factors in the assessment instruments used to evaluate English language learners, or, more inclusively, culturally and linguistically diverse students: the need for multiple measures, especially in the area of language acquisition; the need to consider the multidimensional nature of language and reading, perhaps most crucial in Tier 1 general education programs; the place of progress monitoring in the RTI framework for English language learners; and the way assessment data are used and shared, taking into account the need for second language acquisition and bilingual education specialists on the RTI team.

Phonemic awareness is always a component of current interest in literacy programs. English language learners will often speak English with an accent influenced by the mother tongue. We should consider how important it is that all children hear and produce English sounds in the same way—perhaps it is not terribly important. After all, children from India, Australia, England, Scotland, Ireland, Jamaica, Ghana, Brooklyn, New Orleans, and Boston can look at the same text, read it aloud with widely varying pronunciations, and comprehend it.

RTI and the Gifted

Teachers often conclude that gifted children do not have reading problems. Many or most learn to read at home if parents read to them, and the rest appear to learn to read quickly in kindergarten or the first grade. But Temple, Ogle, Crawford, and Freppon (2011) point out that teachers often make these erroneous assumptions about gifted children:

- *Gifted children don't have reading problems.* The gifted child reading on grade level has a reading problem that should be diagnosed and addressed. Based on expectations, gifted children should be reading above grade level, usually several grades above their age-expected level. Although gifted children probably won't end up in Tier Three of RTI programs, they might appear in Tier Two.
- *Gifted children have mastered the basic skills of reading.* It isn't unusual to observe the fragmentation of basic skills among gifted children—they may have mastered most basic skills, but gaps may appear. They can be integrated into reading groups that are addressing identified areas of weakness at the time an appropriate lesson or lessons are offered, even though those groups are usually working below the levels of these otherwise more capable students.

- *All gifted children speak English well.* Often, gifted children can read in a language other than English, which means that their greatest need is to learn to understand and speak English.

The Role of Technology in RTI

Dorn and Henderson's (2010) Comprehension Intervention Model (CIM) of RTI makes effective use of technology within their strong commitment to professional development. Their website includes a teacher discussion board that is widely used, not only by their own project, but also by school teams from around the country. It has three purposes: offering resources for providing a high-quality general education program at the classroom level; offering information about how to work with struggling readers at the intervention level; and permitting teacher collaboration and problem solving.

Summary

RTI is an approach to identifying and serving students with learning disabilities that is mandated under IDEA and IDEIA. It is designed to assess and predict which students will experience difficulties in learning to read (in the case of this book), to design and implement interventions for those identified students, and to monitor their progress through interventions, adjusting or changing them where indicated by lack of progress.

Most RTI programs are organized around three tiers. Tier One is the general education tier that all children experience. Based on a screening assessment, some students are identified as at risk and receive interventions in Tier Two, usually in small groups, but sometimes in individual settings. When these are not effective and the student does not make satisfactory progress, a student may be diagnosed in depth and then assigned to intensive intervention in Tier Three, which is often conducted by special educators.

Assessment has a strong role in RTI programs, and it is designed and implemented by school teams that generally are made up of classroom teachers and reading specialists or literacy coaches, special educators, school psychologists, building principals or other administrators, and parents.

Interventions, including the general education program in the regular program, are evidence based. There is provision for differentiated instruction in that interventions are not one-size-fits all. Because classroom teachers are frequently expert in the area of literacy, they have a stronger role in RTI programs than in earlier iterations of IDEA.

References

Allington, R. L. (2008). *What really matters in Response to Intervention*. Boston, MA: Allyn & Bacon.

Anderson, K. L. (2010). Spotlight on the interactive strategies approach: The case of Roosevelt Elementary School. In M. Y. Lipson & K. K. Wixson (Eds.), *Successful approaches to RTI: Collaborative practices for improving K–12 literacy*. Newark, DE: International Reading Association.

California State Department of Education. (2009). Response to instruction and intervention (RTI[2]). http://pubs.cde.ca.gov/tcsii/ch2/responsetointerven.aspx

Costello, K. A., Lipson, M. Y., Marinak, B., & Zolman, M. F. (2010). In M. Y. Lipson & K. K. Wixson (Eds.), *Successful approaches to RTI: Collaborative practices for improving K–12 literacy*. Newark, DE: International Reading Association.

Council for Exceptional Children. (2007). *Position on Response to Intervention (RTI): The unique role of special education and special education teachers*. Arlington, VA: Council for Exceptional Children.

Damico, J. S. (1991). Descriptive assessment of communicative ability in limited English proficient students. In E. V. Hamayan & J. S. Damico (Eds.), *Limiting bias in the assessment of bilingual students* (pp. 157–218). Austin, TX: PRO-ED.

Dorn, K. J., & Henderson, S. C. (2010). The comprehensive intervention model: A systems approach to RTI. In M. Y. Lipson & K. K. Wixson (Eds.), *Successful approaches to RTI: Collaborative practices for improving K–12 literacy*. Newark, DE: International Reading Association.

Farrell, M. M., & Phelps, L. (2000). A comparison of the Leiter-R and the Universal Nonverbal Intelligence Test (UNIT) with children classified as language impaired. *Journal of Psychoeducational Assessment, 18*(3), 268–274.

Fuchs, L. S., & Fuchs, D. (2008). The role of assessment within the RTI framework. In D. Fuchs, L. W. Fuchs, & S. Vaughn (Eds.), *Response to intervention: A framework for reading educators*. Newark, DE: International Reading Association.

Fuchs, M. L., & Mellard, D. F. (2007). *Helping educators discuss responsiveness to intervention with parents and students*. Lawrence, KS: National Research Center on Learning Disabilities.

Gelzheiser, L. M., Scanlon, D. M., & Hallgren-Flynn, L. (2010). Spotlight on RTI for adolescents: An example of intensive middle school intervention using the interactive strategies approach-extended. In M. Y. Lipson & K. K. Wixson (Eds.), *Successful approaches to RTI: Collaborative practices for improving K–12 literacy*. Newark, DE: International Reading Association.

Gersten, R., & Baker, S. (2000). What we know about effective instructional practices for English-language learners. *Exceptional Children, 66*(4), 310–322.

Gersten, R., & Dimino, J. A. (2006). RTI (Response to Intervention): Rethinking special education for students with reading difficulties (yet again). *Reading Research Quarterly, 41*(1), 99–108.

Goetze, S. K., Laster, B., & Ehren, B. J. (2010). RTI for secondary school literacy. In M. Y. Lipson & K. K. Wixson (Eds.), *Successful approaches to RTI: Collaborative practices for improving K–12 literacy*. Newark, DE: International Reading Association.

Hill, R., Carjuzaa, J., Aramburo, D., & Baca, L. (1993). Culturally and linguistically diverse teachers in special education: Repairing or redesigning the leaky pipeline. *Teacher Education and Special Education, 16*(3), 258–269.

Individuals with Disabilities Education Act 1997 (Reauthorization), (1997), 20 U.S.C. 1400 et seq.

Individuals with Disabilities Education Improvement Act of 2004. (2004). 108th Congress (2003-2004) H.R.1350.ENR.

International Reading Association. (2009). *Response to Intervention: Guiding principles for Educators from the International Reading Association*. Newark, DE: Author.

International Reading Association and National Council of Teachers of English. (2009). *Standards for the Assessment of Reading and Writing, Revised Edition*. Newark, DE: Author.

International Reading Association—Revised 2010. (2010). *IRA Standards for Reading Professionals*. Newark, DE: Author.

Johnston, P. (2010). An instructional frame for RTI. *The Reading Teacher, 63*(7), 602–604.

Juel, C. (1988). Learning to read and write: A longitudinal study of 54 children from first through fourth grades. *Journal of Educational Psychology, 80*, 437–447.

Klingner, J. K., & Edwards, P. A. (2006). Cultural considerations with Response to Intervention models. *Reading Research Quarterly, 41*(1), 108–117.

Klingner, J. K., Soltero-González, L., & Lesaux, N. (2010). RTI for English-language learners. In M. Y. Lipson & K. K. Wixson (Eds.), *Successful approaches to RTI: Collaborative practices for improving K–12 literacy*. Newark, DE: International Reading Association.

Lyon, G. (1995). Research initiatives in learning disabilities: Contributions from scientists supported by the National Institute of Child Health and Human Development. *Journal of Child Neurology*, 10(Suppl. 1), S120–S126.

Mesmer, E. M., & Mesmer, H. A. E. (2008/2009). Response to Intervention (RTI): What teachers of reading need to know. *The Reading Teacher, 62*(4), 280–290.

Meyer, K. E., & Reindl, B. L. (2010). Spotlight on the comprehensive intervention model: The case of Washington School for Comprehensive Literacy. In M. Y. Lipson & K. K. Wixson (Eds.), *Successful approaches to RTI: Collaborative practices for improving K–12 literacy*. Newark, DE: International Reading Association.

Moore, J., & Whitfield, V. (2009). Building schoolwide capacity for preventing reading failure. *The Reading Teacher*, *62*(7), 622–624.

National Association of School Psychologists (NASP). (2006). *The role of the school psychologist in the RTI Process*. Bethesda, MD: Author.

NEA [National Education Association]. (2004). *NCLB: The intersection of access and outcomes*. Washington, DC: Author.

Peer-Assisted Literacy Strategies (PALS) Series. (2010). http://smu.edu/education/readingresearch/interventions/pals.asp

Scanlon, D. M., & Anderson, K. L. (2010). Using the interactive strategies approach to prevent reading difficulties in an RTI context. In M. Y. Lipson & K. K. Wixson (Eds.), *Successful approaches to RTI: Collaborative practices for improving K–12 literacy*. Newark, DE: International Reading Association.

Taylor, B. M. (2008). Effective classroom reading instruction in the elementary grades. In D. Fuchs, L. W. Fuchs, & S. Vaughn (Eds.), *Response to intervention: A framework for reading educators*. Newark, DE: International Reading Association.

Temple, C., Ogle, D., Crawford, A., & Freppon, P. (2011). *All children read: Teaching for literacy in today's diverse classrooms*. (3rd ed.). Boston, MA: Pearson.

Vaughn, S., & Fuchs, L. S. (2003). Redefining learning disabilities as inadequate response to instruction: The promise and potential problems. *Learning Disabilities Research & Practice, 18*(3), 137–146. doi:10.1111/1540-5826.00070.

Walmsley, S. A., & Allington, R. L. (2007). Redefining and reforming instructional support programs for at-risk students. In R. L. Allington & S. A. Walmsley (Eds.), *No quick fix: Rethinking literacy programs in America's elementary schools* (pp. 19–44). New York, NY: Teachers College Press.

Assessing and Teaching Emergent Readers and Writers

CHAPTER 3

Chapter Outline

Sarah Fellows and Howard Gao teach in a multiage kindergarten and first-grade classroom. Between them, they have 30 children who range in age from five to almost seven years old. Every morning before class begins, the children find cards with their names written on them and place them in the "Look Who's Here Today!" pocket chart. Then the children go to the circle for Morning Message. Children take turns coming forward and choosing the printed cards with the names of the day and the month, and the numbers for the date. There are pictures of a sun, a cloud, snowflakes, and rain that are put on the flannel board to show the weather. Either Sarah or Howard leads an interactive writing session, talking through a preview of the day's events and inviting a child forward to write whole words or fill in letters for some of the sounds.

Both teachers like the multiage arrangement because it helps the children whose emergent literacy has progressed further to read along with a more advanced peer group. Children who are still working on emergent concepts can work with peers as well. But the groups are almost constantly being formed and re-formed based on the two teachers' close observation and periodic assessment of their children.

Emergent Literacy

Understanding Emergent Literacy

In the pages that follow, we will explore many aspects of emergent literacy, along with ways of assessing and teaching them. In the final section of the chapter we will share suggestions for helping children with different levels of preparedness in emergent literacy.

To begin, here are two scenarios:

Forty years ago, a first-grade teacher explained how she decided if a child was ready to learn to read. She asked the child to reach his right arm across the top of his head and touch his left ear. If he could, she invited him to join the reading lesson. If he couldn't, he was allowed to play in the sand box a few more weeks. Her practice was actually based on a theory people believed at the time: Children's mental development was thought to be proportional to their physical development, and since from babyhood to childhood arms grow more quickly than heads, eventually a magic moment comes when—voilá!—a child can reach across her head and touch her other ear; at this moment she is simultaneously thought to be mentally ready for the challenges of reading. In this teacher's view, children reach a moment when they are ready to read, and it is pointless to begin reading instruction before that time. This view of early reading is reflected in the term ***"reading readiness."***

A Head Start program director in our city makes sure every parent of a newborn takes a children's book home from the hospital along with the baby. Why? Because she firmly believes that literacy's beginnings reach back to earliest childhood, and she doesn't want any child to wait even the four short years before preschool begins to have someone read to him.

Science is on the side of that Head Start director. Between birth and the time they enter school, studies show that children learn lessons of language and literacy that may make learning to read a relatively smooth and natural process that easily connects to their experiences in early childhood. Or, if literacy and the elaborated language that comes with it are missing during those early years, learning to read can seem foreign, confusing, unnatural, and embarrassing. The term *emergent literacy* (Clay, 1991; Ferreiro & Teberosky, 1979; Teale & Sulzby, 1986) came into use a few decades ago when educators observed that if children are given exposure to written language and encouragement to explore it in early childhood, they learn many concepts and acquire abilities related to literacy at a very young age. In turn, those concepts facilitate their learning to read and write once they are in school.

Emergent literacy began as a *constructivist* concept; the earliest proponents of emergent literacy supposed that children discover or construct much of their learning about literacy through their own explorations, although with stimulation, encouragement, and modeling of literate practices from those around them (Teale & Sulzby, 1986; Temple, Nathan, & Burris, 1982). But educators soon observed that children do not acquire early literate concepts equally well, and that skillful intervention is necessary to supply those competencies that some children—especially children with socially different or limited early experiences with literacy—may lack when they begin learning to read in school. Learning to read in school without emergent literacy concepts has been described as trying to climb a staircase with the first several steps missing. With insights from studies of children's emergent literacy, we are better able to fill in those missing steps, both by providing emergent literacy curricula that give attention to important aspects of early literacy and by providing interventions to help those children who are lacking emergent literacy concepts.

Aspects of Emergent Literacy

Emergent readers cannot yet read through a line of text—children who know how to do that are considered beginning readers. What emergent readers do have and know are:

- **Concepts about print**—These concepts relate to the nature of the English writing system. Written language represents words, so in order to learn to read, a child needs a concept of word. English writing is alphabetic, which means that letters represent words by their sounds, at the level of their phonemes. Children need to know the identities of those letters—and, even before they learn the whole alphabet, they need to understand that letters represent sounds. They also need an understanding of what people are doing when they read and write.

- **Awareness of sounds in words**—English spelling works by relating letters to sounds; and knowing the letters is not enough without also knowing how the speech stream can be broken into smaller parts that can be matched to letters. We call this *phonological awareness,* because phonology refers to knowledge of the sound system of a language.
- **Oral language (vocabulary, syntax, and decontextualized language)**—At its simplest, reading is rendering print into speech and then understanding speech (Gough & Tunmer, 1986). Thus a child's success in reading and learning to read will be closely related to his capacity at oral language. A child's vocabulary is an important part of her capacity to experience, to learn. Words are tokens of concepts; we can easily think about things we have words for. Vocabulary size is a predictor of success in learning to read (Cunningham & Stanovich, 1997; Snow, Porsche, Tabors, & Harris, 2007). So is knowledge of syntax, or grammar (the rules by which we string words together sensibly), especially with respect to comprehension (Catts et al., 1999; Tomblin, Zhang, Buckwalter, & Catts, 2000). Decontextualized language is a kind of language use that is closely related to reading. Children who are used to hearing words that evoke events that are not present in the here and now also have an advantage when it comes to learning to read (Dickinson & Tabors, 1991; Pellegrini & Galda, 1994; Snow, 1991).
- **Comprehension**—Understanding written texts, even when someone else is reading them aloud, is another aspect of children's emergent literacy. Part of comprehension is the oral language ability we have already mentioned. Comprehension also includes using what we already know to make sense of new information; having questions and getting them answered; and knowing the structures of stories and other kinds of texts and using them to guide understanding.

In the following sections we will discuss ways of assessing these aspects of emergent literacy, sometimes together and sometimes on their own. Then we will describe ways of teaching for emergent literacy—again, sometimes treating aspects individually and sometimes together.

Assessing Emerging Readers

In this section we will look first at the assessment of children's concepts about print. Next we will turn to assessing children's ability to break speech down into small units (phonological awareness). Then we will look at oral language development, and finally, at comprehension.

Assessing Print Concepts

The National Reading Panel (Snow, Burns, & Griffin, 1998, p. 5) stressed the importance of acquainting young children with "the basic purposes and mechanisms of reading." New Zealand educator Marie Clay showed a particular genius for seeing these basic purposes and mechanisms from a child's point of view. One whole set of challenges facing a young child is finding her way around a book. Imagine a child in a reading circle who hears instructions such as these:

> Open the book to the first page. Look at the first word. Go on to the next word. What letter does it begin with? Look at the end of the line: Don't you see that the author is asking a question? Now go on to the next page.

The teacher in this situation is assuming that the child knows how an English book is opened (it's different in Chinese); knows what a "page" is and where to find the "first" one; knows what a word is and that words in written English are arranged on a page from left to right and from top to bottom (not so in Chinese or Hebrew; and in ancient Greek, the words on the same page were alternately arranged from left to right and from right to left); knows what a letter is and that the "first letter" in a word refers to the one farthest to the left; understands marks of punctuation; and so on.

It is unwise to assume that children who are just entering school understand the mechanisms of print. There are many children in kindergarten and first grade who do not, so Clay developed the *Concepts About Print Test* (1979/2000) to assess these aspects of a child's orientation to books and to written language. This test is highly recommended for kindergarten and primary-grade teachers as well as for reading clinics. It comes with one of two reusable books and is available from Heinemann Educational Books.

The aspects of the Concepts About Print Test that are especially relevant to the present discussion of emergent literacy are

- Book orientation knowledge.
- Principles involving the directional arrangement of print on the page.
- The knowledge that print, not the picture, contains the story.
- Understanding of important reading terminology such as *word, letter, beginning of the sentence,* and *top of the page.*
- Understanding of common punctuation marks.

The assessment of orientation concepts about written language can be carried out by using a simple illustrated children's book, one that the child being tested has not seen before. The Concepts About Print Test has two specially made books (*Sand* and *Stones*), but teachers can get much of the flavor of the procedure with a book of their own choosing. The following are some concepts that can be tested and the procedures to use with them:

1. **Knowledge of the Layout of Books.** Hand the child a book, with the spine facing the child, and say, "Show me the front of the book." Note whether the child correctly identifies the front.

2. **Knowledge That Print, Not Pictures, Is What We Read.** Open the book directly to a place where print is on one page and a picture is on the other. (You should make sure beforehand that the book has such a pair of pages and have it bookmarked for

easy location.) Then say, "Show me where I begin reading." Observe carefully to see whether the child points to the print or the picture. If the pointing gesture is vague, say, "Where, exactly?" If the child points to the print, note whether the child points to the upper left-hand corner of the page.

3. **Directional Orientation of Print on the Page.** Stay on the same set of pages, and after the child points at some spot on the printed page, say, "Show me with your finger where I go next." Then observe whether the child sweeps his finger across the printed line from left to right or moves it in some other direction.

Then ask, "Where do I go from there?" and observe whether the child correctly makes the return sweep to the left and drops down one line.

Note that a correct direction pattern is like this:

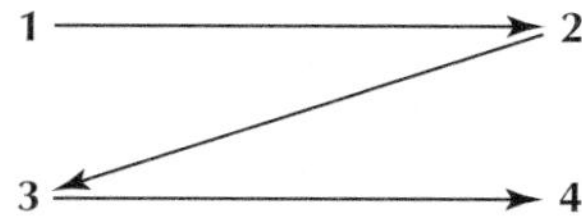

If the child indicates some other directional pattern, make a note of it.

4. **Knowledge of the Concepts of *Beginning* and *End*.** Turning now to a new page, say, "Point to the beginning of the story on this page" and then "Point to the end of the story on this page." Observe whether the child interprets both requests properly.

5. **Knowledge of the Terms *Top* and *Bottom*.** Turning to another pair of pages that have print on one page and a picture on the other, point to the middle of the printed page and say, "Show me the bottom of the page" and then "Show me the top of the page." Then point to the middle of the picture and say, "Show me the top of the picture" and then "Show me the bottom of the picture." Note whether the child responds accurately to all four requests.

6. **Knowledge of the Terms *Word* and *Letter*.** Now hand the child two blank index cards and say, "Put these cards on the page so that just one word shows between them" and then "Now move them so that two words show between them. Now move them again so that one letter shows between them" and then "Now move them so that two letters show between them." Make note of the child's response to all four requests.

7. **Knowledge of Uppercase and Lowercase Letters.** On the same page, point to a capital letter with your pencil and say, "Show me a little letter that is the same as this one." (Beforehand, make sure that there is a corresponding lowercase letter on the page.) Next point to a lowercase letter and say, "Now point to a capital letter that is the same as this one." (Again, make sure that there is one.) Repeat this procedure with other pairs of letters if the child's response seems uncertain.

8. **Knowledge of Punctuation.** Turn to a page that has a period, an exclamation point, a question mark, a comma, and a set of quotation marks. Pointing to each one in turn, ask, "What is this? What is it for?" Note whether the child answers correctly for each of the five punctuation marks.

To follow this assessment procedure efficiently, you will have to choose a book carefully and practice using the assessment questions enough times to become proficient. The procedure is easily carried out with Marie Clay's own test booklet, which is well worth the nominal cost. Alternatively, you can assess a child's concepts about print using any illustrated book that meets these criteria:

1. It should have a fairly large font size—16 points or larger.
2. It should have at least one pair of pages with print on one page and an illustration on the other.
3. It should have one page with at least three lines of print.
4. It should have one page with a single line of print.
5. It should have a page with examples of upper- and lowercase versions of at least two letters.
6. One page should have several marks of punctuation: a period, quotation marks, a question mark, and an exclamation point.

It is advisable to make up a record sheet that provides for the quick recording of information yielded by the assessment.

Alphabet Knowledge

Alphabet knowledge is technically one of the concepts about print, but it is so important that it deserves special treatment.

Alphabet knowledge has two faces: recognizing letters and being able to write them. Kindergartners' ability to recognize letters has been known to be an early predictor of later reading success (Walsh, Price, & Gillingham, 1988). Part of the reason for this, no doubt, is that those children who know more letters have had more exposure to print. But knowing letters is important in itself, for several reasons. First, even children who seemingly learn to recognize words as wholes, rather than analyzing them by their parts, need enough letter knowledge to identify at least a salient part of a word (Ehri, 1991). Second, and related to the previous point, children who voice-point (focusing visually on word units as they recite to themselves a known line of text) seem to rely on at least beginning letters to orient themselves to word units (Morris, 1993). Third, as children start to sound out words, or begin to use their fledgling knowledge of the relations between letters and sounds to read words, they will obviously need to be able to recognize several letters. Fourth, as children begin to invent spellings for words—itself an activity that helps children learn to segment words into phonemes and also to explore the relationships between letters and sounds (Clarke, 1988)—they will need to know how to name and produce several alphabet letters. Indeed, before any direct instruction in reading is likely to be of much benefit to children, those children must be able to recognize and produce most of the letters of the alphabet (Morris, 1990).

Children's ability to write letters should not be neglected. Most children in the primary grades and later who are considered to be disabled writers are hampered by *transcribing skills*—difficulty writing letters. In recent years, handwriting instruction for most children in American schools has been relatively neglected, and the impact on children with less home support for writing can be a serious setback (Graham et al., 1997). All children need a sound program of handwriting instruction beginning in kindergarten and continuing through the primary grades. Children who have special difficulty forming letters should be identified early and given special help.

Assessing Alphabet Knowledge. When testing students' alphabet knowledge, we ask them to recognize all of the letters of the alphabet in both uppercase and lowercase. We also ask them to write all of the letters once each, without specifying uppercase or lowercase. The letters are always presented in a scrambled sequence so that the children cannot use serial order as a cue to identifying a letter.

For a Letter Recognition Inventory, prepare the following letters as a separate display. Prepare another copy to use as a record sheet.

d f t g n b e h l v o y m a
r c q z u p j s i x k w

D F T G N B E H L V O Y M A
R C Q Z U P J S I X K W

As you proceed from left to right across the line, point to each letter and ask the child to identify it. Enter on the record sheet only a notation of what letters were misidentified or unnamed.

Many beginning readers will have difficulty recognizing *Z*, *Q*, *V*, and perhaps one or two letters that they encounter out of sequence. Difficulty with *b*, *d*, *p*, *q*, and *g* is also common because of directional confusion.

Children who confuse letters in isolation might still read them correctly in words, though they will be more uncertain than those who do not confuse them. Children who have difficulty identifying letters other than these will need more experience with print and letters as a top priority.

The Concept of Word

The concept of word is also technically a concept about print; but it may be more resistant to teaching than the other concepts, so we treat it here as a separate topic. The concept of word is the knowledge that spoken language comes in units of words, and that those units are represented in print by clusters of letters with spaces on either side. Having the concept of word enables students to track accurately between the words as they are spoken and the words as they are represented on the page.

Assessing the Concept of Word. To assess a student's concept of word, follow this procedure designed by Morris (1998).

Teach the student to memorize the poem shown below orally, *without showing her the written version.*

My little dog Petunia
Is a very strange dog.
She bellows like a mule
But she leaps like a frog.

Once the student can say the words from memory, show her the written poem and explain that these written words say the poem just learned.

Now, read through the poem at a slow natural rate, pointing to each word with your finger as you read it. Explain that you want the student to read the poem the way you did, but one line at a time.

Ask the student to say or read the first line, pointing to each word as she says it. On the record sheet shown in Figure 3.1, enter a score of 1 under *line-pointing* if she points

Concept of Word Assessment

Student: ______________________ Grade: ______________________

Teacher: ______________________ School: ______________________

Date: ______________________ Examiner: ______________________

	Line Pointing	*Word Pointing*
My little <u>dog</u> <u>Petunia</u> **1 2**	________	________
Is a <u>very</u> <u>strange</u> dog. **1 2**	________	________
She <u>bellows</u> <u>like</u> a mule **1 2**	________	________
But <u>she</u> leaps like a <u>frog</u>. **1 2**	________	________

Word-Pointing: ________ (of 4)

Word Identification: ________ (of 8)

Total Concept of Word (Line Pointing plus Word Pointing):

________ (of 12)

FIGURE 3.1 *Concept of Word Assessment*

to every word in that line correctly, and a score of 0 if she incorrectly points to any word in that line. Next, ask the student to point to the word *little.* Enter a score of 1 under *word pointing* if she points to it and 0 if she does not. Now ask her to point to the word *Petunia.* Enter a score of 1 under *word pointing* if she points to it and 0 if she does not.

Now go to the second line and repeat the process, testing first the student's voice-pointing and then the student's word pointing. Award 1 point if the student points to every word just as she says it, and a 0 if the student makes any errors. Then ask her to point to *very* and then to *strange.* Award one point for each word the student correctly points to, and a 0 for each error. Repeat these instructions for lines 3 and 4.

Phonological Awareness

Phonological awareness is the consciousness of the sounds of language. *Phonology* refers to the sound system of spoken language and is not concerned with written language. Hence phonological awareness does not include phonics because phonics deals with the relationship between alphabet letters and sounds. Phonological awareness includes the awareness of *syllables, onsets and rimes,* and *phonemes.*

- **Syllables** are the pulses of language. They are the "beats" we hear in *table* (two syllables), *heart* (one syllable), and *tricycle* (three syllables).
- **Onsets and rimes** are two parts of most single syllables: The onset is the first consonant sound or sounds, and the rime is the vowel and any consonant that follows. In *car* the onset is /k/ and the rime is /ar/; in *stop* the onset is /st/ and the rime is /op/; in *bee* the onset is /b/ and the rime is /ee/.
- **Phonemes** are the smallest speech sounds in language. *Dog* has three phonemes: /d/, /o/, and /g/. *Fort* has four phonemes: /f/, /o/, /r/, and /t/. (Note that we conventionally represent phonemes with slashes on either side.)

Hall and Moats (1999) present the following as abilities of normally developing children in kindergarten and first grade:

At the End of Kindergarten

- *At the syllable level:* Can identify single-syllable words that rhyme.
- *At the onset and rime level:* Can match a word with a rhyming word.
- *At the phoneme level:* Can pick out words that begin with the same sound and find an "odd word out" that doesn't begin with the same sound as the others.

Two Months into First Grade

- Given two letters (as on Scrabble chips), can combine them and pronounce the word they spell (*in, on, at, it, up*)
- Given a three-phoneme word, can say the word that is left when the first consonant is deleted: *bat/at, sit/it, cup/up.*

By the End of First Grade

- Can pronounce two-phoneme words so as to separate the phonemes: *T–oo; b–y.*
- Given longer words, can separate off the first consonant: *b–utterfly.*
- Given three isolated phonemes, can combine them to make a word: /s/ /i/ /t/ = *sit.*

The Importance of Phonological Awareness. To read in any writing system, a person should be able to make accurate mappings between the spoken units of a language and the written units. A logographic writing system such as that of Chinese is made up of written characters, or *zi,* that correspond to the spoken language at the whole-word level. In a mixed logographic and syllabic writing system, such as that of Japanese, some of the units of written language (the *kanji*) correspond to whole words, and some (the *katakana* and the *hiragana*) correspond to spoken syllables. In an alphabetic writing system, such as we use in English, the units of written language (the letters) correspond to the spoken language at the level of phonemes. Every language has phonemes, of course, but only alphabetic languages base their writing systems on them. This is a mixed blessing.

On the positive side, an alphabetic writing system gives us remarkable economy. We would need to have a million characters at the word level to write our immense vocabulary in English. We would need around 2,700 characters at the syllable level to spell that same vocabulary (Barker, 1986). But by writing our words at the phonemic level, we can make do with 26 letters. However, the economy of alphabetic writing systems is won at a cost, because phonemes are difficult to pay conscious attention to. The fact is, we don't always hear phonemes as isolated sound units. Of the three sounds in the word *cat,* for instance, only the vowel sound between the two consonant sounds is easily identified when the sounds of the word are cut apart and played back individually on a recording system (Lieberman, 1998). The consonant sounds /k/ and /t/ cannot be recognized unless they are pronounced with a vowel sound. We know the consonant sounds are there because we can substitute different consonant sounds and change the words. Changing /c/ in *cat* to /b/ gives us *bat.* Changing the final /t/ for /p/ gives us *cap.* But as the etymology of the word *consonant* (sound + together) makes clear, consonants are clearly perceived only in combination with vowels or with other consonants.

Phonemes may be difficult for children to pay attention to unless they have had rich experience in activities that play on speech sounds, such as reciting jump rope rhymes or nursery rhymes, clapping along to Dr. Seuss, or playing Pig Latin (Bradley & Bryant, 1985). Paradoxically, it may also be hard for children—or even older people—to be fully aware of phonemes unless they have had some experience trying to sound out written words or trying to write them with invented spelling. The awareness of phonemes seems to cut both ways: It helps, and it is helped by, even children's earliest efforts at beginning to read.

Those of us who can read face another challenge as we try to attend to phonemes because our knowledge of spelling may make it difficult to focus on sounds. For instance, we may have difficulty hearing that there are two phonemes in *shoe* (/sh/ is one phoneme, and /ū/ is another) or three phonemes in *thick* (/th/ is one phoneme, /ĭ/ is another, and /k/ is another). *Sing* has three phonemes: /s/, /ĭ/, and /ng/. What may be troubling us are the *digraphs:* the single phonemes that are spelled by two letters. Less troublesome for us are the *consonant blends,* like those spelled by the first three letters in *splash* and *street.* In consonant blends, each separate phoneme is sounded. We may be confused when consonant blends are spelled in ways we don't expect. For instance, *ax* has three phonemes, /a/, /k/, and /s/, and the two consonant sounds are spelled by the single letter X.

If the facts just described are not obvious, it is surely because our awareness of spelling has made it difficult for us to attend to sounds. If we are going to help children make connections between sounds and writing—that is, to read and write—we must push beyond these difficulties and become aware of speech sounds in words.

Note, too, that being aware of the effects of phonemes is different from perceiving them. Most five-year-old children will pick up the cat and not the bat when you ask them to, showing that they can perceive the difference between /k/ and /b/. Most will hesitate, though, if you ask them to tap their finger on the table to each of the three constituent sounds in *cat.* The difference is one of responding to the meaning of language—which young children find relatively natural—and consciously focusing on the sounds of language, or *phonological awareness,* which is much harder for children.

Why does phonological awareness matter? A host of research has pointed to the importance of children's understanding the *alphabetic nature of the English writing system,* or the *alphabetic principle.* As we said above, written English words are spelled by letters and letter clusters that represent individual speech sounds—phonemes. As children begin to read words, they can use their awareness of the alphabetic principle to sound out words by associating letters with the sounds they spell. They can do this matching, however, only if they can break words down into their phoneme constituents. If children are not fully able—and many children are not—to perceive the sound units that make up words, they will not be able to match many letters with sounds. A child who can perceive the beginning consonant sound but not the rest of the sounds in the word *back,* for instance, will read the word as if it were spelled *bxxx.* He may thus read the word as *bike, buck,* or even *ball* or *bust* unless the context helps narrow down his choices.

Other researchers, such as Stanovich (2000) and Iverson and Tunmer (1993), suggest a similar sequence (although they do not stress the concept of word).

Children can be taught to become aware of phonemes. Natural and child-friendly exercises in preschool that use nursery rhymes have been shown to be effective. With kindergarten through second-grade children, more focused sound awareness exercises have been shown to help (Blachman et al., 1995). Also, contextualized practices such as writing with invented spelling have been shown to be worthwhile in helping children develop phonemic segmentation, word reading ability, and spelling ability (Clarke, 1988). Snow, Burns, and Griffin (1998) remarked:

> It is important for parents and teachers to understand that invented spelling is not in conflict with correct spelling. On the contrary, it plays an important role in helping children learn how to write. When children use invented spelling, they are in fact exercising their growing knowledge of phonemes, the letters of the alphabet, and their confidence in the alphabetic principle. A child's 'iz' for the conventional

> 'is' can be celebrated as quite a breakthrough! It is the kind of error that shows you that the child is thinking independently and quite analytically about the sounds of words and the logic of spelling. (p. 102)

In the following pages, we will look first at ways of assessing children's awareness of phonemes and then at ways of helping children develop awareness of them.

Assessing Phonological Awareness. Phonological awareness has many aspects, including the awareness of rhymes and the ability to manipulate phonemes in many ways—isolating them, comparing them, adding them, deleting them, separating them, and more.

Distinguishing rhyming words from non-rhyming words. This is a test that should be administered to an individual child. Say aloud the following pairs of words. Ask the child to say either "They rhyme" or "They don't rhyme."

cat	**rat**	____________	**lid**	**hill**	____________
dog	**log**	____________	**ham**	**lamb**	____________
pick	**bog**	____________	**me**	**heel**	____________
cut	**rut**	____________	**sick**	**lick**	____________
see	**tea**	____________	**peel**	**key**	____________

Score:__________/10.

Producing rhymes. Now ask the student to "Say a word that rhymes with the word I say."

see	____________	**car**	____________
fit	____________	**fill**	____________
pad	____________	**pick**	____________
pat	____________	**say**	____________
cut	____________	**go**	____________

Score:__________/10.

Phoneme isolation. Say the following words aloud. Ask the child to say the first sound in each word.

Example: ***b*** + ***ox*** ➤ ***box***

car	______	**chip**	______
seal	______	**thin**	______
dog	______	**fill**	______
bag	______	**tent**	______
land	______		

Score:__________/10.

Phoneme comparison. Show the child the following sets of four pictures (see Figure 3.2). Ask the child first to say the names aloud (and correct any errors). Then the child should say which word does not begin the same way as the others. Demonstrate the activity with the first set (marked "0").

Phoneme addition. Say these words one at a time. After each word, say, "Add a sound to this word to make a new word." The child may add any sound to make a new word—for instance to *at* she may add *h, c, b, m, p,* etc. Demonstrate with the example first. Write what the child says in the blank and then score each response as correct or not correct.

at	______	**ill**	______
up	______	**ad**	______
all	______	**ad**	______
it	______	**ark**	______
an	______	**ail**	______

Score:__________/10.

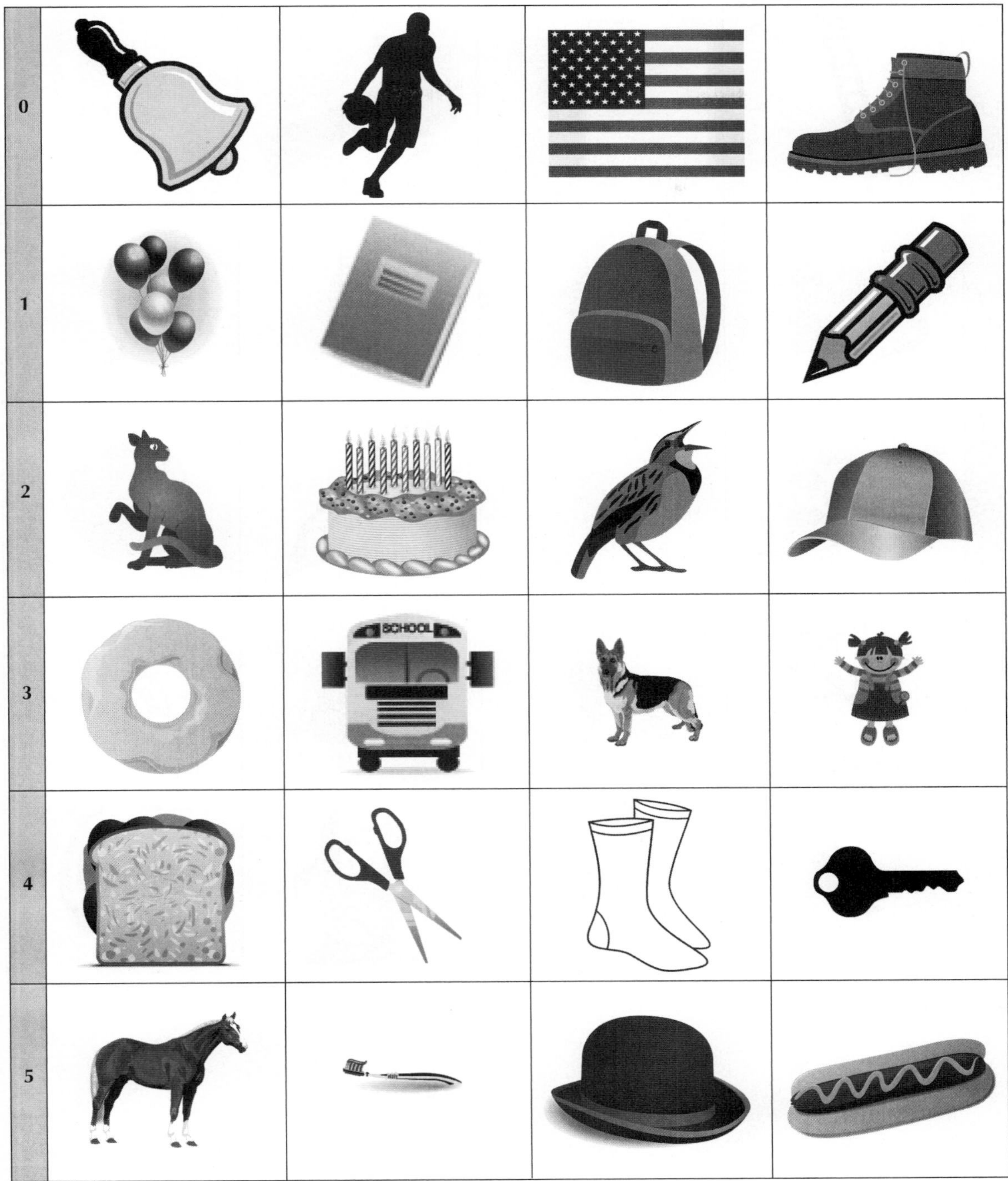

FIGURE 3.2 *Phoneme Comparison*

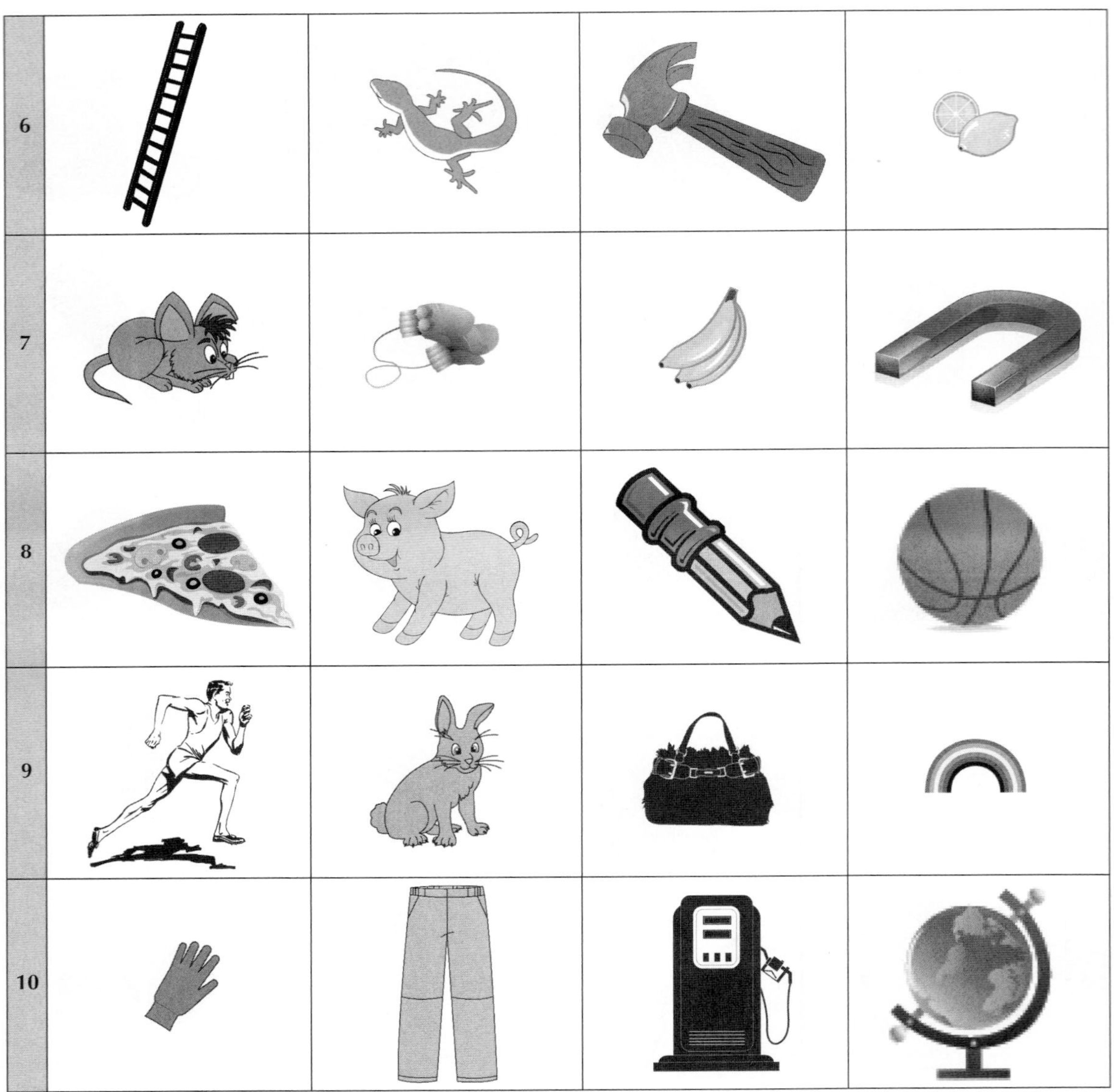

FIGURE 3.2 *Continued*

Phoneme subtraction. Say these words one at a time. After saying each word, say, "Take away the first sound in this word to make a new word." Demonstrate with the example first. Write what the child says in the blank and then score each response as correct or not correct.

Example: ***box – b→ ox***

cat	____________	**raid**	____________
cup	____________	**slip**	____________
ball	____________	**spill**	____________
fill	____________	**spark**	____________
loops	____________	**snail**	____________

Score:__________/10.

Phoneme segmentation. The Yopp/Singer test of phoneme segmentation is done as follows. You say:

> Today we're going to play a word game. I'm going to say a word, and I want you to break the word apart. You are going to tell me each sound of the word in order. For example, if I say *old,* you will say o-l-d. Let's try a few words together. (Yopp, 1988, p. 166)

You follow with three more demonstration words: *ride, go,* and *man.* Praise the child if she is correct and correct her if she is wrong. After the trials, read the 22 words to the child, and have her break each word apart as it is read. You should give praise or correction after each word. Note that the number of phonemes or separate sounds in each word is given in parentheses after the word. Score each word "1" if the child separately pronounces all of the phonemes in the word, or "0" if she does not. The words are in the following list.

dog (3)	______________	**do** (2)	______________
fine (3)	______________	**keep** (3)	______________
she (2)	______________	**no** (2)	______________
grew (3)	______________	**wave** (3)	______________
red (3)	______________	**that** (3)	______________
sat (3)	______________	**me** (2)	______________
lay (2)	______________	**race** (3)	______________
zoo (2)	______________	**three** (3)	______________
job (3)	______________	**in** (2)	______________
ice (2)	______________	**at** (2)	______________
top (3)	______________	**by** (2)	______________

Score:__________/22.

Assessing Phonemic Awareness by Means of Invented Spelling. Another way to observe whether a first-grade child has phonemic awareness is to ask him to spell words that he does not already know. When a child is asked to spell unknown words, he must rely upon his *invented spelling*, the inner capacity to forge connections between letters and sounds. Children have an amazing intuitive ability to invent spellings, and we can learn much about their word knowledge by looking at their invented productions.

A procedure for testing phonemic segmentation (after Morris, 1993), then, is to have the child spell the following list of words as you call them out. Then you can count the number of phonemes the child reasonably attempted to represent. (Guides to scoring each word are presented in parentheses.)

bite	(three phonemes: BIT = 3 points; BT = 2 points, BRRY, etc. = 1 point)
seat	(three phonemes: SET or CET = 3 points; ST, CT = 2 points)
dear	(three phonemes: DER = 3 points; DIR or DR = 2 points)
bones	(four phonemes: BONS or BONZ = 4 points; BOS or BOZ = 3 points)

mint	(four phonemes: MENT or MINT = 4 points; MET or MIT = 3 points; MT = 2 points)
rolled	(four phonemes: ROLD = 4 points; ROL or ROD = 3 points)
race	(three phonemes: RAS, RAC, or RAEC = 3 points, RC or RS = 2 points)
roar	(three phonemes: ROR or ROER = 3 points; RR = 2 points)
beast	(four phonemes: BEST = 4 points; BES or BST = 3 points; BS or BT = 2 points)
groan	(four phonemes: GRON = 4 points; GRN = 3 points; GN = 2 points)
TOTAL:	35 points

Explain to the child that you are going to ask him to spell some words you know he doesn't know how to spell. He will have to figure out the spellings as best he can. After you call out each word (at least twice, and as many more times as the student requests), ask the student to try to spell each sound in the word. If the student says he can't, ask him to listen to the way the word begins. What sound does it start with? Ask him to write down a letter for that sound and letters for any other sounds he can hear. If the student is not sure how to spell a sound, ask him to write a little dash (—).

After reading all 10 words (fewer if the test seems too arduous for a particular child), count the number of reasonable letters the child wrote for each word and compare that to the number of phonemes in the word. A child who consistently writes three or four letters that show some reasonable connection to the sounds in the word appears to be able to segment phonemes. A child who writes nothing or strings together many letters indiscriminately is not yet able to segment phonemes, and a child who writes one or two reasonable letters per word is just beginning to segment phonemes. You might calculate a score for phonemic segmentation by scoring each word according to the guide at the right of each word and then comparing the total number of points the child receives to the total possible.

Oral Language Development

Earlier we mentioned that a simple view of reading holds that a child should be able to render print into speech, and then comprehend the speech. Here we will suggest that in addition to phonological awareness (see above), the aspects of oral language that are most important to reading are vocabulary, syntax, and decontextualized language.

Vocabulary. Vocabulary knowledge is a strong predictor of later reading achievement (Cunningham & Stanovich, 1997). It is also a high divider of children (Hart & Risley, 1995). Studies show huge differences—four-fold differences—between the number of words spoken to children in their years before entering school, and also huge differences in children's vocabulary sizes (at least two-fold) all through the grades (Beck, McKeown, & Kucan, 2002). We also know that there are many words to be known—88,500 different words are contained in all of a typical student's school books through ninth grade (Nagy & Anderson, 1984). Teachers don't need to teach all of those words, fortunately. Beck et al. have found it useful to divide those words into three different levels of vocabulary: tiers I, II, and III. Tier I words are those children learn on their own. Tier III words are technical terms that are almost exclusively seen in specialized subjects. Tier II words are those we should worry about: These are words of wide usage that children might not already know. Beck et al. suggest that teachers can teach Tier II words. They should select them according to three criteria:

1. **Importance and Utility.** They should be words that students will hear and use often.
2. **Instructional Potential.** They should be words that will be fruitful to teach, because they are visible in daily life or they often come up in school contexts.
3. **Conceptual Understanding.** They are words that will help children put names to concepts they are trying to understand.

Assessing vocabulary. Vocabulary assessment is a bit of an enigma. We know that many students need to increase their vocabularies (Weizman & Snow, 2001), and that the U.S. Department of Education lists vocabulary as one of the five essential components of reading (along with phonological awareness, phonics, reading fluency, and comprehension) that deserve concentrated attention from teachers. Teachers are often urged to assess children's vocabulary (see for instance, Silverman & Crandell, 2010). Yet it is not completely clear how teachers should go about making the assessment. There are instruments on the market for assessing vocabulary, but the ones most widely used are quite expensive. For example, the most popular instrument, the Peabody Picture Vocabulary Test, 4th Edition, costs $400, and the training CD is another $150. Besides, the PPVT and other instruments like it are meant to be administered by trained psychologists.

Vocabulary assessment is complicated for several reasons. One is that we mean different things by "knowing" a word. For any word, you can say:

I have never heard of this word.
I have heard of this word, but I'm not sure what it means.
I know generally what this word means—-it is "good" or "bad," for instance.
I know what this word means, and I can use it in a sentence.

Another is that many words—and especially Tier II words!—have multiple meanings. *Drift*, for instance, can mean "to move aimlessly," as in "The canoe drifted off course." But it can also mean "the general idea," as in "I got the drift of what they were saying." *Gee* can be an expression of surprise, or it can be a command to make a mule turn right.

Yet another reason vocabulary can be difficult to measure is that there is a vast number of words that might be learned, but there is no agreement over which words children should learn at any age (Beck et al., 2002). Thus it may be unreliable to test children on a small sample of words and expect their performance to indicate what portion of a larger vocabulary they might know.

With all of those caveats in place, we would suggest you make frequent observations of each student's language use. Your observations might be guided by rubric such as is shown in Figure 3.3.

	Nearly always	Much of the time, but with significant gaps	Almost never
The child uses words with enough precision and clarity that other students understand his or her meaning.			
The child can use words that express her meaning clearly in a range of situations (classroom discussions, social interactions, storytelling).			
The child appears to understand classroom instructions and explanations.			
The child follows read-alouds with apparent understanding.			

FIGURE 3.3 *Observation Rubric*

Keep notes on each child. If you consistently make observations in the columns toward the right, you should discuss the child's case with your school psychologist, since it is likely that more elaborate testing is in order.

Syntax, or Grammar. Syntax is the ability to arrange words in grammatical strings, and also to deploy grammatical morphemes such as plural markers and verb endings. Syntax is not often assessed in isolation by teachers; it may be considered one aspect of a child's difficulty in oral language comprehension. Back in the 1970s, the late Marie Clay and her colleagues developed a simple assessment instrument for children's syntax. They were influenced by the intensive psycholinguistic research going on at the time into children's language acquisition, but their general approach to the assessment of syntax has been supported by a more recent review by a panel of experts (Lust, Flynn, & Foley, 1996). *The Record of Oral Language* was recently published in a new edition by Heinemann (Clay, Gill, Glynn, McNaughton, & Salmon, 2007).

The Record of Oral Language is a sentence imitation task. The teacher reads to the child from several sets of sentences of increasing grammatical complexity:

Level I: My brother's knees are dirty.
Level II: That big dog over there is going to be my brother's.
Level III: Be as quiet as you can when your father's asleep.

The child is asked to repeat each sentence back verbatim. Research has supported the supposition that in order to repeat the sentence, the child has to process that sentence through her or his own understanding of grammar (Lust, Flynn, & Foley, 1996). Thus the child's ability to repeat a sentence verbatim is an indication of her or his development of power over syntax.

The Record of Oral Language contains suggestions for teachers to help children add to their repertoire of sentence structures.

Decontextualized Language. A mother says, "Put that down! Bad boy!" and snatches a cell phone away from a frightened child.

Contrast that scenario with this one: A father sits down with his daughter and says, "Guess what? As I was walking home from work, I heard a buzzing sound up in the sky. I looked up and saw an airplane, flying very slowly. Suddenly, a dark blob fell from the airplane, and then another, and then another. Then bright colors appeared above each dark blob—red, blue, and yellow. They were parachutes! The people in parachutes drifted slowly down until they disappeared behind the trees and I couldn't see them anymore."

The language in the first example is *contextualized:* the child's deed and the cell phone, and the mother's angry tone of voice and frowning face convey virtually all of the meaning. Even if the child doesn't understand the words, he knows what is being communicated.

The language in the second example is *decontextualized.* There is no airplane present, no buzzing, no blobs, and no parachutes to support the meaning of what the father says. The child must depend entirely upon the words her father speaks and her imagination to create an understanding of the scene. This is called decontextualized language because the context in which the language is uttered and heard provides little or no support to the meaning. The words, and the listener, must create understanding on their own.

A child who often hears decontextualized language learns more vocabulary than one who hears mostly contextualized speech (Dickinson & Tabors, 2001). That child also gets more practice in constructing understanding from language—including imaging, following sequences of events, responding with emotions to the contours of a plot, and following the explanations of expository texts (Bus et al., 1995). That child will be well prepared for reading, too, because written language is usually decontextualized. Note that you understood the father's account of the parachutes by *reading* it—without seeing airplanes or parachutes, either.

Assessing for knowledge of decontextualized language. Children's knowledge of decontextualized language is not assessed directly. Rather, the results of having familiarity with decontextualized language will be evident in

- Children's ability to follow stories and other structures of text.
- Children's ability to take part in conversations about things and events outside of the here and now.

Narrative comprehension. Paris and Paris (2001) developed the Narrative Comprehension Scale or NC to assess the narrative competence of children who cannot yet read words. The point of the assessment is to evaluate those "outside-in" factors of emergent literacy that are outside the act of cracking the code. There is an old joke about a silly person who was looking for his car keys under the street light, even though he had dropped them in a dark alley. When someone asked why, the man responded, "Because the light is better here." Paris and Paris surmise that reading experts may be placing undue emphasis on aspects of reading such as phonological awareness and awareness of letter-to-sound relationships (decoding) mainly because we have better measures available for those components. It follows that schools also may be devoting undue amounts of time to teaching these components. Parents, on the other hand, focus on constructing meaning when they read with children—who the characters are, what is happening, and how they feel about it. If Paris and Paris are correct, we may be neglecting the need to develop more holistic approaches to emergent literacy and beginning reading in our push to develop such skills as phonological awareness.

The Narrative Comprehension assessment consists of three parts: a picture walk, a retelling, and a narrative probe. All three are done using a wordless book. The assessment procedure was developed using *Robot-bot-bot* by Fernando Krahn (1979) and *A Boy, A Dog, and Frog* by Mercer Mayer (2003). The procedure can also be done using a highly visual picture book (Pam Conrad's *The Tub People* will work nicely) without emphasizing the words.

Picture walk. The picture walk tasks yields a snapshot of a child's ability to engage with a book. The task may be used by itself as a measure of children's ability to interact with a book, minus the focus on print. Or it may be followed by either or both of the next two tasks—retelling and prompted comprehension—for a more thorough look at children's comprehension of stories.

To carry out the picture walk task, begin by handing a child a wordless picture book or highly visual book, and allowing the child to explore it for a few minutes. Then ask the child to "Say out loud whatever you are thinking about the pictures or the story." Score the child's performance during the picture walk using the rubric in Figure 3.4. The rubric describes five aspects: Book handling, Engagement, Picture comments, Storytelling comments, and Comprehension strategies.

Picture Walk Element	Score Description	Score
1. Book Handling Skills: Orients book correctly, has sense of appropriate viewing speed and order, where viewing errors include skipping pages, speeding through pages, etc.	Incorrectly handles book and makes more than 2 viewing errors	0
	Makes 1–2 viewing errors (i.e., skips pages)	1
	Handles book appropriately, making no viewing errors	2
2. Engagement: Behavioral and emotional involvement during picture walk, as judged by attention, interest in book, affect, and effort.	Displays off-task behavior or negative comments	0
	Displays quiet, sustained behavior	1
	Shows several examples of attention, affect, interest, or effort (i.e., spontaneous comments)	2

FIGURE 3.4 *Assessment and Rubric for the Picture Walk*

Source: Alison H. Paris and Scott G. Paris. *CIERA Children's Comprehension of Narrative Picture Books*, CIERA Report #3-012, Appendix A, http://www.ciera.org. Reprinted by permission of Scott G. Paris.

Picture Walk Element	Score Description	Score
3. Picture Comments: Discrete comments about a picture, which can include descriptions of objects, characters, emotions, actions, and opinions as well as character vocalizations.	Makes no picture comments	0
	Makes 1 picture comment or verbalization	1
	Makes 2 or more comments or verbalizations about specific pictures	2
4. Storytelling Comments: Makes comments that go across pictures which demonstrate an understanding that the pictures tell a coherent story—can include narration, dialogue, using book language and storytelling voice.	Makes no storytelling comments	0
	Provides storytelling elements, but not consistently	1
	Through narration or dialogue, connects story events and presents a coherent story line	2
5. Comprehension Strategies: Displays vocalizations or behaviors which show attempts at comprehension, such as self-corrects, looks back/ahead in book, asks questions for understanding, makes predictions about story.	Demonstrates no comprehension strategies	0
	Exhibits 1 instance of comprehension strategies	1
	Demonstrates comprehension strategies at least 2 or more times	2

Subtotal score:____________/10.

FIGURE 3.4 *Continued*

Story retelling. Immediately following the Picture Walk, the book is taken away from the child, and the child is asked to retell as much of the story as possible. When the child completes the retelling, one prompt is given by asking the child if (s)he can remember anything else about the story. Children's retellings are transcribed, and the information is categorized according to the six following story grammar elements: setting, characters, goal/initiating event, problem/episodes, solution, and resolution/ending. One point is awarded for phrases indicating the presence of each story element. Retelling scores range from 0 to 6, with 0 points demonstrating that the child does not recall any of the story elements and 6 signifying that the child's retelling includes phrases representing all of the elements. Figure 3.5 provides a rubric for assessing story retelling.

Prompted comprehension. For a further assessment of the child's comprehension of the story from the wordless picture book, you may administer a third assessment task, prompted comprehension. Paris and Paris define narrative comprehension as "the construction of meaning from pictures by integrating information across pages so as to create coherent and connected understandings."

Tell the child that you are going to read the book together one more time. This time you guide the page turning, and ask ten prepared questions as you open on each page. Five of the questions will test *explicit comprehension* and five will test *implicit comprehension.* Figure 3.6 provides a rubric for assessing prompted comprehension.

Note that after each question, Paris and Paris recommend giving the child one more prompt to give a more complete answer, such as "Are there any other characters in this story?"

Widely Distributed Tests of Emergent Literacy

Virtually all of the aspects of emergent literacy that have been discussed in this chapter have been incorporated into programmed bundles of instruments. Two that will be reviewed here are DIBELS and PALS.

School districts in many states are using DIBELS, the Dynamic Indicators of Basic Early Literacy Skills, which was developed at the University of Oregon with a federal grant and is available to teachers without cost online. This test begins with a preschool version that assesses initial sounds or *onset fluency.* At the kindergarten level, there are added tests of phonemic segmentation fluency, letter naming fluency, and nonsense word reading fluency. These continue through first grade, where an oral reading fluency measure is also added. It continues through third grade. These are called fluency tests because children's responses are timed, and the speed of the child's responses is noted in addition to accuracy (see **http://dibels.uoregon.edu/measures.php**).

The Phonological Awareness Literacy Survey (PALS) (**http://pals.virginia.edu/**) is provided to school districts in Virginia and is widely used elsewhere as both a screening and a monitoring tool.

The Illinois Snapshot of Early Literacy (**http://www2.nl.edu/READING_CENTER/**) is promoted by that state as a screening tool.

The Texas Education Agency developed the Texas Primary Reading Inventory (**http://www.tpri.org/**), with versions for kindergarten through third grades that can be administered as a screening, diagnosis, and monitoring tool.

Assessment and Rubric for Story Retelling		
Setting	Makes no mention of the place or time the story occurred	**0**
	Mentions the place or time the story occurred	**1**
Characters	Makes no mention of the characters in the story	**0**
	Mentions the characters in the story, either by name or by description	**1**
Goal/initiating event	Makes no mention of the event that sets in motion the main action of the story, or the goal the characters seek to fulfill	**0**
	Mentions the event that sets in motion the main action of the story, or the goal the characters seek to fulfill	**1**
	Mentions the attempts the characters make to reach their goal, or the sequence of actions that follow from the initiating event	**1**
Solution	Makes no mention of the solution to the problem, or the characters' success in reaching their goal	**0**
	Mentions the solution to the problem, or the characters' success in reaching their goal	**1**

Subtotal score:____________/6.

FIGURE 3.5 *Assessment and Rubric for Story Retelling*

Source: Alison H. Paris and Scott G. Paris. *CIERA Children's Comprehension of Narrative Picture Books,* CIERA Report #3-012, Appendix A, http://www.ciera.org. Reprinted by permission of Scott G. Paris.

Explicit Questions			
Question Type	**Description**	**Rubric**	**Score (Circle one)**
1 Characters	[With the book closed, ask] "Who are the characters (or people, or animals) in this story?"	Response indicates the main characters in the story.	**2**
		Response contains at least 2 of the story's characters.	**1**
		Response provides only 1 character or answer is inappropriate.	**0**
2 Setting	[With the book closed, ask] "Where does this story happen (or take place)?"	Response indicates an understanding of multiple settings.	**2**
		Response provides only one setting.	**1**
		Response is not an appropriate setting.	**0**
3 Initiating event	[Point to the picture that shows the initiating event and say] "Tell me what happens at this point in the story. Why is this an important part of the story?"	Response identifies the initiating event and links it with other relevant story information, e.g., with the problem.	**2**
		Response identifies the story element, in this case the initiating event.	**1**
		Response fails to identify the initiating event.	**0**

FIGURE 3.6 *Prompted Comprehension Assessment and Rubric*

Source: Alison H. Paris and Scott G. Paris. *CIERA Children's Comprehension of Narrative Picture Books,* CIERA Report #3-012, Appendix A, http://www.ciera.org. Reprinted by permission of Scott G. Paris.

4	**Problem**	[Point to the picture that shows the problem and say] "If you were telling someone this story, what would you say is going on now? Why did this happen?"	Response identifies the problem and links it with other relevant story information, e.g., with the initiating action.	**2**
			Response identifies the story element, in this case the problem.	**1**
			Response fails to identify the problem.	**0**
5	**Outcome Resolution**	[Point to the picture that shows the resolution of the problem and say] "What happened here? Why does this happen?"	Response identifies the outcome resolution and links it with other relevant story information, e.g., the problem or the initiating action.	**2**
			Response identifies the story element, in this case the resolution of the problem.	**1**
			Response fails to identify the resolution of the problem.	**0**
		B. Implicit Questions		
6	**Feelings**	[Point to a picture where a character or characters are having an emotional reaction and ask] "Tell me what the people are feeling in this picture. Why do you think so?"	Response indicates the inference of appropriate character feelings and connects the feelings to other pages or events.	**2**
			Response indicates the inference of appropriate character feelings.	**1**
			Response is not an appropriate inference of character feelings.	**0**

FIGURE 3.6 *Continued*

7	**Causal Inference**	[Point to a picture that shows an important action and ask] "Why did _____ what she (or he) just did here?"	Response is an appropriate inference that is explained by using events from multiple pages.	**2**
			Response is an appropriate inference that is derived at the page level.	**1**
			Response fails to include an appropriate causal inference.	**0**
8	**Dialogue**	[Point to a picture where people are talking and ask]: "What do you think the people would be saying here? Why would they be saying that?"	Response indicates the inference of appropriate character dialogue and connects the dialogue to other pages or events.	**2**
			Response indicates the inference of appropriate character dialogue.	**1**
			Response does not concern character dialogue or is not appropriate.	**0**
9	**Prediction**	[Point to a picture in the book that precedes an important event and say] "This is the last picture in the story. What do you think happens next? Why do you think so?"	Response represents a prediction that used previous action or pages from the story.	**2**
			Response indicates a prediction that could be made based only on the last picture of the story.	**1**
			Response does not contain an appropriate prediction.	**0**

FIGURE 3.6 *Continued*

10	**Theme**	[With the book closed, ask] "In thinking about everything that you learned after reading this book---," (now frame a question that guides the child to think about and respond to the theme of the book. For *Robot-bot-bot,* Paris and Paris ask "If you knew that your friend's dad was bringing home a robot for his family, what would you tell the dad to help him so that the same thing that happened in this story doesn't happen to him? Why would you tell him that?")	Response indicates the incorporation of multiple events in order to create a narrative-level theme.	**2**
			Response is a simple theme that uses information from one aspect of the story.	**1**
			Response does not indicate an understanding of any theme.	**0**

Subtotal score:_______/20.

FIGURE 3.6 *Continued*

Most of these instruments will offer (for a fee) electronically based data management and reporting services that keep track of children's and schools' scores in comparison to those of other groups. Some also offer instructional suggestions based on the children's scores.

Teaching for Emergent Literacy

The techniques that are used to help each youngster's literacy emerge, whether in a classroom or a clinic, should derive from three guiding principles. First, they should include immersion in real reading and real writing in real contexts, because teachers are unlikely to anticipate all of the things students may need to understand about literacy, so a rich immersion experience is a safe way of offering many lessons at once. Second, they should respond as much as possible to what the child knows and needs to know about reading and writing. And third, they should include targeted instruction, too, on those aspects of literacy we know that children need to develop, even when that includes specific instruction.

Teaching Print Orientation Concepts

How do we help children to develop print orientation concepts? One solution is a big book: a giant, 3-foot-high version of a trade book. The teacher can place a big book on a chart stand, where it can be readily seen by a group of children. The teacher can have them read along as he points out features of print: where the text begins on a page, the left-to-right direction of reading, the return sweep, the spaces that demarcate words, and punctuation.

Big books were originally made by the teacher or a parent volunteer. They might be chosen to accompany a reading series of which the children have copies—that way the children can look for the features on the page in front of them that the teacher points out in the big book. Big book versions are also made up from favorite trade books. When children already know and are excited about the story line, they can more easily pay attention to the way print portrays the text, which is the point of this sort of lesson. Big book versions of children's books are now available from many sources, although many teachers still prepare their own.

Teaching the Alphabet

Many children enter kindergarten knowing most of their letters. Middle-class children are often able to point to and name all but Q, Z, J, and Y—unless, of course, their own names contain some of these letters—and write a dozen or more letters. Some children, however, enter kindergarten knowing very few letters and come to know letters in school only slowly and with difficulty (Ehri, 1989). Although it might be possible to recognize a few words by memorizing their overall appearance (focusing on the "eyes" in *look,* for example), knowing the letters is necessary for learning to read appreciable numbers of words and to write using invented spelling.

Marie Clay's work (1975) and the work of Harste et al. (1985) suggest that many children can invent their way to letter knowledge if they have models of print around them and are given early opportunities to write. However, by kindergarten, and certainly by first grade, those children who do not know most of their letters need more explicit teaching. Indeed, many studies show that children who know many letters in kindergarten are more likely to read by the end of first grade than are children who know few (Walsh et al., 1988).

How can we teach children the alphabet?

Alphabet Books. Alphabet books are arranged A to Z, usually with examples of both uppercase and lowercase letters and an illustrative picture that begins with the sound of the letter. Kate Greenaway's alphabet book, first published a century ago, is still in print, and more and more gorgeous and innovative alphabet books come out every year.

Older children in the school can make alphabet books for younger children. Or younger children can prepare alphabet books themselves, with guidance from the teacher. Either way, it is highly desirable for every preschool and kindergarten child to have a personal alphabet book.

When children take alphabet books home, send along instructions to the parent to take the time to listen to the child read the alphabet book. Remind the parent to make this an enjoyable occasion—certainly not a drill session.

Letter-Matching Games. Once the children know some letters, you can play letter-matching games with them along the lines of the concentration game. First, make up two sets of five different lowercase letters on cards. Turn these cards face down on the table, and turn up a pair. If they are the same, you have to name them, and then you can have them. Work through all of the lowercase letters in this way. Then do the same with the uppercase letters. After children become proficient at matching lowercase letters in this way, they are ready to play with uppercase and lowercase versions of the same letters.

Sounds and Letters. As you will undoubtedly note from the foregoing discussion of concepts about print, the following procedure assumes that children are well along in their awareness of sounds in words and their notions of beginnings and ends of words. For children who have reached these milestones, this procedure, from the work of the McCrackens (1987), is a worthwhile activity.

Working with first graders, they will introduce a letter, say, M:

1. They write M on the board.
2. They pronounce the letter slowly and ask the children to watch their mouths as they say it.
3. They ask the children to pronounce the letter slowly and pay attention to how it feels in their mouths.
4. They ask the children to write the letter on their individual chalk tablets, saying the letter aloud as they do so.
5. Later, they hand the children specially prepared tablets, as shown in Figure 3.7.

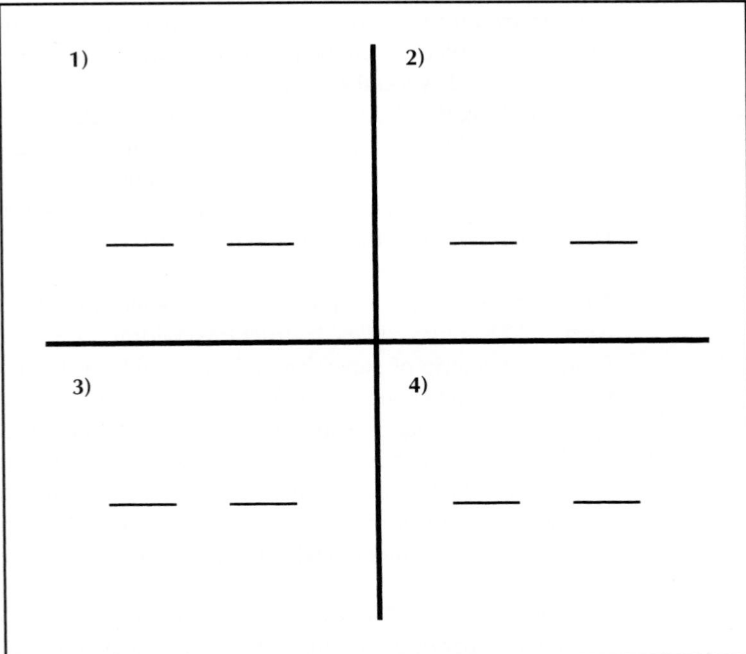

FIGURE 3.7 *The McCrackens' Procedure for Teaching Letters*

The teacher says the word *me* and asks the child to write the letter M in the appropriate slot in the square marked 1. Does the M come at the beginning of the word *me* or at the end? For square 2, the word is *may;* for square 3, the word is *am;* and for square 4, the word is *um.*

Teaching the Concept of Word

The concept of word, as we have seen, is the important ability to relate words in the mind with words on the page. Research by Morris (1981, 1993) has suggested that children need to develop this ability before they will advance very far in their word recognition ability because they need a concept of word to be able to focus their attention properly on word units in print. Several of the tasks that we have already introduced in this chapter as assessment devices work quite well as instructional devices, too.

The Voice-Pointing Procedure. One way to use this procedure is to read a text aloud—say, a big book, or a dictated chant on the chart—pointing to the print, one word at a time. Also, call attention to the word saying, "See? That word is 'fish.' See the F it begins with? That's the word 'fish.'"

When children have memorized a text, as in a little book, encourage them to point to the words as they read.

Cut-Apart Words. Have a child memorize a four- or five-word sentence or a line of poetry. On a piece of tag board, write down the sentence as the child says the words. Read the words several times, pointing to them. Then cut the words apart, scramble them, and ask the child to rearrange them correctly.

If the child can rearrange them successfully, take away a word, and ask the child which word it was. If the child cannot rearrange the words successfully, make a copy of the line, leave it intact, and ask the child to rearrange the cut-apart words underneath by matching them to the words in the intact version.

Dictated Experience Accounts. Write a small version of text and duplicate it so that each child has two copies. Instruct the children to cut the paper so that each sentence is on its own strip of paper. Then they should cut these sentence strips into individual words. The teacher should circulate among them to identify the words they are cutting apart and encourage the children to identify them. Once the words are cut apart, the children should match the cut-apart words with the same words on the other, intact sheet, laying each word above the intact word so that it does not cover it.

Once children can do this sort of activity fairly easily, they can arrange the cut-apart words into sentences without using the intact words as a guide.

Morning Message. The morning message is a limited and more focused version of a dictated experience account. Morning message is both predictable and meaningful because the activity follows the same format every time it is used, yet it has important information. And it builds a sense of community among students and makes children feel important.

Morning message is used to open the day in many kindergarten and first-grade classrooms. The message is written on chart paper and an easel, or on a part of the chalkboard that will not be erased.

A typical message says something like this:

> Today is *(day of the week)*. (The date may be included, too.) The weather today is _______. Our classroom helpers are *(students' names are written)*. Today we will _______ *(a special event is written)*. _______ (the name of a student) has a birthday today.

The teacher has the option of putting words for the day of the week, the month, and the weather on a tag board with pieces of tape on the back for posting on the chart.

After the plan for the day is discussed with the children, the teacher and students together decide what will be written. They say each sentence more than once to fix it in memory. The teacher begins by writing the first few words; then she invites one child at a time up to help with the writing.

Morning message is a fine opportunity to teach about written language: direction of print, concept of word, capitalization, and letters and sounds. The message should be read again and again for practice once it is written and left up so that some children can revisit it.

Teaching to Build Phonological Awareness

Activities to boost phonological awareness are recommended for kindergarten through grade 3 (National Reading Panel, 2000). They may also be recommended for older children whose reading development is considerably delayed. Activities to develop phonological awareness need not take much time during the day. Six or 7 minutes a day yields the 20 hours a year that the National Reading Panel (2000) recommends.

Activities to develop phonological awareness have been shown to be most effective when they work with letters at the same time they call attention to sounds (Blachman et al., 1995; National Reading Panel, 2000). Perhaps this is because letters provide a visual stimulus to accompany an auditory stimulus, but in any case, associating sounds with letters will help children learn to read and spell.

Activities to boost phonological awareness can take place at several levels.

At the Syllable Level

- Children can clap the syllables in their names—"Clau-di-a," "Sha-nee-sha," "Char-lie."
- Children can raise their hands when the teacher says a word with one syllable, two syllables, three syllables.

- The teacher says, "Two syllables!" and calls on children to say words with two syllables. Then he says, "One syllable!" and the children must say words of one syllable, and so on.

At the Onset and Rime Level

- Children are asked to supply rhymes to complete couplets like:

  Ding, dong, dell
  Kitty's in the _______ (well)
  Ding, dong, divver
  Kitty's in the _______ (river)
  Ding, dong, dimming pool
  Kitty's in the _______ (swimming pool)

- Children are told a target word, such as *say*, and asked to raise their hands when they hear a word that rhymes with it, as the teacher says a list of words: "*Be, bet, back, bay.*"
- The teacher says a word such as *hat*. Then she challenges the children to say a new word that begins with the sound she calls out: /s/, /b/, /f/.

At the Phoneme Level

- Sing a song that substitutes the vowel sounds:

  I like to eat, eat, eat, apples and bananas
  I like to eat, eat, eat, apples and bananas.
  I like to oot, oot, oot, ooples and bonoonoos.
  I like to oot, oot, oot, ooples and bonoonoos.
  I like to oat, oat, oat, oples and bononos.
  I like to oat, oat, oat, oples and bononos.

- Practice taking words apart into their phonemes:

  If I say *dog* /d/ /o/ /g/, you say *cat, ball, foot* the same way.

- Say a series of speech sounds and ask children to say the word they form:

  /f/ /i/ /t/ = *feet;* /s/ /o/ /p/ = *soap.*

- Using sound boxes (Elkonin, 1973), have children shove letter markers into boxes as they emphasize the phonemes while saying the words.

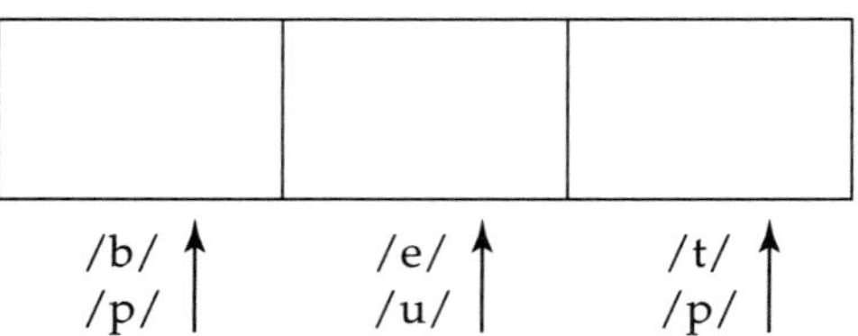

Teaching for Many Things at Once

Many important aspects of emergent literacy are taught in holistic lessons that combine reading and discussing written language. In previous sections we have stressed the importance of oral language development—vocabulary, syntax, and decontextualized language. We have also underscored the importance of comprehension of stories and other structures of text. All of these things can be taught by reading aloud and discussing books, and also by storytelling. However, be alert to the fact that specific language skills such as vocabulary can be taught even more effectively if the book and story discussions are enhanced by targeted teaching strategies (Dickinson, 1994). Later in this chapter, we will give suggestions for such instruction. Also, please note that children's language learning improves even further if the words, concepts, and syntactic structures continue to be used and discussed during the school day, after the reading is done (Silverman & Crandell, 2010).

Reading Storybooks

By paging through and pretending to read favorite storybooks, in imitation of adults they have seen reading, children develop concepts about the form and function of written text and the kind of language that is used in print. Therefore, good instruction for emerging readers will include providing individual books that they will enjoy on their level, with simple text. The teacher introduces the books by reading them to a child or group of children more than once and then giving them to the children and encouraging them to "read" the books to friends or parents. Opportunities for such storybook reading should be provided daily for children on all levels.

Reading Many Books, Repeatedly. Reading to children familiarizes them with books, acquaints them with characters and plots and other patterns of literature, and gradually helps them to learn the elaborated syntax and special vocabulary of written language. Best of all, it helps them come to enjoy books and feel at home with them. Reading six to eight books a day is not too many. Choose books that are simple and highly patterned at first—with rhyming lines, repeated actions, or a strong plot.

It's fine to read the same book through more than once at a sitting. On subsequent days, reread some of the books that you read before. Repeated reading familiarizes the children with the pattern of the book. Some literary patterns are shared by many books, so if children get the pattern, they will appreciate a similar book that much more readily. This is especially true of books by the same author. Bill Martin's *Brown Bear, Brown Bear, What Do You See?* leads nicely into his *Polar Bear, Polar Bear, What Do You Hear?* Each of Cynthia Rylant's *Henry and Mudge* books prepares children for the next, as do Arnold Lobel's *Frog and Toad* series, Norman Bridwell's *Clifford* books, and James Marshall's *George and Martha* books. Folktales can do this, too, such as Ivan Bilibin's collection of Russian folktales, many of which feature magical transformations of the hero and the exploits of the remarkable witch Baba Yaga or the many Anansi stories.

Repeatedly reading the same book serves another purpose, too: Once the children are familiar with a book, you can leave it out and invite them to "reread it" themselves or to other students. By regularly supporting and encouraging them in pretend reading, you are giving them close encounters with literature from which they will gradually learn about print.

Reading Expressively. Listen closely to a parent talking to a baby. The parent's voice makes exaggerated swoops, from high to low, from quiet to loud, from pauses to dramatic emphases. Parents' speech, sometimes called "motherese," is thought to use these exaggerated moves to attract and hold the child's attention and even show the child the significant features of speech (Stern, 1982).

Reading a book to children is like that. As we read through a story, we deliberately exaggerate the changes in our voices: from especially bright and cheerful to doleful and sad, to slow and suspenseful, to rapid and excited. We make the rhythms of language march, and we savor delightful words. By reading that way, we are showing children the dramatic contours of stories, the ebb and flow of emotions, the force and conflicts of characters, the pull of the plot, the music and cadence of rich language. Children might not sense these things unless we make them very clear and put them out there to be appreciated.

If you are new to reading aloud to children, the odds are that you will have to work on your voice to make it as expressive as it should be. Box 3.1 offers suggestions for practicing reading aloud expressively.

BOX 3.1

Ten Pointers for Reading Aloud

1. Read the book to yourself first to get familiar with it. You need to know whether this book is suitable for the children. If it is, you also need to think out how the characters' voices should sound, which parts have suspense, which parts are comical, and which parts are sad.
2. Arrange the children in front of you in a quiet area where they won't be distracted for the duration of the reading.
3. Preview the book for them. Show the cover and a few pictures from inside. Ask children to talk about what they see. Invite them to speculate on what might happen in the story.
4. As you read, go slowly and put animation and drama into your voice. Come up with slightly distinct voices for the characters—but don't overdo them.
5. Stop and show them the pictures. (In fact, you should practice reading books upside down so that you can show children the pictures as you read.) Allow time for the children to talk about what they notice.
6. Stop at the exciting parts and ask the children to predict what they think is going to happen.
7. After you've read on a ways, stop and ask them if their prediction happened. Were our predictions correct?
8. Read the book again, and invite the children to chime in on the repeated parts. Reread it another day, too. It's good for children to really get to know books.
9. Follow up. Ask them what they thought was the best (scariest, funniest, most exciting) part.
10. Leave the book out where they can look at it on their own after you've read it to them.

Shared Reading

Shared Reading (Holdaway, 1979) is a flexible means of working through a text with a student or students, calling the students' attention to the important features of texts, and inviting children's engagement and response. The technique is adaptable because it is based on the needs of the students and on the possibilities presented by the text.

Scaffolding and Shared Reading. The teacher's strategies during a Shared Reading session are summed up by the term *scaffolding* (Collins, Brown, & Newman, 1986). That is, the teacher offers the students just as much help as they need, with the goal that they should function as independently as possible as soon as possible. The teacher withdraws support as soon as it is no longer necessary.

Modeling. In modeling (Roehler & Duffy, 1991), the teacher behaves like a skilled reader who describes her own thinking and perceptual processes as they are practiced. The teacher voices her own questions and lays out her own plans for inquiry. The teacher says what she wonders about and, as naturally as possible, draws out the students' own questions and suppositions: "You know, this title, *Nobody's Mother Is in Second Grade,* makes me think some child's mother is going to come to school, and the child will be embarrassed about it. Think that's what will happen?"

Challenging. Here, the teacher gently challenges the students to practice specific comprehension strategies, especially ones that he has modeled: "I just told you my prediction of what will happen in this story, based on the title. What does the title make you think will happen?"

Praise. The teacher congratulates the student for practicing a specific skill. The praise is highly specific: "Good for you! You got to the end of the sentence, realized that the word you read earlier didn't make sense, and went back and corrected yourself once you knew what the whole sentence was. That's a great strategy!"

Preparing for Shared Reading. The teacher prepares for a Shared Reading session by considering the needs of the student or students who will be participating and the kinds of challenges that the text presents. The teacher needs to make several decisions about ways in which the text will challenge the students, and also help the students grow, in each of the following areas:

1. **Print Orientation.** Do these students need to be reminded that the print "talks," not the picture? Do they need to see the directional layout of print?
2. **Word Recognition.** What word patterns are presented that the children may be working on?
3. **Vocabulary.** What terms will the children need to know in advance, and what terms are they likely to learn from reading the text?
4. **Background Knowledge.** What knowledge will the children need in advance, and what are they likely to learn?

5. **Literary Genre.** Do the children have experience reading text of this type? What can be done to help them follow it successfully?
6. **Comprehension Strategies.** Which of the following comprehension strategies are the students already able to use? Which ones should be demonstrated and practiced in this lesson? *Summoning up background knowledge, setting purposes for reading and asking questions of the text, making predictions, making inferences, monitoring comprehension, visualizing, finding main ideas, summarizing.*

Conducting a Shared Reading Lesson. Shared Reading is best done with a big book with multiple copies of regular-sized versions. It can be done with a whole class or with a smaller group. The teacher should make sure the students are seated comfortably where they can see the book he is holding.

A Shared Reading lesson has a beginning, middle, and end. Teachers have different names for these three phases. Some call them *into, through,* and *beyond.* Others call them *introducing the book, reading and responding to the book,* and *extending the book.* Because we use similar phases with students in higher grades, too, we will use the same three terms for these phases at all levels: *anticipation, building knowledge,* and *consolidation.*

Anticipation is the phase in which the students first approach the text, find out what it is about, consider what they know about the topic, ask questions, and set purposes for reading.

Building knowledge is the phase in which students thoughtfully listen to or read the text, with their purposes and questions in mind, inquiring and seeking answers to their questions and to satisfy our purposes, and also raising new questions as the text suggests them and pursuing new purposes for their listening and reading.

Consolidation is the phase in which students do something with the new information they have gained: respond to it, question it, debate it, apply it, adjust their knowledge of the world in light of it—and decide where their inquiry should take them next.

In the anticipation stage. In this phase, the teacher attempts to arouse the students' interest in the text and get them ready to read meaningfully. The teacher works the following steps into this phase:

1. The teacher encourages the students to inspect what is to be listened to or read, look at the cover, consider the title, peruse a few pictures inside the book, and perhaps listen to or read a few lines. The students' purpose is to determine what topic the book is about and also what form or genre of writing it is (story, informational book, poem, etc.). For younger children, rather than to speak of genre, the teacher can point out who the author is and recall other books by that author that the students have enjoyed. Then the teacher can gently direct their expectations by venturing a question such as, "Do you think George is going to do something goofy, as he did in the other George and Martha books?"

2. The students should be reminded of other books of the genre that they already know, being as specific as they are able. If it is a biography, they should think of other biographies they have read and what kinds of things they found out. If it is a work of fiction, they might want to decide whether the book appears to be fantasy, realistic, or folk literature because answers to these questions shape the expectations they should have for what might happen in the book.
3. If it is an informational book or a work of realistic fiction, the teacher should ask the questions that lead the students to reflect on what they already know about that topic. They should be aware of areas they don't know about or are unsure about that might be informed by this book. Then they should formulate questions about the topic that they hope to have answered by the text.
4. If it is a work of fiction, students should be asked to make predictions about what is likely to happen in the book, given the title, the illustrations, and the notes on the jacket.
5. The teacher should look through the book ahead of time to identify up to four words that the students might not be familiar with. These can be introduced into a discussion of what the book is about and defined in the course of that discussion.

In the building knowledge phase. After the teacher has introduced the text, aroused the students' interest and curiosity about it, and led them to set purposes for their reading, he is ready to lead them into the text in the *Building Knowledge phase* of reading. The teacher can take different approaches here, depending on the students' needs. The teacher might focus on *print orientation*, on *word recognition*, on *language expansion*, or on *comprehension*. The teacher will always focus on enjoyment, keeping the exercise moving ahead at a good pace and showing enthusiasm all the while.

To stress print orientation. If the teacher wishes to stress print orientation and word recognition, a big book should be used. The teacher reads a page of the book, reading very expressively (see the section entitled "Ten Pointers for Reading Aloud," Box 3.1, for read-aloud suggestions). Using a pointer or a finger, the teacher points to each word as it is read, makes the return sweep to the left, and drops down to the next line. If some of the students need extra help with print orientation, the teacher says aloud what he is doing: "Look, I'm going to begin reading up here in this corner. I'm going to read each word across, and then go down to the next word. See?" The teacher is careful not to belabor the talking about the print; it is important that the reading go along quickly so that students do not lose the meaning.

To stress word recognition. The teacher is reading a page of text aloud. She comes to a key word in the text and covers the word with her hand:

> *Ahmed walked along, and walked along, until he came to a* _______ (This word is covered and the teacher skips it) *in the road.*
>
> "Which way do I go?" he said.

Then the teacher asks the students what the word is. After they make several guesses, the teacher uncovers the first letter: f: _______ and again asks students what they think the word is now. If need be, the teacher keeps uncovering letters until they correctly guess the word *fork*.

To stress comprehension. To develop comprehension, the teacher can model questions and comments and offer probes that encourage the students to listen or read to find out. As the teacher or the students read the text, the students are reminded to keep their questions and purposes in mind and to be alert to what they are learning (and not learning). The teacher also encourages the students to visualize what they are reading and to be alert to new directions and new questions that arise from the text.

Working almost conversationally, giving cues to the students and taking cues from them, the teacher works the following steps into the students' activity in this phase:

1. Having begun the lesson by asking the students to venture predictions and raise questions, the teacher encourages the students to read with their predictions and questions in mind.
2. The teacher stops the reading periodically (usually four or five times per session) and asks the students whether their questions have been answered and whether their predictions were correct. The teacher also encourages the students to be alert for other details they have noticed that lead to new predictions and new questions.
3. The teacher reminds students of places where inferences should be made and helps them to make those inferences.
4. The teacher encourages the students to visualize settings or actions that have been described. The children might do this through spontaneous drama, even by reading aloud expressively: "Janet, say those words to George the way you hear Martha really saying them. Bill, show us what George is going to look like while Martha says those things to him."
5. The teacher makes sure the students are aware when they are understanding what the text means: "Jeannie, can you say what the author just said, but put it in your own words?"

In the consolidation phase. After the students have read the book or have otherwise reached a stopping point, the teacher takes steps to get them to talk about the work and to respond to it in other ways. These steps include the following:

1. The teacher might ask for a retelling of the work. The purpose of the retelling is to invite the students to summarize the work.
2. The teacher might ask the students to reflect back on the questions and predictions they posed at the outset and how the material they found in the text answered the questions and fulfilled the predictions. If some questions were not answered, the students can discuss where they can now turn for answers. If the predictions

strayed significantly from what happened in the text, they can discuss what led them astray or what surprises occurred in the text.

3. The teacher might ask the students to say what was the most important idea the author told them in this work. The purpose is to lead students to think about main ideas.
4. The teacher will certainly ask the students for their personal responses to the work, especially if it is fiction or poetry. The teacher uses open-ended questions such as "What is in your mind about this book (or chapter, or passage or reading) right now?" or "What are you feeling right now when you think of this book? Why? What makes you feel that way?" or "What does this book make you think of?" or "What was your favorite part? Why?"
5. The teacher might follow the students' personal responses to the work with two or three interpretive questions. Interpretive questions are open-ended: They invite different answers, yet they are still close to the text. After reading *Where the Wild Things Are,* for instance, the teacher could ask, "Why do you think the supper was still hot?"
6. To help students visualize the work, the teacher might ask students to draw or act out their favorite part or the most important or exciting part.

Dialogic Reading. When working with individual children, one approach to reading called *dialogic reading* helps put the child in the active role as a storyteller and not just a listener. Use of dialogic reading has promoted gains in children's language acquisition and growth in concepts about print (Whitehurst & Lonigan, 2001).

Dialogic reading is intended to be used by parents, teachers, and volunteer tutors, such as college students working in special literacy programs including America Reads or Jumpstart. In some communities, training in dialogic reading is available through family literacy programs offered by public libraries. The training is supported by twenty-minute videotapes. Adult readers are taught to read interactively with the child. Two acronyms, PEER and CROWD, are used to remind the adult readers of the steps. PEER is a mnemonic for a strategy used to nurture language development with younger children as they read a book together with an adult. The letters stand for:

Prompt the child to name objects in the book and talk about the story;
Evaluate the child's responses and offer praise for adequate responses and alternatives for inadequate ones;
Expand on the child's statements with additional words; and afterward
Repeat—Ask the child to repeat the adult's utterances.

CROWD identifies five kinds of questions adults ask:

1. *Completion prompts.* The child is asked to supply a word or phrase that has been omitted. (For example, "I see a yellow duck looking at ___.")
2. *Recall prompts.* The child is asked about things that occurred earlier in the book. ("Do you remember some animals that Brown Bear saw?")

3. *Open-ended prompts.* The child is asked to respond to the story in his own words. ("Now it's your turn: You say what is happening on this page.")
4. *Wh- prompts.* The adult asks what, where, who, and why questions. ("What is that yellow creature called? Who do you think Brown Bear will see next?")
5. *Distancing prompts.* The child is asked to relate the content of the book to life experiences. ("Do you remember when we saw a yellow duck like that one swimming in the lake? Was it as big as this one?")

Teaching to Nurture Vocabulary Development

Reading aloud to children, shared reading, dialogic reading, and storytelling can be rich in vocabulary, sophisticated syntax, and, of course, decontextualized language. But research shows that what the teacher does during those activities can make a sizable difference in how much of those things children take away from the experiences.

During read-aloud time, children have been shown to learn significantly more new words if teachers used certain practices in addition to reading aloud expressively and discussing stories. Noteworthy among these practices are:

1. Introduce a few rich (low frequency) words, and repeat them often during the lesson.
2. Clarify and demonstrate the word meanings by giving definitions and picture clues and using the words in the context of a sentence.
3. Make sure the children understand the meaning of the overall story or text.
4. Discuss deeply the ideas in the text, especially the concepts to which the new words refer (Dickinson & Smith, 1994).
5. Use active listening strategies when children are speaking.
6. Ask questions that elicit recall, predictions, and reactions.
7. Make connections between issues raised in the storybook and life in the classroom (Wasik, Bond, & Hinman, 2006).
8. Show the new vocabulary in print, and encourage children to pronounce the words and pay attention to the letters used in the words (Silverman, 2007).
9. Introduce new words ahead of the reading, and ask children to raise their hands when they hear the words.
10. Talk about the new words in different contexts, and ask questions that encourage children to extend the use of the new word to new situations (Coyne, McCoach, Loftus, Zipoli, & Kapp, 2009).

Focused instruction similar to the recommendations made above with respect to vocabulary can be used to introduce new syntactic structures, too. For example, if you want to introduce children to the present progressive tense ("I am giving my old toys away"), you can use the following strategies:

1. Pick just one syntactic structure and repeat it several times during the read-aloud event.

2. Carefully explain how the structure works in the meaning of a sentence.
3. Introduce the structure ahead of time and ask children to listen for it and raise their hands when they hear it used.
4. Show a sentence with the syntactic structure written down.
5. Explain cases in which the same structure can have more than one meaning (for example, "I am giving away my old toys, too" may either mean "I am doing it right now" or "I intend to do it soon").
6. Ask the children to come up with their own examples using the structure.
7. Deliberately use the structure throughout the rest of the school day, and call children's attention to it when you do.

Some structures that cause non-native English speakers spelling problems are the simple present third person singular *-s*, *-s* as a plural marker, and the possessive (*'s* or *s'*). They can't get the spelling right unless they understand the grammar. The same is true of *there, their,* and *they're* and of *you're* and *your*. The hypercorrect use of the pronoun *I* (as in "Mother gave Jim and I money to buy ice cream.") may be another target for grammar instruction.

Teaching Decontextualized Language

Teaching children to respond to and converse in decontextualized language is an important part of assisting children's emergent literacy. Decontextualized language is a richer means of vocabulary development and a stronger preparation for reading than contextualized language; yet as Dickinson's research shows, it is not used nearly as often in preschool classrooms. He found that "only 20 percent or less of the time children talked with adults in preschool was spent in conversations that went beyond the here and now. The rest of the time teachers were giving directions or asking children for specific information, such as the names of colors or letters" (Dickinson, 2001). Here are some suggestions for developing children's familiarity with decontextualized language in the classroom:

1. Have conversations with children about things that are not in the present space. Talk to them about what they did this morning, or what they will do later today.
2. Read aloud to them. Engage them in the reading by giving them specific targets to listen for.
3. Tell them stories. Invite them to predict what will happen, and to comment on the action. See pages 88–89 for suggestions on learning and telling stories.
4. Invite them to tell stories. Tell several stories about the same characters, such as "Goldilocks and the Three Bears." Make up some new versions yourself. Then invite the children to tell their own versions.

Storytelling for Comprehension. Reading aloud to children has the advantages of introducing children to decontextualized language, expanding their vocabulary, and acquainting them with the patterns of stories and other texts. Storytelling—telling a story to children instead of reading it—offers something more. A teacher who tells a story from memory conveys the story with expressive language and gestures and connects it with each child, inviting even the most reluctant of children into the virtual world of story. That teacher can build a bridge from the decontextualized language found in books to forms of expression that are more familiar to the children. That teacher can use questions, think-alouds, and invitations to participate that can stimulate vocabulary, comprehension, awareness of the structure of stories, and enthusiasm for literature.

Learning stories to tell. Most people who regularly tell stories agree that the way to prepare a story for telling is not to memorize it. Memorizing will make a story sound flat or set the teller up for a mental block during the telling. Besides, the beauty of a told story is that it is forever invented. But a story is not random, either. A well-told story is crisp, with the beginning, ending, and repeated parts told just so.

How do you achieve this crispness without memorizing the story? Here's one way.

Get a dozen index cards, and read through the story four times, each time with a different purpose:

1. On the first pass, read for the sense of the whole tale.
2. Next time, pay close attention to the different events in the story. Jot down each event in a few words on a separate card.
3. On the third read-through, pay close attention to the characters. On a separate card, name each character and make notes about the way she or he should sound and move. Note any gestures that you want to associate with each character.
4. Read through the story again and jot down the beginning and ending, as well as any repeated phrases. This is important. If you know exactly how a story begins, you can launch into it confidently. If you know exactly how the story ends, you can wrap it up crisply. So memorize both. In between, pay attention to repeated phrases (such as "Little pig, little pig, let me come in. Not by the hair on my chinny-chin-chin") or repeated patterns of actions.

Practice the story. Once you have the cards prepared and arranged in the order you find most useful, tell the story repeatedly (to yourself, to a friend, to your dog) until you can tell it confidently without looking at the cards. Later, when you tell the story, keep the cards unobtrusively in your lap—but have them handy in case you begin to forget.

For more suggestions on learning stories, see these sources:

Haven, Kendall, and MaryGay Ducey. (2006). *Crash Course on Storytelling.* Libraries Unlimited.

McDonald, Margaret Read. (1993). *Storytellers' Start-Up Book.* August House.

McGuire, Jack. (1992). *Creative Storytelling: Choosing, Inventing, and Sharing Tales for Children.* Yellow Moon Press.

For collections of stories to tell, probably the best single source is August House (www.augusthouse.com). Their stories are written up specifically for storytelling.

Margaret Read MacDonald, Martha Hamilton and Mitch Weiss (a husband and wife team who are known as "Beauty and the Beast Storytellers"), and David Holt are good names to start with.

Hamilton, Martha. (2005). *How and Why Stories.* August House.
—. (2006). *Scared Witless: 13 Eerie Stories to Tell.* August House.
Hamilton, Martha, and Mitch Weiss. (2006). *Noddlehead Stories.* August House.
Holt, David and Bill Mooney. (1995). *Ready-to-Tell Tales.* August House.
—. (2000). *More Ready-to-Tell Tales from Around the World.* August House.
MacDonald, Margaret Read. (2004). *Twenty Tellable Tales: Audience Participation Folktales for the Beginning Storyteller*—Revised Edition. American Library Association.
—. (2004). *Three Minute Tales.* August House.
—. (2007). *Five Minute Tales.* August House.

Summary

Emergent literacy is the critical phase of reading and writing that children pass through before they enter formal literacy instruction. Or it used to be. Thanks to the discoveries in recent years of the concepts and skills children need to develop in this prefatory phase of literacy, wise teachers are making sure that all children learn these foundational skills and concepts in kindergarten and first grade.

The aspects of emergent literacy that children need to develop include concepts about print, including the nature of reading and writing; the layout of written language; and the concept of word—the idea that spoken language comes to us in units of words and these units are represented on the page by clusters of letters bound by spaces. Emergent literacy also includes certain language skills. Some of these are phonological skills like the ability to break spoken words into smaller units, such as syllables, onsets and rimes, and phonemes. An important language skill is the ability to follow decontextualized language, which uses words to create virtual realities, without reference to the here and now. And another is the ability to comprehend stories by using their narrative structure. Young readers need to develop their vocabulary, too, as well as their grasp of syntax—the grammar of language.

A number of strategies were shared in this chapter to help children develop emergent literacy. Among them were strategies and activities for teaching concepts of print: alphabet knowledge and the nature and layout of printed language. Strategies for teaching several aspects of language were also shared: for teaching phonological awareness (awareness of the sounds in language), vocabulary, decontextualized language, and story comprehension.

References

Barker, C. (1986). *How many syllables does English have?* http://ling.ucsd.edu/~barker

Beck, I. L., McKeown, M. G., & Kucan, L. (2002). *Bringing words to life.* New York, NY: Guilford.

Blachman, B., Tangel, D., Ball, E., Black, B., & McGraw, D. (1995). Developing phonological awareness and word recognition skills: A two-year intervention with low income, inner-city children. *Reading and Writing: An Interdisciplinary Journal, 11,* 273–293.

Bradley, L., & Bryant, P. (1985). *Rhyme and reason in reading and spelling.* Ann Arbor, MI: University of Michigan Press.

Bus, A. G., Van Ijzendoorn, M. H., & Pellegrini, A. D. (1995). Joint book reading makes for success in learning to read: A meta-analysis on intergenerational transmission of literacy. *Review of Educational Research, 65*(5), 1–21. EJ 504 345.

Catts, H., Fey, M., Zhang, X., & Tomblin, J. B. (1999). Language basis of reading and reading disabilities: Evidence from a longitudinal study. *Scientific Studies of Reading, 3,* 331–361.

Clarke, L. (1988). Inventory versus traditional spelling in first graders' writings: Effects on learning to spell and read. *Research in the Teaching of English, 22*(3), 281–309.

Clay, M. (1975). *What did I write?* Portsmouth, NH: Heinemann Educational Books.

Clay, M. M. (1979). *Concepts about print.* Portsmouth, NH: Heinemann.

Clay, M., Gill, M., Glynn, T., McNaughton, T., & Salmon, K. (2007). *The record of oral language.* Portsmouth, NH: Heinemann Educational Books.

Collins, A., Brown, J. S., & Newman, S. (1986). *Cognitive apprenticeship: Teaching the craft of reading, writing, and mathematics* (Report No. 6459). Cambridge, MA: BNN Laboratories.

Conrad, P. (1995). *The tub people.* Illustrated by R. Egielski. New York, NY: HarperCollins.

Cunningham, A. E., & Stanovich, K. E. (1997). Early reading acquisition and its relation to reading experience and ability 10 years later. *Developmental Psychology, 33*(6), 934–945.

Dickinson, D. K. (1994). *Bridges to literacy: Children, families and schools.* Cambridge, MA: Basil Blackwell.

Dickinson, D. K., & Tabors, P.O. (Eds.) (2001). *Beginning literacy and language: Young children learning at home and in school.* Baltimore, MD: Brookes.

Ehri, L. (1989, April). *Research on reading and spelling.* Paper presented at the George Graham Memorial Lectures, University of Virginia, Charlottesville.

Ehri, L. (1991). Development of the ability to read words. In R. Barr, M. Kamil, P. Mosenthal, & P. D. Pearson (Eds.), *Handbook of reading research: Vol. 2.* New York, NY: Longman.

Elkonin, D. (1973). Reading in the USSR. In J. Downing (Ed.), *Comparative reading.* New York, NY: Macmillan.

Ferreiro, E., & Teberosky, A. (1979). *Literacy before schooling.* Portsmouth, NH: Heinemann.

Gough, P. B., & Tunmer, W. E. (1986). Decoding, reading, and reading disability. *Remedial and Special Education,* 7, 6–10.

Graham, S., Berninger, V. W., Abbott, R. D., Abbott, S. P., & Whitaker, D. (1997, March). Role of mechanics in composing of elementary students: A new methodological approach. *Journal of Educational Psychology, 89,* 171–182.

Hall, S. L., & Moats, L. C. (1999). *Straight talk about reading.* Lincolnwood, IL: Contemporary Books.

Harste, J., Woodward, V., & Burke, C. (1985). *Language stories and literacy lessons.* Portsmouth, NH: Heinemann.

Hart, B., & Risley, T. (1995). *Meaningful differences in the everyday experiences of young American children.* Baltimore, MD: Brookes Publishing.

Holdaway, D. (1979). *Foundations of literacy.* Portsmouth, NH: Heinemann Educational Books.

Iverson, S., & Tunmer, W. (1993). Phonological processing skills and the Reading Recovery programme. *Journal of Educational Psychology, 85*(1), 112–126.

Krahn, F. (1979). *Robot-bot-bot.* New York, NY: Dutton.

Lewis, B. A., Freebairn, L. A., & Taylor, H. G. (2000, January-February). Academic outcomes in children with histories of speech sound disorders. *Journal of Communication Disorders 33(1)*, 11–30.

Lieberman, P. (1998). *Eve spoke: Human language and human evolution.* New York, NY: W. W. Norton & Company.

Lust, B., Flynn, S., & Foley, C. (1996). What children know about what they say: Elicited imitation as a research method for assessing children's syntax. In D. McDaniel, C. McKee, & H. Smith Cairns (Eds.), *Methods for assessing children's syntax.* Cambridge, MA: MIT Press.

Mayer, M. (2003). *A boy, a dog, and frog.* New York, NY: Dial.

McCracken, R., & McCracken, M. (1987). *Reading is only the tiger's tail.* Winnepeg: Peguis.

Morris, D. (1981). Concept of word and phoneme awareness in the beginning reader. *Research in the Teaching of English, 17,* 359–373.

Morris, D. (1990). *Case studies in beginning reading: The Howard Street tutoring manual.* Boone, NC: Fieldstream.

Morris, D. (1993). The relationship between children's concept of word in text and phonemic awareness in learning to read: A longitudinal study. *Research in the Teaching of English, 27,* 133–154.

Nagy, W., & Anderson, R. C. (1984). How many words are there in printed school English? *Reading Research Quarterly, 19,* 304–330.

National Reading Panel. (2000). *Teaching children to read: An evidence-based assessment of the scientific research literature on reading and its implications for reading instruction.* Washington, DC: National Institute for Literacy.

Paris, A. H., &. Paris, S. G. (2001). *CIERA Children's comprehension of narrative picture books.* CIERA Report #3-012. http://www.ciera.org/library/reports/inquiry-3/3-012/3-012.pdf.

Pellegrini, A. D., & Galda, L. (1994). Play. In V. S. Ramachandran (Ed.), *Encyclopedia of human behavior* (pp. 535–543). New York, NY: Academic Press.

Roehler, L. R., & Duffy, G. G. (1991). Teachers' instructional actions. In R. Barr, M. Kamil, P. Mosenthal, & P. D. Pearson (Eds.), *Handbook of reading research: Vol. 2.* New York: Longman.

Silverman, R., & Crandell, J. (2010, July/August/September). Vocabulary practices in prekindergarten and kindergarten classrooms. *Reading Research Quarterly, 45*(3), 318–340. doi: 10.1598/RRQ.45.3.3.

Snow, C. E. (1991). The theoretical basis for the relationships between language and literacy development. *Journal of Research in Childhood Education, 6*(1), 5–10.

Snow, C. E., Burns, M. S., & Griffin, P. (Eds.). (1998). *Preventing reading difficulties in young children.* Washington, DE: National Academy Press.

Snow, C., Porche, M. V., Tabors, P., & Harris, S. (2007). *Is literacy enough? Pathways to academic success for adolescents.* Baltimore, MD: Paul H. Brookes.

Stanovich, K. E. (2000). Toward an interactive-compensatory model of individual differences in the development of reading fluency. In *Progress in Understanding Reading.* New York, NY: Guilford Press.

Stern, D. (1982). *The first relationship.* Cambridge, MA: Harvard University Press.

Teale, W. H., & Sulzby, E. (Eds.), *Emergent literacy: Writing and reading.* Norwood, NH: Ablex Publishing.

Temple, C., Nathan, R., & Burris, N. (1982). *The beginnings of writing.* Boston, MA: Allyn and Bacon.

Tomblin, J. B., Zhang, X., Buckwalter, P., & Catts, H. (2000). The association of reading disability, behavioral disorders, and language impairment among second-grade children. *Journal of Child Psychology and Psychiatry and Allied Disciplines, 41,* 473–482.

Walsh, D., Price, G., & Gillingham, M. (1988). The critical but transitory importance of letter naming. *Reading Research Quarterly, 23,* 108–122.

Weizman, Z. O., & Snow, C. E. (2001). Lexical input as related to children's vocabulary acquisition: Effects of sophisticated exposure and support for meaning. *Developmental Psychology, 37,* 265–279.

Whitehurst, G. J., & Lonigan, C. J. (2001). Emergent literacy: Development from prereaders to readers. In S. B. Neuman & D. K. Dickinson (Eds.), *Handbook of early literacy research* (pp. 11–29). New York, NY: Guilford Press.

Yopp, H. K. (1988). The validity and reliability of phonemic awareness tests. *Reading Research Quarterly, 23,* 159–177.

Assessing and Teaching Beginning and Fledgling Readers and Writers

CHAPTER 4

Chapter Outline

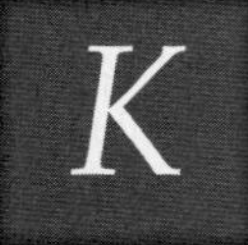

atie Flowers directs a tutoring project for a small liberal arts college. The program has worked continuously for fifteen years, and is very popular with college students. Nearly one hundred of them volunteer each term to go out to a local school and work one on one with a first-, second-, or third-grade student who has been recommended by a teacher for extra help.

At the beginning of each semester, the students are given a couple of hours of training; then they come back periodically for more training during the semester. The students go out to a local school two times each week, both before and after school. Each time the students go out, they follow a lesson plan with five parts. The lesson plan was borrowed from Darrell Morris' Howard Street Tutoring Manual (2006).

1. *Read an easy book to develop fluency.*
2. *Read a harder book to help the children learn new words.*
3. *Do a word study task—phonics or vocabulary.*
4. *Have the child write something.*
5. *Read aloud to the child.*

The students work on affective concerns, too: challenging and encouraging their young tutees.

Katie asks the teachers to fill out feedback forms at the end of each term. Last spring, one teacher reported that over the year, a third-grade student progressed from 58 to 153 words per minute. Another teacher reported a big increase in a child's Lexile score on a commercial reading test. Children enjoy the companionship of the college tutors. "Here come the teenagers!" one excited boy was heard to say, as the tutors trooped off the bus and into the school.

Beginning to read is like beginning to ride a bicycle (though, we hope, not so painful!). The young cyclist has a general idea what bike riding is about, having watched with longing admiration as her older siblings strapped on helmets and rode off for adventures. She has learned most of the separate skills of bike riding—pedaling, steering, braking, and balancing. Her challenge now is to coordinate all of those skills so that she, too, can pedal some wobbly distance down the sidewalk. Likewise, the young beginning reader knows what reading is about (he developed early concepts about reading as an emergent reader), and he has learned or is learning the parts—print concepts, phonics, some memorized words, strategies of comprehension, and the structures of texts. His challenge is to get all of these parts to work together smoothly enough so he can forge his way through a couple of lines of print. Both children have one other thing in common: There is an adult hovering close by, one running alongside and holding up the bike, and the other prodding, supplying hard words, and praising efforts as the child works his way through a line of print.

In more technical terms, **beginning readers:**

- Can read short texts with picture and other contextual support.
- Have a sight word repertoire of around 15 words.
- Have phonological awareness and decoding skills closing in on more sounds in words—the beginning and ending consonants.
- Have limited reading fluency.
- Are more concentrated on reading words than understanding meaning.

Fledgling readers have moved beyond the beginning stage. Fledgling readers can:

- Recognize fifty words or more at sight.
- Read unknown words by onset and rime.
- Read simple texts with less contextual support.
- Read with more fluency.
- Use comprehension strategies (Morris & Slavin, 2002; Tynan, 2009).

The rest of this chapter will be devoted to explaining what these abilities mean, how they are assessed, and how they are taught.

Components of Beginning and Fledgling Reading

The skills that are developed and practiced during the phase of beginning reading include:

- Word recognition, including *sight word acquisition* and *phonics.*
- Comprehension, including vocabulary—the ability to derive meaning from text.
- Fluency, or reading words with reasonable speed, accuracy, and intonation.

Word Recognition

As you read the text on the preceding pages, you probably recognized most of the words without effort. Your eyes made a fixation on each word and collected a chunk of visual information that was transmitted to your brain, where the word was matched to a dictionary or lexicon of words you had stored in your memory along with their meanings. That lexicon is what teachers call a *sight vocabulary,* a collection of words that are recognized "at sight," without a careful examination of their parts. There may have been a couple of words that caused you to take a second look. *Affective* (a psychological term, meaning having to do with feelings) is often confused with *effective* (having results), and readers may need to pause to remember which word is which. *Intonation,* too, might have given you pause, since it was used here as a technical term for the musical side of pronouncing a string of words. But for the most part, you practiced *sight word recognition:* that is, you recognized words as wholes that were already stored in your memory.

Contrast the way you as a mature reader recognize words with what a beginning reader does. The beginner has far fewer words stored in memory. The first words he learns to read are those he sees over and over again and stores away the way you recognize faces. But beyond the first few dozen words he learns as wholes, to grow his reading vocabulary, his word reading will increasingly rely on *decoding*—that is, relating smaller units in the written words to their sound equivalents, merging the several sound units into a spoken word, and then associating that spoken word with a meaning. No wonder his reading is fairly slow and laborious. He will be helped by the encouragement of a teacher or a tutor to keep him going through this challenging work.

Sight Words. The term *sight words* has two meanings. One meaning is "words that have been stored in memory and can be recognized instantly." The other meaning is "the words that are most frequently used in print, and have been compiled into lists to be taught to young readers."

Sight words as learned words. Not all sight words come from these high-frequency lists, of course. As children are exposed to words through reading experiences, they store whole words in memory. When they are first beginning to read, they may store several dozen words as wholes, often seemingly recognizing them by their visual features rather than letter by letter. (To dramatize this point, Phillip Gough [1993] did an interesting experiment in which he asked children to learn words printed on cards. On a few of the cards he planted a seemingly innocent thumb print. The children remembered those words easily—yet when he showed the same words later without the thumb print on the card, they no longer recognized them!)

A generation ago, Russell Stauffer (1975) recommended that teachers wait until children had acquired about fifty sight words, and only after the children knew that number quite well should they be encouraged to analyze those words for their parts. More recent research-based descriptions of children's development of word knowledge have borne out the wisdom of his advice. For practical purposes, students will need about fifty words in memory so they can compare and contrast and categorize them and can learn generalizations about the spelling system of English.

It is essential that children be encouraged to learn and store up a collection of sight words from reading. Their own sight words are especially useful because they are personally interesting to the children and they often are written to spelling patterns that can be generalized to many other words.

High-frequency sight words. There is a surprising amount of repetition in the words children see in print. Just 25 words make up a third of the words children are likely to read in the first few grades, and 220 words comprise half the words they will read. There is obviously some benefit in children being able to read the highest frequency words. Also, because the most commonly used words in English are often not spelled the way they sound (think of *one, only, gone, give,* etc.), it makes sense to teach them as wholes rather than have children decode them.

But having children memorize high-frequency words won't make readers out of them, because so many of the highest frequency words convey less information than lower frequency words. The highest frequency words are often grammatical "glue" words like *the, a, an, but, and, so, also*—or pronouns, or adverbs—that contribute little to our understanding. Because their referents are often less clear, they can be less memorable than low-frequency words and not easy for children to learn. (See Figure 4.1 for an illustration.) Still, the high-frequency words are important for children to know. Stumbling over these words bogs down a beginning reader's progress through a line of print, and failure to read them properly can make understanding break down.

The best known lists of high-frequency words were compiled by Edgar Dolch (1948) and Edward Fry (2004). Dolch's list of 220 words constitutes half of the words children see in print. But there are no nouns on the list, and because it was compiled in 1936 and published in 1948, many of the words are not up to date. Edward Fry's list consists of the 1000 highest frequency words from children's reading and writing, and is the most current list available. The first 300 words from Fry's list can be found later in this chapter (see page 114).

Word Recognition by Decoding. Children normally begin to focus on parts of words after they have learned several words as wholes. Then most children begin to decode the words—that is, pronounce them part by part by relating letters to sounds. Decoding is not as straightforward as it sounds. Let's review some basics about the issue.

- English employs an *alphabetic writing system.* That means that words are essentially represented by their sounds, and the sounds that are represented are the smallest units of speech, the *phonemes.* Phonemes are the sounds spelled by C, A, and T in *cat.* Problems may arise when a child is not able to mentally break a spoken word down into its phonemes—and many children have trouble with this. If the child isn't aware that *-bat-* is made up of the sounds /b/, /æ/, and /t/ (that's the way you indicate speech sounds, according to the International Phonetic Alphabet), he will have difficulty "sounding out" the words—that is, breaking the word into its constituent sounds and matching each one with a letter.
- English words are also composed of *onsets* and *rimes:* a cluster of vowel and consonant or consonants, preceded by a beginning element (examples: *c* + *at* = *cat; b* + *at* = *bat; st* + *itch* = *stitch; w* + *itch* = *witch*). The presence of onsets and rimes means that it may be more useful for a child to recognize *b* and then *–and,* rather than try to sound out *b, a, n,* and *d* as separate units.
- English words are made up of meaningful parts called *morphemes.* Morphemes may be grammatical morphemes, such as *dog* + *s* = *dogs,* or *want* + *ed* = *wanted.* Prefixes and suffixes are called *bound morphemes.* They combine with free morphemes

Read these two passages:

Passage with Only High-Frequency Words

____1____ *AND THE* ____2____

____3____ ____4____ a ____5____ there ____6____ a ____7____ ____8____ who had an only ____9____ ____10____ ____11____. She was very ____12____, for ____13____ had been ____14____, and ____15____ was too ____16____ to work. ____17____ all the ____18____ of the little ____19____ had been ____20____ to buy ____21____, until at last there was nothing left ____22____ ____23____. Only the good ____24____, ____25____, ____26____, and she ____27____ ____28____ every morning, which they took to ____29____ and ____30____. But one ____31____ day ____32____ ____33____ no ____34____, and then ____35____ ____36____ ____37____ ____38____.

Passage with High-Frequency Words Removed

JACK ____1____ ____2____ *BEANSTALK*

ONCE upon ____3____ time ____4____ lived ____5____ poor widow ____6____ ____7____ ____8____ ____9____ son named Jack. ____10____ ____11____ ____12____ poor, ____13____ times ____14____ ____15____ hard, ____16____ ____17____ ____18____ ____19____ young ____20____ ____21____. Almost ____22____ ____23____ furniture ____24____ ____25____ ____26____ cottage ____27____ ____28____ sold ____29____ buy bread, ____30____ ____31____ ____32____ ____33____ ____34____ ____35____ ____36____ worth selling. ____37____ ____38____ ____39____ cow, Milky White, remained, ____40____ ____41____ gave milk ____42____ ____43____, ____44____ ____45____ took ____46____ market ____47____ sold. ____48____ ____49____ sad ____50____ Milky White gave ____51____ milk, ____52____ ____53____ things looked bad indeed.

After reading the two passages, decide which one gave you the information you need to answer these typical comprehension questions.

1. What is the title of the story?
2. Who are the main characters in the story?
3. What is the main problem they have?
4. What did they do to try to solve their problem?
5. What was their situation at the end of the passage?

FIGURE 4.1 *Comparing Words of High and Low Frequency*

to modify their meaning, as in *re* + *tell* = *retell*, *dis* + *own* = *disown*, *thank* + *ful* = *thankful*. Compound words are groups of independent or "free" morphemes joined together, either with no spaces between them or with hyphens: *house* + *boat* = *houseboat*; *mother* + *in* + *law* = *mother-in-law*. Some morphemes are considered "dead": They can't stand on their own as words, but they appear in combinations with other morphemes to make words, such as *micro-* in *micro*scope, *micro*phone, *micro*biology, and *micro*cosm. Most of the dead morphemes in English came from Latin and Greek. Part of the task of recognizing words is to be aware of the morphemes they contain, and to understand their meanings and their effects on the stems to which they are attached.

- English spelling has not kept close to the pronunciation of many words. This is true for a host of reasons. Some of those reasons are arbitrary, such as the B in *subtle* which was introduced by mistake, or the spelling WH, which was originally spelled HW as it sounds, but was reversed to match CH, TH, and SH—which were introduced to spell sounds for which the Roman alphabet had no letters. But most of the reasons for the many mismatches between letters and sounds are logical, according to some linguists (e.g., Chomsky & Halle, 1968), because writers have had to forsake phonetic consistency in order to honor common origins and related meanings of words. Many English words that are closely related to each other in origin and meaning can have very different pronunciations, such as *woman* and *women*, *child* and *children*, *sign* and *signal*. These spellings sacrifice a close tie between spelling and pronunciation in favor of the meaning. Perhaps as many as 80 percent of English words have fairly predictable letter-to-sound relationships, and many of the rest have spellings that make sense on some level. Unfortunately, those with the less predictable spellings are some of the words children see most often, like *said*, *of*, *was*, *one*, *any*, *are*, *been*, *come*, *do*, *from*, *give*, *put*, and many others (including *others*).

Comprehension, the Ability to Derive Meaning from Text

To understand a passage of text requires that the young reader coordinate several kinds of thinking at once. The reader must:

- Know the *vocabulary*, the meanings of the words. Sometimes this is a straightforward act of matching a single meaning with a word, as in "William pulled on his *sweatshirt*." Sometimes it means choosing between more than one possible meaning, depending on the context: "Let's build a fire"; "Hold your fire!" And sometimes it means using the context to help figure out the meaning of an unknown word, such as "The explorer wore a *parka* to keep warm."
- Know the *syntax*, the grammar of the sentences. "The trapper wore a parka, a thick overcoat." "The gold was discovered by an old beggar." Written language relies more heavily on syntax for understanding than does speech. In speech, we rarely use appositives, subordinate clauses that follow nouns and explain them; or passive constructions, word arrangements that put the receiver of the action as the subject

of the sentence and leave the agent or "doer" of the action unclear (unless we're professional spokespersons, trying to sidestep responsibility for something controversial!). These constructions are fairly common in written language, though.

- Form and work from a *schema.* A reader must be able to use words and pictures from the text to construct a schema (Anderson & Pearson, 1984) or an *envisionment* (Langer, 1995)—a scenario of what is going on—and use that schema or envisionment to interpret each new detail. The working of the schema to establish a context in which the subsequent details makes sense is most readily visible when reading fiction: The story begins with a setting and introduces characters, gives them a problem, and makes the reader wonder what solution they will try. But the phenomenon works with informational text, too: The text introduces a topic, raises our curiosity about it, suggests questions that will be answered, and then sets about answering them.
- Generate images. A reader should be able to generate images in her mind in response to descriptive words on the page. If the passage says, "The poor cow had grown so thin you could see every rib on her sides. Her skin hung on her scrawny body like an old tent sagging on a frame," the reader should be able to picture or visualize all that. Imaging is one of the pleasures of reading, but it is also essential to thorough comprehension of text.
- Summarize. A reader should be able to perceive the main idea of a passage and report it in a few words. This is not an ability that comes naturally to young readers, but teachers should keep in mind that it is an eventual goal of reading.
- Draw inferences. Readers should be able to use clues in a text to deduce conclusions. For example, in Harry Allard's ever-popular picture book, *Miss Nelson Is Missing,* a too-sweet school teacher is replaced in the classroom by a fierce substitute named Viola Swamp, whose harsh treatment soon has the children longing for their original teacher. The last frame of the book shows a satisfied Miss Nelson lying in her bed, and behind her in the open closet is shown the substitute's costume. Young readers delight in drawing the inference that Viola Swamp was Miss Nelson in disguise—but the book doesn't explicitly say so.
- Monitor comprehension. We noted earlier that as he begins to read, a reader should form a schema or an envisionment—a conception of what the text is about. The schema forms a context in which subsequent details make sense. Each new sentence, and each new word in a sentence, should add up to something meaningful that fits in the general understanding of the text that the reader is constructing. If it doesn't—if the reader misreads words and the result is nonsense—the reader should be aware of the breakdown in comprehension and be motivated to go back to the point of the misreading and "self-correct." A failure to exercise comprehension monitoring is observable when a child makes an oral reading error and keeps reading without self-correcting.

Reading Fluency

Smooth and accurate word recognition, articulated with meaningful inflections, together form *reading fluency.* Reading fluency is essential to successful reading because it signifies that a reader has sufficient skill at reading a certain level of text that the mind has the capacity available to it to devote to the meaning of the text and the purposes for reading it. Disfluent reading ties up concentration in efforts to decode and pronounce words, and therefore reduces comprehension.

So these are the parts of beginning reading that we will be watching. We turn next to the ways of assessing these factors, and then to ways of teaching them. The discussions that follow will address beginning reading generally—looking at the mix of factors together, because that is the way beginning readers grapple with them. Later we will look in detail at the separate processes and skills of word recognition, comprehension, vocabulary, and fluency so you will know how to help children who have difficulties in these areas.

Assessing Beginning and Fledgling Readers

We will look first at holistic assessments of beginning and fledgling readers. Then we will proceed to more specific assessments, and finally we will set out instructional procedures that are matched to identified needs.

Running Records

Running records of students' oral reading are one of the most widely used ongoing assessments teachers use. Running records are transcripts of reading material that is at a comfortable level of difficulty (the *instructional level*), with the reader's oral reading errors or *miscues*, correction attempts, comments about the text, and other reading behaviors marked using a standardized system of marks (Clay, 1993, 2000, 2005). Taking a running record is very much like marking an oral reading selection in an Informal Reading Inventory, which will be described in Chapter 5. Running records are made periodically to show the reader's mastery of successively difficult texts, types of miscues made, strategies used in figuring out unfamiliar words, and comprehension (Fountas & Pinnell, 1996). Many teachers find running records helpful in documenting a reader's progress at systematic intervals because they are taken during authentic reading tasks without interrupting the flow of a lesson. Dated copies of running records in a reader's assessment file provide concrete documentation of her progress.

Running Records to Document Progress. Running records were first used in conjunction with Reading Recovery, an early intervention program designed by Marie Clay (1993, 2005; Shanahan & Barr, 1995; Swartz & Klein, 2002). Clay devised running records as a way of keeping track of a reader's use of key strategies and growth toward higher levels of difficulty of text on a daily basis. A Reading Recovery teacher takes a running record of the reader's second reading of a new book, done the day after the child has read the new book independently for the first time. Since a new book is introduced daily in a Reading Recovery lesson, running records are taken daily to document the child's progress.

In the years since Reading Recovery's introduction, running records have become widely used in other remedial and tutorial programs and during everyday group instruction. For example, during a guided reading lesson, the teacher takes a running record of one student reading yesterday's new book while the others listen; in this way, each child in the group is assessed about once a week. Other teachers prefer to take a running record every few weeks; for older students, this generally provides sufficient information about reading progress without becoming burdensome for the teacher.

In our own classrooms, we take running records weekly for remedial students who are reading short, easy materials; and monthly or less often for developmental readers who are reading longer texts such as chapter books and novels.

Figure 4.2 shows an example of a running record.

Running Records and Text Difficulty. Another important use of running records is to determine whether readers are self-selecting materials that are too easy, too difficult, or just right. Ideally, students self-select a lot of what they read. Self-selection helps children to read more and encourages them to develop literary tastes and preferences, but it may also mean that what they read is not challenging enough to spur their development.

It's understandable why students would select easy books: Reading them is usually very enjoyable because the reader doesn't have to work very hard at it. Consider your own and other adults' self-selected pleasure reading materials. If you are like most adults, you would rather read popular best-selling fiction and nonfiction than the "good-for-you" novels that your English teachers assigned you.

Children are no different. Leave it entirely up to them, and they'll generally choose the easy, the familiar, and the popular over material that might make them think, wonder, or struggle the least bit. But texts that are a stretch for us help us to become better readers, thinkers, and communicators. Teachers can use running records to check whether the materials students are choosing are very easy for them. If students are reading material orally for the first time (i.e., "reading it cold") at close to 100 percent accuracy with few miscues, then the material represents their *independent level.* The independent reading level is one of three reading levels reading specialists speak off. The other two are the *instructional level* and the *frustration level.* All three levels are defined and explained in Figure 4.3.

Some reading at the independent level is good for you, but a steady diet of reading material on that level will not help you to grow as a reader.

If students are reading at around 90 percent or greater accuracy, making a few miscues that either make sense or are spontaneously corrected, then the material represents their *instructional level* As you saw in Figure 4.3, the instructional level represents material that is comfortably challenging. Material written on this level is ideal for growth in reading. It is easy enough to be read without a struggle but not so easy that it can be done with the mind on automatic pilot.

If students are reading at much below 90 percent accuracy and their miscues generally don't make sense, or if they can't correct their miscues or don't try to correct, then we deduce that the material is at the *frustration level.* Reading at this level is unpleasant

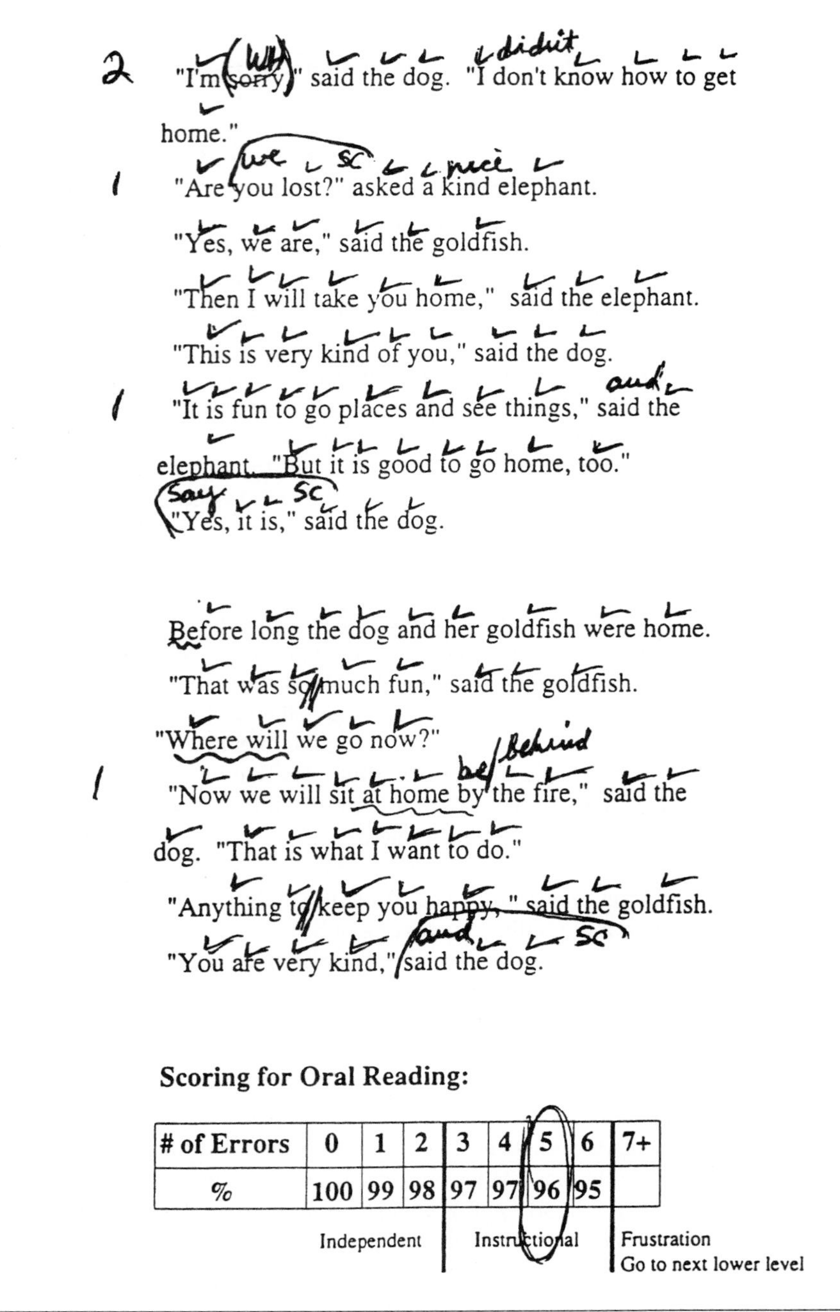

"I'm sorry," said the dog. "I don't know how to get home."

"Are you lost?" asked a kind elephant.

"Yes, we are," said the goldfish.

"Then I will take you home," said the elephant.

"This is very kind of you," said the dog.

"It is fun to go places and see things," said the elephant. "But it is good to go home, too."

"Yes, it is," said the dog.

Before long the dog and her goldfish were home.

"That was so much fun," said the goldfish.

"Where will we go now?"

"Now we will sit at home by the fire," said the dog. "That is what I want to do."

"Anything to keep you happy," said the goldfish.

"You are very kind," said the dog.

Scoring for Oral Reading:

# of Errors	0	1	2	3	4	5	6	7+
%	100	99	98	97	97	96	95	

Independent | Instructional | Frustration Go to next lower level

FIGURE 4.2 *A Running Record*

It is possible to measure children's *reading levels,* the difficulty levels of text they can read for different purposes. To talk about reading levels implies two things: that texts have levels of difficulty and that readers have levels of ability. To speak of levels of difficulty of texts implies that some are written on a first-grade level, some on a second-grade level, and so on. These levels of difficulty are referred to as **readability**. When we speak of the reading levels of individual readers, it helps to ask what the reading task is: Will they be studying a book in a group under the teacher's supervision, reading a textbook for homework, or reading for pleasure? Depending on the answers to those questions, it is proper to speak not of one reading level but three: the *independent level,* the *instructional level,* and the *frustration level.*

INDEPENDENT READING LEVEL. If the child is to read material on his or her own, without the support of a teacher or other more skilled readers, then the material should fall within the child's independent level of reading ability. In material written at the child's independent level, the child should encounter no more than three or four unknown words in a hundred and should enjoy nearly total comprehension.

Books that fall within children's independent level include ones children choose to read for pleasure and textbooks they use independently for homework. Regardless of a child's grade placement, if the books are above the child's independent level, then the child should be given easier books or should be offered support for reading such as buddy reading, study guides, or recorded text. Conversely, teachers sometimes have to prod children to read more challenging material that falls within their independent level.

INSTRUCTIONAL READING LEVEL. In the classroom, teachers often work with children in material that is moderately challenging for them so they will learn from the supported practice. Material used for this purpose should fall within the child's instructional level of reading ability. Such material presents the child with unknown words at a rate of up to one in ten, as well as language and concepts that are not fully comprehended—at least not at first. The intention is that with guided practice in materials written at the instructional level, children will learn the unknown words and come to comprehend the once-challenging language and concepts. The instructional level corresponds to what Vygotsky (1976) called the *zone of proximal development,* the area of moderate challenge that is just at the threshold of a reader's growing abilities. It is here that teachers most often practice *scaffolded instruction,* providing temporary support, including teaching strategies that will help the child learn on his or her own in the future.

Again, a particular child's instructional level often falls above or below that child's grade placement level. Because of the value of working in moderately challenging materials when teaching a child to read, it is very important to locate a child's instructional level wherever it may be.

FRUSTRATION READING LEVEL. If the material is too challenging—that is, if it contains more than one unfamiliar word in ten, in addition to language and concepts that substantially resist comprehension—the material is said to be written at the child's frustration level. The frustration level is not actually a reading level because children do not practice successful reading there. It is used rather to define the limits of a child's instructional level. Teachers can assign reading material during closely supervised instructional tasks that approach, but do not cross into, the frustration level.

As the name implies, frustration level text is so challenging to a child that the challenge of reading it is burdensome and disagreeable. Children will actually progress faster in learning to read and learning to spell when they are placed in instructional level text, even though that is easier than frustration level text.

It is often possible to determine through observation that a child is reading at frustration level. The child exhibits some or all of the following behaviors: laborious word-for-word, or even letter-by-letter, reading with flat intonation; pointing behavior, especially when that is not observed in easier passages; squinting or moving the text very close to the eyes; and rocking back and forth, perhaps kicking the chair or table. Think about what your own physical behaviors would be if you were asked to read aloud from a quantitative chemistry text that you did not understand at all.

FIGURE 4.3 *Functional Reading Levels: Independent, Instructional, Frustration*

The characterization of miscues based on meaning, structural, or visual information is intended to bring to light the kind of information a child is tracking in a text. Clay writes:

Meaning: *Does the child use meaning (M)? If what he reads makes sense, even though it is inaccurate, then he is probably applying his knowledge of the world to his reading.*

Structure: *Is what he said possible in an English sentence (S is for syntactically appropriate)? If it is, his oral language is probably influencing his responding. If it is not . . . [he] is paying close attention to detail, or to word by word reading. . .*

Visual information: *Does he use visual information (V) from the letters and words or the layout of print? [In a footnote, Clay adds, "Whether the child is relating visual information to sounds (phonological information) or to orthography (information about spelling) is a refinement of using visual information not distinguished in this analysis at this time."]*

(Clay, 1993, p. 31)

FIGURE 4.4 *Clay's Classification of Reading Errors*

and discouraging; little is learned from the reading, and negative attitudes about reading might quickly develop.

Clay's formulation of the Running Record invites the teacher to do further analysis of the kinds of word reading errors the child commits. They can count the number of self-corrections the child makes and calculate the percentage of errors that are corrected. And they may make judgments about whether the errors appeared based on "meaning," "structural," or "visual" cues from the text (see Figure 4.4).

Note, however, that the value of both calculating self-correction rates and of classifying reading errors has been called into serious question by Share (1990) and Adams (1999), respectively. Children's rates of self-correction may be more an artifact of the difficulty of the text than an indication of the child's appropriate use of metacognition or comprehension (Share, 1990). As for the classification of errors as meaning-based, structural, or visual, the main problem is that these distinctions seem to date from a time when some experts thought reading was a "psycholinguistic guessing game" in which the best readers made meaning-based guesses at words and the poor readers paid attention to the letters and words and used phonics knowledge to decode them. The overwhelming majority of the evidence now suggests that just the opposite is true (Adams, 1998; National Reading Panel, 1999). That being the case, it is unclear what teachers should do with this information. It may be enough, then, to record how well the student reads the passage and score the results quantitatively.

Further Assessments of Beginning and Fledgling Readers

Running Records measure children's accuracy in reading connected text at their instructional level. When we add timing their reading and asking for and scoring a retelling, Running Records give a measure of their reading fluency and their comprehension also. When you test a child with the Running Record and find he cannot read sentences unaided, though, you should drop back and give the following assessments:

- The concepts about print test (pages 47–49).
- The cluster of assessments that include alphabet knowledge, concept of word, phonemic awareness, and word recognition (pages 49–61).
- The test of listening comprehension (pages 221–225; 230–231).

Going the other way, occasionally even a young child reads the text in the Running Record so fluently that we suspect he or she is no longer a beginner. (Imagine administering a Running Record to Little Man, Cassie Logan's precocious little brother in Mildred Taylor's *Roll of Thunder, Hear My Cry*!) You will need to assess such a child with an Informal Reading Inventory, which is discussed in the next chapter. Informal Reading Inventories can identify children's reading levels over a wide spectrum, and provide additional assessment information of a diagnostic kind.

Assessing Beginning and Fledgling Students' Word Knowledge

Learning to read words accurately and quickly is the main work of beginning and fledgling reading (Morris & Slavin, 2002; Tynan, 2009). Not that comprehension and vocabulary and fluency and the habit of reading aren't important—they all are. But until word reading becomes easy and automatic, figuring out what the words on the page say will occupy most of students' concentration.

There are several things we need to know about students' word recognition.

1. We first need to know how many words they can recognize in the texts they are asked to read. Running Records show us this information fairly well. The Informal Reading Inventory (discussed at length in the next chapter) yields as much or more information about the quantity of words students recognize in different levels of text.
2. Next we need to understand how they think about the structures of words—what Stanovich and his associates (Cunningham, et al., 2011) call *orthographic processing*. As will be seen in Chapter 8, children at one developmental level look at words as wholes. Children at a more advanced level look at the relations between single letters and sounds in words. Later, children look at "chunks" of letters and relate them to larger units of sound. And gradually they become aware of grammatical morphemes and other markers, compound words, and words derived from the same roots. So a second way of looking at word recognition is analytic or qualitative—looking below the surface of children's word reading and word writing errors to try to ascertain how they are processing the spellings of words. To look at children's word knowledge qualitatively, we will present two kinds of assessments in this chapter. One is a test of word knowledge by means of invented or intuitive spelling, the *Monster Test* by Richard

Gentry. The other tests word knowledge through the recognition of novel words: Alan Crawford's *Demtup Names Test*.

3. A third kind of assessment is to see how many high-frequency sight words they know. To measure this, we can ask them to recognize words from Dr. Ed Fry's *Instant Words* list.

Assessing Word Knowledge Through Invented Spelling: *The Monster Test*. It is possible to assess children's word knowledge through their spelling errors when they write words they have not yet learned to spell. Richard Gentry devised a widely used measure for analyzing spelling errors, called the *Monster Test* (see Figure 4.5). The test is intended for young readers: kindergarten through second grade. It consists of only ten words, and is simple to administer. It can be administered to several children at a time—although if it is given to a group, you should take care to have them write their

SPELLING WORD LIST

1. monster	The boy was eaten by a **MONSTER**.
2. united	You live in the **UNITED** States.
3. dress	The girl wore a new **DRESS**.
4. bottom	A big fish lives at the **BOTTOM** of the lake.
5. hiked	We **HIKED** to the top of the mountain.
6. human	Miss Piggy is not a **HUMAN**.
7. eagle	An **EAGLE** is a powerful bird.
8. closed	The little girl **CLOSED** the door.
9. bumped	The car **BUMPED** into the bus.
10. type	**TYPE** the letter on the computer.

FIGURE 4.5 *The Monster Test*

Source: Adapted from "You Can Analyze Developmental Spelling," by J. Richard Gentry in *Teaching/K–8*, May 1985 as appeared in *All Children Read*, 3/e by Charles A. Temple et al. Reprinted by permission of J. Richard Gentry.

answers on numbered lines so you can tell later which written response corresponded with which spoken word.

You will want to reassure the children before testing them, so begin by telling them that you want to see how they spell some new words. You know that the words are too difficult for children their age to spell correctly, so you want them to invent their own spelling, to show how they think the words might be spelled. The activity won't be graded right and wrong; it will be used to see how the children think the words might be spelled.

Read each spelling word and then the exemplary sentence. Give plenty of encouragement; keep the atmosphere light and playful.

In order to interpret the results, read over the examples and descriptions of spelling phases provided by Gentry in Figures 4.6 and 4.7.

DEVELOPMENTAL SPELLING TEST SCORING CHART
Dr. J. Richard Gentry
Professor of Elementary Education and Reading

WORDS	Precommunicative Stage	Semiphonetic Stage	Phonetic Stage	Transitional Stage	Conventional Stage
1 monster	Random letters	Mtr	Mostr	monstur	monster
2 united	Random letters	U	Unitd	younighted	united
3 dress	Random letters	Jrs	Jras	dres	dress
4 bottom	Random letters	Bt	Bodm	bottum	bottom
5 hiked	Random letters	H	Hikt	hicked	hiked
6 human	Random letters	Um	hum	humum	human
7 eagle	Random letters	El	Egl	egul	eagle
8 closed	Random letters	Kd	Klosd	clossed	closed
9 bumped	Random letters	B	Bopt	bumpped	bumped
10 type	Random letters	Tp	Tip	tipe	type

FIGURE 4.6 *Scoring Responses to the Monster Test*

Source: Adapted from "You Can Analyze Developmental Spelling," by J. Richard Gentry in *Teaching/K–8,* May 1985 as appeared in *All Children Read,* 3/e by Charles A. Temple et al. Reprinted by permission of J. Richard Gentry.

1. **PRECOMMUNICATIVE SPELLING** is the "babbling" stage of spelling. Children use letters for writing words but the letters are strung together randomly. The letters in precommunicative spelling do not correspond to sounds.
   Examples: OPSPS = eagle; RTAT = eighty.
2. **SEMIPHONETIC SPELLERS** know that letters represent sounds. They perceive and represent reliable sounds with letters in a type of telegraphic writing. Spellings are often abbreviated representing initial and/or final sound.
   Examples: E = eagle; a = eighty.
3. **PHONETIC SPELLERS** spell words like they sound. The speller perceives and represents all of the phonemes in a word, though spellings may be unconventional.
   Examples: EGL = eagle; ATE = eighty.
4. **TRANSITIONAL SPELLERS** think about how words appear visually; a visual memory of spelling patterns is apparent. Spellings exhibit conventions of English orthography like vowels in every syllable, e-marker and vowel digraph patterns, correctly spelled inflectional endings, and frequent English letter sequences.
   Examples: EGIL = eagle; EIGHTEE = eighty.
5. **CONVENTIONAL SPELLERS** develop over years of word study and writing. Correct spelling can be categorized by instruction levels. For example, correct spelling for a corpus [of] words that can be spelled by the average fourth grader would be fourth grade level correct spelling. Place the word in this category if it is listed correctly.

FIGURE 4.7 *Explanation of Gentry's Stages of Invented Spelling*

Source: Adapted from "You Can Analyze Developmental Spelling," by J. Richard Gentry in *Teaching/K–8*, May 1985 as appeared in *All Children Read*, 3/e by Charles A. Temple et al. Reprinted by permission of J. Richard Gentry.

Compare each child's spellings to the samples given in the chart. If half or more of a child's errors can be matched to any one phase, it is likely to be the child's phase of spelling development. Phases of spelling development and word knowledge will be discussed in detail in the next chapter. For now we will pass along Gentry's description of the spelling stages identified by the *Monster Test*. (See Figure 4.7.)

For more information on the *Monster Test* and teaching procedures that are recommended from it, please see Gentry (2007). For further instructions on administering and scoring the test, including a video, please see Gentry (2008).

Applying the Results of *The Monster Test*. To apply the results of the *Monster Test*, consider what children know and need to know at each level of spelling development.

Children at the precommunicative stage. Children who are what Gentry call precommunicative spellers will need the most basic acquaintance with written words. Teaching with the Language Experience Approach (see pages 127–129) and Shared Reading will be in order. It is also advisable to give them the emergent literacy assessments described in the previous chapter, since these children are emergent readers and not beginning readers.

Children at the semi-phonetic stage. Children at this next stage have discovered the alphabetic principle: Letters represent words via their sounds. They are not yet confident or consistent at representing sounds in words, though. They should be taught phonics combinations at the letter-to-sound level. These children should be given lots of practice reading simply worded texts, particularly texts that contain the phonics patterns they are learning. They should receive instruction that reinforces the concept of word, and also instruction in phonemic segmentation (see the previous chapter for suggestions for both).

Children at the phonetic stage of spelling. Children who are phonetic spellers, as Gentry calls them, are accomplished at dividing words into their phonemes. They have an intuitive idea of how letters represent sounds, but these ideas are often incorrect. They will be helped by instruction in letter-to-sound relationships. The interactive writing task described later in this chapter will also help, since it offers instruction on just those letter-to-sound relationships that they don't yet know. Encouraging writing with invented spelling is still recommended, but these children should also be given dictionaries of words they use frequently so they can practice the correct spellings of them.

Children at the transitional stage of spelling. Transitional spellers have begun to look at words beyond the letter-to-sound level. They are now aware of onsets and rimes, or phonogram patterns. They are also aware of more general rules about spelling, especially the marking of long and short vowels (see next chapter). They are beginning to be aware of morphemes—such as past tense and plural endings. (These are often not spelled as they sound.) These students should be encouraged to write, and to read widely. They should also be given practice with the more advanced word study techniques we will present in the next chapter.

Assessing Word Knowledge by Means of Novel Words: *Demtup Names Test.* Another way to test children's recognition of different letter-to-sound pairings, or elements of phonics, is to ask them to read novel words. The logic here is that children will need to rely upon their knowledge of letter-to-sound relationships, or phonics knowledge, to recognize words they have never seen before. Another part of the logic is that proper names are a familiar type of unfamiliar word. Therefore reading novel words as if they were people's names still falls within the ballpark of a natural act of reading.

Alan Crawford developed the *Demtup Names Test* as part of *The Developmental Literacy Inventory* (Temple, Crawford, & Gillet, 2008). (Figure 4.8 explains how to administer the Demtup Names Test, which follows as Figure 4.9. Figure 4.10 is the scoring sheet for the text.)

The *Demtup Names Test* can be used to examine students' strengths and weaknesses in specific types of phonics skills in words they do not already know. It should be administered in a different sitting from the other parts of the *Developmental Literacy Inventory.*

Getting Ready to Test

Find a quiet place and plan for the time needed. Using the *Demtup Names Test* for the purpose of determining a student's ability to decode unknown words can take about ten minutes.

Arrange the space and assemble the materials. Before you begin, assemble all of the materials you will need:

1. A copy of the *Demtup Names Test* pages for the student to read.
2. A photocopy of the examiner's pages for recording the student's responses.
3. Blank paper and pencils.
4. (Optional) A tape recorder.

Reassure the student. Before beginning, tell the student that you want to know how she figures out how to pronounce new and unknown words. (Avoid using the word "test.") There will be no grade. It is important for the student to do his or her best, although there will be some activities she or he will not be sure about.

Sit beside the student. If you are right-handed, place the student to your left, with your materials for recording placed off to the right and out of the student's view. If you are left-handed, do the reverse.

Assessing Phonics Knowledge in Unknown Words

Begin by reading these instructions to the child: *Demtup is a planet far from Earth. The children there have very strange names. The children look strange, too. Read about the children from Demtup, but be sure to say their names correctly. It hurts their feelings if you don't.*

Then hand the child the student's version of the *Demtup Names Test* and ask the child to read each sentence out loud. Tell the child that the children's names have to be sounded out, but that the rest of each sentence about strange children from the planet *Demtup* is easier to read.

On the score sheet, you will only score the *Demtup* names listed there. Do not score any elements in italics. You will also ignore the part of each sentence that follows each name; those parts are not included on the score sheet. You may help a child with the part of a sentence that follows the *Demtup* names, if necessary, but not with the *Demtup* names themselves. Circle correctly read elements in the *Demtup* names. If the child makes an error, write what the child said above the element not read correctly. If the child successfully self-corrects in a phonics element within a *Demtup* name, you may give full credit. Again, ignore any errors in the part of each sentence that follows the *Demtup* name.

Continue testing until the student is unsuccessful on four consecutive items.

FIGURE 4.8 *Administering the* Demtup Names Test

Suggestion for the Examiner:
When a student makes a response, receive it in a way that is encouraging, but not evaluative: "Thank you. OK, let's go on." Avoid pointing out errors. Also avoid praising a student for correct answers. The tasks will soon get harder, the student will make errors, and the absence of praise may become unnerving to the student!

Suggestion for the Examiner:
At least until you become proficient marking the errors, you may want to tape record the session. If you do, put the tape recorder in an inconspicuous place, and use a long-playing tape so you won't have to change it while you are testing. You will still need to mark the errors while you test. The tape recording will serve as a backup to reinforce your accuracy.

Enter the results on the Score Summary Sheet. Enter the number of correct responses on each line on the Score Summary Sheet. You may sum the scores at the bottom.

Interpreting the Results

The *Demtup Names Test* assesses a sample of phonics elements. The 78 test items provide an overview of a student's ability to decode unknown words that contain a variety of phonics elements ranging from simple letter-to-sound patterns to more complex patterns of onsets and rimes, root words, prefixes, and suffixes. It may be used to observe how the student decodes unknown words that contain major types of phonics elements. You may find, for example, that a student has a good mastery of initial consonant sounds, but that vowel sounds are difficult. You may find that individual consonant sounds are not difficult for a student, but that they are difficult when combined in consonant blends. These results may suggest general areas of phonics instruction that need to be reinforced.

The total score should be considered within the context of the student's grade level. A score of 24 at the end of the first grade may be quite good, but not at the end of the fifth grade. Use the results as a window into your understanding of the student's progress in phonics, not as an absolute goal to be reached immediately at any cost.

FIGURE 4.8 *Continued*

Mab lives on Demtup.

Tep lives there, too.

Gom has three eyes.

Fid has only one eye.

Ret has two noses.

Yob likes to eat candy.

Vax is her friend.

Cim is ten years old.

Mabben laughs at his friend.

Hock has a bicycle.

Rabbitwood has a long name.

Catly runs very fast.

Trin is very happy.

Smet has six arms.

Plun likes to eat wood.

Jath has a dog.

Lupet has four brothers.

Mape lives in a big house.

Tay is green.

Aulon has four ears.

Nur can fly.

Zink is very sad.

Knop can sing well.

Minition likes his name.

Polynough doesn't like his name.

FIGURE 4.9 *Assessing Phonics Knowledge: The* **Demtup Names Test**

Source: Temple, et al., *Developmental Literacy Inventory*, "The Demtup Names Test" pp. 402–405, © 2009. Reproduced by permission of Pearson Education, Inc.

Instructions: As the child reads aloud from the student copy, circle each correct element that is shown below on this scoring sheet. In the event of an incorrect response, write what the child said above the element. The words in the sentences that follow the Demtup names have been eliminated from the scoring sheet. They are not to be scored. Do not score the elements in *italic* type. They duplicate or parallel elements already scored.

Mab	onset /m/	rime /ab/	________/2 points
Tep	onset /t/	rime /ep/	________/2 points
Gom	onset (hard) /g/	rime /om/	________/2 points
Fid	onset /f/	rime /id/	________/2 points
Ret	onset /r/	rime /et/	________/2 points

FIGURE 4.10 *Score Summary Sheet for the* **Demtup Names Test**

Source: Temple, et al., *Developmental Literacy Inventory*, "The Demtup Names Test" pp. 402–405, © 2009. Reproduced by permission of Pearson Education, Inc.

Yob	onset /y/	rime /ob/		________/2 points
Vax	onset /v/	rime /ax/		________/2 points
Cim	onset (soft) /c/	rime /im/		________/2 points
Mabben	short /a/ in stressed syllable			________/1 point
	schwa (ə) in unstressed syllable			________/1 point
Hock	onset /h/	rime /ock/		________/2 points
Rabbitwood	Student should read rabbit and wood as sight words without decoding			________/2 points
Catly	read sight word cat, and suffix ly without decoding			________/2 points
Trin	onset /tr/			________/1 point
Smet	onset /sm/			________/1 point
Plun	onset /pl/			________/1 point
Jath	onset /j/	rime /ath/		________/2 points
Lupet	long /u/ in open syllable			________/1 point
Mape	onset /m/	rime /ape/		________/2 points
Tay Noam	onset /t/	rime /ay/		________/2 points
Aulon	rime /au/	onset /l/	rime /on/	________/3 points
Nur	onset /n/	rime /ur/		________/2 points
Zink	onset /z/	rime /ink/		________/2 points
Knop	onset /kn/			________/1 point
Minition	prefix /mini/ pronounced without decoding	suffix /tion/		________/2 points
Polynough	prefix /poly/	final /ough/		________/2 points
TOTAL POINTS				________/46 points

FIGURE 4.10 *Continued*

Assessing Recognition of High-Frequency Words

To see how many of the highest frequency words a child knows, show the child the words one at a time, and check all correct responses in the record sheet. It may be helpful to print the words on index cards, and show the cards in order. Figure 4.11 is the list of high-frequency words.

Instruction for Beginning and Fledgling Readers

Once we have assessment information on a child, what do we do next? In the following sections, we lay out suggestions for teaching beginning readers and fledgling readers

FRY'S 300 INSTANT SIGHT WORDS

First Hundred

a	before	get	how	many	our	then	were
about	boy	give	I	me	out	there	when
after	but	go	in	much	put	they	which
again	by	good	is	my	said	this	who
all	can	had	it	new	see	three	will
an	come	has	just	no	she	to	with
any	day	have	know	of	so	two	work
are	did	he	like	old	some	up	would
as	do	her	little	on	take	us	you
at	down	here	long	one	the	very	your
be	for	him	make	or	their	was	
been	from	his	man	other	them	we	

Second Hundred

also	box	five	leave	name	pretty	stand	use
am	bring	found	left	near	ran	such	want
another	call	four	let	never	read	sure	way
away	came	friend	live	next	red	tell	where
back	color	girl	look	night	right	than	while
ball	could	got	made	only	run	these	white
because	dear	hand	may	open	saw	thing	why
best	each	high	men	over	say	think	wish
better	ear	home	more	own	school	too	year
big	end	house	morning	people	seem	tree	
black	far	into	most	play	shall	under	
book	find	kind	mother	please	should	until	
both	first	last	must	present	soon	upon	

Third Hundred

along	clothes	eyes	green	letter	ride	small	walk
always	coat	face	grow	longer	round	start	warm
anything	cold	fall	hat	love	same	stop	wash
around	cut	fast	happy	might	sat	ten	water
ask	didn't	fat	hard	money	second	thank	woman
ate	does	fine	head	myself	set	third	write
bed	dog	fire	hear	now	seven	those	yellow
brown	don't	fly	help	o'clock	show	though	yes
buy	door	food	hold	off	sing	today	yesterday
car	dress	full	hope	once	sister	took	
carry	early	funny	hot	order	sit	town	
clean	eight	gave	jump	pair	six	try	
close	every	goes	keep	part	sleep	turn	

FIGURE 4.11 ***High-Frequency Words***

Source: From *1000 Instant Words: The Most Common Words for Teaching Reading, Writing and Spelling* by Edward B. Fry. Copyright © 2000 Teacher Created Resources. Used with permission of Teacher Created Resources, www.teachercreated.com.

who need extra support. A good plan for teaching a beginning or fledgling reader should include a blend of reading activities that provide instruction and practice of most of the components of beginning reading:: word recognition, comprehension, fluency, and vocabulary. Such a plan has been suggested by Darrell Morris in his Early Steps program (Morris et al., 2000). The plan is for a tutoring lesson of 30–40 minutes duration.

Tutoring Lesson

Step One: Read an Instructional Level Book. The first part of the lesson is done with a reading from a book written at each child's instructional level. This portion of the lesson should last eight to ten minutes. Begin by reading a book that the child finds moderately challenging. The point of reading an instructional level book is that it will contain words, phrases, sentence structures, and concepts that the child does not already know, but can learn with the support of the tutor. An instructional level book is one in which the child reads 90–95 percent of the words correctly and comprehends about three quarters of the ideas in the text. The book used in this part of the lesson may be a short "little book," or a section from a longer book. Once a program of tutoring has begun, the book that was previewed in the preceding session will be used for this lesson.

Tell the child that his goal is to read this challenging text so that he can learn new words and new ideas. Remind him that the more he reads, the easier reading will get. You will be there to help him. He should also practice using certain reading strategies as he reads.

Preview the book. Before reading a book, it helps to preview it for several reasons. First, previewing provides a context for the reading that will make it easier to make predictions for what will follow, and also to read unknown words. Second, previewing offers the teacher a chance to teach the child about the parts of a book: the cover, the title, and the author's and illustrator's names. It also affords a chance to pre-teach new vocabulary that will appear in the reading.

To preview the book, the teacher first shows the cover, the title, the author's name, and the illustrator's name (if not the same as the author). The teacher asks or thinks aloud about the author, and reminds the child of other books they have read by the same author. They discuss the illustration on the cover and name the characters and the setting that are depicted; then they begin to make predictions about what will happen in the book.

Next they do a picture walk. Together they page through the book, looking at the pictures, and trying to weave a story across them. In the picture walk, the teacher can carefully name the parts of the plot: the setting, the characters, the problem, the attempts at a solution, and the solution. The picture walk may stop before the final couple of pages, so as not to give away the conclusion of the story. The teacher can raise a question about the ending: What do we think will happen?

The teacher has identified three to five new words in advance. As these words appear in the text during the picture walk:

- The teacher points to the word and reads it aloud.
- The teacher reads the sentence aloud in which the word appears.

- The teacher has the child say the word.
- The teacher explains what the word means.
- The child is asked to repeat the word, and then they move on.

Reading with scaffolding. Reading an instructional level book is challenging by definition, so a teacher must be ready to ease just enough of the burden to keep the reading going forward without over-stressing the child. Some children need more support than others; and the same child may need more or less support depending on the day. It is important not to give the child more support than she needs, so that she will put in a solid effort to read the text.

Scaffolding can take several forms:

- **Offer a prompt for an unknown word.** The best way to do this is to remind the child of a strategy she already has been taught. But you may also tell the child the word if she is unable to figure it out after 15 seconds or so. It is important that the reading keep moving forward, so that the child doesn't lose the thread of the meaning.
- **Offer specific praise.** When the child uses a strategy correctly, it helps for the teacher to praise the child and name the strategy the child used: "Good for you. You went back and corrected your reading of that word. That's what good readers do."
- **Alternate reading with the child.** If the child seems reluctant to read on, offer to read a paragraph, and then have the child read the next one, and so on. Or alternate sentences. Or alternate pages. Slowly phase out your own reading as the child gains confidence.

Reading unknown words. Useful strategies for reading unknown words include looking at a picture for a meaningful context to support the reading, "getting your mouth ready to say it," asking what word would make sense in that place, asking if a pronounced word sounds right, and finding known chunks of words within an unknown word. During each tutoring lesson, the teacher should introduce one strategy and work with the child to practice it over several lessons. Then in a later session the teacher can introduce another strategy, practice that one over several sessions, and introduce another strategy. The strategies can be drawn on a chart on the wall, and also placed inside the cover of a child's reading notebook (see Figure 4.12).

Rereading for fluency. Beginning readers work hard to render groups of letters into sound. In the process, they may pronounce the words oddly, and lose the thread of what the words mean. They may also miss the prosody, or the "music" of the lines. When this happens, the teacher should ask the child to "Go back and read that line again. Make it sound like talk." Repeated exposure to the words is beneficial, first because it aids comprehension, and second because the more times the child fixates on new words in print, the more likely she is to remember them. When he reads, the teacher should also take opportunities to model fluent expressive reading. The teacher can call attention to what he is doing, so the child understands that expressive reading that "sounds like talk" is her goal, too.

Reading and questioning. To keep part of the focus on comprehension, the teacher should think aloud about the meaning—what is going on, what the characters are like,

As the child reads an unknown word, he should be taught to:

- **Look at the picture** for a clue to the meaning.
- **Ask himself: Is it making sense?** If it is not, he should go back and reread a questionable word.
- **"Get your mouth ready to read it."** As the child reads through the line of print, when he gets to an unknown word, he should pronounce the first letter and then try to predict what the rest of the word will be, based on the context of what he has read.
- **Ask himself: Does it sound right?** Sometimes in the efforts to sound out a word, a child will pronounce the letters incorrectly. At those times the child should ask himself, "Does it sound right?" And he should ask if it makes sense.
- **Find chunks.** The child should be encouraged to find parts of a word she already knows within an unknown word. For example, *cart* has *car* in it; *brat* has *rat* in it.

FIGURE 4.12 *A Chart of Word Reading Strategies*

what is likely to happen or be revealed in the next lines. The teacher can offer his or her own ideas or questions, and then invite the child to offer his or hers.

Step Two: Read an Independent Level Book. Text written at children's independent reading level can be read with 95 percent accurate word recognition or higher, and 90 percent comprehension or higher. It may be a book the child has read before. Children need to read independent level books for practice toward fluency. They also are much better able to explore the ideas in the text if they can read the words easily.

For beginning and fledgling readers, reading texts at the independent level allows teachers to introduce and practice more comprehension-oriented reading practices. Some of these are:

- imaging
- predicting and confirming
- inferring
- identifying parts of a narrative
- identifying parts of an informational text

There is something of a natural progression to these strategies. Imaging is not so hard for children to do under a teacher's guidance. Predicting and confirming is an activity that children commonly practice outside of school. Identifying parts of a story or other text is harder than predicting and confirming because it challenges the child to use meta-language—that is, language about language. The parts of stories are easier to learn than the parts of informational text. Learning to do both will make it easier for children to summarize what they have read.

Introduce these strategies one at a time, each one in a single lesson. Give the children guided practice using the strategy in a tutoring or small-group session. Then have them practice using the strategy while reading independently or with a "buddy."

Imaging. Summoning up visions "in the mind's eye" in response to words on the page is a valuable way to savor the experience of a written work. Good readers use books as a way to take themselves to other times and places and to get to know new people. Pearson and Duke (2002) consider imaging to be a key comprehension skill. Authors construct images by using words that appeal to the five senses. The passage below uses many of the senses.

> The next day, Jack was surprised to see a thick green bean vine growing right outside the window where his mama had thrown those beans. Jack looked up. He couldn't see how high the bean stalk went. So he grabbed a leaf stem and pulled himself up. He pulled up on another one. He climbed and pulled and pulled and climbed all morning—and then he looked down. His little cottage looked like a matchbox. The road to the market looked like a crooked string. Then that beanstalk began to sway. It swayed this way, and that way, and all around. Jack clutched the trunk and squeezed his eyes shut. And then he opened them again and started climbing up and up and up. Suddenly fog was everywhere. He felt little dew drops on his cheeks. He climbed on. It got lighter, and then—daylight! Jack was on top of the clouds. He put his foot out and tested one. It held his weight, so he stepped off the beanstalk onto the cloud. It was soft and springy, like walking on a bed. Soon Jack was bouncing across the clouds.

To teach children to image, take advantage of passages like this when you come across them.

1. **Name and explain the strategy.** Tell the children they will be working on the strategy of imaging, or forming a picture in their minds of what the text says. Authors use words that say how things look, feel, sound, smell, or taste. It is a good idea to pause when you read such words and let your imagination bring these images to life in your mind.
2. **Ask children to adopt the point of view of a character.** Children can imagine that they have become a character, and mime the sensations and feelings of the character:

   "Let's put our heads out the window, and look up like Jack did. What do we see? Any idea how tall it is?"
   "Now let's climb up on these leaf stems. Careful—are you sure they will hold our weight?"
   "Look down! What do you see? They're so tiny! How does that make you feel?"
   "Whoa! The beanstalk is swaying! Hold on tight!"
   "Now, do you feel these little cool drops of cloud on your cheek?"

3. **Ask children to assume the posture of a character.** For instance, children may be asked to hunch their shoulders like the mysterious old man, put their fists on their hips and frown in exasperation like Jack's mother, swell their chests like the giant, or shuffle about the kitchen like the giant's wife.

4. **Ask children to draw what they see in their imaginations.** After reading about a scene with sensory language, stop and ask children to draw pictures of what they saw. One at a time they can explain their pictures, while the teacher stresses things they saw, heard, felt, smelled, and tasted.
5. **Remind the children of the name of the strategy—"imaging," review the steps of the strategy,** and suggest that the children use the strategy when they are reading stories on their own.

Predicting and confirming. Making predictions of what will happen requires that children pay attention to the plot: who the main characters are, what their problem is, what they will try to do to solve the problem (and their efforts should be fitting to their characteristics), and what the results are likely to be. The prediction and confirming strategy uses the following steps.

1. **Clearly explain that the children will be learning to use the predicting and confirming strategy.** Explain that the strategy is useful because it helps us understand stories if we make predictions and then check to see if our predictions come true. This is a strategy we can practice when we are reading on our own.
2. **Choose four or five stopping places in advance of the reading.** Each stopping place should appear just after some information has been revealed, and just before more information is about to be revealed (rather like the place where a commercial would come in a television program).
3. **Ask the children to predict what will happen in the next section**: "What will ____ do?" "What will happen to ____?" Then ask, "Why do you think so?"
4. **Receive their predictions and their reasons with encouragement**, but without indicating which ones are more or less likely to be correct.
5. **Indicate where the next stopping place is found, and ask the children to read that far—and no further**. The teacher and the children all read to the next stopping place.
6. When all have finished reading, **ask the children which predictions came true.**
7. **Then ask the children to find the sentence that proved which prediction came true**—or showed what really happened if there were no accurate predictions.
8. **Remind the children of the name of the strategy—"predicting and confirming."** Review the steps of the strategy, and suggest that the children use the strategy when they are reading stories on their own.

The first few times the predicting and confirming strategy is used, the teacher may need to scaffold the procedure. *Thinking aloud* provides the most support. The teacher can venture her or his own predictions of what will happen next in the story, and ask children if they agree. Then they all can read to the next prearranged stopping place, and the teacher can ask the children if the prediction came true. If the children are not yet responsive, the teacher can venture his or her answer. Then the teacher should challenge the children to go back and find the sentence that proves the prediction was or was not correct; if the children seem unsure of themselves, the teacher can find the sentence and read it aloud to the class.

To release more responsibility to the children, the teacher can invite the children to choose between alternative answers. For example, the teacher can ask, "Do you think Jack will climb the beanstalk or stay home?"

Somebody	Wanted	But	So

FIGURE 4.13 *Somebody-Wanted-But-So Chart*

Source: Figure: "Somebody-Wanted-But So Chart" in *Responses to Literature,* Author: James M. Macon, Author: Diane Bewell, Author: Mary Ellen Vogt, Newark, DE: International Reading Association, 1991. Used and reprinted with permission of International Reading Association, www.reading.org.

As the children are able to participate with more confidence, the teacher withdraws support and asks the children to think for themselves.

Identifying Parts of a Story. If the children are reading a well-formed story in a setting with characters who have a problem, face a conflict, and find a solution, the teacher can point out the parts of the story. Probably the simplest description of the structure of common stories is the **Somebody-Wanted-But-So** procedure (Macon, Bewell & Vogt, 1991). The teacher makes a graphic organizer on chart paper or the board as in Figure 4.13.

After they have read a story, the teacher asks the children who the most important character was in the story, and that person's name is written in the "**Somebody**" column. Then the teacher asks the children what that character *wanted.* What was wanted is the goal of the story—the problem that needs a solution—and the answer to that question is written in the **"Wanted"** column. There is usually a problem that makes it difficult for the character to get what she or he wants. That problem is written in the **"But"** column. The characters succeed or fail in getting what they want. Whatever the resolution is at the end of the story is written in the **"So"** column.

The Somebody-Wanted-But-So chart can be posted on the classroom wall. As other stories are discussed and analyzed in this way, their parts are written in the appropriate columns on the chart.

Writing

Writing is a worthwhile skill in its own right. It is also a useful way for children to examine, learn, and practice the relations between letters and sounds or phonics. In the context of a reading lesson for beginners and fledgling readers, we recommend the **shared writing procedure.**

Shared Writing with Individual Children. The child should have something he wishes to communicate in writing. He or she will be asked to write it down, sound by sound, letter by letter, as the teacher offers encouragement, corrections, and instruction. Following are detailed instructions for individual shared writing.

1. **Begin the first few sessions by reminding the child that we get better at writing with practice.** Also, writing gives us a chance to see how letters represent words, and that helps us read.
2. **Prior to this session, ask the child to be thinking of something he or she wants to write at this time.** The child should come to the session ready to write out that idea. It is also a good idea to interview the child at the beginning of the school year, and keep a list of topics in a portfolio for each child. If the child comes to a tutoring session or small-group session without a topic to write about, you can quickly review his list of interests and suggest a topic from that list.
3. **Have the child rehearse the topic.** It is best if the child decides on one sentence to write down. Have the child say that sentence aloud many times so that it can be remembered.
4. **In a notebook that the child will keep all year, turn to a fresh page, date it, and ask the child to write her or his idea on that page.**
5. **Encourage the child to say the first word she or he wants to write, say the beginning sound, and write it down.** Proceed in this way as the child writes the first word.
6. **Have the child place a finger on the page between the first word and the next one, and between each subsequent word.**
7. **If a child makes a spelling mistake, say "That letter doesn't spell the ___ sound in this word.** The way we spell that sound in this word is _____." Have the child write each sound in the word correctly. Continue until the child has finished writing the sentence.
8. **Observe and take notes on the child's letter formation and handwriting.** Does the child form each letter correctly? If not, plan to teach a lesson on forming those letters that are giving trouble. Is the child's handwriting developing normally? Does the child appear to know a system for writing each letter in a way that is legible and easy to replicate? If not, plan to teach or reinforce the teaching of handwriting.
9. **Observe the child's spelling of the words.** Make a list in your portfolio of some key words the child spelled correctly, and also some words he struggled with. Use this information in planning word study lessons.
10. **Congratulate the child on a job well done.** Remind the child that writing and spelling are important, and that the child is learning useful skills.

Interactive Writing with a Small Group

Interactive Writing. If a teacher is working with more than one child, the interactive writing procedure can be used. Developed in London by Moira McKenzie, in *interactive writing* (Fountas & Pinnell, 1996), the teacher and the children "share the pen." The procedure works best if the children are on roughly the same levels of reading and writing ability. Interactive writing uses the following steps.

1. The teacher and a group of three to six children share an experience and agree on a topic that they will write about. The topic may be a retelling of a story, a poem, or a song, the daily news, or an idea under study.
2. The children offer a sentence about the topic. The teacher has the children repeat the sentence many times, and even count the words, to fix them firmly in their minds.

3. The teacher asks the children for the first word, pronounces that word slowly, then writes its letters.
4. The teacher now asks for the next word and invites a child up to write the whole word, or a few letters, or a single letter. The teacher fills in letters the children miss. If the child writes an incorrect letter, the teacher pastes a short strip of correction tape over it and helps the child identify the sound and write the correct letter for it.
5. Each time a word is added, the whole text is read back by the children, with the teacher pointing to the words.
6. After the session, the teacher should take notes on the children's performance—letter formation, handwriting, and spelling. These can be used to inform lessons for the children later on.

Attention to Handwriting. Handwriting has been called a "neglected skill of literacy" (Sheffield, 1996). It is true that nearly all primary school teachers devote time to teaching children to form letters properly and write them legibly and automatically, for an average of 70 minutes of instruction per week. But only one teacher in eight reports being prepared by teacher education courses to teach handwriting (Graham et al., 2008). Moreover, a closer look at handwriting instruction shows that many teachers' handwriting curricula and instruction are not sufficiently preparing students to write fluently and legibly (Van der Hart et al., 2010).

The neglect of handwriting has serious consequences for learners in the primary and intermediate grades. As Troia et al. (2009) point out, the inability to write letters automatically and legibly is a serious impediment to writing fluently and composing thoughtfully:

> If children have difficulty with handwriting and spelling and, consequently must devote substantial effort to transcribing their ideas, they will have fewer cognitive resources left available to engage in effective planning and revising behaviors, and to focus on writing content, organization and style. . . . (p. 99)

We recommend several actions to ensure that all children learn automatic, fluent handwriting.

1. Take care that you are a good model of fluent and legible handwriting yourself. There are several self-help guides available for the many adults, including college students, who were not properly taught to write fluently and legibly. These sources can help:

   Barchowsky, N. J. (2006). *Fix it write*. Swansbury Press.
   Sassoon, R. (2007). *Teach yourself better handwriting*, 3rd edition (2009). McGraw-Hill.

2. Use a program that teaches children to write the letters and practice fluent and legible handwriting. Practice handwriting daily. For manuscript handwriting, there is:

   Norris, J. (2000). *Daily handwriting practice: Traditional manuscript*. Evan Moor.
   Evan Moor (2000). *Daily handwriting practice: Contemporary cursive*. Evan Moor.

   Many schools prefer the D'Nealian handwriting system by Donald Thurber (1993). D'Nealian handwriting begins by introducing letters in a slightly sloping manuscript form that are easily linked together to make a cursive form. D'Nealian practice books and wall charts for children are available in levels from preschool through grade five.

3. Especially for older students, handwriting can be made more interesting by studying different styles of handwriting—taking time, for instance, to teach italic script. Students can also study handwriting analysis. There are a number of books for young people that explore these topics, as a quick search of the Amazon or Barnes and Noble websites will show.

Word Study

A portion of each reading lesson should be devoted to word study. *Word study* is a more general term than phonics instruction. We use it because *phonics* refers to the relation between letters and sounds, and we want children to learn not only phonics but also morphology, word families, and other important information about English words.

In the portion of the lesson devoted to word study, the teacher may choose from the following activities: the sound board, making and breaking words, or push it say it. All three activities are explained below. The teacher may also use the word sort technique or word walls, both of which are explained in the next chapters.

Sound Boards. A *sound board* (Blachman, 2000) is a device for showing children how words are constructed. You can use a commercially available pocket chart, or make your own. To make your own sound board, cut a piece measuring 11 inches by 14 inches from a sheet of poster board; then tape three strips of a different color from the board an inch and a half deep across the long side of the board.

Whether you use a pocket chart or make your own sound board, you will need to make *grapheme cards* on which you will write letters. These should be 1 inch wide by 3 inches high. Write letters or letter combinations exactly the same size on only the top half of each card (the bottom half of the card will disappear into the pocket). Prepare cards with consonant letters on them (written with a broad tip marker in black ink) and other cards with vowel letters and vowel teams (written in red ink).

Single consonant cards should include: **b, c, d, f, g, h, j, k, l, m, n, p, qu, r, s, t, v, w,** and **z.** Digraph consonant cards (a digraph is two letters that spell a single sound) should include **ch, th, sh, wh, ck,** and **ph.**

Vowel cards should contain ***a, e, i, o,*** and ***u.*** Vowel team cards should contain **ai, ay, ey, ee, ea, ie, oo, ou, ow, oi, oy, au, aw,** and **ew.** Vowel plus consonant cards should contain **ar, er, ir, ur,** and also **al** (as in **walk, calm,** and **bald**) (after Blachman, 2000).

The top pocket is for storing learned consonants and the middle pocket is for learned vowels. The bottom pocket is for making words. A manila envelope is attached to the back of the sound board for storing grapheme cards.

To use the sound board, put a consonant such as *s* in the bottom pocket. Pronounce its sound. Then put a vowel letter *a* to the right of it and pronounce its sound. Then put a consonant letter *t* to the right of the vowel and pronounce it. Say all three sounds and then pronounce the word *sat.* Now ask the child to repeat the activity, using the same three letters. Take away the letter *s* and ask him to sound the other two letters out and pronounce the word (*at*). Then pick up a new consonant letter card such as *p* and pronounce its sound. Put the *p* to the left of *a* and *t* and ask the child to pronounce all three sounds and say the word (*pat*).

Making and Breaking Words. As an enhancement of the word study component of the Reading Recovery program™ (see below for a discussion), Iverson and Tunmer (1993) developed a procedure for "making and breaking words." The procedure is carried out with a set of plastic letters and a magnetic board (available in most toy stores) and is conducted one-on-one.

The teacher asks the child to move the letters around to construct new words that have similar spellings and sound patterns. For instance, the teacher arranges letters to make the word *and.* The teacher announces that the letters spell *and* then asks the child what the word says. If the child seems uncertain, the teacher forms the word again, using different letters, says its name, and asks the child to name the word.

As a next step, the teacher scrambles the letters and asks the child to make *and.* Again, if assembling scrambled letters proves difficult, the teacher spreads the letters apart, in the proper order, at the bottom of the magnetic board and asks the child to make the word *and* with them in the middle of the board. When the child has made the word, the teacher asks the child to name the word. If the child responds correctly, the teacher scrambles the letters and asks the child to make the word again and to name the word afterward. The teacher repeats the procedure until the child is readily able to assemble the letters and name *and.*

As a next step, the teacher puts the letter *s* in front of *and* and announces what he has just done. The teacher takes a finger and moves the *s* away and then back and says, "Do you see? If I put *s* in front of *and,* it says *sand.*" The teacher asks the child to read the word *sand,* and the child runs a finger under it. Now the teacher removes the *s* and points out that with the *s* removed, the word is now *and.* With the *s* pushed aside, the teacher asks the child to make *sand.* If the child correctly makes the word, the teacher asks him to name the word he has made.

Next the teacher instructs the child to make *and.* As a next step, the whole procedure is repeated, making *hand* and *band.* Now the teacher can make *sand,* then *band,* then *hand,* and *and,* asking the child to name each word as it is made. When the child can do so successfully, the teacher scrambles the letters *and* on the board, and puts the letters *s, b,* and *h* to one side. Now the teacher challenges the child to make *and.* If the child can do so, the child is then challenged to make *hand, sand,* and *band.* The child is asked to read each word after it is made.

Push It Say It. From Johnston, Invernizzi, and Juel's *Book Buddies* program (1998) comes the *Push It Say It* technique. Here you prepare word cards as follows. One set of cards should be consonants (such as *s, b, c, t, m*), and the other should be rimes or phonogram patterns (such as *at, it, op*). To carry out the activity, first demonstrate it to the child, as follows.

1. Put a consonant card and a phonogram card separately on the table in front of the child. Drawing out the consonant sound ("ssssss"), push the consonant card forward.

2. Then drawing out the sound of the rime ("aaaaaat"), push the rime card forward.
3. Now pronounce the resulting word (*sat*).

Then provide the child a consonant card and a rime card and ask her to repeat what you did.

Teaching High-Frequency Words. As we explained earlier in this chapter, a couple of hundred words account for the majority of the words children see in texts. Many of the highest frequency words have irregular spelling patterns, and they are best learned through repeated exposure and direct teaching. Any Internet search engine will turn up dozens of suggestions for teaching high-frequency sight words (especially since teaching sight words seems to be a popular item with parents who home school their children).

Sight words by their nature need memorization. But memorization is facilitated if the words are seen in a variety of contexts, played with in games, and applied in different tasks.

Word hunts are a way to have the students search for sight words in printed material. Print out two or three sight words on index cards, and have children search for those words in disposable printed matter—newspapers or magazines. Once they find them, they can underline them and later show them to you—reading each word that they found.

Word games can take many forms. Make two sets of the same words printed individually on index cards (or index cards cut into three or four business card-sized pieces). Turn the cards face down on a table, scramble them, and play a game of Concentration. Make three or four sets of six or seven words, deal them out to three or four players, and play "Go Fishing." Make up Bingo cards with sight words printed in the columns and have three or more students play.

Word walls. Word Walls (Cunningham, 1995; Cunningham, Hall, & Sigmon, 2007) are groups of words, arranged in columns on the walls of the classroom in ways that allow the words to be easily seen and accessed. The words have something in common—often a shared spelling pattern, but they may be grouped for other reasons as well.

Here is an example of a Word Wall that features words that begin with the same letter and sound. The teacher tapes scrambled words that begin with two different letters on the Word Wall (see the words on the left, in Figure 4.14). The teacher puts two different words that at the top of the Word Wall and reminds the students of the first sound of each word, and the letter that makes it. The students decide which words go in which column. The teacher and the class arrive at two columns, like those on the right.

Review reading the words in the word wall every day, by pointing to the words as the students read them. Using Word Wall Chants will help students remember the words. As the students and the teacher review the words on the word wall, they may (1) chant the word, (2) chant out each letter, and then (3) chant the word again.

- "The chicken": Flap your arms up and down as you say each letter
- "The opera singer": Sing each letter, and finally the word, in an operatic voice
- "The volcano": Say each letter louder and louder, until you shout the word
- "The nose": Hold your nose as you say the letters and the word
- "The audience": Clap once for each letter until the word is spelled, then clap loudly

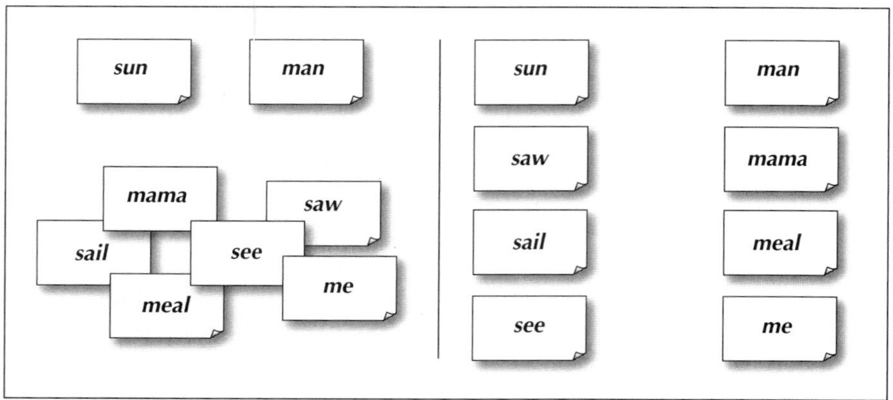

FIGURE 4.14 *Word Wall*

Word Walls have many other uses besides teaching spelling patterns. As Penny Freppon (in Temple, Ogle, Crawford, & Freppon, 2010) suggests, post the words from favorite books, inquiry units of study, and words and pictures with the letters of the alphabet. It is nearly always best if words are put on the wall during the teaching process. As children's development progresses, word walls may change from picture-word walls to word-only walls. Word hunts and word sorts expand the word study. Books are reread to keep a focus on meaningful reading and reading for enjoyment. Imagine the word walls on science and other inquiry work you can have with middle and upper grades. High-frequency sight words can be introduced by the teacher on word walls, along with other "important words" that children may offer during reading activities. The teacher should engage children in doing sight word walls regularly (Cunningham et al., 2007). Here are suggestions for creating and using a sight word wall:

- Add words gradually (about five per week).
- Make words highly accessible by putting them where all students can see them, writing them in large print with big black letters, and using colors for words that are often confused, such as *for, from, that, they,* and *this*.
- Select only the words children encounter most frequently in their reading and the words they use most frequently in their writing. Do not overwhelm them or yourself with too many words. Nothing succeeds like success!
- Practice the words by saying, spelling, and writing them ("do the wall").

Reading Aloud

At the end of the lesson—or at another period in the day if there is no time during the lesson—the teacher reads aloud to the children. There are many reasons for this.

Children who come from families and preschools where reading aloud is a regular feature may experience a shock when they are beginning to read themselves. The first texts they are able to read are nowhere near as sophisticated as what they are used to listening to, and they won't be for a while. Their reading comprehension won't catch up to their listening comprehension until they reach fourth grade (Loban, 1976).

Children who have not been read to extensively are in even greater need of hearing rich written language read to them. The vocabulary and the sentence and text structures of written language are more complex than those of spoken language. Children will face a greater challenge when reading complex text and complex vocabulary if they haven't heard written text read to them.

As important as it is to be read to, some children will not fully engage the listening experience on their own. They will need for their teacher to use strategies that will pull them into the reading. These strategies include think-alouds, predictions, and imaging. (See Chapter 5 for explanations of these and other approaches).

The Language Experience Approach

The Language Experience Approach, or LEA (Crawford et al., 1995; Stauffer, 1975), works well for beginning readers. The LEA is unique in that it uses the student's oral language to teach written language, that is, to teach reading. There are several cumulative steps to take when teaching with the LEA and many variations of it. The following is a step-by-step process we recommend. Use it with a small group or in working with one child.

First Lesson. In the first twenty- to thirty-minute lesson, complete these three steps.

Step 1: Discussion. Talk with students about their experiences (e.g., their favorite foods or birthday parties). Respond positively, be curious about their stories, and value their input. Let the children know that you will write down some things from their stories that they can all read together. In later LEA lessons the discussion topics could be about science or current events.

Step 2: Dictation. Ask the children what to write, select some of their responses, and write them on large chart paper, an overhead, or a computer screen. Be sure everyone can see your writing. Make teaching points about where to begin writing as you think appropriate. Read each sentence and ask them to read it back to you.

Step 3: Reading the text. Now it's time for the children to read their text. But first read it to them again and guide them to watch the words as you run your finger or pointer under them. Then have the children read along with you, and finally ask them to read on their own.

To extend the lesson give the children copies of the text and have them practice in pairs or alone. Emphasize that this is just practice; give the children time and support to engage deeply in reading their own language.

In this initial two-day cycle of LEA, the first lesson consists of motivation and discussion, dictation and reading, and shared reading, as just described. On the following day, there are several additional steps.

Second Lesson

Step 1: Reading the text. Read the text again and prompt careful watching of the words as you point to them. Then have the children read with you. Practice this as much as needed. When reading sounds somewhat fluent, have the children take turns reading on their own. Include everyone. Every child can read even if it is only a word or two with your support.

Step 2: Reassembling the text. Before step 2, make copies of the sentences on sentence strips in the order they appear on the original text. Begin the lesson by having the children look at the whole text and then have them look for the first sentence. As children point out each sentence, put them in a sentence strip holder or adjustable pocket chart one at a time and practice reading them together. Each time, read the sentence and then read the entire text. Again, children can take turns reading individually as they are able. You can also ask children to point at the sentence that tells [fill in blank].

This two-day cycle is repeated once or twice every week with a new theme for each set of lessons. Children will not learn all the words at first, but keep developing new charts for them to maintain interest. Be sure to keep copies available so children can practice. When you notice that children have learned a number of words, you can add a third lesson on sight vocabulary and move on to a three-day LEA cycle.

Third Lesson

Step 1: Reassembling the words into sentences. Before step 1, cut each sentence strip made for the second lesson into individual words. Place the words in the pocket chart or even on the chalk rail. Place them in a random order and support the children in reassembling the words into sentences. Have the original story nearby so they can refer to it as needed. Build independence by asking children, "If you don't know a word, can you find it in our story? Now read the sentence. Can you read the word?" As sentences are reassembled, guide the reading of the whole text from time to time. Finally, you can implement other word activities. Here are a few ideas:

- Give word cards from the sentences to the children, and ask them to find the words in the text.
- Say, "Here is the word _____. Find the same word in the text."
- Make a large chart paper copy of one of the texts with some words left out. Tell the children that some words are missing and ask if they can identify them. Read with the children, pausing when you come to a missing word. Support them in "guessing the missing word" and write it in.
- Guide the children to write and keep a personal file collection of the words they learn. Begin with a few words and encourage building the collections and game playing with the word cards.

For further support of word recognition, you might color code sentence strips and word cards. Or various colors might be marked on the back of cards. Word cards are inevitably mixed up as children work with them at their desks or tables. They are easily sorted back into word groups of original sentences according to the colors on the reverse side.

Several weeks or even months after the third lesson activities, children will likely show signs of recognizing using letter/sound correspondences in words. This is a signal to add a fourth day to the cycle, a day for word analysis using the context of words the children now recognize at sight.

Fourth Lesson

Word recognition study. Have the children read the story and find words that begin alike, as you support their learning to associate letters and sounds using words they

READING LESSON FORM

Child's name: ______________________

Date: ______________________

PHASE OF THE LESSON	WHAT WE DID	HOW IT WENT
The child reads a book at the instructional level.	Name of book: Strategies used:	
The child reads a book at the independent level	Name of book:	
The child performs a writing task.	What the child wrote (transcribe the sentence here as the child wrote it):	Word patterns the child used correctly: Word patterns the child needs to learn:
The child carries out a word study task.	Word patterns used: Activity:	
The teacher reads aloud to the child.	Name of book: Strategies used:	
Observations:		

FIGURE 4.15 *Planning and Record-Keeping Form*

already know. Guide the children to draw conclusions, that is, phonic generalizations out of their observations of letters and corresponding sounds. Continue to use the written language, the words, sentences, and whole texts that have evolved from the children's oral language dictations. This makes powerful use of their background knowledge and helps them to extend their knowledge of sounds and letters in known words to new words. You can also bring out old LEA charts from time to time for review lessons and practice.

Repeated readings develop fluency and automaticity (when children recognize words automatically). As word recognition becomes easier and easier, they are able to focus attention on comprehension (Samuels, 2006).

Planning and Record Keeping

It is important to make every lesson count when we are teaching struggling readers (and anyone, for that matter). A good way to take care of both planning and record keeping for ongoing assessment is to write up a plan for each child's lesson that allows a space to keep records on the child's response to each part of the lesson.

The lesson we have outlined in this chapter consists of these parts:

- The child reads a book at the instructional level.
- The child reads a book at the independent level.
- The child performs a writing task.
- The child carries out a word study task.
- The teacher reads aloud to the child.

The planning and record-keeping form can look like the one shown in Figure 4.15 on page 129.

Summary

Beginning readers have moved beyond the emergent stage and are now able to read lines of print—but for short periods of time, and with adult support. Fledgling readers are able to read for longer periods of time, and are practicing reading to gain fluency. While all of the aspects of literacy are being developed—fluency, comprehension, vocabulary, and writing—much of the teaching emphasis at this level will go to helping children recognize words accurately and automatically. That is because rapid word recognition has been shown repeatedly to be the gateway to fluent reading with comprehension. Fluency and comprehension should not be neglected, of course. Some strategies for promoting both were shared in this chapter, and many more will be presented in the next chapter.

Just as automatic word recognition should be stressed with beginning and fledgling readers, fluent and automatic handwriting should be practiced, too. As we will see throughout this book, learning to write supports learning to read. Many struggling readers are held back from fluent and thoughtful writing because they cannot form letters quickly and easily.

For assessment of literacy at the beginning and fledgling stages, we introduced Running Records, the *Monster Test,* and the *Demtup Names Test.*

References

Adams, M. J. (1998). The three-cueing system. In F. Lehr & J. Osborn (Eds.), *Literacy for all: Issues in teaching and learning* (pp. 73–99). New York, NY: Guilford Press.

Anderson, R. C., & Pearson, P. D. (1984). A schema-theoretic view of basic processes in reading comprehension. In P. D. Pearson (Ed.), *Handbook of reading research* (pp. 255–291). New York, NY: Longman.

Blachman, B. (2000). *An overview of the STARS program.* Syracuse, NY: Syracuse University School of Education, Syracuse Reading Project.

Chomsky, N., & Halle, M. (1968). *The sound pattern of English.* New York, NY: Harper & Row.

Clay, M. M. (1993). *Reading Recovery: A guidebook for teachers in training.* Portsmouth, NH: Heinemann.

Clay, M. M. (2000). *Running records for classroom teachers.* Portsmouth, NH: Heinemann.

Clay, M. M. (2005). *An observation survey of early literacy achievement* (2nd ed.). Portsmouth, NH: Heinemann.

Cunningham, P. M. (1995). *Phonics we use.* New York, NY: HarperCollins.

Cunningham, P. M. Hall, D. P., & Sigmon, C. M. (2007). *The teacher's guide to the four blocks.* Greensboro, NC: Carson-Dellosa.

Dolch, E. (1948). *Problems in reading.* Chicago, IL: American Book Company.

Fountas, I. C., & Pinnell, G. S. (1996). *Guided reading: Good first reaching for all children.* Portsmouth, NH: Heinemann.

Fry, E. (2004). *1000 Instant words: The most common words for teaching reading, writing and spelling.* Westminster, CA: Teacher Created Materials.

Gentry, J. R. (2007). *Breakthrough in beginning reading and writing*. New York, NY: Scholastic.

Gentry, J. R. (2008). *Step-by-step assessment guide to code breaking*. New York, NY: Scholastic

Gentry, J. R., & Gillet, J. W. (1993). *Teaching kids to spell.* Portsmouth, N.H.: Heinemann.

Gough, P. B. (1993, June). The beginning of decoding. *Reading and Writing*, *5*(2), 181–192.

Graham, S., Harris, K. R., Mason, L., Fink-Chorzempa, B., Moran, S., & Saddler, B. (2008, February). How do primary grade teachers teach handwriting? A national survey. *Reading and Writing: An Interdisciplinary Journal*, *21*(1–2), 49–69.

Iverson, S., & Tumner, W. (1993). Phonological processing skills and the Reading Recovery program. *Journal of Educational Psychology*, 85(1), 112–126.

Langer, J. (1995). *Envisioning literature: Literary understanding and literature instruction.* New York, NY: Teachers College Press.

Loban, W. (1976). Language development: Kindergarten through twelfth grade. Urbana, IL: NCTE.

Morris, R. D. (2006). *The Howard Street Tutoring manual* (2nd ed.). New York, NY: Guilford Publishing.

Morris, R. D., Tyner, B., & Perney, J. (2000). Early steps: Replicating the effects of a first-grade reading program. Journal of Educational Psychology, 92(4), 81–93.

Morris, R. D., & Slavin, R. (2002). *Every child reading.* Boston, MA: Allyn and Bacon.

National Reading Panel. (1999). *Teaching children to read: Report of the National Reading Panel.* Washington, DC: National Research Press.

Pearson, P. D., & Duke, N. K. (2002). Comprehension instruction in the primary grades. In C. C. Block & M. Pressley (Eds.), *Comprehension instruction: Research-based practices* (pp. 247–258). New York, NY: Guilford.

Samuels, S. J. (2006). Toward a model of reading fluency. In S. J. Samuels & A. E. Farstrup (Eds.), *What research has to say about fluency instruction* (pp. 24–46). Newark, DE: International Reading Association.

Shanahan, T., & Barr, B. (1995). Reading Recovery: An independent evaluation of the effects of an early instructional intervention for at-risk learners. *Reading Research Quarterly*, *30*, 958–995.

Share, D. L. (1990). Self correction rates in oral reading: Indices of efficient reading or artifact of text difficulty? *Educational Psychology*, *10*, 181–186.

Sheffield, B. (1996, January). Handwriting: A neglected cornerstone of literacy. *Annals of Dyslexia*, *46*(1), 21–35.

Stauffer, R. G. (1975). *The Language-experience approach to the teaching of reading.* New York, NY: HarperCollins.

Swartz, S. L., & Klein, A. F. (2002). *Research in reading recovery: Vol. 2.* Portsmouth, NH: Heinemann.

Temple, C., Crawford, A., & Gillet, J. (2009). *Developmental literacy inventory.* Boston, MA: Allyn & Bacon.

Temple, C., Ogle, D., Crawford, A. & Freppon, P. (2010). *All children read* (3rd ed.). Boston: Allyn and Bacon.

Thurber, D. (1993). *D'Nealian handwriting.* Glenview, IL: Scott Foresman.

Troia, G., Lin, S-J, Monroe, B. W., & Cohen, S. (2009). The effects of writing workshop instruction on the performance and motivation of good and poor writers. In G. Troia (Ed.), *Instruction and assessment for struggling writers.* New York, NY: Guilford Press.

Tynan, B. (2009). *Small group reading instruction.* Newark, DE: International Reading Association.

Van der Hart, N., Fitzpatrick, P., & Cortesa, C. (2010, July). In-depth analysis of handwriting curriculum in four kindergarten classrooms. *Reading and Writing: An Interdisciplinary Journal*, *23*(6), 673–699.

Vygotsky, L. (1976). *Thought and language.* Cambridge, MA: MIT Press.

CHAPTER 5

Assessing and Teaching Developing Readers

Chapter Outline

Carl Hardy's friends kid him that his third-grade classroom looks like one of those corner grocery stores way up on Broadway in New York City where he teaches. Every possible inch is crammed with something. The walls are hung with columns of words written on tag board. There is a reading corner near the bookshelf with the classroom library. There is a listening center hung with sets of headphones. There is even a puppet theater for acting out stories. A colorful chart of the reptile family hangs on the wall opposite a large map of the world, with flags taped to the countries where his students came from. The students' own map of the neighborhood has push pins marking the places where they live. Prints of works by this month's artist, Pablo Picasso, hang from wires stretched below the ceiling. Carl's desk is pushed to the side of the classroom to make room for the carpeted circle area where classroom community meetings and large- and small-group lessons are conducted. On his desk is a thick American Heritage Dictionary*—Carl Hardy loves words.*

In a file cabinet is a folder for each student in the class. It holds the students' work samples, Carl's observational notes of their reading and learning, and results from several kinds of reading assessment. The Informal Reading Inventory scores gave him an initial idea of what level of book in which to place each student, and also each child's strengths in different aspects of reading: word recognition, fluency, and comprehension. There are also more frequently administered monitoring assessments to keep track of the students' reading success.

The students' reading ability spreads across four grade levels, and that means that not only will the books be on different levels, but the strategies for word study will differ as well.

In this chapter we look at developing readers, those children who are reading more and more text and rapidly learning sight words. According to some experts, these readers will fall into two categories: *transitional readers* and *independent readers* (Morris, 2008). Normally, such readers are found from late second grade through fourth grade. However, when children experience difficulty, this period of developing reading may begin later and last longer.

As part of the public awareness campaign surrounding the No Child Left Behind Education Act, the U.S. Department of Education adopted from the National Reading Panel (2000) five essential components for reading instruction: *phonemic awareness, phonics, fluency, vocabulary,* and *comprehension processes* (see Figure 5.1). We will add

Five Essential Components of Reading

The National Reading Panel (2000) identified five essential components of reading that children must be taught in order to learn to read. Adults can help children learn to be good readers by systematically practicing these five components:

1. *Recognizing and using individual sounds to create words, or phonemic awareness. Children need to be taught to hear sounds in words and that words are made up of the smallest parts of sound, or phonemes.*
2. *Understanding the relationships between written letters and spoken sounds, or phonics. Children need to be taught the sounds individual printed letters and groups of letters make. Knowing the relationships between letters and sounds helps children to recognize familiar words accurately and automatically and to "decode" new words.*
3. *Developing the ability to read a text accurately and quickly, or reading fluency. Children must learn to read words rapidly and accurately in order to understand what is read. When fluent readers read silently, they recognize words automatically. When fluent readers read aloud, they read effortlessly and with expression. Readers who are weak in fluency read slowly, word by word, focusing on decoding words instead of comprehending meaning.*
4. *Learning the meaning and pronunciation of words, or vocabulary development. Children need to actively build and expand their knowledge of written and spoken words, what they mean, and how they are used.*
5. *Acquiring strategies to understand, remember, and communicate what is read, or reading comprehension strategies. Children need to be taught comprehension strategies, or the steps good readers use to make sure they understand text. Students who are in control of their own reading comprehension become purposeful, active readers.*

FIGURE 5.1 *Five Essential Components of Reading*

another: a positive attitude toward reading, which leads to the habit of reading—because without extensive practice, the other components of reading won't have a chance to develop (Wilson, Anderson, & Fielding, 1986).

Several of the strategies and instruments for assessing reading that we have introduced in the previous chapters of this book are useful for developing readers, too. Some devices such as the Informal Reading Inventory are used periodically to assess many aspects of a child's reading ability, including word recognition (in isolation and in context), reading fluency, and comprehension (both while reading and while listening). More frequently administered assessments such as the running record and observational procedures can be used to monitor children's progress in learning to read, particularly their word recognition and fluency, but also their comprehension and even their interest in reading.

Now we will focus on what to do with all of this information. How do we teach children so as to help them develop the aspects of reading ability that need strengthening?

Phonics and Word Knowledge for Developing Readers

In Chapter 3, we treated phonemic awareness in some detail. In this chapter we focus on phonics, vocabulary development, fluency, and comprehension.

Word Knowledge at Different Levels

In popular parlance, phonics is sometimes described as the cure-all for literacy problems. Understanding the ways letters and print relate to each other is surely important in learning to read. But to be useful, phonics instruction should be tailored to what the child already knows about words. And what children know about words is different at different stages of development.

When we are observing children's attempts to read words that are just beyond their reach, we see different children using different strategies. One child will look at the first letter and say nearly any word that comes to mind that begins the same way. Another child will sound out every letter in the word, as if that letter announced an individual sound that had nothing to do with either the sound that came before or the one that came after it. Another child will pronounce the first part of the syllable and then the latter part, as if they were two parts of the whole, and then say the whole word. Still another child will explain, if asked, that she sees a word she knows as part of the longer word. How would you teach "phonics" to all of these children? Differently, of course!

The German researcher Uta Frith (1985) observed that children pass through four stages as they learn to recognize words. Her stages are summarized in *The Handbook of Reading Research, Vol. 3,* by Usha Goswami (2000). Frith's stages are called *logographic, transitional alphabetic, alphabetic,* and *orthographic.* To these we have added one more stage: *derivational reading.*

Logographic Reading. Preschool and kindergarten children who are just beginning to see familiar words around them tend to recognize words as whole displays. Children recognize McDonald's restaurants by their golden arches. They may recognize the word *look* by associating the two O's with eyes. Children in this stage may call the same word by different but related names, calling a Crest toothpaste label at one time "Crest" and at another time "toothpaste" (Harste, Woodward, & Burke, 1985). They are not yet focusing on the parts of the words, but are trying to find any identifiable feature that will help them remember them. This isn't a very powerful strategy, and logographic readers often give no response at all when faced with a word they do not know because they do not yet have strategy for sounding out words.

Because young children often look at a word and call it by the few names of words they know, Marsh et al. (1981) called this stage of word recognition "glance and guess." We shouldn't belittle this stage, though. Many teachers advocate encouraging children to learn to recognize several dozen words as wholes before they begin to call their attention to the parts of the words.

Transitional Alphabetic Reading. Once they have sufficient practice with words as wholes, more advanced children—usually in early first grade—begin to focus on the letters in words and use their knowledge of the letters' sounds to read them. At first, they may pay attention to the first and last consonants, and later pay attention to the vowel that comes in the middle. Some teachers advocate having children at this level read *decodable texts,* which contain words composed of the most reliable spelling patterns. The trade-off is that we want children to expect texts to mean something. Some excellent versions of decodable texts exist, though. Nancy Shaw's *Sheep* books are good examples.

Alphabetic Reading. By the middle of first grade and into early second grade, most children begin to read more and more letters in words. When they attempt to read a word, rather than calling out the name of another word that begins the same way, a child might sound out every letter, even if it means pronouncing something that doesn't make sense. A child might say, "We went to the fire sta-t-yon" instead of "fire station." With practice, students produce fewer nonsense word readings and read words more accurately.

Children are acquiring a growing body of *sight words* that they can read accurately and quickly without having to decode them. This rapid word identification occurs after a period of sounding out the words, or *phonological recoding,* as linguists call it. Ehri (1991) suggests that the earlier practice of reading words alphabetically—figuring them out letter by letter—lays down pathways to the memory that makes it easier for children to recognize the words when they see them later. Ehri (1991) writes:

> When readers practice reading specific words by phonologically recoding the words, they form access routes for those words into memory. The access routes are built using knowledge of grapheme-phoneme correspondences that connect letters in spellings to phonemes in the pronunciation of words. The letters are processed as visual symbols for the phonemes, and the sequence of letters is retained as an alphabetic, phonological representation of the word. The first time an unfamiliar word is seen, it is read by phonological recoding. This initiates an access route into memory. Subsequent readings of the word strengthen the access route until the connections between letters and phonemes are fully formed and the spelling is represented in memory. (p. 402)

Orthographic Reading. By late first grade to the middle of second grade, most children are looking at words in terms of spelling patterns—not just one letter to one sound, but also familiar patterns such as *ake, ight,* and later *tion.* Children who can separate words into *onsets and rimes* and who are taught by means of *word sorts* (Bear, Invernizzi, Templeton, & Johnston, 2012) can read by *analogy;* that is, if they can read *bake* and *take,* they can also read *rake* and *stake.* As they move further into the orthographic phase, children read not just by phonogram patterns, or onsets and rimes, as Trieman (1985) calls them, but increasingly by *root words* and even *historical morphemes.*

Derivational Reading. From about fourth or fifth grade and up, normally advancing readers enter a phase of word recognition that we call *derivational reading.* Readers from late first grade and second grade recognize that words like *firehouse* and *grounds-keeper* contain within them other words they know. From fourth grade and later, more proficient readers recognize that words like *telegraph, telephone, biology,* and *biography* also contain word parts that they recognize: *graph,* from a Greek word meaning "to write"; *tele* from another Greek word meaning "at a distance"; and *bio-* from a Greek word meaning "life." They recognize that *sanity* is related to *sane* and that *sign* is related to *signal.* Derivational reading thus combines something of word recognition and vocabulary.

Having laid out these stages that children are thought to pass through as they learn to recognize words, it is clear that children will need different instruction at the different stages.

Teaching Phonics

Phonics is an important part of instruction for emergent and beginning readers, and in Chapter 3 we laid out steps for teaching children to pay attention to words, the sounds in words, and the relations between letters and sounds. Refer back to Chapter 3 for a complete discussion of teaching phonics to emergent and beginning readers. Here we offer a set of principles for such teaching.

Steven Stahl (1992) suggested ten components of effective phonics teaching. According to Stahl, exemplary phonics instruction:

1. **Builds on What Children Already Know.** It builds on what reading is about, how print functions, what stories are and how they are worded, and what reading is for. This knowledge is gained by being read to, by shared reading of predictable books (see Chapter 3), by experience with dictated stories, and by participation in authentic reading and writing tasks before reading begins. These are components of both whole language and traditional instruction in preschool, kindergarten, and primary grades.

2. **Builds on a Foundation of Phonemic Awareness.** Phonics instruction builds on a child's ability to perceive and manipulate sounds in spoken words. Phonemic awareness includes being able to think of words that rhyme; perceiving that some words have the same or very similar sounds at the beginning, middle, and end; and being able to segment and blend sounds in spoken words. A further explanation of phonemic awareness follows in a subsequent discussion.

3. **Is Clear and Direct.** Good teachers explain exactly what they mean, while some phonics programs appear confusing and ambiguous. Some years ago, debate raged about whether a phoneme, or letter-sound, had any existence outside of the spoken word. Teachers and programs that were influenced by this argument hesitated to pronounce any sounds in isolation—for example, never explaining that *b* produced the /b/ sound at the beginning of words such as *box, bear,* or *bed.* Of course, we want to avoid inaccurate pronunciations such as "buh-eh-duh" for *b-e-d,* but more harm is done when

we beat around the bush and never directly show at least the common and predictable consonant sounds.

4. **Is Integrated into a Total Reading Program.** Phonics instruction should not dominate, but instead should complement, the reading instruction children receive. The majority of time should be spent in reading real texts, discussing them, acting them out, writing about them, and interpreting them. Phonics instruction should spring from the words that children need to read in real texts, not from a preset hierarchy of skills or a scope-and-sequence chart. Stahl (1992) suggests that a maximum of 25 percent of instructional time be spent on phonics. On many days, even this will be excessive. In addition, the phonics skills that are taught should be directly applicable in the text being read at that time. A criticism of many basal phonics strands is that the skill being presented has only limited application in the accompanying story. Trachtenburg (1990) suggests using high-quality children's literature that features a particular phonics pattern to illustrate and practice the pattern, for example using *The Cat in the Hat* and *Angus and the Cat* to illustrate the short-*a* pattern. A fuller description of children's literature/phonics connections follows in a subsequent section.

5. **Focuses on Reading Words, Not Learning Rules.** Effective readers use patterns and words they already know that are similar, rather than phonics rules, when they decode. Most teachers already know that rules have so many exceptions that they are rarely useful, yet many phonics programs continue to stress them as though they were "golden rules." If a child can't decode *rake*, it is more helpful to point out that it has the same pattern as *make* and *take* than to cite the "silent *e* makes the vowel long" rule. Many poor readers can recite phonics rules fluently, but cannot apply them in reading.

6. **May Include Onsets and Rimes**. Onsets (beginning sounds), and rimes (the part of the word or syllable from the vowel onward), have long been taught under the more common name of *word families.* Teaching children to compare words using onsets and rimes helps them to internalize patterns and use known words, such as *make* and *take* in the previous example, to decode the unfamiliar *rake.* It is certainly more productive than having children sound out letters in isolation.

7. **May Include Invented Spelling Practice.** It has been widely recognized that when children are encouraged to invent spellings for unfamiliar words that they write, using the sounds in the words as they are pronounced, they practice decoding strategies within the context of real language use. Encouraging invented spelling has become a widely used and welcome aspect of primary literacy instruction.

8. **May Include Categorization Practice Such as Word Sorting**. The practice of word sorting is a series of exercises in which children group together words with common phonic features, such as beginning consonants, phonogram patterns, and other spelling dynamics. Word sorting encourages students to study the words they know and to abstract features from them that they can then use to read and spell words that they do not know. Word sorting is given book-length treatment in a book by Bear et al. (2012).

9. **Focuses Attention on the Internal Structure of Words.** Good phonics instruction helps children to see and use patterns in words. Whether they use individual letter sounds, similar words with the same rime, or invented spelling, children are encouraged to look closely at the patterns in words. We learn to read and spell not word by word, but pattern by pattern.

10. **Develops Automaticity in Word Recognition.** The purpose of all phonics instruction is not to be able to sound out words or "bark at print," but to be able to quickly and accurately "unlock" unfamiliar words so that the reader's attention may be reserved for understanding and enjoying what is read. Strict decoding emphasis programs of the past, such as DISTAR, encouraged children to learn to decode at the expense of comprehension; they failed because they created "word-callers" rather than effective readers. Effective phonics instruction today encourages automaticity (LaBerge & Samuels, 1974) in word recognition so that the mind may be freed for comprehension (Perfetti & Zhang, 1996).

Word Study at More Advanced Levels

Beyond the early stages of beginning to read, the kind of knowledge required to read words accurately changes in complex ways. Now it is more appropriate to speak not of phonics alone but also of children's word knowledge. The word *phonics* refers to the relationships between letters and sounds, but the word knowledge required for developing readers to recognize and understand words deals with several additional matters. In the case of developing readers, children's learning about words encompasses knowledge of

- Phonogram patterns.
- Grammatical affixes.
- Derivational affixes.
- Compound words.
- Homophones and homographs.
- Etymologies.

Phonogram Patterns. Phonogram patterns, which were mentioned above, are the rhyming parts of words like *bake* and *cake, dance* and *prance*. They are clusters of vowels or of vowels and consonants that are found in many words. They are also called *onsets and rimes*. Some years ago Wylie and Durrell (1970) identified 37 common spelling patterns that form the basis of word families in English. Those patterns account for more than 500 common words. They are:

ack	**all**	**ap**	**aw**	**est**	**igh**	**ing**	**ock**	**ot**	**un**
ain	**ame**	**ash**	**ay**	**ice**	**ill**	**ink**	**oke**	**uck**	
ake	**an**	**at**	**eat**	**ick**	**in**	**ip**	**op**	**ug**	
ale	**ank**	**ate**	**ell**	**ide**	**ine**	**it**	**ore**	**um**	

But Wylie and Durrell's list is not exhaustive. For example, *alk, ish, eed, eel, oak, old, ow,* and *y* are also phonogram patterns whose word families have many members.

Words with Grammatical Affixes. An *affix* is a part of a word that usually cannot stand alone and is added to a base word to change or modify its meaning. English words add grammatical affixes to show the grammatical function of the word. The most common grammatical affixes are listed below.

- The affix *-s* can mark the plural form of a noun or the third-person singular present tense form of a verb. Note that the ending *-s* has two different pronunciations: /s/, as in *rocks,* and /z/, as in *trees.* With words that end in *-es* there may be a third pronunciation of /iz/, as in *wishes.*
- The affix *-ed* marks the past tense of verbs and also regular past participles (verb forms that function as adjectives), as in "She wanted to go home" and "She had dyed hair."
- The affix *-ing* marks the present progressive form of verbs or present participles, as in "He was running" and "The stream was full of running water."
- The affixes *-er* and *-est* are the comparative (meaning "more") and superlative (meaning "most") forms of adjectives, as in "Akeesha was a fast*er* runner than Juan, but Maya was the fast*est* in the class."

Words with Derivational Affixes. Another class of affixes that change a word from one part of speech or function to another are *derivational affixes.* We call them *derivational* because they serve to derive one word from another. Recognizing derivational affixes and base words can give children a clue to both the reading of a word and its meaning. Once the child recognizes *-or* and *-er* as markers meaning "one who ______s," they may more easily read a word like *actor* by reading the word in parts: *act* + *or.*

Derivational markers that young readers encounter are *-er* and *-or* (*sleeper, teacher, creeper, actor*), *-ful* (*careful, wonderful, frightful*), *-ly* (*slowly, loudly, awfully*), *un-* (*unkind, unlucky*), and *re-* (*rerun, recycle, rewrite*).

Some derivational markers that older readers encounter are *-ment* (*pavement, government, treatment*), *-ist* (*racist, aerialist, cyclist*), *-ism* (*racism, alcoholism, feminism*), *-ant* (*triumphant, compliant, defiant, militant*), and *inter-* (*international, interaction*).

Being aware of derivational affixes helps children read words and to understand their meanings.

Compound Words. English has three kinds of compound words. Some words have been used together so frequently that they are written together: *shotgun, nightgown, afternoon.* Some compound words are joined by hyphens, especially when they are used as adjectives: *pig-stealing great-grandfather, self-cleaning oven, mother-in-law.* Some pairs of words are considered as compounds but are written separately: *shoe shine, boa constrictor, mail carrier.* For readers, the compounds written together are challenging, and children can be helped if asked "to find two words in this word." For spellers, compound words present quite a different challenge. Children may be unsure which compound words to write together, which to join with hyphens, and which to write separately.

Homophones and Homographs. Two or more words that are pronounced the same but spelled differently are called *homophones. Waste* and *waist; to, too,* and *two*; and *road* and *rode* are examples. Two or more words that are spelled the same but pronounced differently are called *homographs. Lead* (as in "to guide") and *lead* (the heavy metal) are examples. So are *read* (present tense) and *read* (past tense).

Readers need to learn to attach the correct meaning to a homophone. They also need to pronounce homographs correctly. In both cases, the context of the passage helps.

Etymologies. Another aid in recognizing words—in pronouncing them and knowing their meanings—is to know their etymologies, or histories. Take, for example, the words *telescope* and *telephone*. By normal pronunciation patterns, *tele* should be pronounced like *teal*. But the word stem *tele,* which comes from an ancient Greek word, is always pronounced like "telly," and it has the meaning of "far" or "at a distance." Similarly, the word *photograph* contains the *ph* grapheme, which, in words from ancient Greek, is pronounced like /f/. In words from Old English, though, such as *shepherd,* the *ph* has a different pronunciation. *Graph* comes from a Greek word meaning "to write or draw," and *photo* comes from a Greek word meaning "light." A *photograph,* then, is "written with light" (which you will know is literally true if you have ever worked in a darkroom). Even knowing just these few word stems would enable a reader to figure out the meanings of *telegraph* and *phonograph*.

Guiding Word Study

At the developing reader level, students' word knowledge can be nurtured by some of the means we saw in the previous chapter as well as by some new methods.

Teaching Words with Shared Phonogram Patterns

Words that share phonogram patterns, or word families, can be readily taught through the *word sort procedure*. In making a word sort, words from more than one word family are written on word cards, scrambled, and sorted into two or three columns on a desk, according to their families. It is best to make sure that the children know at least one and preferably two words from each family. Thus, if the first word in a column is the known word *bunk,* the child may place the unknown word *skunk* underneath it by making a visual match—and then, after reading *bunk,* the child can be encouraged to pronounce /sk/ and add the rest of the rime, *unk,* and finally read *skunk*. The teacher or tutor must demonstrate this strategy several times before most children get it, but once they do, children can do word sorting in small groups, in pairs, or alone.

Word Hunts. These present another way to work with word families. Especially after you have introduced the word family through a word sort procedure, children can be sent to look for other words from the same family in an old newspaper or magazine, cut them out, and paste them onto a page.

Word Family Walls. These are adapted from Patricia Cunningham's *word walls* (1999). After a word family has been introduced and worked with, make a poster for the word family, beginning with three or four examples. Then, as children come across other members of that family in their reading, add those words to the Word Family Wall, with ceremony and flourish!

Word Family Dictionaries. Children can make personal dictionaries of the words they find for each family. Have each child bring a small (3 inch by 5 inch) spiral notebook—bound note cards are preferable because they are more durable. Label the top of each page with a guide word for each word family. You may begin with three or four families and add more families over time. As children do word sort activities and word hunts, have them write new words on the page for each family.

Spelling. Put at least two words from each word family on a spelling list for children to study. Test them on the words each week.

Word Games. Since so many games work with groups of items, word families lend themselves to games like Go Fish! Once children have learned at least six word families, make a card deck with four word cards from each family. Deal out two-thirds of the cards to the players and put the other third in the Go Fish! pile. The players group the cards in their hand according to a word family. Then one at a time they say to one player, "Give me all your cards that rhyme with ______." If the other player has the card, she hands it over. If not, she says "Go Fish!" and that player draws a card from the pile.

Teaching Words with Grammatical Affixes and Derivational Affixes

Words with grammatical and derivational affixes, as well as compound words and even words with ancient roots such as we saw in the section on etymologies, can all be studied by means of word building exercises.

Word Building. Word building can be done to help children work with grammatical affixes. For each child in a small group, prepare a set of cards with word stems such as *truck, cat, dog, bark, purr,* and *shout* on them, and another set with grammatical affixes such as *-ed,* and *-s* on them. Tell the children to join a word stem and an affix to put together words for:

More than one furry animal that purrs
Made that sound yesterday
More than one eighteen-wheeler
Spoke loudly yesterday
More than one animal that barks

Word building can also help children work with derivational affixes. For each child in a small group, prepare a set of cards with word stems such as *write, play, true, glad, thank, train,* and *quick* on them, and another set with grammatical affixes such as *-er, re-, un-,* and *-ly* on them. Tell the children to join a word stem and an affix to make a word for:

Someone who helps athletes get ready
Another word for an athlete
What you shouldn't believe
To do something, feeling happy about it
To make marks on paper for the second time
To do something without wasting time

Teaching compound words with the word building activity proceeds the same way. Prepare cards with single parts of the compound words on them, and prepare hints to guide students to construct the target words.

Teaching Homophones and Homographs

Read Fred Gwynne's *The King Who Rained* (1988) to introduce the children to the idea of homophones: words that have the same sounds but different meanings and different spellings. Prepare cards with pairs of homophones, one set for each student in the group. Call out a definition and ask the children to hold up the correct card. Some useful homophones are:

rain, rein, reign
two, to, too
road, rode, rowed
waste, waist
eight, ate
tacks, tax
die, dye

Have the children prepare homophone pages in their word study notebooks. To teach homographs, prepare ahead of time a list of words that are homographs and write them on the chalkboard. For example:

read
lead
produce
conduct

Prepare clues to the pronunciation of different versions of the words. For example, "Yesterday I opened my book and I _____." The children raise their hands and provide the correct pronunciation as you point to the word.

Developing Sight Vocabulary

Individual words become *sight words* (recognized immediately without analysis) when they are seen repeatedly in meaningful context. Many youngsters acquire some sight words before school entry, and without direct teaching or drill, by looking at the same favorite storybooks many times over. First they learn what words are on the page as they hear the same story read to them again and again. Soon they can recite the words along with the reader; soon after that, they can recite independently, role-playing reading as they turn the pages.

If at this point the reader casually points to the words as they are read, the child begins to associate the word spoken with its printed counterpart. This speech-to-print matching is an important foundation for learning to recognize words in print.

It is essential for readers to have a large sight vocabulary so that they can move through print quickly and efficiently. Youngsters who have only a small store of sight words are forced to read very slowly, with frequent stops to figure out words; these stops interrupt their comprehension and interfere with their getting meaning. Many youngsters read poorly for this reason. Increasing their sight vocabularies is mandatory for their reading improvement. This can be accomplished by a number of means.

Dictated Stories and Language Experience

Dictated stories are a part of the language experience approach to beginning reading (Temple, Ogle, Crawford, & Freppon, 2011). The method of using dictated stories to teach reading has been used for many years. In fact, a variation of it was used in Europe by John Amos Comenius in the 1600s! The method works as follows. An individual or small group dictates an account to someone who writes down the account verbatim. The account is reread chorally until the students can recite it accurately and point to the individual words while reciting. Then parts, or the entire account, are read individually, and words that can be immediately recognized first in context, then in isolation, are identified. These new sight words go into the students' word banks, collections of sight words on cards or in a notebook.

It was long held that the value of dictated stories lay in the preservation of children's natural language, which might differ considerably from "book language." This is important, but a greater usefulness of dictated words for developing sight vocabulary lies in the repeated rereading of the material. Students might reread dictated stories more willingly than other material because the stories concern experiences the students have had themselves. Rereading the stories chorally and independently, regardless of the topic or syntax used, reinforces the recognition of the words in other contexts.

As the students' sight vocabularies grow and their word banks come to contain about 100 or more words, this is a sign that they will have an adequate sight vocabulary to read other kinds of texts. Now the dictated stories are usually phased out, and other material is introduced. Dictation works best as an initial means of establishing and fostering sight vocabulary and also as a confidence-building transition into reading.

When dictated stories are mentioned, some teachers of older poor readers associate the practice with very young children. They might immediately presume that older poor readers will be put off by what they assume is a juvenile practice. Although language experience is common in primary classrooms, it need not be reserved for little children. In fact, with many older and adult poor readers, what they dictate might be about the only print they can read successfully.

With young children, you need a concrete stimulus, or experience, to talk about: an object, picture, storybook, or immediate event. With older students, past or future experiences, hopes, fears, reminiscences, content-area subjects, and abstract concepts can serve as topics. Older students can usually move through steps more quickly than younger ones and can usually skip the voice-pointing step entirely. Older students often work best with this procedure individually or in pairs or threes rather than in large groups. A word notebook might replace the word bank card collection. And if the teacher presents the activity with a businesslike air and explains why it is being done, the experience need not feel like a juvenile one.

Figure 5.2 lists the steps in using dictated stories with younger and older students, in groups or individually.

Support Reading: Echo Reading and Choral Reading

Support reading means helping readers get through text that is too difficult for them to read independently. Although students should never have to read material at their frustration levels without support, sometimes it is necessary for them to get through some difficult material. This is most often the case with older poor readers who are expected to get information from a content-area textbook that is beyond their instructional level. If appropriate material at their instructional level is not available, you can help them through difficult text using support-reading methods.

In *echo reading,* the teacher reads a sentence or two aloud, and the student immediately repeats what the teacher read while looking at and, if necessary, pointing to the words. Only one or two sentences, or even one long phrase, are read at a time to allow students to use short-term memory as they "echo." Older students might use specially prepared tapes, with pauses for repetition, to practice echo reading independently. Echo reading is an intensive support measure that is best used with short selections and material that is quite difficult or unfamiliar. Sometimes, it might be sufficient to echo-read only the beginning of a longer passage to get students started. One important characteristic of echo reading is that it allows the teacher to model fluent reading and the students to practice it.

Choral reading means reading aloud in unison. It is somewhat harder to choral-read than to echo-read, so this procedure is best for material that is easier or for text that has been silently previewed or echo-read first. Choral reading, with the teacher's voice leading and providing the model, is an excellent way of practicing oral reading without the anxiety of a solo performance. Complicated or unfamiliar text should be read aloud

WITH YOUNGER PUPILS:

1. Present a concrete stimulus—an object or event—to discuss.
2. Encourage describing and narrating so that the students will have plenty to say about it.
3. Tell students you will help them write the story using a chart tablet, transparency, or the board.
4. Ask for volunteers to contribute sentences for the story.
5. Print the account verbatim, allowing students to make changes or additions. Read aloud what you have written, including amended portions.
6. Read the completed account to the group.
7. Lead the group in choral recitation, pointing quickly to the words as you read. Repeat until the whole account can be recited fluently.
8. Ask for volunteers to read one or more sentences alone, pointing to the words as in step 7.
9. Ask for volunteers to point out and identify words they know. Keep a list of these for review.
10. Provide individual copies of the story for rereading and sight word identification.
11. Any words that a child can identify out of the story context can go into the child's word bank, to be used for sorting and other word study activities.

WITH OLDER PUPILS:

1. Work with groups of three or fewer.
2. Suggest, or allow students to suggest, a topic.
3. Lead discussion of the topic, encouraging as rich language use as possible.
4. Take the dictation as above, making minor word changes or additions as necessary to keep the story fluent. Cursive writing may be used instead of printing. Use a regular size sheet of paper if you wish.
5. Lead the choral rereading as above. Students might prefer to do more individual than group reading.
6. Provide an individual copy for each student, typed if possible, for practice rereading and word identification. Encourage rereading to a partner or someone else.
7. As individuals read to you and identify newly acquired sight words, have them enter the words in a sight word notebook. Older students might prefer a notebook to a traditional word bank.

FIGURE 5.2 *Steps in Using Dictated Stories*

1. Introduce the material by briefly discussing the topic with students.
2. Read the material aloud expressively.
3. Read the material a second time while children follow along in a large copy of the material (chart tablet sheet, transparency, or Big Book).
4. Choral-read the material several times until it is very familiar.
5. Begin adding pauses, sound effects, movement, tonal variety, or other expressive aspects to the reading.
6. Practice often so that all children feel very comfortable with it.
7. Ask children to suggest ways in which they can share their choral-readings with others, and follow up on their ideas.

FIGURE 5.3 *Choral Reading Poetry or Predictable Books*

Source: Joyce K. McCauley and Daniel S. McCauley. Adapted from "Using Choral-Reading to Promote Language Learning for ESL Students," *The Reading Teacher*, Vol. 45, No. 7 (March 1992); 526–533. Reprinted with permission of the International Reading Association.

to the students first and may be echo-read initially as well. Again, tapes can be used effectively for independent practice.

Choral reading is a superb way to enjoy poetry. Poetry deserves to be read aloud; many poems that are read silently are only pale shadows of what they are when rendered aloud. Add a little movement, a sound effect or two, and a bit of variety with voices (high/low, loud/soft, fast/slow) and you have more than a poetry reading—you have a performing art! Choral reading of poetry and prose is a low-anxiety experience; children's individual mispronunciations or lapses disappear into the sound of the collective voices, while everyone gets to experience fluent reading. It encourages the rereading of text, which contributes to fluency and sight-word acquisition, while students barely recognize that they have read the same text many times over. Choral reading has been shown to particularly help children who are nonfluent English speakers (McCauley & McCauley, 1992). Figure 5.3 shows procedures for choral reading of poetry or other predictable text.

Developing Word Analysis Strategies

Immediate, accurate recognition of more than 90 percent of the words in running text is necessary for effective instructional level reading. As students read more widely and sample various kinds of text, they will necessarily encounter words that they do not recognize on sight. The role of teaching word analysis is to help students acquire efficient strategies for figuring out unrecognized words.

Using Context

In addition to rapid, accurate decoding, good readers use the context of an unfamiliar word to help figure it out. Most words have meaning in isolation, but some have no real meaning, only a function in sentences; who can define *the*, for example? Many other words, including some of the most frequently occurring words, have many meanings, and only sentence context helps us to choose the right one; for example, there are at least six different meanings for *run:* a rapid gait, a tear in a stocking, a jogger's exercise routine, a small creek, a sequence of events, and a computer operation. Sentences have more meaning than the sum of meanings of their component words. For example, even if you know what *time, a, saves, stitch, in,* and *nine* mean, it is only when they are combined in a sentence, *A stitch in time saves nine*, that comprehension can occur. Sentences have meanings beyond the meanings of individual words; paragraphs and larger units of text have meanings beyond that of individual sentences. In language, the whole is indeed more than the sum of its parts.

Using these larger meanings to help make "educated guesses" about what an unfamiliar word might be involves using context as a word recognition strategy. It requires a reader to ask the mental question "What would make sense here?" Several strategies may be taught to help students use context effectively.

Cloze procedures are a means of identifying students' reading levels in relation to a particular text. They are also useful teaching tools for helping students to use context. To complete a cloze passage, students must think along with the author, so to speak, using prior information, the meaning suggested by the entire passage, and grammatical and meaning clues provided by the words preceding and following the omitted words. Systematic practice with cloze procedures helps readers to become sensitive to "context clues" and use them when reading.

For teaching, it is not necessary to delete every fifth word as you do when making a cloze passage for assessment. It might be better to delete fewer words and leave more of the text intact. Particular types of words, such as pronouns or verbs, could be deleted to highlight their function. Allow students to insert their best guesses; then discuss their choices. Discussion should guide students to consider how several alternatives might make good sense in one instance, whereas only one possible choice would make sense in another instance, and how different choices can lead to subtle but important changes in meaning. Cloze passages should be accompanied by discussion; their effectiveness is reduced if they are used as worksheets to be completed individually. Older students or more fluent readers may use text they have not read before; then compare their efforts to the original text. Younger students or less fluent readers might be more comfortable, and more successful, with text that they have read or heard before, such as dictated stories, predictable books, and familiar rhymes.

Confirming from text involves covering part of the text as it is read, predicting what might come next, and then uncovering the hidden portions and proceeding. Whole words, parts of words following an initial letter, word groups, or phrases may be covered, depending on what cues you want your students to use as they read the passage. Big books and stories that are put on transparencies or chart tablets work best for this activity.

If you are using a transparency, use a paper or tag board strip to cover part of the text, have students read up to the covered part (and even a bit beyond it, in some cases), and ask them to predict what might come next. If you have covered a whole word, you might now uncover the initial letter or letters and have them predict again. Then slide the strip back and continue reading. At the end of the sentence, have students tell what clues they used to help them guess. If you are using a big book or chart tablet, words can be covered with small sticky notes, and phrases or lines on a tag board strip can be held in place with paper clips. Keep the activity moving so that students don't get bogged down, and don't cover so many words so that context is lost. It is better to do a little of this activity fairly often than to do it infrequently and drag it out too long.

Approaching Word Attack Strategically

Students read many words every day that they must come to either recognize immediately or figure out through some kind of analysis. One team of researchers put the number of different words students will encounter in their school reading by the ninth grade at 88,500 (Nagy & Anderson, 1984). Since more and more of those words are encountered when students are reading independently, the average student must identify more than a dozen new words every day. Students need to become strategic in their word recognition, which means both that they must be disposed to solve the problem of unlocking words and that they must possess the strategies for doing so.

J. David Cooper (1993) arrived at a set of six strategies that can be taught to students explicitly. The number of strategies can be reduced and their directions simplified when they are used at lower grade levels.

1. When you come to a word you do not know, read to the end of the sentence or paragraph and decide whether the word is important to your understanding. If it is unimportant, read on.
2. If the word is important, reread the sentence or paragraph containing the word. Try context to infer the meaning.
3. If context doesn't help, look for base words, prefixes, or suffixes that you recognize.
4. Use what you know about phonics to try to pronounce the word. Is it a word you have heard?
5. If you still don't know the word, use the dictionary or ask someone for help.
6. Once you think you know the meaning, reread the text to be sure it makes sense. (p. 202)

Figure 5.4 shows a simplified version of these strategies for primary-grade students.

FIGURE 5.4 *Strategy Poster for Inferring Word Meanings*

Assessing Reading Fluency

Reading fluency has moved from being a neglected skill to an area of intense interest. In *Put Reading First*, Armbruster, Lehr, and Osborne (2001) define reading fluency this way:

> Fluency is the ability to read a text accurately and quickly. When fluent readers read silently, they recognize words automatically. They group words quickly in ways that help them gain meaning from what they read. Fluent readers read aloud effortlessly and with expression. Their reading sounds natural, as if they are speaking. (p. 22)

Reading fluency is most simply measured by counting the number of words children read per minute, minus the errors. A more complete measure of reading fluency takes into account a reader's expressiveness and phrasing. This yields a measure called Words Correctly Read per Minute, which is calculated using this formula:

$$\frac{\textbf{(Total words read, minus words read incorrectly)} \times \textbf{60}}{\textbf{Reading time in seconds}} = \textbf{WCPM}$$

Thus, for example, if a third grade student reads 125 words in one minute, but makes five reading errors, we would calculate her fluency rate of Words Correctly Read per Minute.

$$\frac{(125 - 5) \times 60}{60} = \frac{120 \times \cancel{60}}{\cancel{60}} = 120 \text{ WCPM.}$$

According to the data in Figure 5.5, this would be an acceptable reading rate for a mid-year third grader.

Reading fluency consists not only of speed and correctness, but also of reading with expression and proper phrasing. Zutell and Rasinski (1991) developed the Multi-dimensional Fluency Scale (see Figure 5.6) to help teachers observe several dimensions of fluency at once.

Those factors were expression and volume, phrasing, smoothness, and pace. The scale is a rubric to guide teachers' judgment. In order to carry out the procedure, the teacher selects a passage of at least 100 words that should be written at the student's instructional level and listens and marks the rubric as the child reads. It certainly helps to tape record the child's reading, so you can go through and mark one feature at a time.

Developing Reading Fluency

Tim Rasinski suggests that teaching reading fluency should include these four emphases:

1. Model good oral reading.
2. Provide oral support for readers.
3. Offer plenty of practice opportunities.
4. Encourage fluency through phrasing. (Rasinki, 2003)

Modeling Fluent Oral Reading

Teachers should be careful to provide models of fluent reading for their students. We mean this in two senses. First, teachers should actually demonstrate the concept of fluent versus disfluent reading. Second, teachers should frequently read aloud to students and entice them with examples of rich language that is read well.

The following oral reading fluency norms were developed by Hasbrouck and Tindal (1992).

Grade	Percentile	Fall WCPM	Winter WCPM	Spring WCPM
2	75	82	106	124
	50	53	78	94
	25	23	46	65
3	75	107	123	142
	50	79	93	114
	25	65	70	87
4	75	125	133	143
	50	99	112	118
	25	72	89	92
5	75	126	143	151
	50	105	118	128
	25	77	93	100

(50th percentile for upper grades: 125–150 WCPM)

FIGURE 5.5 *Oral Fluency Norms*

Source: Table 1 from "Curriculum-Based Oral Reading Fluency Norms for Students in Grades 2 Through 5" by J. Hasbrouck and G. Tindal, *Teaching Exceptional Children*, Vol. 24(3), 1992, p. 42.

To introduce the very concept of fluent reading, begin by reading a passage to the students two ways. First read it haltingly and uncertainly, in a voice that suggests you are concerned with slashing your way through the words and getting a disagreeable experience over with: In other words, read disfluently. Then read it again, but this time with your voice full of expression and interest, with pauses and emphases. Show that you are enjoying the message of the text and not simply struggling to pronounce the words: That is to say, read fluently. Then ask the students which reading they preferred and why. In the discussion that follows, call attention to the qualities of fluent reading:

- The reader is thinking about the message and not just about pronouncing the words.
- The reader varies her voice between loud and soft, and between faster and slower.
- The reader groups words meaningfully.
- The reader may show emotion—enjoyment, surprise, and excitement—as she reads.

	1	2	3	4
Expression and Volume	Reads in a quiet voice as if to get the words out. The reading does not sound natural like he is talking to a friend.	Reads in a quiet voice. The reading sounds natural in part of the text, but the reader does not always sound like he is talking to a friend.	Reads with volume and expression. However, sometimes the reader slips into expressionless reading and does not sound like she is talking to a friend.	Reads with varied volume and expression. The reader sounds like she is talking to a friend with her voice matching the interpretation of the passage.
Phrasing	Reads word by word in a monotone voice.	Reads in two- and three-word phrases, not adhering to punctuation, stress, and intonation.	Reads with a mixture of run-ons, mid-sentence pauses for breath, and some choppiness. There is reasonable stress and intonation.	Reads with good phrasing, adhering to punctuation, stress, and intonation.
Smoothness	Frequently hesitates while reading, sounds out words, and repeats words or phrases. The reader makes multiple attempts to read the same passage.	Reads with extended pauses or hesitations. The reader has many "rough spots."	Reads with occasional breaks in rhythm. The reader has difficulty with specific words and/or sentence structures.	Reads smoothly with some breaks, but self-corrects with difficult words and/or sentence structures.
Pace	Reads slowly and laboriously.	Reads moderately slowly.	Reads fast and slow throughout reading.	Reads at a conversational pace throughout the reading.

FIGURE 5.6 *Multidimensional Fluency Scale*

Source: J. Zutell and T. Rasinski, 1991.

Later, read aloud to the students again, reading as fluently as you can, and "thinking aloud" as you read, that is, pausing to explain to the students of a decision you just made—such as where to pause, what words to group together, or how to read a character's voice—in order to read fluently. When you read a text aloud to your students, you should take steps to call attention to your fluent reading. Make sure to point out to students how you

- Match the emotional qualities of the passages—serious, humorous, exciting, urgent—with your tone of voice.
- Stress the important words in the passages.

- Honor the punctuation—pausing at commas, stopping at periods, and raising your voice at the ends of sentences with question marks.
- Read the dialogues as if people were actually talking.

Providing Oral Support for Reading

Providing oral support for students' reading means having them read a text aloud at the same time they hear others reading it fluently. This may be accomplished several ways.

Choral Reading. Choral reading happens when groups of students read the same text aloud. It can happen with poetry, or with speeches or other texts. When they are choral reading poetry, readers should practice over and over again to get the sounds right. Texts may be broken up for reading, with lines, phrases, or individual words read

- By the whole chorus, by individuals, by pairs, or by two alternating sections.
- In loud or soft voices.
- Rapidly or slowly.
- Melodiously, angrily, giggling, or seriously.

You should prepare the children to choral-read a text by discussing the circumstances or the context in which it might be said, so the text is read meaningfully. For example, the following poem, "The Grand Old Duke of York," has a martial rhythm. Invite the children to imagine they are a platoon of soldiers marching along a road. From a single vantage point, they are very quiet when they are heard from a distance, then louder as they approach, then very loud when they are right in front of the person, then quieter until they are very quiet. Have them practice reading the poem in unison, going from very quiet to VERY LOUD to very quiet again.

THE GRAND OLD DUKE OF YORK (TRADITIONAL)

The Grand Old Duke of York
He had ten thousand men.
He always marched them up the hill
Then he marched them down again.
And when they were up they were up.
And when they were down they were down.
And when they were only halfway up
They were neither up nor down.

Paired Reading. Students can practice reading a text in pairs, too. It is good practice to pair students with different reading abilities—but not too different. For example, if you group your students, groups 2 and 4 pair up. They take turns reading the same text aloud, alternating sentences or paragraphs.

Recorded Texts. Individual students can read along with recorded text, wearing headphones so as not to disturb others. Remind them to read in quiet voices. Recorded versions of children's books are available from www.Audible.com and other sources. More elaborate computer-based programs are also available—at proportionately higher costs—with texts read at varying rates, and with provisions for students' own reading to be recorded and timed, via speech recognition software. Insights Reading Fluency software (www.charlesbridge.com) and other programs have these features.

Providing Practice in Oral Reading

Rereading is the strategy of reading the same material more than once. Rereading helps students to gain fluency, bolsters students' self-confidence as readers, assists students in recognizing familiar words at sight, and helps students use phrasing to support the meaning of what they read. It need not mean drudgery for students, however. There are a number of ways in which we can integrate rereading into our teaching.

1. Have students read material silently before oral reading or discussion. If you will use predictive questions in your discussion, have them read silently up to a stopping point.
2. Encourage oral rereading for real purposes: to prove a point in a discussion, to role-play a dialogue, or to savor an effective descriptive passage, among other purposes.
3. Encourage the rereading of familiar or completed stories as seatwork or independent work or during free reading or sustained silent reading periods.
4. Use buddy reading: Select or have students choose reading partners or buddies, and then reread completed stories or books aloud to their partners.
5. Encourage children to take home familiar books to reread to family members. Since rereading is usually more fluent than the initial reading, children can show off their fluent reading at home this way.
6. Encourage rereading of favorite stories by revisiting old favorites when you read aloud to the class.
7. Have students listen to recorded material, either professionally produced or done by you or other volunteers. After listening and silently following along, have students imitate the reader as they listen, and then eventually read the material alone. Record their readings for self-critique.
8. Act out favorite stories using the technique of reader's theater, in which scripts are always read instead of memorized and recited.
9. Use choral reading frequently and perform for others.

Repeated Reading for Fluency

Repeated reading refers to a systematic practice of using timed oral rereadings to develop reading fluency. Described by Samuels (1979), the method involves helping the student select an instructional level passage and a reading rate goal, timing the first

1. Choose, or help each student to choose, a fairly comfortable, interesting selection to practice reading. It should be too long to memorize: 100 or so words for younger children, 200 or more words for older ones. Trade books and previously read basal stories are good.
2. Make up a duplicated chart for each pupil (see Figure 5.8). Omit the accuracy axis if you want to simplify the task.
3. Time each reader's first, unrehearsed oral reading of the passage. Mark the chart for Timed Reading 1.
4. Instruct the readers to practice the passage aloud as many times as possible for the next day or two. Let them practice in pairs, independently, and at home.
5. Time the reading again and mark the chart for Timed Reading 2. Show the students how to mark their own charts.
6. Continue timing at intervals of several days. As the rate increases for the first passage, help each child to set a new rate goal.
7. When the reader reaches the goal set, begin a new passage of equal (not greater) difficulty. Successive portions of a long story are perfect. Repeat steps 3 through 6.

FIGURE 5.7 *Steps in Using Repeated Reading*

unrehearsed oral reading of the passage and successive readings after practice, and keeping a simple chart of the student's rate after successive timings. When the student is able to read the passage at or beyond the goal rate, a new passage of equal (but not greater) difficulty is begun.

This method of repeated reading is not intended to directly aid comprehension, but rather to help students acquire sight words and practice reading fluently and confidently. As they practice rereading their passages for timing, their reading rate for that passage climbs dramatically; keeping a chart that shows these increases is highly motivating, especially for older poor readers.

Of course, we are not surprised that their rates climb as they practice reading the same passage. What is surprising, and what is the real benefit of this practice, is that their reading rates also increase on each successive unrehearsed oral reading. This increase occurs because all of the rereading has enabled them to acquire more sight words and has helped them learn to read aloud fluently and confidently. Figure 5.7 shows the steps in using the timed repeated reading method, and Figure 5.8 shows a partially completed chart.

Of course, it matters a great deal what students have to read. Expecting students to read frequently, copiously, and repeatedly in material that is at their level of competence assumes that plenty of lively and interesting reading material will be available at many different levels of difficulty. Fortunately, this is true.

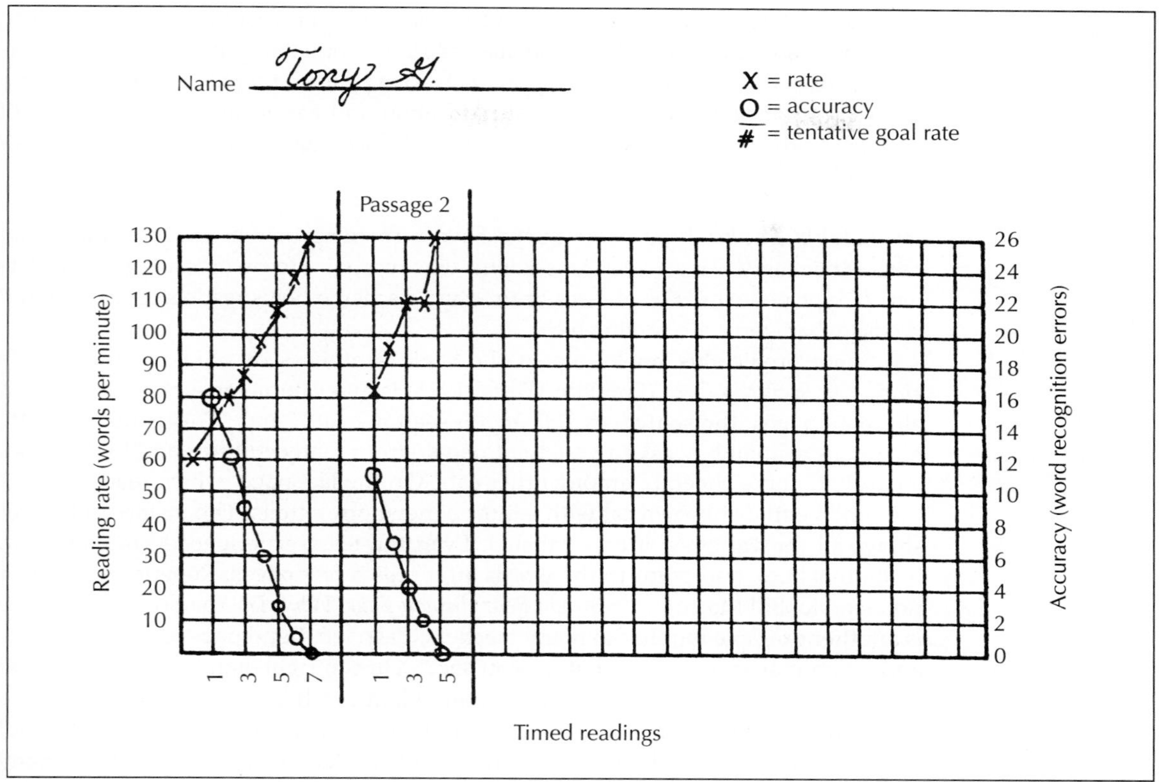

FIGURE 5.8 *Sample Repeated Reading Chart*

Predictable Books, "Easy Readers," and Other Easy Reading Fare

If we acknowledge that "children learn to read by reading" (as reading guru Frank Smith put it), then children need material that they can and will read. Such material must be available at all reading levels, and it should appeal to a range of interests. Some of it should appeal to more mature interests, even though its difficulty level is low.

It used to be that there were relatively few such books available. Primer-level basals were written in straight narrative style, and for that reason, dictated accounts and simple poems were often used in their place. Today, however, as the field of children's trade books has exploded to meet the demands of families and classrooms, more attention is being paid to the needs of developing readers. There are many wonderful predictable books for young readers, many of them available in big book format for group instruction. Some publishers, such as The Wright Group (www.wrightgroup.com) and Rigby books (www.harcourtachieve.com), have built their product lines around the use of predictable books in both big book and individual book formats. Many of the large commercial publishing houses, too, have special lines of books for young developing readers. In addition, a number of smaller education-oriented publishers publish collections of books that were written especially to appeal to students in the elementary grades and beyond who need special motivation and easier fare. Three varieties of such books that are discussed here are *predictable books, easy readers,* and *high-interest/ low-reading-level books.*

Predictable Books. Predictable books have a rhyming or repetitious element that makes them easy to read, even for students who recognize few words at sight. The pattern of repeated words or phrases or the rhyme scheme helps readers remember and predict what words are coming next.

Some predictable books repeat the same sentences or phrases. Eric Carle's *Have You Seen My Cat?* (Franklin Watts, 1973) is an example of such a pattern. On alternate pages, the sentences "Have you seen my cat?" and "This is not my cat!" repeat, as a small boy asks a variety of people from many cultures and finds a lion, a panther, and a cheetah, among other cats. On the last page, which reads "This is my cat!" he finds his own cat with a litter of newborn kittens. The inside back cover shows all the varieties of cats, labeled. Even the least-experienced prereader can recite this book and point to the words after only a few pages. Repetition makes it predictable. Bill Martin, Jr.'s *Brown Bear, Brown Bear, What Do You See?* (Holt, 1983) is another example familiar to many teachers. Each left-hand page identifies a color and an animal and asks, "What do you see?" On the right-hand page, the animal answers, "I see a _____ looking at me," and identifies the next color and animal: a yellow duck, a blue horse, a green frog, and so forth. Again, the last page lists all the animals cumulatively with small copies of the larger illustrations. Like many others, these books are available in big book, standard trade book, and miniature versions. Eric Carle's *The Very Hungry Caterpillar* (Philomel Books, 1969), *The Grouchy Ladybug* (Harper & Row, 1977), and *The Very Busy Spider* (Philomel Books, 1984) are other examples.

Some predictable books rely on rhyme rather than repetition. Nancy Shaw's *Sheep in a Jeep* (Houghton Mifflin, 1986) is an example. Although it has few words, the hilarious antics of the sheep that go for an ill-fated joyride make it appropriate for a wide range of ages. It sounds like this: "Uh-oh! the jeep won't go. Sheep leap to push the jeep. Sheep shove, sheep grunt. Sheep don't think to look up front." It is a great source of rhyming words, those that share the same spelling pattern (*sheep/jeep*) as well as those that don't (*grunt/front*), and colorful sound words (*splash! thud!*). The rhyming adventures of the sheep continue in *Sheep on a Ship* (Houghton Mifflin, 1989) and *Sheep in a Shop* (Houghton Mifflin, 1991).

Predictable books also serve as jumping-off places for students to create their own original books. Changing the topic and illustrations, while retaining the original pattern, can result in wonderful original versions that children enjoy reading as much as, or more than, the original version. For example, after mastering *Brown Bear, Brown Bear, What Do You See?* a group of first graders created *The Vegetable Book:* "Green pepper, green pepper, what do you see? I see a red tomato looking at me," and so forth. With the basic pattern written on chart paper and blanks for the color words and nouns, the group chose the vegetable theme and volunteered the word pairs to fill the blanks: *brown potato, orange carrot, purple eggplant,* for example. Each couplet was then printed on a separate sheet, and pairs of students were assigned to illustrate each page. The resulting big book was stapled together and reread numerous times. Meanwhile, the text was typed on individual pages with space for illustration, duplicated, and stapled into individual copies. Each student then illustrated his or her own copy to keep. (During this time, the class brought in samples of the various vegetables for exploring and tasting.) Another group followed the same procedure with *Have You Seen My Cat?*, creating their original *Have You Seen My Dog?* and illustrating it with different breeds and colors of dogs. (This effort involved looking at numerous books about dogs to learn about different breeds.) These books remained very popular all year long for independent reading.

Both commercial and student-written predictable books are extremely useful for independent reading and as springboards for creative writing. They help students to acquire and reinforce sight words while providing successful reading practice for even the least fluent reader.

Easy Readers. Children's books have been available in the United States for more than 200 years, but it is only in the past several decades that quality works that children could read themselves have become regularly available. Traditional picture books were written to be read to children by adults and only rarely by children (Temple et al., 2010), so there has long been a need for accessibly written works that appealed to children's desire for interesting fare. Now many of the major trade publishers put out series of easy readers. The Putnam and Grosset Group publishes the *All Aboard* reading series. Dial Press has the *Easy-to-Read* series. The series from Random House is called *Step into Reading,* and HarperCollins publishes *I Can Read.* In conjunction with Bank Street College, Bantam publishes the *Bank Street Ready-to-Read* series. Although Macmillan has no particular name for its easy reader offerings, it has published more than a dozen easy readers about *Henry and Mudge* by Cynthia Rylant.

Easy readers have been produced by some of the best children's authors and illustrators we have. Cynthia Rylant has won Newbery and Caldecott Awards. Other award-winning children's authors such as Dr. Seuss, James Marshall, Tomie dePaola, Arnold Lobel, Lee Bennett Hopkins, and Joanna Cole have also written easy readers. An excellent source of reviews of easy readers is the *Adventuring with Books* series, published approximately every four years by the National Council of Teachers of English and containing nearly 2,000 annotated listings of books by topic and by difficulty level for students in grades pre-K through 6.

High-Interest/Low-Reading-Level Books and Magazines. Since the 1960s, several educational publishers have produced works specifically for reluctant readers. The early efforts were not of particularly high quality (Ryder, Graves, & Graves, 1989), but the books have improved since. The books' strengths are also their weaknesses, note

Ryder et al. To be "relevant" to reluctant readers, earlier versions of hi-lo books often highlighted the experiences of boys in the inner city who (if they come from minority groups) were African American or Hispanic. Other students felt as distant from the characters in these books as they did from white youths in gated suburbs. Also, to be more readable, the books have limited their vocabulary and sentence length, sometimes at the expense of comprehensible text.

Contemporary high-interest/low-reading-level materials are diverse and interesting. Some even come in computer-based formats. Susan Jones's Resource Room online is a good guide to hi-lo materials for readers at the sixth-grade level and above (http://www.resourceroom.net/comprehension/hilow.asp).

Developing Readers' Vocabulary

Vocabulary is important in reading. As Carl Smith puts it, "Most people feel that there is a common sense relationship between vocabulary and comprehension—messages are composed of ideas, and ideas are expressed in words" (1997, p. 1). But the relationship between children's vocabulary and their reading comprehension points in more than one direction, and the means of helping children develop vocabulary have been subject to dispute, even while the teaching of vocabulary has not commanded much attention from elementary teachers (Beck et al., 2002). Before going on, then, we must pause to discuss vocabulary instruction and reading.

Vocabulary development interacts with word recognition, as children try to recognize in print words they already know—or partially know—in speech. But although younger children have most of the words in their spoken vocabulary that they are likely to encounter in print, there are still many words that occur in young children's picture books that children don't hear in the spoken language around them (Stanovich, 1992). If you need convincing on this point, read William Steig's *Sylvester and the Magic Pebble* (1987). By fourth grade, the vocabulary found in books is considerably richer than the words children use in speech.

Certainly, children can grow larger vocabularies from doing wide reading (Stanovich, 1992). As Nagy et al. (1985) point out, however, readers who encounter 100 unknown words will learn perhaps 5 of them. Children must do a great deal of reading, in at least moderately challenging texts, to acquire large vocabularies from reading. But there are huge disparities in the amount of reading children do. As we saw in Chapter 1, in one study (Wilson, Anderson, & Fielding, 1986), the top 20 percent of a fifth-grade class read twenty times as much as the bottom 20 percent. The bottom 20 percent read very little. If we count on children to learn vocabulary from reading, we will surely continue to see the huge disparities in vocabulary size described above.

One way to help children learn vocabulary is to show them how to learn more words from context (Szymborski, 1995). Another way we can help their vocabularies grow is to give them systematic vocabulary instruction (McKeown & Beck, 1988). We will look at both approaches next.

Levels of Vocabulary Knowledge

What do we mean by *knowing* vocabulary? Beck et al. (2002) suggest a continuum of word knowledge that looks like this:

- No knowledge.
- General sense, such as knowing *mendacious* has a negative connotation.
- Narrow, context-bound knowledge, such as knowing that a *radiant bride* is a beautifully smiling happy one, but being unable to describe an individual in a different context as *radiant.*
- Having knowledge of a word but not being able to recall it readily enough to use it in appropriate situations.
- Rich, decontextualized knowledge of a word's meaning, its relationship to other words, and its extension to metaphorical uses, such as understanding what someone is doing when she is *devouring* a book. (p. 10)

Knowing vocabulary well means not just understanding what words in a book mean, then, but knowing words in a range of contexts, in associations with other words, and in connection with our own experience—to have words as one's own.

Dissecting Children's Vocabulary

Teaching vocabulary is a serious job. Nagy et al. estimate that by ninth grade, students have to cope with a written vocabulary of 88,500 words (Nagy & Anderson, 1984). Were we to try to teach all those words, the prospect of helping children learn nearly 10,000 words a year would be daunting indeed. But as we saw earlier in this book, Beck et al. (2002) have found a useful way to break down those numbers.

Tier One Words. There are several thousand words already in children's spoken vocabulary that we won't usually have to teach. Beck et al. call these Tier One words, and they include examples like *mother, clock,* and *jump.*

Tier Three Words. Then there are many more thousands of words that are so highly specialized that they are almost never used outside of the disciplines where they are encountered. These Tier Three words—like *monozygotic, tetrahedron,* and *bicameral*—are best learned in the science, social studies, and other classes where they are tied to the content under study.

Tier Two Words. That leaves the Tier Two words, those with wide utility that most children don't have in their spoken vocabularies—words like *dismayed, paradoxical, absurd,* and *wary*. Beck et al. (2002) estimate that there may be about 7,000 Tier Two words, and even if we teach children half of them—or about 400 words a year—we will have gone a long way toward growing children's vocabularies and equalizing children's access to learning.

Approaches to Teaching Vocabulary

There is a wide consensus among researchers that vocabulary is best learned in the context of ideas under consideration, that learners should be actively involved in making meaning with new vocabulary, and that vocabulary should be related to other words and new words should be tied to the learners' own experience (Smith, 1997).

Word Conversations. When young readers (kindergarten and first grade) are learning new words, Beck et al. (2002) suggest that teachers conduct a rich discussion of words, which includes these six steps:

1. Contextualize words, one at a time, within a story. For example, with kindergartners, the authors use Don Freeman's perennially popular *A Pocket for Corduroy* as a pretext for introducing the words *insistent, reluctant,* and *drowsy.* The teacher says, "In the story, Lisa was *reluctant* to leave the laundromat without Corduroy (her new teddy bear)."
2. Ask the children to repeat the word, so as to make a phonological representation of it.
3. Then explain the meaning of the word in a child-friendly way: "*Reluctant* means you are not sure you want to do something."
4. Now provide examples of the word in other contexts. "I am *reluctant* to go swimming in the early summer when the water is cold."
5. Next, ask children to provide their own examples: "What is something you would be *reluctant* to do?"
6. Now, ask the children to repeat the word they have been talking about, so as to reinforce its phonological representation.

Word conversations work best when they are prepared in advance. The teacher may choose the book to provide a meaningful context for introducing the vocabulary. Or, if the book is rich in many vocabulary words, the teacher locates the Tier Two words in advance and decides which ones will be most useful. The teacher thinks carefully about how to explain the meaning of each word in a child-friendly way. She carefully plans questions to relate the words to the children's experience. And she is careful to remind the children of the words they are studying, giving them several opportunities to pronounce them (see Beck et al., 2002, for further discussion of this approach).

Exercises for Second Grade and Up

Activities to teach vocabulary should relate words to a meaningful context, to other words, and to the students' own experience. The following exercises satisfy these requirements.

Semantic Maps. There are several ways to use *semantic maps*. The most open-ended way is to draw a circle on a page and write a topic-word in it. Then, together with the students, you think of aspects of the topic and come up with examples or aspects of that subtopic (see example for *dolphins* in Figure 5.9).

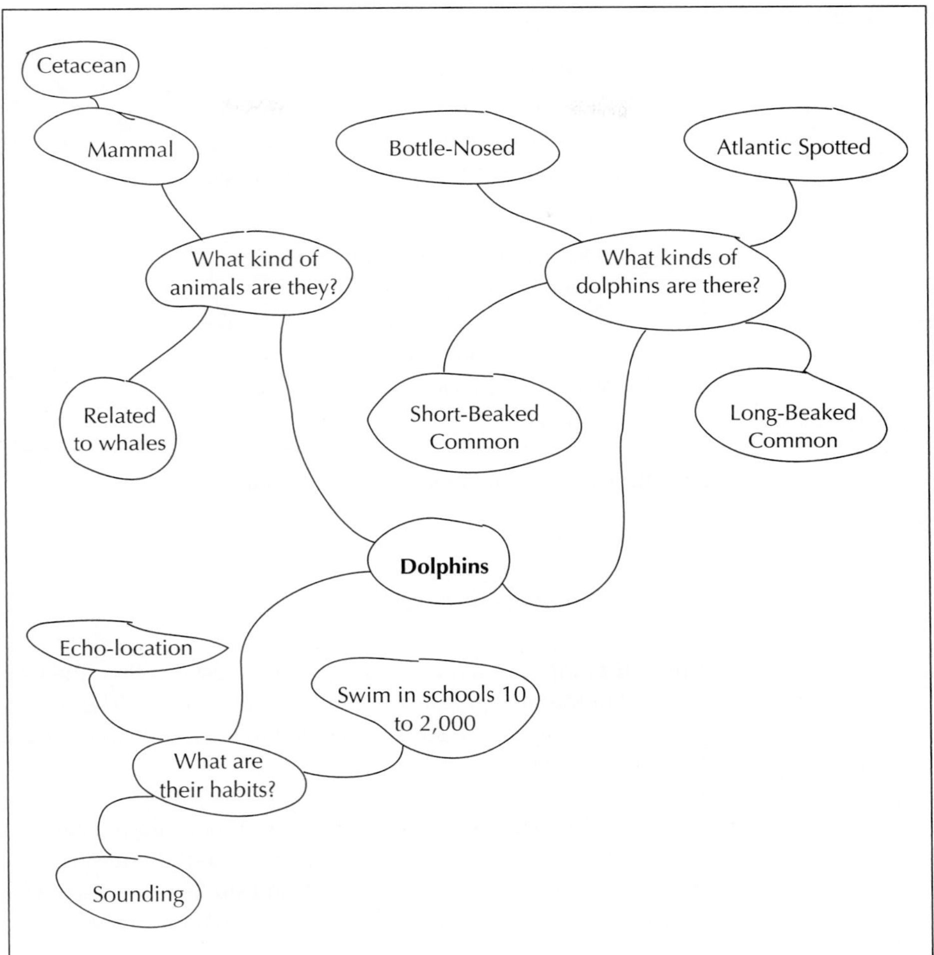

FIGURE 5.9 *A Semantic Map: Dolphins*

A particular approach to semantic maps is the *character web*. The name of a character is written in the circle in the middle of the display. Words that describe the character are written as satellites around the character's name; then examples that illustrate each attribute are written as satellites around the descriptive words.

Webbed Questions. Schwartz and Raphael (1985) suggest guiding the students' responses to a semantic map, asking them to offer answers to three questions asked about the target word (see Figure 5.10, where this technique is applied to the dolphin example of Figure 5.9):

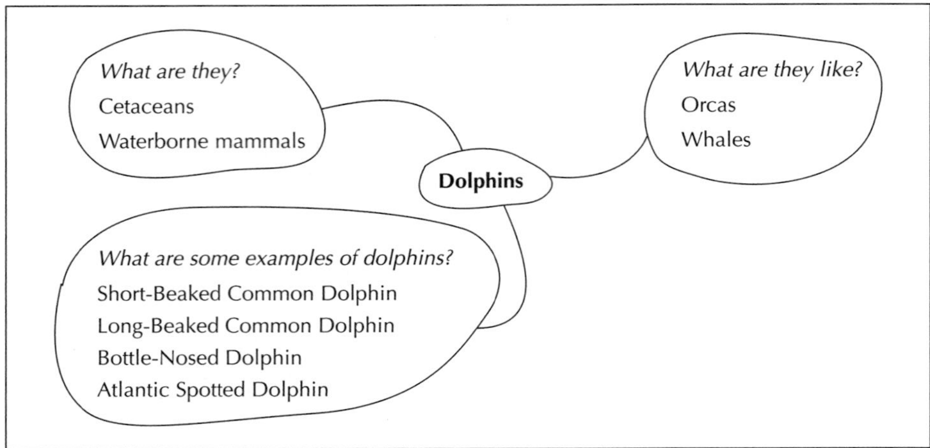

FIGURE 5.10 *Webbed Questions: Dolphins*

What is it?
What is it like?
What are some examples of it?

Concept Ladder. A more elaborate set of questions than the webbed questions above is found in the *concept ladder* (Temple & Gillet, 1984). The concept ladder is used with terms for concepts. The students are led to answer a structured set of questions about the concept (see Figure 5.11).

Semantic Feature Analysis. *Semantic feature analysis* enables students to compare several terms at once and make judgments about the terms. The terms are placed in a grid like the one shown in Figure 5.12, and students are asked to write in a + sign if the answer to the question is positive and a – sign if the answer is negative.

What kind of thing is this? ______ ______	What is it a part of? ______ ______	What causes it? ______ ______
What are the kinds of it? ______ ______	What are its parts? ______ ______	What does it cause? ______ ______

FIGURE 5.11 *A Concept Ladder*

	Bear live young	*Have gills*	*Cold-blooded*	*Have milk*
SHARKS				
DOLPHINS				

FIGURE 5.12 *Semantic Feature Analysis*

M-Charts. A word has a *denotation*, which is its literal meaning, and a *connotation*, which comprises the attitudes it conveys or evokes. According to their connotations, words can have a positive or a negative "ring." To call attention to the connotations of words, you can use an M chart (see Figure 5.13). Put a target word in the middle and ask the students to provide terms that convey both positive and negative connotations. Write those terms in the left- and the right-hand columns. To personalize these words, ask the students to think of times when people might have thought they or someone else was *timid* when they were really being *cautious.*

Positive	*Neutral*	*Negative*
CAUTIOUS	*Reluctant to act*	*TIMID*
PRUDENT		*COWARDLY*

FIGURE 5.13 *An M-Chart for Connotations*

Teaching the Use of Context Clues to Vocabulary

As we said above, learning words from context is usually inefficient. We can boost students' success in learning words from context by making them aware of the recurring kinds of clues to the meanings of words in context. There are four kinds of context clues:

1. **Definitions and Explanations**. Writers who are aware of their readers' needs for information often explain the meaning of a word or phrase right after the word is introduced. For example:

> Dolphins use *echo-location*, <u>which is the use of sound to locate objects</u>, as they hunt schools of herring on which to feed.

2. **Restating the Term in Other Words.** An uncommon word may be restated or followed up by words that give clues to its meaning. For example:

> Because they are *herbivores*, elephants <u>eat only leaves and branches of trees.</u>
>
> The phrase <u>eat only leaves and branches of trees</u> suggests that *herbivores* are creatures who eat such things.

3. **Providing Contrasting Words or Antonyms**. An unknown word may be followed by its opposite, its *antonym*. If the student knows the meaning of the antonym, he may find a clue to the meaning of the unknown word by reversing the meaning of the antonym. For example:

> Shirley was a prompt worker, not a *procrastinator*.
>
> The phrase prompt worker is offered as the opposite of the term *procrastinator*. Therefore, *procrastinator* might mean someone who does not get her work done promptly.

4. **Providing Examples**. If an unknown word is the name of a category, followed by a list of examples, some of which are known, the examples provide a clue to the meaning of the unknown word. If the name of the category is known, it may also give a clue to the meaning of unknown examples. For instance:

> There was nothing on the table but *hors d'oeuvres* such as crackers and cheese, pickled cauliflower, and deviled eggs.
>
> The items crackers and cheese, pickled cauliflower, and deviled eggs, give a clue to the meaning of *hors d'oeuvres*.

Teachers can find passages in books to read aloud to students to practice using context clues such as these to approach the meanings of unknown words. They can be asked to be on the lookout for context clues in their own reading.

Developing Reading Comprehension

Throughout this book, we have noted that comprehension is an active process of making meaning. Good comprehenders summon up their prior knowledge about the topic of a reading, they ask questions about the topic before and during the reading, they make appropriate inferences when ideas are not explicitly stated, they find main ideas, they summarize, and they make mental images from the words in the text.

According to this view, comprehension requires an active reader, one who is confident and curious enough to bring her own ideas to the reading and to question the ideas in the text. However, in a decade-long study of what happens when elementary-grade students read textbooks, Beck and McKeown (1994) did not find many such readers. Traditional teaching required students to read and later answer factual questions about what they had read; and it seemed these questions were more often intended to prove that students had understood the reading rather than to draw out their thinking about the subject matter. Too many students approached comprehension as if it worked by passively ingesting ideas from the text.

Since, as Isabel Beck's work suggests, the teacher's approach influences what students do when they attempt to comprehend, it is critically important that the instruction teachers provide for students guides them into cognitive activities that bear fruit. In this section, we describe several strategies for instruction that have been tested by research and practice.

We divide our treatment of comprehension into three phases, related to what should be done before, during, and after a reading. We call these the phases of *anticipation, building knowledge*, and *consolidation*, respectively.

For the Phase of Anticipation

As you recall, anticipation is the phase in which students inspect a text, remind themselves of what they already know about it, raise questions or make predictions about what they will find out from reading it, and set purposes for their reading.

Developing Prior Knowledge. Prior knowledge is what we already know or have experienced, directly or vicariously, that we bring to the act of reading. When we can somehow relate what we read to our prior knowledge, we understand and remember more clearly. When we lack prior knowledge to relate to what we read, chances are that we will become confused, misunderstand, and forget what we read. In this situation, we might also become disinterested in what we are reading, calling it boring or dull. And if our need is great to remember it, as in preparation for a test, we might resort to inefficient strategies such as memorizing. Helping students to develop, organize, and become aware of their prior knowledge is critical to improving their reading comprehension.

But two problems are associated with prior knowledge. One is that we might lack sufficient prior knowledge about a topic, not having heard or read of it before. A second problem is that much of our prior knowledge about a given topic might not be readily accessible; it has been buried, so to speak, under other information, and we can't summon it up and think about it readily. Because we can't bring it to mind immediately, we think we've forgotten it or never had it. Activities that develop prior knowledge center on helping students to establish some basis for classifying new information and helping them to remember and organize prior knowledge that is not readily accessible.

Webbing. A simple way to help students begin to recall prior knowledge and form relationships is to use *webbing*, an exercise in which the teacher writes a topic or term on the board, students offer terms or phrases that might be related, and the teacher draws lines connecting associated terms with each other. In the subsequent reading, terms and relationships are noted, and the web may be revised to reflect new information required. The webbing exercise serves to help students remember old information related to the reading and to form expectations about what they will be reading.

For example, let's say that Ms. Brown, a fourth-grade teacher, plans to have her students read a nonfiction basal selection about how museums are organized and the jobs museum workers perform. She suspects that some of the students have never visited a museum and that the topic is relatively unfamiliar to many of them. She begins, then, with a web to explore with them what they already know.

First, she writes *museum* on the board and begins a brainstorming session, in which every student in turn offers a word or phrase related in some way to *museum.* Because some students look apprehensive, she suggests some questions to help get them started:

What is a museum for?
What are the names of some museums?
What might be in them?
What work do people do in museums?

As each student responds, Ms. Brown writes the response on the board around the key word. Because this is brainstorming, all responses are accepted without comment or evaluation. She notices that the first few responses appear to remind others of things they might have forgotten and that many appear excited as their turn nears. After everyone has responded once, volunteers might offer other suggestions until their information begins to wane. Then she reads over all the suggestions from the board.

The next step is to help students organize this seemingly random collection of terms into categories. One way Ms. Brown could do this is to use different colors of chalk to draw connecting lines, but because there are a lot of items on the board, this might not help to clarify. So she selects one term, writes it below the web, and says, "What other words go with this one?" Items are checked off and listed in categories, with students explaining why these items go together. These categories resulted:

paintings
scientists
mummies
statues
suits of armor
rockets
airplanes
old cars
Indian stuff
animals and birds
furniture
old cars
dinosaur bones

scientists
guards
guides

set up exhibits
clean up
take tickets
tours

Smithsonian
Museum of
Natural History

Students then suggest names for these categories: *things in museums, museum workers, jobs in museums,* and *names of museums.* Ms. Brown then says, "We're going to read an article about how museums are organized and what kinds of work must be done. As you read, watch for mention of the names of famous museums, their collections, and museum workers' jobs. Let's see which of the things we mentioned are in the article."

After the reading is completed, Ms. Brown leads her students in reinspecting the web, adding to the appropriate categories items from the article that the students had not mentioned and marking those not appearing in the article for later research in another source.

A webbing activity like this is effective for several reasons. One is that it encourages all students to draw on whatever prior knowledge they have, no matter how extensive or limited, and apply it to the reading task. Another is that hearing others' ideas often triggers a forgotten bit of information in a person's mind, so all benefit from sharing of information. A third is that seemingly unrelated information is directly organized so that relationships are sought and explored. A fourth is that prereading participation fosters curiosity and gives readers something to watch for as they read, and a purpose for reading. A fifth is that the exercise helps the teacher to realize what prior knowledge, if any, students have on the topic before they begin reading.

Previewing. Another way to help students organize their prior knowledge and develop expectations about what they are going to read is to let them quickly *preview* a reading selection and predict what kinds of information they might find in it.

When students preview a reading selection, they do not begin to read it; rather, they scan each page, looking at illustrations and text features such as boldface print and headings. The time that is allowed for this is very short, so that they can get an overall general idea of the content, just enough to begin to predict about specifics. Depending on the length of the selection, two minutes or less are usually sufficient. Previewing is effective with both fiction and nonfiction, as we will see in these examples.

Mr. Talbott works with a group of fifth graders reading at a third-grade instructional level. He has selected a basal story for them to read and discuss that deals with events surrounding the celebration of the Chinese New Year. Because this holiday and Chinese American customs in general are unfamiliar to his students, he uses previewing to help them form a basis for their reading. He tells the group to find the first and last pages of the story and then to look at the title and the pictures, but not to begin reading yet. He gives them 30 seconds to do so, telling the group when to begin and stop. Then he asks them to close their books and tell him what they saw in the pictures. He lists all the responses on the board:

Chinese people
a parade
fireworks
people in costumes
people wearing masks
some kind of big snake or dragon
people inside a dragon suit
some children looking scared
people eating
a building with a funny roof

Then he asks, "What do you think is going on in this story? What could be happening?" Again he lists responses:

party
celebration
parade
holiday

Then he introduces some terms from the story and encourages predictions about what they might mean and how they might be related to the story: *festival, calendar, temple, parade,* and *feast*. The students' predictions begin to form around the idea that a Chinese holiday celebration is occurring in which people prepare special foods, observe religious customs, wear ceremonial clothing, and participate in a street procession with costumes and fireworks. From this basis of information, Mr. Talbott guides his students to reexamine the illustrations and predict what might happen in the story—for example, who might the children be who are pictured several times? Why might they be frightened in this picture? What might happen at the end?

At this point, the students have developed a good basis of information and expectation and are ready to begin reading. Their previewing has helped them to develop a context for the story's events, introduced some of the story's key vocabulary, and helped them to set purposes for their reading.

Ms. Niles works with older poor readers from several grades. Seven of her students must read an earth science selection on glacier formation, but a prereading discussion reveals that both prior information and interest in the topic are lacking. She uses previewing to help overcome both problems.

First, she asks the group to tell what they already know about glaciers. Other than that they are made of ice, her question is met with shrugs and blank looks. "All right," she says, "you have exactly two minutes to look over these pages and find out as much as you can, and we'll see who is able to gather the most information. Sally and Becky, you look at headings and boldface print. Maurice and John, you look at maps. Sam and Daniel, you look for topic sentences at the beginnings of each major section. Jessica, you look at photographs and their captions. All set? Begin!"

Ms. Niles has adapted the previewing task to fit the special informational demands of this selection and has given each student a specific task. She has also used a team approach and introduced an element of competition to arouse the students' interest in the task. After two minutes of silent study, she asks each student or pair to report on the specified area and begins listing terms, topics, and descriptions on the board under general headings. She compliments each responder on the amount of information gathered, without designating any "winner." After a quick review of the lists on the board, the students begin to read the selection, armed with an array of facts, terms, and concepts they had not possessed before, as well as with some confidence that they can read the chapter successfully.

Previewing is an effective means of helping students to acquire some prereading information on topics about which they have little prior knowledge and to set some expectations about the text that they can compare to what the selection conveys. The previewing time should be kept short, and the discussion period should be conducted in an accepting, encouraging manner. Reading should begin when interest is aroused and some basis for reading has been established.

Developing Predictions. Closely related to the topic of prior knowledge is the process of *prediction*, in which students compare what they already know or remember to what they think they are going to read. Prediction requires that students relate their prior knowledge to the reading task at hand and form expectations that they will apply to the reading. Thus, prediction forms the connection between students' prior knowledge and the new information.

For the Phase of Building Knowledge

Building knowledge is the phase of reading and finding out. Suggested activities for this phase are the Directed Reading Activity, the Directed Reading-Thinking Activity, the Know-Want to Know-Learn method, Questioning the Author, and Reciprocal Teaching.

The Directed Reading Activity. The Directed Reading Activity (DRA) is a strategy that gives the teacher a broad opportunity to guide students' thought processes toward the aspects of comprehension that were discussed earlier in this chapter. The steps to the procedure are described below.

Before the lesson begins, the teacher chooses four or five stopping points in the text for each class period in which it will be discussed. Then, to begin the activity, the teacher does a prereading introduction of the text, pointing out the title, the author, and the genre; showing pictures if there are any; and inviting students to venture what they think the text may be about. The teacher may use think-alouds to show the way to making predictions and comments.

Before the students read the first marked-off section, the teacher puts a question to them, to give them a purpose for their reading. "Read this section to see who this story is going to be about, and what kind of situation she is in," the teacher might ask. The students read to find answers to the question. After they have read, they share their answers. The teacher may challenge them to go back and read the passages on which they based their answers.

Before they read the next section, the teacher asks students to read to find the answer to another question, and the reading proceeds in this scavenger hunt fashion.

What kinds of questions should the teacher ask? Research has shown that questions are most helpful when they follow the contours of the *format* and *genre* of the text. That is, the questions should help readers follow the presentation of information that is particular to the kind of text the students are reading.

If the students are reading a narrative text, these questions usually contain a predictable set of elements: the *setting*, the *characters*, the *problem*, *attempts at solutions*, the *consequences of the actions*, and the *theme or message* of the story.

Questions about *settings* may lead students to notice what sensory words the author used to evoke images: "Read this next section and pay attention to what the author wants you to hear, smell, and feel." Questions may ask students to predict what kinds of events might take place in such a setting.

Questions about *characters* similarly call attention to how the author helps the reader know the characters, sense the tensions between the characters, and understand the kinds of problems the main character might have and what kinds of actions they might take.

Questions about the *problem*, the *attempts at solutions*, and the *consequences of the actions* can guide readers to follow the plots of stories. Readers can be asked to note the main character's problem and to predict how she or he will attempt to solve it, given what they know about the character (and what they could predict from the kind of story they are reading). They can also be asked about the consequences of the actions, and how the situation at the end of the story differs from the situation at the beginning.

Themes or messages of stories can be examined in several ways. Students can be asked what the story meant to them. They can also be asked why they would or would not agree with the message the story seems to convey—because many popular stories suggest ways of living to which we shouldn't readily subscribe—that one must be beautiful or very aggressive in order to be successful, for instance.

Teachers may ask questions when using the Directed Reading Activity with other genres of text, such as informational and persuasive texts.

Directed Reading-Thinking Activity. Not to be confused with the DRA or Directed Reading Activity, the *directed reading-thinking activity* (DRTA) is a guided group discussion activity that focuses on the formation and testing of prereading predictions. In essence, it is a set of procedures for guiding prereading predictions. In a DRTA, children develop critical reading and thinking by predicting possible story events and outcomes, and then reading to confirm or disprove their hypotheses. As described by Stauffer (1975), who developed the strategy, in a DRTA, the students form a set of purposes for reading, processing ideas, and testing answers by taking part in a predict-read-prove cycle. The teacher *activates thought* by asking, "What do you think?"; *agitates thought* by asking, "Why do you think so?"; and *requires evidence* by asking, "How can you prove it?" (Stauffer, 1975, p. 37). The DRTA format helps students to read more critically and with improved comprehension because it engages them in this process of fluent reading in a structured fashion, slowing down and making concrete the phases of the prediction process.

Students might be asked to form tentative hypotheses about a story from the title, cover art, or first illustration. They might be asked to look at other illustrations or to read the first sentence, paragraph, or page. They are asked to predict what might happen in the story and how it might end up and to justify their predictions on the basis of what they have seen, read, and already know or believe. At preselected points in the story, they are asked to stop reading, review predictions and change them if necessary, form new predictions about upcoming material, and continue reading. Predictions might be recorded on the board to aid in recalling them later. Predictions that are disproved by later story events or that students no longer think are likely may be erased or crossed out. Students are continually asked to justify their positions on the basis of what they have already read. They may reread orally to back up their points. The predict-read-prove cycle continues through the story; as students get closer to the end, their predictions become more convergent as more and more of the story is revealed. At the story's end, predictions and clues may be reviewed or other kinds of follow-up questions may be asked.

K-W-L: Active Reading of Nonfiction. *K-W-L* stands for the three questions readers should ask themselves as they read a nonfiction selection: "What do I *know?* What do I *want* to learn? What did I *learn* from this?" The first two questions are asked before reading; the third is asked after the reading. They correspond to the mental operations of accessing prior information, determining reading purposes, and recalling information (Ogle, 1986). The procedure has three steps.

1. **Step K:** Before reading, the teacher guides students in brainstorming what they already know about the topic of the reading. The teacher records this information on the board or on a transparency. After the brainstorming, students are asked to use their prior information to predict what general types or categories of information they might expect to encounter when they read the passage. For example, if the topic is Columbus's voyage to the New World and students have recalled prior information about three ships, cramped quarters, and inadequate food, the teacher might lead them to identify categories of information such as "how they got there," "what the ships were like," and "what they ate and drank on the voyage." Since students often find this step difficult, the teacher needs to model and demonstrate this step numerous times until students begin to be able to perceive categories themselves.

2. **Step W:** As students complete the first step, disagreements and uncertainties will arise. These form the basis of the "What do I want to learn?" step. The teacher's role here is to highlight disagreements and gaps in prior information, raising questions that will help students to focus on the new information they will encounter. Students should write down the specific questions they want to have answered, thus making a personal commitment to the information. Students might be given a K-W-L worksheet to use for note taking, with the three questions as headings. An example of a completed worksheet is shown in Figure 5.14.

3. **Step L:** After completing the reading, whether they read the whole article or a portion of it, students should write down the information they recall from the passage. They should check their written questions to see whether they found answers to them; some questions might require further reading or checking of other sources. The teacher guides a discussion of the questions generated and the answers students found, including areas of disagreement; students refer to the passage to resolve disputes. Carr and Ogle (1987) developed K-W-L Plus, an enhanced K-W-L with two additional steps for secondary students. After the reading and the use of the three steps, students engage in concept mapping and summarizing. A *concept map* is a graphic organizer that allows students to group pieces of information gleaned from the text, which helps them to see associations and relationships among various pieces of information. This process is considered important because many students, particularly poor readers, acquire information from text only as isolated facts, failing to organize them into any coherent units of meaning. Practice in organizing information into main ideas or topics and supporting details improves overall comprehension. An example of a concept map is shown in Figure 5.15. The concept map is then used as the organizer for a written summary, which requires students to reflect on information gleaned and to express it in their own words

Topic: Crocodiles

K What We Know	W What We Want to Find Out	L What We Learned
eats people	do they eat people?	Do eat people
eats meat	What do they eat?	Also eat bugs, fish, ducks, birds, antelope
reptile	How do they get their food?	Actively hunt with others
lays eggs	How big are they?	Herds fish with tail
about 6 feet long	How does it have its babies?	Shares its food
leaves its babies	How many babies at one time?	Live in groups
solitary		6–15 feet long
vicious		most common 6–8 feet
has about 6 babies		female digs a nest
		uses same nest year after year
		guards the nest
		helps babies dig out
		helps babies break shell
		father crocodile helps
		can help break eggs
		protects babies for 12 weeks

Categories of Information:

Diet
Getting Food
Size
Reproduction
Family Life

FIGURE 5.14 *K-W-L Worksheet*

in a logical and readable form. Practice in summarizing helps students to organize and include all the important information from a text, not just the facts they found most memorable or interesting.

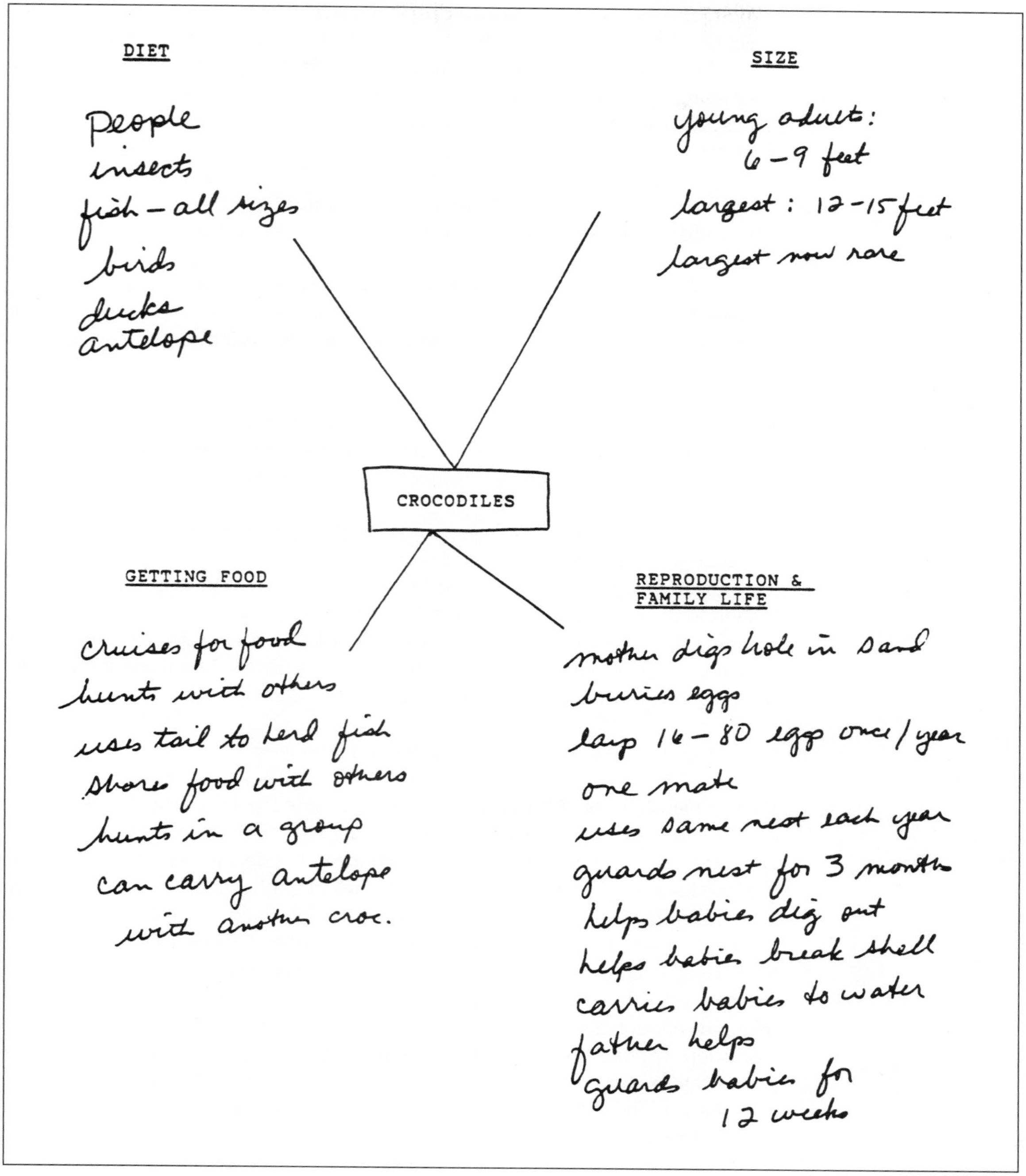

DIET

people
insects
fish – all sizes
birds
ducks
antelope

SIZE

young adult:
6–9 feet
largest: 12–15 feet
largest now rare

CROCODILES

GETTING FOOD

cruises for food
hunts with others
uses tail to herd fish
shares food with others
hunts in a group
can carry antelope
with another croc.

REPRODUCTION & FAMILY LIFE

mother digs hole in sand
buries eggs
lays 16–80 eggs once/year
one mate
uses same nest each year
guards nest for 3 months
helps babies dig out
helps babies break shell
carries babies to water
father helps
guards babies for
12 weeks

FIGURE 5.15 *K-W-L Plus Concept Map*

Questioning the Author: Close Reading for Comprehension. Students in the Beck and McKeown (1994) study also viewed the text as infallible, even when the text did not state ideas clearly or when it asked for prior knowledge that the students were not likely to have. Summing up their findings, McKeown, Beck, and Sandora (1996) concluded that "textbooks . . . are not serving students well [and] students often react to inadequate text presentations by developing a view of themselves as inadequate readers" (p. 97).

Beck, McKeown, and Kucan (1997) saw breakdowns at each point in the process of comprehension: The students often did not have sufficient prior knowledge, they did not make necessary inferences, and they did not come away with important ideas.

Beck et al. (1997) developed a comprehensive teaching strategy that would, first, reorient the students' thinking about texts and, second, lead them into using the kinds of thinking processes needed to understand the texts. They call their strategy *questioning the author*, or QtA (Beck et al., 1997).

Preparing for a QtA Lesson. The teacher prepares for a QtA lesson by deciding on a portion of text that can support intense questioning for a reasonable period of time, perhaps 20 to 30 minutes. Then the teacher follows three steps:

1. Reading through the text in advance and identifying the major understandings that the students should engage in this text.
2. Planning stopping points in the text that occur often enough to give adequate attention to the important ideas and inferences in the passage.
3. Planning the queries (probing questions) to be asked at each stopping point. (These are tentative plans only. The teacher will take his cue for the actual queries from the students' own comments and questions.)

Conducting a QtA Lesson. The lesson proceeds in two stages:

1. *Prepare the Students' Attitudes.* The teacher begins the lesson by discussing the idea of authorship and explaining that texts are written by human beings who are not perfect people, and therefore, their texts are not perfect works. Things might be unclear. Ideas might have been left out. Things might be hinted at, but not stated. It is the readers' job to question the author. It might help to remind the students of what happens in a writing workshop (Calkins, 1986; Graves, 1982; Temple, Nathan, Temple, & Burris, 1992). When we listen to a classmate sharing her writing in a writing workshop, we know that sometimes she will mention something without telling us enough about it or even describe some things inaccurately. In a writing workshop, we question the author so that we can understand the writing better and also to help the author make the writing clearer. In a QtA session, students also question the author—but since the author isn't present in the classroom, the class will have to answer for the author.
2. *Raise Queries about the Text.* Next, the teacher has the students read a small portion of the text. When they stop, the teacher poses a query about what they have read. The kinds of queries the teacher might use are shown in Figure 5.16.

INITIATING QUERIES

What is the author trying to say here?

What do you think the author wants us to know?

What is the author talking about?

FOLLOW-UP QUERIES

So what does the author mean right here?

That's what the author said, but what did the author mean?

Does that make sense with what the author told us before?

How does that fit in with what the author has told us?

But does the author tell us why?

Why do you think the author tells us that now?

NARRATIVE QUERIES

How do you think things look for the character now?

How does the author let you know that something has changed?

How has the author worked that out for us?

Given what the author has already told us about this character, what do you think he's up to?

How is the author making you feel right now about these characters?

What is the author telling us with this conversation?

FIGURE 5.16 *Sample Queries for Questioning the Author*

Source: From *Improving Comprehension with Questioning the Author: A Fresh and Expanded View of a Powerful Approach* by Isabel L. Beck and Margaret G. McKeown. Copyright © 2006 by Isabel L. Beck and Margaret McKeown. Reprinted by permission.

The Role of the Teacher in QtA. The earlier research by Beck, McKeown, and their colleagues suggested that the kinds of tasks teachers set and the kinds of questions they ask have a strong influence on how students approach the cognitive activity of comprehension. This influence can lead students in productive directions, or it can lead them toward passive and inefficient practices.

In QtA, the teacher is knowledgeable about what comprehension is and how it should be approached. The teacher understands that comprehension requires activity on the part of the students, and conducts discussions that require students to think and construct meaning. The teacher understands the difference between important ideas and details, so, in the words of Beck et al. (1997),

> he asks questions that focus . . . on meaning rather than on locating text information; for example, asking, "What did Tony mean when he said that to his brother?" rather than simply "What did Tony say to his brother?" (p. 114)

An Example of a QtA Discussion. In the following example, a class is discussing a single sentence from *Ben and Me* (Lawson, 1988). The sentence, which is narrated by a fictitious mouse named Amos, reads, "This question of the nature of lightning so preyed upon his mind that he was finally driven to an act of deceit that caused the first and only rift in our long friendship."

Teacher: What's the author trying to say about Ben and Amos?
Temika: That their friendship was breaking up.
Teacher: Their friendship was breaking up? OK, let's hang on to that. What do you think, April?
April: I agree with the part that their friendship did break up, but, um, I think that they got back together because when you are reading um, further, it said that he was enjoying the mouse.
Alvis: I think that um, Amos is just, Amos is just lying because in the story it said if they weren't good friends, why would um, um, Ben build a um, kite for, build a kite for him so he could have fun?
Teacher: OK, so Alvis is telling us that, why would Ben go to all that trouble and build that beautiful kite if they weren't friends? A lot of people agreed that their friendship is broken up. Alvis doesn't think their friendship is broken up. Can somebody help me out? What's the author want us to figure out here? (Beck, McKeown, & Kucan, 1997, p. 110)

Reciprocal Teaching. Reciprocal teaching (Brown, Palincsar, & Armbruster, 1984) is a method for demonstrating and developing reading comprehension in a group setting. The teacher models a systematic way of approaching a passage by using a sequence of comprehension processes: *summarizing, questioning, clarifying,* and *predicting.* After the teacher models these processes in four steps, students take turns following the same steps and leading the others in discussing the passage they read. This procedure is useful with any kind of text; it is particularly useful with nonfiction, which often contains a great many facts and pieces of new information. Following are the steps for using reciprocal teaching.

1. The teacher divides the passage to be read into fairly short sections; depending on the total length of the selection, one or two paragraphs at a time might be sufficient. For long selections such as whole chapters, long chapter sections, and longer stories, several pages might be better. Or the teacher might wish to start the procedure with short sections, and then make them longer as the reading progresses.

2. The teacher asks everyone to read the passage silently. To avoid having some students waiting for slow readers, the teacher should assign the reading before the activity begins. In this case, all students should quickly reexamine and review the passage before the discussion begins.

3. After the reading is completed, the teacher models the comprehension process by following these four steps:

a. Summarize the section in one or a few sentences.
b. Ask the group one or two good questions, avoiding picky details.
c. Identify a difficult part of the passage and clarify it by explaining, giving examples, drawing analogies, or making other clarifying statements.
d. Predict what the next section might be about or what might be learned from it.

4. The teacher should repeat steps 1 through 3 until the pattern is familiar to all students. Afterward, she can take turns leading the discussion steps previously mentioned: teacher-student-teacher-student or teacher-student-student. The teacher modeling and continued teacher involvement is critical to the students' success with the procedure.

Here is an example of how a teacher might use reciprocal teaching with a nonfiction passage: Ms. Brown has chosen an article about penguins from a nature magazine to supplement a science lesson with her fifth graders. The article is three pages long, with lavish illustrations, so she divides the reading into passages of several paragraphs each. First, she distributes copies of the article with the stopping points marked on them. (If she were using a textbook, she would have each student locate the stopping point and mark it with a strip of paper across the page.) She directs students to read the first three paragraphs, which contain general information about the penguins' habitat, habits, and diet. Then she models the use of the comprehension steps in this way:

> First, I'll summarize this passage. In these paragraphs, we read that penguins are large birds that are unusual because they do not fly, but they are excellent swimmers. Their wings are specially shaped like flippers to help them swim very fast and over long distances. They live in icy frozen areas of the world where there is little or no plant life. They live on a diet of fish.
>
> I would ask these questions about these paragraphs:
>
> - In what ways do we know penguins are different from other birds? (Students answer that they do not fly, they swim very skillfully, and they live in icy places where there are no plants.)
> - In what ways do you think penguins are like other birds? (Students answer that they have wings, other kinds of birds also eat fish, and they lay eggs.)
> - In what ways might their environment affect how they survive? (Students discuss the lack of plant life for making nests, and the dangers of cold.)
>
> I thought that the paragraph telling about their environment was a little difficult. The passage used some complicated words like *barren*, *Antarctic*, and *ice floes*, which might need discussion. Let's write these on the board and discuss what each one means. (Discussion follows about the meaning of these terms; one student gets a dictionary, and they refer to it.)
>
> In the paragraphs to follow, I predict that we will find out more about how penguins adapt to extreme cold temperatures and find out how they raise their young in this environment.

Ms. Brown then directs students to read to the end of the next section, and she again models these four steps. After the class reads the third section, she calls on a volunteer to follow the same steps: summarize, ask a couple of good questions, clarify a part or term, and predict what might be coming up. When the article is finished, students briefly discuss the main points of the article and evaluate how well they answered questions and followed the steps in the comprehension process.

Reciprocal teaching helps students learn how effective readers approach challenging texts and helps them develop systematic ways of dealing with the information in them. After a number of repetitions, students might begin to internalize the comprehension steps and apply them independently to other text material.

Reciprocal Question-Answer Relationships. Successful readers use a variety of strategies to maximize their comprehension of text: They monitor their own comprehension, they self-question, they mentally summarize, and they seek relationships among ideas and facts presented in what they read. Unsuccessful readers often do not do these things; they tend to focus more on pronouncing the words and answering the teacher's questions, but they have few strategies for predicting what questions might be asked or for finding answers. Helfeldt and Henk (1990) propose an instructional strategy that helps at-risk readers use self-questioning to improve their comprehension. They call it *reciprocal question-answer relationships* (ReQAR). The procedure consists of four general steps: explaining what the students will do, reciprocal questioning (in which students and teacher take turns asking each other questions about a passage that was just read and answering each other's questions), categorizing questions and their answers according to where the information is found ("in the book" or "in my head"), and finally combining steps 2 and 3 by combining reciprocal questioning and categorizing the answers. In this step, students ask the teacher a question about the material, and the teacher answers it and categorizes the answer as "in the book" or "in my head"; then roles are reversed, with the teacher asking and the student or students answering and categorizing.

For the Phase of Consolidation

Consolidation is the phase of looking back on the meaning, questioning it, interpreting it, applying what was learned, or reexamining one's ideas about the topic in light of it.

Story Mapping. A good way to have students reflect on and consolidate their understanding of a story they have read is to have them construct a *story map.* A story map is a graphic representation of the parts of a story that shows how the story parts are related. Story maps "provide a practical means of helping children organize story content into coherent wholes" (Davis & McPherson, 1989, p. 232). "Story mapping," wrote Boyle and Peregoy (1990), "helps children use story grammar for comprehension and composing" (p. 198). Story maps can be used to help readers perceive and understand plot structure and a variety of text structures such as literal and implied information, cause and effect, sequential ordering, and comparison and contrast (see Figure 5.17). They are similar to other graphic organizers such as structured overviews, story diagrams, and webs.

Figure 5.18 shows a sample story map for the Aesop's fable "The Crow and the Water Jug." This story map emphasizes the essential story structures described in the previous section: setting, initiating event or "problem," internal response or "goal," attempts and outcomes, and consequence or "resolution." Figure 5.19 shows another kind of story map, devised by Boyle and Peregoy (1990). In this model, the essential story grammar is boiled down to SOMEBODY . . . WANTED . . . BUT . . . SO (see Chapter 3, page 120 for more discussion). Under each of these headings, the teacher or students list the character or characters and their problems, their goals, and their means of achieving them. Other story maps might compare the advantages and disadvantages of some story action, the causes and effects of certain story events, or aspects of the various characters in a story.

To construct a story map, first think about the kinds of information or story structures you want to emphasize in your lesson. Make some notes about how this information might be arrayed. For example, comparison and contrast may be illustrated by listing items in two vertical columns; sequential order of story events might lend itself to a linear or timeline arrangement; details of characterization might be illustrated by a web-style arrangement of circles connected to a central circle with short lines; or the comparison of two stories or characters might be shown by two intersecting circles, sometimes called a *Venn diagram.* Examine your story map to make sure it emphasizes the logical flow of information. Don't make it too technical or detailed; emphasize just one pattern of organization at a time.

To teach with a story map, it is best to start with a straightforward, literal map of story events. Introduce it after the story has been read to help students recall and reconstruct what happened. When students are somewhat familiar with the story map and its use as a postreading activity, you might begin using story maps as a prereading organizer. Students might be given some minimal information and asked to predict story events, or they might be shown a partially completed story map and asked to predict what else might occur. Such prereading prediction has a positive effect on later recall and comprehension, just as it does with directed reading-thinking activities, K-W-L, and other related prediction strategies. After reading a portion of the story, the story map can be modified, and students can continue reading and changing the map until the story is completed. Story maps may also be used as a postreading activity, with students reconstructing a map individually or in cooperative learning groups; they may also complete partially filled in maps, which Davis and McPherson (1989) call "macro cloze story maps."

Retelling. We know that retelling stories helps children to understand and remember stories and develop a sense of story. Retelling requires readers or listeners to organize information and make inferences about it based on text information and their own prior information by constructing a personal rendition of the text. Thus, retelling focuses children's attention on relevant text information, sequences, and causes and effects. It requires that they organize that information into a coherent structure for retelling to

Story maps can take many forms. At their simplest, story maps can ask children to reflect on and record what happened at different points of a story. More complex story maps lead children to think about story elements.

Introduce story maps by talking through a simple story with the children, such as the Aesop fable, "The Crow and the Water Jug." Involve the students in answering the questions as you write up their answers for all to see. Once they understand how to complete the story map, they can write them individually. It helps if you prepare and duplicate a form for them to complete, such as one of the following.

A Simple Story Map

What happened at the beginning?	**What happened in the middle?**	**What was the climax?**	**What was the conclusion?**
______	______	______	______
______	______	______	______
______	______	______	______
______	______	______	______

A More Complex Story Map

Your Name: ______________________ Story Name: ______________________

Describe the setting and the characters.

What is the main problem at the beginning of the story?

What goal do the characters set?

What *attempts* are made to reach the goal? What are the *outcomes*?

Describe the conclusion. What is the *resolution* of the problem?

FIGURE 5.17 *Story Maps*

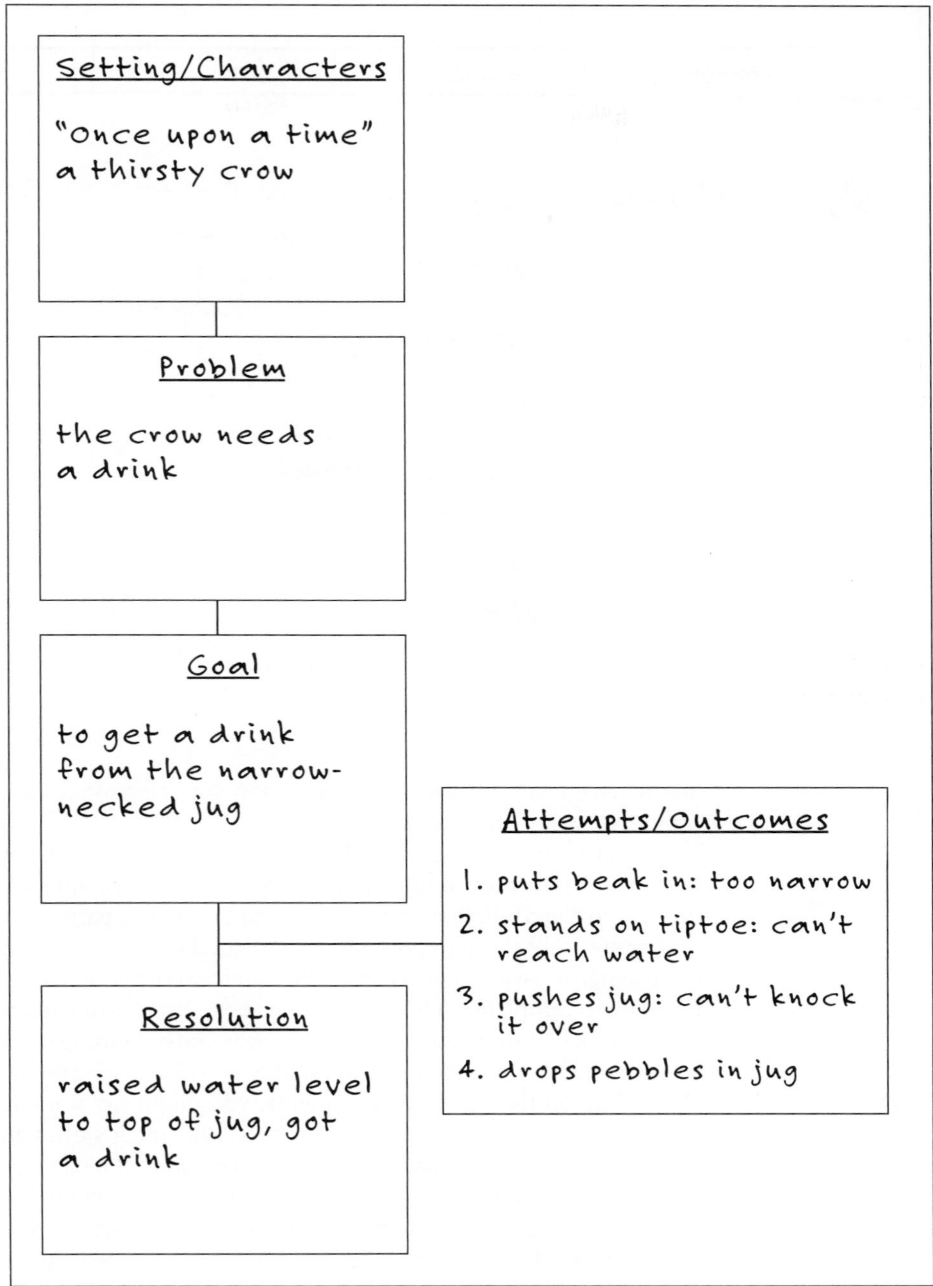

FIGURE 5.18 *Story Map for "The Crow and The Water Jug"*

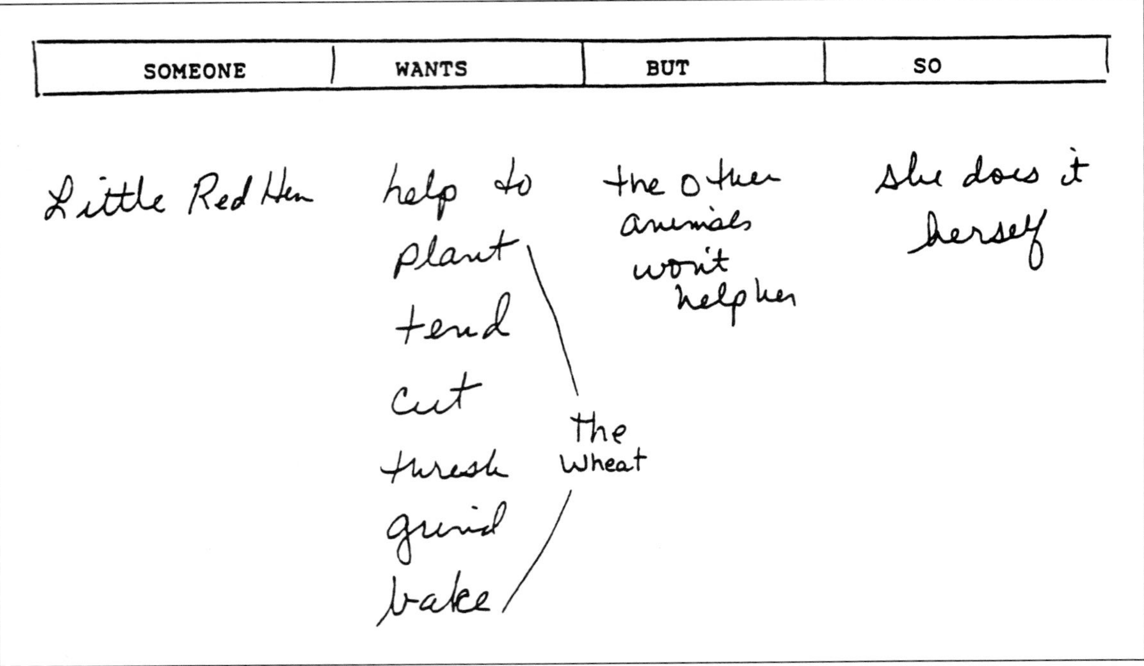

FIGURE 5.19 *Story Map for "The Little Red Hen"*

another. You can use retelling strategies in your classroom to help all readers to improve their story comprehension.

In its simplest form, a retelling activity involves two students working together during direct instruction time or independent work time; one reads or listens to a portion of a text or a whole story and then teams up with a partner to retell the story. Since the listener's role is an important one and good listening is active, rather than passive, the listener is asked to provide helpful questions or comments to the teller and may be asked to complete a retelling reaction sheet. Before students begin this activity, you need to model it so that they will have a clear understanding of what they are to do and why they are doing it. First, explain simply and clearly why retelling is a useful activity. Depending on the age of your students, you might say something like, "Retelling a story you have read or listened to helps you remember stories and helps you check to see if you understand what you have read or heard. It also helps you to learn to be a good storyteller. I will show you what to do to practice retelling stories and how to be a helpful listening partner. Then you will have time to practice retelling with a partner."

Model retelling by announcing to students what you are going to do: "I'm going to read a short passage from this story. Then I'm going to retell it to you without looking at the story. I'm going to try to include all the important areas and information. As I read it, listen for the important ideas."

Narrative Text

Who are the main characters?

When did the story take place?

Where did the story take place?

What important events happened in the story?

How did the story end?

Expository Text

What is the topic of the selection?

What are the important ideas in the selection?

FIGURE 5.20 *Prompts for Encouraging Retelling*

Source: Figure: "Prompts for Encouraging Retelling" from "Retelling: A Strategy for Enhancing Students' Reading Comprehension," Author: L.B. Gambrell, Author: B.S. Heathington, Author: B.A. Kapinus, Author: P.S. Koskinen, in *The Reading Teacher*, May 1988, 41(9), 892–896, The International Reading Association. Used and reprinted with permission of the International Reading Association, www.reading.org.

Next, read aloud a fairly short passage from a story or nonfiction text or a short, complete story. Afterward, retell the story or passage in a few sentences, including the most important information, sequences, and other details. Then ask students for feedback on the retelling by asking them whether you included all the important ideas, accepting their contributions or suggestions. Immediately after the modeling, students can read a short passage from a basal reader, textbook, or other material that they all have. Guide them in group retelling by having volunteers retell to the group, using question prompts that are appropriate for the type of text with which they are dealing (see Figure 5.20).

When children seem to have the idea of retelling, which might be after more than one model and group practice, create opportunities for students to practice retelling to a partner. In this practice, one student silently reads a passage or text for retelling, and then retells it to a partner. Both students need not have read the same material; if the partner has not read the story and has trouble understanding it from the retelling, this is a good indication that more practice retelling is needed. This is an excellent opportunity for students to read and share trade books they are reading in class. Students might practice reading and retelling during independent work time or free reading time. They should do this regularly, several times a week.

Retelling is more effective for both students involved if the listener has an active role. Good listening is active and responsive, not passive. The student who is the listening partner should have something to do besides just listen. With guided practice, the listening partner can learn how to ask helpful questions by using the prompts referred to in Figure 5.20 or by suggesting other important information that the teller omitted, if any. Students can also complete a retelling reaction guide, such as the one in Figure 5.21.

Name ____________________ Date ____________

I listened to _____

I chose one thing my partner did well. _____

He or she told about the characters. _____

He or she told about the setting. _____

He or she told about the events in the story. _____

His or her story had a beginning. _____

His or her story had an ending. _____

I told my partner one thing that was good about his or her story. _____

FIGURE 5.21 *Example of a Retelling Reaction Sheet*

Source: Figure: "Example of a Retelling Reaction Sheet" from "Retelling: A Strategy for Enhancing Students' Reading Comprehension," Author: L.B. Gambrell, Author: B.S. Heathington, Author: B.A. Kapinus, Author: P.S. Koskinen, in *The Reading Teacher*, May 1988, 41(9), 892–896, The International Reading Association. Used and reprinted with permission of the International Reading Association, www.reading.org.

This procedure focuses on positive responses rather than criticism, which is very important. Providing this task for listeners helps them to set a purpose for listening and helps keep them focused on the task. Giving students systematic, structured opportunities to talk about what they have read helps develop comprehension and oral expression skills and provides teachers yet another way to incorporate fiction and nonfiction trade books in their regular instruction program.

Summarizing. Sometimes called *summarization*, summarizing is the activity of reducing a presentation to its essentials. A student who can summarize a passage she has just read has understood the passage and made a judgment about what is most important about it. As anyone knows who has listened to a seven-year-old recount a movie she just saw ("And then, and then, and then—but wait—and then . . . ") knows that summarizing doesn't come naturally to students. In fact, Hickman (1992) found just the opposite: When she asked children of different ages to summarize a story that had been read to them, five-year-olds recounted exciting but not essential events, seven-year-olds recited one event after another in undifferentiated strings, and eleven-year-olds reduced the story to its main point.

But children and older students can be taught to summarize, and doing so makes them better at comprehending what they read (Biancarosa & Snow, 2006; Duke & Pearson, 2002) and also better at writing (Graham & Perin, 2007).

With emergent and beginning readers, retelling is the first step to summarizing. The teacher can guide the retelling by asking the children to remember and say all of the things that happened in the text and helping them put those points in the correct order. These points are placed on chart paper, to focus children's attention and show them the words in print. The points can also be written on sentence strips and organized in order in a pocket chart.

Setting	
Characters	
Problem	
Actions	
Solution	

FIGURE 5.22 *A Story Map*

With fledgling and early developing readers, those who are reading lines independently with more fluency and expression, the teacher can use story structures and other text structure guides. The SOMEBODY . . . WANTED . . . BUT . . . SO . . . strategy (see page 120) is a way to do this. Story maps—graphic organizers consisting of the main parts of a story, can be used to guide a whole-class or small-group summary, and can be reproduced and distributed for students to complete on their own (see Figure 5.22).

For texts with different structures, other graphic organizers may be used, such as a sequence of events (see Figure 5.23), cause and effect (see Figure 5.24), a taxonomy or classification scheme (see Figure 5.25), or an argument—point of view with support, and opposing views (see Figure 5.26).

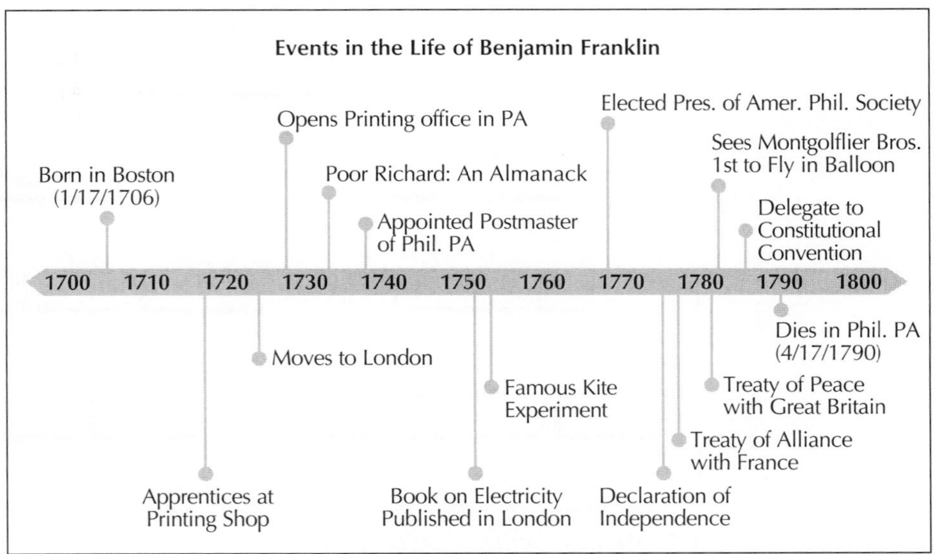

FIGURE 5.23 *Sequence of Events or Time Line Chart*

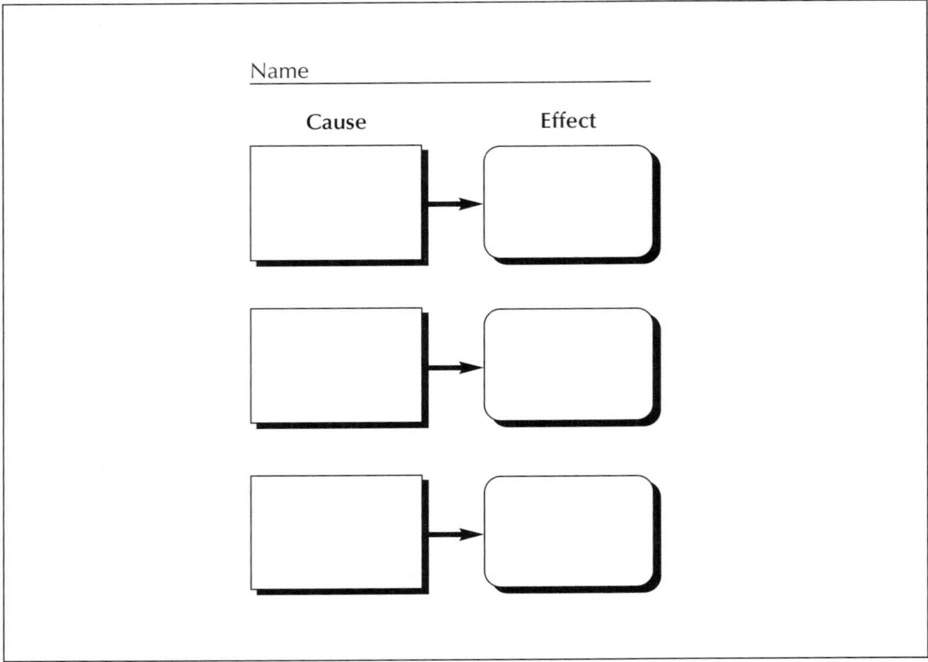

FIGURE 5.24 *Cause and Effect Chart*

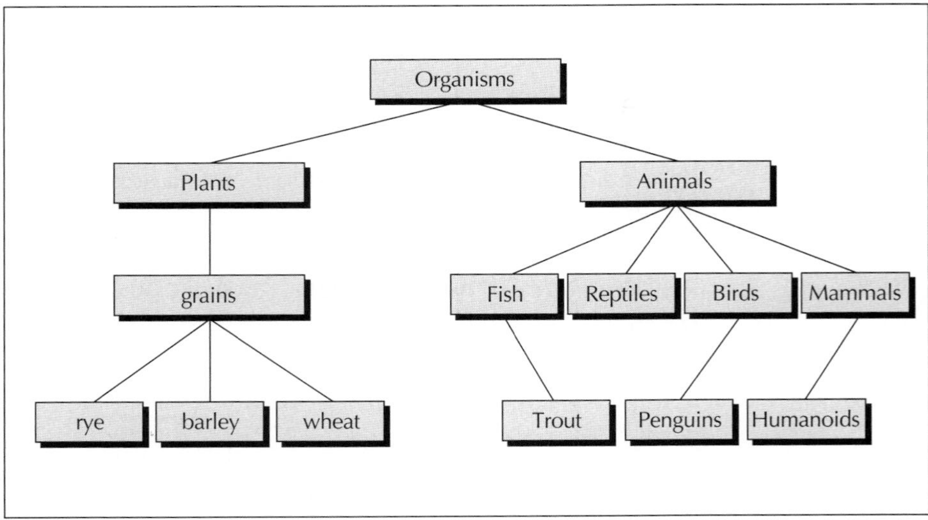

FIGURE 5.25 *A Classification Chart*

Argument Chart

Viewpoint	Support	Opposing Viewpoint
Teacher's Comments		

FIGURE 5.26 *Argument Chart*

Developing Listening Comprehension

Listening comprehension is related to reading ability in that students who are not yet fluent, mature readers can usually listen to and comprehend text that is read to them that they cannot yet read for themselves. The most common example of this is with emergent and beginning readers, who can listen to and understand a wide variety of materials but who might not yet be able to read anything for themselves.

As students' reading abilities develop and their instructional levels go up, the gap between their instructional reading level and their listening level might begin to close, and by the time they have become fluent, mature readers, there might be no difference between what they can listen to and what they can read successfully. For much of the time before a student has reached this zenith in reading development, however, there will be a gap between these two levels.

Experience is an important factor in listening comprehension. Even if all other things are equal, a student who has been read to and whose school and home environments are rich in oral language (regardless of dialect or language origins) has an advantage over the student who has not had this experience. In the same way, students who can read fairly effectively have a greater store of information, concepts, and vocabulary than illiterate students or very poor readers, and the first group's listening comprehension levels are more likely to be higher.

A student's listening comprehension level is important because it shows us how closely his or her ability to understand written text approaches the grade-level demands and gives us an indication of how much potential for reading improvement the student has at this point in time. We must remember that unlike IQ or other intelligence measures, the listening level is not fixed; as the student's reading ability improves and he or she reads more, the listening level also rises. Thus, progress today paves the way for more progress tomorrow.

A directed listening-thinking activity (see pages 171–172) is a good alternative to straight reading aloud. So is the Questioning the Author technique (see pages 176–178)—done with the teacher reading the text aloud. The Directed Reading Activity (not to be confused with the Directed Reading-Thinking Activity) can also be used as the teacher reads aloud (see page 172).

Immersion in a rich language environment also means that students should be actively engaged in oral discussions and conversations. They must be guided to do more than just answer questions, the most common form of classroom talk. They should also describe, summarize, persuade, and argue, using as specific, vivid, and precise vocabulary as possible. Many of the typical composition activities that are suggested in reading and English books, such as making up stories, recounting real events and reminiscences, describing objects, persuading others to some action or belief, arguing for or against some course of action, and composing directions, are just as useful for oral language and listening development. Speaking and listening cannot be separated; they will develop together. Students with underdeveloped listening comprehension need daily experience with both.

Oral reading by students for other students can be useful, too, but must be used with care. All oral reading should be rehearsed and prepared by the reader beforehand. No one is served by listening to someone stumble through text. Material for oral reading should be read silently several times, and then read aloud for practice before the final reading. Also, oral reading should be done for some purpose, not as an end in itself. Some material deserves to be read aloud, and enjoyment of it is enhanced by being effectively read: Poetry, vivid descriptions, and good dialogue are examples. The purpose of oral reading should be to share and enhance such material, not just to practice reading aloud.

Again, we return to the point of teacher modeling. The teacher sets the tone and provides the model by which students judge what is useful and important. Without dominating activities, teachers must show students by their modeling what they want them to be able to do. As teachers, we should prepare in advance what we read aloud to the class so that our reading will be fluent and expressive. We should share portions of material we find appealing or especially effective with them and work to make our descriptions and summaries colorful and precise. We should exhibit interest in and curiosity about words and expressions and share with students interesting and unusual language in texts we read. We should respond to students' efforts to use language more effectively with sincere interest, attention, and positive reinforcement. We should listen more to what they say than to how they say it, and we should respond first to their message.

The more direct experience with language students have, the more their language use will expand. The more it grows, the more their listening comprehension will improve. The more listening comprehension develops, the more they will be able to bring to reading, and thus their reading will improve. The roots of reading ability are buried deep in oral language, and we cannot overlook this foundation if we wish to help our students read better.

Time Spent Reading

So far in this chapter, we have concentrated on methods and issues that are related to reading instruction: helping students to develop sight recognition of words, use word analysis strategies fluently and effectively, organize and apply prior knowledge to new information acquired from reading, and use a variety of reading processes and skills to become more fluent and comprehend better. It might be thought that effective reading depends on instruction, and indeed, good instruction is an absolute requirement in helping children grow as readers. In spite of all the instructional techniques we apply, however, there is another factor that is critical: To become a good reader, a child must spend a lot of time reading.

This point seems self-evident. But how much time do children actually spend reading? A number of research studies have been conducted in attempts to determine this, and the results of these studies are disturbing. Walberg and Tsai (1984) studied the out-of-school reading behavior of 2,890 U.S. thirteen-year-olds. They found that the median child in their sample read 7.2 minutes per day and that the median child reported reading on about one day out of five. Forty-four percent of the subjects in the study reported spending no time reading for enjoyment, while only 5 percent reported spending three hours or more. Not surprisingly, these researchers found that frequency and amount of reading were related to reading achievement. Anderson, Wilson, and Fielding (1988) found that the average fifth grader read about five minutes outside of school.

For comparison, consider the amount of media (television, DVDs, video games) that the average young person aged 8 to 18 uses. One study put the figure at four hours. These findings reveal, in Paul Wilson's words, "a bleak picture" of most children's voluntary reading habits (Wilson, Anderson, & Fielding, 1986, p. 76). We already know that in spite of our instruction, children generally do not do very much reading of connected text in school; of the hours they spend in school, only a few minutes a day are usually spent actually reading text. A study by Taylor et al. (1990) found that fifth and sixth graders reported reading an average of 15.8 minutes per day in a 50-minute reading class, and 15 minutes per day at home. With the explosion of hand-held electronic media since these studies were done, there is little chance students are spending any more time reading books.

Summary

Good teaching is directed toward supporting a student's strengths while teaching and practicing skills and strategies the student needs. From diagnostic data, strengths and needs are identified and priorities are established. Instructional time is planned to fulfill priorities and provide instructional balance.

Readers can develop *sight vocabulary* when they see the same words repeatedly in meaningful contexts. *Dictated stories* feature rereading until students achieve fluency and can identify individual words in and out of context. *Support reading* helps students to get through difficult text and reinforces word recognition. Support reading includes *echo reading* and *choral reading*. *Predictable books* are useful because the same words appear repeatedly and help to build readers' confidence.

Fluency contributes to comprehension and is developed when students reread material.

Word analysis strategies are needed when students do not recognize a word at sight. Although debate still rages over the role of phonics instruction in learning to read, a growing body of evidence suggests that good readers are able to use decoding strategies automatically and accurately during reading, thus freeing the mind for comprehension. It also suggests that all students learn letter-sound relationships as part of learning to read. Exemplary phonics instruction builds on what students already know about letters, sounds, and words; emphasizes phonemic awareness; is clear and direct; is integrated into a total reading program; focuses on reading words rather than learning rules; includes the use of onset and rimes; focuses on the internal structure of words; and develops automaticity in word recognition. *Phonemic awareness* is the ability to manipulate speech sounds in words; it contributes to the ability to rhyme and use phonics. Phonics instruction may be integrated with literature by using trade books that feature particular phonic patterns. Using *context* is also an important word analysis strategy. *Cloze procedures* and *confirming* help students to develop facility with context. *Word sorting* helps students to apply phonic regularities by categorizing words sharing a similar word feature.

We divided our treatment of reading comprehension into three phases: *anticipation, building knowledge,* and *consolidation.* In the *anticipation phase,* we presented teaching strategies focusing on readers' use of *prior knowledge, webbing, previewing,* and *prediction.* For the *building knowledge phase,* we presented the strategies of the *directed reading activities, directed reading-thinking activities, K-W-L* and *K-W-L Plus,* and also *reciprocal teaching, reciprocal question-answer relationships,* and *questioning the author. Story mapping, retelling,* and *summarizing* were presented as activities for the consolidation phase. (Many more strategies for this phase will be found in Chapter 8.)

Listening comprehension supports and promotes reading comprehension. The *listening level* provides an estimate of the reader's present potential for reading improvement. Means of developing students' listening comprehension include *reading to students, directed listening-thinking activities,* and *teacher modeling.*

A host of studies have shown that most students do little, if any, reading outside of school. Yet they also show a significant relationship between *time spent reading* and *reading achievement*. All students, especially poor readers, must increase their time spent reading; ways of doing so are discussed in this chapter.

References

Anderson, R. C., Wilson, P. T., & Fielding, L. G. (1988). Growth in reading and how children spend their time outside of school. *Reading Research Quarterly, 23*(3), 285–303.

Armbruster, B., Lehr, F., & Osborne, J. (2001). *Focus on fluency.* Washington, D.C. US Department of Education, National Institute for Literacy. http://www.nifl.gov/partnershipforreading/publications/reading_first1.html

Bear, D., Invernizzi, M., Templeton, S., & Johnston, F. (2012). *Words their way: Word study for phonics, vocabulary, and spelling* (5th ed.). Upper Saddle River, NJ: Merrill.

Beck, I. L., & McKeown, M. G. (1994). Outcomes of history instruction: Paste-up accounts. In J. F. Voss & M. Carretero (Eds.), *Cognitive and instructional processes in history and the social sciences* (pp. 237–256). Hillsdale, NJ: Erlbaum.

Beck, I., McKeown, M., & Kucan, L. (1997). *Questioning the author: An approach for enhancing student engagement with text.* Newark, DE: International Reading Association.

Beck, I., McKeown, M., & Kucan, L. (2002). *Bringing words to life.* New York, NY: Guilford Press.

Biancarosa, C., & Snow, C. E. (2006). *Reading Next—A vision for action and research in middle and high school literacy: A report to Carnegie Corporation of New York* (2nd ed.). Washington, DC: Alliance for Excellent Education.

Boyle, O., & Peregoy, S. E. (1990). Literacy scaffolds: Strategies for first and second language readers and writers. *The Reading Teacher, 44*(3), 194–200.

Brown, A. L., Palincsar, A. S., & Armbruster, B. B. (1984). Instructing comprehension—Fostering activities in interactive learning situations. In H. Mandl, N. L. Stein, & T. Trabasso (Eds.), *Learning and comprehension of text.* Hillsdale, NJ: Erlbaum.

Calkins, L. (1986). *The art of teaching writing.* Portsmouth, NH: Heinemann.

Carr, E., & Ogle, D. M. (1987). K-W-L Plus: A strategy for comprehension and summarization. *Journal of Reading, 30*(7), 626–631.

Cooper, J. D. (1993). *Literacy: Helping children construct meaning.* Boston, MA: Houghton Mifflin.

Cunningham, P. (1999). *Phonics they use* (3rd ed.). Boston, MA: Allyn and Bacon.

Davis, Z. T., & McPherson, M. D. (1989). Story map instruction: A road map for reading comprehension. *The Reading Teacher, 43*(3), 232–240.

Duke, N. K., & Pearson, P. D. (2002). Effective practices for developing reading comprehension. In A. E. Farstup & S. J. Samuels (Eds.), *What research has to say about reading instruction* (pp. 205–242). Newark, DE: International Reading Association.

Ehri, L. C. (1991). Development of the ability to read words. In R. Barr, M. L. Kamil, P. B. Mosenthal, & P. D. Pearson (Eds.), *Handbook of Reading Research: Vol. 2* (pp. 383–417). White Plains, NY: Longman.

Frith, U. (1985). Beneath the surface of developmental dyslexia. In K. E. Patterson, J. C. Marshall, & M. Coltheart (Eds.), *Surface dyslexia* (pp. 301–330). London: Erlbaum.

Goswami, U. (2000). Phonological and lexical processes. In M. L. Kamil, P. B. Mosenthal, P. D. Pearson, & R. Barr (Eds.), *Handbook of reading research: Vol. 3.* Mahwah, NJ: Erlbaum.

Graham, S., & Perin, D. (2007). *Writing Next: Effective strategies to improve writing of adolescents in middle and high schools:* A report to Carnegie Corporation of New York (2nd ed.). Washington, DC: Alliance for Excellent Education.

Graves, D. (1982). *Writing: Teachers and children at work.* Portsmouth, NH: Heinemann.

Gwynne, F. (1988). *The king who rained.* New York, NY: Alladin.

Harste, J., Woodward, V., & Burke, C. (1985) *Language stories and literacy lessons.* Portsmouth, NH: Heinemann.

Helfeldt, J. P., & Henk, W. A. (1990). Reciprocal question-answer relationships: An instructional technique for at-risk readers. *Journal of Reading, 33*(7), 509–514.

Hickman, J. (1992). What comes naturally. In C. Temple & P. Collins (Eds.), *Stories and readers.* Norwood, MA: Christopher-Gordon.

Koskinen, P. S., Gambrell, L. B., Kapinus, B. A., & Heathington, B. S. (1988). Retelling: A strategy for enhancing students' reading comprehension. *The Reading Teacher, 41*(9), 892–896.

LaBerge, D., & Samuels, S. (1974). Toward a theory of automatic information processing in reading. *Cognitive Psychology, 6,* 293–332.

Lawson, R. (1988). *Ben and me.* Boston, MA: Little, Brown.

Marsh, G., Friedman, M., Welch, V., & Desberg, P. (1981). A cognitive-developmental theory of reading acquisition. In G. MacKinnon & T. Waller, *Reading research advances in theory and practice.* New York, NY: Academic Press.

McCauley, J. K., & McCauley, D. S. (1992). Using choral reading to promote language learning for ESL students. *The Reading Teacher, 45*(7), 526–533.

McKeown, M. G., & Beck, I. L. (1988). Learning vocabulary: Different ways for different goals. *Remedial and Special Education (RASE), 9,* 142–146.

McKeown, M. G., Beck, I. L., & Sandora, C. (1996). Questioning the author: An approach to developing meaningful classroom discourse. In M. Graves, P. Van den Broek, & B. Taylor (Eds.), *The first R: Every child's right to read.* New York, NY: Teachers College Press.

Morris, R. D. (2008). *The diagnosis and correction of reading problems.* New York, NY: Guilford.

Nagy, W., & Anderson, R. (1984). How many words are there in printed school English? *Reading Research Quarterly, 19,* 304–330.

Nagy, W. E., et al. (1985, December). *Learning word meanings from context: How broadly generalizable?* (Technical Report No. 347). Urbana, IL: Center for the Study of Reading.

National Reading Panel. (2000). *Teaching children to read: An evidence-based assessment of the scientific literature on reading and its implications for reading instruction.* Washington, DC: National Institute for Literacy.

Ogle, D. M. (1986). K-W-L: A teaching model that develops active reading of expository text. *The Reading Teacher, 38*(6), 564–570.

Perfetti, C., & Zhang, S. (1996). What it means to learn to read. In M. Graves, P. Van den Broek, & B. Taylor (Eds.), *The first R: Every child's right to read.* New York, NY: Teachers College Press.

Rasinski, T. V. (2003). *The fluent reader: Oral reading strategies for building word recognition, fluency, and comprehension.* New York, NY: Scholastic.

Ryder, R., Graves, B., & Graves, M. (1989). *Easy reading: Book series and periodicals for less able readers.* Newark, DE: International Reading Association.

Samuels, S. J. (1979). The method of repeated reading. *The Reading Teacher, 32*(4), 403–408.

Schwartz, R. M., & Raphael, T. (1985). Concept of definition: A key to improving students' vocabulary. *The Reading Teacher, 39,* 198–205.

Smith, C. (1997). *Vocabulary instruction and reading comprehension.* Bloomington, IN: ERIC Clearinghouse on Reading, English, and Communication.

Snow, C., & Burns, S. (Eds.). (1998). *Preventing reading difficulty in young children.* Washington, DC: National Academy Press.

Stahl, S. A. (1992). Saying the "P" word: Nine guidelines for exemplary phonics instruction. *The Reading Teacher, 45*(8), 618–625.

Stanovich, K. E. (1992). Are we overselling literacy? In C. Temple & P. Collins (Eds.), *Stories and Readers.* Norwood, MA: Christopher-Gordon.

Stauffer, R. G. (1975). *Directing the reading-thinking process.* New York, NY: Harper & Row.

Szymborski, J. A. (1995). *Vocabulary development: Context clues versus word definitions.* M.A. Project, Kean College of New Jersey.

Taylor, B., Frye, B. J., & Maruyama, G. M. (1990, June). Time spent reading and reading growth. *American Educational Research Journal, 27*(2), 351–362.

Temple, C., & Gillet, J. (1984). *Language arts: Learning processess and teaching practices.* Boston, MA: Little Brown.

Temple, C., Martinez, M., & Yokota, J. (2010). *Children's books in children's hands: An introduction to their literature* (4th ed.). Boston, MA: Allyn & Bacon.

Temple, C., Nathan, R., Temple, F., & Burris, N. (1992). *The beginnings of writing* (3rd ed.). Boston, MA: Allyn & Bacon.

Temple, C., Ogle, D., Crawford, A., & Freppon, P. (2011). *All children read: Teaching for literacy in today's diverse classrooms* (3rd ed.). Boston, MA: Allyn & Bacon.

Trachtenburg, P. (1990). Using children's literature to enhance phonics instruction. *The Reading Teacher, 43*(9), 648–654.

Trieman, R. (1985). Onsets and rimes as units of spoken syllables: Evidence from children. *Journal of Experimental Child Psychology, 39,* 161–181.

Walberg, H. J., & Tsai, S. (1984). Reading achievement and diminishing returns to time. *Journal of Educational Psychology, 76*(3), 442–451.

Wilson, P. T., Anderson, R. C., & Fielding, L. G. (1986). Children's book-reading habits: A new criterion for literacy. *Book Research Quarterly, 2*(3), 72–84.

Wylie, R. E., & Durrell, D. D. (1970). Teaching vowels through phonograms. *Elementary English, 47,* 787–791.

Zutell, J., & Rasinski, T. (1991). Training teachers to attend to their students' oral reading fluency. *Theory Into Practice, 30*(3), 211–217.

Informal Assessments of Reading

CHAPTER 6

Chapter Outline

u Kyen Sung, a fourth-grade teacher, keeps an assessment folder for each student in her class. Each student's folder contains different kinds of assessment information collected over the course of the year. It is early October, and Mu Kyen is preparing for a conference with Ben's parents. During the conference, she will explain how Ben's growth and progress have been assessed this fall and will answer his parents' questions about assessment results and implications. At various points during the coming year, Mu Kyen will add new assessment information and will be able to show Ben's parents how his progress has been documented. At another formal conference in the spring, she will share end-of-year assessment results including his achievement of state-mandated goals for all students in his grade.

A review of Ben's various assessments will help Mu Kyen to be fully informed for the conference. Also, it allows us a chance to peer over her shoulder, so to speak, and consider the kinds of literacy-related assessments—both formal and informal, periodic and ongoing—that are typically used with students.

First, Mu Kyen scans a sheet that contains all of Ben's standardized achievement test scores. On the reading section of the test given at the end of third grade, Ben's scores fell in the 30th percentile, with subtest scores ranging from the 16th to the 41st percentile. Mu Kyen looks at this sheet first, but it is not the most important; in fact, she considers these standardized test scores to be among the *least* informative to her in teaching Ben. However, she reviews them because she knows that standardized test data have great importance to her principal, as well as to Ben's parents.

These results indicate that Ben is functioning significantly below average in reading in comparison to others of his age and grade in the norm group and in the local group being tested at the same time; in fact, they show that Ben performed as well as or better than only about 30 percent of other third graders taking the test, while about 70 percent performed better than Ben. His performance was also below the *mean,* or average, score that was at about the 50th percentile. In addition, Ben failed to meet state-required standards in reading and writing at the end of third grade.

Mu Kyen next turns to other informal assessments she gave Ben during the first weeks of this year. These include:

- *Running records,* or annotated copies of material Ben has read aloud, with miscues and other reading behaviors noted.
- An *Informal Reading Inventory* given at the beginning of the year, showing Ben's oral and silent reading rates, his oral reading accuracy, the types of miscues that occurred as he read, and his comprehension after oral and silent reading of passages at successive grade levels.

- *Observation records,* or notes Mu Kyen took while she observed Ben working in a variety of learning situations.
- *Cloze procedures,* or reading passages with words systematically deleted and replaced by blanks to be filled in by the reader.
- *Spelling records* showing patterns and high-utility words Ben has mastered and the dates they were successfully tested.
- *A list of books read* so far this year.
- *A writing progress inventory,* showing Ben's progress in using various forms and voices in writing.
- *A reading attitude survey* that she will discuss with Ben, to see what they can do to help him get more enjoyment from both recreational reading and school-based reading.
- *A portfolio* that Ben has just begun, containing work samples he chose that show what he is learning and work he is proud of.

Informal Assessment in the Classroom

Mu Kyen Sung's choice of assessments demonstrates her well-considered beliefs about reading and teaching. Her use of different measures and samples of reading and reading-related behaviors shows her understanding that reading is not a single operation, nor is reading the same each time it occurs; rather, reading changes according to the material being read and the reader's purposes. In Mu Kyen's use of multiple sources, information from one source builds on, or is contrasted by, information from other data sources. The result is a multidimensional picture of the student's reading performance in a variety of situations and with different kinds of materials: an authentic, dynamic portrait of a reader.

Mu Kyen Sung knows that reading is not just the sum of all its parts, but the result of the *interaction* of all the necessary operations, in concert with each other, combined with what the reader knows and brings to the reading, his or her motivation and purposes for the reading, and the complexity of the text being read, in authentic (not test-like) reading situations. So when preparing an assessment picture of a reader, she prefers to use a variety of behavior samples in real reading acts, combined with her informed observations of the reader in authentic learning situations, to strengthen and support the instructional decisions she makes. And she makes sure that the data she collects are gathered at regular, frequent intervals so that an accurate record of the reader's progress is developed. Without the ongoing assessments that Mu Kyen provides, the picture of Ben's achievement would be one-sided and unnecessarily grim.

Informal Reading Inventories

An Informal Reading Inventory, often called an IRI, consists of reading passages corresponding in difficulty to materials at grade levels from primer through high school along with questions for each passage that are intended to test readers' comprehension after reading. Passages are arranged in order of difficulty from easiest ("primer"—or kindergarten—and primary grades) to hardest (usually ninth grade or beyond). There are usually at least two relatively equivalent passages at each grade level, and sometimes more. Some Informal Reading Inventories, such as the *Developmental Literacy Inventory* (Temple, Crawford, & Gillet, 2008), contain passages written in different genres (narrative and expository). IRIs usually also contain a Word Recognition Inventory—lists of individual words arranged in levels of difficulty like those of the reading passages. In addition, many stand-alone IRIs have supplementary tests such as phonics inventories, cloze tests, and spelling inventories.

Figures 6.1 and 6.2 show a student page and corresponding examiner's pages from an IRI.

Many language arts textbook series provide an IRI to be used diagnostically and for placement within that series. IRI passages are selected from that series. Other IRIs are stand-alone assessments and are not related to any particular set of materials. Passages in such IRIs are either selected from different sources or are specially written for the test. Passages are typically 50 to 250 words long. An IRI consists of a student's copy of the reading passages and an examiner's copy of the instrument. The examiner's copy contains the reading passages and the corresponding comprehension questions with their correct answers.

To assess oral and silent reading separately, an IRI should have two or more different passages at each grade level. The passages should be from different texts, but comparable in difficulty. The grade levels that are represented should range from preprimer or primer (kindergarten and early first grade) through at least sixth-grade text, preferably higher; text typical of middle and high school reading is very useful.

Like all assessment devices, IRIs have both advantages and disadvantages. They offer the teacher a complete set of materials ready to reproduce and use. Multiple forms at each grade level allow assessment of oral and silent reading and retesting later with new material. IRIs are not difficult to administer, score, or interpret, with a little practice. They are readily adaptable to use in the classroom since they can be administered a little at a time over a period of days if necessary and they do not require strict administration procedures like formal tests. They are cost-effective and widely available.

They may have shortcomings, however. When an IRI from a language arts series is made up of passages from that series, students may have previously read some of the stories. Their comprehension scores on those passages may then be falsely inflated. Sometimes those passages are "reserved," meaning that teachers are told not to teach those stories, but students might have read them in another school or on their own.

Stand-alone IRIs have passages that are specially written to conform to readability levels or passages selected from other sources, but the quality of such passages can vary widely. For example, very short passages limit the number of ideas available to the reader as well as the number of questions. If an IRI carries on the same story from passage to passage, it is difficult to omit the lower levels or move

Great Shellfish Bay

One of the most beautiful bodies of water in the United States is the Chesapeake Bay. A bay is a part of a sea or lake that cuts into a coastline. The name *Chesapeake* came from a Native American word that means "Great Shellfish Bay." The Chesapeake Bay also has inlets that go into the shore. An inlet is a narrow opening in a coastline. An inlet is smaller than a bay. The state of Maryland surrounds part of Chesapeake Bay. The other state that borders the Chesapeake Bay is Virginia. The Chesapeake Bay plays an important part in the history of both of these states. For example, the first capital of Maryland was St. Mary's City, and the first capital of Virginia was Jamestown. Both settlements were built on inlets from the Chesapeake Bay.

The Chesapeake Bay is rich in crabs, oysters, clams, and other shellfish. About two hundred different kinds of fish live in the bay as well. Because of this abundance of seafood, many families in the Chesapeake Bay area earn their living harvesting the sea. The people who fish the bay are called watermen. These men and women gather different kinds of seafood in different seasons.

The watermen are also known for their contribution to American history. During the Revolutionary War, they helped the French fleet, guiding their ships around the complicated waterways of the bay. With this help, American and French forces were able to trap the British army.

Watermen who catch crabs are called "crabbers." Crabbers fish for crabs in the summer using crab pots. A crab pot isn't really a pot at all—it is a large wire cage with several sections. Crabs can swim into the pot, but they cannot swim out of it. To harvest crabs, a crabber pulls the crab pot into the fishing boat, empties the pot, and sorts the catch by size and type. Then the crabber takes the catch to market.

FIGURE 6.1 *Commercial IRI Pupil Page*

Source: Temple. Charles, Crawford, Alan & Gillet, Jean Wallace. (2008). *Developmental Literacy Inventory*. Boston: Allyn & Bacon.

from a higher to a lower level during assessment. A passage may be taken from the middle of a story with no introduction provided to help the reader understand what came before. Some IRIs use factual recall questions almost exclusively without adequately sampling other aspects of comprehension. If you have to choose a stand-alone IRI, the following section will help you evaluate the most important aspects of these instruments.

Social Studies Sixth-Grade Level: Great Shellfish Bay

Introduction: *Now you're going to read a passage about a large bay in the eastern part of the United States. You will find out how it got its name. Read carefully because I will ask you questions about it after you finish.*

Record the time at the beginning: _____.

Great Shellfish Bay

One of the most beautiful bodies of water in the United States is the Chesapeake Bay. A bay is a part of a sea or lake that cuts into a coastline. The name *Chesapeake* came from a Native American word that means "Great Shellfish Bay." The Chesapeake Bay also has inlets that go into the shore. An inlet is a narrow opening in a coastline. An inlet is smaller than a bay. The state of Maryland surrounds part of Chesapeake Bay. The other state that borders the Chesapeake Bay is Virginia. The Chesapeake Bay plays an important part in the history of both of these states. For example, the first capital of Maryland was St. Mary's City, and the first capital of Virginia was Jamestown. Both settlements were built on inlets from the Chesapeake Bay.

The Chesapeake Bay is rich in crabs, oysters, clams, and other shellfish. About two hundred different kinds of fish live in the bay as well. Because of this abundance of seafood, many families in the Chesapeake Bay area earn their living harvesting the sea. The people who fish the bay are called watermen. These men and women gather different kinds of seafood in different seasons.

The watermen are also known for their contribution to American history. During the Revolutionary War, they helped the French fleet, guiding their ships around the complicated waterways of the bay. With this help, American and French forces were able to trap the British army.

Watermen who catch crabs are called "crabbers." Crabbers fish for crabs in the summer using crab pots. A crab pot isn't really a pot at all—it is a large wire cage with several sections. Crabs can swim into the pot, but they cannot swim out of it. To harvest crabs, a crabber pulls the crab pot

FIGURE 6.2 *Commercial IRI Examiner's Pages*

Source: Temple. Charles, Crawford, Alan, & Gillet, Jean Wallace. (2008). *Developmental Literacy Inventory*. Boston: Allyn & Bacon.

into the fishing boat, empties the pot, and sorts the catch by size and type. Then the crabber takes the catch to market.

Record the time at the end: _____.

326 words

890 L (6th grade)

Questions

1. According to this passage, how did Chesapeake Bay get its name? (from a Native American word for "Great Shellfish Bay") **Recall**

2. According to this passage, how are inlets and bays similar? How are they different? [must answer both parts correctly] (similar: both are parts of the sea or a lake that cut into the shore; different: inlets are usually smaller than bays) **Recall**

3. In the sentence, "Because of this abundance, many families earn their living from the sea," what does *abundance* mean? (richness; lots and lots of something, in this case fish and seafood) **Vocabulary**

4. According to this passage, how did watermen help win the Revolutionary War? (guided the French fleet to defeat the British) **Recall**

5. According to this passage, how does a crabber use a crab pot? (the pot is a cage that he puts in the water; the crab swims in but can't swim out; the crabber pulls the pot back into the boat and takes out the crabs) **Recall**

6. Why is the Chesapeake Bay a good place to make a living from the sea? (because many kinds of fish and shellfish live there; because the fish and shellfish are so abundant) **Inference**

7. Why might Chesapeake Bay watermen be interested in keeping the bay free of pollution? (to protect the fishing; to protect their livelihood; so they could keep making a living from the sea) **Inference**

8. Why do you think watermen catch different kinds of shellfish at different times during the year? (some things may not be ready to catch, or large enough, at certain times of the year; they need to catch different kinds of shellfish so they don't catch too many of one kind) **Inference**

Words in passage: 326 Errors in Oral Reading Accuracy: _______
Correct Comprehension Responses: _______

(Continued)

FIGURE 6.2 *Continued*

SCORING GUIDE FOR ORAL READING AND COMPREHENSION

(Circle the Boxes That Correspond to the Student's Scores)

	Oral Reading Accuracy	*Reading Comprehension*	*Listening Capacity*
Independent level:	13 or fewer errors	7–8 correct responses	
Instructional level:	14–33 errors	6–7 correct responses	6–7 correct responses
Frustration level:	34 or more errors	5 or fewer correct responses	

Comprehension Scores, by Type

	Recall questions	*Inference questions*	*Vocabulary questions*
Student's correct answers			
Total possible correct answers	4	3	1

Reading Rate Scoring Guide for Sixth Grade (Mid-year)

	Below average reading rate (150 wpm or less)	*Average reading rate (175 wpm)*	*Above average reading rate (200 wpm or more)*
Reading rates for this passage	More than 130 seconds? Enter the time below:	Around 110 seconds? Enter the time below:	Less than 98 seconds? Enter the time below:
Number of seconds the student takes to read the passage			

FIGURE 6.2 *Continued*

Selecting a Stand-Alone Informal Reading Inventory

To choose the best IRI for your needs, examine and compare several; then select the one you believe has the most strengths and will serve your diagnostic needs best. The following aspects are important in choosing an IRI:

- **Literary quality of reading passages.** Passages in IRIs are usually written expressly for each test, to rule out the possibility that students have seen the materials elsewhere. But test authors are not necessarily skilled writers; so it is important to check to make sure that the passages are clearly written and well-structured. If students are to be tested on their understanding of a passage, it is important that the passage be understandable.
- **Clarity and relevance of questions.** It should be clear what the question is asking, and the wording of the question should be appropriate to the level of understanding demanded by the passage.
- **Balance of explicit and implicit question types, requiring a variety of comprehension skills.** Skilled readers should be able to recall information from a passage, and they should also be able to make inferences, and infer meanings of words from context. Questions should ask them to do all of these.
- **Convenient format.** It is helpful if you can easily find your way around a test booklet, from students' passages to testers' passages, and from one form to another.
- **Complete instructions, including examples.** If the test scores are to be meaningful, the test must be given properly, and for it to be given properly, the instructions for administration, scoring, and interpretation must be clearly understood by everyone who works with the test.
- **A balance of both narrative and expository passages, ideally featuring use of both types at each level.** Reading a story and reading an explanation of scientific phenomena put different demands on readers. It is useful to know if a reader can handle the challenges of narrative and expository texts.

The following list contains some currently available stand-alone IRIs:

Applegate, M. D., Quinn, K. B., & Applegate, A. J. (2007). *The critical reading inventory.* Upper Saddle River, NJ: Pearson/Merrill/Prentice Hall.

Burns, P. C., & Roe B. D. (2010). *Informal reading inventory* (7th ed.). Boston, MA: Houghton Mifflin.

Cooter, R. B., Jr., Flynt, E. S., & Cooter, K. (2007). *Cooter/Flynt/Cooter comprehensive reading inventory.* Upper Saddle River, NJ: Pearson/Merrill/Prentice Hall.

Ekwall, E., & Shanker J. L. (2005). *Ekwall-Shanker reading inventory* (4th ed.). Boston, MA: Allyn & Bacon.

Johns, J. L. (2009). *Basic reading inventory*. Dubuque, IA: Kendall/Hunt.

Leslie, L., & Caldwell, J. (2005). *Qualitative reading inventory 4.* Boston, MA: Pearson/Allyn & Bacon.

Silvaroli, N. J., & Wheelock, W. H. (2003). *Classroom reading inventory* (10th ed.). New York, NY: McGraw-Hill.

Stieglitz, E. L. (2002). *Stieglitz informal reading inventory* (3rd ed.). Boston, MA: Allyn & Bacon.

Temple, C., Crawford, A., & Gillet, J. (2008). *Developmental literacy inventory.* Boston, MA: Allyn and Bacon.

Woods, M. L., & Clark, K. J. (2010). *Analytical reading inventory.* Upper Saddle River, NJ: Pearson/Merrill/Prentice Hall.

Administering an Informal Reading Inventory

Giving an IRI generally takes 30 to 50 minutes, but the duration depends on how well the student reads, how many passages are read, and how many parts of the IRI are used. It does not all have to be done in one sitting. If you are giving an IRI during regular instruction time, break up the testing into a number of short sittings, with the student reading one or two passages at a time and finishing the IRI over a period of several days. This allows you to give an individual test without taking too much time away from other students or activities. You will need a student copy of the passages, an examiner's copy for recording each student's responses, pencils, and a stopwatch for timing the reading.

Sit beside the student with the student to your left if you are right-handed, or to your right if you are left-handed. Keep your recording materials convenient to your writing hand, but out of the student's line of sight. Students may get distracted if they see you recording their responses.

Tell the student that you want to see him or her read. There will not be a grade. The student should do his or her best, but not worry when the test gets difficult.

Where to Start. One of the first questions IRI users ask is, "Where should I begin testing?" It would not be economical to begin at the lowest level and proceed upward until the frustration level is reached. Where to begin depends in part on your assessment purpose. If you are testing to see whether material at a particular level of difficulty would be comfortable reading, begin there. If the reader is successful, you may proceed to higher levels or stop. If the reader is unsuccessful, you should drop down to a lower level.

Many experts advocate giving the word recognition test, leveled lists of single words, as a way of determining where to start. Administration procedures for the word lists are included in the section entitled "Assessing Recognition of Words in Isolation." In essence, the word lists are given first, and the examiner begins giving the reading passages at the level where the reader began to read fewer than 90 percent of the words on the list correctly. This is a very common procedure, and the most common use for the graded word lists. However, it often happens that students can recognize words with accuracy, but cannot comprehend text at the same level of difficulty. When this happens, we end up starting the IRI considerably above the reader's real instructional level. For that reason, some teachers don't give the word recognition inventory until after they have assessed oral reading, reading comprehension, and listening comprehension. There are good reasons for either method.

Starting with word lists. Let's say that you have been taught to use the graded word lists as the initial assessment. You may start with the easiest level, preprimer or primer (pronounced "primmer"), or a level one or two grades below the reader's present grade, and proceed to successive lists until the student begins to miss many of the words. (This is a very general statement, but the specific guidelines are contained in a subsequent section.) You then begin administering passages at the highest level in which the reader scored 90 percent or higher, representing the independent level. But what if the student recognized individual words well, but had poor comprehension of passages at the same level? You will have to drop down to lower level passages until you find the student's instructional level. You will read more about the specifics of word list administration in a section to follow.

Starting with passages. Another way to begin is to start with reading passages you think will be easy, move up or down as needed, and administer the word lists later. Let's say that a new child has just been enrolled in your third-grade class. Records from his previous school may take some time to arrive; even with them, you wish to form your own judgment of his instructional level, so he can be appropriately placed immediately. So your first, most general question might be, "Is he instructional at grade level?" You begin the IRI with a third-grade passage. His oral reading is fairly fluent and largely correct, with some miscues that mostly make sense. He answers seven of nine comprehension questions correctly. He also reads another third-grade passage silently within a reasonable length of time, and again answers most of the questions accurately. You decide that third-grade material is comfortable for him, a good instructional level. Your first diagnostic question has been answered. You can, for the time being, stop giving the IRI and place him temporarily in a group that is reading material at grade level.

However, you still don't know several things: Is his instructional level significantly above grade level? What is his approximate listening level? Later, perhaps in the next week or so, you will want to continue IRI testing with this student, determining his independent level by administering passages below his instructional level, determining his frustration level by continuing to give successively harder passages until the frustration level is reached, and determining his listening level by reading successively harder passages to him until he can no longer answer questions about what he has listened to. These procedures are detailed in the sections to follow.

Your assessment purpose might not be to determine whether a reader is instructional at grade level, but more generally to determine just where his instructional level is. Let's return to our example of the new student in your class. Perhaps your first diagnostic question is not, "Is he instructional at third grade?" but rather, "What is this child's instructional level?" You can start with third-grade passages, or you can begin lower. Let's say that you begin with a second-grade passage. His oral reading is rapid, expressive, and accurate, and his comprehension excellent; he answers correctly all questions and occasionally supplies details not called for in the answers. Second grade seems like his independent level, doesn't it? You'll proceed upward then; you could skip the second-grade silent passage for the moment and go on to third grade, or you could even skip third and go to fourth if you thought his reading was that strong.

But let's change the scenario a bit. When he reads the second-grade passage, he struggles with it, reading fairly slowly with numerous miscues, many of which don't make any sense. In this case, of course, you will want to move down, to first-grade passages and lower if necessary, until you determine a level that is comfortable and successful for him. With an IRI, you can move in either direction with ease, or even skip a level and come back to it later if necessary.

Where to Stop. Once you've started, by either method described above, your next question is bound to be, "When should I stop testing?" Most IRIs feature a scoring key after each passage that allows you to determine whether the passage represented the reader's independent, instructional, or frustration level without having to compute any percentages.

For example, look again at Figure 6.2, "Great Shellfish Bay." After the comprehension questions, you'll see a box that tells you how many miscues may be made for this 326-word passage to fall within each reading level; in this case, up to 13 miscues represent an independent level, from 14 to 33 miscues represent the instructional level, and 34 or more miscues represent the frustration level.

Next to the boxes for recording the number of miscues, you'll see another box into which you enter the number of comprehension questions the reader answered correctly, regardless of their type. In this example, answering 8 questions correctly indicates the independent level, 6 or 7 correct answers indicate the instructional level, and 5 or fewer correct answers indicate the frustration level.

If the IRI you're using does not contain such a feature, you will have to quickly figure the percentage of accuracy for the comprehension questions on the spot. When the reader's comprehension score reaches about 50 percent, the frustration level has been reached. (We discuss scoring procedures in more detail in a section to follow.)

When the quality of the reading shows that the grade level just read was clearly at the frustration level, you should stop the reading portion of the testing. If you are not sure whether the reader can go any further, another level may be given then or in another sitting. When the reader's frustration level has been reached, the listening comprehension portion of the assessment begins. This procedure is detailed in the section "Assessing Listening Comprehension" later in this chapter.

Step-by-Step Administration. In this section we go back over the general procedures we described above and fill in the details.

1. You may give the Word Recognition Inventory first in order to find out where to begin, or begin at a level at which you think the student will be able to read easily. (If you overestimated, you can drop back to lower levels.) This practice is discussed in the section "Assessing Recognition of Words in Isolation" later in this chapter.
2. At each level, give the oral reading passage next. Show the student where to begin reading and where to stop and say, "Please read this passage out loud to me. When you are finished, I will ask you some questions about what you have read." Be sure to record the time the student began reading, in minutes and seconds, and keep a watch with a second hand nearby.
3. Follow along on your copy and carefully mark down the miscues, or divergences, from the text. Later they will be analyzed to provide information about the reader's use of word analysis, syntax, and meaning during oral reading. Marking of miscues is discussed in the section "Marking Oral Reading Miscues" later in this chapter.
4. When the oral reading is completed, write down the ending time, in minutes and seconds, before doing anything else. Then remove or cover the passage and ask

the comprehension questions. Jot down key words or phrases from the student's answers. Within reason, you can probe for more information or ask a student to explain or justify an answer.

5. Give the silent reading passage for the same level. Show the student where to begin and stop reading. Remove or cover the passage when the reader is finished. Then ask the comprehension questions for that passage as above.
6. If the student answered 50 percent or more of the comprehension questions correctly or is within the instructional-level criteria for the test you're using, proceed to the next level. In general, it's best to test both oral and silent reading at each level—but not always. If oral reading comprehension scores are low, but silent reading comprehension is still above 50 percent, discontinue the oral reading but continue silent reading at higher levels until these scores also drop below 50 percent and remain there. If the student shows poor silent comprehension, but oral comprehension scores are still above 50 percent, discontinue the silent reading but continue the oral reading. Discontinue the reading portion of the IRI when both oral and silent reading comprehension fall to the frustration level. If you're not sure, give one more level.

Reinspection and comprehension. Most often, a reader's comprehension of IRI passages is assessed by asking comprehension questions and by expecting *unaided recall;* that is, answers given without referring back to the passage. Most IRI directions tell you to cover or remove the passage after reading so the student can't look back at it. But there are drawbacks to this approach.

- When *reinspection* (looking back to the passage) is not allowed, both recall and comprehension are being tested. Readers might comprehend, but fail to recall information, causing the examiner to underestimate their comprehension.
- Readers may fail to include information in a response because, to the reader, it appeared obvious, redundant, or secondary to other information. Reinspection tends to encourage more complete answers.
- Recall without reinspection is more a test-taking skill than an everyday reading strategy. In classroom reading, students usually discuss material and answer questions with the material before them rather than with books closed. In real, everyday reading, we are typically able to look back at, or reread portions of, material we did not understand.

When we do not allow readers to reinspect an IRI passage when they answer questions, we place an unreasonably heavy burden on the process of recall and short-term memory (Gipe, 2006; Rubenstein, Kender, & Mace, 1988). But most IRI directions clearly state that students should not look back, except when specifically asked to do so in a question assessing their locational skills (for example, "Find and read me the sentence that tells you the goldfish was happy.").

Therefore, we must face the question of whether we are testing reading comprehension, which surely involves memory but includes other factors as well, or whether we are instead testing the reader's short-term memory.

One of our reasons for using an IRI is to assess students' reading in as natural a way as possible; however, disallowing reinspection appears to run counter to what people really do when they read. You can incorporate reinspection fairly easily into standard IRI administration by directing the reader to locate some specific information in the passage after the retelling and questioning.

Some stand-alone IRIs have reinspection or "look-back" items included in the comprehension questions, but many do not. In this case, it is a simple procedure to direct the reader to "Look back and find the place where it says that . . ." or the like, noting whether the reader is able to scan for the desired information or must begin reading all over again and whether the information can be located. One reinspection item per reading passage is probably enough. If the IRI you're using doesn't have such items, you may want to add one to each passage, adjusting the scoring criteria to accommodate an additional item.

Retelling and comprehension. Another issue involves the use of questions alone, rather than allowing students to *retell,* or recall in their own words, what they remember from passages. By asking questions, we shape students' comprehension; questions provide clues to what we believe is important for readers to remember and include in their answers. Because of this, an effective way to learn more about students' comprehension is to ask them to retell what they read and either record what each student tells you or use a checklist of all of the information in a passage, allowing the student to use her own words in recalling these items. Retelling should be done *before* asking any comprehension questions.

Some stand-alone IRIs include retelling in their comprehension assessment. Figure 6.3 shows an examiner's page from one that does. You will see that both a checklist for retelling and a set of questions is included for each passage. Students are asked to retell the passage without prompting or probes before questions are asked. Even when a retelling checklist is included, not all teachers use them. They add considerably to administration time and are not included in scoring.

In retellings, readers are not expected to recall verbatim, and few do. The examiner decides if the retelling matches the information in the passage. Information that is recalled may be checked off on the list, or items may be numbered in the order in which the reader recalled them. The second method helps the examiner to determine if the reader recalled information in roughly the same order as it occurred in the passage or if the retelling was not sequentially ordered. Information that is included in a retelling but is not in the passage may be noted as well. Retellings are not scored, but they are evaluated subjectively based on the quantity, completeness, and accuracy of the most important information or ideas in the passage. Although these judgments may contribute to our diagnosis and implications for instruction, they are typically not included in determining overall reading levels.

An important qualification to this statement, however, is that the widely used Developmental Reading Assessment (DRA2) (Beaver, 2006) features retelling as a key component of determining the reader's performance level. After the student reads the passage and before questions are asked, the student is directed to "tell in your own

Level: Two

Retelling Scoring Sheet for "Whales and Fish"

Main Idea

_____ Whales
_____ and fish both live
_____ in the water
_____ but they are different
_____ in many ways.

Details

_____ Whales are large
_____ animals.
_____ They must come
_____ to the top
_____ of the water
_____ to get air.
_____ Whales breathe
_____ in air
_____ through a hole
_____ in the top
_____ of their heads.
_____ At the same time,
_____ they blow out
_____ old air.
_____ Fish take in air
_____ from the water.
_____ Mother whales give birth
_____ to live whales.
_____ The baby whale comes
_____ to the top
_____ of the water
_____ right away
_____ for air.
_____ The baby drinks milk
_____ from its mother
_____ for about a year.
_____ Most mother fish lay eggs.
_____ The babies are born
_____ when the eggs hatch.
_____ Right after they are born,
_____ the baby fish must find their own food.

Main Idea

_____ Whales
_____ and fish are alike
_____ in some ways too.

Details

_____ Whales
_____ and fish have flippers
_____ on their sides.
_____ They have fins
_____ on their tails.
_____ Flippers
_____ and fins help whales
_____ and fish swim.
_____ Fins move
_____ and push the water away.

49 Ideas

Number of ideas recalled _____

Other ideas recalled, including inferences:

Questions for "Whales and Fish"

1. What is this passage mainly about?
   Implicit: how whales and fish are alike and different

2. According to the passage, how are whales and fish different?
   Explicit: whales breathe air and fish take in air from the water; whales give birth to live babies and fish lay eggs; baby whales get food from their mother, and baby fish have to get it for themselves

FIGURE 6.3 *Commercial IRI Retelling Scoring Sheet*

Source: Leslie and Caldwell, *Qualitative Reading Inventory-4*, p. 218, © 2006. Reproduced by permission of Pearson Education, Inc.

words what happened in the story starting at the very beginning." The examiner's copy lists the characters, setting, and story events. The teacher checks off whether characters, important details, and vocabulary or special phrases from the passage, setting, ending, and story events were included in the recall and if story events were recalled in sequence or out of sequence.

If the initial retelling is complete, the teacher may move to another passage or stop. If the retelling is incomplete, the teacher gives a general prompt by saying, "Tell me more." If the student adds information about the previously omitted elements of the story, no further questioning is done. But if the retelling is still incomplete, the teacher asks specific questions to elicit omitted information, such as "Who had to stop? Why did the police officer tell the bus to stop? Where did Mother Duck and her babies go?"

This instrument assesses comprehension both by retelling and by responding to questions, which makes it unique among IRIs. At any grade level, a student's performance may be rated as 4/Proficient, 3/Basic Understanding, 2/Partial Understanding, or 1/Minimal Understanding. A score of 4 or 3 is required for the student to be instructional at that level. A score of 4 is achieved when the student's retelling is spontaneous and is accomplished with only one general prompt or one comprehension question. A score of 3 is achieved when the student's retelling is done with the use of more than one general prompt or one question. A score of 2 is achieved when the retelling is done with prompts and/or questions that elicit some, but not all, of the additional correct information, while a score of 1 is achieved when the student provides little correct information even when prompts and questions are used (Beaver, 2006; Seattle Public Schools, 2006).

Marking oral reading miscues. While the student is reading aloud, you will mark all of the oral divergences from the text, or miscues, on your copy of the passage. These important reading behaviors are considered in two ways; they are *counted* to determine the reader's degree of oral reading accuracy and *analyzed* to determine what word attack strategies the reader used during the oral reading.

Miscues include:

- *Substitutions* of real or nonsense words.
- *Insertions* of extra words.
- *Omissions* of whole words or phrases.
- *Self-corrections* occurring immediately or later during the reading.
- *Words provided* by the examiner.
- *Reversals* of word order.

Very long *pauses* and *repetitions* of words or phrases may also be marked, but are not counted as errors.

Box 6.1 contains a simple coding system that will allow you to record all miscues accurately. Most stand-alone and reading series IRIs will have a suggested system for marking miscues; these are usually very similar. There may be small differences; for example, some systems show self-corrections marked with a check; some with the letters

BOX 6.1

A System for Marking Oral Reading Miscues

1. *Substitution of a word or phrase:* the student's word written over a word in text

   The doll fell from the shelf.

2. *Insertion of a word not in text:* a word written in over a caret or small arrow

   The doll fell from the shelf.

3. *Omission of a word or phrase:* the omitted element circled

   The big dog ran away.

4. *A word given by the examiner:* parentheses placed around that word

   The climbers were assisted by (Sherpa) tribesmen.

5. *Miscue spontaneously corrected by the reader:* check mark next to original coding

   The big dog ran away.

   or © next to original coding

   The big dog ran away.

   or sc with line showing corrected element

   The big dog ran away.

6. *Reversal of order of words:* proofreader's symbol of inversion used

   "Let's go," shouted Sally.

7. *Repetition of word or phrase:* wavy line under repeated element

   The climbers were assisted . . .

8. *Pauses longer than normal:* slashes for pauses, one per second

   The / / controversial theory . . .

SC and a line showing which part of the word, phrase, or sentence was corrected; and some with a C in a circle. All these marks mean the same thing. Small differences are unimportant, but it is important to be able to read what another examiner has marked. It's best if everyone uses the same system, but if everyone using IRIs in your school or team doesn't use the same marks, be sure you are familiar with the variations.

Figure 6.4 shows a sample passage with miscues marked.

Assessing listening comprehension. When the student can answer correctly only about half of the questions for a passage, functional reading has broken down. One very important aspect remains to be tested, however: the student's listening comprehension.

Narrative First-Grade Level: Jack's Dinner

Introduction: *Sometimes it's hard to stop what you are doing when you are called to dinner. Read to find out what happened when Jack was busy at dinner time. I will ask you questions about the passage after you finish reading.*

Record the time at the beginning: _____.

Jack's Dinner

"Come to dinner," said Jack's Mother.

Jack didn't want to come.

He was busy.

He was bending wire. He was pounding nails. He was mixing paint. He was making a toy.

"I don't care if you're busy. Come now." Mother sounded cross.

"Just one more minute," said Jack. He kept bending wire. He kept pounding nails. He kept mixing paint.

"Now, Jack," said Mother. "Your dinner will be cold."

Jack came to dinner.

He showed Mother his toy truck.

"That's so cool!" said Mother. "I didn't know you could make a toy truck."

Record the time at the end: _____.

FIGURE 6.4 *Sample IRI Passage with Miscues*

Source: Temple, et al., *Developmental Literacy Inventory*, Narrative 1st Grade Level: Jack's Dinner, p. 146, © 2009 Pearson Education, Inc. Reproduced by permission of Pearson Education.

As we discussed earlier in this chapter, the listening level, the highest level of text a reader can comprehend when listening to someone read aloud, provides a rough estimate of a student's potential for reading improvement. It helps us to form reasonable expectations for growth in reading.

When reading comprehension scores indicate that the reader has become frustrated (scores 50 percent or less), read one of the next level passages aloud to the student and then ask the comprehension questions. Before you read, say something like,

"You've worked hard and the last passage was difficult. This time I want you to listen carefully while I read out loud. Afterward I'll ask you questions as I did before." Read normally, not too slowly or with exaggerated expression. If the student gets more than half of the questions correct, read a passage from the next level in the same way. Proceed until you reach a level at which the student gets 50 percent or fewer of the questions correct; then stop.

Calculating the reading rate. Reading rate is usually measured in Words Read Correctly Per Minute, or WCPM. Reading rate and accuracy are not all there is to reading fluency—prosody and intelligent phrasing are also important—but it is often counted as an index to stand for the other factors as well.

Reading rate as WCPM can be determined in the following way:

1. Subtract the number of words read incorrectly from the total number of words in the passage. For testing purposes, words are read incorrectly when:
   - other words are substituted for the correct word
   - a correct word is omitted, or
   - an additional word is inserted in the sentence.
2. Subtract the beginning time from the ending time, and convert the result to seconds.
3. Calculate the result according to this formula:

$$\text{Reading Rate in WCPM} = \frac{(\text{Total words read} - \text{reading errors}) \times 60}{\text{Total time taken to read (in seconds)}}$$

Some IRIs do much of this calculating for you. The *Developmental Literacy Inventory* provides ranges of reading times that correspond to an average, above average, or below average reading rate for that grade, for that time of year (see Figure 6.5).

Assessing recognition of words in isolation. A component of an IRI that is used to assess recognition of words in isolation (words in lists, not in context) is the *Word Recognition Inventory (WRI).* This instrument consists of graded lists of individual words, usually primer level through grade 6, typically included in stand-alone IRIs.

The WRI is used to assess sight recognition and some aspects of phonic and structural analysis. Since the words appear in isolation, the WRI is not used to assess how students recognize words in context or to measure comprehension in any way.

As was mentioned previously, a secondary purpose of the WRI is to help determine where to begin administering the reading passages of the IRI. For this purpose, the WRI is given before the IRI, and the examiner begins having the student read story passages at the grade level at which he first began to miss some words. When it is used only to provide information about the student's word recognition, the WRI can be given after the rest of the IRI.

The WRI consists of graded word lists for the student to read and a corresponding set of examiner's pages for the teacher to mark and score. Figure 6.6 shows a word list from a stand-alone WRI. The student's copy (not shown in the figure) contains only the

If the results computed just above show that the student read this passage at his independent level, you may wish to calculate his reading rate and compare it to those of other readers at his grade level.

1. Here is the number of words in this passage: 197
2. Write the number of words read incorrectly here: ______
3. Subtract #2 from #1 and write the answer here: ______
4. Using a calculator, multiply #3 by 60 seconds and write the answer here: ______
5. Write the student's reading time in seconds here: ______
6. Using a calculator, divide #4 by #5 and write the answer here: ______

The answer in #6 is the reading rate (words read correctly) per minute.

To interpret this number, first locate the column in the chart below that represents the time of the year when this test was administered. Then circle the reading rate that most closely matches your student's reading rate for this passage. Read across to the left to find the student's percentile rank—that is, an estimation of where that reading rate falls within the range of rates of other students at that grade level at that time of year.

Oral Reading Fluency Norms for Grade 2

Percentile	Fall WCPM	Winter WCPM	Spring WCPM
90	106	125	142
75	79	100	117
50	51	72	89
25	25	42	61
10	11	18	31

From Hasbrouck and Tindal, 2004.

FIGURE 6.5 Temple, et al., *Developmental Literacy Inventory*, "Reading Rate Scoring Guide for Grade 2" pp. 149–150, © 2009. Reproduced by permission of Pearson Education.

individual words, arranged in lists. On the examiner's copy, each word is followed by two blanks for filling in what the reader said when errors occurred.

Typically, each word in succession is shown to the student for a very brief exposure of less than one second; the word is uncovered for a longer look if it is not identified im-

3rd	*Flashed*	*Untimed*
station		
ought		
idea		
coach		
type		
damp		
elbow		
mystery		
yourselves		
midnight		
motorcycle		
insect		
study		
easier		
headache		
match		
quit		
alive		
moment		
range		
Total Errors:		

0–2 errors = Independent Level

3–6 errors = Instructional Level

7 + errors = Frustration Level

FIGURE 6.6 *Word Recognition Inventory, Examiner's Page*

Source: Temple, et al., *Developmental Literacy Inventory*, Examiner's Page 3, p. 77, © 2009 Pearson Education, Inc. Reproduced by permission of Pearson Education.

mediately. There are several similar ways to reveal each word for only a brief exposure. One is to use an index card to cover each word, drawing the card down the list to briefly reveal each word as the student reads down the list; another is to use two index cards, moving one to briefly uncover the word, then covering it again with the other card; a third is to use a card with a small rectangular window cut in it and slide the card down the list so that each successive word appears briefly in the window. Most teachers find that with a bit of practice, one or another of these methods is most comfortable for them. How the words are shown is less important than whether each word is revealed briefly yet completely and whether the administration is smooth and fluid. This might take a little practice.

Words that the reader recognizes immediately and accurately are checked off on the examiner's copy; words that are incorrectly identified or sounded out are noted in the blanks following each word. Some stand-alone IRIs have only one column of blanks, but most have two; those that have two blanks after each word are providing spaces for the examiner to note if the word was recognized automatically or had to be decoded by the reader. Percentages of accuracy are derived for each list of words by counting the errors made.

Deriving percentages is really academic since we are not interested in setting a functional reading level from reading word lists but rather in analyzing the student's word recognition strategies and assessing how well the student recognizes words automatically. Scores for each list may be entered on the IRI record sheet.

To summarize, the steps in administering an IRI are shown in Box 6.2.

Scoring an Informal Reading Inventory

Scoring procedures for an IRI are fairly simple. Word recognition in isolation, oral reading accuracy, and comprehension are scored by percentages, which help the teacher determine the student's independent, instructional, and frustration reading levels. See the next page for an explanation of these three reading levels.

BOX 6.2

Steps in Administering an Informal Reading Inventory

1. Begin the assessment one or two grade levels below the student's present grade or basal level or at a level you think will be easy for the student. Remember, you can move back as well as forward in the IRI if the reading is still too difficult.
2. Administer the first oral reading passage. Mark the miscues during the oral reading. You may tape-record the oral reading for greater accuracy if it does not distract or annoy the reader. Record the retelling. Ask the comprehension questions and record the gist of the answers.
3. Administer the silent reading passage at the same level. Ask the comprehension questions and record the gist of the answers.
4. If the student was not reading comfortably and successfully at this level, move back to a lower level and administer the oral and silent reading passages as before. Then continue to move forward in the IRI, skipping the level that you already administered when you come to it.
5. If the student was reading comfortably at the level on which you began testing, continue to move forward in the IRI, giving oral and silent passages as above, until the comprehension scores drop to 50 percent or less.
6. When you have located the frustration level, read one of the next-level passages aloud to the student and ask the comprehension questions as before. Continue assessing listening with one passage per level until the listening comprehension score drops below 50 percent. Then stop the IRI.

Levels of Reading Ability. Usually the statements and questions we hear about reading levels assume that a reader has one single reading level, but, this is an oversimplification. Most readers who have progressed beyond beginning reading can be said to have three reading levels. Each level is appropriate for reading different kinds of texts for different purposes. Each has important instructional implications.

The independent level. At the independent level, students can read *easily,* without help. Comprehension is generally excellent, and silent reading is rapid because almost all the words are recognized and understood at sight. Students rarely have to stop reading to analyze an unfamiliar word. Oral reading is generally fluent. Occasional *miscues,* or divergences from the written text, rarely interfere with comprehension. Independent level reading is easy and typically enjoyable for readers, and most readers self-select material at their independent level. Independent-level reading is not hard work; it is recreational.

In the classroom, we want students to read at their independent levels for enjoyment and practice. Anything they have to read and understand on their own, such as tests, homework, and centers, should ideally be at students' independent levels. Harder material will make it difficult for them to complete this reading without help.

Beginning readers, regardless of their age, may not have an independent reading level. That is, they may not be competent enough readers to find any level of material easy to read. Readers who are beyond the beginning reading stage typically have an independent level a grade or two below their present grade placement.

The instructional level. At the instructional level, the material is not easy but is still *comfortable.* Students are comfortably challenged and will benefit most from instruction. When we refer to a student's reading level, we mean his *instructional* reading level. Students whose instructional level is the same as their present grade placement are considered to be reading "at grade level" and to be progressing satisfactorily.

At the instructional level, comprehension is good, but help may be needed to understand some concepts or vocabulary. Silent reading is rapid enough to allow for good comprehension, though somewhat slower than at the independent level.

Some word analysis is usually necessary, but most words are recognized on sight; when an unfamiliar word must be decoded, the reader can usually do this successfully within a few seconds. Oral reading is fairly smooth and accurate, and miscues usually make sense in the context and do not cause a loss of meaning. For example, a student reading aloud at her instructional level may read *grandfather* as *grandpa* or *did not* as *didn't.* Occasional miscues that interrupt the flow of meaning do occur, but they are rare enough that the reader can maintain adequate to good comprehension.

The instructional level is the highest, or most difficult, level of text a reader can read comfortably and comprehend satisfactorily. This is the level most appropriate for instruction. Textbooks, basal readers, instructions, and anything else a student reads with instruction or help available should be at his instructional level. Students self-select material at their instructional level if their interest in the subject is high.

The frustration level. At the frustration level, the material is *too difficult* for successful reading. Comprehension is poor, with major ideas missed, forgotten, or misunderstood. Both oral reading and silent reading are typically slow and labored, with frequent stops to analyze unknown words. Attempts to figure out unfamiliar words are often unsuccessful. Oral reading miscues are frequent and serious, causing the reader to lose the sense of what was read. This level is so named because it is frustrating for students to attempt to read such material for sustained periods of time, and their efforts often fail. This level is to be avoided in instruction.

We want students reading at the instructional level in materials for direct instruction such as trade books, language arts or reading basals, subject-area textbooks, study guides, workbooks, skills activities, and worksheets that are read in class, where the teacher can provide help and guidance. But to do so, we must determine which material represents the frustration level. This means that we must have students attempt to read difficult material. Unless we explore the limits of students' reading ability, we will not know how far they can go. We have to see what strategies students can use when pushed and what strategies continue to serve well. After the frustration level has been determined, readers should not be assigned to read material that difficult.

Figure 6.7 shows the characteristics of each level and some typical kinds of reading a student might do at each level.

	Characteristics	*Typical Reading*
Independent Level: Easy	Excellent comprehension Excellent accuracy in word recognition Few words need analysis Rapid, smooth rate Very few errors of any kind	All pleasure reading All self-selected reading for information Homework, tests, seatwork, learning centers, and all other assigned work to be done alone
Instructional Level: Comfortable	Good comprehension Good accuracy in word recognition Fairly rapid rate Some word analysis needed	School textbooks and basal readers Guided classroom reading assignments Study guides and other work done with guidance Forms and applications
Frustration Level: Too hard	Poor comprehension Slow, stumbling rate Much word analysis necessary	No assigned material Reading for diagnostic purposes only

FIGURE 6.7 *Functional Reading Levels*

The listening level. Although it is not a reading level, there is one more level of text difficulty that is important because it relates to a student's reading abilities: the listening level. This is the most difficult text material that a student can understand when she listens to it. The listening level provides an estimate of the student's immediate potential for reading improvement.

Prior to fourth or fifth grade, most readers can understand material that is read to them more easily than material they read for themselves. That is because before it becomes largely automatic, the act of reading words takes up concentration that might otherwise be devoted to comprehending the message. Still, students may differ in the ratio of their listening comprehension to their reading comprehension. The difference can matter. For example, consider two students in sixth grade. Both have been identified with reading difficulties. Sarah has average word recognition but low reading comprehension. Her listening comprehension is low, too—about the same as her reading comprehension. Beatrice, on the other hand, has below average word recognition and also low reading comprehension. But her listening comprehension is much higher than her reading comprehension.

Sarah, the first student, appears to need help with language comprehension in general, including vocabulary and background knowledge. She needs a rich and informative curriculum and lots of opportunities to talk and think about it. Beatrice, the second student, urgently needs help in word recognition. It is the mechanics of recognizing words and making meaning, rather than language comprehension, that appears to be holding her back.

The Usefulness of Reading Levels. Because of the tremendous variety of reading materials used in almost every classroom today, it is more important than ever to know what difficulty of texts students can read comfortably and successfully. This allows us to help students select books they can read with good comprehension and enables us to provide the support they need to learn from required texts that might be overly difficult. When we match, or *target,* readers with texts that they can read with a high degree of comprehension, students "report confidence, capability, and control when reading. [T]argeted readers choose to read, and thus read more and read better. Targeted reading is self-reinforcing, pleasurable, and productive. Poorly targeted reading can be discouraging or worse; it can produce frustrated students who do not choose to read or like to read" (Stenner, 1999, p. 2).

Because IRIs are often used to determine a student's independent and instructional levels, the criteria for setting these levels are very important. IRIs have been widely used since the 1940s, when Betts (1941, 1957) and others popularized their use, and the criteria for setting levels were derived largely from clinical experience. For many years, the minimum instructional level criteria attributed to Betts—95 percent oral reading accuracy and 75 percent comprehension—were widely accepted.

Today some authorities still use the Betts criteria, although 70 percent comprehension is most often used. However, the long-standing oral reading accuracy criteria have been challenged as too stringent. Ninety percent is widely accepted as the lower end of the instructional range for oral reading accuracy (Johns & Magliari, 1989) and for taking a running record to determine whether a student is reading instructional level material (Clay, 2000).

Oral Reading Accuracy

For each oral passage that was read, score the oral reading accuracy by counting the uncorrected miscues, which are shown in Box 6.1 on page 211.

The issue of whether to count miscues that the reader corrected is an important one. Many clinicians do not count self-corrected miscues because self-correction shows that the reader is monitoring whether the passage makes sense. But some count all miscues, corrected or not, and some stand-alone IRIs instruct users to do so. In informal assessment there are some issues on which practitioners disagree. You should discuss these issues with experienced IRI users along with your colleagues and use your best judgment as a teacher.

While you are learning to give and score an IRI, it is helpful to record the oral reading so that you can replay it and be sure you caught all the miscues. It might also help you to make a check or tally mark at the end of each line of print, one for each uncorrected miscue in that line. It makes counting up easier.

To obtain a reader's total accuracy score, you must know not only how many miscues occurred, but also how many words are in the whole passage. In other words, what percentage of the total words does each individual word contribute?

Most stand-alone IRIs do the math for you, providing a box or chart showing how many miscues represent the independent, instructional, and frustration levels for that passage. As we mentioned in the previous section on administration, if you look back at Figure 6.2, you will see a box at the end of the passage indicating how many miscues may be made for the passage to fall within each reading level; in this case, up to 13 miscues represents an independent level, from 14 to 33 miscues represents the instructional level, and 34 or more miscues, the frustration level. (These scores do not reflect whether the miscues made sense within the passage; that issue is discussed in a later section entitled "Qualitative Analysis of Oral Reading Miscues." This discussion refers only to the total accuracy of the oral reading.)

If you are using an IRI that provides you only the total number of words in the passage, you will have to calculate the oral reading accuracy score.

Let's use the marked oral reading passage in Figure 6.4, "Jack's Dinner," as an example. This passage contains 93 words. The reader made five uncorrected miscues.

To calculate oral reading accuracy:

1. Determine the number of words that were read correctly by subtracting the number of miscues from the number of words in the passage.
2. Divide the number of words in the passage into the number of words correct.
3. Multiply the resulting decimal number by 100 to get the total accuracy score. Round off to the nearest whole number.

By making 5 uncorrected miscues in a passage of 93 words, the reader read with 95 percent accuracy.

1. 93 – 5 = 88
2. 88/93
3. .95 × 100 = 95%

As you score each oral reading passage, write the percentage of accuracy on the examiner's copy of the passage. The oral reading accuracy scores will contribute to your determination of the student's independent, instructional, and frustration levels.

The most widely accepted criteria for oral reading accuracy are these:

Independent level: 97 percent or higher
Instructional level: 90–96 percent
Frustration level: below 90 percent

If these criteria seem high, remember that sentence context provides a powerful word recognition aid. In sentences, words are constrained by their grammatical usage and meaning. An unknown word in a sentence does not appear there arbitrarily, as it might in a list, but because it fits grammatically and semantically. The number of alternatives for any individual word in context is therefore small. When a student misses more than about 1 in 10 running words, comprehension will be affected.

Reading and Listening Comprehension

Score the silent and oral reading comprehension questions separately for each passage and determine the percentage of questions answered correctly. Do the same for any passages you used for listening comprehension. These passages are all scored in the same way.

If the IRI that you are using does not have a box for checking off the number of correct answers and the corresponding level, you will have to determine the percentage of correct answers, as you would if you were grading a test or quiz. To determine how much each question counts, divide the number of questions into 100. The answer represents the percentage each question counts. Multiply this number by the number of correct answers to obtain the comprehension score for each passage.

Jot down the score for each passage on the examiner's copy of that passage. Repeat the same procedure for all passages that were read to the student. The comprehension scores will contribute to your determination of the reader's independent, instructional, frustration, and listening levels.

The most widely accepted criteria for reading and listening comprehension scores are these:

Independent level: 90 percent or higher
Instructional level: 70–89 percent
Frustration level: below 70 percent

In our discussion of administering IRIs, you were told to continue testing until a score of 50 percent or lower was attained. By doing so, you can be sure that the frustration level has been reached.

Scoring the Word Recognition Inventory

The WRI is easy to give and to score. When a word is correctly identified during the brief exposure, it is checked off in the column labeled *Automatic* (or whatever the designation is on your IRI for the brief exposure of each word) on the examiner's sheet; if an error is made, the error is written on the blank instead of a check. Then the word is uncovered for a longer exposure, and the student's second attempts are written in the column labeled *Decoded* (or whatever the designation is on your IRI for the longer, or untimed, exposure of the word). If the reader corrects the error after looking at the word again, a check may be placed in that blank.

Each column is scored separately for each level. Some WRIs like the one shown in Figure 6.6 show you how to derive an independent, instructional, or frustration level from these scores. If not, you will derive a percentage score for each column, as though you were grading a quiz.

The most widely accepted criteria for word recognition in isolation are these:

Independent level: 90 percent or higher
Instructional level: 70–89 percent
Frustration level: below 70 percent

These levels are most useful when the WRI is used to show where to begin the reading passages. You will not determine a functional reading level from reading word lists alone, but you will use this information in analyzing the student's word recognition strategies and assessing how well the student recognizes words automatically.

Keeping Track of Scores

After you have derived scores for word recognition in isolation, oral reading accuracy, oral and silent reading comprehension, and listening comprehension, enter the scores on a record sheet, which can be stapled to the front of the examiner's copy of the student's IRI. Having all the pertinent scores and observational notes you made during the testing on one sheet aids in interpreting the student's performance. (Interpreting IRI results is discussed in the next section.)

A model score record sheet is shown in Figure 6.8. On this sheet are spaces for recording all scores from the IRI and WRI, notes, observations, and information about the student such as age and grade.

The necessary scores for determining the functional reading and listening levels from an IRI are summarized in Table 6.1. If the IRI that you prefer to use specifies somewhat different score criteria, use those given in the IRI instructions.

Interpreting an Informal Reading Inventory

As with all assessment procedures, IRI scores are not an end in themselves. They should be interpreted and then applied in instructional planning. To do so, the student's functional reading levels must be determined, and patterns of strength and need must be noted and addressed.

Student ______________________ Age ______ Grade ______
Date tested ______ Tested by ______________________

	WORD RECOGNITION INVENTORY		ORAL READING		COMPREHENSION		
Level	Automatic	Decoded	Total Accuracy	Total Acceptability	Oral Reading	Silent Reading	Listening
P							
1st							
2nd							
3rd							
4th							
5th							
6th							
7th							
8th							
9th							

READING LEVELS
Independent ______________________
Instructional ______________________
Frustration ______________________
Listening ______________________
Retelling ______________________

Strengths: ______________________

Needs: ______________________

Prior Knowledge: ______________________

Recommendations: ______________________

FIGURE 6.8 *Informal Reading Inventory Record Sheet*

TABLE 6.1 *Criterion Scores for Establishing Reading and Listening Levels with an IRI*

	Oral Reading	*Comprehension*
Independent Level	97%	90%
Instructional Level	90%	70%
Frustration Level	below 90%	below 70%
Listening Level	—	70%

Establishing Reading and Listening Levels. The scores that are derived from the oral reading and comprehension measures are used to determine overall levels. Scores for both oral reading accuracy and comprehension should meet the criteria for the instructional level to be sure that the reader will be comfortable at that level.

Figures 6.9 and 6.10 show examples of oral reading and comprehension scores for a second grader and a sixth grader. Let's consider what the scores tell us about each student's reading levels.

The child whose scores are shown in Figure 6.9 reads easily at the primer (P) level, with accurate word recognition and excellent comprehension. All scores are at the independent level.

At the first-grade level, her oral reading accuracy is still good, although she made more miscues, and comprehension is good in both oral and silent reading. An oral reading accuracy score of 94 percent and comprehension scores of 75 percent and 80 percent are within the instructional level. First-grade material represents a good instructional level for this youngster. In second-grade material, both word recognition and comprehension break down. Second-grade material represents her frustration level.

The listening comprehension score of 80 percent at third grade shows that this second grader can listen to and understand material at a third-grade level of difficulty, while the listening score of 60 percent at fourth grade shows that this level of material is presently too hard for her to understand adequately even when she hears it. The

		Comprehension		
Grade	*Oral Reading*	*Oral*	*Silent*	*Listening*
P	97	100	100	—
1	94	75	80	—
2	88	60	50	—
3	—	—	—	80
4	—	—	—	60

FIGURE 6.9 *Sample IRI Scores for a Second Grader (in Percentages)*

Grade	Oral Reading	Comprehension		
		Oral	*Silent*	*Listening*
2	99	100	90	—
3	94	85	80	—
4	91	70	70	—
5	86	50	55	—
6	—	—	—	90

FIGURE 6.10 *Sample IRI Scores for a Sixth Grader (in Percentages)*

80 percent score at third grade also represents this youngster's *potential* reading level; that is, she has the vocabulary and verbal concepts to understand material appropriate for third graders when she hears it. This is a positive sign; she has considerable potential for improving her reading. However, she presently is able to read only first-grade material.

In Figure 6.10, the student's scores at second grade are within the independent level. (Since independent-level scores were obtained at second grade, first-grade and primer levels were not assessed.) His scores at both third and fourth grades fall within the instructional range, so we can say that fourth-grade material represents his highest instructional level; his instructional reading level actually includes both third- and fourth-grade material.

Since all fifth-grade scores are in the frustration range, we conclude that fifth-grade material is too difficult for this student to read, but the 90 percent listening comprehension score at sixth grade shows he can understand material at his present grade level when he hears it. This sixth grader's listening comprehension score shows that he has the ability to read at grade level, although he is presently instructional at a fourth-grade level.

The process of deriving percentages of correct responses and using these scores to determine reading levels is called *quantitative analysis.* It is useful, but it is incomplete because it lacks the essential element of in-depth analysis of the student's responses. To determine what the reader knows and where help is needed, we must determine the strategies underlying the correct and incorrect responses. From this perspective, *how many* correct responses the student made is less important than *which* responses were right and *why.* This assessment is termed *qualitative analysis* because it focuses on the quality of responses and the strategies that the reader demonstrated.

Quantitative analysis helps us determine the levels of difficulty of text the reader can deal with successfully. Qualitative analysis helps us determine what the student has mastered and what skills and processes are lacking. Both analyses are needed to develop a prescriptive program for a reader.

Qualitative Analysis of Oral Reading Miscues. The context in which a word occurs is a powerful aid to word recognition, but context is provided only by connected text. When we make a transcript of the oral reading of IRI passages, we can analyze word recognition within the real act of reading. Therefore, accurate marking and analysis of miscues are important.

Even very fluent readers make occasional miscues, especially when the material is unfamiliar. Some miscues change the meaning of the sentence or passage very little; others change the author's meaning significantly and can interfere with the reader's comprehension. By examining and evaluating a reader's miscues, we can better understand what the reader is doing while reading. We can see more than just whether the reading is highly accurate. We can see, through the miscues themselves, whether the reader is using context and sense-making strategies to actively construct meaning. Students who generally make acceptable, or qualitatively "good," miscues need a different kind of word-attack instruction to help them read more accurately than those whose miscues generally don't make sense.

Comparing Miscues. Let's say two readers read the following three sentences aloud:

> The day was warm and sunny. Tom and Mandy packed a lunch. They brought ham sandwiches, chips and pickles.

One student reads:

> "The day was *hot* and sunny. Tom and Mandy packed *their* lunch. They brought ham sandwiches, chips and *peaches.*"

The other student reads:

> "The day was warm and *sandy.* Tom and Mandy *picked* a lunch. They brought ham sandwiches, chips and *pirckles.*"

Each reader made three uncorrected miscues. Their overall accuracy scores for this paragraph would be the same, but the first reader's miscues more nearly preserved the meaning of the paragraph, whereas the second reader's miscues made less sense and probably interfered more with her comprehension.

Hot and *warm,* when discussing weather, are closer in meaning than *sunny* and *sandy.* It makes better sense, and is more like the meaning of the text sentence, to say the day was *hot and sunny* than *warm and sandy.* Although it isn't grammatically correct, "packed *their* lunch" is closer to the original meaning of the sentence than "*picked* a lunch." *Peaches* aren't much like *pickles,* but they are at least both foods that might be found in a picnic lunch; *pirckles* is a nonsense word, even though it looks and sounds more like *pickles* than *peaches* does. Although both readers made three miscues, the first reader's miscues were qualitatively better, in the sense of preserving the intended meaning, than the second reader's.

Scoring Miscue Acceptability. When considering the quality of miscues, we reread the passage as the reader read it, with all the miscues just as we marked them, and decide

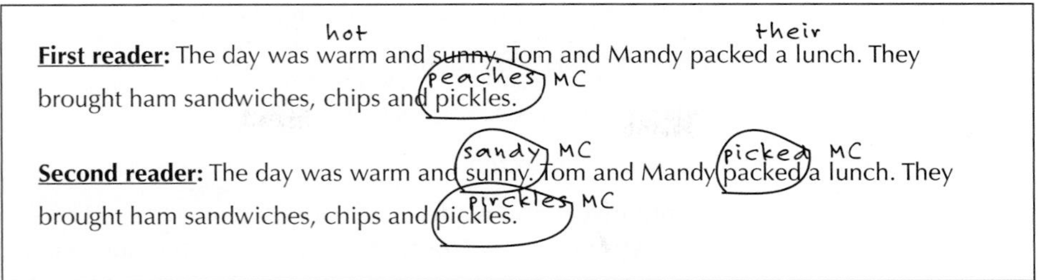

FIGURE 6.11 *Two Readers' Meaning-Changing Miscues*

whether each miscue significantly changes the meaning of the passage or sentence in which it occurs. We do not look only at the individual word, but at the miscue within the phrase, sentence, or passage context. Circle, highlight, or write MC for Meaning Change over miscues that significantly change the meaning of the context. If we were marking the sentences read in the foregoing examples, we would mark only the first reader's *peaches* as a meaning-change miscue, and all three of the second reader's miscues as meaning changes, as shown in Figure 6.11.

What makes a miscue acceptable? At this point, you might wonder how much a miscue must change meaning to be considered significant. It can be argued that any change in the author's words, no matter how small, changes the author's meaning. But we are not concerned here with tiny or subtle meaning changes. Instead of asking ourselves, "Does this miscue change the meaning?" we ask, "Does this miscue change the meaning *significantly?* Is this a *big* meaning change?"

Whether the meaning is changed a lot, a little, or hardly at all depends on the miscue *and its surrounding context.* That's why miscues must be considered in their context, not taken out of context, placed in a list, and evaluated, as some IRI instructions say. We try not to split hairs, in terms of meaning, but rather to be aware of big changes in meaning. A word, phrase, or sentence can make good sense even when it is grammatically incorrect, so we avoid making hard-and-fast rules such as "changes in parts of speech always result in meaning change."

With experience, we've found that there isn't much ambiguity about most miscues; it's clear either that little or no meaning was lost or that the miscue changed the meaning a great deal, and the ones we have to puzzle over are rare. With these, we usually consult someone else and read what the sentence was supposed to say and what the reader said, and ask whether they think the miscue was significant.

Dialects and miscues. An important issue in miscue analysis is the role of nonstandard English dialects in oral reading accuracy. As we have seen, counting all the miscues and deriving an accuracy score do not take into account whether the reader's errors make sense. Nor does this process take into account whether the reader is translating standard English text into her own familiar, albeit nonstandard, oral dialect.

For example, let's say the sentence reads like this:

Rose said, "This is my mother."

The reader, a dialect speaker, reads this:

Rose say, "This my mother."

Quantitatively, the reader has made two uncorrected miscues: the omission of *is* and the substitution of *say* for *said.* Qualitatively, the oral reading does not correspond exactly to the written words, but it does represent an accurate translation into a widely used nonstandard dialect, with no loss of meaning. In most dialects it is grammar, not meaning, that differs from the written text (McWhorter, 2000).

It is important not to confuse dialect miscues with true word recognition errors because doing so results in underestimating the word recognition abilities of many dialect speakers. Likewise, it is not helpful to assume that all miscues produced by dialect speakers will be acceptable and not provide the help they may need to develop greater accuracy and automaticity in word recognition. By listening closely to the informal speech of your dialect-speaking students, you will gain enough familiarity with its conventions to recognize true dialect miscues, which are generally acceptable, from those that interfere with comprehension.

When you are marking a dialect speaker's oral reading, it's best to mark what the reader says, then rescore the passage for acceptability. If they are dialect usages, most of the miscues will be insignificant.

What about names? Names are especially tricky for readers. Often, students stumble over names in a passage even when they read harder words correctly. We generally don't count names as miscues more than once in a passage, provided that the reader calls the character by the same wrong name each time. That is, if *Phillip* is read as *Phil,* or even as *Pillip* throughout a passage, we count it only the first time. If *Phillip* were read as *Phil* a few times, then changed to *Flip,* we'd count each change once.

Some people count name miscues as a separate error each time; this seems excessively strict. Others count it if the name seems to change the gender (calling *Phillip Phyllis,* for example). Check the instructions for administering your IRI and follow what the authors recommend if it makes sense to you.

Analyzing Reading Comprehension. By looking at oral and silent comprehension scores across several grade levels, we can determine if the reader's comprehension during either oral or silent reading is particularly weak or strong, and whether such patterns are age-appropriate. We can also look at responses to the different types of comprehension questions within or across grade levels to see whether the student has particular strengths or weaknesses in the comprehension skills required by the questions.

If readers consistently demonstrate better comprehension after oral reading and lower comprehension scores after reading silently, we can conclude that they need to hear themselves say the words aloud to understand what they are reading. Such readers translate, or *recode,* print into speech and derive meaning from the spoken words.

This is typical of many beginning readers, especially those whose early reading instruction has been primarily oral.

When they read silently, they sometimes lose their place in the text because their voices help "anchor" them in the print. It is not surprising when they show consistently better oral than silent comprehension. However, when an older student reads this way, we are concerned. Fluent silent reading for meaning is needed to keep up with the amount of reading that is required in upper grades.

Readers beyond the beginning stage can read faster silently than orally. Oral reading speed is limited by how clearly we can speak; about 200 words per minute is very rapid speech, and even fluent oral readers do not read aloud that fast. However, fluent silent reading may vary from 200 to 400 or more words per minute depending on the difficulty and familiarity of the material and the reader's purpose. Fluent adult readers read challenging material silently at about 250 words per minute (Perfetti, 1985), and they read easy interesting material for pleasure even faster, up to 600 words per minute. By the end of second grade, fluent readers read at about 90 words per minute, and rates increase by about 20 words per minute each year until sixth grade, when fluent readers read at about 180 words per minute (McCormick, 2003).

Somewhere between second and fourth grade, most readers begin this shift toward more silent reading and characteristically show better silent comprehension. This is developmentally appropriate; it certainly does not indicate that these older students show an oral reading weakness or that they should begin a lot of remedial oral reading. On the contrary, in the upper grades oral reading should be deemphasized while silent reading is emphasized.

Comprehension Skill Patterns. Some readers have consistent difficulty with a particular kind of comprehension question. For example, one might have little difficulty with questions requiring direct recall of explicitly stated information, but have much more difficulty with inferences, main ideas, or vocabulary items. If we go back to the comprehension questions following the reading passages and consider each kind of question, we can see whether there was a particular type of question with which a student had consistent difficulty. Figure 6.12 shows the major types of questions that usually appear in IRIs.

By systematically looking across grade levels, we can see what, if any, pattern emerges. Was there a type of question that repeatedly gave the student difficulty at different levels or one that the student consistently answered correctly? Looking for individual patterns in comprehension responses allows us to design appropriate comprehension activities for students according to their individual needs.

However, we must be certain that the questions really tap the comprehension skills that they say they do. IRI questions are notoriously hard to classify. Even experienced teachers attempting to classify comprehension questions by type often classified questions quite differently from the authors of a particular IRI (Gipe, 2006).

Unquestioning acceptance of IRI question categories, or of all IRI questions as good questions, is unwise. Comprehension patterns can often be discerned, however, and helpful teaching strategies devised from these judgments, if teachers continually use critical judgment. Don't take either the quality of questions or the way the author

Literal Comprehension (Answers to questions explicitly stated in passage)

Topic:	What event was this story about? What was this passage mostly about?
Main Idea:	What was the most important thing the author said about dogs? What was the most important information in this passage?
Important Detail:	What kind of animal was Nitwit? What did Bob do when he got home?
Sequence:	What happened after Jill heard the window break? Where did the children go first?
Characterization:	What did Ms. Willis do that showed she was angry? How did Bruce act when he saw Jamie again?
Re-Inspection:	Find the sentence that describes Ben's new bike and read it to me. Find the place in the story where the children began to argue and read it out loud.

Interpretation and Judgment (Answers to questions not explicitly stated in passage)

Inference:	Why do you think Jim spoke roughly to the dog? What makes you believe Cathy might enjoy flying?
Vocabulary:	What did Rita mean when she said "I'm simply green"? What is a "chopper" in this story?
Prediction:	What could happen if the delivery boy loses the package? If Shana runs away, where might she go?

FIGURE 6.12 *Sample Comprehension Questions*

classified them on faith. Read the passages and each of the questions, and consider carefully whether you think the questions are appropriately labeled by type. Then, if you discern a consistent pattern in a student's response to particular question types, you have a working hypothesis about the student's needs.

Begin instruction based on your hypothesis that a student needs practice in particular areas, but continue to evaluate on the basis of how the student responds to that instruction. Only further teaching will reveal whether your working hypotheses were accurate.

Patterns in Listening Comprehension. If students achieve 70 percent or better on the comprehension questions after listening to a passage read aloud by the examiner, we assume that they can understand similar concepts and vocabulary when they hear it, although they cannot read that level of material for themselves. We refer to the highest grade level at which the student had 70 percent or better as the student's *listening comprehension level.* This level is important because it helps us to determine what we can expect this student to achieve; thus, the listening level makes it possible to set reasonable instructional goals.

As we discussed earlier in this chapter, most students who are not fluent, mature readers can listen to someone else reading aloud and understand material that they cannot yet read successfully. Most of them, especially the younger ones, are still learning and developing as readers, whereas they have been competent listeners and language users for a lot longer. Therefore, their listening levels are somewhat above their instructional reading levels, which is predictable, for it shows that they are not yet able to read as well as they can think.

Some youngsters will have instructional reading and listening comprehension levels that are the same. Material too difficult for them to read is also too difficult for them to understand on an auditory basis. This is fine. This shows that they are reading just as well as they can and that at this present time, there is not much room for improvement. These students are reading right at their potential, using all their ability to read as well as they can. They need support and further instruction, but if they are poor readers, they will probably make steady but not spectacular gains in reading. The listening comprehension level represents a sort of overall goal in reading improvement.

The listening comprehension level is dynamic, not fixed. As children grow older and have more experiences, they can understand more difficult material because they have gained knowledge and experiences to which new information and experiences can be related. The average seven-year-old can listen to and understand stories that are appropriate for second or third graders and understand them, but ninth-grade material would be too difficult conceptually. By the time the child is twelve or thirteen, however, ninth-grade materials might well be comprehensible because vocabulary, store of concepts, and experiences have grown in those intervening years. The listening level represents an estimate of *present* functioning. Establishing a student's listening level once and using it as an ongoing standard, however, is no more appropriate than expecting last year's instructional level to be the same next year.

Here are three examples, all second graders:

> Jenny
>
> Jenny's listening comprehension level is late second grade. Since she is in second grade, we infer that her verbal intelligence is roughly average for her age and that she has the necessary concepts and vocabulary to learn to read second-grade material successfully, although presently, she has a first-grade instructional level. Although her instructional level is low, she can improve her reading with appropriate instruction and support.
>
> Matt
>
> Matt has a listening comprehension level of sixth grade. He has the concepts and vocabulary to listen to and understand very advanced material, and he is obviously very bright. In spite of his potential, he is achieving at grade level and has an instructional level of late second grade. Therefore, his achievement is average for his grade, although he has the potential for higher achievement. The finding that Matt is not performing at his full potential is not necessarily negative. If he is comfortable, motivated, and interested, there is no need for concern. If he appears to be apathetic, bored, or frustrated, then he certainly needs greater intellectual challenge.

Sandy

Sandy has an instructional level of first grade, and his listening level is also first grade. Although Sandy's achievement is below grade level, it is in line with his present potential. Sandy might be a slow learner or of below-average verbal intelligence; he might have learned to read later than others, or he might have a limited background of experience with print. At any rate, his performance and potential appear to be in line at the present. Sandy needs much support and instruction, and as he becomes a more proficient reader, his listening level will increase. This in turn will make further reading improvement possible.

Analyzing Word Recognition in Isolation. As we discussed in earlier sections, the Word Recognition Inventory, consisting of graded lists of words, is used to assess students' automatic recognition of words at each level, as well as some aspects of word analysis and decoding. Since words appear in isolation rather than in context, the student's use of context and word meaning as a cue to recognition is not assessed with this device. The WRI is administered by showing each word for a very brief exposure, using either an index card or a card with a window cut in it, to briefly reveal each word. Words that are not recognized immediately or that are misidentified are shown for a longer, untimed exposure.

The student's immediate sight word recognition is assessed by the Automatic, or timed exposure, portion of the instrument. A large sight vocabulary forms the basis of fluent, effective reading. A reader who has a good sight vocabulary of common, frequently occurring words will usually score around 90 percent or better on automatic recognition of words, at least at the lower grade levels. At any grade level, scores much below 70 percent indicate that the student probably does not recognize enough of the words to read fluently and effectively at that level of difficulty.

The responses in the Decoded, or untimed, columns give us information about the phonic and word analysis strategies that a student can use when he does not recognize a word immediately. Students who typically correct an initial error when decoding the word show us that though their sight recognition is weak, their decoding skills are stronger. Students who make unsuccessful attempts to decode unrecognized words but who typically preserve the initial consonant or blend sounds in their attempts show us that they have a grasp of initial sounds but may be weak in decoding middle or final sounds. By looking for patterns in both correct and incorrect responses, we can begin to determine what word attack skills need to be reviewed or taught.

Observations of Reading Behaviors and Strategies

Classroom-centered observations assist teachers in making instructional decisions and help parents and students better understand student achievement. In this model the teacher, rather than the test, is the tool. The informed teacher is ideally placed to observe and collect information about students continuously, unobtrusively, and interactively, and to make sense of classroom events (McCormick, 2003; Owocki & Goodman, 2002). But observation doesn't just happen; it must be planned and carried out systematically and accurately, or valuable opportunities to learn about students will be lost. In the following sections you will learn about various ways to carry out effective student observations.

Observing Readers

The classroom teacher is in the best possible position to observe and record students' daily interactions with text. These observations can be very helpful in communicating to parents, completing report cards and progress reports, talking with students about their progress, and meeting instructional needs.

The lists that follow show many of the behaviors that we would want to observe in our work with students. You can add other behaviors you observe.

Physical Behaviors

- Points to words accurately during reading (for beginners).
- Appears to be very absorbed in reading for pleasure; is not distracted by environmental activity during reading.

Cognitive Behaviors

- Predicts easily about material to be read.
- Recalls directly stated information easily.
- Demonstrates understanding of cause-and-effect relationships.
- Produces inferences, conclusions, applications easily.
- Offers personal opinions and/or experiences related to the reading.
- Uses background knowledge or prior information to understand text.
- Responds critically to aspects of plot, characters, author's style, illustrations.
- Draws comparisons between this material and other texts.
- Expresses enjoyment of an activity or text or pride in success.

Reading Strategies Observed

- Uses one or more strategies spontaneously before seeking assistance.
- Tries another strategy when the first attempt isn't successful.
- Uses context or sense making and decoding together.
- Reruns or rereads to get past a difficult part or to self-check.
- Indicates with words or gestures when reading doesn't sound right or doesn't make sense ("What?" "Huh?" "Wait a minute," a puzzled look, etc.).
- Attempts self-correction, whether successful or not.
- Effectively uses text aids like headings, bold print, charts, maps, tables, and summaries.

Recording Observations

One way to keep track of your observations while ensuring that you observe each student systematically is to make copies of an observation record sheet marked with a square for each student like the one in Figure 6.13. The squares should be large enough to accommodate a sticky note. Each square is labeled with a student's name. Observations are noted on the sticky notes, which are then attached to the student's square.

Blair Jan. 12 – Made two self-corrections during reading.	**Brianna**	**Vincent**	**Luke**
Raquel	**Lauren**	**Carla**	**Richard**
Antoine	**Kevin**	**Carlos** Jan. 16 – Volunteered to read first today!	**Marisa**
Scott Jan. 9 – Helped Huang check spelling during writing.	**Terri**	**Sherita**	**Denzel**
Anthony	**Jamahl**	**Huang**	**Paula** Jan. 10 – Used a dictionary for first time, self-initiated.

FIGURE 6.13 *Observation Record Sheet with Sticky Notes*

SEPTEMBER

Sunday	Monday	Tuesday	Wednesday	Thursday	Friday	Saturday
1 Last Quarter	2 Blair LABOR DAY	3 Brianna 9/8 Self-corr. during reading	4 Vincent	5 Luke	6 Raquel	7
8 New Moon GRANDPARENT'S DAY	9 Lauren ROSH HASHANAH	10 Carla	11 Richard	12 Antoine	13 Kevin 9-13 Begin-ning to space bet. words	14
15 First Quarter	16 Carlos	17 Marisa 9-17 Volunteered to read for first time CITIZENSHIP DAY	18 Scott YOM KIPPUR	19 Terri	20 Sherita	21
22	23 Denzel Full Moon FIRST DAY OF AUTUMN	24 Anthony 9-19 Has much difficulty pointing to each word	25 Jamahl	26 Huang	27 Paula	28
29	30				AUGUST S M T W T F S 1 2 3 4 5 6 7 8 9 10 11 12 13 14 15 16 17 18 19 20 21 22 23 24 25 26 27 28 29 30 31	OCTOBER S M T W T F S 1 2 3 4 5 6 7 8 9 10 11 12 13 14 15 16 17 18 19 20 21 22 23 24 25 26 27 28 29 30 31

FIGURE 6.14 *Observations on Calendar Page*

As additional observations are made, the notes are stacked one atop the other. Many observations can be kept on one sheet, and there is no need to transfer your comments to another sheet. A drawback of this system is that sticky notes may fall off.

Another way to record observations is to write them directly on a calendar page with a student's name in each weekday square; the month is already printed on it, and dates are jotted in each student's square as they occur, as shown in Figure 6.14. Or you can make a number of blank sheets with the squares ruled. Notes are made directly on the sheet, with the date marked. This system eliminates having to recopy notes onto the sheet, but space for comments is limited.

A third system involves making notes on index cards that may be carried in a pocket or on a clipboard, as in Figure 6.15. Index cards allow room for numerous or extended comments, but the notes have to be transferred to another sheet for permanence.

A fourth system involves keeping a separate observation sheet for each student like the one shown in Figure 6.16. This system is convenient for monitoring a few students,

Lauren Wells

9-12 Lauren points accurately to each one-syllable word but gets "off" on multi-syll. words

9-17 Lauren struggled w/pointing as she read "hippopotamus" — wants to make it two words - but got it right after 3 tries!

9-26 Pointing is more accurate — self-corrects errors as they occur.

Patrick Logan

9-8 Doesn't attend closely to print — takes a quick look and guesses wildly.

9-17 Tried self-correction w/o reminder for the first time!

9-24 Self-correcting, or attempting to, about half the time, usually successful.

FIGURE 6.15 *Observation Index Cards*

such as members of a remedial group or mainstreamed students with special needs. Sheets may be kept in daily work folders, in a binder, or on a clipboard. This system is cumbersome for large groups but allows plenty of room for each observation and eliminates recopying.

Whatever system you choose to record your observations, you must be careful of several issues: using objective language, observing every student, and including observation time in your plans.

Student: Denzel Miller **Grade:** 1

Date	Observed Behavior
9/6	Denzel uses random letters to write. Letter formation shaky, no spaces. Could not read what he had written to me.
9/17	Denzel still uses random letters if he writes alone, but with encouragement he used a few beginning sounds today: M (mom), B (basketball)
9/26	Beginning sounds are appearing w/more regularity; random letters are beginning to drop out
10/13	Observed Denzel sounding out beginning sounds to himself as he wrote today! First time w/o being reminded!

FIGURE 6.16 *Individual Student Observation Sheet*

1. ***Use Objective Language.*** Record what occurred in factual terms, rather than your interpretation of the behavior. Write *what* the behavior is, or *how often* or *in what circumstances* the behavior occurs. For example, "Richard repeatedly pulled the book away from his reading partner" tells what occurred; "Richard has trouble sharing a book with a partner" is unspecific and judgmental. "Joanne looks out the window for most of the sustained reading period" is factual; "Joanne wastes her reading time" is judgmental. Record what the student said or did, not what he or she *is.* Avoid sweeping generalizations such as "Justin hates to read," "Nakia works well in groups," or "Timmy is uncooperative."
2. ***Observe Every Student.*** You might sometimes observe certain students more often than others, especially if they are having particular difficulty or showing a growth spurt, but in general you should make sure you observe every child before starting another round of observations. The record-keeping systems shown in Figures 6.13 and 6.14, in which all notes are kept on one sheet with labeled squares, help you to keep track of which students you have observed recently. An empty square indicates that you need to observe that individual.

   If you don't pay attention to this, you may unwittingly observe some students many more times than others. There are many reasons for this, some better than others. Students who are having great difficulty, are discipline problems, or are just more engaging or likeable than others tend to be observed more often. Whatever the reason, it is unfair to observe some students often and others infrequently.

3. ***Plan Observation Time.*** Plan systematically for student observations. Whether it's daily, once a week, or every other week, block off observation time in your schedule. If you don't, observation can get pushed aside by the daily demands of teaching. If you look at your last observation notes and find that it's been longer than a few weeks since you kept any observation records, you'll know that you need to carve out some time on a more regular basis.

Monitoring Types and Difficulty of Texts Read

Another important record to keep is what texts students are reading, what types or genres are preferred, and how difficult the texts are. These are most important in programs in which students are self-selecting at least a portion of what they read, as they should be. But required or teacher-selected material should also be documented.

One way to do this is to keep a running list in each child's work folder or in a binder that shows the materials being read, their genres, and some indication of their difficulty. Another way is for students to keep such a list individually and share it with you in periodic conferences. Older students can easily keep their own records; they should record the title and author, the type of material (joke book, short story collection, historical or contemporary fiction, biography, science, etc.), and their self-assessment of its difficulty for them (easy to read, pretty hard book, over 100 pages long, etc.). For longer works that take more than a day or so to finish, the starting and ending dates may be recorded.

Such lists show you at a glance how much and what kind of reading the child is doing. If a student appears to be reading one kind of material exclusively, consider encouraging him to try another author, topic, or genre. If only very easy books are attempted, introduce the student to a little more challenging material; for the one who always chooses too-difficult, discouraging texts, give guidance about selecting more manageable books. The student who takes months to read a single book needs to be led to shorter works or material at a lower readability level, or she needs to increase her time spent reading.

These records can also be very effective in demonstrating to parents just what their children are capable of and interested in. This can help them provide appropriate materials for reading at home. Also, most students enjoy getting a panoramic look at what they are reading, and they gain satisfaction in watching their lists grow and change. Such information can help students become more reflective and self-evaluative. You will read more about helping students become self-evaluative in the sections to follow about portfolios.

There are several ways to informally determine the difficulty level of different materials. These include using the book's guided reading level, the readability level, Lexiles, and cloze procedures. Each of these methods is discussed in the sections to follow.

Guided Reading Levels

One way of determining text difficulty is to refer to the guided reading level for a book. *Guided reading* (Fountas & Pinnell, 1996, 1999, 2001) is a literature-based approach in which books of many types and genres are grouped in general categories of difficulty. Factors such as length, print size and layout, vocabulary and concepts, language structures used, text structures, genre, predictability and supportive patterns within the text, and illustration support (Fountas & Pinnell, 1996, p. 114) are used to assign books to levels that are identified by the letters A through Z, corresponding roughly to kindergarten through sixth grade.

Fountas and Pinnell refer to this as developing a *text gradient,* which they describe in this way: "A gradient of text reflects a defined continuum of characteristics related to the level of support and challenge the reader is offered. . . . A gradient of text is not a precise sequence of texts through which all children pass. Books are leveled in approximate groups from which teachers choose particular books for individuals or reading groups" (1996, p. 113).

Guided reading levels A through C represent books that are very easy to read. They typically focus on one idea or have one very simple story line; have one or two lines or sentences per page; feature large, well-spaced print; and have very high illustration support; that is, there is a direct correspondence between the picture and the words on each page. Patterns, repetition, and topics familiar to young children (playing, getting dressed, bedtime, etc.) make these texts very supportive for the youngest readers.

Levels C through I roughly correspond to first-grade material. Story lines become gradually more complex, with more words and longer sentences used. Vocabulary becomes progressively more challenging, and inflectional endings such as *-ed* and *-ing* are common. A full range of punctuation is used, including quotation marks, question marks, commas, and exclamation marks. By Level G, most pages have four to eight lines of print, and sentences are longer. Stories have multiple events and characters, new vocabulary is introduced, and the words rather than the illustrations carry the story line.

Levels I through M roughly correspond to second-grade material. There is considerable overlap between typical second-grade and third-grade reading, and Levels M through P roughly correspond to third-grade reading. At these levels texts are longer, with more sentences per page and unusual or challenging vocabulary appearing. Genres include realistic fiction, informational nonfiction, folktales, and fantasy. Some books at these levels are beginning chapter books that allow readers to read longer selections and sustain interest and comprehension through longer texts. Stories have multiple characters and episodes, there may be fewer illustrations, and there are more abstract concepts and themes presented.

Levels P through Z represent typical material for fourth through sixth grades. As readers progress to higher levels, they find the texts are gradually becoming longer, more complex, more challenging to read and understand, and much less dependent on illustrations. By Level P, many books no longer have illustrations at all. Literary language, figurative language, literary devices (such as flashbacks), and dialogue become more challenging; topics are more specialized; and themes and ideas are more mature. Figure 6.17 shows the typical text gradient of guided reading levels by grade level. Many publishers of trade books for classroom and library use now list the guided reading level for many of their titles in their catalogs. Fountas and Pinnell also list hundreds of titles by level in their books on guided reading: *Guided Reading: Good First Teaching for All*

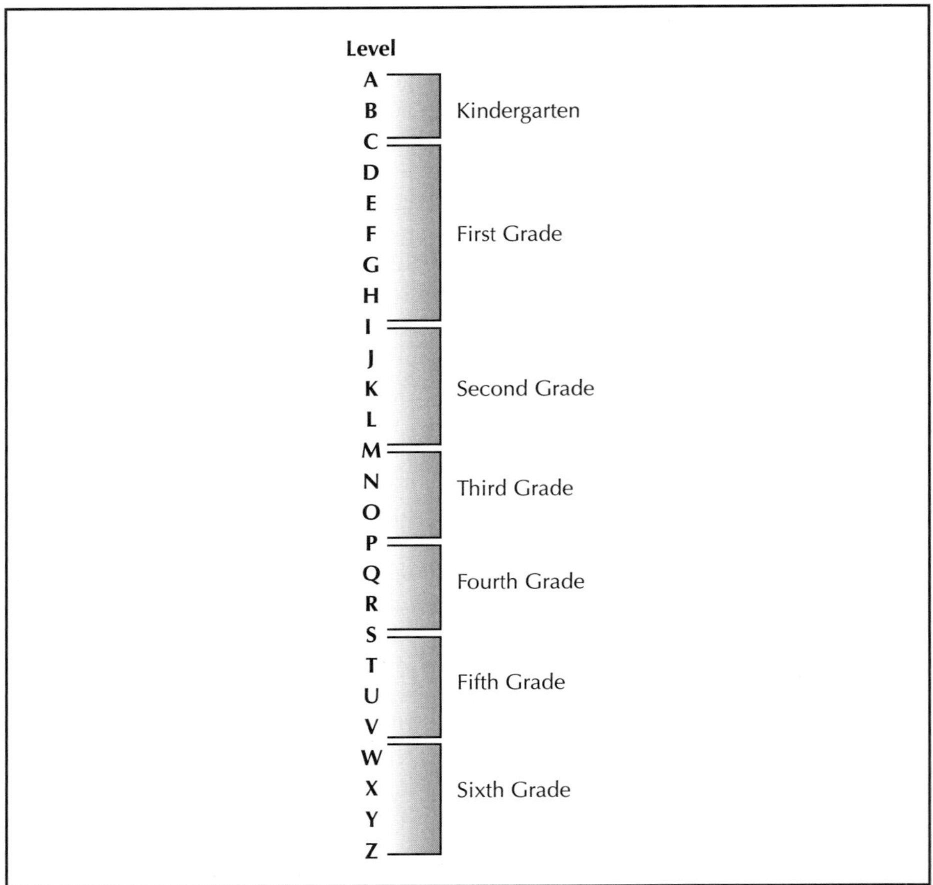

FIGURE 6.17 *Text Gradient for Guided Reading Levels*

Source: Adapted from Fountas and Pinnell (1996, 1999, 2001).

Children (1996), *Matching Books to Readers: Using Leveled Books in Guided Reading, Grades K–3* (1999), and *Guiding Readers and Writers Grades 3–6: Teaching Comprehension, Genre, and Content Literacy* (2001). Finally, many teachers level their own books, following guidelines suggested by Fountas and Pinnell (1996) for establishing grade level and reader expectations.

Readability Estimates

Teachers can also use the publisher's estimate of the text's readability, often shown on the back or front cover. Readability estimates are determined by using arithmetic readability formulas, and are expressed as decimal numbers showing the estimated grade level of difficulty in years and months. A reading level, or RL, of 4.0, for example, is read as fourth grade, no months, or the beginning of fourth grade; a reading level of 4.5 is read as the fourth grade plus five months, or about mid-fourth grade. Above sixth grade, readability levels may simply be expressed as MS, or middle school, HS, or high school, or YA, or young adult (usually middle to older teens). Conversely, materials for beginning readers may be marked P, or primer, or Beginning Reader, or the like.

Difficulty of text is considered to be a function of word and sentence length, rather than of the information conveyed. The assumption behind readability formulas is that easy-to-read texts have short words and many short sentences, whereas harder-to-read texts have many longer words and fewer, longer sentences. Many school media specialists have simple computer programs that compute the readability level of texts using several comparable formulas when three 100-word samples are typed in. It is also possible, although cumbersome, to compute these levels by hand using readability formula charts. Following is an example of a widely used device.

The Fry Readability Chart

1. Select three 100-word samples, one each from the beginning, the middle, and the end of the passage or book. Count proper nouns, dates (1776), numerals (5,380), number words (5th), acronyms (NATO), and symbols (+, &) as single words. Mark the text after the 100th word.
2. Count the **number of sentences** in each 100-word sample, estimating to the nearest tenth of a sentence in the case of an incomplete sentence at the end of a passage. Average these three numbers by adding them and dividing by 3.
3. Count the total **number of syllables** in each 100-word passage. Do so by reading the words *aloud;* there is a vowel sound in each syllable of a word. Do not be misled by how a word looks; *idle* is short but has two syllables, but *through* is long and has only one. For dates, acronyms, symbols, and the like, count each *character* as a syllable; 1918 has four, GNP has three, and = has one. Average the number of syllables by adding them and then dividing by 3 as above.
4. Plot on the graph shown in Figure 6.18 the location of the average number of syllables and the average number of sentences. Most will occur near the heavy curved line on the graph. The perpendicular lines show the approximate grade-level areas. If the syllable and sentence averages fall outside or at the extremes of a grade-level band, check your arithmetic for error and, if necessary, recalculate using three new samples.

Lexiles. Another determiner of the difficulty or readability of texts is a measure called a *Lexile.* A Lexile is a number assigned to a text that indicates the difficulty of the text based on sentence length and word frequency. The Lexile system was developed in the late 1980s using sophisticated statistical procedures that measure the average length and complexity of sentences and the familiarity, or frequency of occurrence, of each word (Chall & Dale, 1995). Instead of yielding a grade-level equivalent, Lexile measures yield a number on a scale from 200 to 1700. A Lexile of 200 corresponds to the simplest

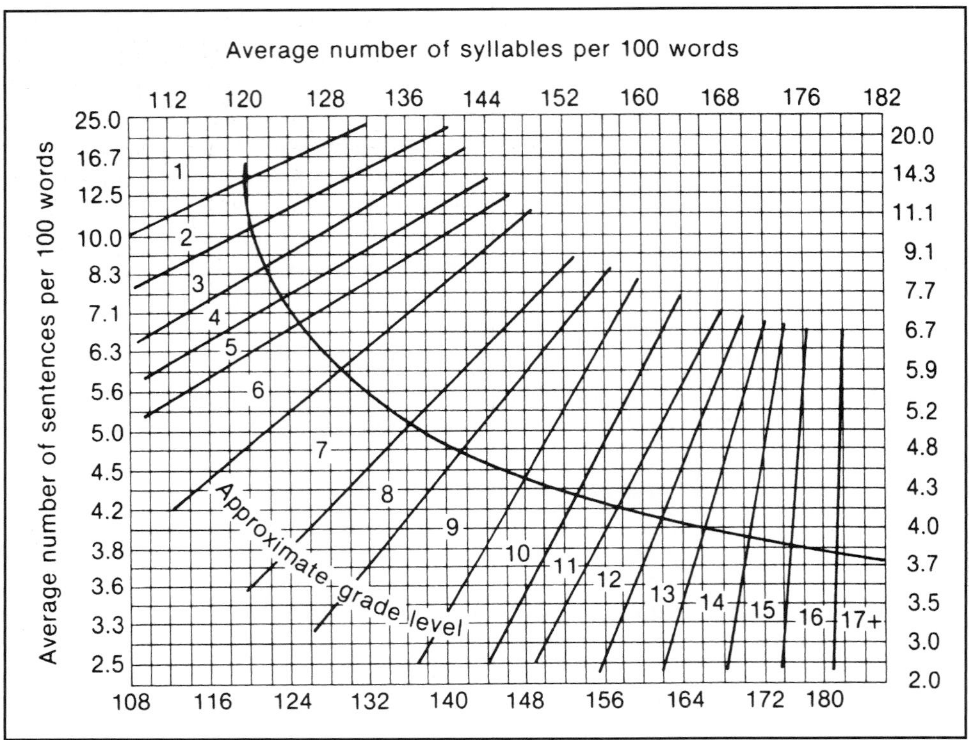

FIGURE 6.18 *Fry's Graph for Estimating Readability—Extended*

Source: Fry, Edward, "Fry's Graph for Estimating Readability," Elementary Reading Instruction, The McGraw-Hill Companies, 1977. Reproduced with permission of The McGraw-Hill Companies.

primer-level materials, while a Lexile of 1700 represents the most challenging technical text one might encounter in graduate school. Figure 6.19 shows how Lexile levels correspond to grade-level equivalents.

An additional feature of Lexile measurement is that Lexiles also represent a student's reading comprehension level. Thus, both a book and a reader have a Lexile. The same scores are used to measure the difficulty of texts and the reading ability of readers, which allows teachers to closely match readers with texts they can read comfortably and successfully. This practice of matching students to texts based on Lexile measures is referred to as *targeting:* that is, matching readers with books that are appropriately challenging, that match readers' interests and reading purposes, and that have a high probability of being read with good comprehension and enjoyment (Stenner, 2001). When students read material at or near their Lexile level, we can expect them to read with about 75 percent comprehension. If they read materials that are 250 or more Lexiles below their level, their comprehension increases to about 90 percent or better. But if they read materials that are about 250 Lexiles above their current level, comprehension drops to about 50 percent. Thus, by knowing both a reader's Lexile and that of various

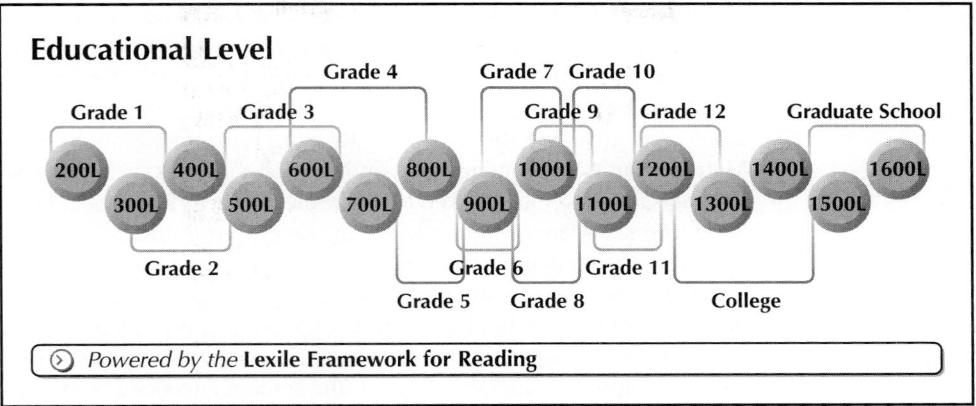

FIGURE 6.19 *The Lexile Framework*

Source: Reprinted from Scholastic Reading Counts! Website by written permission of Scholastic, Inc.

books, we can aim readers toward materials they can read successfully, comfortably, and confidently (Stenner & Wright, 2002).

Like other readability measures, the Lexile measure uses sentence length as one of the two criteria for difficulty. Intuitively, we know that longer sentences are harder to read; this may have to do with both sentence complexity and the demands longer sentences place on the reader's short-term memory. But whereas classic readability formulas also measure average word length, the Lexile measure uses the frequency of occurrence of words in print (it matches words in a text against an enormous computer-based dictionary) as an indicator of how common or familiar the words are likely to be to readers.

Many consider Lexiles a better way than grade equivalents of representing both a reader's instructional level and the difficulty of material. Grade equivalents are hard to interpret. What does it mean if we say that a reader is presently reading at, say, a fourth-grade level? If the reader is a fourth grader, the interpretation is that the reader is doing fine. But if the reader is in a higher grade, the interpretation is negative; here's an older student who is able to read like someone only in the fourth grade. Many older students are embarrassed, even angered, by grade-level equivalents. They resist our efforts to get them to read materials at their instructional level because they feel they are too old for such books, even if the topic is interesting and the difficulty level is appropriate.

In contrast, Lexiles sound more objective. Instead of comparing the reader's performance to those of other students, the performance is measured in terms of a scale of text difficulty that is independent of grade-level expectations. We can tell a parent, "Your child is reading at a Lexile level of 600. To read successfully at the next grade level, he needs to increase his Lexile level to about 700. He should be reading at least three hours a week at home in order to make this progress. Here are some books at about a 600 Lexile level that he could read comfortably and successfully." We can tell a student, "Since the beginning of the year, you have increased your Lexile level from 800 to 870. This shows that you're making steady progress in reading. Choosing books with Lexiles between 860 and the low 900s will help you continue to improve. These books might have been too hard for you a few months ago, but you're ready for them now." We can give parents suggested reading lists corresponding to students' Lexile levels, thus giving parents much-needed help in providing books for home reading.

A reader's Lexile measure can be determined in several ways. A number of stand-alone tests including the Scholastic Reading Inventory; Stanford 9 Achievement Test, Metropolitan Achievement Test 8, and various state tests such as the North Carolina End of Grade Test have been linked to the Lexile framework and yield Lexile levels as well as other forms of scores. Informally, we can determine a student's approximate Lexile level by having the student read a page or two from several books with known Lexile levels. If the reading proceeds smoothly and with good comprehension, we infer that the student reads at least at that Lexile level. If the reading is not fluent or the reader does not comprehend the text easily, we try a lower-Lexile text. Usually two or three samples will give us an approximate Lexile level. If the student chooses a book at a comfortable Lexile level and reads it with enjoyment and good comprehension, we have confirmation of our estimate. The key to this procedure is to know the Lexile level of various books. Presently tens of thousands of books have Lexile measures that are available to teachers. Many publishers of trade books provide the Lexile for individual titles in their catalogs.

Cloze Procedures

A cloze procedure is another way of matching readers and texts. First developed in the early 1950s as an instructional alternative to readability formulas (Taylor, 1953), a cloze procedure shows how well students can read a particular text or selection by having them supply words that are systematically deleted from the text. The result is an estimate of whether an individual, group, or class is likely to find the material too easy, comfortable, or too hard. Teachers have used cloze procedures for decades to select materials and plan instruction because cloze assessment is authentic, requiring readers to read and make sense of real text, and because passages are easy to devise and score. They are often used when teachers are evaluating textbooks, supplemental materials, or classroom magazines for purchase, or forming groups for differential instruction. Figure 6.20 shows part of a cloze passage developed for a reading class.

Constructing a Cloze Passage

1. Choose a text selection of about 275 to 300 words that students have not read.
2. Leave the first sentence intact (or the first two sentences, if the first sentence is very short). Randomly select one of the first five words in the next sentence and delete every fifth word thereafter, replacing it with a blank. Make each blank the same size. If a word to be deleted is a proper noun, skip it and delete the next word.
3. Continue in this fashion until you have 50 blanks. Finish the sentence in which the 50th deletion occurs and include one more intact sentence. Make a separate answer sheet or have students write answers directly on the passage.

Administering a Cloze Passage

1. Show students how to complete a cloze passage, using example sentences or short paragraphs. Encourage them to use what they already know as well as language

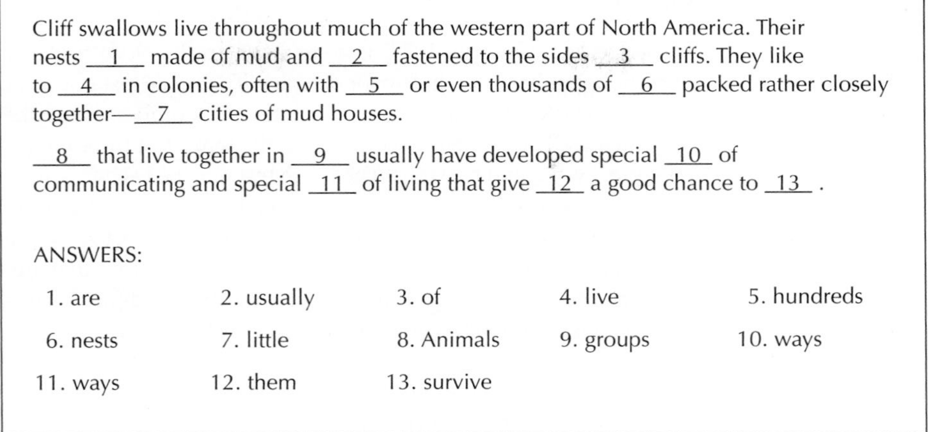

Cliff swallows live throughout much of the western part of North America. Their nests __1__ made of mud and __2__ fastened to the sides __3__ cliffs. They like to __4__ in colonies, often with __5__ or even thousands of __6__ packed rather closely together—__7__ cities of mud houses.

__8__ that live together in __9__ usually have developed special __10__ of communicating and special __11__ of living that give __12__ a good chance to __13__ .

ANSWERS:

1. are	2. usually	3. of	4. live	5. hundreds
6. nests	7. little	8. Animals	9. groups	10. ways
11. ways	12. them	13. survive		

FIGURE 6.20 *Portion of a Cloze Passage*

in the passage to try to figure out the *exact word* that belongs in each blank. Some classes or groups may need extended practice before doing the "real thing."

2. Explain that no one will get every word correct, and that getting about half of the words right is a good score. If they don't know this in advance, students can get very anxious and some might give up in frustration.
3. Allow as much time as needed to complete the passage individually without rushing. This is not a timed exercise.

Scoring and Interpreting a Cloze

1. Count as correct every *exact* word from the text, even if it is misspelled. Don't count synonyms, even if they make sense. Doing so will affect the score criteria, which were developed using exact replacements only. Also, students will argue endlessly about what is "close enough."
2. Multiply the total number of correct replacements by 2 to determine each student's score on the 50-item passage.
3. Create three lists:
   - Students whose score was *above 60 percent correct.* The material is at or close to their *independent* reading level. They can probably use this material without guidance or support.
   - Students whose score was *between 40 and 60 percent correct.* The material probably represents their *instructional* reading level. They can read it most effectively if they are given support and guidance such as visual organizers, study guides, or directed discussion.
   - Students whose score was *below 40 percent correct.* The material is likely at their *frustration* level and is too difficult for them to read. More suitable material should be found for them. If they are required to read that material, they will need extensive support and guidance such as listening to the material read aloud and direct experience with the topic.

Maze Tests

The maze test (Guthrie, 1974) is a variation on the cloze test that is gaining popularity, even though it has been in use for decades. The maze test is a sort of cloze procedure that leaves out every Nth word (where N is a random number, usually between five and seven). But instead of leaving the space blank, in the maze test three choices of words are given—the correct word and two foils. The maze test may be less stressful for the student than the cloze test. Some students may be frustrated by the fact that it is virtually impossible to get a perfect score on a cloze test, but on a maze test a perfect score is possible. The drawback to the maze test is that different test writers may write foils that are more or less obviously incorrect, thus introducing some unreliability into the difficulty level of the test.

To construct a maze test, follow these instructions.

1. Find a passage of about 220 words.
2. Leave the first sentence intact.
3. Then go through and underline every fifth word until you have underlined ten words.
4. Then leave one more sentence intact.
5. For each underlined word, add two foils, and scramble the order of the three choices.
6. Each word choice will be worth ten points out of a possible score of 100.

Longer passages will yield more reliable scores, so for older students, you may use a passage of 450 words, and put in 20 choice words.

For older students, a maze test is available online from the Aimsweb program. Aimsweb's maze tests offer choices of every seventh word. Their passages range between 300 and 400 words in length. (See http://www.aimsweb.com/measures-2/maze-cbm/.)

See Figure 6.21 for a sample maze test based on the same passage used in the cloze test in Figure 6.20.

A Portion of a Maze Test

Instructions: Circle the word from each set of three that makes the most sense.

Cliff swallows live throughout much of the Western part of North America. Their nests (run, are, bird) made of mud and (into, very, usually) fastened to the sides (into, of, dirt) cliffs. They like to (forget, mile, live) in colonies, often with (hundreds, never, not) or even thousands of (rot, nests, rocks) packed rather closely together–(people, softly, little) cities of mud houses.

(Cheerful, Animals, Even) that live together in (groups, seas, terrible) usually have developed special (food, calling, ways) of communicating and special (each, ways, friends) of living that give (eagles, owners, them) a good chance to (sell, survive, often).

FIGURE 6.21 *A Portion of a Maze Test*

Student Portfolios

A *portfolio* is a collection of materials that demonstrates how each student is progressing in learning content, mastering operations, broadening and refining tastes and interests, and moving toward more mature or complex developmental stages. Portfolios represent *authentic assessment*, or analyzing how students demonstrate learning by performing meaningful, purposeful real-life tasks (Ediger, 2003; McCormick, 2003).

Students and teachers systematically collect representative samples of work over time and reflect on what the samples show about the students' achievement, goals, and capabilities. Portfolios can be used with any grade level and subject to showcase achievement, document progress over time, demonstrate effort, and foster students' decision making, self-evaluation, and reflection (Cohen, 2006; Gipe, 2003; Jasmine, 1992; McMahan & Gifford, 2001).

Showcasing Achievement

One purpose of portfolios is to showcase one's best work. Students might choose work that they believe represents the pinnacle of their achievement in one or more curricular areas. The emphasis is on products, rather than processes. For example, a student may select his best spelling papers, perfect math tests, or best pieces of writing. Another way students can think about their best work is to consider pieces that they feel particularly proud of. These pieces might not necessarily have received the highest grades, but they represent results students are especially pleased with. For example, in selecting work for a math portfolio, a sixth grader included several pages of algebra problems that were not all solved correctly. She explained that she was proud that her teacher had included her in an advanced group that was studying beginning algebra, even though the work was not easy for her.

Documenting Progress

Another purpose of portfolios is to show progress in a particular subject area, skill, or process. For this purpose, students choose work samples that show increasing complexity, mastery, or difficulty (McMahan & Gifford, 2001). For example, a student might select first drafts of original stories at monthly intervals, dated spelling tests showing mastery of increasingly difficult patterns, or math worksheets moving from simple to complex computations. Such examples are particularly useful for communicating with both students and parents about students' developmental progress.

Demonstrating Effort

Another useful purpose is to demonstrate areas or processes in which the student might not excel but is putting forth considerable effort. For example, reluctant writers might feel discouraged about the amount of writing they can produce, but they might be surprised to see that over time their written pieces are growing longer and more readable. Likewise, a writer might choose to include a composition that represents a great deal of work, even though the final product was not outstanding. Or a student who rarely persists long enough to finish a project might be encouraged to select work that demonstrates perseverance and completion.

Fostering Self-Evaluation and Reflection

Another important function of portfolios is to help students develop the objectivity to step back from their own work, reflect on its quality and importance to them, and evaluate their own strengths and abilities (Galley, 2000). When students do this, they move toward becoming independent learners, able to rely on their own judgments rather than being bound by what teachers or peers think of their work. This is particularly valuable for adolescents, who can be devastated by peers' harsh judgments. Self-evaluation helps students to value their own instincts and judgments and retain self-respect even when others don't value their work. It also enables students to feel ownership of and responsibility for their work (Hansen, 1994, 1996; Temple, Ogle, Crawford, & Freppon, 2011).

Kinds of Portfolios

Before you can determine what will go into students' portfolios, you must decide the purpose for keeping them. The content of a portfolio depends on

- The intended audience.
- The purpose for developing a portfolio.

A simple *collection portfolio* contains a wide variety of work because its purpose is to form a pool of materials. From it, certain pieces or samples may be drawn for other purposes, such as to create another kind of portfolio, demonstrate growth in different areas, or familiarize students with the fundamentals of portfolio collection. Its audience is the teacher and student. This kind of portfolio is sometimes referred to as a *work folder* or *drop file* and is widely used in many classrooms, even where teachers don't think they are using portfolios.

A *showcase* or *display portfolio* contains examples of the student's best work, chosen specifically to show growth and achievement in a particular subject area in which the student excels, such as math, art, or writing. Its purpose is to display the depth and breadth of the student's talents. The audience is the student, teacher, parents, and others whom the student wants to impress, such as college admissions officers, competition judges, or leaders of selective programs. Showcase portfolios are fairly common in high schools and in programs for gifted and talented students.

The *progress* or *assessment portfolio* is the most familiar type of student portfolio. This portfolio contains examples of the student's best work and work that shows marked growth, as does the showcase portfolio. However, it also contains selected work in progress, work that represents significant effort even if the product is not extraordinary, and copies of relevant assessment devices. These may include chapter and unit tests, standardized achievement tests, interest and attitude inventories, developmental checklists, lists of achievement benchmarks, lists of books read, running records of oral reading, videotapes and/or audiotapes, students' goal statements and written self-evaluations, teachers' evaluations and anecdotal records, notes on student-teacher portfolio conferences, and parent comment sheets. The purpose of an assessment or progress portfolio is to demonstrate progress, achievement, and effort. Its audience is the student, teacher, and parents.

What Goes into a Portfolio?

Here is a list of possible inclusions in a reading-writing portfolio. Some items listed may not be available or are not used in your classroom or school; some items you consider important may not be listed. Adapt it to fit your purposes and students.

- ***Baseline or Beginning Samples.*** These are the students' earliest samples of work in any area, such as reading journal entries, running records, recordings of oral reading, and first writings. These are collected to establish a baseline with which to compare later work.
- ***Reading Journal Entries.*** Reading journals, also known as *reading response logs* and *literature logs,* are notebooks that students use to record their responses to what they are currently reading. Simple summaries should give way to more thoughtful responses such as character studies, opinions about the characters' actions, and so forth. Reading journal entries can be collected quarterly, monthly, or at other intervals to show growth in critical thinking and types of literature selected.
- ***Learning Log Entries.*** Like reading journals, learning logs are often used to have students respond in writing to topics in science, math, and social studies. For example, students may write their thoughts or opinions about subject-area topics like pollution, rain forest preservation, or the dangers of smoking; describe the steps to be followed in solving a math problem; or summarize the new information they learned from a reading assignment, discussion, or demonstration. Periodic sampling from the learning log helps develop a picture of the student's growth in thinking, writing clarity, and subject-matter knowledge.
- ***Writing Samples.*** A common component of elementary portfolios is the sampling of students' writing at periodic intervals. Earlier writings can be contrasted with later efforts to show growth in any or all of the writing areas: use of prewriting strategies, development of early and later drafts, use of strategies to clarify and extend content, sentence formation, standard English usage and grammar, spelling, punctuation, and so forth. In addition to selecting pieces from different times of the year, students should be guided to select pieces written for different purposes and audiences: original stories, retellings of familiar stories, nonfiction or expository writing, persuasive pieces, letters, poetry, and so forth. At least twice a year, they should choose pieces that illustrate the steps in the writing process, from

prewriting through successive revised drafts to editing, polishing, and sharing of the completed piece. In doing so, students and parents can observe the process of composing as well as the final product, the various ways writing is used in everyday life, and their growth in many areas.

- ***Records of Oral Reading.*** Many teachers use periodic running records to determine the accuracy and fluency of students' oral reading and their use of decoding, syntax, and context strategies to identify unfamiliar words as they progress to more challenging reading levels. Teachers use a system of conventional marks to record what a reader says while reading a portion of text aloud at a comfortable level of difficulty. Recordings of the student reading aloud at timely intervals may also be included, as they graphically demonstrate to the student and parents how the student's oral reading fluency and accuracy are progressing.
- ***Lists of Books Read.*** Each student should keep a list of books read in and out of school, noting the title, author, number of pages read, genre, and beginning and ending dates. At intervals such as quarterly or at the end of a grading period, students can evaluate their reading habits in a number of ways. They can graph the number of books read each month or quarter, or the amount of time they spend reading. They can evaluate whether they are developing balance in their reading habits by selecting various genres or authors and set appropriate goals for the next period. Lists of books read help students, parents, and teachers see what and how much students are reading and whether they are developing wide reading habits.
- ***Text Samples with Written Responses.*** Periodically, students can choose a current or recently completed book and photocopy a page or two to illustrate the types and difficulty of text they are reading. This makes a good accompaniment to the list of books read, which might not convey much to parents if the books are unfamiliar to them. Students should include a written rationale for their choices, a response to an open-ended question about the text, a summary or critique of the book up to that point, or other written commentary.
- ***Recordings of Oral Presentations.*** Recordings are useful for capturing students' story retellings, oral reports, and book talks as well as oral readings. They are an excellent way of documenting students' growth in oral language use, fluency, vocabulary development, and sentence structure.
- ***Video.*** Video is invaluable in offering students a chance to observe and evaluate their reading, speaking, and listening skills. It also offers parents and others a unique opportunity to see students in classroom situations they would otherwise miss and provides a way to include three-dimensional projects in portfolios that otherwise could not be included. Video can be used to record drama activities such as improvisations, reader's theater, skits and plays, presentation of projects and research, book talks and read-aloud activities, poetry readings, dramatic choral readings, debates, panel discussions, and so forth.
- ***Photographs.*** Although they are less compelling than video, photographs are simpler and less expensive to use while still offering a way to capture students' projects, plays, and other strictly visual work. Photographs can be useful in documenting learning activities like plays, skits, artwork, science projects, animal care, and constructions.

- ***Conference and Student Self-Evaluation Records.*** These include forms used to document when the student and teacher met to discuss the portfolio and students' written reflections on their progress and achievements. These inclusions document students' ability to reflect on their strengths, make decisions, set goals, and work toward achieving them.
- ***Assessments.*** These may include results of standardized tests, classroom tests, Informal Reading Inventories, interest inventories, anecdotal records, skills or benchmark checklists, and so forth. These document student achievement and progress that may be mandated by the school or district and are more informative to teachers and parents than to students. Some teachers prefer to keep assessments in private folders that are separate from students' daily work, shared with parents at conferences, and transferred with portfolios to the next grade at the end of the year.

These inclusions are summarized in Box 6.3.

BOX 6.3

Possible Inclusions in Reading-Writing Portfolios

Baseline or entry writing samples, running records, reading inventories, other assessments
Interest inventories
Lists of books read
Book reports or reviews
Book summaries
Reading response journal entries
Running records of oral reading
Literature logs
Character studies
Personal journal entries
Original creative writing: stories, poetry, plays, etc.
Successive drafts of work showing the writing process
Subject area reports and projects
Photographs, audiotapes, and/or videotapes of student work
Teacher-student conference records
Student self-evaluations and goal statements
Parent review and comment forms
Records of extracurricular achievements

Organizing a Portfolio Program

Most teachers already have some system of keeping track of students' work, such as work folders into which students keep current work to collect and send home, a drop file in which graded student work is kept for displays and parent conferences, or even a bulletin board of excellent work.

The first thing you will need to decide is how comprehensive your portfolios should be. What subject areas or skills do you want to document in this way? If you have never used portfolios before, it may be best to keep things simple at first. You might decide to choose one particular area, such as reading, writing, or math, and include only materials related to that area at first. Whether you choose to include one subject area, several, or all areas, avoid trying to do too much at once. If students are new to the portfolio process, it is easier to start simply and add complexity than to have to cut back or streamline later.

At the beginning, you will need to organize storage materials and communicate what you are doing with students and their families (Cohen, 2006). You should also inform your administrator that you are trying a new way of documenting student progress that will supplement your classroom grades, standardized test scores, and other numerical data.

First, each student needs a sturdy folder. Many teachers use cardboard folders with pockets or expanding file folders that can hold a lot. Regular open-sided file folders can't hold very much, and papers begin to spill out. Also, they are not useful for storing nonpaper materials, such as artwork, recordings of oral reading, and so forth. Students can decorate or otherwise make their folders unique.

Next, find an accessible place for portfolio storage. Plastic milk crate boxes, plastic storage tubs, or even a cut-down cardboard box can house the folders, as long as it is easily accessible to students. File cabinets can be dangerous as they can tip over if students lean on an open drawer while looking for their folders.

In classrooms in which teachers have job charts or rotating duties, a new job may be added: portfolio helper, who makes sure the portfolios are neatly stored in alphabetical order at the end of the day. For students who may not have mastered alphabetical order, each student can be assigned a number and folders arranged in order. Checking folder order daily reinforces alphabetical and numerical ordering, and each student will get this practice in turn.

Next, prepare a letter to parents explaining that students will collect much of their work in a special folder to document what they are doing and how they are progressing. Explain that students will be asked to share the responsibility for choosing what work goes into their portfolios, and that such choices require students to consider what may be their best work, their most challenging work, work of which they are most proud, and so forth. Invite parents to view the collected work at conferences, at open houses, and during visits to the classroom. Figures 6.22 and 6.23 are sample parent letters for primary and middle grades.

Next, explain to students what they will be doing. If possible, have another teacher who already uses portfolios come to your room, perhaps with a few of her students, to

Dear Parent or Guardian,

Welcome to the new school year! Our classroom will be an exciting place to grow and learn this year.

This year students will keep portfolios of their work in several subjects. It will be easy for students, other teachers, and you to see how your student is progressing. Students and I will work together to choose work to be included and to evaluate the work.

I will explain more about student portfolios, and show you some examples, at Back-to-School Night. If you would like to know more before then, please call me at school or stop by our classroom. We would love to show you our work!

Sincerely,

FIGURE 6.22 *Sample Parent Letter, Primary Grades*

show what portfolios look like and why students keep them. Or borrow a few portfolios from another classroom—with students' permission—to demonstrate. Explain that many professionals, such as artists, photographers, actors, and models, compile portfolios that visually represent their experience and achievements and that the students' portfolios will likewise show their talents and progress. Pass out the empty portfolios

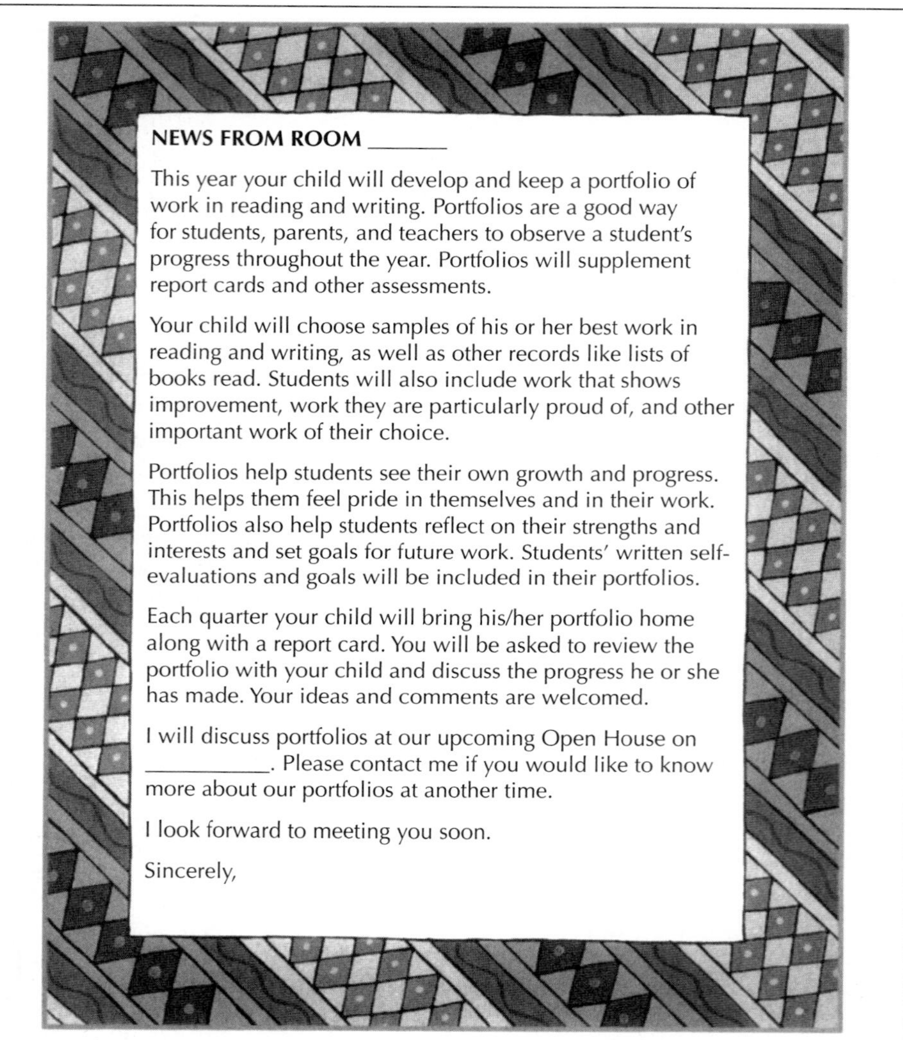

NEWS FROM ROOM ______

This year your child will develop and keep a portfolio of work in reading and writing. Portfolios are a good way for students, parents, and teachers to observe a student's progress throughout the year. Portfolios will supplement report cards and other assessments.

Your child will choose samples of his or her best work in reading and writing, as well as other records like lists of books read. Students will also include work that shows improvement, work they are particularly proud of, and other important work of their choice.

Portfolios help students see their own growth and progress. This helps them feel pride in themselves and in their work. Portfolios also help students reflect on their strengths and interests and set goals for future work. Students' written self-evaluations and goals will be included in their portfolios.

Each quarter your child will bring his/her portfolio home along with a report card. You will be asked to review the portfolio with your child and discuss the progress he or she has made. Your ideas and comments are welcomed.

I will discuss portfolios at our upcoming Open House on __________. Please contact me if you would like to know more about our portfolios at another time.

I look forward to meeting you soon.

Sincerely,

FIGURE 6.23 *Sample Parent Letter, Middle Grades*

for personalization, show how they are to be stored, and perhaps ask students to find one or more current pieces of work to be included.

All work should be dated. Dating all work helps students see their progress across time, as well as how long a particular project took. Many teachers use rubber stamps for this purpose. Office-type date stamps work well and look very official. Some use different stamps to indicate the stage of some written work: "1st Draft," "Revised," "To Be Edited," and "Completed" are useful categories, with space for the student to write in the date.

Finally, an overall plan for reviewing portfolios, selecting work, and reflecting on it should be developed. Work may be reviewed and selected monthly, quarterly, or at the end of each report card period, depending on the grade level, subject area, type of work being done, and other defining characteristics of the class. For example, young students might benefit from more frequent reviews; important work that takes a long time to complete, like research reports, projects, and ambitious writing efforts need fairly long intervals between reviews; and students with low self-esteem may need frequent reviews to feel successful.

Let's say, for example, that you decide to have your third-grade class select work in reading and writing on a monthly basis. You have reviewed the list of possible inclusions found in the previous section and posted a list of the things students will be selecting to include. You have sent a letter home informing parents, introduced your class to the concept and purpose of portfolios, had students personalize folders, and taught them how portfolios are to be stored, ordered, and retrieved.

The first entries in portfolios will be the baseline samples referred to in the previous section. In each area, have students collect their first pieces of work: for example, their initial writing samples, reading journal entries, reading response log entries, and first recorded oral readings. (If students use composition books for reading response logs and learning logs, as most do, they will include dated photocopies of their first entries.) In the first weeks you will add each student's first running records, Informal Reading Inventory, interest inventory, skills checklist, and so forth.

One way to organize the baseline samples is to have each student use a construction paper pocket or mini-folder, a 12-inch X 18-inch sheet of construction paper folded in half and stapled on the sides with the date or month on the front. This keeps all the baseline samples together. Another way is to separate the samples into areas (such as reading, writing, and assessments), place them in separate mini-folders, and add related samples to them later.

Now, at monthly intervals, you will plan for students to review their current work, select samples to add to their portfolios, and compare earlier and later work. Using the same organizational scheme, students may collect all of that month's samples in a mini-folder of a different color, dating the front, or they may add later samples to the separate mini-folders they are keeping for each subject area. Whatever organizational scheme you use, remind students to date everything and to refrain from including items in their portfolios with the intention of organizing it later. Portfolios can quickly become chaotic! Allow time for your "organizationally challenged" students to sort and arrange their portfolios frequently.

Along with the selection of work, students will engage in self-evaluation, goal setting, and portfolio conferences with the teacher. Evaluation and conferring with students and parents are discussed in sections to follow.

Primary Grades. Primary graders' portfolios will necessarily be simpler than those of older students. A simple drop file, into which students drop all of their current work in the chosen subject, works well. At regular intervals, say, once each week, time should be set aside for students to look at everything in their folders, choose particular pieces on the basis of some general criteria, and remove other pieces. The pieces that are removed can be sent home immediately.

For example, a first-grade teacher using portfolios for the first time set aside time on Friday afternoon for portfolio review. Students were to look at everything in their folders and set aside several work samples:

- Their best writing done that week
- Something they had worked very hard on
- Something they were very proud of

Other work was put into large, sturdy envelopes to take home that afternoon. Parents were to review the work, sign the empty envelope, and return it to school on Monday. Work that was selected to be included in portfolios was briefly shared and discussed either with the whole class, a small group, or a friend or with the teacher in a brief portfolio conference. Here is an example of part of a quick whole-group sharing:

Teacher: As we go around the circle, hold up one piece you chose and tell us why you chose it. Amanda, will you begin?

Amanda: I chose this story about my dog because I think it's a good story and because I drew a picture of my dog on the back.

Bruce: I chose my word study test because I got all the words right.

Middle and Upper Grades. Older students can take more responsibility for selecting work to be included, keeping some of their own records, and responding thoughtfully to their own work and effort. They can also arrive at more sophisticated judgments about how their work is changing and how they are progressing (Graves & Sunstein, 1992; Paris, 2001). If students are inexperienced in keeping portfolios, they will need a hands-on demonstration of what portfolios are, just as younger students do. Again, bringing in samples can be very helpful. At one middle school, the art teachers visit each language arts class to show their own and others' professional art portfolios. They explain how artists use portfolios to visually demonstrate their talents and invite students to draw comparisons between an artist's portfolio and a student's language arts portfolio. Students from other classes can also share their portfolios and their part in the evaluation process.

If portfolios are to follow students from one grade to the next, a selection of the previous year's portfolios can be studied. On the other hand, if portfolios are routinely returned to students at the end of the year, other teachers might have a few that they kept as samples from students who moved out of the district or for other reasons.

Teachers who are new to the portfolio process might make a note to keep one or two portfolios for this purpose, perhaps photocopying the contents at year's end so the students can keep theirs. Another way is to build a sample portfolio by photocopying exemplary pieces from a variety of students' work. Protect students' privacy by securing permission from them and by removing names from photocopied work.

Evaluating Portfolios

Portfolios are more than a way to document progress. They are also an effective way of helping students become reflective and self-evaluative. After your baseline samples have been selected, begin teaching students how to self-evaluate and set goals for themselves. After they master these processes, they will use them each time they select new material to be included in their portfolios. Students of all ages, even the youngest, can learn to evaluate their own work and set goals for themselves (Galley, 2000).

Teaching Self-Evaluation. Teach students to self-evaluate the same way you would teach any new operation: by defining what students are to do, modeling the operation for them, having them practice the operation in small groups and discuss what they did, and having them practice the operation individually. This is the basic scaffold for teaching self-evaluation in any subject area.

Let's say, for example, that you want students to practice self-evaluating their writing. You would define the criteria for evaluating a composition by listing with students the things that make writing effective; these would include the writing skills that are appropriate for your grade. With the whole group, compare a sample you made up or one from a previous year with the listed criteria and note its strengths. This whole-group modeling may be repeated with other samples until students are comfortable with it.

In another lesson, present small groups with a composition similar to the one you used for your demonstration. Have each group use the criteria chart to write an evaluation stating the strengths of the sample. (Young students can share their findings orally.) Repeat as necessary, changing the composition of each group so that students work with a variety of peers. When they are able to do this easily in small groups, they can work individually on a sample you provide. Or they can apply what they have learned in an individual evaluation of a current composition of their own. For their first time doing this individually, baseline samples are fine. Self-evaluation cards like those shown in Figure 6.24 can be used to begin the process of student self-evaluation.

Students can also learn to self-evaluate their selections of other kinds of work. After they have learned how to self-evaluate their writing samples, they can practice the same process using selections from their reading response journals and learning logs, selections of content-area work, and so forth. You might need to reteach the process for each different kind of portfolio selection, or your students might need only to review the procedure described above and develop criteria charts for good work in each area.

For example, criteria for effective literature responses might include writing the date, title, author, and copyright date; describing a character and the reasons for certain actions; explaining a conflict and its resolution; discussing the author's writing style or use of dialogue, narration, and so forth; and using correct writing mechanics. Criteria for effective learning log entries might include writing the date and subject area, writing the question or issue being responded to, using correct sentence structure and mechanics, and including drawings or diagrams to illustrate the entry. Criteria for effective research might include selecting a topic of interest to the researcher, using various sources of information, taking notes, creating an outline, organizing information, and producing an edited final draft.

Student Self-Evaluation Card

Name Steve Date

Think About: Why did I choose this piece?

My Self-Evaluation This is my best poem. I used good words and made word pictures. I read it to my friends.

Student Self-Evaluation Card

Name Irma Date

Think About: How does this report compare to your first one?

My Self-Evaluation I put in lots more information. I used more books and I used two encyclopedias. My spelling was better too.

FIGURE 6.24 *Student Self-Evaluation Cards*

Criteria charts should be developed with students and displayed for them to refer to when they are evaluating their portfolio selections. As time passes, the charts can be updated and additional criteria can be added. As students become more proficient at self-evaluation, they will begin to internalize the criteria for good work, and will have less need for charts and prompts.

Teaching Goal Setting. After students have practiced self-evaluation and are comfortable finding their own strengths, they are ready to begin setting goals by finding areas for improvement. Self-evaluation helps students see the positives and feel pride in their work. Goal setting helps them strive toward greater challenge, growth, and mastery. The criteria charts for effective work are used again, this time to find things that students need to continue practicing.

Goals should be realistic and specific. You might list some hypothetical needs, followed by examples of goal statements that are either vague or unrealistic.

Consider the example of a student who doesn't read very much. A goal for him might be to read more. "I will read more," however, is too vague, while "I will read 100 pages every day" is unrealistic. Students can brainstorm better goals for this example: "I will read for 20 minutes every night," "I will read five books this month," or "I will finish reading (title) by (date)."

You can then return to the criteria chart developed for a particular area, review how a selection may be evaluated for its strengths, and then extend the lesson by having students brainstorm how it could be improved. As a class or in small groups, have students write specific, reasonable goals as if the piece were their own. Repeat this process until students are able to confidently find strengths, then areas of need, and write one or two meaningful goals for sample selections.

Then have students write goals for improving their own selections. Have volunteers share their initial goals and invite peer feedback, so that students practice writing goals that they really can work toward. Here are some examples of specific, realistic goals:

- "I want to make my stories more interesting by using more colorful words."
- "I will use an outline to help me organize my next report."
- "My goal is to have a punctuation mark at the end of each sentence."

Remind students that working toward one or two goals at a time is enough; trying to master too many things at once can be discouraging, even overwhelming. Reviewing goals and how students are working toward them is discussed in the section entitled "Portfolio Conferences."

Teacher Evaluations. Teachers' evaluations of students' strengths and needs are a fundamental part of the portfolio process. First, these evaluations provide important information about students' abilities and progress. Second, you validate students' efforts, helping them to see their achievement and growth and guiding them to explore new areas and interests. Third, your evaluations help you evaluate and modify your instructional program;

awareness of students' strengths and needs gives direction to instructional change. There are several ways you can use the portfolio process to document students' achievement, progress, and needs (Graves & Sunstein, 1992; Jervis, 1996).

One way is through *portfolio conferences* (see page 262 for a detailed discussion). Your input in these conferences and your records of their content provide crucial documentation of students' progress and effort, their growth in goal setting and decision making, and your attention to individual instruction.

A second important source of teacher evaluations is *anecdotal records.* This term refers to notes teachers make while they are observing students in various classroom situations, sometimes referred to as *kidwatching* (Owocki & Goodman, 2002). Kidwatching includes two perspectives: *involved observations,* which take place while the teacher is actively working with students, and *objective observations,* which take place while students work independently. Anecdotal records are notes kept during kidwatching or shortly thereafter while the observation is fresh in the teacher's mind. They should report, rather than judge or interpret; they are intended to document what students do and say, thus forming an objective record of students' day-to-day operations.

Earlier in this chapter we suggested several ways to keep anecdotal records systematically: using a grid with a square for each student and carrying the clipboard around the room, keeping an index card for each student and making dated entries on each card, using a calendar page with a student's name on each square and recording observations on sticky notes, and so forth. You may want to review Figures 6.13 through 6.16. We also discussed how to organize classroom observations and how to use specific, objective language in recording what you observe.

A third way of incorporating teacher evaluations into portfolios involves traditional *grading.* In a sense, report card grades and portfolios are like oil and vinegar; they share fundamental characteristics but don't mix very well. In salad dressing, oil and vinegar contribute different but compatible flavors to the salad; in student evaluation, traditional grades and portfolio documentation contribute different but compatible information to the portrait of students' progress.

Grades show where students are in comparison to others. When they are compared to their peers, we may think of this as "grading on a curve," or determining where the individual stands in comparison to a distribution with the performance of the lowest and highest students as the boundaries. When students are compared to a set of pre-established criteria, as on a criterion-referenced test or a teacher-made test for which the teacher knows what a "typical" class might do, they are being compared to a hypothetical peer group or to a set of expectations designed to fit a hypothetical group of peers. Either way, students are compared to each other. Portfolios, on the other hand, allow comparison of students to themselves, since earlier and later works by the same student are being compared. Both kinds of comparisons are valid; both communicate to students, parents, and other teachers, and both contribute to each other.

Many teachers believe that work selected to be included in a portfolio should not be graded since the portfolio is intended in large part to be a celebration of the student's unique abilities, achievements, and progress. Instead of assigning a letter grade, such work might be evaluated in narrative form, with comments attached to the work. Since the portfolio is designed to hold only a sampling of a student's work, other similar work can be graded and sent home to parents.

Comments attached to portfolio work samples may vary in length, but should be concise and positive, noting specifically what the student did well and, as necessary, indicating areas for possible further practice. Such evaluations should be done after students have self-evaluated the sample, to avoid influencing what students think of their own work. The student "owns" the portfolio, so comments should be addressed to the student by name and should be written on cards or notes attached to the work, not directly on the work itself.

In the beginning, you may find that writing a comment for each selected sample is time-consuming, but with practice you will find that it takes less time to write more meaningful, less general comments. For one thing, not every work sample needs to be accompanied by a teacher comment. Often students' self-evaluations, plus comments you make about the sample in a conference with the student, are sufficient. Also, a few minutes is not too long for you to spend commenting on work that may have taken the student days or even weeks, to complete. As a general rule, the longer it took the student to complete the work, the more time its evaluation deserves. Samples that were quickly completed, like a worksheet, spelling quiz, or Math Minute, can be evaluated quite quickly: for example, "Look how many more problems you completed this time, Liz!" or "Alex, this sample shows me how hard you've worked on spelling vowel sounds," are sufficient for short assignments. Figure 6.25 shows some sample narrative comments that are more substantive.

Parent Evaluations. Parents' input into their children's portfolios is valuable for several reasons. First, their comments show that they are aware of at least some of the things their children do in the classroom.

Second, parents' comments show whether they understand some of the fundamentals of today's instruction, like the importance of home reading, children's use of invented spelling, and the stages of the writing cycle. Parents' comments can show you where you need to make an explanatory phone call, invite parents in to observe or talk informally, send samples home more often, plan a parent education event, or make other efforts to better inform parents.

Third, parents' comments can give you valuable insight into variables in the children's lives outside of school that may bear on their interests, difficulties, areas of strength, behavior, and motivation. Your awareness of home influences in the child's life helps you teach the whole child.

Fourth, parents' comments can be very validating and encouraging to the student. Parents welcome opportunities to observe their children's progress and development. Portfolios offer the perfect opportunity to inform and involve them. Parents can gain a clearer understanding of their children's strengths and weaknesses from seeing sequential work samples than from test scores or grades. Parents also appreciate that teachers see their children as unique individuals, too. And parents become active participants in their children's education, even if they cannot participate in traditional parent activities like classroom volunteering or parent-teacher organizations.

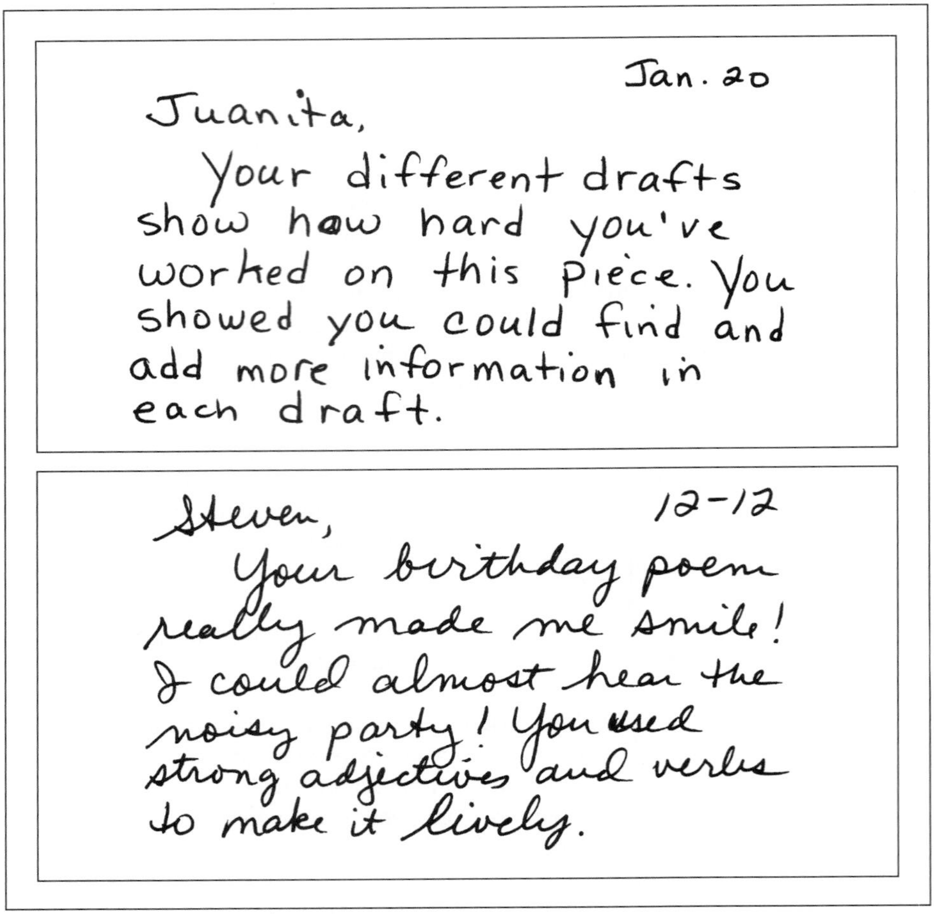

Jan. 20

Juanita,

Your different drafts show how hard you've worked on this piece. You showed you could find and add more information in each draft.

12-12

Steven,

Your birthday poem really made me smile! I could almost hear the noisy party! You used strong adjectives and verbs to make it lively.

FIGURE 6.25 *Sample Teacher Evaluation Comments*

One way parents can contribute to the evaluation process is by completing a *parent response form* to be returned to school with the portfolio or selected samples after review at home. Figure 6.26 shows two samples of this kind of form. They should be kept short and simple, but allow room for parents to write their comments.

Parents should be invited to review their children's portfolios regularly, whether during a scheduled conference, an open house, a classroom event, or a drop-in visit. Questions and concerns can be addressed in conferences or on the phone. You will read more about portfolio conferences with parents in the next section.

Portfolio Conferences. Students' evaluation and goal setting culminate in portfolio conferences. When teachers and students confer, they become collaborators in the

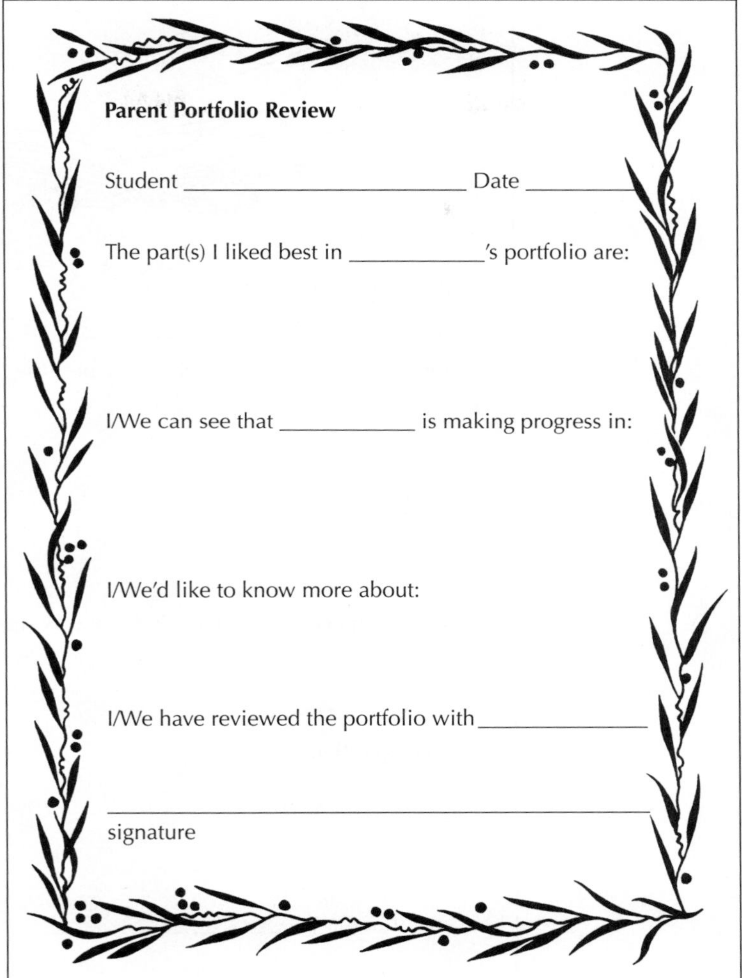

Parent Portfolio Review

Student ______________________ Date ________

The part(s) I liked best in __________'s portfolio are:

I/We can see that __________ is making progress in:

I/We'd like to know more about:

I/We have reviewed the portfolio with ____________

____

signature

FIGURE 6.26 *Two Sample Parent Response Forms*

evaluation process. When students confer with peers about portfolio selections, they give and receive encouragement on their efforts and achievements and gain awareness of their strengths. When students and teachers confer with parents, they can help parents gain a comprehensive view of the student's work and abilities and a better understanding of their child's development.

Teacher-Student Conferences. Formal teacher-student conferences often occur in the later part of the quarter or report card period. However, informal conferences may occur much more often at your discretion. Conferences vary in length depending on the

Parent Response Form

Student ____________________ Date __________

Student comments: I chose this work because . . .

It shows my progress because . . .

Parent comments: I/We think that this work shows . . .

Parent questions:

Parent(s) signature ________________________

FIGURE 6.26 *Continued*

student's age, the portfolio contents, and other factors; however, 10 minutes or so for most elementary students is a fair estimate. Conferences with middle and high school students may take longer, unless the conference is limited to discussing one sample or goal. Some teachers post lists showing which students will have their conferences that day, and hold conferences while students are working independently or in small groups. Students should review their portfolios prior to the conference so they can discuss their progress and goals.

Teacher-student conferences typically have three main parts:

1. *The teacher compliments* the student on some aspect of the portfolio, such as organization, selection of samples, thoughtful self-evaluations, and so forth. The conference should begin on a positive note.
2. *The student recognizes areas of growth* shown by selected samples and discusses his reading and writing progress with the teacher. This may include discussion of how previous goals have been met or worked toward.
3. *The student sets goals* for the next interval, with the teacher's help if necessary.

You can see why students need time to review their portfolios before conferences and to know what they should look for. If you need to draw a student out during a conference, you can use questions like these:

- How does your portfolio show what you are learning?
- How can you tell from your work that you are growing as a reader (writer, etc.)?
- What can you do well in writing?
- What might your portfolio convey about you to a person who didn't know you?
- What kinds of things do you like to read (write) about?
- What does this piece tell about you as a reader (writer)?
- How have you worked toward the goal(s) you set for yourself last time?

These open-ended questions are intended to get the student thinking and talking about the work. The student should talk more about the work than the teacher does. Avoid dominating the conference or cross-examining the student.

Students should review their previous goals and reflect on how they are meeting them. This will help them set goals for the next interval. Some students may need help in setting realistic or attainable goals. Those students who set ambitious or long-range goals may continue working toward them. Not every student will have attained the previous goals or set new ones, but it is important for each one to reflect on her progress toward attaining them. It may be helpful for the student to write what her most recent goal was and how she has attained it.

Portfolio conference records should reflect the dates of student-teacher conferences, areas discussed, goal setting, and other relevant comments. Figure 6.27 shows a cumulative portfolio conference record on which the teacher has listed the dates, topics, and goals of Kendra's conferences with her. Figure 6.28 shows an individual conference form completed after one conference with Carrie.

Peer Conferences. Peer conferences are for sharing selected work, explaining choices and goals, and getting helpful feedback from others. Like other examples of cooperative learning, peer conferences can be beneficial for both parties; the owner of the portfolio gets to show off some of his best work and accomplishments, and the portfolio partner gets to see what others are including in their portfolios and offer encouragement.

Student Kendra Teacher Mrs. Gillet

Date	Selection	Observations	Goals
9-16	"My Dog"	Baseline story-3 sents. Took 25 mins.	Fluency
10-11	"Puppies"	First attempt at expository. Knows a lot! 9 sentences	encourage her to write about what she knows
11-20	"Barry"	Response to reading *The Bravest Dog Ever.* She loved the story! Wrote 1½ pp.	continue topic-related reading

FIGURE 6.27 *Cumulative Conference Form*

Students need to be taught, however, how to make these conferences positive and helpful. Demonstrate with one student how to listen attentively, make positive comments about specific aspects of the work, and ask thoughtful questions. Then let students practice conferring with a partner and evaluate what they did in groups before you have students schedule peer conferences. Students could create a class list of Peer Conference Do's and Don'ts to which they could refer as they work together. Figure 6.29 shows a sample partner review form.

Parent Conferences. Portfolios can be invaluable in helping you to explain to parents what their children are working on, where their academic strengths lie, what skills and processes they need to develop, and how they are progressing. Portfolios give parents a "bird's-eye view" of their children's work that report cards, test scores, and other evaluative information cannot provide.

Student-Teacher Portfolio Conference

Student Carrie M. Date 11-12

Student Comments/Evaluation:

"... my best story so far."
(what makes it good?)
it's long
I've been working a long time on it
I just like it

Student Goals:

finish it
publish it

Teacher Comments/Evaluation:

Carrie spoke w/great enthusiasm about this piece; shows real pride. Her comments show awareness of her effort. Goals vague — doesn't yet have clear idea of what's next.

Student signature ______

Teacher signature ______

FIGURE 6.28 *Individual Conference Form*

Portfolio Partner Review

Name ____________________ Date of review ______

I reviewed ___________'s work sample.

I think this sample shows that ____________ can . . .

I think ____________ did these things well in this sample:

I think ____________ learned . . .

And I learned . . .

Signature __________________________________

FIGURE 6.29 *Portfolio Partner Review Form*

When you confer with parents, begin by highlighting the student's strengths and using portfolio samples to show how far the student has progressed to date. It is much easier for parents to understand their child's needs after they have heard you acknowledge the child's strengths. Portfolio samples can be used to show areas in which students need to practice and to interpret test scores, report card grades, and other evaluations. Goal statements and conference records document students' active role in learning.

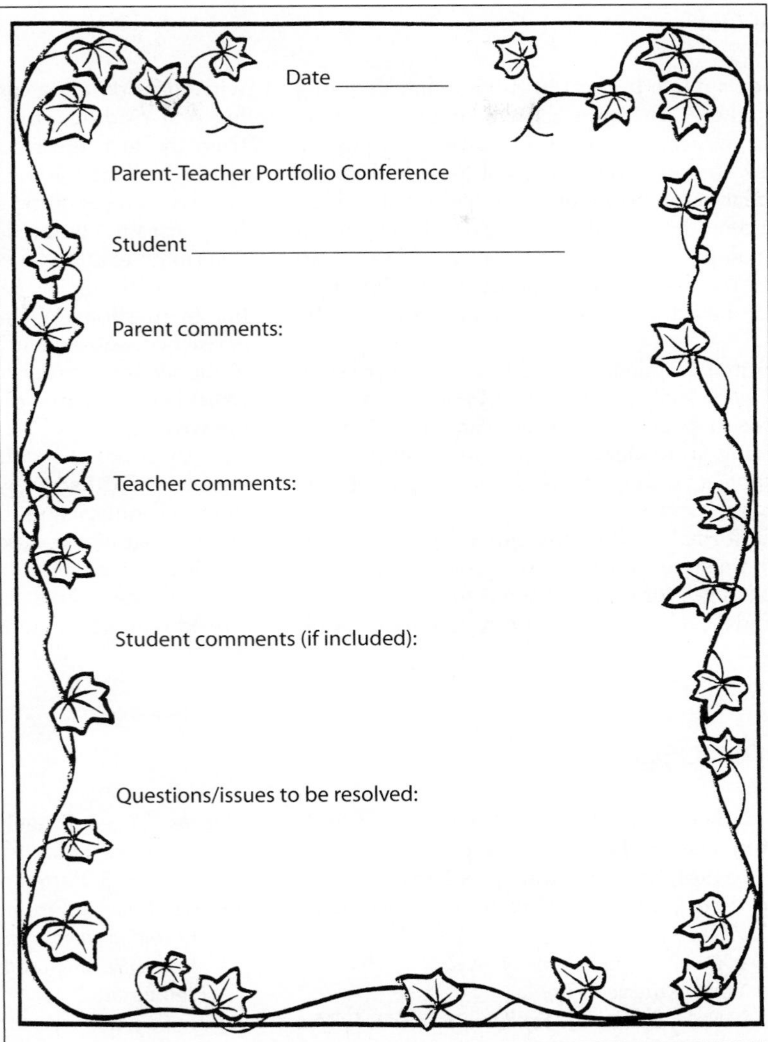
Date ___________

Parent-Teacher Portfolio Conference

Student ______________________________

Parent comments:

Teacher comments:

Student comments (if included):

Questions/issues to be resolved:

FIGURE 6.30 *Parent-Teacher Conference Form*

Parents' comments and concerns should be noted on the teacher's copy of the parent-teacher conference form you use to document such conferences; if your school does not already have such a form, you can adapt the one shown in Figure 6.30.

Summary

As students move beyond beginning and fledgling reading, there are more aspects of their reading available for teachers to examine, and support as necessary. Teachers want to have tools and strategies available for assessing students' reading ability, including their reading levels, word recognition ability, comprehension, and fluency, This chapter discusses the assessment of students' reading performance based on informed judgments by the teacher.

Informal diagnostic procedures make possible the *qualitative* analysis of reading behaviors as well as the use of *quantitative* scores. They are useful in determining a reader's *independent*, instructional, and *frustration* reading levels and reading strengths and needs.

An Informal Reading Inventory (IRI) is individually administered for these purposes. IRIs consist of text passages for oral and silent reading, at escalating grade levels from primer through high school, with corresponding comprehension questions. During oral reading, students' *miscues*, or divergences from the text, are recorded, counted to determine a reader's oral reading fluency, and analyzed to reveal word recognition strategies and use of context. Responses to comprehension questions are used to determine reading levels and reveal comprehension skills and strategies. *Retellings* may be used in addition to questions. When the frustration reading level is reached, subsequent passages may be read aloud to the reader in order to determine his *listening comprehension* level, an indicator of potential for reading improvement.

An informal *Word Recognition Inventory* consisting of graded lists of words may be used to assess sight vocabulary and decoding skills out of context. Sight recognition is assessed by exposing individual words for a very brief instant, and phonic and structural analysis skills are assessed by reexamining missed words in an untimed exposure.

References

Beaver, J. (2006). *Developmental reading assessment 2.* Boston: Pearson Learning Group.

Betts, E. A. (1941, June). Reading problems at the intermediate grade level. *Elementary School Journal, 40,* 737–746.

Betts, E. A. (1957). *Foundations of reading instruction.* New York: American Book.

Chall, J., & Dale, E. (1995). *Readability revisited: The new Dale-Chall readability formula.* Cambridge, MA: Brookline Books.

Clay, M. (2000). *Running records for classroom teachers.* Portsmouth, NH: Heinemann.

Cohen, L. (2006, April). The power of portfolios. *Early Childhood Today.*

Ediger, M. (2003). Data driven decision making. *College Student Journal, 37*(1), 9–15.

Fountas, I. C., & Pinnell, G. S. (1996). *Guided reading: Good first teaching for all children.* Portsmouth, NH: Heinemann.

Fountas, I. C., & Pinnell, G. S. (1999). *Matching books to readers: Using leveled books in guided reading, grades K–3.* Portsmouth, NH: Heinemann.

Fountas, I. C., & Pinnell, G. S. (2001). *Guiding readers and writers grades 3–6: Teaching comprehension, genre, and content literacy.* Portsmouth, NH: Heinemann.

Galley, S. (2000). Portfolio as mirror: Student and teacher learning reflected through the standards. *Language Arts, 78*(2), 121.

Gipe, J. P. (2003). *Multiple paths to literacy: Assessment and differentiated instruction for diverse learners, K–12* (6th ed.). Upper Saddle River, NJ: Pearson/Merrill/Prentice Hall.

Gipe, J. P. (2006). *Multiple paths to literacy assessment and differentiated instruction for diverse learners, K-12* (6th ed.). Upper Saddle River, NJ: Pearson.

Graves, D., & Sunstein, B. (Eds.). (1992). *Portfolio portraits.* Portsmouth, NH: Heinemann.

Guthrie, J. (1974). The maze technique to assess monitor reading comprehension. *The Reading Teacher*. 28(2), 161–168.

Hansen, J. (1994). Literacy portfolios: Windows on potential. In S. Valencia, E. Hiebert, & P. Afflerbach (Eds.), *Authentic reading assessment: Practices and possibilities*. Newark: DE: International Reading Association.

Hansen, J. (1996). *Doing what counts: Learners become better evaluators.* Portsmouth, NH: Heinemann.

Jasmine, J. (1992). *Portfolio assessment for your whole language classroom.* Huntington Beach, CA: Teacher Created Materials.

Jervis, K. (1996). *Eyes on the child: Three portfolio stories.* New York: Teachers College Press.

Johns, J. L., & Magliari, A. M. (1989). Informal reading inventories: Are the Betts criteria the best criteria? *Reading Improvement, 26*(2), 124–132.

McCormick, S. (2003). *Instructing students who have literacy problems.* Upper Saddle River, NJ: Pearson.

McKenna, M. C., Kear, D. J., & Ellsworth, R. A. (1995). Children's attitudes toward reading: A national survey. *Reading Research Quarterly*, 30, 4, 934–956.

McMahan, G. A., & Gifford, A. P. (2001). Portfolio: Achieving your personal best. *Delta Kappa Gamma Bulletin, 68*(1), 36–41.

McWhorter, J. (2000). *Spreading the word: Dialect and language in America.* Portsmouth, NH: Heinemann.

Owocki, G., & Goodman, Y. (2002). *Kidwatching: Documenting children's literacy development.* Portsmouth, NH: Heinemann.

Paris, S. (2001). Classroom applications of research on self-regulated learning. *Educational Psychologist, 36*(2), 89.

Perfetti, C. A. (1985). *Reading ability.* New York: Oxford University Press.

Rubenstein, H., Kender, J. P., & Mace, F. C. (1988). Do tests penalize readers for short term memory? *Journal of Reading, 32*(1), 4–10.

Seattle Public Schools. (2006). *Developmental Reading Assessment, grades K-3: Guide to administering and scoring the DRA.* Seattle: Seattle Public Schools.

Stanovich, K. E. (1992). Are we overselling literacy? In C. Temple & P. Collins (Eds.), *Stories and readers.* Norwood, MA: Christopher Gordon.

Stenner, J. (1999). *Matching students to text: The targeted reader.* New York: Scholastic Center for Literacy and Learning.

Stenner, A. J. (2001, January). The Lexile framework: A common metric for matching readers and text. *California School Library Association Journal, 25,* 41–42.

Stenner, A. J., & Wright, B. D. (2002, February). *Readability, reading ability, and comprehension.* Paper presented to the Association of Test Publishers, San Diego.

Taylor, W. (1953, Fall). Cloze procedure: A new tool for measuring readability. *Journalism Quarterly, 30,* 415–433.

Temple, C., Crawford, A., & Gillet, J. (2008). *Developmental literacy inventory.* Boston, MA: Allyn and Bacon.

Temple, C., Ogle, D., Crawford, A., & Freppon, P. (2011). *All children read: Teaching for literacy in today's diverse classrooms* (3rd ed.). Boston, MA: Allyn & Bacon.

Yopp, R. R., & Yopp, H. K. (2004). Preview-predict-confirm: Think aloud about the language and content of informational text. *The Reading Teacher 58*(1), 79–83.

Assessing and Teaching Middle and Secondary School Readers and Writers

CHAPTER 7

Chapter Outline

Fermina Sanchez is principal of an urban middle school, where the students' families run the gamut from recent immigrants from Central America to the middle to lower middle class, to working class. Some families who have been hit hard by the loss of industrial jobs in the community are on public assistance. There is increased pressure because of the results from new state reading tests at the middle school level. Over half of the students are not meeting grade-level standards for reading. The teachers in her school are committed to their students, and they are looking for the best ways they can help them. They are grateful to Fermina for advocating to the district administrators for more funds for their school. In the past decade, the district made a large push to help younger students get off to a good start in reading, and the larger share of the district's funding for reading programs went into that effort. The effort had done some good—now, more of the students coming into the middle school are better prepared in reading. But the majority of them still don't read well enough, and the teachers have the feeling that time may be running out for those whose needs are most severe.

Fermina is working with a committee of her teachers on a bold plan that makes all of the faculty teachers of reading. Those students who need greater levels of help in reading will get it, with some of them having frequent classes intended to teach them what they need to know to become successful readers. This will be an ambitious undertaking, since attention must be paid to assessing the students at many points, providing materials at different reading levels, arranging and scheduling small and intense reading classes, training the faculty, and keeping everyone on the same page.

The Reading Issues of Older Students

If you have been teaching in a middle or secondary school in recent years, you may have been wondering why so much of the emphasis on reading has been shifting away from your level and onto students in the early primary grades. There are reasons, of course. First, there is evidence that intensive reading instruction in the early grades may go a long way toward heading off later reading failure. Second, there are early intervention programs such as Reading Recovery and Book Buddies that are showing success in helping young at-risk students get off to a better start in reading. And third, the widespread testing required by the No Child Left Behind Act began at third grade and worked upwards, so a great many school districts put their resources where needs were so publicly exposed. But none of this means that students in America's middle and secondary schools don't need help in reading and writing. On the contrary: The literacy levels of our post-primary students are, if anything, cause for alarm.

Seventy percent of students in grades four through twelve do not read proficiently (NAEP, 2005). That's 8,700,000 students. A fourth of the students in that age group—more than 3,000,000—lack basic reading skills. Taken separately, nearly half of the African American and Hispanic students lack basic reading ability. The reading problems of students above the primary grades in some ways may be more serious than those of younger students. Younger students in the United States outscored most industrialized countries in the world on tests of reading ability, but older students lagged behind most countries in their comparison group (OECD/PISA, 2009). Moreover, while the reading problems of younger students are centered on word recognition and phonics, problems with word recognition affect only one older student in ten. Older students' problems lie in other areas where improvements may be harder to come by.

- **Most older students don't read enough.** A famous study of the amount of reading done by fifth graders (Anderson, Wilson, & Fielding, 1988) showed them reading an average of fewer than ten minutes per a day. The more avid readers managed about an hour, while many students devoted a minute or less to reading. Given that the average student watches more than two hours of television per day, the scant time spent reading cannot be attributed to a lack of leisure (see Figure 7.1).

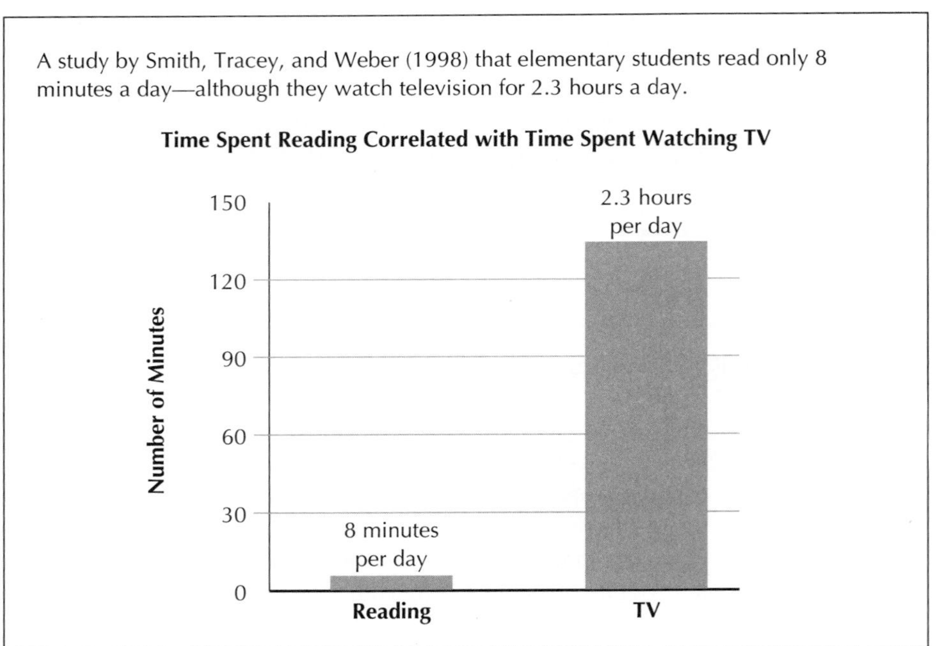

FIGURE 7.1 *Time Spent Reading*

Source: Smith, C., Tracy, E., & Weber, L. (1998). *Motivating Independent Reading: The Route to a Lifetime of Education*. Masters Action Research Project, 40–143.

Students' voluntary reading has declined significantly in recent years. In 1984, 9 percent of high school students in a national survey reported that they never read for pleasure. That figure had doubled by 2004 (Rich, 2008).

- **Many older students don't understand what they read.** The main problem older students have is not understanding what they read. This matters more for older readers than for younger ones, because beyond fourth grade so much of what students must learn comes to them through reading. Older students must read many different kinds of text, most of it for information.
- **Most older students don't write well, either.** A national report recently published by the Carnegie Corporation claimed that 70 percent of America's students in the fourth through twelfth grade are deficient writers, and half of them don't write well enough to meet the demands of the first year in college.

Why Should We Be Concerned about Older Students' Reading Ability?

Teachers who worry about older students' reading ability may find themselves in a lonely spot, because many, perhaps most, of the students who need help learning to read don't readily admit or even realize that they need help. For example, a very large national survey of adult literacy found that most of the poorest readers nevertheless claimed that they could read adequately. Few of even the poorest readers said they ever asked others to help them read important documents. In the case of older students in school, so many of their peers read poorly that it should not be surprising that they do not see reading deficits as cause for concern.

But it should be. Low reading ability not only affects grades in language arts; it also limits what students can learn in other school subjects. As soon as students leave school it predisposes them to a host of unpleasant outcomes. Poor readers are far more likely than other teens to become involved with the penal system. As we saw in Chapter 1 of this book, among adults, there is a strong association between reading ability and the likelihood of employment, the kind of job a person gets, a person's income, and a person's participation in civil society.

Responding to the Needs of Readers Beyond the Primary Grades

In a report for the Carnegie Corporation entitled *Reading Next*, Biancarosa and Snow (2004) recommend several strategies to improve adolescent literacy, and those that were directed to the classroom include these:

1. **Direct, explicit comprehension instruction,** which is instruction in the strategies and processes that proficient readers use to understand what they read, including summarizing, keeping track of one's own understanding, and a host of other practices

2. **Effective instructional principles embedded in content,** including language arts teachers using content-area texts and content-area teachers providing instruction and practice in reading and writing skills specific to their subject area
3. **Motivation and self-directed learning,** which includes building motivation to read and learn and providing students with the instruction and supports needed for independent learning tasks they will face after graduation
4. **Text-based collaborative learning,** which involves students interacting with one another around a variety of texts
5. **Strategic tutoring,** which provides students with intense individualized reading, writing, and content instruction as needed
6. **Diverse texts,** which are texts at a variety of difficulty levels and on a variety of topics
7. **Intensive writing,** including instruction connected to the kinds of writing tasks students will have to perform well in high school and beyond
8. **A technology component,** which includes technology as a tool for and a topic of literacy instruction
9. **Ongoing formative assessment of students,** which is informal, often daily assessment of how students are progressing under current instructional practices
10. **Extended time for literacy,** which includes approximately two to four hours of literacy instruction and practice that takes place in language arts and content-area classes. (Biancarosa & Snow, 2004).

But which students need what kind of help? Linda Diamond (2006), writing for the American Association of School Administrators, suggests that we think of these older readers in four different categories, for the sake of giving them appropriate help:

> **Advanced Learners** are those who are reading at or above grade-level standards (which puts them ahead of most of their peers, you will remember). They may already know much of the content of their courses, and often appear bored in classes. The challenge for teachers of these students will be to provide them with enrichment opportunities within the regular curriculum, or to organize advanced classes for them where possible.
>
> **Benchmark Learners** are average learners who can meet learning standards, especially if they are given encouragement and suggestions for organizing themselves for learning. They should have their learning progress assessed at least three times per year, and they should have frequent instruction in strategy instruction and vocabulary. They should also be encouraged to write.
>
> **Strategic Learners** are those who fall below the norm, testing between the 30th and 49th percentile. These students are taught in regular classes, but they do not perform well without regular help. They have difficulty learning from their textbooks, so there are significant gaps in their knowledge that may impair further learning. For example, because they may not know which countries are in Europe, or when the Civil War and the World Wars occurred or who the combatants were, they may have trouble following class discussions or reading assignments in social studies. These students may be pulled out into a resource room or special reading

class for part of the year and given intensive instruction in reading comprehension and vocabulary. Their learning should be assessed monthly, in order to make sure that the reading interventions are yielding progress.

Intensive Intervention Students typically test below the 30th percentile on reading measures, show low performance in their courses, regularly fail to turn in homework, and may miss a fair amount of school. They might best be served in special reading classes instead of their English classes. Like special intervention classes for younger students, such as Reading Recovery, these reading classes should be considered short-term fixes: They are not warehouses for failed students, but should provide intensive experiences and tailored support to equip students to cope with the reading demands of the regular curriculum.

A Range of Responses to Older Students' Reading Needs

Most troubled readers beyond the primary years need to improve their comprehension and vocabulary (Biancarosa & Snow, 2004), and these abilities can be developed and supported in the subject areas (particularly English language arts, social studies, science, and health). The students who have greater reading needs, though, will need more focused help to develop skills of comprehension and vocabulary, and even word recognition. In the following sections, we will begin with a section that suggests strategies that nearly all teachers can use to support older students' reading. Then will come a section of more focused strategies that teachers can use with those students who need intensive reading support.

Reading Strategies for Use across the Curriculum

Instruction that supports students' understanding (a) connects with students' prior knowledge and encourages them to ask questions and set purposes for learning; (b) guides their inquiry and helps them make sense of the materials under study; and (c) helps them reflect on what they have learned, and consider its implications, interpret it, debate it, apply it, and extend it. These three phases of learning were called the ABC model elsewhere in this book (see Chapter 5). ABC stands for **anticipation, building knowledge,** and **consolidation** (Crawford, Saul, Mathews, & MaKinster, 2005).

Anticipation

Learning begins when students get curious about a topic, when they activate their prior knowledge of the topic and prepare to make sense of the contents of the lesson. Thus in the first, "anticipation," phase of a lesson, teachers give enticing previews of a topic and then ask students what they already know about the topic, encouraging them to raise questions about the topic and set purposes for reading. They may preview the important vocabulary items in the text that students might not know. They hope that awakening the students' curiosity, thoughts, and questions will prepare them to enter the next stage, **building knowledge**, with alert and active minds.

Building Knowledge

Once their curiosity has been piqued, their questions have been raised, and their purposes have been set, students select from a number of ways to explore the topic—or, in psychological terms, to assimilate the new information to their old knowledge structures. These many ways of making meaning include the comprehension strategies of visualizing, detecting the structure of the text and following it to guide understanding, finding main ideas, understanding the meanings of words from the context of the passage, making inferences, and predicting what is to come.

Consolidation

In the consolidation phase, students look back over what they have made sense of, consider what they knew about the topic at the outset and what they know now, think about the implications of what they have found out, and reassess their assumptions about the topic in light of what they have just learned. Again, in psychological terms, students are now asked to go back and reassess or update their knowledge structures (ideas, beliefs, and attitudes) to accommodate their old ways of thinking to the new insights they have gained. In the reflection phase of learning, students use strategies of making interpretations, responding to literature, applying ideas from the text to new situations, and debating what has been presented.

Teachers of all subjects can support students' reading with understanding if they will approach reading, and especially reading comprehension, using strategies drawn from each of the phases of the ABC model.

Strategies for the Anticipation Phase

Activities in the anticipation phase of a lesson are meant to summon up the students' prior knowledge about a topic, arouse their curiosity, and lead them to set purposes for their further studies. Strategies to accomplish these purposes are advance organizers, anticipation guides, brainstorming, terms in advance, think/pair/share, free writing, and semantic maps. In addition, the "know/want to know/learn" strategy begins in this phase.

The amount of emphasis given to the anticipation phase can vary according to the students' needs. For example, if the lesson treats an area in which the students are likely to have many misconceptions, the teacher may invest more time in the anticipation portion of the lesson in order to tease out those misconceptions so that students can correct them.

Advance Organizers

The educational psychologist David Ausubel (1978, 1979) developed the idea of the advance organizer, with the thought that beginning a lesson with a brief explanation of a topic to give students "the lay of the land" could help them make better sense of the information that was coming. So, for example, before having students read a passage about Marco Polo, the teacher talks briefly about the geography of Europe and Asia and the state of transportation in the late Middle Ages. The talk would give some context for the students' understanding of the passage on Marco Polo.

The Anticipation Guide

An anticipation guide (Vacca & Vacca, 1989) also activates students' prior knowledge and stimulates predictions about the text. An anticipation guide is a set of statements about the text that students respond to and discuss before they begin reading the text. The teacher's role is to create the anticipation guide, accept a broad range of student responses, and facilitate discussion before reading. After reading the text, the teacher should lead students in a discussion in which they contrast their own predictions with the author's stated meaning. Vacca and Vacca (1989, p. 145) provide guidelines for constructing and using anticipation guides:

1. Analyze the material to be read. Determine the major ideas—implicit and explicit—with which students will interact.
2. Write those ideas in short, clear, declarative statements. These statements should in some way reflect the world that the students live in or know about. Therefore, avoid abstractions whenever possible.
3. Put these statements into a format that will elicit anticipation and prediction making.
4. Discuss readers' predictions and anticipations before reading the text selection.
5. Assign the text selection. Have students evaluate the statements in light of the author's intent and purpose.
6. Contrast readers' predictions with the author's intended meaning.

A sample anticipation guide appears in Figure 7.2.

Once they have read the text, students return to their anticipation guides and compare what they know now with their original ideas.

Group Brainstorming

The teacher sets out a topic and asks the class to brainstorm—that is, to think of everything that comes to mind about a topic in a fixed period of time—say, five minutes. The

Directions: Before you read the article on mummies, mark those statements that you think are true *T* and those statements that you think are not true *NT*. Then discuss your responses with class members. After you read, mark the statements again using the information that you learned.

Before		**After**
1. _____	Egyptians believed everyone had a *ba* and a *ka*.	_____
2. _____	Bodies that were not preserved were said to be mummified.	_____
3. _____	People believed that Pharaohs became gods when they died.	_____
4. _____	To make mummies, embalmers took out the inner organs.	_____
5. _____	The embalmers did not take the brain out through the nose with hooks.	_____
6. _____	*Shabits* are magical figures that were tucked into the mummy's wrappings.	_____
7. _____	Everyone who died in ancient Egypt became mummies.	_____

FIGURE 7.2 *Anticipation Guide: Mummies in Egypt*

teacher lists these ideas on the board. The teacher might help the students to arrange their ideas into categories to elicit better coverage of the topic. In the case of Marco Polo, for example, the categories might be "Who?" (Who was Marco Polo? Who else is involved in his story?), "What?" (What did he do?), "Why?" (Why did he do what he did?), and "So what?" (What was important about his accomplishments? Why is he remembered?).

Then the teacher has the students read a text (or listen to a lecture or watch a video) and see which of their ideas were borne out by the material they encountered.

Paired Brainstorming

This activity is similar to the one above, except that pairs of students list on a sheet of paper the facts and ideas that they know or think they know about a topic. They may also list questions to be answered in a reading. Teachers set a time limit for this activity—usually five minutes or less. Again, it might help if the teacher has students arrange their ideas into categories.

Terms in Advance

In advance of a lesson, the teacher might choose four or five key terms from a text and write them on the board. Pairs of students are given five minutes to brainstorm how those terms might be related, how they will be related—in a historical chronology, in the explanation of a scientific process, or in a work of fiction—in the text they are about to read. Once the pairs have agreed on a set of relationships among the terms, the teacher asks them to consider the text carefully to see how those same terms played out in the text. After they have read the text, the teacher will ask them to review their original answers and find out how similar they were to what the text actually said.

Think/Pair/Share

Think/Pair/Share (Slavin, 1996) is an engaging strategy that can be used at any point in a lesson in which we want students to think about issues. To use a Think/Pair/Share in the anticipation phase of a lesson, the teacher thinks of a discussion question that bears on the topic and that can be talked about briefly. The question might ask students to list what they know about a topic, recount a personal experience that has bearing on a topic, or reflect on a philosophical issue that relates to a topic.

During a period of four or five minutes, the teacher puts that question to the class and asks each student to prepare an answer. Then each student shares that answer with a partner and listens carefully to the partner's answer. The two of them may next prepare a joint answer. The teacher calls on three or four pairs to give a 30-second summary of their discussions.

The Think/Pair/Share strategy can be used at any point in a lesson, of course, and not only during the anticipation phase.

Free Writing

The teacher can invite students to write for five minutes, without stopping, everything that comes to mind on a topic about which they are going to read (Elbow, 1989). When the five minutes are up (it's advisable to call time after five minutes and give the students one more minute to finish up, as good ideas often come out under pressure), the teacher might ask the students to read their paper aloud to a partner.

At this point, many options are available. Pairs can be invited to share ideas with the whole group, as in the group brainstorming, or students can underline the ideas in their paper that they are least sure about and pay close attention to the reading to learn whether it sheds light on their areas of uncertainty.

Free writing also can be used at any point in a lesson and not only during the anticipation phase. It makes a useful activity in the middle of a lesson to summarize responses to what has been learned so far, and to predict what might come ahead. It can also be used at the end of a lesson as a way of reflecting back on what was learned.

Semantic Maps

Semantic maps or semantic webs are ways of previewing ideas that students already hold about a topic, so that they can identify gaps in their knowledge as well as questions they want to have answered through the reading. Semantic maps can also be used to introduce new vocabulary that students will need in order to understand the reading.

As was shown in Chapter 5, the teacher guides the students in making a semantic map by writing the name of the topic in the center of the chalkboard and then inviting students to say what they know about the topic. As the students suggest ideas, the teacher adds them to the chart by making satellites around the original topic. The teacher can organize the students' ideas into logical categories, and then ask the students what other information they can offer to fill out a category. Semantic maps can be used in other places in the lesson besides the anticipation phase. They can be used during the building knowledge phase of a lesson to collect ideas as they occur to the readers, and in the consolidation phase to help sum up what was learned.

Know/Want to Know/Learn

The K-W-L strategy (Ogle, 1986) asks students **what they already know** about a topic and what they **want to know**. Then the students read a text or otherwise investigate the topic, and later report on **what they learned.** As you can see, the first two parts of the K-W-L strategy take place in the anticipation phase of a lesson. The K-W-L strategy can be combined with other strategies described in this chapter. For example, students might first brainstorm ideas about a topic and share their ideas with a partner, or create a semantic map (also called a "web") of their prior knowledge, before offering their ideas to be added in a K-W-L activity. Note that while the K-W-L strategy appears here as an anticipation activity, it also spreads across the other two categories of building knowledge and consolidation. See Chapter 5 for more information about the K-W-L strategy.

Strategies for the Building Knowledge Phase

Once students have summoned up their prior knowledge, examined what they were sure of and not so sure of, raised questions, and set purposes for learning, they are ready for the building knowledge phase of learning. Depending on the students' needs and the purposes of the lesson, more or less time may be devoted to this phase of the lesson. If the reading material is especially dense, or if the students will be expected to understand the material to the point of mastery, more time may be devoted to building knowledge.

The I.N.S.E.R.T. Model

I.N.S.E.R.T. (Vaughn & Estes 1986) stands for Instructional Note-taking System for Enhanced Reading and Thinking. The device is used in two parts. Only the first is relevant to the building knowledge phase of a lesson. Here, students are given a system for marking the text as they pursue different kinds of information in it:

√ A check mark indicates a statement that confirms an idea they already knew.
– A minus sign (–) marks a passage that contradicts something they thought they knew.

+ A plus sign (+) marks a passage of interesting information that they had not anticipated.
? A question mark (?) goes next to a passage that they would like to know more about.

As students read the assigned text, they place the appropriate mark in the margin next to relevant passages.

Since the categories of information that students will be marking in the text relate back to what they knew or thought they knew about the topic of the text, the I.N.S.E.R.T. system works best when preceded by an anticipation activity that asks students to summon up their prior knowledge about the topic. Brainstorming or paired brainstorming works well for this purpose.

Text Coding

There are other ways to mark particular elements in texts in addition to the I.N.S.E.R.T. method. The teacher can ask the students to read in order to find a set of aspects of the text that will guide their comprehension. For example, if the text explains a procedure, ask them to write lightly with a pencil a "P" beside the procedure being described, and number 1, 2, 3, and so on for the steps of the procedure. They can mark with a "C" any cautions that are given.

If they are reading a text that contains—

- **a sequence of events,** they can identify and number the events.
- **a persuasive argument,** they can mark the claim, the reasons that support the claim, and the evidence that supports each reason.
- **a descriptive paragraph,** they can mark the details that appeal to each of the senses.
- **a story,** they can make a mark next to the characters, the setting, the problem, the attempts at a solution, and the conclusion.
- **a poem,** they can make a mark next to the images, the metaphors and similes, the symbols, the repetitions, and the examples of onomatopoeia.

Study Guides

Study guides help to direct students' processes of inquiry even when the teacher is not present, as when students are reading an assigned text independently. The sample three-level study guide in Figure 7.3 is intended to direct the students' attention to certain ideas that are woven through a lengthy text on the topic of corn. The students are expected to think about the questions as they read the whole piece and write down their answers either as they read or after they read. Answers to the first two questions are woven through many parts of the assigned text. The third question asks readers to engage in higher-order thinking about the insights they were guided to assemble in the first two questions. Later, students' answers to the questions can frame a whole-class or small-group discussion about the topic of the text.

1. In what ways have humans adapted corn to our own uses?
2. How long have humans been manipulating corn plants for their own purposes?
3. Some people claim that it is unnatural, and therefore wrong, for people to "tinker" with nature. Using what you know about corn, construct an argument that agrees or disagrees with that position.

FIGURE 7.3 *Three-Level Study Guide: "Corn: What Good Is It?"*

For the purposes of promoting critical thinking, study guides work best when they:

1. Help students to follow intricate patterns of thought or subtle ideas that they probably would not have reached on their own, but do not serve as a substitute for a careful reading of the text.
2. Invite critical or higher-order thinking at every step.
3. Are used as a springboard to discussion or writing, and not as an end in themselves.

A three-level study guide such as Figure 7.3 asks questions of this form (Vaughn & Estes, 1986):

1. What did the author say?
2. What did the author mean?
3. What can we do with the meaning?

In preparing a study guide, the teacher often proceeds in reverse order. That is, we decide what is the most important use of the meaning in the reading and we formulate a question or questions about it. Next, we decide which concepts or insights a student would have to have reached to get the main benefit from the article. Then, we decide what facts the students would have to have noticed to derive those concepts or insights. Finally, we present the questions the right way around.

Study guides may take other forms, too. Pattern guides are specially constructed to call students' attention to the ways different genres of text organize information. An example of a chronological pattern guide is given in Figure 7.4. Other pattern guides will be considered later in this chapter when we discuss patterns of text organization.

Dual-Entry Diaries

Dual-entry diaries (Berthoff, 1981) are ways for readers to closely link material in the text to both their own curiosity and their own experiences. They are especially useful when students are reading longer assignments, outside of class.

To make a dual-entry diary, the students should draw a vertical line down the middle of a blank sheet of paper. On the left-hand side, they should note a part of

A. Fill in the blanks with an event or events that happened in Burton in each time period.

Before A.D. 800	After A.D. 870	Tenth Century	Eleventh Century	Seventeenth Century
____________	____________	____________	____________	____________
____________	____________	____________	____________	____________
____________	____________	____________	____________	____________

B. Fill in the blanks with a brief description of what the town of Burton might have looked like in each period.

Before A.D. 800	After A.D. 870	Tenth Century	Eleventh Century	Seventeenth Century
____________	____________	____________	____________	____________
____________	____________	____________	____________	____________
____________	____________	____________	____________	____________

FIGURE 7.4 *A Chronological Pattern Guide for "Burton"*

the text that struck them strongly. Perhaps it reminded them of something from their own experience. Perhaps it puzzled them. Or perhaps they disagreed with it. On the right-hand side of the page, they should write a comment about it: What was it about the quote that made them write it down? What did it make them think of? What question did they have about it? As they read the text, they should pause and make entries in their dual-entry diaries. Some teachers assign a minimum number of dual-entry diary entries: a certain number of entries for every ten pages read, for example.

As we shall see, reviewing the students' entries to their dual-entry diaries later in class can structure a whole-class discussion.

Cooperative Learning: Jigsaw II

Jigsaw II is a popular cooperative learning technique developed by Robert Slavin et al. (1992).

The teacher should go through the text in advance and prepare four different expert sheets, which are sets of questions that relate to the most important points in the reading passage that will be assigned. (One suggestion for an expert sheet would be a study guide, such as the one discussed above.)

The lesson should proceed as follows:

1. **Set the Stage.** Explain that the class will be doing a cooperative learning activity called Jigsaw II. Announce the topic of the lesson and explain that everyone will be responsible for learning all parts of the text, but each person will become an expert on one part of the text and will teach others about it.
2. **Assign Students to Home Groups.** Assign students to home groups of four or five members.
3. **Read the Text.** Distribute copies of the text to all students. Also distribute to each student in a home group a different expert sheet, often a set of questions about the text. If there are more than four people in a home group, distribute copies of more expert sheets, so that not more than two people have the same expert sheet.

   The expert sheet has questions to guide that person's reading of the text. The expert sheets differ, because later, each person will be responsible for helping the others in the home group to learn about the aspects of the reading covered by his or her expert sheet.

   Allow an adequate amount of time for everyone to read the passage. Everyone should read the whole text but should pay special attention to the material that answers the questions on his or her expert sheet. If people finish early, they should take notes on portions of the text that pertain to the questions on their expert sheet.

4. **Study the Text in Expert Groups.** Set up four tables or clusters of chairs to seat four expert groups. If there are more than six students in any one expert group, divide that group into two groups. Appoint a discussion leader for each expert group. Spend a few minutes going over the rules of participation:

   a. "Everybody participates. Nobody dominates."
   b. "The group agrees on what the question means, or what the task is, before answering."
   c. "When you are not clear about something that is said, restate it in your own words."
   d. "Everybody sticks to the task at hand."

   Explain that the expert groups will have twenty minutes to discuss their questions and to formulate answers to them. They should already have located answers to the questions in the text, and they should take notes on answers their group offers to the questions. Also, they should decide how they are going to teach their material to their home groups. The teacher should circulate among the expert groups to help them stay on task.
5. **"Experts" Teach the Text to Home Groups.** When the study period is up, have the students leave the study groups and return to their home groups. Now each student should take about five minutes to present to the home group what she or he learned in the expert group. The "expert's" task is not just to report, however, but to ask and entertain questions from the group, to make sure everyone learned his or her piece of the text.

6. **Evaluate the Process.** Ask each person to write about what he or she contributed to the discussion and what could make the activity go better.

Strategies for the Consolidation Phase

Many of the strategies that are followed during the anticipation and building knowledge phases are designed to culminate during the consolidation phase. Here are several that do.

The Discussion Web

An active discussion can cover a lot of ground, and it's not unusual for students to remember only the last things said or the ideas that were put forth most forcefully. Graphic organizers might help with this problem. Graphic organizers, written aids to capture and display the results of students' thinking, are useful at all stages of a discussion. They can help to frame a question, record and keep preliminary thoughts available for review, and communicate the group's findings to others.

One particularly useful graphic organizer, the discussion web, was published by Donna Alvermann (1991). The discussion web is used to organize a five-step lesson, arranged around any text or topic that invites controversy (the taking of two different points of view):

1. The teacher prepares the students to read the selection by setting up the appropriate exploratory activity, that is, by giving them whatever background knowledge, vocabulary, or predictive questions they are likely to need.
2. After the students have read the selection and perhaps have had an opportunity to share their personal responses with a partner or in a small group, the teacher assigns the students to pairs and asks each pair to prepare a discussion web like the one shown in Figure 7.5. The teacher should point out that the students will be asked to take sides on a question that is specific to the text. After reading Walter Dean Myers' *Monster*, for instance, and considering the evidence presented in the book, students might be asked, "Was Steve Harmon guilty of murder?"

   The discussion web has two columns, marked "Yes" and "No," and the pairs are asked to think of as many good reasons pro and con as they can—reasons why Marty was justified in keeping the dog and reasons why he was not. The students should try to list an equal number of reasons in each column.
3. After a few minutes, each pair is asked to join another pair and pool their reasons, pro and con. After they have considered all of the reasons, the foursomes are asked to reach a consensus agreement on an answer. They should write that answer at the bottom of the web, in the space marked "Conclusion," and also write the best supporting arguments. The teacher should remind them

"Was Steve Harmon guilty of murder?"

YES	NO
______________________	______________________
______________________	______________________
______________________	______________________
______________________	______________________

Conclusion:

____

____

____

FIGURE 7.5 *Discussion Web for* Monster

that individuals may dissent from the consensus, but they should try to keep an open mind.

4. When each foursome has arrived at a consensus, the teacher gives each of them three minutes to share their conclusion with the class and to discuss which of their reasons best supports their finding.
5. The teacher concludes the activity by asking students to write their own answers to the question, taking into account the other arguments they have heard. The teacher posts these answers on a bulletin board so that students can read what others have written.

The discussion web may stand on its own. It may also be used as a springboard for writing (have the students write a short essay in which they take and defend a side of the argument) or as the warm-up to a debate (have the class divide between those who are pro and con, with "undecideds" in the middle). In both of these cases, it is preferable to stop the discussion web activity before step 3—that is, leave it to the individuals to reach their conclusions either in writing or by means of the debate.

Academic Controversy

Academic controversy (Kagan, 1992) is another cooperative learning activity that follows a pattern similar to that of the discussion web. But unlike the discussion web, students are responsible for finding reasons to support only one side of an argument at a time. We have found that for some students, this is easier than listing arguments for both sides during the same step. Also, the procedure includes an explicit invitation for students to step out of their roles and argue what they really believe—an opportunity that most students enjoy. The activity proceeds as follows:

1. The teacher assigns a reading, preferably one that raises an issue that invites diverse responses.
2. The teacher prepares at least one issue for discussion, stated in a form that is likely to elicit at least two justifiable positions from students (for example, "Was Jack justified in stealing from the giant?").
3. Students are assigned to groups of four.
4. Within the groups, pairs of students are assigned a position on the issue that they must defend.
5. The pairs list reasons that support their position.
6. The pairs temporarily split up and form new pairs with classmates who are defending the same positions. They share the reasons each of the original pairs listed in support of the position.
7. Students return to their original partners and set out a position statement followed by supporting reasons: "We want to argue for _____ because of X, Y, and Z."
8. Each pair presents its argument to the other pair within their group while the latter pair listens and takes notes.
9. The two pairs then debate.
10. Optionally, the pairs within each group may now be told to switch positions and repeat steps 4 through 8.
11. Finally, the students stop defending any point of view and construct the position on which they can find consensus, supported by the best reasons that came to light in the previous discussion.

Providing Close Support for Students' Reading Development

Earlier in this chapter we suggested that as teachers decide how to provide help to older readers, they divide the student population into *advanced readers, benchmark readers, strategic readers,* and *readers needing intensive support.* In the case of the first two groups, instruction that will help them grow as readers can be provided in the context of the regular subjects—not just English language arts, but also social studies, science, health, and other subjects. It is the last two groups of readers—strategic readers and those needing intensive support—who concern us here. Both groups need focused instruction in reading. The difference is that strategic readers can make do with a couple of periods of instruction each week for short durations—perhaps a semester each year—whereas readers needing intensive instruction may require daily focused instruction on reading, normally for most of the school year or for several years.

Organizing Focused Strategic and Intensive Instruction

The principle behind focused instruction is that it should be just that: intensive and focused teaching that gives students what they need in order to be able to read successfully and to cope with the academic demands of the school curriculum. Such instruction should incorporate the following features. The plan of instruction should:

- be based on detailed information about the student's reading ability
- provide help to the student in demonstrated areas of need
- work in materials at each student's instructional and independent reading levels
- follow a consistent plan of activities over which the student can gain some control
- provide a variety of activities in order to maintain the student's interest
- provide emotional support and motivation for learning
- be supported by close and ongoing monitoring of the student's learning

Assessing Readers for Focused Instruction

A *screening assessment* is normally done at the beginning of the school year or at the end of the previous one. Screening assessments for older students may be standardized tests, administered to many students at once. If a group-administered test is used, though, caution is advised in interpreting the results, as older low-performing readers are not reliable test-takers. In any case, scores on screening tests are usually complemented by a teacher's recommendation, based on observation of the student's work in class.

Once a student has been identified for special help by the screening assessment, there is still a need for *diagnostic assessment* of the student's specific reading abilities. A diagnostic procedure such as an informal reading inventory will be able to bring to light the student's

- independent, instructional, and frustration reading levels
- strengths in word recognition
- reading fluency
- comprehension ability, including his or her relative strengths in getting main ideas, making inferences, and inferring vocabulary from context
- listening capacity, as compared to his or her reading comprehension

All of this is information that a teacher will need in order to plan instruction for the student. Still, even an Informal Reading Inventory, however well administered, is never a perfect predictor of how a particular student will respond to instruction, so during the first several lessons the teacher should be "roaming around the known" as Marie Clay puts it (Clay, 2000)—that is, teaching experimentally and observing closely to see how the student responds to different kinds of reading tasks.

Once instruction has begun in earnest, the teacher will periodically perform *monitoring assessments* to see how the student is progressing and to determine which instructional procedures seem to be working. In one sense, monitoring assessment occurs almost constantly, especially if teachers keep observational notes on how the lessons go and record the levels of texts the student is reading. Nonetheless, it is recommended that a more formal stock-taking be done once each month, and more often for readers with disabilities. These monitoring assessments might consist of a careful reading of an extended passage of text written at a known reading level, in which the teacher

- records the percentage of words read correctly (word recognition in context).
- invites the student to retell the passage, or asks comprehension questions to measure comprehension.
- measures the student's fluency and reading rate.
- asks the student what is working and what is not

Planning Lessons for Readers with Disabilities

Students differ in the amount of time they are able to pay attention to learning tasks. Readers with disabilities may have attention spans that are shorter than those of other students. There is also usually a menu of skills students with disabilities will need to develop. So a teacher should plan a typical 50-minute lesson to include three to five different activities. The plan might proceed as follows:

1. **Focused lesson.** Here the teacher introduces a strategy that can be used to read better. Of course, there are many points that can be taught in a focused lesson, but some likely ones are these:
   - **Previewing a text.** How to examine the title, any illustrations, headings, and the first paragraphs of a text to decide what it is about, to think about what we already know about it, and to raise questions and set purposes for reading.
   - **Searching for answers.** Once questions have been set, how to read and look for answers to them.
   - **Summarizing what has been said.** After a section has been read, saying in a few sentences the main ideas of the text.
   - **Perceiving and following patterns.** Perceiving the way the text is organized and predicting how the information will be presented based on that organization.
   - **Visualizing details.** As the text uses words to describe something, calling up in "the mind's eye" the images that the words evoke.
   - **Understanding vocabulary.** Using the context to approximate the meanings of unfamiliar words.
   - **Making predications.** Having read the first sections in the text, predicting what will come next.
   - **Noting important points for later studying.** Paying attention to main ideas, noting them down, and rehearsing them for later recall.

   A focused lesson may take no more than 10 to 15 minutes. The strategy used in the focused lesson can be utilizing a *think-aloud, Questioning the Author, visualizing,* or using a *graphic organizer,* all of which are explained later in this chapter. The teacher makes sure that the student is aware of the strategy and is able to articulate the steps necessary to apply it.

2. **Guided practice.** Following the focused lesson, the student is asked to read a text and practice the strategy that was introduced in the focused lesson. The student may be asked to *think aloud* or use the *ReQuest procedure, reading and questioning, reciprocal teaching,* or *repeated reading* or *reader's theater* for fluency (all are described below). Guided practice may be done in moderately challenging reading material, text written at the student's instructional level.
3. **Independent reading.** The student should read some interesting text at her or his independent level. The reading may be supported by *audio books* and may be followed by a discussion. (Several discussion strategies were presented earlier in this chapter.)
4. **Vocabulary.** Poor readers typically have smaller vocabularies than proficient readers, and their limited vocabulary imposes limits on their comprehension—not only of written texts but also of the information encountered in daily life. Vocabulary lessons should cultivate a respect for words, should share strategies for learning new words, and should teach the "tier two words" or "frontier vocabulary": high-utility words that students will frequently encounter.
5. **Writing.** Some writing should be included in nearly every lesson. Tasks for writing can include written responses to the reading or a learning log in which the student writes down the most important thing learned from today's lesson, or one thing she or he wants to be sure to learn in future lessons. Or the writing task can follow the writing workshop format of rehearsing, drafting, revising, editing, and sharing.

Teaching Strategies to Build Reading Competence

A daily lesson such as the one outlined above may use activities drawn from those described below.

Thinking Aloud

Imagine learning to be a proficient skier if all you saw were people wiping out on the slopes; or becoming a proficient singer if all you heard were people who couldn't carry a tune or keep the beat. In most domains we seek out skilled models to imitate so that we can develop skills ourselves. That's true of reading, too. Imagine that you wanted to *show* students how to read well. You would demonstrate each step that good readers take as they work through a text. To think aloud, then, the teacher:

- Surveys the topic, the title, and the genre, and says what she or he expects to find in a text.
- Comments after reading the beginning about what the argument, the topic, or the main problem of the text is.

- Makes predictions of what will come in the text.
- Visualizes what the text describes.
- Confirms or disconfirms the predictions after reading ahead in the text.
- Makes inferences where ideas are implied.
- Clarifies the meanings of rare words that can be explained from context.
- Summarizes from time to time what has been read.
- Suggests implications of what the text says.

The teacher asks the student or students to join in on these activities, following her or his model.

ReQuest Procedure

When students need support in reading text for information, one way to structure a reading so that they give each other that support is to use the ReQuest Procedure (Manzo, 1979, 1991). In this procedure, two students read through a text, stop after each paragraph, and take turns asking each other questions about it.

For example, after reading the first paragraph (silently) in an informational text, the teacher asks Juana several good questions about that paragraph. She asks her questions about main ideas. She asks about nuances. She asks what importance some item in this paragraph might come to have later in the text. (She is trying not only to get Juana to think about the text, but also to model for Juana the kinds of questions she might ask when it comes to be her turn.) Juana has to answer those questions as well as she can. After Juana has finished answering the teacher's questions, it is her turn to ask the teacher questions about the same paragraph, and the teacher has to answer them. When Juana and the teacher have both brought to light the important information of that paragraph, they read the next one. After that paragraph is read, Juana now gets the first turn at asking the teacher all the good questions she can think of about that paragraph. When she is finished, the teacher gets to ask her questions. When both are finished, they read the next paragraph, and so on.

After the teacher has introduced the activity by being a questioning partner, the teacher sets up pairs of students to read and ask questions of each other.

Visualizing

Good readers form pictures in their "mind's eye" of what is described in the text. You can help students visualize settings and events in a text by first modeling visualizing by means of a think-aloud. Then you can guide students through the process by evoking images that appeal to each of their senses.

For example, the teacher reads aloud the following text:

> *Along the north coast of Scotland, the winter wind howls through dark nights and gray days, and towering seas smash against black rocks. But in summer, the sea calms, and the days grow long, until the daylight lasts through twenty-four hours. Then the few fishermen who live on that remote coast row their nets out into the sea, to catch their livelihood. Even in summer, a sudden storm may overtake them; or a silent fog may creep upon them*

and make them lose their way. Then their loved ones go down to the shore, and gaze for some sign at the mute waves, perhaps to see a seal stare back with big sad eyes. The people see the seals, and they wonder . . .

The teacher says, "The first words make me hear the wind howling and shrieking. It must really wear down the people to hear it all night and all day. I can picture the fisherman's door banging in the wind when he tries to close it behind him, and see his hand reaching out of the cottage to pull it shut. I see the fisherman's wife bent low in the fierce wind as she picks her way along the rocky ground toward the cottage. I imagine that she feels hard bits of cold rain hurled by the wind."

Then the teacher points out to the students how she has used the senses of hearing, sight, and feeling to evoke the scene in her mind's eye. Next the teacher tells the students that she will read them another passage. The passage will be chosen from another text that is at or slightly above the students' reading level. Any vocabulary that is likely to be unfamiliar to the students should be explained to them.

The teacher tells the students to close their eyes and try to picture, hear, and feel what the words suggest to them. They should imagine a movie in their heads as the words are read to them.

Following the reading, the teacher asks individual students to say aloud what they visualized. The teacher specifically praises any visualizations that seem accurate, and asks a student to rethink any that seem off the mark—rereading the relevant parts of the text to guide the student in adjusting the visualization.

Questioning the Author

Even good readers tend to blame themselves when they fail to understand a text, even though the text itself may be unclear (McKeown, Beck, & Sandora, 1996). Students who are less skilled readers are even more likely to feel inadequate and to grow discouraged when faced with a difficult text. After studying many students' failure to make sense of informational text, McKeown, Beck, and Sandora (1996) concluded that "textbooks . . . are not serving students well [and] students often react to inadequate text presentations by developing a view of themselves as inadequate readers" (p. 97). Beck, McKeown, and Kucan (1997) saw breakdowns at each point in the process of comprehension: The students often did not have sufficient prior knowledge, did not make necessary inferences, and did not come away with important ideas. In response to this problem, these researchers developed a comprehensive teaching strategy that would reorient the students' thinking about texts and show them how to use thinking strategies to understand the texts. They called their strategy *questioning the author,* or *QtA* (Beck et al., 1997).

The teacher prepares for a QtA lesson by deciding on a portion of text that can support intense questioning for a reasonable period of time, perhaps twenty to thirty minutes. Then the teacher follows three steps:

1. Reading through the text in advance and identifying the major understandings that the students should engage in this text.
2. Planning stopping points in the text that occur often enough to give adequate attention to the important ideas and inferences in the passage.

3. Planning the queries (probing questions) to be asked at each stopping point. (These are tentative plans only. The teacher will take his or her cue for the actual queries from the students' own comments and questions.)

The lesson proceeds in two stages:

1. *Prepare the Students' Attitudes.* The teacher begins the lesson by discussing the idea of authorship and explaining that texts are written by human beings who are not perfect people and their texts are not perfect works. Things might be unclear. Ideas might have been left out. Things might be hinted at but not stated. It is the readers' job to question the author. But since the author isn't present in the classroom, the class will have to answer for the author.
2. *Read a short section of the text.* Next, the teacher has the students read a small portion of the text, and when they stop, the teacher poses a query about what they have read. The kinds of queries the teacher might use are shown in Figure 7.6.

INITIATING QUERIES

What is the author trying to say here?

What is the author's message?

What is the author talking about?

FOLLOW-UP QUERIES

So what does the author mean right here?

Did the author explain that clearly?

Does that make sense with what the author told us before?

How does that connect with what the author has told us here?

But does the author tell us why?

Why do you think the author tells us that now?

NARRATIVE QUERIES

How do you think things look for the character now?

How does the author let you know that something has changed?

How has the author settled that?

Given what the author has already told us about this character, what do you think he [the character] is up to?

FIGURE 7.6 *Sample Queries for Questioning the Author*

Source: Figure: "Initiating queries, follow-up queries, narrative queries," in *Questioning the Author: An Approach for Enhancing Student Engagement with Text,* Author: Isabel L. Beck, 1997, International Reading Association. Used and reprinted with permission of the International Reading Association, www.reading.org.

The earlier research by Beck, McKeown, and their colleagues suggested that the kinds of tasks teachers set and the kinds of questions they ask have a strong influence on how students approach the cognitive activity of comprehension. This influence can lead students in productive directions, or it can lead them toward passive and inefficient practices.

In QtA, the teacher is knowledgeable about what comprehension is and how it should be approached. The teacher understands that comprehension requires activity on the part of the students, so he or she conducts discussions that require students to think and construct meaning. The teacher understands the difference between important ideas and details, so, in the words of Beck et al., "He asks questions that focus . . . on meaning rather than on locating text information; for example, asking, 'What did Tony mean when he said that to his brother?' rather than simply 'What did Tony say to his brother?'" (1997, p. 114).

Reading and Questioning

Reading and Questioning (Temple, 2003) is a procedure that is aimed at helping students learn from an informative text. The procedure helps students read carefully and study materials with a partner (working together can be more motivating than working alone). The method is suitable for any content subject in which the information from a text is to be understood and remembered. In terms of grouping, Reading and Questioning will work with an unlimited number of pairs. Each pair will need at least one text between them. The activity may take half an hour to complete. Often it is done by students independently, outside of class time.

Here is how it is done. The students take turns reading an assigned text in sections. The first student reads a section aloud, from one heading to the next heading. Then both students decide on key terms to write in the margin of the text. Both students make up several questions about the text, using the terms from the margins. The questions should resemble test questions the students think might appear on an examination covering the material. They write the questions on index cards or sticky notes. The students take turns answering each question. If both students agree on the answer, they write the answer to the question on the other side of the index card. They continue to trade roles until the assigned text is read.

In the days after the activity, the students continue to quiz each other on the assigned material, using the cards or slips of paper with the questions and answers on them.

Reading and Questioning can be done by the whole class, with students divided into pairs. The first time you do the Reading and Questioning procedure with the full class, it is advisable to stop after the students have finished reading and questioning the first section of the text. Then review their terms, questions, and answers, and suggest corrections as necessary. Thereafter, you should circulate among the students and listen to their questions and answers. Also, before the students study from their questions and answers, it is a good idea for you to review the questions and answers to make sure they are adequate and accurate.

Reading and Questioning can also be done with a tutor, or it can be recommended for students to use either by themselves or in pairs outside of class.

Audio Books

Many popular books for older students, young adults, and mature readers are available in audio book versions. Public libraries stock many audio books, and, increasingly, school libraries do, too. Older students can listen to an audio book as they read the printed version. Hearing the book read aloud can open up for young readers the pleasures of literature, pleasures that have been denied to them since the earlier school years when teachers more commonly read aloud to students. Listening to books read aloud can also build vocabulary and familiarity with written language. After listening to an audio book, students can participate in many of the discussion activities described earlier in this chapter.

Introducing and Focusing Attention on New Vocabulary

Research suggests that students who are not proficient readers usually have smaller vocabularies than students who read well—perhaps only half as many words on average. That matters, because larger vocabularies make it easier to notice things and to learn about new things. As we saw earlier in this book, the total number of words students encounter in their school books through ninth grade is enormous: 88,500 words, according to one careful estimate (Nagy & Anderson, 1984). That potentially works out to 10,000 words to be learned each year, or 50 words each school day, if the whole sum of words had to be taught from first grade through ninth. But Beck and her associates (2002) have reminded us that we don't have to teach all of these words in a reading class. As we saw in Chapter 3, Beck et al. suggest we think of the total vocabulary in three tiers:

> **Tier I** words are the everyday words students already know, that don't need to be taught: **mother, house, football,** etc.
> **Tier III** words are specialized terms that are learned in the context of science, math, and social studies classes: **bicameral, monozygotic, hypotenuse,** etc.
> **Tier II** words are those in between: They are useful words that are found in many contexts, but that are probably not yet part of students' vocabularies. Tier II words, what some call "frontier vocabulary," are the words we usually focus on in reading classes.

Activities that are useful for teaching vocabulary, particularly Tier II words or "frontier vocabulary," include vocab-o-grams, character clusters, webbed questions, and the Frayer Model—all presented in the following pages.

Vocab-o-gram

Words that will figure prominently in a work of fiction or a narrative poem can be introduced and practiced by means of a vocab-o-gram (Temple, Ogle, Crawford, & Freppon, 2011). A vocab-o-gram is a graphic organizer with cells designated for the important parts of a story: setting, characters, problem, solution, and emotional tone. An "other"

A Vocab-o-Gram

Instructions: Before you read Eleanor Updale's *Montmorency: Thief, Liar, Gentleman,* try to predict the way each of the following terms will be used. Write each word in the box where you think it best fits. We will review your choices from time to time as we read the book. Here are the words: ***discomfort, prisoner, cunningly, habitual thief, exposure, manhole, redeemed, transformation, finery.***

Characters	Setting	Problem
Feeling or Tone	**Solution**	**Other Words**

FIGURE 7.7 *A Vocab-o-Gram*

category is created for important words that don't obviously fit in one of the foregoing cells (see Figure 7.7).

Vocab-o-grams can be created with other categories besides the elements of a story. They might be *sources of pollution, effects of pollution, ways of reducing pollution,* and *chemical processes of pollution,* for example.

Character Cluster

When a semantic map is applied to a character in a story, it is a *character cluster.* A character's name is written in the central circle. Then words that describe the character are written as satellites around the character's name, and examples that illustrate each attribute are then written as satellites around the descriptive words.

The Frayer Model

The Frayer Model is a graphic organizer for relating a word for a concept to other words (Buehl, 2001). The Frayer Model directs students to think of essential and non-essential characteristics of a concept, as well as examples and non-examples of it. The model is best used to name a common concept that has many characteristics and examples. That way the students get to consider a larger number of words in context (see Figure 7.8).

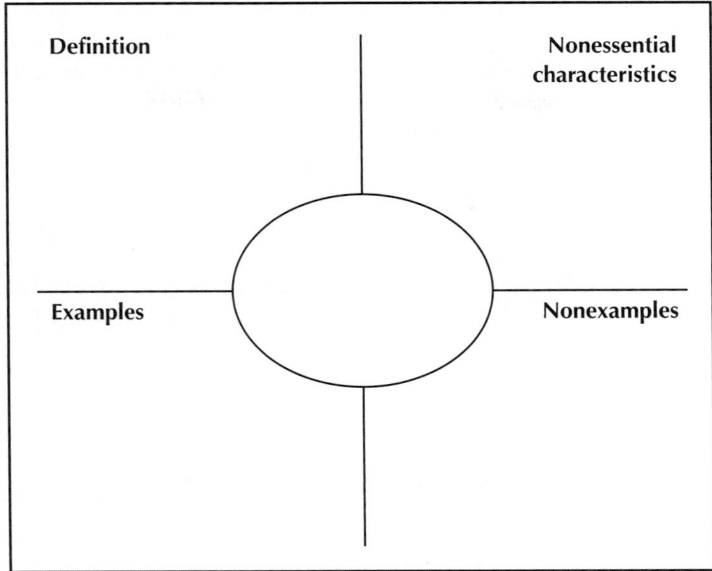

FIGURE 7.8 *The Frayer Model*

Helping Older Students Write

Comprehending and composing are reciprocal activities: two sides of the same coin. As students write—as they practice formulating main ideas and setting them forth on paper with the support of details, in a structure that includes an introduction, a body, and a conclusion—they are working with just those aspects of a text that are used in understanding a text when it is read. Moreover, writing enables students to capture their ideas on paper so they can return to them, reflect on them, and pursue their insights to more depth. In these and other ways, writing develops students' ability to understand written language.

In 2007, the Carnegie Corporation published a report on the state of adolescent students' writing in the United States. Steve Graham and Dolores Perin surveyed the writing achievements and deficiencies of U.S. students in grades 4–12 and produced *Writing Next: Effective Strategies to Improve Writing of Adolescents in Middle and High Schools.*

The report begins with a list of "causes for alarm": shortcomings of U.S. high schools students' writing abilities. Here are a few of them:

Cause for Alarm

- *Seventy percent of students in grades 4–12 are low-achieving writers* (Persky et al., 2003).
- *Every school day, more than 7,000 students drop out of high school* (Pinkus, 2006).

- *Only 70 percent of high school students graduate on time with a regular diploma, and fewer than 60 percent of African-American and Latino students do so* (Greene & Winters, 2005).
- *Students who enter ninth grade in the lowest 25 percent of their class are 20 times more likely to drop out than are the highest-performing students* (Carnevale, 2001).
- *College instructors estimate that 50 percent of high school graduates are not prepared for college-level writing* (Achieve, Inc., 2005).
- *U.S. graduates' literacy skills are lower than those of graduates in most industrialized nations, comparable only to the skills of graduates in Chile, Poland, Portugal, and Slovenia* (OECD, 2000).
- *The knowledge and skills required for higher education and for employment are now considered equivalent* (ACT, 2006; American Diploma Project, 2004) (Graham & Perin, 2007, pp. 7–8).

Graham and Perin assembled a list of recommendations that all teachers, and not just teachers of language arts, should follow.

Eleven Elements of Effective Adolescent Writing Instruction*

This report identifies eleven elements of current writing instruction found to be effective for helping adolescent students learn to write well and to use writing as a tool for learning. It is important to note that all of the elements are supported by rigorous research, but that even when used together, they do not constitute a full writing curriculum.

1. **Writing Strategies,** which involves teaching students strategies for planning, revising, and editing their compositions
2. **Summarization,** which involves explicitly and systematically teaching students how to summarize texts
3. **Collaborative Writing,** which uses instructional arrangements in which adolescents work together to plan, draft, revise, and edit their compositions
4. **Specific Product Goals,** which assigns students specific, reachable goals for the writing they are to complete
5. **Word Processing,** which uses computers and word processors as instructional supports for writing assignments
6. **Sentence Combining,** which involves teaching students to construct more complex, sophisticated sentences
7. **Prewriting,** which engages students in activities designed to help them generate or organize ideas for their composition
8. **Inquiry Activities,** which engage students in analyzing immediate, concrete data to help them develop ideas and content for a particular writing task
9. **Process Writing Approach,** which interweaves a number of writing instructional activities in a workshop environment that stresses extended writing opportunities, writing for authentic audiences, personalized instruction, and cycles of writing

---

*From Graham, Steve and Delores Perin (2007), *Writing Next: Effective Strategies to Improve Writing of Adolescents in Middle and High Schools* pp. 4–5. A Report to Carnegie Corporation of New York, Washington, DC: Alliance for Excellent Education, 2007. Reprinted by permission. A full-text PDF of this document is available for free download from www.all4ed.org/literacy.

10. **Study of Models,** which provides students with opportunities to read, analyze, and emulate models of good writing
11. **Writing for Content Learning,** which uses writing as a tool for learning content material (Graham & Perin, 2007, pp. 4–5).

In the following sections are teaching suggestions that incorporate most of Graham and Perin's points.

Teaching Writing Strategies and Teaching the Writing Process Approach

Writing strategies and the writing process approach can be taught together in language arts classes. Prewriting and collaboration can be combined with them, too. The writing process approach put forward by Pulitzer Prize–winning journalist and writing teacher Donald Murray (2003) and language arts specialist and researcher Donald Graves (1982) guides writers through five steps or phases as they produce their works: *rehearsing, drafting, revising, editing,* and *publishing.* We will describe each below.

Rehearsing. Rehearsing means preparing to write by gathering information and collecting one's thoughts. Student writers think of what they might like to write about, survey what they know about the topic, and begin to plan a way to write about it. Several strategies are available that can teach students to rehearse their ideas before writing:

- *Brainstorming and clustering.* Students can jot down in list form their ideas about a topic before embarking on writing about it. As a more elaborate version of the brainstorm, they create a graphic organizer, such as a cluster or semantic map, with the topic listed in the center connected to "satellites" around it.
- *Interviewing each other to find the story.* Students can interview a partner. Regardless of whether a writer has already prepared a semantic map of the topic, it often helps if another student asks the writer questions about the topic to help him or her "find the story." The student asks questions such as the following:

  "Why did you choose this topic?"
  "What most interests you about the topic?"

  The student also asks questions about details, things that the writer might not realize other people will want to know.
- *Researching the topic.* One of the more enjoyable parts of writing is collecting information about a topic. Students might need to read up on it or interview experts about it, or they might observe carefully and collect details about it. If they are engaged in long-term writing projects, they may keep notebooks or journals for gathering observations.

Drafting. Drafting involves setting ideas out on paper. Drafting is tentative and experimental. Students write down their ideas so that they can see more of what they have to say about their topic; often their best ideas do not occur to them until they begin committing thoughts to paper. According to writing process experts, the phase of drafting is not the time to be critical about spelling and handwriting, because a concern with correctness can inhibit the flow of ideas. They believe such mechanical concerns are better dealt with later; drafting is the time for students to focus on getting their ideas onto the page. In a social studies or science class, however, there is rarely an "other" time to attend to spelling, grammar, and handwriting—so teachers are not as prone to relax their insistence on correctness.

Revising. After their thoughts have been written out in draft form, students can be encouraged to think about stating their ideas more clearly. Many older students still need to be shown ways that writing can be improved: by having clear beginnings, middles, and ends; by finding a topic and sticking to it; by showing and not telling; and the like. Teachers can demonstrate these points through focused lessons (discussed later) and help writers internalize them by means of conferences. Teachers use two main kinds of conferences in teaching writing.

Teacher-led conferences. Conferences allow the teacher to help students clarify their writing and also to model for them ways to ask questions that will encourage other struggling writers—their peers. The teacher needs to ask questions that teach, pulling solutions from the students themselves and always respecting the students' ownership of their writing. The teacher asks students questions to help them focus on areas to improve their writing, and provides checklists of things to watch out for.

Peer conferences. Once the teacher has modeled the process, students can hold conferences with each other. Because many conferences may be going on in the room at one time, it helps if students understand their tasks clearly. The teacher can put together a checklist of good questions to ask as the students review their works-in-progress with each other, such as the following:

- Did my opening lines interest you? How might I improve it?
- Do I need more information anywhere? That is, where could I be more specific?
- Do you ever get lost while reading my draft?
- Do I stay on topic?
- Do I come to a good conclusion?

Editing or Proofreading. Once a paper has been drafted and revised, it needs to be reviewed for mistakes. Proofreading is often held off for last because whole paragraphs might be cut or added in the revising stage. The habit of proofreading must be taught. It consists of three things:

- Caring that the paper be correct
- Being aware of particular errors
- Knowing how to set those errors straight

A caring attitude toward writing is probably best developed by publicly sharing what students write. Students are most likely to care about correctness once they realize that writing is not simply done for a grade, but that their works must pass the scrutiny of others, who will be distracted from their ideas if the papers are marred by flaws in spelling, grammar, and handwriting.

After clearly teaching students to be aware of different kinds of errors and showing them how to repair them, the next step is to get the students to proofread their own work. Give them a checklist to guide their proofreading, such as the one shown in Figure 7.9. Each point on the checklist should be carefully introduced, explained, and practiced before students are sent off to use it on their own. Several versions of the checklist might be introduced during the year as new points for correction are added to the students' repertoires. Once the checklist has been introduced, students should practice using it with a partner to go over each other's papers before they are ready to use the checklists by themselves.

Publishing. Publishing is the final stage of the writing process and actually drives the whole endeavor. The prospect of sharing what they have to say with an audience makes many students want to write, rewrite, and smooth out and refine, especially if they have seen other students' work received with appreciation and delight. Publishing also lets students see what others are doing. A good idea is contagious; and anything from an interesting topic to a plot structure, to the form of a poem may be shared from one student to another through the process of publishing.

Focused Lessons. Focused instruction shows students strategies for writing. These lessons may focus on any aspect of writing, from mechanical issues such as spelling and punctuation; to word-choice issues such as showing, not telling, to write vividly and clearly; to composition-related issues such as ways to write strong introductions and closings. Focused lessons also may highlight the writing process itself, showing students how writers get ideas and narrow them, how writers put ideas into words, how writers go back and make the work better, and how writers share their work and learn from their peers' comments.

The goal of all focused lessons is for students to internalize the main points and use them while they are writing their papers, and also when they are reviewing their peers' papers and their own. Focused lessons follow a five-part model for teaching skills in context: showing a model of the skill in context, teaching the students the skill with explanation and demonstration, giving students exercise in using the skill, giving them guided practice, and independent use. In the writing workshop, focused lessons use those five parts in the following ways.

1. **Showing a model that demonstrates a point or skill you want to teach.** For example, if you want to show students how to combine short sentences to make more complex and "literate-sounding" ones, you may take a passage from Eleanor Updale's *Montmorency: Thief, Liar, Gentleman:*

   > The only hint of kindness came from Professor Humbley. He was a philosopher, who had just given a lecture on logical reasoning, which Montmorency had found more entertaining than he had expected. (Updale, 2003, p. 28)

A Proofreading Checklist

Paragraphs:

- ❑ Begin every paragraph on a new line
- ❑ Indent the first line of every paragraph
- ❑ Go through and take out any sentences that lead readers away from the topic of the paragraph

Sentences:

- ❑ Capitalize the first word of every sentence
- ❑ End every sentence with the right punctuation mark
- ❑ Rewrite pronouns that don't have clear referents (Unclear "it" or "this")
- ❑ Correct run-on sentences (For example, "however" can't join two sentences)
- ❑ Correct sentence fragments (*These are. Sentence fragments.*)

Verbs:

- ❑ Make sure you have a subject and verb in every sentence
- ❑ Make sure subjects and verbs agree ("Those guys was bad" may sound OK in speech, but it doesn't look good in print)
- ❑ Keep verb tenses consistent (*"Gaul was the ancient name for France. It has three parts"* doesn't work)

Check your punctuation and capitalization:

- ❑ Capitalize proper nouns and proper adjectives (*France, French; Germany, German*)
- ❑ Enclose direct quotes, but not indirect quotes, in quotation marks (*He said, "I'm sad." He said he was sad.*)
- ❑ Use commas at both ends of clauses to set them off (*Paris, the capital of France, is beautiful*).
- ❑ Use commas to separate city names from state names (*She lives in Baton Rouge, Louisiana*).
- ❑ Use commas to set off the name of someone addressed directly (*"May I help you, sir?"*)
- ❑ Use commas to set off days from months in dates (*June 1, 2014*)

Spelling:

- ❑ Remember that computer spell checkers can miss incorrect homonyms (watch out for *"to," "too,"* and *"two"* and *"they're," "there,"* and *"their"*)
- ❑ Use an apostrophe in contractions (*don't, can't*) and in possessive nouns (*the person's name*) --but not in its (*The cat stretched out its claws*)

FIGURE 7.9 *A Proofreading Checklist*

Source: Adapted from Hershey (PA) High School http://www.hershey.k12.pa.us/560370819115234/FileLib/browse.asp?A=374&BMDRN=2000&BCOB=0&C=51592

2. **Teaching the students the skill with explanation and demonstration.** Updale's second sentence in that passage could have been combined from some five shorter "kernel" sentences:

   a. He [Professor Humbley] was a philosopher.
   b. He had just given a lecture.
   c. The lecture was on logical reasoning.
   d. Montmorency found it entertaining.
   e. It was more than he had expected.

   The teacher shows the students how those kernel sentences can be combined into a complex sentence:

   He was a philosopher + he had just given a lecture →
   He was a philosopher who had just given a lecture

   He was a philosopher who had just given a lecture + The lecture was on logical reasoning →
   He was a philosopher who had just given a lecture on logical reasoning

   He was a philosopher who had just given a lecture on logical reasoning + Montmorency had found it entertaining →
   He was a philosopher who had just given a lecture on logical reasoning which Montmorency had found entertaining

   He was a philosopher who had just given a lecture on logical reasoning which Montmorency had found entertaining + it was more than he had expected →
   He was a philosopher, who had just given a lecture on logical reasoning, which Montmorency had found more entertaining than he had expected

3. **Giving students exercises in using the skill.** The teacher now gives the students kernel sentences to practice combining into longer ones. Depending on the skill levels of the students, they may be asked to combine just a couple of the kernel sentences, or they may combine more.

   Montmorency was a thief.
   He was the best in London.
   He had a trick.
   He knew the pathways of the sewers.
   The sewers were new.

4. **Giving the students guided practice.** The teacher asks students to pair up and look at one student's paper at a time. They find at least two examples of short choppy sentences that can be combined into longer, more smoothly flowing sentences.
5. **Independent use.** So that the points taught in the focused lessons enter students' repertoire of writing skills, you might add each point to a writing rubric or editing checklist or to your guidelines for good writing. You can also add that point into rubrics used to evaluate students' writing or into the checklists they use to edit their own and each other's drafts.

Before we move on, we should note that this lesson demonstrated three of the recommendations from *Writing Next* (Graham & Perin, 2007): It provided a *model* of good writing to be imitated, it engaged students in *collaboration*, and it taught *sentence combining.*

Having Goals for Writing

One of the eleven recommendations in *Writing Next* that could easily be overlooked is having the students set goals, and periodically reviewing together their progress toward meeting those goals. Troia and his associates (2009) conducted an elaborate study of the effects of writing process approaches on good and poor writers. Their findings were sobering. The workshop approaches alone were not effective in helping either proficient or poor writers write better. One recommendation they made was for teachers to explicitly teach skills of writing—from spelling to sentence construction to paragraph construction. Another was to have students set concrete goals for their writing. These goals could relate to both the quantity—how many pages the students will write during a week and during a marking period, and quality—improvements students aim to make as measured, for example, on the Six Traits rubric (see pages 335–338).

Keyboarding Skill

An observation that will not be surprising to special education teachers is that children and older students who struggle to write don't just have trouble conceptualizing ideas or composing fluent sentences and paragraphs. They also lack *transcribing skills*—the ability to render what they want to say into print. It may well be that handwriting has been a neglected skill in American schools. (Google "handwriting" and "neglected" to read plenty on the subject.) In any case, students who labor to form letters on the page certainly carry a heavier burden than those who write fluently and effortlessly. Add to those troubles lack of skill in spelling, and you have two heavy burdens that stand between the less well prepared students and those who write fluently. Teaching students to write on the computer can go a considerable way toward easing both burdens. Computers eliminate the struggle to form letters legibly and quickly. Computer programs also point out incorrect spellings. Special word processing programs for school use go beyond most spell-checkers and point out potential problems with homonyms—a source of most spelling errors that slip past spell-checkers (Troia, 2010).

Writing for Inquiry

Writing for inquiry—sometimes referred to as writing across the curriculum or writing to learn—can boost students' learning in any class, and also improve their writing ability at the same time. Several strategies for inquiry-oriented writing are explained below.

Ten-Minute Essays and Other Free Writes. Following a reading or a class discussion, students can be helped to collect their thoughts if they are asked to write a ten-minute essay, using the free write technique. To set up a ten-minute essay, the teacher asks students to write without stopping on the topic of the reading and discussion.

Some writing teachers insist that the act of writing itself can open up wells of creativity in the mind that are unlike the more deliberate sort of thinking that we do when we plan what we are going to write (Elbow, 1989). Thus, in producing a free write, students write continuously without stopping. If they can't think of anything to write, they write "I can't think of anything to write." The point is to keep the writing coming out without going back over it, examining it, or being critical of it.

Many teachers occasionally follow free writes with the invitation to go back through the free write, choose the most promising ideas, and craft a new essay, using these insights as the core of the paper—and eliminating all of the other chaff that usually comes out in a free write.

The Five-Minute Essay. The five-minute essay is used at the end of class to help students to get closure on their thoughts about the topic of study and to give teachers a better connection to the intellectual happenings of the class. The five-minute essay asks students to do two things: Write one thing you have learned about the topic and write one question you still have about the topic.

The teacher collects these essays as soon as they are written and might use them to plan the next day's lesson.

Three-Part Diaries. Students need to interact with both the material and the teacher regarding the material if their inquiry is to be powered by personal curiosity, yet also have the benefits of a wise guide. For that reason, teachers use the three-part diary.

The diary is used throughout a whole course, and it is useful for shaping and recording a student's inquiry from day to day, as an aid to study, as a means of linking the student's learning in the course to his or her life outside of class, and as a means to frame longer written compositions. The three sections of the diary have different functions. The first section is used for the student to write his or her responses to the readings and discussions. A dual-entry diary format (see the discussion earlier in the chapter) is often used for this section; the student divides each page down the middle with a vertical line and writes notations on one side and comments on the other.

The second section is left for the student's own impressions and associations about the topic. The student is encouraged to record thoughts that occur to him or her and notes from informal readings and other conversations—in short, any information and insights that further the student's understanding and appreciation of the topic of study. The material in this section will be used to inspire the writing of formal papers later on, but it will take some work by the teacher to make this happen. The teacher keeps his or her own three-part diary and, from time to time, reads to the class from the notes entered in this middle section. "Thinking aloud," the teacher demonstrates how he or she finds recurring patterns of interest or ideas strong enough to inspire further inquiry. The teacher then encourages students to do the same with this section of their diaries, meeting individually with students when there is time and encouraging students to interview each other about their entries in this section. The goal, again, is to find the thread of an inquiry, a recurring pattern of curiosity, an insight that is trying to be born.

The third part of the diary is reserved for letters to the teacher. Every month, at least, the students are asked to write the teacher a letter in which they comment on the class and their work in it, raise questions they have had, express hopes for their learning, and describe their own experience of learning in that course: What were their thoughts in the beginning? What goals do they have for themselves? How have they experienced growth in learning? What impediments are they facing? What would help?

The teacher collects the diaries (on a staggered schedule) every month and responds in writing to each student's letters.

The I-Search Paper. One popular kind of research project that highlights the process of research and stresses students' personal connection to the topic is the "I-Search" Paper, developed by Ken MacRorie (1988). The I-Search Paper is developed in six stages:

1. *The students formulate questions about a topic.* After they have been immersed in a topic, the students are helped to search their knowledge and curiosity and formulate a researchable question.
2. *The students make a research plan.* The plan might incorporate several kinds of sources, including not only books and magazines, but interviews, surveys, and Internet-based searches.

   The plan might include a graphic organizer such as the one shown in Figure 7.10.

3. *The students gather and record information.* Students should be given instruction in all of the ways they may do the research: methods of finding resources in the library, procedures for arranging and conducting interviews, and standards for discriminating between different sources on the Internet. They should also be taught

	Source #1	Source #2	Source #3	Source #4
Question #1				
Question #2				
Question #3				
Question #4				

FIGURE 7.10 *A Graphic Organizer for Sources of Information*

note-taking and outlining skills, as necessary. They may be taught to use graphic organizers as a way of visualizing their information before writing it up.

4. *The students write their paper.* The paper should be formatted according to the outline given in the next section, "Layout of the I-Search Paper."
5. *The students present their papers.* The students submit the written papers and may also give oral presentations or poster sessions on the papers.
6. *The paper is evaluated.* The evaluation of the paper is conducted according to criteria that are tied to the process and form of the paper, and that are communicated to the students in advance—usually by means of a rubric.

Layout of the I-Search Paper

Questions. In this section students will describe what they already knew about this question when they began their search, what associations they had for the topic, in what context the topic arose, and why they cared about their question.

The search process. In this section, students will describe the sequence of steps in their search for answers to their question. For example, students can describe what sources they began with and how these led to further sources. They can recount problems they encountered and breakthroughs in their search. They can describe their personal experience and say when they became more interested in the topic, when they were disappointed, and what made them decide to focus the inquiry in a particular way. They can tell how their questions changed or expanded as a result of the search process. They should also acknowledge any help they received from others as they pursued answers to their questions.

What was learned. Here students will present on the main findings of their research. They should support the findings with examples, stories, tables of data, or arguments that will help the reader understand how they arrived at their conclusions. They should include any analyses they carried out that led to their conclusions; for example, they can list effects and their causes, arguments for and against a proposition, comparisons of phenomena, or sequences of steps. They should connect their findings with their original questions. They might also suggest further questions they may want to explore in the future.

Lessons for the writer. This section will give students a chance to describe how they have developed as researchers. They will answer the question, "What do you now know about searching for information that you didn't know before?" To answer this question, students will describe those findings that meant the most to them. They might also discuss how their newly found knowledge will affect the way they act or think in the future. Finally, they might want to talk about the skills they have developed as researchers and writers.

References. This section will contain all of their references, following whatever format (APA, MLA, or Chicago) has been assigned in advance.

The I-Search procedure can be done by small teams of two or three students or by individuals. The topic can vary between those that require students to go to written sources (such as the Kosovo War) and those that require them to do more direct observation and interviewing (such as what advice people over 70 have for young people's character development). Either way, the format and procedures of I-Search make it an engaging and enjoyable exercise for writers—and also a natural impediment to plagiarizing. (Because the papers are highly personal, it won't work for students simply to download material from the Internet and pass it off as their own.)

Motivational and Emotional Issues of Adolescent Students with Literacy Problems

By the time students reach adolescence, their teachers and peers expect them to be able to read and write independently. If adolescents lack the ability to read at grade level, they risk falling behind their literate peers academically. This often leads to other problems with social relationships and can ultimately result in severe behavior problems and finally students dropping out of school.

The tasks of the teacher who works with adolescent students who are far behind their age group in reading and writing are extensive, and they often go well beyond instruction in comprehension, vocabulary, word attack, writing, and other skills associated with literacy. The first step is often simply rebuilding the students' trust in the educational system.

This section addresses ways of meeting the needs of adolescent students who have reading problems. First, we present the principles and theories that guide our decision making about assessment and instructional procedures. We then present three case studies that illustrate ways to deal with adolescent students who have reading, writing, and motivational problems.

Guiding Principles and Theories

Our approach is based on five principles:

1. Establishing trust
2. Providing literal role models
3. Reducing the feelings of learned helplessness or passive failure
4. Legitimizing personal knowledge and experiences
5. Developing a learning environment

Establishing Trust

The keystone for success with adolescent students with reading problems is the establishment of trust between the student and teacher. Without trust, students do not view the teacher, or anyone in authority, as a credible source of information. Erikson (1963) proposed that as early as infancy, individuals begin to develop trust or mistrust in others. This early trust is based on having general survival needs met.

The family is perhaps the earliest influence—positive or negative—on trust. The trust that is established during infancy can be enhanced or diminished as people grow and have experiences outside the family. Their initial experiences with schooling also can enhance or diminish trust.

Many adolescent students with literacy problems have a basic mistrust of authority, whether from family or school experiences. Without this trust, the outlook for subsequent positive social and academic development is poor (Erikson, 1963). However, trust can be established between adolescents with literacy problems and their teachers. With this trust, teachers have a solid base upon which to address the problems of literacy for adolescents. Trust will foster risk-taking in the adolescents' writing and reading efforts.

Providing Literate Role Models

One reason students fail to develop the ability or motivation to read by the time they reach adolescence is the lack of literate role models in their lives. When we think back over our own academic histories, we often find that there were very few occasions on which we observed teachers reading silently. If adolescents have no literate role models in their homes and have had few opportunities to observe teachers or peers reading silently, there is little reason to expect that reading will be a normal part of their lives.

To address the lack of role models for literacy, the classroom environment must be one in which reading and writing are pursued for pleasure as much as for formal school tasks. Students and adolescents model behavior they observe in trusted adults and peers (Bandura, 1986). This modeling extends beyond fashion and social behavior to the areas of reading and literacy in general.

Reducing the Feeling of Learned Helplessness or Passive Failure

Adolescents who meet with repeated failure due to the lack of literacy skills often resist the most well-intentioned attempts at assessment or instruction. At the extreme, this results in learned helplessness. Learned helplessness is a sense that no matter what one does, nothing will help. We see this in adolescents with literacy problems when they honestly believe that no amount of effort will bring about escape from a cycle of failure. They see all their attempts at success as leading to failure. Harter (1992) proposed that students and adolescents who feel as though they have little or no control over their successes or failures in school often attempt to evade tasks that might result in failure. These young people tend to make excuses for their failures based on either an external or an internal failure. Some students will blame the test or the teacher for failure. This kind of helplessness provides some protection against an additional example of personal inadequacy and reflects the view that forces outside the students control their fates. Other students will sit quietly and whisper "I knew I was going to fail, I'm just too dumb." This kind of helplessness represents a sense that internal forces are limiting the students' performances. Perhaps the most depressing combination of the reasoning behind success and failure in school is for students to attribute failure to the lack of ability (internal inadequacy) and success to the fact that the test was "so easy anyone could pass it" or "I was just lucky" (external control).

Johnston and Winograd (1985) used the phrase *passive failure* to describe the way in which students who have feelings of learned helplessness view literacy. They suggest that readers and writers who exhibit passive failure are not aware of the relationship between effort and success; they attribute success in literacy tasks to luck or simplicity of task; they attribute failure to their lack of ability; and they generally fail to persist in difficult tasks. Adolescents who are experiencing passive failure are not moved by simple cheerleader-type statements such as "You can do it; all you have to do is try." They have heard that statement, they have tried, and they have failed.

One way in which learned helplessness and passive failure can be overcome is through modeling. Over time, modeling by a trusted and respected individual can be a strong motivation. If adolescents observe a trusted individual (e.g., a peer, a volunteer, or a teacher) modeling literate behavior and successfully reading a book or tackling a difficult writing assignment, they are more likely to attempt tasks involving literacy. When these attempts are used as building blocks instead of measuring sticks, the adolescents begin to overcome passive failure and learned helplessness. Some of the building blocks include:

- Being able to read a printed version of a short dictated story.
- Coming to class.
- Opening a book or magazine.
- Asking for help reading a personal letter.
- Listening to a story that is read to the class and asking questions.
- Attempting to write.

Some of these might appear insignificant. However, the goal is to recapture the adolescent as a learner and overcome passive failure.

Legitimizing Personal Knowledge and Experiences

Classrooms today are much more culturally diverse than those of a decade ago. This trend will increase in the future as more students come to school with greater cultural and social differences. These differences are also seen between students and their teachers. This diversity can lead to the selection of inappropriate materials, inappropriate topics, and the misinterpretation of word meanings.

Adolescents with literacy problems reflect this broad diversity of cultural and personal experiences and knowledge. Reading and writing instruction are particularly suited to the use of students' cultural and personal experiences to enhance instruction. A teacher can create opportunities for students to use their personal knowledge and experiences through self-selection of topics for writing, reading, and class discussion, thus legitimizing personal knowledge and experiences.

In summary, adolescents with reading problems learn best in an instructional environment in which:

- A trusting relationship exists between the teacher and students.
- Literacy is modeled.

- Learned helplessness and experience of passive failure are replaced by a willingness to try and opportunities for success.
- Personal knowledge and experiences are valued and used.

These guiding principles lead us to an environment in which a variety of print material is available. It is structured to allow teachers and other literate participants to model reading and writing. When possible, students select their own writing topics, reading materials, and classroom talks. Within these tasks, there are ample opportunities for legitimate successes in which efforts are related to outcomes. Finally, the students and teacher develop a trusting relationship through a freedom to express feelings, ideas, and opinions in a non-evaluative atmosphere.

Developing a Learning Environment

Davidson and Koppenhaver (1988) suggest that programs that have been successful in fostering literacy among adolescents

1. Spend a high proportion of time on reading and writing.
2. Teach skills in context.
3. Stress silent reading.
4. Teach strategies for reading comprehension.
5. Build on background information and experience.
6. Integrate speaking and listening with reading and writing.
7. Focus on writing.
8. Use modeling as a teaching technique.
9. Use involvement or experience-based curriculum approaches that foster conceptual development.
10. Facilitate discussions rather than lead them.
11. Give students access to a wide variety of materials.
12. Use varied groupings and value collaborative learning. (pp. 184–189)

The methods by which each characteristic is realized and the specific strategies that are taught should be based on students' needs, interests, and abilities. Teachers typically can seize the teachable moment and create instructional lessons that are based on legitimate tasks such as preparing for driver's license examinations, writing birthday cards for friends, or completing job applications.

Discussions of topics that are currently on the minds of adolescents also provide the basis for many literacy lessons in these classrooms. For example, child abuse, drug addiction, and teen pregnancy can be key topics for many readings, class discussions, and written and dictated compositions. In this way, the classroom provides an opportunity not only for fostering literacy but also for addressing pressing social issues in the lives of adolescents. Within such a classroom, a variety of approaches can be implemented to address the complex needs of adolescent students with reading problems.

Summary

Older readers—those beyond the primary grades—need our attention, too. Even though much of the current emphasis in literacy skills improvement has been placed on early intervention to help young students avoid reading and writing failure and learn along with their peers, there is plenty of evidence that older readers need attention, too: as many as 70 percent of them read below grade level and are also deficient writers, according to national studies. Indeed, as the testing mandated by No Child Left Behind legislation works its way up through the grades, the reading problems of older students will surely become even more apparent.

In this chapter we have distinguished between readers who are reading above and at or near grade level expectations, and those who fall below those expectations. For all of them we have recommended instructional procedures that can be embedded in the teaching of all subjects. But for the lower achieving students, such instruction will be helpful but not sufficient. They need focused instruction in reading that will give them the skills necessary to cope with academic challenges. This instruction should be based on careful assessment of the students' reading-related strengths and weaknesses. We have argued that such instruction should be focused and, to the extent possible, short term. Several teaching procedures, as well as a set of general principles for assessment and instruction, were shared in this chapter. As students grow beyond the primary grades, those who experience difficulty learning to read almost invariably suffer the emotional consequences from not succeeding at a skill that is so centrally valued by schools. These consequences include embarrassment, anger, withdrawal, and what psychologists call learned helplessness. This chapter closes by exploring ways teachers can reach through students' emotional and motivational difficulties and help them learn to read.

As Steve Graham and Dolores Perin pointed out in their report for the Carnegie Corporation, *Writing Next* (2006), we have as many students in this country who are in need of focused attention to their writing as students who need help with reading. They are often the same students. Graham and Perin set out eleven recommendations to teachers so that we can help those students, and they were listed and discussed in this chapter. The chapter then set out suggestions for Teaching Writing Strategies and Teaching the Writing Process Approach, for helping students set goals for writing, for improving keyboarding skill, and for writing for inquiry.

References

Achieve, Inc. (2005). *Rising to the challenge: Are high school graduates prepared for college and work?* Washington, DC: Author.

ACT. (2006). *Reading between the lines: What the ACT reveals about college readiness in reading.* Iowa City, IA: Author. Retrieved from http://www.act.org/path/policy/pdf/reading_report.pdf

Alvermann, D. (1991, October). The discussion web: A graphic organizer for learning across the curriculum. *The Reading Teacher, 45*(2), 92–99.

American Diploma Project. (2004). *Ready or not: Creating a high school diploma that counts.* Washington, DC: Achieve, Inc.

Anderson, R. C., Wilson, P. T., & Fielding, L. G. (1988). Growth in reading and how children spend their time outside of school. *Reading Research Quarterly, 23*(3), 285–303.

Ausubel, D. P. (1979, March). *The use of ideational organizers in science teaching.* Occasional Paper 3. Columbus, OH: ERIC Information Analysis Center for Science Education.

Ausubel, D. P. (1978, Spring). In defense of advance organizers: A reply to the critics. *Review of Educational Research, 48*(2), 251–257.

Bandura, A. (1986). *Social foundations of thought and action: A social cognitive theory.* Englewood Cliffs, NJ: Prentice Hall.

Beck, I. L., McKeown, M.G., Hamilton, R., & Kucan, L. (1997). *Questioning the author: An approach for enhancing student engagement with text.* Newark, DE: International Reading Association.

Beck, I., McKeown, M., & Kucan, L.. (2002). Bringing words to life. New York: Guilford Publications.

Berthoff, A (1981). *The making of meaning: Metaphors, models, and maxims for writing teachers*. Portsmouth, NH: Boynton/Cook.

Biancarosa, C., & Snow, C. E. (2006). *Reading Next—A vision for action and research in middle and high school literacy: A report to Carnegie Corporation of New York* (2nd ed.). Washington, DC: Alliance for Excellent Education.

Buehl, D. (2001). *Classroom strategies for interactive learning*. Newark, DE: International Reading Association.

Buell, D. (1998). *Fifty reading strategies*. Newark, DE: International Reading Association.

Carnevale, A. P. (2001). *Help wanted... college required.* Washington, DC: Educational Testing Service, Office for Public Leadership.

Clay, M. M. (2000). *Reading Recovery*. Portsmouth, NH: Heinemann.

Crawford, A., Saul, W., Mathews, S., & MaKinsater, J. (2005). *Lessons from the Thinking Classroom.* New York: IDEA.

Crawford, A., Saul, W., Mathews, S., & MaKinster, J. (2005). *Teaching and learning lessons from the thinking classroom.* Budapest: Central European University Press.

Davidson, J., & Koppenhaver, D. (1988). *Adolescent literacy: What works and why.* New York: Garland.

Diamond, L. J. (2006, April). Triage for struggling adolescent readers. *The School Administrator*. Retrieved from: http://www.aasa.org/publications/saarticledetail.cfm?ItemNumber=5870&snItemNumber=&tnItemNumber

Elbow, P. (1989, Fall) Toward a phenomenology of freewriting. *Journal of Basic Writing, 8*(2) 42–71.

Erikson, E. H. (1963). *Childhood and society*, 2d ed. New York: Norton.

Graham, S., & Perin, D. (2007). *Writing next: Effective strategies to improve writing of adolescents in middle and high schools – A report to Carnegie Corporation of New York.* Washington, DC: Alliance for Excellent Education.

Graves, D. (1982). *Writing: Teachers and children at work.* Portsmouth, NH: Heinemann.

Harter, S. (1992). The relationship between perceived competence, affect, and motivational orientation within the classroom: Process and patterns of change. In A. K. Boggiano & T. S. Pittman (Eds.). *Achievement and motivation: A social-developmental perspective.* New York: Cambridge University Press.

Johnston, P. H., Winograd, P. N. (1985). Passive failure in reading. *Journal of Reading, 17*(4), 279–301.

Kagan, S. (1992). *Cooperative learning*. San Juan Capistrano, CA: Kagan Cooperative Learning.

MacRorie, K. (1988). *The I-Search paper*. Portsmouth, NH: Boynton/Cook.

Manzo, A. V. (1979, Winter) Reading and questioning: The ReQuest procedure. *Reading Improvement, 7*(3), 80–83.

Manzo, A. V. (1991, Summer). Training teachers to use content area reading strategies: Description and appraisal of four options. *Reading Research and Instruction 30*(4), 67–74.

McKeown, M., Beck, I., & Sandora, C. (1996). Questioning the author: An approach to developing meaningful classroom discourse. In M. Graves, P. Van den Broek, & B. Taylor (Eds.), *The first R: Every child's right to read.* New York, NY: Teachers College Press.

Murray, D. (2003). *A writer teaches writing, Revised edition.* Belmont, CA: Wadsworth.

Nagy, W. E., & Anderson, R. C. (1984). How many words are there in printed school English? *Reading Research Quarterly, 19,* 304–330.

OECD (Organization for Economic Cooperation and Development). (2000). *Literacy in the information age: Final report of the international adult literacy survey.* Paris, France: Author. Retrieved from http://www1.oecd.org/publications/e-book/8100051E.pdf

Office of Economic and Community Development. (2009). PISA: Program of International Student Achievement. Retrieved from: http://www.oecd.org/document/53/0,3746,en_32252351_46584327_46584821_1_1_1_1,00.html

Ogle, D. (1986). K-W-L: A teaching model that develops active reading of expository text. *The Reading Teacher, 39,* 564–570.

Persky, H. R., Daane, M. C., & Jin, Y. (2003). *The nation's report card: Writing 2002.* (NCES 2003–529).

Pinkus, L. (2006). *Who's counted? Who's counting? Understanding high school graduation rates.* Washington, DC: Alliance for Excellent Education.

Rich, M. (2008). Literacy debate: Online, r u really reading? *The New York Times*, July 27, 2008.

Schwartz, R. M., & Raphael, T. (1985). Concept of definition: A key to improving students' vocabulary. *Reading Teacher, 39*(2), 198–205.

Slavin, R. E. (1996, March–April). Cooperative learning in middle and secondary schools. *Clearing House 69*(4), 200–204.

Slavin, R., et al. (1992, September). Putting research to work: Cooperative learning. *Instructor, 102*(2), 46–47.

Smith, C., Tracy, E., & Weber, L. (1998). *Motivating independent reading: The route to a lifetime of education.* Master's Action Research Project, 440-143.

Temple, C. (2003). *B/C Teachers' Upgrade Programme.* Dar es Salaam, Tanzania: Tanzanian Ministry of Education and Culture and UNESCO.

Temple, C., Ogle, D., Crawford, A., & Freppon, P. (2011). *All children read,* 3rd ed. Boston, MA: Allyn and Bacon.

Troia, G. (Ed.). (2010). *Instruction and assessment for struggling writers: Evidence-based practices.* New York, NY: Guilford.

Troia, G., Lin, S-j. C., Monroe, B. W., & Cohen, C. (2009). The effects of writing workshop approaches on the performance and motivation of good and, poor writers. In G. A. Troia (Ed.), *Instruction and assessment for struggling writers*. New York, NY: Guilford.

Updale, E. (2003). *Montmorency: Thief, liar, gentleman.* New York: Scholastic.

U.S. Department of Education. (2005). *National Assessment of Educational Progress.* Retrieved from: http://nces.ed.gov/nationsreportcard/

U.S. Department of Education (1993). *National Adult Literacy Survey.* Retrieved from: http://www.literacycampus.org/download/NALS.pdf

Vacca, R., & Vacca, J. (1989). *Content area reading,* 3d ed. Glenview, IL: Scott, Foresman.

Vaughn, J., & Estes, T. (1986). *Reading and reasoning beyond the primary grades.* Boston, MA: Allyn and Bacon.

Assessing Spelling and Writing

CHAPTER 8

Chapter Outline

eading, writing, and spelling are interrelated processes that support and enhance each other. Readers apply what they know about spelling to recognize unfamiliar words, and what they know about writing to construct meaning from someone else's written language. Writers apply what they know about language and speech sounds to spell, what they know about spelling and vocabulary to select just the right words to express their meanings, and what they know about written language to put their messages into written language.

Monitoring Spelling Progress and Problems

Spelling counts. Shakespeare may have signed his name many different ways, but after printing became widespread, words were spelled consistently, rapid (and silent) reading became possible—and "good" and "poor" spelling became grounds for low grades in school and for embarrassment out in the world at large. (Who can forget the Vice President of the United States who tried to correct a child in a spelling bee for not putting a final E on "potato"?)

Spelling counts for more than good grades and social propriety, though. Special educators note that *transcribing skills*—meaning both fluent handwriting and easy and automatic spelling—contribute greatly to students' skill as writers and constitute extra burdens on students with low levels of literacy. Invented spelling may have its place in the early stages of learning to read and write, but for older students, wondering how words might be spelled and working them out letter by letter takes up concentration that might have been devoted to thinking through what they want to say.

Spelling also counts because learning to spell contributes to learning to read. Spelling and reading—or more specifically, word recognition—appear to draw on the same store of orthographic representations in the brain (see Cunningham et al., in press, for a review).

Learning to read words requires the operation of recognition; learning to spell them requires the more difficult, but related, operation of production. Thus, children's ability to read words usually outstrips their ability to spell them; this generally holds true for adults as well. (You can probably read any number of words that you might have difficulty spelling correctly. However, it's unlikely that you could spell a word you couldn't read.)

For beginning readers, spelling attempts can be windows that reveal the child's growing phonemic segmentation ability. Phonemic segmentation, or phonemic awareness, is a key component of early literacy. It means the ability to break a spoken word into its component phonemes, or speech sounds, and to hold these sounds in memory while searching for a letter or letter combination to represent them in writing. Young children's phonemic segmentation ability may be assessed by having them try to write unfamiliar words or whole sentences and then looking at how many phonemes they represent accurately or acceptably. A dictation test is part of the Diagnostic Survey for Reading Recovery (Clay, 1993), in which children are asked to write as much of a standard sentence as they can; there are five different sentences, each consisting of 37 phonemes. Children who can represent at least half of the sounds in one of these sentences are considered to be well on their way to developing phonemic segmentation ability. Figure 8.1 shows a first grader's performance on a sentence dictation task in September and in April.

For fledgling and transitional readers, spelling both draws upon and reveals their knowledge of the structures of words beyond letters and sounds: onsets and rimes, morphemes, and roots that are shared among families of words. Thus teachers need to be aware of the processes and stages of children's spelling development, as well as the signs of that development. And they need to have tools to help learners consolidate their learning at every stage and move on to more advanced stages.

Developmental Spelling Stages

Years of spelling research have shown that young children apply systematic strategies to relate speech sounds to letters and words and that these strategies develop in a sequence of predictable stages, each stage marked by typical misspellings (Ganske, 2000; Gentry, 1997, 2006; Henderson, 1990; Henderson & Beers, 1980; Read, 1971, 1975; Templeton & Bear, 1992). As children mature and gain more experience with print, their temporary spellings approximate correct spellings more and more closely. These developmental stages are described below.

Nonalphabetic Stage

The precursor to writing, this stage is represented by writing that contains no letters or letter-like forms, but is typically made up of lines of squiggles that look like writing to the child. The writing is definitely communicative; the writer can "read" it to you, although the message is usually different each time it is read. The intent is to communicate, but the writer has not discovered that writing is made up of letters and that the message is the same each time it is read. Nonalphabetic writing doesn't last very long, but it is an important prewriting stage, similar to babbling in learning to talk. Figure 8.2 shows an example of nonalphabetic writing by Leslie, then 2 years old. The letter-like forms at the top and bottom are attempts to write her name. The body of the writing is a letter to her grandmother.

Early Emergent Stage

Children have enough experience with print to know that it is made up of letters and that it conveys a message, but they do not yet understand that letters represent speech sounds. At this stage letters are used randomly, representing a message only the writer can read. Numerals and other characters are sometimes included. Early emergent writing is usually written in horizontal lines but without spacing.

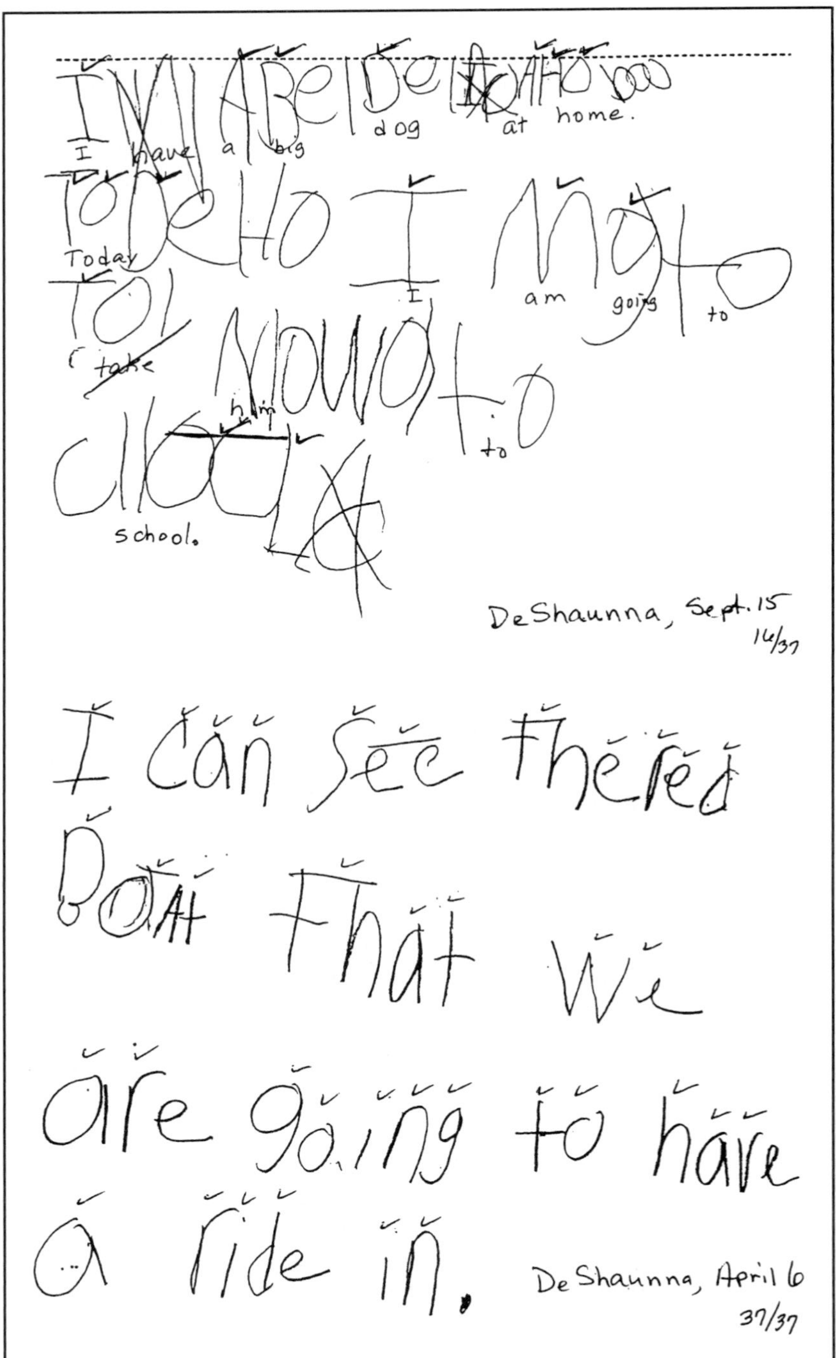

FIGURE 8.1 *Sentence Dictation Test*

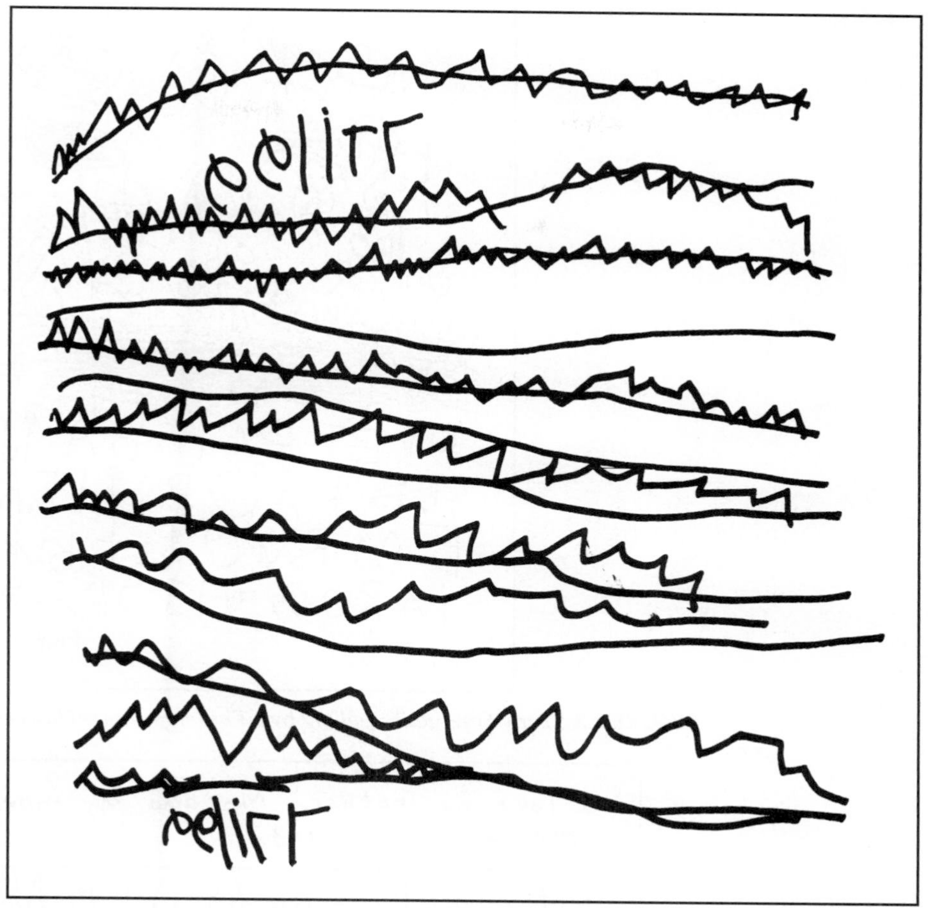

FIGURE 8.2 *Nonalphabetic Writing by a 2-Year-Old*

Figure 8.3 shows a sample of early emergent spelling by Phillip, then in kindergarten. Phillip drew an elaborate picture of flowers, birds, and butterflies and wrote four lines of random letters beneath it. When asked to read his writing Phillip talked about the picture without reference to the writing.

Later Emergent Stage

As children are taught the alphabet, they begin to recognize that letters have sounds associated with them. They begin to try out this concept by representing one or more sounds, usually the initial and sometimes the final sound, with letters that have that sound. Whole words may be represented with one or two letters. Spaces between the units intended for words may appear late in this stage.

Figure 8.4 shows a classic later emergent piece written by a first grader to describe his drawing; it reads, "I love my mother. Me and my mother. Me and my dog." The

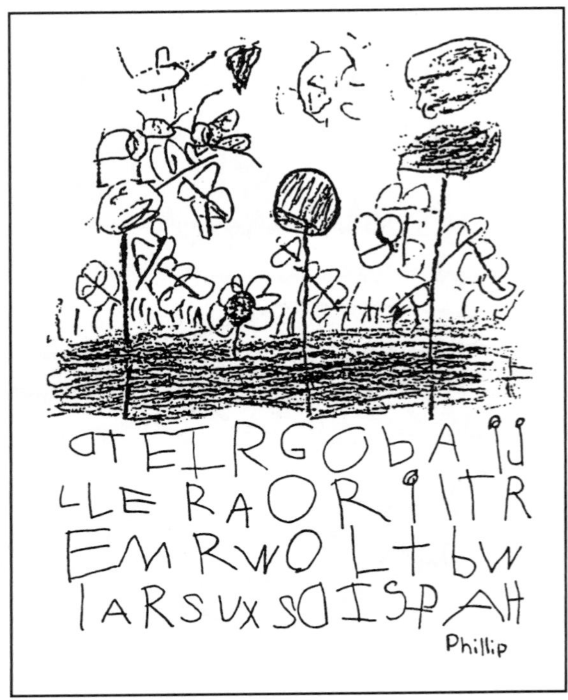

FIGURE 8.3 *Early Emergent Spelling by a Kindergartner: "Flowers"*

FIGURE 8.4 *Partial Alphabetic Spelling, First Grader: "I love my mother"*

FIGURE 8.5 *Later Emergent Spelling*

Source: J. Richard Gentry and Jean Wallace Gillet. Reprinted with permission from *Teaching Kids to Spell*.

writer used a single letter for the first sound in all but two of the words; he used the first and last sounds to represent "mother" and the entire word "dog," the only word he knew how to spell already. Figure 8.5 shows another first grader's later emergent piece, a caption for her picture that reads, "Ideas of Quilts."

Letter-Name Stage

As children move into beginning reading, they learn more and more about the ways in which letters represent sounds in written words, and they use this information both to decode in reading and to encode, or spell, in writing. First, inventions become more word-like, with more consonant sounds represented, as in LFNT for *elephant*. Then vowels begin to appear; first the long vowels since they "say their names," as in EGL

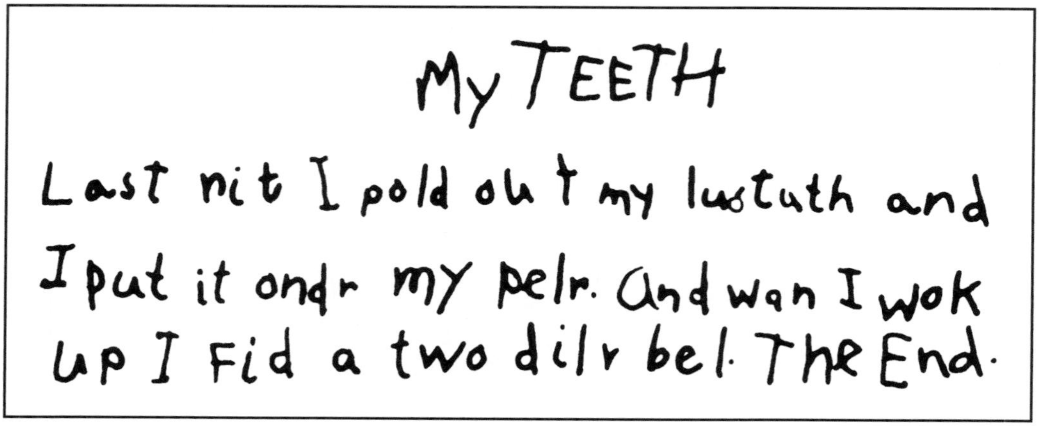

My TEETH

Last nit I pold out my lustuth and I put it ondr my pelr. And wan I wok up I Fid a two dilr bel. The End.

FIGURE 8.6 *Letter-Name Spelling, First Grader: "My Teeth"*

for *eagle* or BOLN for *bowling*. Finally, short vowels appear; they are usually misspelled because children try to use the *name* of the letter to approximate its sound, which works with long vowels and most consonants, but rarely works with short vowels. Typical letter-name spellings are HIT for *hot* and BAT for *bent*.

Figure 8.6 shows a typical letter-name speller's piece. Spellings such as LUS for *loose*, WOK for *woke*, DILR for *dollar*, and FID for *found* are exemplary of spelling at this developmental stage. Billy's uses of I for the vowel sounds in *dollar* and *found* are especially intriguing; they represent the use of the letter name I, which sounds like "ah-ee" if you say it slowly, for the short *o* sound in *dollar* and the *ow* sound in *found*. Similarly he used the letter name U, "yoo," for the *oo* sounds in *loose* and *tooth* that a more mature speller would represent with *oo*.

Figure 8.7 shows another first-grade letter-name speller's work. Leslie's spellings are quite complete, with all syllables represented. Long vowel sounds are represented by the vowel letter's name, as in VARE for *very*, RANBO for *Rainbow*, and NIS for *nice*. Reduced vowel sounds in unaccented syllables, sometimes referred to as *schwa* sounds, and vowel digraph sounds are not represented but collapsed into the consonant sound, as in BRN for *born*, TIGR for *Tiger*, and SANFLAWR for *Sunflower*. Irregular vowel substitutions for short vowel sounds show up in WAN for *when*, GAT for *got*, and SAN for *Sun* in *Sunflower*. A few high-utility learned words are present in *is, we, was, not, he, she*, and *loved*.

Within-Word Pattern Stage

This stage encompasses strategies of growing sophistication and is typical of many second and third graders. As their reading abilities grow and they experience more decoding and spelling instruction, children gradually move away from the primarily phonemic, or sound-based, spelling on which they previously relied. "Rather than relying on letter-by-letter and sound-by-sound processing, learners at this stage are able to chunk parts of words and process them in a more automatic fashion" (Ganske, 2000). They begin to

FIGURE 8.7 *Letter-Name Spelling, First Grader: "Guinea Pigs"*

develop strategies for spelling whole syllables and word parts, silent letter patterns, and entire words, as well as a visual memory for hundreds of words. They now learn words by patterns, as most spelling programs advocate, and can generate many words based on learning common patterns like CVC/*get*, CVCe/*cake*, CVVC/*hear*, and so forth.

Spellers at this stage are deeply involved with pattern mastery. As a result, their once-logical letter-name spellings, like RAN for *rain* and FITN for *fighting*, no longer look right. Learning word families and rules for dividing words into syllables allows writers to spell many words correctly and to produce very readable spelling errors. Within-word errors often result from overusing or misusing spelling rules, particularly those governing the spelling of long vowels. Within-word spellers often use the right strategy in the wrong word. Homophones, with their different spellings of identical-sounding words like *tale/tail* and *threw/through*, are particularly troublesome. Examples of within-word errors are WEAKE for *weak*, OWNLEY for *only*, HERT for *hurt*, and WRIGHT for *write*. Letter reversal errors like GRILS for *girls* are also common at this stage, and, if not corrected, they can become habitual problems.

Figure 8.8 shows another first grader's spelling representing within-word patterns. Josiah's directions for making a vest are very readable. He has used "the right spelling in the wrong word" in several cases. MEATIUM for *medium*, EATHER for *either*, and NEADLES for *needles* show his overuse of the *ea* pattern for long *e* sounds. MATEERIAL for *material* shows another long *e* strategy, again a correct strategy but not for this word. BUTTENS for *buttons* shows a typical representation of the reduced vowel sound in an unaccented syllable. SOING for *sewing* is a typical homophone-related error. Josiah's spelling is advanced for a first grader and is typical of many second- and third-grade spellers.

Make a vest.
If you want to make a rest, you hare
to get some meatium-size
buttens and then some neadles
a nd threds and then some
light Mateerial for the back
Make sureit is White matee
and Make Sure that theves
is brown or tan then start
Soing. Make sure it has
no arms eather. Make sureit
has three buttens then you hare
a rest to wear.
You will Know how to make a vest

Josiah

FIGURE 8.8 *Within-Word Spelling, First Grader: "Make a Vest"*

Syllables and Affixes Stage

This stage is seen by some as an extension of the within-word stage. Certainly it encompasses many similar features and confusions. Syllables and affixes spellers are usually proficient readers who read many genres of texts and write at least fairly comfortably for different purposes. Spellers at this stage are usually in the intermediate grades, from fourth to sixth or beyond.

Syllables and affixes spellers usually have mastered the patterns necessary to spell most single-syllable words correctly and are concerned now with the rules and patterns for spelling polysyllabic words. They must apply what they know about spelling patterns across syllable boundaries, which can cause new confusions. Doubling errors at syllable boundaries, like SILLENT for *silent* and BAGAGE for *baggage*, are common.

Spellers who can spell single-syllable base words correctly now wrestle with rules about consonant doubling, dropping of silent *e*, and adding of affixes. As a result, errors like HOPEING for *hoping*, DRAGED for *dragged*, REALY for *really*, MISPELL for *misspell*, and STANDDING for *standing* often occur.

Syllables and affixes spellers also struggle with issues involving stressed and unstressed syllables, especially vowel sounds in unstressed syllables. In stressed syllables, the vowel sound is usually fairly obvious. However, in unstressed syllables the reduced vowel sound, which is called a *schwa*, sounds like "uh." This reduced vowel sound can be spelled with any of the five vowel letters as in *again*, *agent*, *pencil*, *complete*, and *focus* or with vowel combinations like in *numerous* (Ganske, 2000, p. 20). A wide variety of unstressed-syllable errors can occur, such as APPAL for *apple*, PENCEL for *pencil*, SQUIRILL for *squirrel*, TRAMPUL for *trample*, and REGULER for *regular*. Learning how to add affixes to base words and how to deal with unstressed syllables are the big challenges of this stage.

Derivational Constancy Stage

In this final stage of spelling development, typical of adolescence and adulthood, individuals grapple with spelling unusual or infrequently occurring words and their related forms, or *derivations*. Negotiating this final developmental stage requires that spellers develop a sense of how words are related by meaning and by their historical, or *etymological*, roots so that spelling patterns can be preserved across these *derived forms*. For example, derivational stage spellers may confuse *-tion* and *-sion*, as in CONSTITUSION for *constitution*, but they are unlikely to spell this affix as it sounds, as a syllable juncture speller would with CONSTITUSHUN. Common derivational errors are confusing *-ily* and *-aly*, *-tion* and *-sion*, and so forth, and failing to preserve the *derivational constancy* of related words like *sign/signal* and *decide/decision*, which can include changes in pronunciation while maintaining the spelling pattern.

Success at this stage requires that spellers develop a keen visual memory for words and a sound understanding of the meaning units, or *morphemes*, that many words contain, rather than relying on how words sound. For example, the common misspelling CONFRENCE is attributable to not relating it to its base word, *confer*; likewise, HASEN occurs when the speller forgets that the base is *haste*, and CRITTASIZE and CRITUSIZE occur when the speller forgets the base, *critic*. Studying the common Greek and Latin bases that many words contain as well as all the related or derived forms of a single base word (*critic*, *critical*, *criticize*, *criticism*, *critique*) are most helpful to spellers at this advanced stage.

Assessing Spelling Progress

With the stages of spelling development in mind, it is useful to monitor and document students' progress by periodically having them attempt to spell a group of unfamiliar words. This provides information about how they handle different common spelling features like vowel patterns, blends and digraphs, prefixes and suffixes, consonant doubling, derivational forms, and so forth. A list of words containing targeted spelling features that is used for assessment is referred to as a *spelling features list*. In the sections that follow, we describe how to use a Word Knowledge Inventory we have developed, and also several other spelling inventories.

The Word Knowledge Inventory

For an introduction to the practice of assessing students' spelling development, we have included the Word Knowledge Inventory (see Figure 8.9). This is a spelling test that consists of 25 words, five groups of five words. The words are arranged from easy to hard.

To administer the test, call out the first five words. Check and see if a student or group of students has spelled two or more words in the first group correctly. Any student who has spelled two words correctly should be asked to spell the next group. Continue up through the groups of five words until the student can spell no more than one word in a group. Then stop testing that student. Consider a student's spelling level to be the highest group of words *before* the level where you stopped testing.

More elaborate devices to assess students' levels of spelling development have been created by Donald Bear and his colleagues (2007), and also by Kathy Ganske (1999). Both are accompanied by extensive and informative materials on teaching the students at their identified spelling development levels. We highly recommend both.

Developmental Spelling Analysis

A commercial spelling assessment procedure composed of feature lists is Ganske's Developmental Spelling Analysis (DSA) (Ganske, 1999, 2000). The DSA inventory is made up of two lists of 25 words each for each developmental stage from Letter Name to Derivational Constancy (emergent spellings are not assessed). The two lists for each stage are alternate forms that contain different words, each having the same target feature. A 20-item Screening Inventory is given to determine each speller's present stage of development, so that the appropriate stage list can be administered.

After the student's initial placement in a stage based on the screening inventory, one of the two lists for his given stage is administered and the list is scored for completely correct spellings as well as for correct spelling of the target feature in each word, even if the entire word is not spelled correctly. For each stage list of 25 words, a *stage score* is derived based on the number of completely correct words. A stage score of 12 to 21 correct spellings indicates that the student is at that stage of spelling development. At that stage, the student understands enough about the features presented to benefit from instruction, but does not have a complete grasp of those features. Instruction is "within the learner's zone of proximal development" (Ganske, 2000, p. 36) and will likely be most beneficial.

Knowing the student's present developmental stage is one piece of the puzzle. Knowing what specific features of that stage each student has mastered or has yet to master is the other important piece. Each student's spelling strengths and weaknesses

Word Knowledge Inventory

The Word Knowledge Inventory (after Ganske, 2001) is a means of testing students' levels of word knowledge. This assessment procedure can yield information for the teacher to use in teaching individual students and groups of students to read and write words more proficiently: that is, it can point the way for the teacher to help students improve both their word recognition and their spelling ability.

Begin by reassuring the student that you want to ask her or him to spell some words to see how she thinks about spelling. The student will not be graded on what he or she writes. The student should attempt to spell words even if not sure how they are spelled. Explain that you are interested in how the student thinks the words *might* be spelled.

Administering the Inventory

Start by asking the student to spell the first word and continue testing the words until the student misspells three words in any group of five, then stop. *Pronounce the words normally, without exaggerating their sounds.*

The lowest level (A, B, C, or D) in which the student misspells three or more words is considered the student's **placement level**. For an example, the student may correctly spell five words in the second group of five (List B), so the assessment continues to the next group of five words (List C). The student misspells two words in this group, so the assessment continues to the fourth group of words (List D). Here the student misspells three words, so the assessment stops. The fourth group of words (List D) indicates the student's placement level.

Placement List A

1. little	The child was too *little* to stay alone. *Little.*
2. chip	She ate a potato *chip. Chip.*
3. rained	It *rained* every day for a week. *Rained.*
4. truck	The woman drove a *truck. Truck.*
5. lend	Please *lend* me a pencil. *Lend.*

Placement List B

6. peeked	She saw me because she *peeked. Peeked.*
7. sailed	The boat *sailed* away. *Sailed.*
8. shove	Don't *shove* you neighbor in the lunch line. *Shove.*
9. sitter	My mother went out and left me with a *sitter. Sitter.*
10. batted	The third baseman *batted* last. *Batted.*

Continued

FIGURE 8.9 *Word Knowledge Inventory*

Placement List C

11. special	She kept her money in a *special* place. *Special.*
12. design	The *design* on his shirt looked like an owl. *Design.*
13. bomber	A *bomber* is an airplane that drops bombs on targets. *Bomber.*
14. fractions	In fourth grade math class, they are learning about *fractions. Fractions.*
15. doubting	There is no *doubting* who will win this game. *Doubting.*

Placement List D

16. physician	The *physician* wore a white coat. *Physician.*
17. biographical	This is a *biographical* novel about a football player. *Biographical.*
18. sympathy	The mother showed *sympathy* for the sick child. *Sympathy.*
19. adjourned	The meeting *adjourned* at 5 o'clock. *Adjourned.*
20. beautician	A *beautician* works with hair and applies make-up. *Beautician.*

Interpreting the Scores

Note the lowest leveled group of words (A, B, C, or D) in which the student misspells three or more words. If it is:

Level A, then the student is in the **letter name stage** or the **emergent stage** of spelling.

Level B, then the student is in the **within-word pattern stage** of spelling.

Level C, then the student is in the **syllable juncture stage** of spelling.

Level D, then the student is in the **derivational constancy stage** of spelling.

FIGURE 8.9 *Continued*

are determined by analyzing how the student handled each of the five features characteristic of that developmental stage. Of the 25 words on each list, there are 5 words that contain each specific feature. Each word containing that feature is examined to see if the particular feature is spelled correctly, even if errors occurred in other parts of the word, and a point is given for each correct target feature. A score of 4 or 5 correct on any feature is a sign that the student has mastered that feature; a score of 3 or fewer indicates that the student has not mastered that feature and needs instruction there. While the stage score tells the teacher what developmental stage a student presently occupies and facilitates creating instructional groups, feature scoring allows the teacher to pinpoint what word features the student has mastered and which need to be taught and practiced.

For each of the four developmental stages, five spelling features are analyzed. They are as follows (Ganske, 2000):

Letter-Name Stage

- Initial and final single consonants
- Initial consonant blends and digraphs
- Short vowels
- Affricate sounds (sounds of /*j*/, /*ch*/, "soft" sound of /*g*/, and sound of /*tr*/ and /*dr*/ blends)
- Final consonant blends and digraphs

Within-Word Stage

- Long vowels (vowel-consonant-silent *e*)
- R-controlled vowels
- Other common long vowels (such as *ai, ay, ee, oa, igh, i*-consonant-consonant)
- Complex consonants (three-consonant blends, *ck, kn, dge, qu*)
- Abstract vowels (vowel diphthongs such as *oi, oy, ou, ew;* vowel pairs *oo, au, aw*)

Syllables and Affixes Stage

- Doubling and *e*-drop with *-ed* and *-ing* (*baking, tapped*)
- Other doubling at the syllable juncture (*silent, cabbage, rabbit, habit*)
- Long vowel patterns in stressed syllables (*tulip, patient, complain*)
- R-controlled vowels in stressed syllables (*disturb, sheriff*)
- Unstressed syllable vowel patterns (*person, sugar, legal, governor*)

Derivational Constancy Stage

- Silent and sounded consonants (*hasten, muscle, condemn, exhibit*)
- Consonant changes (*office/official, explode/explosion*)
- Vowel changes (*define/definition, relate/relative, produce/production*)
- Latin-derived suffixes (*-able, -ible, -ant, -ance, -ent, -ence, -ary, -ery, -ity*)
- Assimilated prefixes (*in-, im-, ir-, il-, com-, con-, dis-, sub-, re-, bi-, tri-*)

Ganske's DSA is a system for periodic ongoing assessment that yields an abundance of specific information about each individual's strengths and weaknesses in spelling and word knowledge. It does, however, require considerable time and experience to interpret, and it yields information that is more detailed than some teachers want or need. Unlike spelling basal placement tests, students are not placed at grade levels, but rather placed in a developmental sequence at which instruction is most likely to be helpful to them. Students can be grouped for differential instruction and weekly word lists tailored to their specific strengths and weaknesses. Ganske's book *Word Journeys* (2000) contains a wealth of specific teaching strategies, word lists, and student examples that support instruction based on this assessment. Another highly recommended resource for instruction is Bear,

Invernizzi, Templeton, and Johnston's *Words Their Way: Word Study for Phonics, Vocabulary, and Spelling Instruction* (2007).

The Gentry Spelling Grade-Level Test

Richard Gentry, a spelling series senior author and spelling authority, has developed a graded list of spelling words that allows teachers and parents to determine a student's "spelling grade level" without analyzing the student's errors or stage of spelling development (Gentry, 1997). The test consists of eight lists of 20 words each for grades 1 through 8. Words selected are those that students in a particular grade often misspelled at the beginning of that grade but typically spelled correctly by the end of that grade. A student who spells 50 percent or more of the words on a particular list is said to be spelling comfortably at that grade level. This is a quick screening device that can be useful in placing students in a commercial spelling series and in determining if further spelling analysis is indicated. The Gentry Spelling Grade Level Test is shown in Figure 8.10.

Monitoring Writing Progress

Assessing students' writing and providing ongoing feedback are critical in encouraging young writers' progress. However, it is important to remember these points about writing assessment:

- Not everything should be assessed or evaluated. Most of children's writing should be for the purpose of communication, not evaluation.
- Assessment should teach; that is, children should learn about writing from the assessment of their work.
- Criteria for assessment should be clear and explicit.
- Children should be involved in the assessment of their writing.
- Assessment should show strengths and progress as well as needed improvement. (Temple, Ogle, Crawford, & Freppon, 2011)

As with spelling, many teachers find it useful to monitor and document students' progress in composition and the use of writing strategies across the year. One way to do so is to collect dated writing samples for comparison across time; another is to compile a checklist of writing features and strategies that students might reasonably be expected to gain facility with across time.

Writing Samples

Collecting dated writing samples is easy, and you can either set aside time for everyone to write a piece to be collected or select and photocopy a piece from each student's writing folder or portfolio at intervals. When you set aside time for everyone to write an

GRADE ONE

1. all
2. me
3. do
4. come
5. play
6. at
7. yes
8. on
9. the
10. and
11. one
12. be
13. like
14. am
15. you
16. see
17. is
18. ten
19. was
20. no

GRADE TWO

1. jump
2. apple
3. five
4. other
5. that
6. more
7. house
8. fine
9. off
10. bell
11. say
12. part
13. like
14. brown
15. hope
16. much
17. seven
18. egg
19. sometime
20. wall

GRADE THREE

1. spring
2. helps
3. farmer
4. people
5. bones
6. saved
7. roof
8. placed
9. below
10. walked
11. also
12. often
13. wrong
14. things
15. airplane
16. learn
17. those
18. cream
19. eight
20. carry

GRADE FOUR

1. worry
2. twenty
3. you're
4. dozen
5. thumb
6. carried
7. surprise
8. blame
9. wreck
10. November
11. loud
12. wasn't
13. finish
14. middle
15. wrote
16. iron
17. fifth
18. tomorrow
19. writing
20. frozen

Continued

FIGURE 8.10 *The Gentry Spelling Grade Level Placement Test*

Source: J. Richard Gentry. Reprinted with permission from *My Kid Can't Spell!* Copyright © 1997 by J. Richard Gentry. Published by Heinemann, Portsmouth, NH. All rights reserved.

GRADE FIVE

1. neighbor
2. parties
3. rotten
4. worst
5. laid
6. manners
7. parents
8. hungry
9. subject
10. claim
11. unknown
12. American
13. officer
14. prove
15. library
16. yawn
17. midnight
18. steady
19. prepare
20. village

GRADE SIX

1. jewel
2. thief
3. avenue
4. arrangement
5. theme
6. system
7. written
8. depot
9. ruin
10. yield
11. seize
12. difference
13. interview
14. zero
15. hymn
16. lettuce
17. burden
18. canvas
19. grocery
20. lawyer

GRADE SEVEN

1. possession
2. yacht
3. thorough
4. gymnasium
5. interrupt
6. athletic
7. secretary
8. agriculture
9. scientist
10. anchor
11. announce
12. revenue
13. patient
14. pressure
15. straighten
16. establish
17. laboratory
18. cashier
19. wrath
20. intelligent

GRADE EIGHT

1. fierce
2. analyze
3. committee
4. predominant
5. pursue
6. chemically
7. financial
8. appropriateness
9. cheetah
10. schedule
11. autobiographical
12. executive
13. coincidence
14. seniority
15. restaurant
16. alliteration
17. grievance
18. vengeance
19. guarantee
20. columnist

FIGURE 8.10 *Continued*

assessment sample, you can assign a general topic or form of writing or you can allow students to choose. Letting them choose their own topics makes the writing somewhat more authentic, but asking everyone to write on the same generic topic (e.g., a lost pet, a description of an object or picture, a holiday celebration) or to produce the same form of writing (e.g., a letter, a story from the imagination, a descriptive paragraph) makes it easier to compare each writer's samples.

Some teachers resist assigning writing topics or styles even for assessment, or prefer writers to select their own pieces. In this case, reviewing each student's writing folder or portfolio at intervals and selecting pieces to compare is the course to follow. Students can share in the selection process. The samples collected are more likely to represent authentic writing in which the writer has some investment, but they should represent what the writer typically produces. The purpose of this sampling is not to showcase the student's best writing, but to show growth from one part of the year to another.

When we collect dated samples across a school year, we write comments either on a copy of the sample or on an attached comment sheet. We usually note how the student appears to be managing tasks such as selecting a topic; forming sentences and paragraphs; using the writing cycle to first develop and elaborate on ideas, then check for mechanical problems; and aspects of writing mechanics such as capitalization, punctuation, and spelling. We also note things that we observed during the writing, if possible, such as difficulty finding a topic, ease and fluency of the writing, the writer's degree of independence during the writing, ability to reread the piece, and what the writer had to say about the topic or the piece.

Writing Checklists

A checklist of writing skills and strategies can also be used to show how and when students achieve certain benchmarks of writing across the school year. When used with dated samples, this provides comprehensive documentation of the student's writing progress.

Figures 8.11 and 8.12 are examples of writing progress checklists that can be adapted for a range of grades. The benchmarks are typical of students' writing at different ages, but you might have different expectations for your students that can be incorporated into your own checklists. These lists are for primary and elementary grades; middle school teachers could easily adapt the elementary standards for middle school grades.

Six Traits Writing Evaluation

The Six Traits model for writing assessment (Spandel, 2005) highlights six key aspects of writing: *ideas and content*, *organization*, *voice*, *word choice*, *sentence fluency*, and *conventions* (Temple et al., 2011).

1. *Ideas and content* means having something to say and saying it clearly to the reader. This trait includes knowing something about the topic before writing about it, having an original point of view, and providing details that engage the reader's interest.

	October	February	May
Composing Easily thinks of topic Can talk about topic before writing Maintains focus Expresses complete thoughts Produces at least 3 related sentences/ thought units			
Style Has a personal "voice" Uses vivid vocabulary Uses descriptive words Organization appropriate to topic and genre			
Usage Inflects plurals Inflects verbs Uses pronouns Subject-verb agreement Complete sentences, not fragments or run-ons			
Mechanics Beginning capitals Proper noun capitals, including I End punctuation Indented paragraphs Spelling checked			

FIGURE 8.11 *Writing Benchmarks for Primary Grades*

2. *Organization* means the writing has a beginning, middle, and end. It may include supporting main ideas with details, sticking to the topic, and making clear transitions from one point to another.
3. *Voice* means using words that express ideas well, even if the writer isn't sure how to use or spell them. Writing with a well-developed voice approaches the writer's oral fluency and expressiveness. If a piece has voice, you can hear the person behind the writing.
4. *Word choice* shows the writer's meaning with precise words and specific, memorable details. The writer uses fresh ways of expressing ideas, avoiding clichés.
5. *Sentence fluency* means a reader can easily read the work aloud. There are sufficient numbers of sentences to convey the meaning, and the sentences are varied in their length and form.
6. *Conventions* include correct spelling, capitalization, punctuation, and grammar. It also includes sentence and paragraph construction.

	October	February	May
Composing Establishes topic easily Topic sentence Supporting sentences Concluding sentence Minimum of one complete paragraph Maintains focus			
Style Has a personal "voice" Maintains voice throughout Vivid vocabulary Uses descriptive adjectives/adverbs Organization appropriate to topic and genre Varied sentence length and style			
Usage Inflects plurals correctly Inflects verbs correctly Pronoun-referent agreement Subject-verb agreement Complete sentences Some evidence of subordinate clauses in sentences Vocabulary appropriate for topic, audience, and genre			
Mechanics Capitalization correct End punctuation correct Commas correct within sentences Quotation marks in dialogue Indented paragraphs High-utility words spelled correctly Spelling appropriate for age/grade			

FIGURE 8.12 *Writing Benchmarks for Elementary Grades*

Writers of different ages and levels of development will be more or less advanced in their performance within each trait. Spandel and her associates have listed behavioral descriptors at four levels of development:

- *Exploring writers* are young writers who are experimenting with the whole enterprise of making meaning with graphic communication. Thus, within the trait of ideas and content, exploring writers might use pictures and scribbles to express ideas.

- *Emerging writers* are still young writers, but they have advanced to the point at which they are starting to work the features of conventional writing into their graphic productions. Thus, within the trait of ideas and content, emerging writers may use pictures or both pictures and mock writing in such a way that a reader might be able to guess an approximate meaning.
- *Developing writers*, through a mix of their own inventions and discoveries and overt teaching, can produce written messages that convey clear meaning, with the beginnings of formal organization and attention to some of the conventions of spelling and capitalization. Thus, within the trait of ideas and content, developing writers create stand-alone messages that are more readily decipherable. Their works show some attention to detail.
- *Fluent/experienced writers* express meanings more eloquently in print and take advantage of many features of fluent writing within all six traits. Thus, within the trait of ideas and content, fluent writers create works that show advancing mastery of qualities of writing, including the ability to say things clearly and in fresh and interesting ways, honoring more and more of the conventions of writing.

Six Traits writing evaluation can guide you in evaluating and grading children's written works. But it has another, equally valuable purpose, which is to call children's attention to the things they are doing well and point the way toward improvement. One highly effective way of showing children what they are doing well and what they can do to improve is to use rubrics.

Writing Rubrics

Rubrics are detailed presentations of quality criteria. Rubrics address several aspects of writing at once, and they explain clearly what constitutes a good job. Rubrics may be constructed by the teacher or by a collaboration between the teacher and the students. Rubrics should be closely connected to the qualities of writing that have been stressed in the focused lessons and any checklists that have been used to guide the students' revising and editing. Students should be fully aware of the meaning of each criterion, or aspect of quality, on the rubric before they produce the work that will be assessed.

Here are the steps for using rubrics:

1. Choose four to eight qualities of writing to assess. (Consider having the students suggest qualities of good writing.)
2. Make sure the qualities of writing you assess have been carefully explained.
3. Describe good work according to each quality. You may also describe fair and poor work.
4. Share the rubrics with the students before they write the works that will be assessed.
5. Use the rubrics often so that students learn what they mean and are able to use their criteria to guide them when they write.

A sample rubric for middle elementary grades, which was adapted from the Six Traits writing evaluation, is shown in Figure 8.13.

Ideas and Content:

Clear ideas. It makes sense. __________
The writer has narrowed the idea to a manageable topic. __________
Good information—from experience, imagination, or research. __________
Original and fresh perspective. __________
Details that capture a reader's interest. Makes ideas understandable. __________

Organization:

A snappy lead that gets the reader's attention. __________
Starts somewhere and goes somewhere. __________
The writer continually makes connections within the work. __________
Writing builds to a conclusion. __________
The writer creates a memorable resolution and conclusion. __________

Voice:

Sounds like a person wrote it. __________
Sounds like this particular writer. __________
Brings topic to life. __________
Makes the reader respond and care what happens. __________
The writer has energy and is involved. __________

Word Choice:

Words and phrases have power. __________
Word pictures are created. __________
Thought is crystal clear and precise. __________
Strong verbs and precise nouns. __________

Sentence Fluency:

Easy to read aloud. __________
Well-built sentences. __________
Varied sentence length. Some long sentences, some short. __________

Conventions:

Looks clean, edited and proofread. __________
Free of distracting errors. __________
Easy to read. __________
No errors in spelling, punctuation, grammar and usage, capitalization, and indentation. __________

FIGURE 8.13 *A Rubric for Assessing Writing: Six Traits Writing Evaluation Sheet*

Source: Temple, et al., *All Children Read*, Fig. 8.13 "A Rubric of Assessing Writing" p. 332, © 2005 by Pearson Education, Inc. Reproduced by permission of Pearson Education.

Summary

Spelling progress and development can be assessed using a *dictated sentence task* or a *developmental spelling inventory.* A sentence dictation task may be used with young children or emergent and beginning readers to show their ability to segment phonemes in spoken utterances. Developmental spelling inventories may be used for beginning and developmental reader/writers, to show their mastery of the successive developmental stages of spelling acquisition. The developmental spelling stages (*early emergent, later emergent, letter-name, within-word patterns, syllables and affixes,* and *derivational constancy*) are described and illustrated. Classroom spelling inventories are included, with directions for administering the inventories and classifying student's misspellings by word features and the speller's developmental stage. Determining a student's developmental stage and what word features have been mastered helps teachers provide differential instruction.

Growth in writing can be documented by collecting *writing samples* for comparison over time and by using *writing checklists* and *rubrics,* included in the chapter, that show how and when each student has achieved certain *benchmarks* of writing development. Six Traits assessment evaluates six key aspects of writing, including *ideas and content, organization, voice, word choice, sentence fluency,* and *conventions.* A Six Traits rubric is included.

References

Bear, D. R., Invernizzi, M., Templeton, S., & Johnston, F. (2007). *Words their way: Word study for phonics, vocabulary, and spelling instruction* (4th ed.). New York: Pearson.

Clay, M. M. (1993). *Reading Recovery: A guidebook for teachers in training.* Portsmouth, NH: Heinemann.

Cunningham, A. E., Nathan, R., & Schmidt, K. (in press). Orthographic processing: Issues and relationships to phonological processing in beginning word recognition. In M. L. Kamil, P. D. Pearson, E. B. Moje, & P. Afflerbach (Eds.), *Handbook of reading research, Vol. IV.* Mahwah, NJ: Erlbaum.

Ganske, K. (1999). The developmental spelling analysis: A measure of orthographic knowledge. *Educational Assessment, 6*(1), 41–70.

Ganske, K. (2000). *Word journeys: Assessment-guided phonics, spelling, and vocabulary instruction.* New York: Guilford Press.

Gentry, J. R. (1997). *My kid can't spell!* Portsmouth, NH: Heinemann.

Gentry, J. R. (2006). *Breaking the code: The new science of beginning reading and writing.* Portsmouth, NH: Heinemann.

Gentry, J. R., & Gillet, J. W. (1993). *Teaching kids to spell.* Portsmouth, NH: Heinemann.

Henderson, E. H. (1990). *Teaching spelling* (rev. ed.). Boston: Houghton Mifflin.

Henderson, E. H., & Beers, J. W. (Eds.). (1980). *Developmental and cognitive aspects of learning to spell: A reflection of word knowledge.* Newark, DE: International Reading Association.

Read, C. (1971). Preschool children's knowledge of English phonology. *Harvard Educational Review, 41,* 1–34.

Read, C. (1975). *Children's categorization of speech sounds in English.* Urbana, IL: National Council of Teachers of English.

Spandel, V. (2005). *Creating writers through 6-trait writing assessment and instruction* (4th ed.). Boston: Allyn & Bacon.

Temple, C., Ogle, D., Crawford, A., & Freppon, P. (2011). *All children read: Teaching for literacy in today's diverse classrooms* (3rd ed.). Boston: Allyn & Bacon.

Templeton, S., & Bear, D. (Eds.). (1992). *The development of orthographic knowledge and the foundations of literacy: A memorial festschrift for Edmund Henderson.* Hillsdale, NJ: Erlbaum.

Working with Culturally and Linguistically Diverse Students

CHAPTER 9

Chapter Outline

orace Tovey teaches third grade in the K–12 school in Swan Quarter, North Carolina. The local economy in Swan Quarter was traditionally based on farming and fishing, as well as staffing the ferry that runs between the mainland and the Outer Banks, offshore islands that are a tourist destination in the summer months. But the opening of a new chicken processing plant three years ago brought an influx of workers from Mexico and Korea—an entirely new development in a rural community where for generations, "everybody knew everybody."

Of Horace's 24 students, five speak Spanish at home and two speak Korean at home. The two Korean girls, Baye and Chin Hwa, have parents that can speak English moderately well. Two of the Spanish speakers' parents speak some English; the others apparently do not. Leona and Sean are African American twins whose family moved to Swan Quarter two years ago. The other 15 boys and girls are white.

Horace's classroom reflects his students' diversity. At first sight, the student work displayed on the walls is what one would expect to see in a third-grade classroom—one-page, handwritten texts accompanied by illustrations; at a closer look, though, some of the texts turn out to have two versions, one in English and one in Spanish or Korean. The word wall has a column labeled "Cognates," and the chalk board has one labeled "Phrase of the Day," where each day one of the English language learners writes a common expression in Spanish or in Korean. Each morning, Horace and his students spend the first five minutes of class learning the phrase of the day and practicing previously learned expressions in Spanish and Korean. The classroom library has a host of multicultural children's books, some of which are English-Spanish or Korean-Spanish bilingual books.

The class has finished reading The Giving Tree *and the students are now responding to the story by writing their own texts titled "My Giving Tree." The two Korean girls sit next to each other; they write in silence, looking words up in their bilingual dictionaries and talking to each other briefly in Korean from time to time.*

Anita, the Spanish-speaking student who arrived in the United States six months ago, has written a first draft in Spanish and is now working with Ofelia, who is fluent both in Spanish and in English, on an English version of her writing piece. While laboring over her first sentence ("My giving tree is my family: my mother, my father, my sisters and brothers, my godmother, my grandparents, my uncles and aunts, and my neighbors back home."), Anita learns from Ofelia the English words "family" and "neighbor." With a broad smile on her face, she goes to the word wall and writes "family = familia" in the "Cognates" column.

The twins have written their first paragraph jointly. It reads, "We were five when our father died, and all we did was cry and cry. But then Noah, our ten-year-old brother came and said, Why you cryin'? You ain't alone. You got mama and me. We gonna look after you. And they did." "Great job," says Horace, reading over their shoulders. "Just remember your quotation marks."

In the last thirty years, the demographics of the United States have changed dramatically, primarily because of an increase in immigration. The 2000 U.S. census data show that in 1998, 63 percent of Asian Americans and 35 percent of Latinos were foreign born, while estimates based on the census data predict that by the year 2100, Latinos alone will represent 33 percent, and non-Whites 60 percent of the U.S. population (Riche, 2000).

Along with the rise in the immigrant population has come a sharp increase in the number of immigrant students in American public schools, with most of these students coming from non-English speaking countries. According to the National Clearinghouse for English Language Acquisition (2008), the number of students with limited English proficiency grew by 149 percent from the 1989–1990 to the 2005–2006 school year. If in 1979 one in 20 children and youth in American schools came from a family where a language other than English was spoken, by 2004 the ratio had risen to one in seven, and the numbers of our English language learners (ELLs) more than doubled, from 6 million to 14 million (August & Shanahan, 2006).

The proportion of English language learners is much higher in some states than in others, with California, Texas, Florida, New York, Illinois, and Arizona enrolling the largest numbers of ELLs in public schools (August & Shanahan, 2006). But English language learners are also appearing in large numbers in new locations. States such as North Carolina, South Carolina, Tennessee, and Indiana have seen an increase from 300 percent in 1996 to nearly 700 percent in 2006 in the numbers of children from homes where English is not the first language (Goldenberg & Coleman, 2010). In these states English language learners may be found in small rural areas as well as in cities.

Educating immigrant students as well as those who, even though they were born in the United States, speak a language other than English or a non-standard English dialect at home is a growing challenge, especially since their academic achievement tends to lag behind that of their English-speaking, white peers. The 2009 National Assessment of Educational Progress (NAEP) reports a significant score gap in reading between white fourth-grade students and Black and Hispanic fourth-grade students; white students had an average score of 230 points, whereas Black and Hispanic students had an average score of 205 points. According to NAEP (2009), eighth graders in all ethnic groups made gains in reading since 2007; however, white students scored higher on average than Black, Hispanic, and American Indian/Alaska Native students, with significant score gaps persisting between white students and their Black and Hispanic peers. Although some progress was made by English language learners on state reading and mathematics tests, a 2010 analysis by the Center on Education Policy (CEP) also reports very large differences in reading proficiency (45 percentage points) between high school English language learners and other students.

What can be done to close this achievement gap? As Gay (2010) points out, scores on standardized tests are symptoms of, not causes of or remedies for the problem. In order to remove the obstacles to high achievement faced by culturally and linguistically diverse learners, teachers need to understand what is interfering with students' performance. A first step toward developing such an understanding involves an examination of the characteristics of culturally and linguistically diverse (CLD) students, and of the ways in which these characteristics may influence students' academic progress.

Culture and Schooling

In discussing cultural differences, we will use the term *culture* to refer to the social values, cognitive and communicative codes, behavioral standards, worldviews, and beliefs (Delgado-Gaitan & Trueba, 1991) that are shared by an ethnic group and that, despite individual variations, distinguish the group's members from those of another ethnic group. Each of us is born and socialized into a particular culture that becomes a lens through which we perceive and make sense of our life and of the lives of others, and which determines how we think, act, and speak. Importantly, the lens is invisible. "As we learn and use culture in daily life, it becomes habitual. Our habits become for the most part transparent to us . . . We do not think much about the structure and characteristics of culture as we use it, just as we do not think reflectively about any familiar tool in the midst of its use" (Erickson, 2010, p. 35).

Culture affects the ways in which we teach and learn. "The beliefs, attitudes, and values that each of us holds not only shape our perceptions of the world around us, they also make it easier or more difficult for us to build new knowledge" (Hamayan, Marler, Sanchez-Lopez, & Damico, 2007, p. 185). This means that learning will be easier for those children whose cultural background matches the school culture, and more difficult for the children whose home culture diverges from that of the school.

The culture of American schools is primarily of European and middle-class origins (Boykin, 1994); therefore what most educators, who are themselves products of the American education system, consider to be "normal," or "right," or "appropriate" ways of doing things in school will reflect predominantly European middle-class values, standards, vantage points, and beliefs—any of which may be at odds with those that children socialized in non-mainstream cultures bring to school. Because of such mismatches, and often in spite of the efforts of well-meaning teachers, these children may find the classroom to be a hostile, incomprehensible, and exclusionary environment.

In order to prevent or alleviate such feelings and to work effectively with their CLD students, teachers need more than good intentions. First and foremost, they need to be aware of cultural differences that may exist in the classroom—some of which we will discuss in the next section.

Cultural Differences in the Mainstream Classroom

In addition to obvious differences in food, clothing, music, and traditions, cultures also differ from one another along the following dimensions (Brown & Lundrum-Brown, 1995):

- ***Axiology***—the interpersonal values held by members of a cultural group (e.g., competition versus cooperation; emotional restraint versus open expression of emotions; direct versus indirect verbal expression)
- ***Ethos***—the beliefs that guide social interactions among members of a cultural group (e.g., that people are independent or interdependent beings; that one's first allegiance is to oneself or to one's family; that all members of the group are equal or that there is a hierarchy of status)
- ***Epistemology***—ways of knowing and learning (e.g., by relying on one's intellectual abilities or on one's affect and intuition; by questioning, discovering, and making sense of things on one's own or by absorbing the wisdom and knowledge of the past)

Where a particular culture is situated along each dimension will influence, among other things, its *conceptualization of literacy* and the *communication style* of its members.

Conceptualizing Literacy

Different cultural groups assign different meanings to the term *literacy,* have different understandings of the purposes of literacy, engage in different literacy practices, and differ in their involvement in children's literacy development and schooling. For example, many Puerto Ricans and Dominicans believe that literacy means learning the letters and knowing how to combine them; that the meaning of texts is fixed and not open to negotiation; that becoming literate involves memorizing and reciting passages as well as copying teachers' notes from the chalkboard with attention to penmanship; and that the primary purpose of literacy is to facilitate access to God's word (Rubinstein-Avila, 2007; Volk & de Acosta, 2001). Often, Bangladeshi children learn to read and write in Bengali and Koranic Arabic through formal and rigid instruction aimed primarily at developing their sense of belonging to their religion and community (Gregory, 1994). Pakistani Muslim parents believe that they should trust teachers to do the teaching and that going to school to inquire about their children's progress would be inappropriate (Huss-Keeler, 1997).

It is easy to see how such beliefs about literacy and schooling diverge from those that inform classroom instruction in American schools, and how they can cause mismatches between the expectations of students and their families for schooling and those of teachers. For example, if learning to write is understood by a child's family to mean developing good penmanship and orthography, the teacher's encouraging students to experiment with invented spelling is likely to be frowned upon by the child's parents. Conversely, parents' not coming to school out of respect for teachers' authority may be interpreted by teachers as lack of interest and involvement in children's learning. Finally, the students may be confused and frustrated until they figure out how school works, as the words of a Dominican student suggest:

> In Santo Domingo, they expected us to learn and remember the information straight from the book or from copying the teacher's notes [on the board], but *here* I am not sure what exactly we should be learning. They sometimes say, "Write about what you think". . . They say, "Go get information on the Internet," or they say "The answers are all in the chapter." It's confusing . . . What I find [on the Internet] is . . . It's not always the same as what it says in the [text]book. And also, what *I think* may not be correct. (Rubinstein-Avila, 2007, p. 584)

Communication Styles

The values and beliefs of a cultural group also influence the communication practices and behaviors, or *communication styles,* of its members and, by extension, the effectiveness of teacher-student and student-student communication and interaction in the classroom. For example, Asian American cultures encourage respect for authority, obedience, self-restraint in expressing emotions, and indirectness in expressing thoughts and opinions, so many Asian American students find it hard to engage spontaneously in classroom discussions or debates that require questioning others' ideas or expressing opposing views (Fox, 1994; Pai, Adler, & Shadiow, 2006). Also, because in many Asian countries teachers have a highly formal relationship with their students and students are expected to learn individually by listening and memorizing, Asian students often experience discomfort with the informality of student-teacher relationships and with the expectations for student participation and group work in American classrooms (Nieto, 1996).

Unlike Asian Americans, African American students tend to value the overt expression of feelings and emotions, both in student-student and in teacher-student interactions. In the African American community, teachers show that they care for their students by "exhibiting personal power; establishing meaningful personal relationships; displaying emotion to garner student respect" (Delpit, 1995, p. 142).

Following is a description of Mexican students' communication style grounded in an analysis of their home culture:

> Indirect, implicit, or covert communication is consonant with Mexicans' emphasis on family harmony, on 'getting along' and not making others uncomfortable. Conversely, assertiveness, open differences in opinions, and demands for clarification are seen as rude or insensitive of others' feelings . . . Mexican Americans . . . often make use of allusions, proverbs, and parables to convey their viewpoints, which

may leave an impression of guardedness, vagueness, obscurity, or excessive embellishment, obsequiousness, and politeness. (Falicov, 1996, p. 176*)

Additional differences between the norms for mainstream classroom communication and the communication styles of non-mainstream cultural groups involve *participation structures, task-engagement preferences,* and *discourse organization* (Gay, 2010).

Participation Structures. Two types of classroom participation structures have been identified in the literature on ethnic communication styles: a *passive-receptive participation structure* typical of mainstream classrooms and a *participatory-interactive structure* observed in classrooms with African American, Latino-American, and Native Hawaiian students (Gay, 2010; Kochman, 1985). The former requires that students listen while the teacher talks and then respond in some prearranged way—by asking or answering questions in complete sentences, by being brief and to the point, by talking one at a time and taking teacher-regulated turns at speaking, and by making eye contact with the interlocutor. By contrast, in participatory-interactive discourse structures, listeners are expected to engage with the speaker through vocal or motion responses. In the African American culture, this kind of speaker-listener relationship is referred to as "call-response," and it consists of the speaker issuing a "call" (that is, making a statement) to which the listeners respond by giving encouragement, commentary, praise, or even criticism *as the speaker is talking,* so that the discourse is co-constructed by the speaker and the audience. Similar to the African American "call-response" is the Hawaiian "talk-story," in which children talk together to tell a story or formulate an idea as a group (Au, 1993).

Task Engagement Preferences. Related to communication styles are the *task engagement preferences* of various ethnic groups. While in many mainstream classrooms students are expected to "get down to work" as soon as a task is assigned and to "stay on task," in cultures that value collaboration over individual performance, the task needs to be placed in a social context before it is performed (Gay, 2010). For example, Latino adults will first inquire about their colleagues' families and well-being before engaging with a task; prior to making a presentation, African American speakers tend to inform the audience of their emotions, values, or beliefs.

Children coming from these cultures may be doing essentially the same kind of contextualization work when they spend seemingly unnecessary time socializing with their peers instead of beginning to write an essay or take a test. Yet this kind of "preparation before performance" may serve "a purpose in learning similar to a theater performer doing yoga exercises before taking the stage. Both are techniques the 'actors' use to focus, to get themselves in the mood and mode to perform" (Gay, 2010, p. 109). Following is an example of task contextualization by a Latina student. Notice how, in response to the teacher's question, "How can we know when a tornado is coming? How can we find that out?" the student shares personal experience before answering the question.

The other day, we almost had a small one. Here at school, we were in math class. And when one looked at the sky, the clouds that got all black and ugly. And that created like a small drop and we all got scared. We went to see the science teacher,

---

*From "Mexican Families," by C. J. Falicov in *Clinical Handbook of Marital Therapy,* M. McGoldrick, J. Giordano and J.K. Pearce, Eds., 1996, New York: Guilford Press, p. 176. Reprinted by permission of Guilford Press.

> and she helped us. She had a weather map for us, and nothing was happening, except for the clouds which were getting formed, but nothing serious. So I learned that it was the way how it got formed when we could see the clouds, that ugly and everything, and all colors like this dark. (Lee & Fradd, 1996, p. 284)

Just as they engage with learning tasks differently, members of various cultures also engage with the issues involved in a learning task differently. European Americans tend to relate to issues as reporters, focusing on the accuracy of facts and on the intrinsic value of ideas, and trying to entertain multiple points of view in an objective manner that does not leave room for the expression of personal emotions (Kochman, 1981). By contrast, African Americans tend to adopt an advocacy stance when engaging with an issue, so they combine facts, opinions, and emotions in discussing ideas (Gay, 2010). African, Asian, Latin American, and Middle Eastern students value group harmony, modesty in self-presentation, and restraint in taking an oppositional stance; therefore they tend to express ideas indirectly, through subtle implications and imprecise commentary, to provide excessive background information in elaborate introductions, to avoid declaring personal positions and to invoke the wisdom of the past instead (Fox, 1994).

Discourse Organization. The way ideas are organized and presented in spoken or written discourse also varies from one culture to another. European Americans (and most classroom teachers) prefer a *topic-centered discourse* (Cazden, 2001) that focuses on one topic at a time, is organized linearly and "logically," and has a clear beginning, middle, and end. African American, Latino American, Native American, and Native Hawaiian cultures, however, favor a *topic-associative* (Gay, 2010) or *episodic* (Cazden, 2001) *discourse* in which several issues are addressed at once, and which unfolds in a circular, rather than linear, manner, with relationships among the episodes assumed rather than stated explicitly. Look at the following two excerpts of classroom discourse produced during sharing time—one by a white first-grader, Carl, and the other by an African American student, Deena (Cazden, 2001, pp. 12–15).

Topic-Centered Discourse: *A Hundred Dollars*

Carl: Well / last night my father was at work /
he / every Thursday night they have this thing /
that everybody has this dollar /
and it makes up to a hundred dollars /
and my / and you've gotta pick this name out /
and my father's name got picked /
so he won a thousand dollars // a hundred dollars //
Teacher: Tell us what he's gonna do with it //

Episodic Discourse: *Deena's Day*

Deena: I went to the beach Sunday /
and / to McDonald's / and to the park /
and I got this for my / birthday // [*holds up purse*]
my mother bought it for me /
and I had two dollars for my birthday /

> and I put it in here /
> and I went to where my friend / named Gigi /
> I went over to my grandmother's house with her /
> and she was on my back . . .
> **Teacher**: OK I'm going to stop you //
> I want you to talk about things that are really, really very important //

You may have noticed that the teacher responded differently to the two children's stories. The question she asked after Carl's sharing not only pushed the child to extend his discourse by providing an ending to his story, but also contained implicit positive feedback, as it suggested that the teacher had been following the narrative and wanted to find out more about the event. By contrast, Deena's story was cut short and the events that she had narrated were dismissed as unimportant. This happens because to those unfamiliar with it, the episodic or topic-associative discourse sounds "rambling, disjointed, unfocused, and as if the speaker is unprepared and never ends a thought before going on to something else" (Gay, 2010, p. 111).

These examples illustrate how teachers' lack of awareness of the communication norms sanctioned by non-mainstream students' home cultures makes it hard for the children to demonstrate what they know and can do, and for teachers to effectively assess and develop students' knowledge and skills. Aspects of students' communication styles that deviate from the mainstream norms are likely to be misinterpreted or banned from the classroom as inappropriate or simply wrong. For example, an Asian student's reluctance to participate in a debate may be erroneously interpreted as a symptom of disengagement, lack of interest, or unwillingness to cooperate. The viewpoints in a Mexican student's writing, when expressed indirectly, through allusions and parables, may be labeled unclear or vague; those expressed by African American students orally may be deemed too emotional, too personal, or too aggressive. The participatory-interactive communication style can easily be viewed as rude, inappropriate, and inconsiderate in classrooms where the passive-receptive style is the norm. Finally, the "preparation for performance" of a classroom task, especially when it takes the form of side talk, may be frowned on as a waste of precious instructional time, and therefore forbidden.

Yet the communication styles of culturally and linguistically diverse students are "intimately connected to loved ones, community, and personal identity. To suggest that (they are) 'wrong' . . . is to suggest that something is wrong with the student and his or her family" (Delpit, 1995, p. 55). Whether intentional or not, whether overt or covert, such a suggestion is likely to do great damage to a child's sense of self-worth and to have a negative impact on that child's classroom participation, engagement, and achievement. No teacher would deliberately choose to do that to a child! But how can it be avoided? Some suggestions follow.

Accommodating Cultural Differences in the Classroom

Accommodating culturally and linguistically diverse students' communication styles in the classroom poses a serious teaching dilemma: "How to validate a student's present meaning, often grounded in personal experience, while leading the child into additional meanings, and additional ways with words for expressing them that reflect more public and educated forms of knowledge" (Cazden, 2001, p. 22); in other words, how to help a child learn to communicate according to the norms of the mainstream culture while still valuing his or her home-based communication style.

A wonderful example of how a knowledgeable teacher can overcome this dilemma is Carol L. Lee's Cultural Modeling approach (2007). Lee designed a six-week experimental intervention for 109 low-achieving African American high school students in which she used *signifying* as the entry point for developing the students' critical thinking and literary analysis skills. A discourse technique typical of the African American communication style, *signifying* is "a genre of talk that involves ritual insult" (Lee, 2007, p. 13) performed through humor, insinuation, irony, and metaphor.

The intervention was carried out in stages. First, the students analyzed samples of African American signifying dialogues, in order to develop awareness of their own communication style. Next, they read and discussed two professional articles that described the characteristics of signifying and used their understandings to create their own signifying dialogues working in small groups. Following this activity, the students read two novels in which they had to identify and interpret figurative language, irony, and allusions, thus performing a close textual analysis of the works. By the end of the intervention, the students had made substantial improvement in their literary analysis skills, particularly in their ability to infer different types of relationships in literary texts.

Generalizing from experiments such as the Cultural Modeling approach, Geneva Gay (2010) proposes that in order to work successfully with CLD students, teachers should first learn about general communication patterns in different ethnic groups so they will be able to recognize and correctly interpret their students' ways of communicating in the classroom. Further, teachers should examine their own communication style to determine how students from different ethnic groups might respond to it. "The purposes of these analyses are to identify: (1) the habitual discourse features of ethnically diverse students; (2) conflictual and complementary points among these discourse styles; (3) how, and whether, conflictual points are negotiated by students; and (4) features of the students' discourse patterns that are problematic for the teacher. The results can be used to pinpoint and prioritize specific places to begin interventions for change" (Gay, 2010, p. 126), that is, for creating a classroom environment that is conducive to learning for all students.

To find information about their students' cultural backgrounds, teachers can do several things:

- Read about students' home cultures and about the educational and social situations in the students' countries of origin.
- Talk with family members to find out about their home literacy practices and their expectations for schooling.
- Talk with community members or colleagues who are familiar with students' home cultures to find out about cultural differences that are particularly relevant to the classroom (such as differences in communication styles).

- Have students write "identity texts" (Cummins et al., 2005), that is, brief descriptions of themselves, their families, their life and school in their home country, and their experiences in their new culture—in English or in their home language, or both (see page 368 for a discussion of three students' creation of an identity text).

Teachers can use information thus gathered to avoid miscommunication and misinterpretation of culturally and linguistically diverse students' participation (or lack thereof) in the classroom. They can also refer to it when formulating and communicating their expectations for classroom participation to students and parents (clearly and explicitly!). At such times, demonstrating knowledge of students' home cultures and awareness of the fact that different cultures "do school" differently will be a sign of caring, respect, and true appreciation of differences.

Consider the following example. How might the teacher have dealt differently with Alexander's classroom participation?

> Alexander is a Romanian third-grader attending a public school in upstate New York, where he and his family arrived two months ago, when his father, a Fulbright scholar, started his one-year appointment at the local university. Alexander, a top student in Romania, speaks, reads, and writes English well enough to cope with the academic demands of the new school setting; yet his teacher, Mrs. Johnson, is so frustrated with the way he acts in class that she decides to call his father. During the conversation Mrs. Johnson expresses astonishment at the quality of Alexander's written work and at his reading ability in English; at the same time, she expresses bafflement at his classroom participation: "He never responds to anything that his classmates say . . . he doesn't even look their way when they're talking. And he only responds to my questions if I call on him. At those times, he always stands up and answers in one complete sentence, with a very serious look on his face, whether I ask him if he likes hamburgers or why polar bears are white." Equally baffled, Alexander's father replies, "I'm sorry, I'm afraid I don't understand. Is he doing something wrong?" "Well," says Mrs. Johnson, taken aback, "why does he stand up every time I call on him? I was just wondering if he was somewhat retarded . . . "

Cultural differences should not be overemphasized—after all, there are many more commonalities among cultures than there are differences—but they should not be a taboo in the classroom either. In an attempt to make their non-mainstream students comfortable, many teachers avoid talking about cultural differences (at least beyond those regarding food or traditional celebrations, which, more often than not, serve to reinforce stereotypes instead of dismantle them). Yet, if we want all our students to learn to value other cultures, they first need to become aware of them. Therefore (some of) the times when students' classroom participation diverges from the norm can be used, tactfully and thoughtfully, as "teachable moments" in which differences between mainstream American culture and students' home cultures can be discussed openly and non-judgmentally. During such discussions it is important that students assume the role of experts in their home cultures, and that the teacher assumes the role of learner, demonstrating interest, willingness to learn, and appreciation of students' cultures.

Similar "teachable moments" can be created by including *multicultural books* in the curriculum and by inviting students whose home culture is depicted in a book to use their knowledge of that culture in interpreting the text. Chances are that they will identify meanings in the text that readers less familiar with the culture would have missed, and/or that they will identify points of difference between their own cultural practices and the ones depicted by the text. Needless to say, teachers should take the time and find the means to encourage these students to express their thoughts, and to use students' insights to trigger whole-class conversations about similarities and differences between cultures, about stereotypes and prejudice, and about the value of biculturalism.

One of many children's books that can be used as a starting point for such conversations is Hristo Kyuchukov's (2004) *My Name Was Hussein,* a story in which a Roma child talks about Muslims in Bulgaria who had to give up their identities and choose Christian names. Although the circumstances described are specific to a particular place and time, the racial and religious prejudice underlying the story is likely to be noticed and recognized as such by immigrant students from many parts of the world, and the identity issues raised in the narrative are bound to resonate deeply with mainstream and non-mainstream students alike.

Linguistic Differences in the Mainstream Classroom

Cultural diversity usually goes hand in hand with linguistic diversity. It is common knowledge that different ethnic groups speak different languages or different varieties of a language (commonly referred to as *dialects*). Equally well known is the fact that while in school, children need to learn to speak (and understand, and read, and write) Standard English. Less well known, however, may be the fact that Standard English is itself a dialect of the English language and, further, that the distinction between languages and dialects is often an arbitrary one. We will begin our discussion of linguistic diversity in the classroom by clarifying the relationship between languages and dialects.

Languages and Dialects

Linguists define a dialect as a subordinate variety of a language (Romaine, 1994; Wardaugh, 2002), and identify *regional dialects,* associated with a place (e.g., Bostonian English or Appalachian English); *ethnic dialects*, spoken by various ethnolinguistic groups (e.g., Jamaican English); and *social dialects,* associated with a certain social class (e.g., the Queen's English in the UK, which used to be the dialect of the upper classes in Southern England). These distinctions are not always clear-cut. For example, among older European-American speakers in Charleston, South Carolina, the absence of *r* in words such as *bear* and *court* is associated with the dialect spoken by aristocratic, high-status groups, whereas in New York City, the same pronunciation is associated with the dialect of working-class, low-status groups (Wolfram, 2004).

How dialects relate to language is an interesting question. People generally assume that dialects are mutually intelligible varieties of a language. Many counterexamples contradict this assumption, though. For instance, a speaker of Cockney, a variety of English spoken by working-class East Enders in London, UK, may find it difficult to communicate with natives of South Carolina. Does this mean that they speak different languages? In China, speakers of both Cantonese and Mandarin will claim that they speak Chinese, albeit using different dialects; yet spoken Cantonese and Mandarin are not mutually intelligible. (If the speakers are literate, they will be able to communicate with each other through a shared logographic writing system.) Conversely, Danish, Norwegian, and Swedish are considered to be different languages even though they are mutually intelligible (Wardaugh, 2002).

An interesting perspective on the relationship between dialects and languages can be gained by examining the linguistic situation in the former Yugoslav republics. Within the pre-1991 country of Yugoslavia, Serbo-Croatian was the official language and the language spoken in three of the eight provinces that made up the country (Serbia, Croatia, and Bosnia). There were differences among the varieties (or dialects) of Serbo-Croatian spoken in the three provinces, but they involved different preferences for vocabulary rather than differences in pronunciation or grammar (Wardaugh, 2002). After 1991, during the Yugoslav wars, the eight provinces seceded and formed independent states. One outcome of the secession was that Serbian, Croatian, and Bosnian became separate languages in their respective states. This illustrates that the difference between a dialect and a language is often not linguistic, but social, and having to do with the power of its speakers; in Weinreich's words, "a language is a dialect with an army and a navy" (see Romaine, 1994, p. 12).

From a linguistic point of view, dialects differ from one another in terms of phonology and pronunciation, vocabulary, and sometimes syntax, but they are all rule-governed, legitimate linguistic systems; therefore, no one dialect is inherently "better" than another. Nevertheless, people often reserve the term *dialect* for language varieties that are socially stigmatized, and the term *language* for the standard variety.

Standardization involves the selection of a dialect, its subsequent "codification" through grammars, dictionaries, and literature, and its use in courts, education, administration, and commerce (Wardaugh, 2002). Importantly, the selection of a particular variety as the standard "means favoring those who speak that variety. It also diminishes all the other varieties . . . and those who use those varieties. The chosen norm inevitably becomes associated with power and the rejected alternatives with lack of power. Not surprisingly, it usually happens that a variety associated with an elite is chosen" (Wardaugh, 2002, p. 34). Once a variety has become the standard, it becomes *the* language—what is taught to foreigners, what individuals' oral or written communication is gauged against, and, even more importantly, what the society at large considers to be a neutral (i.e., power free) code.

The Ebonics Debate. Understanding the power relationships that undergird the process of standardization of a dialect and the subsequent enforcement of the standard by the institutions of the state helps put into perspective the Ebonics debate—the debate that occurs periodically in the United States over the place and function of African American English (also referred to as Ebonics, African American Vernacular English, or African American Language) in school programs and practices. One such debate took place in 1996–1997 in California, in the Oakland public school district. It was prompted by a resolution of the district's Board of Education to recognize Ebonics as a language, to recognize African American students as bilingual, and to use Ebonics in teaching African American students as a means of supporting their acquisition of Standard Academic English and their academic achievement in general. The resolution was vehemently criticized not only by various European Americans, but, ironically, by several African American political leaders as well, and resulted in anti-Ebonics legislation being proposed in five states and passed in three (Smitherman, 2000).

We may speculate that one explanation for the strong reaction against the content of the resolution had to do with the relative power associated with the terms *language* and *dialect.* Considering Ebonics a *language,* as opposed to a *dialect* of English, and using it as one of the languages of instruction in schools would give it equal status to Standard English and would empower its speakers. Perhaps we, as a society, are not ready for that yet.

Another possible explanation for the resistance to the suggestion that African American students should be educated in their home language as a way to support their academic achievement may lie in the widespread misconception that speaking another language interferes with the acquisition of English. This is an argument often used by opponents of bilingual education. Paradoxically, nobody ever makes the opposite argument—that speaking English interferes with learning another language. On the contrary, more and more middle-class parents are placing their children in two-way immersion programs (usually offered by private schools) so they can become competent bilinguals and thus have better chances of succeeding in an increasingly globalized world, where proficiency in more than one language is valued (Garcia, 2009).

Meanwhile, many educators who will readily admit that learning proceeds from the known to the new and that teachers should always try to build on students' prior knowledge view their ethnic minority students' home dialect or language as a deficiency, as something that needs to be eradicated in order for them to learn Standard English. "But what better way to make a person or a people voiceless, invisible, and powerless than to invalidate their self-selected or cultural communicative means of speaking their thoughts, their ideas, themselves?" (Gay, 2010, p. 87)

Welcoming students' home languages, dialects, and cultures into the classroom should not be viewed as jeopardizing either their acquisition of Standard English or their becoming functional in the American mainstream culture. Standard English is a code of power and there are sound reasons for making it accessible to minority students. Although mastering Standard English does not guarantee educational, social, or economic success, it nevertheless increases one's chances for such success. Similarly, learning to function in the school culture and, by extension, in the mainstream culture, increases culturally and linguistically diverse students' opportunities for academic achievement and offers them a wider range of professional options.

However, teaching these students Standard English should not be done at the expense of or as a replacement of their home languages; nor should teachers' familiarizing their students with the norms of the school culture become an attempt at assimilation, that is, at leading them to forsake their home cultures and take on the ways of the mainstream culture. Rather, we propose that teachers take Ogbu's advice and increase "students' adoption of the strategy of 'accommodation without assimilation' . . . or 'playing the classroom game.' The essence of this strategy is that students should recognize and accept the fact that they can participate in two cultural or language frames of reference for different purposes without losing their cultural or language identity or undermining their loyalty to the minority community" (Ogbu, 1992, p. 12).

Ogbu suggests that teachers support their culturally and linguistically diverse students in becoming bicultural and bilingual (or bidialectal). We suggest that teachers should help them become biliterate as well. In order for teachers to aim for biculturalism, bilingualism/bidialectalism, and biliteracy, they need to view their students' cultural and linguistic backgrounds as strengths rather than deficiencies, and to use them as springboards for these students' adding new discourses to their repertoire, that is, new "ways of acting, interacting, feeling, believing, valuing, and using various sorts of objects, symbols, tools, and technologies—to recognize (themselves) and others as meaning and meaningful" (Gee, 2006, p. 7) in different contexts. The following section describes an instructional approach informed by these goals.

Accommodating Non-Standard Dialects in the Mainstream Classroom. Similar in its underlying premises and design to Lee's (2007) Cultural Modeling approach, the Awareness Approach described by Siegel (2006) views students' home varieties of language as a resource to be used for learning the standard dialect. The Awareness Approach has three components: a sociolinguistic component, an accommodation component, and a contrastive component. In the sociolinguistic component, students learn about languages and dialects, and about how one dialect becomes the "standard." In the accommodation component, students study literature written in their home dialect and respond to it, orally or in writing, either in the standard dialect or in their home dialect, depending on the task. Finally, in the contrastive component, students examine the phonological, morphological, syntactic, and pragmatic features of their home dialects compared to one another and to the standard.

The Awareness Approach has been used in programs involving speakers of Hawaiian Creole, speakers of Caribbean English creoles, and speakers of African American Vernacular English, and has been found to be successful in achieving higher scores in tests measuring reading and writing skills in *Standard English* as well as in improving students' motivation and overall academic achievement. There are several probable reasons for its success.

"First, the sociolinguistic component promotes acceptance of language (and cultural) diversity as 'normal,' and values students' home varieties. This can only lead to more positive attitudes in both teachers and students. Second, the accommodation component may increase students' motivation and participation by including aspects of their home language and culture in the curriculum. Third, the contrastive component makes learners aware of differences between their own varieties and the standard that they may not otherwise notice" (Siegel, 2006, p. 165).

An additional reason for the success of the Awareness Approach is that while it supports the acquisition of the standard dialect by children who speak a different dialect at home, it also supports students' maintenance, and even development, of their home language; that is, it supports bidialectalism. In subsequent sections, we will lay out more instructional ideas for attaining the goals of bidialectalism, bilingualism, and biliteracy for culturally and linguistically diverse students. Before we do that, though, we will continue to examine the linguistic diversity of today's classrooms by focusing on English language learners.

English Language Learners in the Mainstream Classroom

English language learners are by no means a homogeneous group. Some were born in the United States and are second- or third-generation immigrants, yet they speak a language other than English at home. Others are new immigrants who differ in their age of arrival, in their families' reasons for immigration (war, religious or political persecution, poverty, etc.), in their experiences of coming to and living in the United States, in their socioeconomic background, and in their parents' levels of education and proficiency in English. English language learners also differ in their level of proficiency in English and, perhaps even more importantly, in their educational backgrounds.

Some English language learners have had strong academic experiences in their home countries and are often ahead of their new schools' curricula, especially in mathematics and science; they are highly literate in their first language and may have studied English as a foreign language. With proper instruction, these students are most likely to achieve academic success. Due to war in their native countries or to the rural location of their homes, other English language learners (of varied ages) arrive with very limited or interrupted formal schooling and with little or no literacy in their first language; these English language learners are most at risk for educational failure.

Finally, English language learners differ in the languages that they speak at home. Some of the approximately 460 languages that are spoken by students in American schools (Kindler, 2002) are closer to English than others. For example, Spanish is closer to English than Hebrew is, because both Spanish and English belong to the Indo-European language family, whereas Hebrew belongs to the Semitic language family. This means that there are more similarities between Spanish and English than between Hebrew and English, and that consequently English is likely to be easier to acquire by speakers of Spanish than by speakers of Hebrew. Nevertheless, even languages that are highly similar may differ at different levels (phonological, morphological, syntactic, semantic, or pragmatic) or in the characteristics of the writing systems that they use. A basic understanding of the differences between English and other languages is likely to help teachers get a better sense of the challenges that English language learners may face while learning English. We will illustrate some of these differences next.

How Does English Compare to Other Languages?

Some say that English is easy to learn; some say it's hard. The assessment usually depends on how similar English is to one's first language. Even those learners who find it easy, though, will find some aspects of it more difficult to learn than others.

Phonology. English *phonology* may be quite challenging for Spanish speakers, for example, due to certain differences in the phonological systems of the two languages. For example, Spanish has five vowels, whereas English has thirteen. In addition, some phonemes are not common to both languages; for example, the first consonants in the English words *they* and *zeal* are not part of the phonemic inventory of Spanish. Spanish-speaking children who are beginning to learn English will encounter difficulties discriminating the English phonemes that do not exist in Spanish and interpreting the meaning of words that contain these phonemes. Thus, the words *seat* and *sit* will sound the same to such children, because the distinction between the two vowels is not phonemic (i.e., it does not affect word meaning) in Spanish.

Phonological differences between the two languages are also going to affect children's pronunciation. In the beginning stages of learning English as a second language, children will substitute phonemes from their first language for the English phonemes that they are not familiar with. Thus, a Spanish-speaking child will most likely pronounce *sit* the same way as *seat, they* as *day,* and *zeal* as *seal.* Also, because no Spanish words begin with an *s* followed by a consonant, native speakers of Spanish tend to say "I espeak Espanish." Phonological differences are therefore likely to cause both communication problems and reading comprehension problems.

Morphology. Various *morphological* features of English are sources of difficulty for learners of English as a second language. For example, the English articles (*a/an, the*) are particularly troublesome for English language learners whose first language does not have articles (e.g., Bosnian or Chinese). Even at advanced levels of English oral proficiency, many Chinese learners still struggle with the *-s* that marks the plural of nouns in English, most likely because Mandarin Chinese does not have an equivalent morpheme. Many languages (e.g., German or Russian) do not have a progressive aspect (the verb form that shows that an action is in progress); in such languages therefore, there is only one way of saying, "I work" and "I am working." In many languages (e.g., Italian, Spanish, French, or Romanian), the verb forms used to say "I have done my homework" and "I did my homework" are the same. For speakers of these languages, learning the distinction between the present perfect and the past tense in English will take many years.

Syntax. Certain English *syntactic structures* are also likely to cause problems for various English language learners. For example, a "complete" sentence in English needs a subject and a verb; yet in many languages (e.g., Albanian, Arabic, Hindi, Japanese, Portuguese), the subject pronoun of a sentence may be omitted because it is included in the ending of the verb. In English, adjectives are placed before the noun they determine; in other languages (e.g., Romanian or Spanish), they are placed after the noun.

The word order in a well-formed declarative English sentence is subject-verb-object, as in *The children in the house want that puppy.* The same sentence in Hindi has a completely different word order: *House in children that puppy want are* (Lightfoot & Fasold, 2008, p. 122).

Pragmatics. Languages also differ at the level of *pragmatics,* that is, in the ways language is used in different social contexts. Some ways of using language may be considered context appropriate in one language but not in another. Errors caused by first-language transfer in the area of pragmatics can easily lead to misinterpretation and miscommunication because native speakers are inclined to attribute them to personality factors not to the learner's incomplete knowledge of the second language. Consider the following situation:

> *A native speaker of Hebrew promised to return a textbook to his American classmate within a couple of days, but held onto it for almost two weeks. The classmate says, "I'm really upset about the book because I needed it to prepare for last week's class." The non-native speaker replies, "I have nothing to say."* (Gass & Selinker, 2008, p. 288)

The non-native speaker's response suggests an unwillingness to apologize and therefore sounds rude to a native speaker of English. However, as Gass and Selinker (2008) explain, what the speaker meant was the literal translation of a Hebrew phrase that means *I have no excuse.*

Writing Systems. Some languages that ELLs speak have a writing system; some do not. The writing systems may be *alphabetic,* like that of English; *logographic,* like that of Chinese; or *syllabic,* like that of Japanese. This means that speech is represented in print differently: In an alphabetic script, the symbols (letters) represent phonemes (sounds that differentiate meaning in the spoken language); in a logographic script, they represent morphemes (meaningful word parts); and in a syllabic script, they represent syllables. Compared to English language learners who are not literate in their first language, a student who can read and write in a language that uses a logographic writing system is at an advantage when learning to read in English because she understands that writing represents speech; nevertheless, she will still need to acquire the alphabetic principle—a challenging task even for native speakers of English.

Other characteristics of various writing systems may facilitate or complicate English language learners' English literacy development. For example, *the directionality of print* in some languages (e.g., English or Spanish) is from left to right, whereas in others it is from right to left (e.g., Hebrew or Arabic), and in still others, such as Chinese, it is top to bottom. Therefore, children who are literate in Hebrew, Arabic, or Chinese will have to "reset" this parameter of their writing.

Finally, some languages that use alphabetic writing systems have a *shallow orthography,* in which the relationship between phonemes and letters is highly consistent (e.g., Spanish); this means that a phoneme is almost always represented by the same letter(s). Other languages, such as English, have a *deep orthography,* in which a phoneme may be represented by various letters or letter combinations or, conversely, the same letter or group of letters may represent various phonemes. For example, the underlined letters in the English words *see, sea, ceiling, amoeba, meter,* and *marine* all represent the phoneme /i/. The "ie" digraph in *pie, friend,* and *pier,* on the other hand, is pronounced in three different ways. English language learners who can read and write in a language whose writing system has a shallow orthography are likely to be good decoders of English words that have regular spellings; however, they are going to be baffled by the deep orthography of English and will try to impose regularity on it, which will result in reading and spelling errors.

Given all the ways in which English language learners' linguistic backgrounds may differ from one another, it is obvious that there is no one-size-fits-all way of educating them effectively; rather, teachers have to realize that these students are going to have different instructional needs, and that teachers must find individual pathways to academic success for them. In order to do that, teachers need to have some familiarity with their students' first languages. This does not mean that they should be fluent in those languages; however, a basic understanding of the phonology, morphology, syntax, pragmatics, and writing system of students' home languages is likely to make a huge difference in teachers' ability to (a) understand the difficulties that English language learners encounter in the mainstream classroom and (b) design effective instruction for these students. The following section contains some useful tips for adapting instruction to accommodate linguistic differences in the mainstream classroom.

Accommodating Linguistic Differences in the Mainstream Classroom. When designing instruction for a classroom that includes English language learners, teachers need to remember two things: (1) that no child comes to school as a blank slate—if a child has not had literacy experiences in her first language, she most certainly has had life experiences and linguistic experiences (albeit oral) that should be valued and drawn upon in order for that child to thrive in school; and (2) that the one thing that all English language learners need, irrespective of varied differences in their backgrounds, is English language development.

Instruction that is appropriate for English language learners (as well as for children who speak a non-standard dialect at home, for that matter) needs to build on the experiential, cultural, and linguistic resources that these students bring to school; at the same time, it needs to focus not only on disciplinary content, but also on supporting students' acquisition of English as a second language (or of Standard English as a second dialect) *in all subject matters*. This idea is clearly underscored by the Common Core State Standards Initiative (see Figure 9.1).

Here are some things that you, as a mainstream classroom teacher, can do to plan and implement such instruction (adapted from Cloud, Genesee, & Hamayan, 2009):

- Learn about students' home languages, paying particular attention to similarities and differences with English. This can be done by consulting references and/or people who have been educated in those languages (preferably language teachers).
- Draw students' attention to language in the texts they read. If you are familiar with the students' home language, you can point out similarities and differences with English (e.g., in the directionality of print, in spelling, in punctuation, in word formation, in vocabulary, etc.); if not, students can be asked to work in groups to

To help ELLs (English language learners) meet high academic standards in language arts it is essential that they have access to:

- Teachers and personnel at the school and district levels who are well prepared and qualified to support ELLs while taking advantage of the many strengths and skills they bring to the classroom;
- Literacy-rich school environments where students are immersed in a variety of language experiences;
- Instruction that develops foundational skills in English and enables ELLs to participate fully in grade-level coursework;
- Coursework that prepares ELLs for postsecondary education or the workplace, yet is made comprehensible for students learning content in a second language (through specific pedagogical techniques and additional resources);
- Opportunities for classroom discourse and interaction that are well-designed to enable ELLs to develop communicative strengths in language arts;
- Ongoing assessment and feedback to guide learning; and
- Speakers of English who know the language well enough to provide ELLs with models and support.

FIGURE 9.1 *Application of Common Core ELA Standards for English Language Learners*

identify similarities and differences between the two languages. Like the contrastive component of the Awareness Approach (Siegel, 2006) discussed earlier, such activities are going to develop English language learners' metalinguistic awareness, and will increase their ability to use their first language as a support for learning English.

- Teach students to experiment and take risks with applying what they know about reading and writing in their home languages to learning to read and write in English.
- If they make a "mistake," ask students why they did what they did; often, it will be due to the influence of the first language. Importantly, such "mistakes" should not be penalized; instead, they should be publicly acknowledged as an indication of resourcefulness and effort.
- Observe students who speak the same home language to notice common patterns of errors caused by first language influence. Plan mini-lessons that focus explicitly on those patterns and teach them in the context of what students are reading or writing about. For example, if they are reading *The Cat in the Hat*, explain that the letter *h* is always pronounced at the beginning of English words, unlike in Spanish, where it is silent.

Achieving academically is even harder for English language learners than for other students because they need to learn English as a second language *while* also developing literacy and/or learning content in English. It is not unusual for these students to do well in their ESL classes and to be quite fluent in informal interactions with native English speakers, yet to have trouble with reading or learning academic content (Pritchard & O'Hara, 2008). Linguist Jim Cummins explains that this occurs because these children actually have to develop two kinds of proficiency in English: proficiency in the *social language* of everyday interactions, which he calls Basic Interpersonal Communication Skills (BICS); and proficiency in the *academic language* of school subjects, or Cognitive-Academic Language Proficiency (CALP) (Cummins, 1979, 1981).

Most English language learners acquire Basic Interpersonal Communication Skills in natural, context-rich settings, without formal instruction, and much faster than they acquire the academic language needed for reading and writing in the content areas, which is more decontextualized, more complex, and required for performing more cognitively challenging tasks. The latter, however, is the language that English language learners need to become skilled at in order to succeed academically. This is also true of students who speak a non-standard dialect at home and who, while being at an advantage compared to English language learners in that they are already conversant in the social language of everyday interactions, may still need help in developing proficiency in academic language. In order to help language minority students develop such proficiency, teachers should have a basic understanding of the process of second language acquisition.

How Do People Learn a Second Language?

To some of our readers' disappointment, we must begin to answer this question by admitting that the process of second language acquisition (just like the process of first language acquisition, for that matter) is not yet completely understood. The good news is, however, that the little that we do know about it can be used to inform our instructional practices.

Several psychological, psycholinguistic, and linguistic theories of first and second language acquisition have been proposed over the last seven decades. In the remainder of this section, we shall summarize the most influential ones and describe some approaches to language teaching that the different theories have inspired.

For the longest time, second or foreign languages were taught using the *grammar translation approach.* Originally devised for the study of classical languages and literatures and not based on any theory of language acquisition, this approach did not aim to develop students' ability to speak the language; rather, it consisted of presenting learners with vocabulary lists and grammar rules, both of which they were expected to use in reading and translating classical texts. Needless to say, while the learners did get a relatively good grasp of the grammar and vocabulary of the language they were studying, they did not develop fluency in the language.

In the 1940s and 1950s, *behaviorism* was a highly influential theory of learning, especially in the United States. With regard to first language acquisition, behaviorists hypothesized that children learned to talk by imitating the language produced by those around them and by forming "habits" of correct language use. They also postulated that a person learning a second language would start off with the habits formed in his or her first language and *transfer* them to the second language. At the points where the two languages were similar, transfer would result in correct forms in the second language; at the points where the two languages were dissimilar, transfer would result in incorrect second-language forms.

Inspired by the behaviorist perspective of second language acquisition, the *audio-lingual approach* to teaching second and foreign languages was based on mimicry and memorization of scripted dialogues. Students were rarely allowed to use the language spontaneously because speaking freely was likely to result in errors, which, in turn, were likely to become "bad" language habits. All errors were corrected as soon as they were committed in order to avoid this risk. In classrooms, the audiolingual approach did not lead to students' developing fluency in the second language, which explains why it was replaced by communicative language teaching approaches, inspired by innatist theories of first and second language acquisition.

The *innatist* view of first language acquisition was first articulated by Chomsky (1959), who, in reaction to the behaviorist view, argued that children are not born blank slates to be filled by imitating others' language; rather, they are born with an innate ability to discover for themselves the rules of the language(s) to which they are exposed. The way children do this is by (unconsciously) formulating and testing hypotheses about the rules that govern the language(s) they are learning. Thus, rather than being a matter of imitation, language acquisition is a process of creative construction.

Based on Chomsky's model of first language acquisition, Krashen (1982) proposed that if learners received sufficient "comprehensible input" (language that is just one step ahead of their current competence), they would acquire a second language without explicit instruction. Krashen's hypotheses gave rise to a host of *communicative approaches* to second and foreign language teaching. In these approaches there is little, if any, explicit language instruction and little concern with accuracy (i.e., there is little correction); instead, there is a great deal of comprehensible input (language to which the children are exposed that is made comprehensible through visuals, gestures, body movements, slow pace of delivery, simplified syntactic structures, paraphrase, etc.). The emphasis is on comprehension of the second language as opposed to its production.

Linguists working from an *interactionist* perspective (e.g., Long, 1996; Swain, 1985) argued that while comprehensible input was a necessary condition for second language acquisition, it was not a sufficient one, and that, in addition to being exposed to comprehensible input, learners also needed to interact in the second language in order to develop competence in it. In this view, the "negotiation of meaning" that occurs in the course of conversational interactions (through comprehension checks, clarification requests, repetitions, paraphrase, etc.) is particularly conducive to language development for two main reasons: (1) because it makes input comprehensible and (2) because it is likely to focus learners' attention on new language forms or on forms that they are not using in a native-like manner, especially when meaning breaks down. In other words, when learners must produce language that their listeners can understand, they become aware of features of the second language that they have not mastered yet, and then they are likely to acquire them (Swain, 1985).

The idea that second language learners cannot begin to acquire a new language feature until they have become aware of it has received support from both linguists and psychologists (e.g., Gass & Selinker, 2008; Schmidt, 2001), leading applied linguists (e.g., Spada & Lightbown, 2008) to conclude that *second language instruction is most effective when it includes attention both to meaning (through the provision of comprehensible input and through opportunities for meaning-focused interaction) and to linguistic form (through explicit teaching of, and corrective feedback on the language structures that learners seem to fail to acquire through mere exposure)*. The next section contains some useful tips for translating this conclusion into instruction that supports English language learners' language development in the mainstream classroom.

Supporting English Language Development in the Mainstream Classroom. Mainstream classroom teachers do not need to become language teachers or skilled linguists in order to include attention to language in their instruction. What they do need to do, though, is be constantly aware of the fact that the language of the classroom can be an obstacle to English language learners' mastery of the content, and plan and implement instruction so as to overcome this obstacle. Here are some ways for doing it.

A. Make the classroom a space that is conducive to learning for English language learners.

- Make sure English language learners are seated where they can hear you well and where you can see them at all times. Many of them will try to become invisible by sitting at the back of the classroom, so they will not be called on. Explain to them that it is important that they can hear you and that you can see them in order to monitor their comprehension.
- Encourage ELLs to let you know when they do not understand you and to ask for clarifications as needed. For those who may be reluctant to do it out loud, you may devise a "secret" signal (e.g., drawing a question mark in the air) that they can use to alert you to their comprehension difficulties.
- Make both bilingual and monolingual dictionaries available to your English language learners.

B. Provide "comprehensible input."

- Speak audibly, clearly, and unhurriedly.
- Augment your spoken language with gestures and actions that help clarify the meaning of your words.
- Use visuals and graphics to provide alternative representations of important terms, concepts, and relationships.
- Repeat important ideas.
- If students are literate, write important points or words on the board and draw their attention to them.

C. Encourage language production by English language learners.

- Do not let English language learners sit silently unless they are at the very beginning stages of learning English. Give them plenty of opportunities to interact in pairs and in small groups as well as with you, during whole-class discussions. In this latter kind of interaction, you will be modeling strategies for negotiating meaning that your native-English speaking students can use when working in groups with their non-native peers.
- Do not correct English language learners' language errors explicitly in front of the class; ask questions to clarify the meaning of their contributions instead. Remember to praise their efforts to communicate, so their classmates will learn that succeeding in conveying meaning in a second language is a strategic accomplishment even if the language is not perfect.
- Provide peer support for reading and writing activities. If possible, pair up two English language learners with different levels of English proficiency. The one whose English is stronger is likely to help the other to cope with linguistic challenges while also showing empathy.

D. Draw English language learners' attention to linguistic forms.

- Study your instructional materials and assess their language and literacy demands. You may need to modify the materials (by skipping certain passages or rewriting others) to make them more manageable. Identify key vocabulary and sentence structures that you should teach so that your English language learners will understand the material and be able to talk and write about it.
- With the selected key vocabulary and structures in mind, formulate language objectives in addition to content objectives when planning your lessons (Echevarria, Vogt, & Short, 2010). What do you want your students to be able to do by the end of the lesson *in English*?
- Preteach the key vocabulary that students need in order to understand the lesson using multiple ways of illustrating meaning (visual, kinesthetic, etc.).
- Help English language learners identify *cognates* (words that have similar spellings and meanings in both languages) in the text and encourage them to use a dictionary to verify that the meaning of a potential cognate is the same in English and in the home language. Your Spanish-speaking students may discover that the English verb *attend* means *asistir* and not *atender,* that the Spanish verb *atender* means "serve" or "attend to" in English, or that the English *assist* is *ayudar* in Spanish.
- If your students do not know how to use a dictionary, teach them!
- Directly teach the grammatical structures that are particularly salient in a text that students will read, and that you want students to be able to use in their own oral or written texts (see Appendix A at the end of this chapter for an example).
- Plan for contextualized language practice in every lesson, so your English language learners will get multiple opportunities to use the new language structures in speaking and writing about the topic of the lesson (see Appendix A at the end of this chapter).

- Use graphic organizers to raise English language learners' awareness of text structure and to scaffold their writing of particular text types. For example, if they are reading or writing a story, have them complete a story map while reading the story or before writing it. If they are reading or writing a text that compares mammals to birds, have them fill out a Venn diagram while reading or before writing.
- Teach them to identify common transition words that occur with particular text structures (e.g., *although, and yet, as opposed to, but, by contrast, however, like, nevertheless, not only . . . but also, on the other hand,* and *similarly* are commonly found in texts that have an underlying compare/contrast structure).
- Offer feedback to written work that focuses on both content and language. Remember to praise the content even if the language needs improvement.
- Observe students who speak the same home language and read their written work with an eye to common patterns of first language influence; when the opportunity arises, focus feedback explicitly on points of difference between the students' home language and English. For example, if all or most of your Chinese students consistently omit the *-s* ending of plural nouns in speaking and/or writing, you may want to teach a mini-lesson to clarify the fact that, unlike Chinese, English has a grammatical morpheme that indicates whether the speaker/writer is referring to one person/thing or to more than one.

This is certainly a long list, and many mainstream classroom teachers may feel overwhelmed by so many suggestions, some of which may sound more within reach than others. In order to implement as many of these suggestions as possible, we advise classroom teachers to collaborate with the ESL teachers in their schools. ESL teachers are trained to provide English language instruction that supports English language learners' learning across the curriculum. They are skilled at identifying the language demands of texts and at designing activities that help these students learn content and language simultaneously. Therefore, co-planning and co-teaching with an ESL teacher is likely to relieve some of the burden from the mainstream teacher's shoulders and to result in more effective instruction *not only for English language learners, but also for all culturally and linguistically diverse students.*

One last piece of advice: Use English language learners' first language as a springboard for the acquisition of English language and literacy. Especially at the beginning stages of acquiring a second language, the first language functions as a cognitive crutch that learners use, consciously or not, and whether encouraged or not, to support their comprehension of oral or written second-language texts and to cope with the challenges of communicating, orally or in writing, in the second language. As we will show in the next section, the knowledge and skills acquired in the first language transfer, at least to some extent, to the second language.

The Role of the First Language in Second Language and Literacy Development

Recent research on first language and literacy transfer (or cross-linguistic relationships) among children and adolescents learning to read and write in English (Genesee, Geva,

Dressler, & Kamil, 2006) shows that children's first language and literacy knowledge is going to influence their second language and literacy learning. At times this influence will facilitate learning; at other times it will interfere with it.

For example, English language learners with high levels of *phonological awareness* in their first language also have relatively high levels of phonological awareness in English. However, English language learners' *developmental patterns of phonological development* differ from those of native English speakers, reflecting influences of their first language, and even resembling those of children with speech impairment (see the following section for more details). This is an important research finding to remember, so that English language learners will not be judged to be impaired based on what research shows to be normal development patterns in their second language.

The *phonological processes underlying word recognition* in second language learners are influenced by the orthography of the first language. For example, a Spanish speaker may read the word *hit* as *heat,* since the phoneme represented by the letter *i* in Spanish is closer to the phoneme represented by the digraph *ea* in English. Conversely, English language learners' *spelling errors* can be traced to differences between the phonology of their first language and English phonology (see the section on assessment of culturally and linguistically diverse students).

The first language may positively influence second-language *vocabulary development,* particularly when the two languages are related, by allowing learners to recognize cognates. It is nevertheless true that the first language may also negatively influence vocabulary learning, as in cases when meaning is assigned to words erroneously based on first-language syntax. For example, a child who speaks a language in which the adjective follows the noun instead of preceding it may interpret the phrase "military intelligence" as "intelligent military" and conclude that "intelligence" is an adjective.

Reading comprehension ability, reading strategies, and *writing skills* (including both emergent skills and higher order skills having to do with discourse structure) developed in the first language transfer to the second language. In other words, once developed in one language, such strategies and skills do not need to be relearned.

Finally, let us remember that the *communication styles* of various ethnic groups involve culture-based norms for using language that are going to influence students' speaking, writing, and interacting in the classroom. Just as children's home languages and dialects are more or less similar to English or to Standard English, their communication styles are more or less congruent with the mainstream style; therefore, like linguistic transfer, cultural transfer will sometimes facilitate minority students' participation in classroom communication, while at other times it will result in cultural "errors."

Regardless of whether it facilitates the learning of the second language and literacy, English language learners are going to rely on their first language as they try to cope with the social and academic challenges of schooling. Therefore "errors" caused by first language transfer should not be penalized; rather, they should be viewed as strategic attempts by students at "filling in gaps in their English by drawing on corresponding skills and knowledge from the home language" (Cloud et al., 2009, p. 84). Such "bootstrapping" (August & Shanahan, 2006; Genesee et al., 2006) or use of the first language to support the learning of a second should be encouraged in the classroom because:

(1) its encouragement signals to students that the teacher understands and appreciates their efforts to learn and communicate in English; (2) strategically resorting to one's first language in learning another promotes bilingualism and biliteracy, both of which are valued in today's globalized world; and (3) students' resorting to their first language when their knowledge of English proves to be insufficient allows them to demonstrate what they know even before they have become fully functional in English. By contrast, banning the home language or dialect from the classroom will highlight what culturally and linguistically diverse students do *not* know, and will send the message that they are, at least in some ways, deficient. Some suggestions for including students' home languages in the mainstream classroom are outlined in the next section.

Including English Language Learners' Home Languages in the Mainstream Classroom. Although some familiarity with students' home languages can be a huge help in working with English language learners, you do not need to be bilingual or biliterate in order to welcome languages other than English to your classroom. Here are some things you can do to that end.

Create a multilingual classroom environment. One way in which students' home languages can be welcomed to the classroom is by *making the classroom environment bilingual or multilingual,* that is, by displaying print in English language learners' home languages alongside print in English. Teachers should enlist students' help in creating such an environment. For example, the classroom can have a "World News" corner, where students can take turns periodically posting articles about events in their home countries that they find particularly relevant. The articles should be written in the students' home languages and accompanied by a translation or summary in English. The student that posted the article can be asked to summarize it orally and then discuss its contents with his/her classmates and with the teacher; next, he or she can be asked to talk about one aspect of the language of the article that was problematic in translating or summarizing it. Such discussions will not only raise all students' awareness of other parts of the world (something that we, as a society, badly need), but also enhance their metalinguistic awareness.

Make room for translation in the classroom. Because of the failure of the grammar-translation method to produce fluent speakers of a second language, *translation* has been stigmatized as a counterproductive language learning strategy. However, research shows that, particularly for students with lower levels of proficiency in a second language, mental translation supports reading comprehension as they try to understand difficult passages (Kern, 1994). Also, translation or paraphrasing has been found to be a common family literacy practice in immigrant households, often performed by children who are quasi-fluent in English for their non-English speaking family members (Orellana, Reynolds, Dorner, & Meza, 2003). Therefore, making room for translation in the classroom would validate a language and literacy skill that only bilingual people have.

Teachers can encourage English language learners to use this skill by bringing authentic reading materials into the classroom that are likely to be of interest to students' families. For example, in an interdisciplinary unit on "Health," students can read fliers from the local hospital that advertise various services the hospital provides (perhaps including services for people who do not have health insurance). In addition to other tasks that the whole class may perform, English language learners can be asked to translate those materials for their families and to write a paragraph explaining which services their family members were interested in and why. Alternatively, if a flier is already available both in English and in students' first language, English language learners can be asked to read both versions and critique the non-English text.

Make bilingual books available. Another way of creating a multilingual classroom environment is by including bilingual books in the classroom library—whether they are commercially produced or written by English language learners. Commercially produced bilingual books should be purchased only in consultation with someone familiar with both their language and their cultural content to make sure that neither is distorted. Once purchased, the books should be displayed alongside English books in the classroom library, so they will be visible, and "new arrivals" should be signaled to the students.

Here are some sources for bilingual books and materials:

www.bilingualbooks.com
www.cultureforkids.com
www.mantralingua.com
www.panap.com

Bilingual books produced by the students should follow the layout of commercially produced bilingual books; that is, the text on the left page should be in one language, and the text on the right page should be in the other language. Students should be allowed to mix the two languages only when the context calls for it, for example, when there is a direct quote (Cloud et al., 2009).

Producing bilingual books that they can share with their teacher, classmates, and family gives English language learners a much needed sense of empowerment (Cummins et al., 2005) and is an activity that supports biliteracy and develops metalinguistic awareness—two reasons that it should be encouraged in the classroom. The following description recounts three students' process of creating a bilingual book based on an "identity text," that is, on a text in which an immigrant child writes about her immigration experience (Cummins et al., 2005).

> When she was in 7th grade—and less than a year after arriving in Canada—Madiha coauthored a 20-page English-Urdu dual language book titled The New Country . . . Together with her friends, Kanta and Sulmana, also originally from Pakistan, she wrote about "how hard it was to leave our country and come to a new country" . . .
>
> The students collaborated on this project in the context of a unit on migration . . . They researched and wrote the story over the course of several weeks, sharing

> their experiences and language skills. Madiha spoke little English but was fluent in Urdu; Sulmana was fluent and literate in both Urdu and English; Kanta, who was fluent in Punjabi and English, had mostly learned Urdu in Toronto. The girls discussed their ideas primarily in Urdu but wrote the initial draft of their story in English. Sulmana served as a scribe for both languages. (Cummins et al., 2005, p. 39)

If you are a monolingual English teacher who not only encourages your English language learners' production of bilingual books, but also tries to read such books, you can become a wonderful role model for all your students—by trying to figure out what the non-English version of the book is saying and by thinking aloud while doing so; by resorting to the English version only when you have exhausted all other possibilities of making sense of the text; by asking students who speak the other language to help you when your comprehension breaks down; and, above all, by being excited about the challenge of making sense of a text written in a language that you do not know.

Bilingual books can be used in the mainstream classroom in many ways (Cloud et al., 2009). For example, they can be used to promote metalinguistic awareness and cross-linguistic comparisons. In order to do that, you can ask English language learners to compare the two versions of the text and do one of the following (as a homework or extra-credit assignment that can be then shared with the rest of the class):

- Have students decide if the tone of the text is the same in the two languages. If not, what accounts for the difference?
- Ask students to consider translation equivalents for certain words, to try to guess why those particular words were chosen, and to consider alternatives.
- Have students evaluate the translation and suggest changes that would improve it.

Bilingual books can also be used to prepare English language learners for various instructional tasks. For example, they can preview a story or an expository text in the home language while the other students preview the English text. Alternatively, bilingual books can be used to help English language learners consolidate their learning by reading a text related to the topic being taught in their first language.

Engage students in producing multilingual newsletters. Another suggestion for making students' home languages more prominent in the school is to create newsletters in multiple languages by involving English language learners in writing the home-language versions of the information. Such newsletters are a clear sign that students' families are appreciated, and they are more likely to be read by English language learners' parents than newsletters written in English only. In addition, involving English language learners in the production of the newsletters will give these students a much needed opportunity to demonstrate their bilingual competence—one that is often overlooked in mainstream classrooms and that is severely devalued by current assessment practices.

Assessment of Culturally and Linguistically Diverse Students

It is a well known fact that as a result of the increased accountability of schools for student achievement brought about by the No Child Left Behind Act (2001), students are tested more often than in the past. English language learners are tested even more than other students because, in addition to having to take all the standardized tests that are mandatory for all students at different grade levels, their English proficiency is also assessed for identification and placement purposes upon school enrollment, and then annually for reclassification purposes.

Research on the use of wide-scale reading and content area tests in English has revealed that CLD students' performance is adversely affected by the fact that these tests are often linguistically and/or culturally biased. These tests are designed for monolingual speakers of (Standard) English and do not take into account minority students' diverse backgrounds (e.g., Abedi, 2002; Garcia, 1991; Pomplun & Omar, 2001; Stevens, Butler, & Castellon-Wellington, 2000). For example, one of the factors that negatively affect minority students' performance is their lack of familiarity with the passage topics and vocabulary of the test questions. If they were given the opportunity to respond to test questions in their home language or if the questions were posed to them in their first language, English language learners might demonstrate much greater comprehension of the test passages than indicated by their answers on a standardized test (Garcia, 1991).

English language learners tend to perform better in science and mathematics than in reading, a difference that may be attributed to the higher language demands of reading tests compared to science and mathematics tests. Nevertheless, the linguistic complexity of test questions adversely affects these learners' performance even on mathematics tests (Abedi, 2002).

Such findings raise a serious question about the validity of standardized tests when used with culturally and linguistically diverse students. Do these tests really measure what they claim to measure—that is, reading comprehension or knowledge in the content areas—or do they measure students' proficiency in academic English and familiarity with mainstream American culture? Admittedly, it is hard to devise test questions even in science and mathematics that do not require knowledge of the language of the test, just as it is virtually impossible to design a reading comprehension test that is culture-free. Nevertheless, the question remains, and can be asked not only of standardized tests, but of classroom assessments as well. The following examples of test items from an eighth-grade mathematics classroom test illustrate the two types of bias—linguistic and cultural.

Question 1: *The larger of two numbers is 1 less than three times the smaller. If three times the larger is 5 more than eight times the smaller, find both numbers.*

Question 2: *In bowling leagues, some players are awarded extra points called their "handicap." The "handicap" in Anthony's bowling league is 80% of the difference between 200 and the bowler's average. Anthony's average is 145. What is Anthony's "handicap"?*

At first sight, both questions seem to test students' knowledge of solving algebraic equations. They test more than that, though, since both ask that students first convert the problems into symbolic equations before solving them. In order to do that for question (1), students need to understand the (apparently simple) wording of the problem. However, an English language learner who does not know how comparison is expressed in English (i.e., does not know terms such as *more, less,* or *than,* or the meaning of *-er* attached to an adjective) will not be able to make sense of the question even though she may be perfectly capable of solving equations. For such a student, this question tests her knowledge of English, not of mathematics.

The second question is a "word problem," that is, one in which mathematical relationships are embedded in a real-life context. Besides its potential linguistic challenges, this question is potentially problematic for all culturally and linguistically diverse students because it assumes familiarity with the context it presents. Lack of knowledge of the rules and terminology of bowling (which, by the way, is considerably less popular in other parts of the world than it is in the United States) is likely to impede students' comprehension of the context of the problem and obscure the mathematical relationships embedded in it; if non-mainstream students are not completely prevented from solving the problem, at the least, they will have to spend extra time making sense of the problem-situation.

What can be done to reduce the linguistic and cultural bias of tests? First and foremost, English language learners must be included in the design and piloting of these tests (Abedi & Lord, 2001). Then, testing accommodations must be provided for them. The most common accommodations include modifications in the following areas of test administration (Rivera & Stansfield, 2000):

- *presentation* of the test (e.g., repetition, explanation, or simplification of the test questions, translation of the test into students' home languages, or administration of the test by a bilingual specialist)
- *response* to test questions (e.g., the response may be dictated by the student, given in her home language, or displayed using alternative forms of representation)
- *setting* (e.g., individual or small-group administration, administration in a separate location, or administration in multiple sessions)
- *timing/scheduling* (e.g., additional time to complete the test)
- *reinforcement* (allowing the use of glossaries or of monolingual and/or bilingual dictionaries)

Research has shown that the one accommodation that narrows the gap between English language learners' test performance and that of other students is the *linguistic modification of test questions with excessive linguistic demands;* other accommodations increase scores for *all* students (Abedi, 2004; Abedi, Hofstetter, & Lord, 2004). Figure 9.2 includes a list of guidelines for simplifying test questions that can be used both by test designers and by classroom teachers in constructing tests (adapted from Cloud et al. 2009).

- Replace low-frequency words (e.g., *depreciate*) with common words (e.g., *lose value*).
- Repeat words and avoid synonyms. (For example, in the problem, "Daniel's print shop bought a new printer for $3,500. Each year it depreciates at a rate of 5%. What will its value be at the end of the fourth year? How much value will it have lost by then? If the printer were to be sold after three years and a new one were to be purchased for $3,000, how much money would Daniel have to spend?" the word *depreciates* can be replaced by *loses value*, and the word *purchased* by the word *bought*.)
- Make sure that all pronouns have clear antecedents; that is, it should be apparent which noun a pronoun refers to. (For example, in "Daniel bought a new $3,500 printer for his print shop, which depreciates each year at a rate of 5%," it is not clear whether the pronoun *which* refers to *the printer* or to *the print shop*. To avoid the ambiguity, the sentence can be rewritten as "Daniel's print shop bought a new printer for $3,500. Each year it depreciates at a rate of 5%.")
- Remove unnecessary expository material. (For example, in "[Daniel owned a print shop that had to replace its printers every 3–4 years. One year,] Daniel's print shop bought a new printer for $3,500...," the words in brackets are unnecessary for students' understanding of the question.)
- Replace passive structures (e.g., *If the printer were to be sold after three years and a new one were to be purchased*) with active structures (e.g., *If Daniel sold the printer after three years and bought a new one*).
- Separate long sentences into shorter ones. (For example, the sentence "If the printer were to be sold after three years and a new one were to be purchased for $3,000, how much money would Daniel have to spend?" could be rewritten as, "After three years Daniel wants to sell the printer and buy a new one. The new printer costs $3,000. How much money will Daniel have to spend?")

FIGURE 9.2 *Guidelines for Simplifying Test Questions*

For mathematics and science tests, using symbols instead of, or in addition to, words in order to clarify terminology and relationships is yet another way of reducing the language demands of test questions (see Figure 9.3).

To avoid linguistic bias when assessing English language learners' listening or reading comprehension, teachers can use close-ended or limited-response formats that make minimal demands on students' expressive skills (e.g., providing illustrations of possible answers that students need to choose from), and that allow teachers to determine whether students understand what they read even though they cannot express their understanding orally or in writing. If teachers speak the students' first language, they may also choose to allow English language learners to answer comprehension questions in that language.

More often than not, teachers assess their English language learners' literacy skills and development using assessment instruments that have been devised for monolingual

Original Test Question

The larger of two numbers is 1 less than three times the smaller. If three times the larger is 5 more than eight times the smaller, find both numbers.

Modified Test Questions

Version A:
A and B are two numbers. A is 1 less than 3 X B. 3A is 5 more than 8 X B. Find A and B.

Version B:
A=3B-1

3A=8B+5

A=?

B=?

FIGURE 9.3 *Linguistic Modification of a Test Question*

English children. While understandable, this practice may be nevertheless problematic because it ignores certain characteristics of bilingual children's knowledge and development and thus yields inaccurate assessment information.

For example, if an English language learner's vocabulary is assessed using an English vocabulary test, the results will indicate the child's vocabulary knowledge *in English* as opposed to her overall vocabulary knowledge, since bilingual children often know different words in each of their languages (Fernandez et al., 1992). Similarly, using running records or informal reading inventories with English language learners may lead to misleading conclusions about children's reading ability if, for example, pronunciation errors are marked as miscues. Such errors may be due to phonological or orthographic differences between English and a child's first language, and they do not necessarily indicate that the child does not recognize or understand the mispronounced words.

Assessment results yielded by fluency measures such as the DIBELS should also be interpreted with caution. Because English language learners often struggle with the pronunciation of English words (even when they know the words' meaning), their fluency rates often lag behind those of native speakers, even though they may have good comprehension (Lems, Miller, & Soro, 2010). The reverse may also be true, in that some students may be misidentified as good readers based on their scores on fluency measures, when in fact their comprehension of the text may be low (Samuels, 2007).

When assessing English language learners' spelling, teachers may benefit from being familiar with some of the ways in which English language learners' spelling development differs from that of monolingual English children (adapted from Helman & Bear, 2007):

- English language learners progress through the same stages of spelling development as English-speaking children; however, because they are also learning the language as they are learning to read and write, their progress through the stages takes longer than that of their monolingual English peers.
- Some of the misspellings of English language learners may be standard developmental errors, whereas others may mirror phonological and orthographic differences between English and the students' first languages. For example, spelling *hot* as *hat* may occur because the vowel sound in *hot* is represented by the letter *a* in a child's first language. Consonant sounds that do not exist in learners' first languages are also likely to be misspelled (e.g., *than* may be spelled as *van* or *dan* by speakers of many languages).
- Presumably because of the phonological system of their first language, English language learners often do more sounding out than native English speakers, which results in certain words being spelled with more letters than expected. For example, the vowel sound in *blade* is perceived as a diphthong (a combination of two vowels) and represented by two letters (*ei* or *ey*) in Spanish, which may account for a Spanish-speaking child's spelling the word *lady* as *leidy*.
- Because of the differences between the English vowel system and that of other languages, and because internalizing the English vowel sounds takes a long time, there is greater variability in the vowel substitutions that English language learners make as compared to those of native English speakers. For example, a Spanish-speaking child may spell the word *dirt* as *dart*, *dert*, or *durt*, substituting Spanish vowels for the English vowel in *dirt*, which does not exist in Spanish.
- Grammatical morphemes (e.g., the past tense ending *-ed* or the plural ending *-s*) may be omitted in English language learners' spelling before the grammatical structures that the morphemes represent become part of children's oral language.

In conclusion, when assessing English language learners' literacy skills, teachers need to be very clear about what it is that they want to find out; aware of the ways in which these students' literacy development may differ from that of monolingual English children; alert to possible cross-linguistic influences; and careful in interpreting and using the assessment results. This is particularly important in situations in which students are considered for special education services. Those English language learners who are poor readers and writers because of their limited English proficiency can easily be labeled as having a learning disability, even though what they need is not special education, but oral language development and literacy instruction that matches their level of English language proficiency. Figure 9.4 contains a list of questions that teachers and reading specialists should consider when implementing RTI models (described in Chapter 2) with English language learners (adapted from Klingner, Soltero-Gonzalez, & Lesaux, 2010).

If standardized tests often fail to reveal the progress made by English language learners in developing English language and literacy skills, the insights yielded by ongoing assessments and captured in teacher observations, samples of student work, and student portfolios (described in Chapter 6) can be extremely useful in documenting such progress. These insights should be shared with the students, their parents, other teachers, and school staff and administrators when making program placement decisions for English language

Questions related to Tier One:

- Am I well prepared to work with English language learners?
- Are English language learners receiving effective instruction?
- Is students' first- and second-language proficiency considered in planning instruction, assessment, and decision making?
- Do instruction and assessment take into account students' cultural and linguistic backgrounds?
- Am I using the literacy skills that students have developed in their first language to support their development of English literacy?
- Do I encourage students to use their first language strategically to cope with learning challenges?
- Are most English language learners thriving in the classroom/the program?

Questions related to Tier Two:

- Are Tier Two providers well qualified to work with English language learners?
- Does the system for progress monitoring include multiple types of assessments?
- Are teachers and staff with expertise in students' home languages and cultures involved in designing assessments, interpreting assessment data, planning instruction, and reassessing the criteria for entry into and exit from Tier Two?
- Do interventions and assessments take into account students' cultural, linguistic, and literacy backgrounds?
- Do interventions and assessments take into account students' levels of proficiency in their first and second languages?
- Do students receive intervention that has been validated with similar students in similar contexts?
- Are individual students making progress compared to their peers?

Questions related to Tier Three:

- Are Tier Three providers well qualified to work with English language learners?
- Are multiple types of ongoing assessments being used to document students' progress?
- Are students' home languages and cultures considered when planning instruction, designing assessments, and interpreting assessment data?
- Are students' proficiency levels in English and in the home language considered when assessing progress?
- Have all in- and out-of-school factors been considered in accounting for a student's progress (or lack thereof)?
- Are all service providers (general education teachers, special education teachers, ESL teachers) collaborating to ensure that students receive instruction that includes special education support, English language development, and access to general education content?
- How does each student progress compared to his or her peers?

FIGURE 9.4 *Implementing RTI with English Language Learners*

learners. Unlike standardized tests, they will often show that English language learners *are* making progress even though their test scores may not demonstrate it. Moreover, ongoing assessments are likely to be much more useful than standardized tests in helping teachers make informed instructional decisions for their English language learners.

Instructional Suggestions

One of the major findings of the review of research on literacy development in second-language learners carried out by the National Literacy Panel on Language-Minority Children and Youth (August & Shanahan, 2006) was that, much like English-speaking children, English language learners need high-quality instruction in five components of literacy: phonological awareness, phonics, fluency, vocabulary, and comprehension. Another equally important finding was that, "for language-minority children, word-level components of literacy (e.g., decoding, spelling) either are or can be (with appropriate instruction) at levels equal to those of their monolingual peers. However, this is not the case for text-level skills, like reading comprehension, which rarely approach the levels achieved by their monolingual peers" (August & Shanahan, 2006, p. 13). According to the Panel, English language learners' low levels of reading comprehension can be attributed at least in part to their low levels of oral language development in the areas of vocabulary knowledge, listening comprehension, and syntactic skills.

In this section we will share several instructional ideas that teachers may find useful in developing these five components of literacy among their English language learners. Most of the instructional strategies described in previous chapters can be used successfully with these students. Therefore, rather than reiterating them, we will highlight ways in which some strategies can be adapted for English language learners. In keeping with the findings of the National Literacy Panel on Language-Minority Children and Youth, we will place special emphasis on strategies for teaching listening comprehension, phonemic awareness, and vocabulary. To conclude the section, we will describe some techniques that we consider useful in developing English language learners' awareness of text structure and in supporting their writing development.

Strategies for Developing Listening Comprehension

Reading aloud (described in Chapter 3) is as beneficial to English language learners as it is to their monolingual English peers, since it develops listening comprehension, vocabulary knowledge, familiarity with the patterns of stress and intonation (or the prosody) of English, and a sense of story structure. However, English language learners will need extensive preparation and support in order to understand and learn from a story that the teacher reads aloud.

Chang and Read (2006) have shown that the most effective type of listening support for second language learners is providing information about the topic, followed by repeated listening. Teachers can prepare their students for a read-aloud by previewing the book or doing a picture-walk, which activates students' background knowledge of the topic. Sometimes English language learners will have virtually no prior knowledge of the topic. For example, a refugee child from Bosnia may know little, if anything, about American Boy Scouts. Teachers need to be alert to such a possibility and, in these cases, construct, rather than activate, the background knowledge that students need in order to understand the story.

Regardless of whether English language learners are familiar with the topic, vocabulary that is critical to understanding the story needs to be taught both during the preview and while reading the story (by using illustrations, gestures, movements, objects, or verbal explanations). It is important for teachers to remember that pronouncing a new word *once* and explaining its meaning orally or pointing to a picture will not be enough for their English language learners to retain the word. These students need to hear the new word several times, pronounce it, and then use it in sentences of their own (in response to questions posed by the teacher) in order to remember it.

Even more than English-speaking students, English language learners benefit from listening to the same story several times. Especially if they are at the beginning stages of learning English, the first time they listen to a story, they will understand its gist at best. During subsequent listenings, they can be guided to pay attention to more and more details, until an acceptable level of comprehension is achieved. Teachers need to prepare tasks that scaffold students' comprehension of the story by setting clear and increasingly challenging purposes for each listening. Without such scaffolding, English language learners may be overwhelmed and, as they attempt to understand everything, they may end up comprehending very little.

Prior to the first read-aloud and after previewing the book with the class, the teacher can give students a set of pictures that illustrate the main events of the story and tell them that, after listening to the story, they will have to arrange them in the order in which the events occur. To make the task easier, the teacher can pause after reading each section of the text, to give students time to select the picture that corresponds to it.

Before the second read-aloud, the teacher can give the students a list of True/False questions related to details in the story. After going over the questions with the class to make sure that everybody understands them, the teacher tells the students that they are going to listen to the story again and, as they do so, write *T* or *F* next to each statement, and then check their answers with a partner.

Before the third read-aloud, the teacher can give students a list of comprehension questions that require not only recall but also inferencing, and that they will answer individually or with a partner after listening to the story again. After the students complete each task, there should be ample class discussion of the answers. The degree to which English language learners will participate in these discussions is going to vary depending on their level of English proficiency, but once they have completed the tasks, they will be able to follow the conversation at least to some extent.

As a culminating activity, students can be asked to retell the story orally and/or in writing. The pictures used for the first read-aloud can then be glued to the pages of a "little book," and the students can write a sentence (or more) that describes each picture—either in English or in their home language, or in both, depending on the languages in which they are literate.

It is a good idea to provide English language learners with recorded versions of the stories that they have listened to in class and to encourage them to listen to those stories again at home. If they are literate, encouraging them to read along as they listen is likely to benefit both their listening comprehension and their reading development.

Strategies for Developing Phonological Awareness and Phonics Knowledge

Most of the strategies for developing phonological awareness and phonics described in Chapters 3 and 4 can be used successfully with English language learners. For example, *clapping games* will develop students' awareness of English syllables; *rhyming games* will develop their awareness of English onsets and rimes; and activities using *Elkonin boxes, phoneme segmentation, phoneme combination,* and *phoneme deletion* will develop their awareness of English phonemes. *Picture sorts* and *word sorts* will enhance their knowledge of phonics. However, one word of caution is in order at this point.

In previous chapters we have suggested that a whole-part-whole model of reading instruction, in which children focus first on the meaning of a text, then on a particular skill or language feature present in the text, and then back on meaning, is more conducive to overall literacy development than decontextualized phonological awareness or phonics instruction. While such an instructional model benefits *all* children, it is especially useful for English language learners.

Developing phonological awareness and phonics knowledge ultimately means developing awareness of patterns and rules that govern speech and its representation in print. In order to be able to discern these patterns and extract these rules, though, one needs to have access to a large number of language samples. Unlike their English-speaking peers, who have relatively large vocabularies when they come to school, English language learners do not; therefore, before they can develop awareness of the rules of English phonology and spelling, these students need to develop a minimal vocabulary in English.

The whole-part-whole instructional model allows English language learners to learn new words and develop phonological awareness and phonics skills at the same time. In the meaning-focused ("whole") components of the model, students learn and practice using new words in meaningful contexts. Once they have learned the words in context, they can focus on them out of context and analyze their phonological and orthographic features in the form-focused ("part") component of the lesson. If the words selected for phonological awareness or phonics practice are not in English language learners' vocabularies, then asking these students to manipulate their subcomponents will be an utterly meaningless activity, one that will develop neither their language nor their literacy in English. Therefore, we suggest that phonological awareness and phonics activities should always be embedded in whole-part-whole lessons using Shared Reading, Guided Reading, Shared Writing, the Language Experience Approach, or Writing Workshop formats, as described in previous chapters.

When focusing on "parts," teachers of English language learners should remember to *draw students' attention to similarities and differences between English and their first languages*. For example, since we know that the first consonant sound in the word *they* does not exist in Spanish, Turkish, Russian, or Swahili and that speakers of these languages tend to replace it with /*d*/ or /*v*/, the teacher can explain that English has a sound these languages do not have, that is different from both /*d*/ and /*v*/. Further, the teacher can ask the students to listen to several words that she pronounces (e.g., *van, than, then, den, they, day*) and raise their hands when they hear a word that begins with the same sound as the word *they*. Such an activity is likely to help English language learners perceive the unfamiliar phoneme. The teacher can pronounce the same words a second time, pausing after each word and asking students to use it in a sentence, so they will practice producing the different sounds and noticing the difference in meaning that they make. If the students are literate, the teacher can also tell them that the sound they have been focusing on is always spelled by the letters *th*.

The same activity can be used to help English language learners become aware of differences between English vowels that may not exist in their first languages. If the students are literate, the oral discrimination activity can be followed up with a word sorting activity to draw students' attention to the spelling of the different vowels. The following sets of words can be used for such activities.

seat, sit; fit, feet; lip, leap; neat, knit; leak, lick
sat, set; met, mat; bet, bat; sand, send; band, bend
cot, cut; hot, hut; cup, cop; shut, shot; nut, not

When designing activities for their English language learners, teachers must remember that those students who are already literate in a language that has an alphabetic writing system will learn to read and spell decodable English words fairly fast, whereas students who are literate in a language that uses a logographic or syllabic writing system will take longer to do that, and will rely predominantly on sight words in reading and spelling (August & Shanahan, 2006). This means that while all English language learners benefit from phonological awareness and phonics instruction, they also benefit from *sight word learning*, albeit for different reasons. Those who are already familiar with the alphabetic principle will attempt, in all likelihood, to apply letter-sound relationship rules to decoding and spelling English words whose spelling is irregular (e.g., to read *bread* as /*brid*/, or to spell *weigh* as *way*); therefore, they need to learn that the rules do not always apply and that there are words in English whose spelling needs to be memorized. Those children who are literate in a language that uses a non-alphabetic writing system, while taking longer to acquire the alphabetic principle, will nevertheless be able to read and spell quite a few words that they have learned as sight words, regardless of whether these words are decodable.

Used in thoughtful and varied ways, *word wall, word bank,* and *word sorting activities* can be extremely useful for developing both phonics knowledge and sight word learning. For example, the words on a word wall can be arranged in two columns: decodable words (e.g., *men, ten, when, then, den*) and words with irregular spellings that contain the same vowel sound (e.g., *friend, instead*). As they learn new words in which the vowel /*e*/ occurs, English language learners can be asked to add them to the column where they

Bee	*Be*	
Ate	*Eight*	
Way	*Weigh*	
Hi	*High*	
Hole	*Whole*	
By	*Buy*	*Bye*
Rite	*Right*	*Write*

FIGURE 9.5 *Homophones for a Word Sorting Activity*

belong. For a word sorting activity, the teacher can provide cards with words like the ones in Figure 9.5 written on them, ask the students to find pairs of words that have the same pronunciation but different spellings (homophones), and then sort them into two columns: decodable words and words with irregular spelling.

Strategies for Developing Reading Fluency

Fluency instruction has been included in reading instruction because it has been shown to support reading comprehension for English-speaking children and English language learners alike. For the latter, fluency instruction contributes to reading comprehension in at least three specific ways (Lems et al., 2010):

- It helps develop *chunking*, or "the ability to separate or combine written text into meaningful phrases or clause units" (p. 156). Also known as "phrasing" (Rasinski, 2003), chunking helps readers parse the text—not word for word, the way English language learners often try to do—but by larger units of meaning, making comprehension easier. Native speakers develop the ability to chunk speech naturally, as they listen to and speak the language, and transfer their knowledge of how words cluster together in speech to chunking written texts. Fluency instruction can help English language learners develop this skill, too.
- It helps develop knowledge of English prosody, or "the vocal patterns and inflections that people use when speaking and reading aloud" (p. 156). Knowledge of prosody includes knowing when to make adequate pauses, change the intonation for questions, or stress certain words but not others. Non-native speakers are often said to have an "accent" not so much because of their pronunciation, but because of prosodic features of their speech that are different from those of native speakers.
- Fluency practice provides repeated exposure to vocabulary and thus supports English language learners' vocabulary development.

Choral reading, echo reading, paired reading, and *repeated reading* (see Chapter 5) can all be used successfully for developing English language learners' reading fluency. Before the students can engage in these practice activities, though, they need plenty of good models of fluent reading. Teachers should remember to explain the concept of fluent reading and to model it in their reading of the texts that the students will use for fluency practice.

Reader's Theater is a highly enjoyable strategy for fluency practice that can be easily integrated into a lesson with a whole-part-whole format. To prepare for Reader's Theater, the teacher needs a copy of a fictional text that contains dialogue, preferably among several characters.

To prepare for and conduct a Reader's Theater:

- Read through the text and mark the parts that should be read by different readers.
- Put brackets around each part and write the name of the reader to whom it will be assigned next to the bracket.
- Strike through the words that do not need to be read (e.g., "He said," or "She replied").
- Model reading the text fluently several times as the students read along silently.
- Then, have the students practice reading their parts aloud, to prepare for the "performance."
- Offer individual coaching at this point, asking students questions such as, "What is your character feeling? How do you sound when you feel that way?"
- Finally, read the whole text with the class, with each student reading his or her part.
- Offer praise, comments, and suggestions for improvement, and then invite the students to re-read the text.
- Repeat the performance-feedback cycle several times, until everybody is happy with the outcome.

Aaron Shepard's website (www.aaronshep.com) has a wealth of stories from around the world with versions adapted for Reader's Theater.

Reader's Theater develops all aspects of reading fluency, including chunking and prosody, but it works best with fictional texts. Yet English language learners also need to learn to read informational texts fluently. Because informational texts tend to pack information tightly into relatively long sentences, readers need the ability to chunk sentences into units of meaning in order to understand them. To support students in developing this ability, *segment informational text* into lines that break at natural phrase endings (see Figure 9.6 for an example).

Students should look at both the original and the segmented texts; then the teacher should explain how they are different and why it is important that readers chunk texts when reading. Before the students practice reading the second text aloud, the teacher models reading it several times, asking the students to pay attention to the natural pauses after each chunk. When they can read the segmented text fluently, they can practice reading the original text.

When students have developed some familiarity with chunking, they can try to segment texts on their own. Such an activity is also a good opportunity for reinforcing knowledge of punctuation.

Original text

Animals have certain characteristics, behaviors, and adaptations that help them survive, such as mimicry and camouflage. By mimicking something that predators avoid, an animal has a better chance of survival. Camouflage is an adaptation that helps animals to avoid predators by blending in with their surroundings. For example, predators will eat light-colored moths rather than dark-colored moths because the latter are harder to see against a dark background.

Segmented text

Animals have certain characteristics,
behaviors,
and adaptations
that help them survive,
such as mimicry and camouflage.
By mimicking something
that predators avoid,
an animal has a better chance of survival.
Camouflage is an adaptation
that helps animals to avoid predators
by blending in with their surroundings.
For example,
predators will eat light-colored moths
rather than dark-colored moths
because the latter are harder to see
against a dark background.

FIGURE 9.6 *Informational Text Segmented for Fluency Practice*

Strategies for Developing Vocabulary

In Chapter 5 we suggested that vocabulary instruction should focus primarily on Tier Two (or general academic) words that have wide utility across the subject areas, arguing that by the time children come to school, they already have thousands of Tier One words in their spoken vocabularies (Beck, McKeown, & Kucan, 2002). This is true of English-speaking children, but less true of English language learners, many of whom may not know common English words; vocabulary instruction for these learners should therefore include Tier One words as well.

Mainstream classroom teachers need to be constantly alert to the possibility that English language learners may not be familiar with Tier One words that may be critical to their listening or reading comprehension of a text. For example, if a child does not know the word *moth*, she will not understand the example that illustrates the meaning of the Tier Three (specialized, discipline-specific) word *camouflage* in the text on animal adaptations (see Figure 9.6 above); if she does not know what it means for something to *blend in* with its surroundings, she will not understand the explanation of the term *camouflage* either.

Divide the class into two teams. Display two guide words from a dictionary page (the first and the last words on the page) and ten other words, some of which appear on that dictionary page and some that do not. Have the two teams check each other's answers against the dictionary page and award a point for each word correctly classified as appearing on the page or not. Here is an example:

Guide Words: *beak* *bear*

beaker

beard

bar

beer

bean

bake

beam

bead

be

beach

FIGURE 9.7 *Dictionary Practice Activity: Guide Word Race*

While it is virtually impossible for teachers to anticipate which Tier One words their English language learners may not know, they can nevertheless check students' comprehension frequently and, when identifying a Tier One word that is an obstacle to comprehension, clarify its meaning right away. Fortunately, the meanings of Tier One words are usually easy to explain—with gestures, pictures, objects, actions, or by resorting to paraphrase or synonyms. English language learners should nevertheless be encouraged to check their understanding of the meaning by looking up the words in their bilingual dictionaries, and then adding them to their glossaries for subsequent study.

We have already emphasized the importance of teaching English language learners how to use dictionaries (see Figure 9.7 for a dictionary practice activity adapted from Nessel & Dixon, 2008) and of encouraging them to do so in the classroom and at home. In the case of Tier One words, dictionaries can be misleading or confusing because many Tier One words are *polysemous* (i.e., they have different meanings in different contexts). English language learners need to be warned of this risk and to be taught how to use the context in which a word occurs to select the meaning that the word has in a particular text. The first step in this process involves determining the part of speech (that is, whether the word is a noun, a verb, an adjective, an adverb, etc.); the second step consists of mentally replacing the unknown word with its dictionary definition and deciding whether it makes sense in the context of the sentence.

Semantic maps (described in Chapters 5 and 7) can be used to illustrate the multiple meanings and uses of polysemous words. For example, the word *will* can be placed in the center of a semantic map. One branch can show the definition of *will* as an auxiliary verb signaling future tense (e.g., in Robert Frost's line, *Some think the world* ***will*** *end in fire*); another can show its definition as a modal verb indicating a high degree of certainty (e.g., in, *I heard somebody knocking at the door. It* ***will*** *be Will*); a third branch can define *will* as a noun meaning *determination* (e.g., *You need a strong* ***will*** *to climb Mount Kilimanjaro*); and a fourth branch can define it as a legal document that people create to distribute their property after their death (e.g., *The man's children were not mentioned in his* ***will****; all his wealth went to a charity*). Branching out from each definition should be the sentence that illustrates that particular meaning.

One category of Tier One words that is particularly troublesome for English language learners, yet highly useful in everyday communication as well as in reading, is that of *phrasal verbs* (e.g., *come across, look forward to, run into*) and *idioms* (e.g., *add fuel to the fire, call the shots, make waves*). When the students are working with authentic texts (e.g., song lyrics or newspaper articles), teachers can assist their vocabulary development and reading comprehension by highlighting such vocabulary items in the texts. English language learners can be asked to infer their meaning from context and to think of an equivalent expression or word in their home language, while their monolingual English peers can be asked to provide Tier Two synonyms or paraphrases (e.g., *determine* for *figure out; ignore* for *give the cold shoulder*).

While discussing the meaning of phrasal verbs or idioms, teachers should also discuss the contexts in which their use is appropriate. For example, in what contexts would it be appropriate to use each of the following synonymous words and phrases: *die, pass away, expire, perish, decease, kick the bucket, go the way of all flesh*? The students can also use such a list to order the vocabulary items along a register scale ranging from most formal to least formal:

Most Formal *expire, decease, perish, die, pass away, go the way of all flesh, kick the bucket* **Least Formal**

Unlike Tier One words, which are often taught spontaneously, as the need arises, Tier Two words (general academic vocabulary that is useful across the disciplines) should be taught in a planned and thorough manner. Word Conversations (Beck et al., 2002), which have been described in Chapter 5, are a useful instructional strategy for teaching Tier Two words to all students, including English language learners, especially if enough opportunities are provided for students to repeat the words and use them in sentences of their own.

Morpheme analysis (the study of the smallest word parts that have meaning) is recommended by many scholars (e.g., Grabe, 2009; Lems et al., 2010) as a highly effective way to develop English language learners' vocabulary and to boost their listening and reading comprehension. As Lems et al. (2010) explain, "the power of knowing morphemes is that changes in phonemes and graphemes may mislead students, but once they learn to identify morphemes, even with spelling and pronunciation changes, they will have a steadfast compass that points them towards the meaning of a word" (p. 106). An activity that can be used to give students practice with morpheme analysis is the Word List Contest.

Word List Contests (Lems et al., 2010) are activities that develop students' awareness of prefixes and suffixes. To set up a word list contest, the teacher puts students in small groups, each of which designates one of its members as the secretary. Next, the teacher calls out and/or writes a prefix (e.g., *un-*) or a suffix (e.g., *-er*) on the board. The groups have five minutes to generate as many words as they can that contain the prefix or the suffix. When the time is up, the groups take turns reading out their lists of words. Any word that has been listed by another group is crossed out, and the winner is the group with the most words that the other groups did not list.

If the teacher writes the words on the board as the groups are sharing, she can then involve the class in morpheme analysis by asking questions such as, "What does this morpheme mean?" "How does this morpheme change the meaning of the word to which it is attached?" "What parts of speech is it attached to?" "Does it affect the spelling or the pronunciation of the words to which it attaches?" "Does it have an equivalent in other languages?" Such questions are going to develop students' metalinguistic awareness, reveal regularities in the spelling of English that may otherwise be obscured by pronunciation, and support students' reading comprehension and writing.

Depending on the students' level of English proficiency, reading development, and instructional needs, the Word List Contest can be played with lexical prefixes and suffixes, as described above, with grammatical suffixes (e.g., *-ed*), or with compound words. For example, students can be given a word that combines with many other words (e.g., *board, home, man, stop*) and asked to generate as many compound words as they can. The activity should be followed again by a discussion of the ways in which the morphemes in compound words change their pronunciation in English (compare the pronunciation of *board* in isolation and in the compound word *cupboard,* for example), since this phenomenon does not happen in many other languages.

While engaging students in the study of word parts, teachers can also introduce them to the study of etymology. Stirring curiosity about the origins of English words is beneficial for all students; for English language learners it may be even more so, especially if their home languages are related to English. For example, you can ask your students to explore the etymology of the word *bankrupt.* Once they realize that the morpheme *rupt* comes from the Latin word *ruptus* (broken), they will find it easier to figure out the meaning of words such as *rupture, disrupt,* or *interrupt.* Additionally, English language learners may become aware of cognates during such an activity. A speaker of Romanian, for example, will realize that the English words *rupture* and *interrupt* have the same meanings as the Romanian words *ruptura* and *intrerupe.*

Developing Reading Comprehension

The ABC instructional model and the comprehension strategies presented in previous chapters can be used successfully with English language learners in mainstream classrooms. In this section, we will describe two additional sets of strategies for supporting these students' reading comprehension—one meant to develop knowledge of English syntax, and the other meant to enhance awareness of text structure.

The correlation between syntactic awareness and reading comprehension in the first language has been documented by recent research (e.g., Cain, 2007; Nation & Snowling, 2000). Studies of the relationship of second language syntactic awareness and second language reading comprehension (e.g., van Gelderen et al., 2004) also suggest that the former is a prerequisite for the latter.

These findings are not surprising since "syntactic processing builds the phrasal and clausal units that support the construction of semantic propositions" (Grabe, 2009, p. 200). In other words, syntax helps readers to chunk texts into units of meaning. Knowledge of syntax also helps disambiguation processes. For example, in the sentence, "She was followed by her husband and son," syntax helps us determine who was following whom—that is, that the husband and the son were following the woman and not the other way around, even though the subject of the sentence is *she*. Further, syntactic awareness helps us to track referents (words to which other words refer). For instance, when reading the sentences, "Rob himself said that Charlie liked him" and "Rob said that Charlie liked himself," it is our knowledge of syntax that allows us to understand that in the first sentence, the pronoun *himself* refers to Rob, while in the second it refers to Charlie. All of these syntactic processes (and many others) contribute to reading comprehension.

Children learn the syntax of their first language naturally, as they learn to talk. All native English speakers therefore have unconscious knowledge of the syntax of English; English language learners do not. They acquire much English syntax by being exposed to spoken English and by interacting with English speakers; however, some of the aspects of English syntax are acquired earlier than others, and those that have not been acquired yet are likely to cause English language learners to have reading comprehension problems. For this reason, mainstream teachers working with English language learners should be prepared to help these students with certain aspects of English grammar.

Strategies for Teaching Grammar. As we have suggested earlier, mainstream classroom teachers who do not feel comfortable teaching grammar should enlist the help of ESL teachers in identifying the grammatical demands of a text or of a writing task and in explicitly teaching the grammatical features that may cause comprehension problems for their English language learners or that may prevent these students from completing the task successfully.

Mainstream classroom teachers who want to teach certain grammatical structures that they feel are particularly important for students' reading comprehension or writing should take the steps described in Figure 9.8 when preparing and teaching a lesson with a grammar component. For a sample ABC lesson plan with a grammar component, see Appendix A.

Mainstream classroom teachers who may not feel comfortable teaching grammar explicitly can nevertheless help their English language learners develop awareness of English syntax by using the strategies suggested by Nation (2009), which are described

A. Preparation

- Identify a particularly salient grammar structure in the text that the students will read.
- Consult resources (a grammar of the English language or Internet resources) to make sure that you understand the grammar structure well enough to explain it to others.
- Design a lesson plan that follows a whole-part-whole model or the Anticipation-Building Knowledge-Consolidation (ABC) model, and in which the new grammar structure is taught in the context of the text that the students are reading. This will make your grammar instruction more of a discourse-analysis activity than a decontextualized structural activity (Grabe, 2009).

B. Implementation

- Have the students read the text for gist and for important details, focusing on its meaning.
- When a satisfactory level of text comprehension has been achieved, focus students' attention on the grammar structure (for example, by writing a few sentences from the text on the board and underlining the new grammar structure, or by highlighting the structure in the text).
- Ask questions that will help students to analyze the grammar structure in terms of its meaning (e.g., "What kind of action does this verb form express?"), form (e.g., "How do we form it?"), and use (e.g., "What other words are used with it?" "When would we choose to use it instead of another structure?").
- After the students have answered these questions, have them practice using the new form by talking/writing about the topic of the lesson.

FIGURE 9.8 *Teaching Grammar*

below and illustrated in Figures 9.9–9.13 with application to the following excerpt from a text about the Civil Rights Movement.

> [1]On May 17, 1954, the Supreme Court unanimously ruled in *Brown v. Board of Education of Topeka, Kansas* that it was unconstitutional to separate schoolchildren by race. [2]Even though the Court's decision in *Brown v. Board of Education* applied only to public schools, it had the much greater effect of threatening the entire system of segregation. [3]The ruling convinced many African Americans that the time had come to oppose other forms of discrimination as well but at the same time angered many white southerners, who became more determined to defend segregation, no matter what the Supreme Court ruled.
>
> [4]In 1955 the Supreme Court followed up its decision in *Brown v. Board of Education* with another ruling that called on school authorities to make plans for integrating races in public schools, and ordered that integration was to be carried out "with all deliberate speed"—as fast as reasonably possible. [5]Some schools integrated quickly. [6]However, in parts of the South, local leaders vowed to keep African American children out of white schools, which made a clash between the federal government and these states seem more and more likely.

Directions: Find the verbs or verb-related words in the list below in their corresponding sentences of your text. Underline them. For each underlined word, ask yourselves, "What does what?" or "What is what?" and write a complete sentence that contains the word.

(sentence 1) *unconstitutional*

(sentence 2) *threatening*

(sentence 3) *oppose*

(sentence 3) *defend*

(sentence 4) *integrating*

(sentence 6) *likely*

Possible answers:

Separating children by race is unconstitutional.

The Court's decision threatens the entire system of segregation.

African Americans oppose other forms of discrimination.

White southerners defend segregation.

School authorities integrate races.

A clash between the federal government and the southern states is more and more likely.

FIGURE 9.9 *What Does What?*

What does what? This strategy helps readers become aware of the noun-verb relationships that may be obscured by the word order of a passage, especially if the noun and the verb are separated by other words. To help students see these relationships, the teacher chooses verbs, or words related to verbs, from the passage that the students are reading and writes them as a list, with sentence numbers next to them, on the chalk board. The students are asked to find these words in the passage, ask themselves the question "What does what?" or "What is what?" and write out the subjects and objects (if any) of the verbs as nouns. Figure 9.9 illustrates this strategy.

Part of speech activity. For this activity, the teacher chooses words from the passage that the students are reading and writes them with their sentence numbers on the chalk board. The words chosen should be words that can function as different parts of speech in different contexts. The students find each word in the passage and determine from context whether it is a noun, a verb, an adjective, or an adverb by writing *n., v., adj.,* or *adv.* after it. After identifying the parts of speech of the words in the text, the students can be asked to create sentences in which the same words function as different parts of speech.

Being able to recognize the parts of speech is valuable for at least three reasons: "First, when trying to guess the meaning of a word from the context, knowing the part of speech of the word will make sure that the meaning guessed is the same part of speech. Second, it makes looking up the word in a dictionary much easier because the

Directions: Find and underline the words below in the corresponding sentences of your text. Then, determine what part of speech each word is in the sentence in which it occurs.

(sentence 2) *effect*

(sentence 2) *threatening*

(sentence 3) *angered*

(sentence 3) *determined*

(sentence 4) *ruling*

(sentence 5) *integrated*

(sentence 6) *clash*

Answers:

(sentence 2) *effect (n.)*

(sentence 2) *threatening (v.)*

(sentence 3) *angered (v.)*

(sentence 3) *determined (adj.)*

(sentence 4) *ruling (n.)*

(sentence 5) *integrated (v.)*

(sentence 6) *clash (n.)*

FIGURE 9.10 *Parts of Speech Activity*

meanings of words are usually classified according to the part of speech of the word. Third, if a sentence is difficult to understand, it might be because the learners are applying the wrong meaning or function to one or more of the words in the sentence. By checking the part of speech of the words, the learners may be able to understand the sentence" (Nation, 2009, p. 40). Figure 9.10 contains some words extracted from the text about the Civil Rights Movement that can be used for a Parts of Speech Activity.

Coordination activity. This activity consists of simplifying sentences. As Nation (2009) explains, often when there is *and, but,* or *or* in a sentence, the sentence has two parts that are somehow related or parallel. The activity unfolds like this: The teacher writes the numbers of the sentences that include *and, but,* or *or* on the board and asks the students to underline the parallel parts and rewrite the sentence as two or more sentences (see Figure 9.11). Alternatively, the teacher can instruct students to follow these steps:

- Find the words *and, but,* and *or* in the text.
- Look at what follows.
- Find a similar part of speech in front of *and, but,* or *or.*
- Rewrite the sentence as two (or more) sentences, so that each sentence contains the common part plus one of the similar parts.

Conjunctions:

(sentence 3) *but*

(sentence 4) *and*

Possible answers:

The ruling convinced many African Americans that the time had come to oppose other forms of discrimination. At the same time, the ruling angered many White southerners. (The common part is "the ruling," and the similar parts are "convinced" and "angered.")

In 1955 the Supreme Court followed up its decision in Brown v. Board of Education with another ruling that called on school authorities to make plans for integrating races in public schools. The Supreme Court ordered that integration was to be carried out "with all deliberate speed"—as fast as reasonably possible. (The common part is "the Supreme Court," and the similar parts are "followed up" and "ordered.")

FIGURE 9.11 *Coordination Activity*

Identifying noun groups and head nouns. Noun groups that contain items following the head noun add to the difficulty of a sentence. Teaching students to look for the head noun in a noun group and to find the beginning and end of noun groups in long sentences is likely to help them chunk such sentences more easily. To do that, the teacher chooses the head nouns of noun groups from a passage that the students are reading and writes them with sentence numbers on the board. The students find these words in the passage, underline them, and draw a bracket at the beginning of the noun group and another one at the end. Figure 9.12 contains an example of such an activity, based on the text about the Civil Rights Movement.

Identifying pronoun referents. Referents are words to which pronouns such as *he, she, it, they, his, her, its, their, this, that, these, those, who, which, one, ones, the same, the other, the former, the latter* refer. Pronouns are a very important device for text cohesion, which is why the ability to identify their referents supports comprehension over larger units of text. Each pronoun has its own grammar, which can be explained fairly easily. For example, *their* can only refer to plural nouns or to two or more related singular nouns; *he* refers to a singular male person; *this* can refer to a singular noun, a phrase, a clause, or a group of clauses or sentences; *the former* refers to the first item in a sequence of two items.

To give students practice identifying pronoun referents, the teacher writes several pronouns from the text the students are reading on the board, with sentence numbers next to them. The students are asked (a) to locate the pronoun in each sentence, (b) to find its referent, and (c) to substitute the referent for the pronoun to see if the sentence makes sense. Figure 9.13 contains a list of pronouns and their corresponding referents taken from the text about the Civil Rights Movement.

Directions: Find the following head nouns in the text and underline them. Then, draw a bracket at the beginning of the noun group and another one at the end.

Head nouns:

(sentence 2) *effect*

(sentence 4) *ruling*

(sentence 6) *clash*

Noun groups:

[the much greater effect of threatening the entire system of segregation]

[another ruling that called on school authorities to make plans for integrating races in public schools]

[a clash between the federal government and these states]

FIGURE 9.12 *Head Nouns and Noun Groups*

Strategies for Developing Awareness of Text Structure. *Text structure* refers to the ways in which different types of texts are organized. A chapter in a science textbook looks very different from a folk tale, and both look different from an informal letter. In addition, each of the three text types has its own conventions for ordering information—and, as we have shown earlier in the chapter, these conventions may be culture specific. Therefore, while awareness of text structure is likely to benefit all students' reading comprehension and writing, it is especially beneficial for culturally and linguistically diverse students.

Directions: Find the pronouns listed in the left column in the text and underline them. Find the referent of each pronoun and circle it. Mentally substitute the referent for the pronoun to see if the sentence makes sense. Write the referent of each pronoun in the right-hand column.

Pronouns	Referents (to be supplied by students)
(sentence 2) *it*	The Court's decision
(sentence 6) *which*	Local leaders vowing to keep African American children out of white schools
(sentence 6) *these* (states)	The Southern states where local leaders vowed to keep African American children out of white schools

FIGURE 9.13 *Identifying Pronoun Referents*

Teachers can begin to raise students' awareness of the structure of the text they will be reading at the *Anticipation* phase of the lesson, by *previewing* the text. If the text is an informational one, organized by sections and subsections, students can be asked to read the headings and subheadings to get an idea of the main points they will be learning about. As they do this, they can use the headings and subheadings to create an outline of the text, to which they can add details during the *Building Knowledge* phase of the lesson. If the text does not have sections and subsections or if it is a short piece of fiction, students can be asked to read its title and the first sentence of each paragraph and to predict what it will be about. The teacher should explain that, in English, paragraphs often begin with a topic sentence (the sentence that expresses the main idea developed in the paragraph), and that therefore, by reading the first sentence of each paragraph they are likely to get a quick overview of the main ideas in the text.

Teachers can include activities that raise students' awareness of text structure in the Building Knowledge phase of the lesson as well. Constructing or filling out *graphic organizers* such as those described in previous chapters (e.g., semantic maps, story maps, Venn diagrams) as they read the text will support students' understanding of the relationships expressed. These graphic organizers can be revisited (modified or elaborated) at the *Consolidation* phase of the lesson or used as supports for writing activities.

A graphic organizer that can be used as an alternative to creating an outline is the *T-chart* (see Figure 9.14). Students list the headings and subheadings or, alternatively, the main ideas of a text in the left-hand column of the T-chart, and details pertaining to each heading/subheading/main idea in the right-hand column.

Graphic organizers that illustrate cause-effect relationships can be useful in all content areas. The simplest cause-effect relationship, in which one cause has one effect, is illustrated by an arrow that links the cause to its effect (see below). When one cause has multiple effects or, conversely, when several causes lead to one and the same effect, the graphic organizer should be adjusted accordingly.

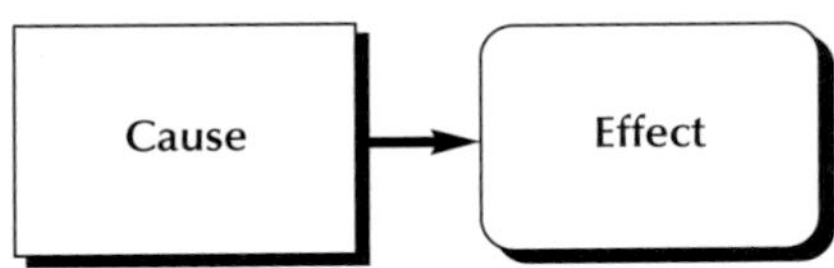

English language learners benefit from *explicit instruction* of text structure (Cloud et al., 2009; Grabe, 2009; Lems et al., 2010). Therefore, while having them work with graphic organizers, teachers should also name the different patterns of text organization that various texts use, such as enumeration, main idea/supporting details, chronological sequence, definition/examples, cause and effect, compare and contrast, problem and solution. At the same time, teachers should draw students' attention to

Headings and Subheadings	Details
Heading 1	
Subheading 1	
Subheading 2	
Heading 2	
Subheading 1	
Subheading 2	

FIGURE 9.14 *T-chart*

signal words (i.e., words that signal particular text structures or relationships among ideas). Figure 9.15 contains lists of signal words commonly associated with certain text structures, and graphic organizers that will help students visualize those text structures.

Text Structure	Graphic Organizer	Signal Words
Enumeration	Bulleted List	*first, second, third, next, then, last, finally, one… another, also*
Main idea/supporting details	T-Chart, Concept Map	*for example, another, in addition to, moreover, not only … but also*
Chronological sequence	Timeline	*first, next, initially, before, after, when, earlier, prior to, later, afterwards, subsequently, while, during, at the same time, finally, eventually*
Compare/contrast	Venn Diagram	*Both … and, neither, like, likewise, similarly, unlike, as opposed to, by contrast, however, but, and yet, on the other hand, neither… nor, similar/identical to, as … as, less/more … than*
Cause/effect	Cause-Effect Graphic Organizer	*because, consequently, therefore, since, if … then, as a result, thus, due to*

FIGURE 9.15 *Text Structures, Graphic Organizers, and Signal Words*

Original text with signal words underlined:

Are Whales Fish?

Whales live in the ocean, can stay underwater for long periods of time, and have strong tails to propel themselves. So do fish. So, are whales fish?

No, whales are not fish. Whales are mammals. They are warm-blooded, give birth to live young, nurse their young, breathe oxygen from air, and have hair. Unlike whales, fish are cold-blooded, reproduce by laying eggs, take in oxygen from the water through their gills, and do not have any hair. While whales move their tails up and down, fish move theirs from side to side, which causes the fish's whole body to undulate. An additional difference is that whales have smooth skin, whereas the body of fish is covered with scales.

Re-written text with signal words underlined:

Are Whales Fish?

Both whales and fish live in the ocean, can stay underwater for long periods of time, and have strong tails to propel themselves. So, are whales fish?

No, whales are not fish. Whales are mammals. They are warm-blooded, give birth to live young, nurse their young, breathe oxygen from air, and have hair. By contrast, fish are cold-blooded, reproduce by laying eggs, take in oxygen from the water through their gills, and do not have any hair. Unlike whales, who move their tails up and down, fish move theirs from side to side, which causes the fish's whole body to undulate. Moreover, while whales have smooth skin, the body of fish is covered with scales.

FIGURE 9.16 *Compare/Contrast Text*

To give students practice using signal words and identifying text structures, teachers can include varied activities in the Building Knowledge and Consolidation phases of the lesson. For example, after reading the original text in Figure 9.16 and completing a Venn diagram, students can be asked to reread the text, underline the signal words in it, and then replace them with other signal words without altering the relationships among ideas. Notice the additional changes that occur in the rewritten text when signal words are replaced by equivalents.

This can easily become an exercise in style, since the changes that students make in the signal words may affect the tone or the register of the text. The activity can also be used as an opportunity to teach punctuation and even grammar, as some signal words require particular syntactic patterns. For example, English language learners may not know that a sentence that contains the phrase *not only . . . but also* requires a comma before *but* and subject-verb inversion in the first clause (e.g., *Not only* ***can he*** *sing well, but he can also dance like Fred Astaire*).

Grabe (2009) suggests additional practice activities for developing awareness of text structure and of signal words:

- Unscrambling sentences in a paragraph
- Unscrambling paragraphs in a text
- Determining which sentence does not belong in a paragraph
- Locating paragraph breaks in a text that has been rewritten without paragraphs
- Identifying the functions of paragraphs in a text
- Making headings for sections of text

Awareness of text structure and signal words is likely to support not only ELLs' reading comprehension, but also their writing development.

Strategies for Supporting Writing Development

Those of us who have learned a foreign language know that writing one paragraph in a language that you do not speak well can be a daunting, time-consuming, and often frustrating task, and that writing a five-paragraph essay is at least five times worse. This is why English language learners need extra support if they are to engage effectively with the challenge of writing in English.

One way in which teachers can provide such support is by giving students models of expected performance. For example, before asking them to write a paragraph about their favorite animal, share a paragraph that you have written on the same topic. Spend time discussing with the students what makes that paragraph good (e.g., its organization, its word choice, the information included, etc.) and teach students whatever they may need in order to write an equally good one (e.g., English paragraph structure, key vocabulary, or sentence combining).

Next, have students brainstorm names of animals they may want to write about and information they have about them. Ask them to jot down their thoughts in their notebooks. Allow them to do this in English, in their home language, or in both, as they choose. The purpose of the brainstorming is for students to generate ideas, and it may be easier for them to do it with the help of their first language. Once they have decided what animal they want to write about, they can start writing their first draft—mostly in English, except for words they may not know, and that can still be in their first language. For those English language learners who may need additional scaffolding, provide a frame or template like the one below:

> *My favorite animal is ________. The (name of animal) is _______, _______, and _______. It has ______ and ______. The (name of animal) lives in _______. It eats _______, _______, and _______. One interesting thing about (name of animal) is that ________. I like (name of animals) because they _______.*

Such templates can be successfully used with older ELLs in the content areas as well. For example, a sentence frame such as

> ________ *is* _________ *that* ________.

can be used to teach students to write definitions (e.g., *A thesaurus is a book that lists words grouped together according to similarity of meaning.*).

After the students have finished their drafts, have them revise what they have written—add or delete details, or reorganize the information. At this point, English language learners should also work with their bilingual dictionaries to find English equivalents for the words that are still in another language in their texts. When they are happy with the content of their paragraph, they should edit it for spelling, punctuation, and grammar, and then "publish" their writing by sharing it with the rest of the class or by displaying it in the hallway. If the teacher chooses to do the latter, the students may wish to type up and/or illustrate their paragraphs.

You may have recognized the stages of the *writing process* in the description of this activity. Taking English language learners through these stages allows teachers to provide the additional support that these students need when writing in English.

A writing activity that allows students to use their knowledge of text types and that can be adapted to include students' home languages and cultures is the *RAFT* procedure (Santa, 1988). RAFT is an acronym for Role, Audience, Format, and Topic. The procedure consists of asking students to adopt different roles with respect to the topic of the lesson and then to write a text for an audience of their choice using a format that is consistent with their role and appropriate for their audience. Students can be encouraged to choose members of their home culture as their audiences, which will allow them to include features of their home-based communication styles and language in their writing. When sharing these texts with the class, students should be encouraged to explain their choices of language and style in terms of the expectations of their imaginary audience.

Helping culturally and linguistically diverse students succeed in the mainstream classroom is every teacher's responsibility. In order to fulfill it, the first step you need to take is to find out what these learners' strengths and instructional needs are; the second is to find ways to build on those strengths and to meet those needs. This chapter has attempted to help you begin to gain an understanding of how you can do both and, hopefully, has succeeded in making your responsibility appear less daunting.

Summary

Every year the students in American classrooms are more diverse in terms of the cultures in which they grew up and the languages they speak at home. This is true in many regions of the United States. To teach the increasingly diverse student populations of our public schools, teachers need to have a good understanding of their students' cultural backgrounds. Such an understanding includes awareness of how cultures differ in the way they use literacy, as well as an understanding of how the values and beliefs of a cultural group influence the ways its members communicate—ways that may differ from the traditional norms of most classrooms. Such differences should be viewed as strengths, accommodated in the classroom, and used as stepping stones in the process of familiarizing culturally and linguistically diverse students with the school culture.

Children coming from non-mainstream cultures often speak languages other than English or dialects other than Standard English at home. While schools do and should strive to help these students learn Standard English, this should not be done at the expense of, or as a replacement for students' home languages or language varieties. Rather, teachers should promote bilingualism and biliteracy among language minority students by including students' first language in the mainstream classroom. To do that, teachers need to have basic knowledge of the relationship between languages and dialects; of similarities and differences between English and other languages; of second language acquisition; and of the role of the first language in the learning of a second language.

Awareness of students' cultural and linguistic backgrounds will allow mainstream classroom teachers to avoid cultural and linguistic biases in designing assessments and in interpreting assessment results. That, in turn, is likely to result in better decisions for matching students with instructional services and teaching ethnic minority students. At the same time, such awareness will enable teachers to support these students' academic achievement by planning and implementing instruction that includes English language development.

References

Abedi, J. (2002). Assessment and accommodations of English language learners: Issues, concerns, and recommendations. *Journal of School Improvement 3*(1), 83–89.

Abedi, J. (2004). The No Child Left Behind Act and English language learners: Assessment and accountability issues. *Educational Researcher 33*(1), 4–14.

Abedi, J., Hofstetter, C. H., & Lord, C. (2004). Assessment accommodations for English language learners: Implications for policy-based empirical research. *Review of Educational Research 74*(1), 1–28.

Abedi, J., & Lord, C. (2001). The language factor in mathematics tests. *Applied Measurement in Education 14*(3), 219–234.

Asher, J. (1988). *Learning another language through actions: The complete teacher's guidebook.* Los Gatos, CA: Oaks.

Au, K. H. (1993). *Literacy instruction in multicultural settings.* New York: Harcourt Brace.

August, D., & Shanahan, T. (Eds.) (2006). *Developing literacy in second-language learners: Report of the National Literacy Panel on Language-Minority Children and Youth.* Mahwah, NJ: Lawrence Erlbaum.

Beck, I., McKeown, M., & Kucan, L. (2002). *Bringing words to life.* New York: Guilford.

Boykin, A. W. (1994). Afrocultural expression and its implications for schooling. In E. R. Hollins, J. E. King, & W. C. Hayman (Eds.), *Teaching diverse populations: Formulating a knowledge base* (pp. 243–256). Albany, NY: State University of New York Press.

Brown, M. T., & Lundrum-Brown, J. (1995). Counselor supervision: Cross-cultural perspectives. In J. P. Ponterotto, J. M. Casa, L. A. Suzuki, & C. M. Alexander (Eds.), *Handbook of multicultural counseling* (pp. 263–287). Thousand Oaks, CA: Sage.

Cain, K. (2007). Syntactic awareness and reading ability: Is there any evidence for a special relationship? *Applied Psycholinguistics, 28*, 679–694.

Cazden, C. B. (2001). *Classroom discourse: The language of teaching and learning.* Portsmouth, NH: Heinemann.

Center on Education Policy (CEP). (2010). *State Test Score Trends through 2007–2008, Part 6: Has Progress Been Made in Raising Achievement for English Language Learners?* Retrieved from http://www.cep-dc.org/document/docWindow.

Chang, A. C., & Read, J. (2006). The effects of listening support on the listening performance of EFL learners. *TESOL Quarterly, 40*(2), 375–397.

Chomsky, N. (1959). Review of "Verbal Behavior" by B. F. Skinner. *Language, 35*(1), 26–58.

Cloud, N., Genesee, F., & Hamayan, E. (2009). *Literacy instruction for English language learners.* Portsmouth, NH: Heinemann.

Crawford, J. (1999). *Bilingual education: History, politics, theory, and practice* (4th ed.). Los Angeles, CA: Bilingual Educational Services, Inc.

Cummins, J. (1979). Linguistic interdependence and the educational development of bilingual children. *Review of Educational Research, 49*(2), 222–251.

Cummins, J. (1981). The role of primary language development in promoting educational success for language minority students. In Office of Bilingual Bicultural Education, *Schooling and language minority education: A theoretical framework* (pp. 3–49). Sacramento, CA: State Department of Education.

Cummins, J., Bismilla, V., Chow, P., Cohen, S., Giampapa, E., Leoni, L., Sandhu, P., & Sastri, P. (2005). Affirming identity in multilingual classrooms. *Educational Leadership, 63*(1), 38–43.

Delgado-Gaitan, C., & Trueba, H. (1991). *Crossing cultural borders: Education for immigrant families in America.* New York: Falmer.

Delpit, L. (1995). *Other people's children: Cultural conflict in the classroom.* New York: The New Press.

Echevarria, J., Vogt, M., & Short, D. J. (2010). *Making content comprehensible for secondary English learners: The SIOP model.* Boston, MA: Allyn & Bacon.

Erickson, F. (2010). Culture in society and in educational practices. In J. A. Banks & C. A. M. Banks (Eds.), *Multicultural education: Issues and perspectives* (7th ed., pp. 33–56). Hoboken, NJ: Wiley.

Falicov, C. J. (1996). Mexican families. In M. McGoldrick, J. Giordano, & J. K. Pearce (Eds.), *Clinical handbook of marital therapy* (pp. 429–450). New York: Guilford Press.

Fernandez, M. C., Pearson, B. Z., Umbel, V. M., Oller, D. K., & Molinet-Molina, M. (1992). Bilingual receptive vocabulary in Hispanic preschool children. *Hispanic Journal of Behavioral Sciences, 14*(2), 268–276.

Fox, H. (1994). *Listening to the world: Cultural issues in academic writing.* Urbana, IL: National Council of the Teachers of English.

Francis, D. J., Lesaux, N., & August, D. (2006). Language of instruction. In D. August & T. Shanahan (Eds.), *Developing literacy in second-language learners: Report of the National Literacy Panel on Language-Minority Children and Youth* (pp. 365–415). Mahwah, NJ: Lawrence Erlbaum Associates.

Garcia, G. E. (1991). Factors influencing the English reading test performance of Spanish-speaking Hispanic children. *Reading Research Quarterly, 26*(4), 371–392.

Garcia, O. (2009). *Bilingual education in the 21st century: A global perspective.* Malden, MA: Wiley-Blackwell.

Gass, S. M., & Selinker, L. (2008). *Second language acquisition: An introductory course* (3rd ed.). New York: Routledge.

Gay, G. (2010). *Culturally responsive teaching: Theory, research, and practice.* New York: Teachers College Press.

Gee, J. P. (2006). *An introduction to discourse analysis: Theory and method* (2nd ed.). New York: Routledge.

Genesee, F., Geva, E., Dressler, C., & Kamil, M. (2006). Synthesis: Cross-linguistic relationships. In D. August & T. Shanahan (Eds.), *Developing literacy in second-language learners: Report of the National Literacy Panel on Language-Minority Children and Youth* (pp. 153–175). Mahwah, NJ: Lawrence Erlbaum Associates.

Grabe, W. (2009). *Reading in a second language: Moving from theory to practice.* New York: Cambridge University Press.

Gregory, E. (1994). Cultural assumptions and early years' pedagogy: The effect of the home culture on minority children's interpretation of reading in school. *Language Culture and Curriculum, 7*(2), 111–124.

Goldenberg, C., & Coleman, R. (2010). *Promoting academic achievement among English learners: A guide to the research.* Thousand Oaks, CA: Corwin Press.

Hamayan, E., Marler, B., Sanchez-Lopez, C., & Damico, J. (2007). *Special education considerations for English language learners: Delivering a continuum of services.* Philadelphia: Caslon.

Healey, J. F. (1995). *Race, ethnicity, gender, and class: The sociology of group conflict and change.* Thousand Oaks, CA: Pine Forge Press.

Helman, L. A., & Bear, D. R. (2007). Does an established model of orthographic development hold true for English learners? In D. W. Rowe, R. Jimenez, D. L. Compton, D. K. Dickinson, Y. Kim, K. M. Leander, & V. J. Risko (Eds.), *56th Yearbook of the National Reading Conference* (pp. 266–280). Oak Creek, WI: National Reading Conference.

Huss-Keeler, R. L. (1997). Teacher perception of ethnic and linguistic minority parental involvement and its relationship to children's language and literacy learning: A case study. *Teaching and Teacher Education, 13*(2), 171–182.

Kern, R. (1994). The role of mental translation in L2 reading. *Studies in Second Language Acquisition, 16*, 441–461.

Kindler, A. L. (2002). *Survey of the states' limited English proficient students and available educational programs and services. 2000–2001 summary report.*

Washington, DC: National Clearinghouse for English Language Acquisition.

Klingner, J. K., Soltero-González, L., & Lesaux, N. (2010). RTI for English-language learners. In M. Y. Lipson & K. K. Wixson (Eds.), *Successful Approaches to RTI: Collaborative practices for improving K–12 literacy*. Newark, DE: International Reading Association.

Kochman, T. (1981). *Black and White styles in conflict.* Chicago: University of Chicago Press.

Kochman, T. (1985). Black American speech events and a language program for the classroom. In C. B. Cazden, V. P. John, & D. Hymes (Eds.), *Functions of language in the classroom* (pp. 211–261). Prospect Heights, IL: Waveland.

Krashen, S. (1982). *Principles and practice in second language acquisition.* Oxford: Pergamon.

Kyuchukov, H. (2004). *My name was Hussein*. Honesdale, PA: Boyds Mills Press.

Lee, O., & Fradd, S. H. (1996). Interactional patterns of linguistically diverse students and teachers: Insights for promoting science learning. *Linguistics and Education, 8*, 269–297.

Lee, C. D. (2007). *Culture, literacy, and learning: Taking bloom in the midst of the whirlwind.* New York: Teachers College.

Lems, K., Miller, L. D., & Soro, T. M. (2010). *Teaching reading to English language learners: Insights from linguistics.* New York: Guilford.

Lightfoot, D., & Fasold, R. (2008). The structure of sentences. In R. W. Fasold & J. Connor-Linton (Eds.), *An introduction to language and linguistics* (pp. 97–137). Cambridge, UK: Cambridge University Press.

Long, M. (1996). The role of the linguistic environment in second language acquisition. In W. Ritchie & T. Bhatia (Eds.), *Handbook of second language acquisition* (pp. 413–468). New York: Academic Press.

Nation, I. S. P. (2009). *Teaching ESL/EFL reading and writing*. New York: Routledge.

Nation, K., & Snowling, M. (2000). Factors influencing syntactic awareness skills in normal readers and poor comprehenders. *Applied Psycholinguistics, 21*, 229–241.

National Center for Educational Statistics (NCES). (2009). *Reading 2009: National Assessment of Educational Progress at Grades 4 and 8.* Institute of Education Sciences. NCES 2010-458. Washington, DC: U.S. Department of Education.

National Clearinghouse for English Language Acquisition (NCELA). (2008). *NCELA frequently asked questions.* Retrieved from www.ncela.gwu..edu/expert/faq/08leps.html

Nessel, D. D., & Dixon, C. N. (2008). *Using the Language Experience Approach with English language learners.* Thousand Oaks, CA: Corwin Press.

Nieto, S. (1996). *Affirming diversity: The sociopolitical context of multicultural education* (2nd ed.). NY: Longman.

No Child Left Behind Act of 2001. 107th Congress of the United States of America. Retrieved from www.ed.gov/legislation/ESEA02/107-110.pdf.

Ogbu, J. U. (1992). Understanding cultural diversity and learning. *Educational Researcher, 21*(8), 5–14.

Orellana, M. F., Reynolds, J., Dorner, L., & Meza, M. (2003). In other words: Translating or "paraphrasing" as a family literacy practice in immigrant households. *Reading Research Quarterly, 38*(1), 12–34.

Pai, Y., Adler, S. A., & Shadiow, L. K. (2006). *Cultural foundations of education* (4th ed.). Upper Saddle River, NJ: Merrill/Prentice Hall.

Pomplun, M., & Omar, M. H. (2001). The factorial invariance of a test of reading comprehension across groups of limited English proficient students. *Applied Measurement in Education, 14*(3), 261–283.

Pritchard, R., & O'Hara, S. (2008). Reading in Spanish and in English: A comparative study of processing strategies. *Journal of Adolescent and Adult Literacy, 51*(8), 630–638.

Rasinski, T. V. (2003). *The fluent reader: Oral reading strategies for building word recognition, fluency, and comprehension.* New York: Scholastic.

Riche, M. F. (2000). America's diversity and growth: Signposts for the 21st century. *Population Bulletin, 55*(2), 3–38.

Rivera, C., & Stansfield, C. (2000). *An analysis of state policies for the inclusion and accommodation of English language learners in state assessment programs during 1998–1999* (executive summary). Washington, DC: The George Washington University Center for Equity and Excellence in Education.

Romaine, S. (1994). *Language in society: An introduction to sociolinguistics.* Oxford: Oxford University Press.

Rubinstein-Avila, E. (2007). From the Dominican Republic to Drew High: What counts as literacy for Yanira Lara? *Reading Research Quarterly, 42*(4), 568–589.

Samuels, S. J. (2007). Afterword for B. W. Riedel. The relation between DIBELS, reading comprehension, and vocabulary in urban first-grade students. *Reading Research Quarterly, 42*(4), 546–567.

Santa, C. M. (1988). *Content reading including study systems: Reading, writing, and studying across the curriculum*. Dubuque, IA: Kendall Hunt.

Schmidt, R. (2001). Attention. In P. Robinson (Ed.), *Cognition and second language instruction* (pp. 3–32). Cambridge, UK: Cambridge University Press.

Short, D. J. *Designing Comprehensive Course Assessment Prompts, Portfolio Tasks, and Exhibition Projects for ELLs.* Paper presented at Secondary ESL Institute, Pawtucket, RI, December 2007.

Siegel, J. (2006). Language ideologies and the education of speakers of marginalized language varieties: Adopting a critical awareness approach. *Linguistics and Education, 17*, 157–174.

Smitherman, G. (2000). African American student writers in the NAEP, 1969–1988/89 and "The Blacker the berry, the sweeter the juice." In *Talkin that talk: Language, culture, and education in African America* (pp. 163–194). New York: Routledge.

Spada, N., & Lightbown, P. M. (2008). Form-focused instruction: Isolated or integrated? *TESOL Quarterly, 42*(2), 181–207.

Stevens, R. A., Butler, F. A., & Castellon-Wellington, M. (2000). *Academic language and content assessment: Measuring the progress of English language learners* (CSE Technical Report No. 552). Los Angeles: University of California, National Center for Research on Evaluation, Standards, and Student Testing.

Swain, M. (1985). Communicative competence: Some roles of comprehensible input and comprehensible output in its development. In S. Gass & C. Madden (Eds.), *Input in second language acquisition* (pp. 235–253). Rowley, MA: Newbury House.

van Gelderen, A., Schoonen, R., de Glopper, K., Hulstjn, J., Simis, A., Snellings, P., & Stevenson, M. (2004). Linguistic knowledge, processing speed, and metacognitive knowledge in first- and second-language reading comprehension: A componential analysis. *Journal of Educational Psychology, 96*, 19–30.

Volk, D., & de Acosta, M. (2001). "Many differing ladders, many ways to climb . . . ": Literacy events in the bilingual classroom, homes, and community of three Puerto Rican kindergartners. *Journal of Early Childhood Literacy, 1*(2), 193–224.

Wardaugh, R. (2002). *An introduction to sociolinguistics* (4th ed.). Malden, MA: Blackwell.

Wolfram, W. (2004). Social varieties of American English. In E. Finegan & J. R. Rickford (Eds.), *Language in the USA: Themes for the twenty-first century*. Cambridge, MA: Cambridge University Press.

Appendix A
Reading Comprehension Lesson with a Grammar Component

Text to be used:

Ellis Island

Ellis Island was an immigrant processing center that was open from 1892 until 1952. During that time, over 12 million immigrants entered the United States through Ellis Island. Today more than four out of every ten American people can trace their roots to an ancestor who entered America through Ellis Island. Built to process 5,000 new immigrants each day, it often processed twice that number.

Once the immigrants stepped off their boats, large numbered tags were tied to their clothing. They were taken to the registry hall where, after waiting in long lines, they were examined by doctors. Chalk marks were put on their clothing if any medical problems were suspected. Anyone whose clothing was marked was detained for further examination. About one out of every six people were delayed for as long as four days because of medical problems, and one out of ten of those delayed were sent back to their homelands because the problems were judged to be serious. Those who made it past the medical examination were then questioned by a government inspector. If any answer was suspect, the person would face a board of special inquiry who would decide if the person could stay. If all tests were passed, the average stay on Ellis Island was about five hours.

Lesson Plan

Topic: Ellis Island (second lesson in a unit on immigration)

Grade: 5th

Objectives: Students will be able to

- Scan the text and answer true/false questions
- Match words to definitions by inferring word meanings from context
- Answer comprehension questions
- Use passive sentences to describe the steps of immigrant processing on Ellis Island
- Talk about how immigrants felt on Ellis Island
- Write a letter from the perspective of an immigrant describing the Ellis Island experience

New language structures:

- Vocabulary: *examine, question, pass/fail a test/an examination, suspect* (noun, adjective, verb)
- The Passive Voice

Students' prerequisite knowledge: reasons for immigration and parts of the world from which immigrants came to the US in late 19th and early 20th century

Materials: Ellis Island text; handouts; pictures

ANTICIPATION PHASE

Teacher leads a whole-class introductory conversation in which topics discussed in the previous lesson (reasons for immigration and parts of the world from which immigrants came to the US at different times in history) are reviewed.

Teacher shows a world map and points to New York City, explaining that boats carrying immigrants from Europe often ended their trip there.

Students are asked to hypothesize what immigrants did once they got off the boat. The new vocabulary is introduced during the conversation to help students express their predictions. The predictions are written on the board.

Teacher shows pictures of Ellis Island, explaining that it was an immigrant processing center where newly arrived immigrants were examined and interrogated by American government officials. Teacher announces that the students are going to read a short text about it.

BUILDING KNOWLEDGE PHASE

Task #1 (reading for gist):
Teacher hands out copies of the Ellis Island text and asks students to skim it for 2–3 minutes to check their predictions. Follow-up: whole-class discussion in which students revisit the list of predictions and decide which were confirmed by the text.

Task #2 (reading for detail):
Teacher gives students a list of sentences (see handout 1 below) and tells them they will scan the text and decide if the sentences are true or false. Before scanning the text, the students are asked to read the sentences and make sure they understand them. Potential comprehension difficulties are resolved.

Handout #1

Scan the text and, working with your partner, decide if the following sentences are true or false.

Example: Ellis Island was an immigrant processing center. – True

1. *The immigrant processing center on Ellis Island was closed down in 1952.*
2. *40% of American people are descended from immigrants who entered the US through Ellis Island.*
3. *Up to 10,000 immigrants were processed on Ellis Island each day.*
4. *All the immigrants were examined by doctors.*
5. *All the immigrants with medical problems were sent back to their home countries.*
6. *All the immigrants that passed the medical examination were questioned by a board of special inquiry.*
7. *No immigrant spent more than five hours on Ellis Island.*

Follow-up: Students share their answers in a whole-class discussion. They are asked to justify their answers by referring to the text.

Task #3 (vocabulary practice):

Handout #2

Directions: Find the words in column A in the text. Read the sentences in which they occur. Then, draw a line from each word to its definition in column B.

A	*B*
trace one's roots	*to keep back*
ancestor	*card or piece of paper tied to something as a label*
tag	*to find one's origin*
detain	*one from whom a person descends*
inquiry	*interrogation; investigation*

Follow-up: Whole-class discussion of the answers. Teacher has students use the words in sentences to talk about their own origins and about immigration procedures on Ellis Island.

Task #4 (comprehension questions):

Handout #3

Directions: In pairs, read the text again and answer the following questions:

1. *On average, how many immigrants entered the US through Ellis Island each year between 1892 and 1952?*
2. *Ellis Island was an immigrant processing center. What does the word "process" mean in this context?*
3. *According to the text, Ellis Island was built to process 5,000 immigrants each day, but it often processed twice that number. Why do you think that happened? (Think of major events in world history that took place in the first half of the 20th century.)*
4. *What percentage of immigrants were sent back to their home countries for medical reasons?*
5. *What might have been "serious medical problems"? Why do you think immigrants with such problems were not admitted into the US?*
6. *What questions do you think the government inspector asked the immigrants?*
7. *What might have been a "suspect answer"? What/who were the Americans suspicious of?*

Follow-up: Whole-class discussion of the answers.

Task #5 (identifying the new grammar structure in the text):

Teacher writes on the board:

Doctors examined the immigrants.

Then, teacher directs students to find the sentence in the text that has the same meaning and writes it on the board:

The immigrants were examined by doctors.

Task #6 (co-constructing the meaning, form, and use of the new grammar structure):

Students are asked to determine the subject, verb, and direct object in the two sentences. Teacher leads a discussion on the function of the subject and of the object in the first sentence (the subject performs the action expressed by the verb, i.e., is the agent of the action; the direct object is affected by the action of the subject) and in the second sentence (the subject is affected by the action of the agent). Teacher explains that the first sentence is called an "active sentence" because its subject does the action (is the agent of the action); and that the second sentence is called a "passive sentence" because its subject does not do anything; rather, the subject is that to whom/which something is done.

Students are led to identify the structure of a passive sentence:

Subject + BE + Past Participle (+ by + Agent)

Teacher writes another sentence on the board:

The immigrants were taken to the registry hall.

Students are asked to identify the subject, the verb, and the agent in the passive sentence. Teacher asks students to hypothesize why the agent is not expressed in this sentence (because it is not important).

Students are asked to scan the second paragraph of the text, underline the passive sentences that they find, and read them aloud. Teacher asks why they think there are so many passive sentences in this text. How are active and passive sentences different? (In a passive sentence, the emphasis is not on the agent, but on the object of the action. The emphasis of the text is on the immigrants, not on the Ellis Island staff.) In what kind of texts would passive sentences be more appropriate—in personal narratives or in science reports?

CONSOLIDATION

Task #1 (Guided Practice):

Handout #4

What were the steps Ellis Island officials took in processing immigrants? With your partner, number the sentences below to establish the correct sequence. Refer back to the text if you need to.

a. The board of special inquiry interrogated the suspect immigrants.

b. Doctors examined the immigrants.

c. A government inspector questioned the immigrants that passed the medical examination.

d. Ellis Island officials tied numbered tags to the immigrants' clothing.

e. The board of special inquiry decided whether an immigrant could enter the US or not.

f. If a government inspector found an immigrant's answers suspect, he referred the immigrant to a board of special inquiry.

Next, write out the steps of immigrant processing on Ellis Island in the correct sequence using passive sentences.

Follow-up: Whole-class discussion.

Task #2 (Making Connections):

In groups of four, students discuss the following questions:

Handout #5

1. *How do you think the immigrants felt when they arrived on Ellis Island?*
2. *How do you think the immigrants felt when numbered tags were tied to their clothing?*
3. *How do you think the immigrants felt when they were examined by doctors and questioned by government inspectors?*
4. *How do you think those immigrants who were sent back home felt?*

Follow-up: Whole-class discussion of students' answers. Teacher asks if any students would like to share their experience of immigrating to the US.

Task #3 (Writing Activity):

Handout #6

Directions: Imagine that it's the year 1945. You are an immigrant who has just been admitted into the US. Write a letter to your family back home in which you

- *Explain your reasons for emigrating to the US.*
- *Briefly describe your trip to the US.*
- *Describe your experience on Ellis Island (include every step of the process).*
- *Describe your feelings while you were on Ellis Island.*

Formal Measures

CHAPTER 10

Chapter Outline

his chapter is devoted to formal measures of reading. Two principal types of formal measures are norm-referenced standardized tests and criterion-referenced tests. Most students encounter these formal measures in the form of group achievement tests administered during the elementary and secondary grades and in college admissions tests such as the Scholastic Aptitude Test. The results of formal assessments of reading are often used to evaluate school, district, or state reading programs; to identify areas of strength and weakness within a curriculum; and to compare achievement patterns of schools, districts, and states.

This chapter provides information to assist you in determining the appropriateness of formal assessments for particular uses and interpreting their results. To use and interpret test scores, teachers must be knowledgeable about characteristics of tests in general and also of specific tests. Without this knowledge, interpretations can be difficult at best and inaccurate at worst.

Understanding Formal Measures

For decades, formal tests were used to quantify student achievement and to assess instructional effectiveness. They are still used for these purposes. However, in recent years, criticism of the validity and authenticity of formal tests has increased. Today, most schools and school divisions are required to administer and interpret formal measures and to supplement them with a variety of informal and observational assessments. What are the major criticisms of formal tests, particularly reading tests?

First, formal reading tests do not reflect what we know about the reading process. We know that reading is a complex, constructive process in which meaning results from interaction among the reader, the text, and the context in which the reading occurs. The prior experiences, background knowledge, interests, motivation, and knowledge of the reading process are reader factors. The amount and nature of the information conveyed, organizational structures, vocabulary, grammatical complexity, writing style, and even size and clarity of type are text factors. The setting in which the reading takes place, the purpose for the reading, the locus of purpose setting (i.e., whether the purpose is set by the text, the reader, or another person), the frequency of interruptions during reading, and so forth are context factors. These factors combine to enable the reader to actively construct meaning from text.

But formal reading tests most often treat reading as a series of isolated, discrete skills. Test results show how readers perform on one separate skill after another, and these scores are generally added together to yield a global or overall reading score. This practice is a holdover from the traditional view that effective reading requires mastery of a set of discrete skills, each of which can be taught, practiced, and mastered in isolation. This model of reading has largely been replaced by the interactive, constructivist model of learning to read.

Second, formal reading tests typically do not assess reading in authentic ways. In real life, comprehension is often demonstrated by doing something with the information that is gained. But in testing reading, comprehension is usually demonstrated by answering questions about a brief passage, often in a multiple-choice format. In real life, readers often read fairly lengthy selections, including whole stories, chapters, and entire books. In testing reading, selections are usually much shorter; they may be as short as a single sentence, and are rarely longer than a single page.

In real life, reading is rarely timed, and the reader determines how quickly or slowly to read the material. In testing reading, most selections are timed, and readers who don't finish the section are penalized. Most educators agree that formal tests create artificial contexts for effective reading.

Third, formal reading tests often do not match the goals of instruction. Most are geared toward retention of a quantity of factual information, which may be thought of as the product. Yet most instructional programs emphasize process as much as product. Especially in the elementary grades, we are as interested in teaching students the process of learning as we are in teaching information, and we are as concerned with the learning process as we are with the products of such learning. But formal tests do not take process into account; indeed, they can create the appearance of a lack of success.

For example, imagine a class of low-achieving, reluctant readers and writers. Their teacher hopes that their test scores will increase this year; but she is even more hopeful that the students will modify their negative attitudes about reading, spend more time reading and enjoy it more, and use writing more effectively for communication and self-awareness. As the year progresses, she documents dramatic increases in the amount of reading and writing her students are doing. Their reading habits and their comments about reading reflect increasingly positive feelings about reading and about themselves as readers. However, end-of-year standardized achievement tests show only a modest increase in average reading level. If only these scores were available, it might appear that the class had made little progress in reading improvement. In this case, the formal measures that the school division used were incompatible with the goals of instruction.

Finally, formal tests most often measure skills and operations that are easily quantified and tested. Frequently, students are required to recognize, rather than produce, correct information. For example, they might be asked to choose the best title for a paragraph from several alternatives rather than to create a good title for it, or to choose the correct spelling from several misspellings rather than to spell the word correctly. Recognition is easier than production; it is easier to do, to score, and to measure. But it is generally not what we want students to learn. We teach spelling so students can spell words correctly, not so that they can merely recognize misspellings. We teach them to recognize main ideas so that they can use the information gained by reading, not so they can choose the main idea from a list. The operations that result in increased test scores might not result in real, useful learning.

In spite of these criticisms of formal tests, their widespread use continues. Why? Communities expect their schools to do an effective job of teaching young people the information and skills necessary to live productive lives and be good citizens. When students reach high school, or leave it, lacking basic skills in reading, writing, science, and mathematics, communities are rightfully concerned. They seek to make their schools accountable in a variety of ways. Most of these ways depend on achieving test scores that show what students have mastered.

Formal tests don't measure all of the things we want students to know or do, but they do show mastery over certain kinds of information and operations. They yield numerical results that are fairly easy to interpret and compare. They are more economical of time and effort than many informal measures. And because they have standardized administration procedures that everyone must follow to the letter, they ensure that all students will have the same instructions, examples, time limits, and so forth. This makes it easier to compare scores from one locality to another.

Finally, the idea that "numbers don't lie" dies hard. Numerical scores seem less subjective than other results. Many people feel more comfortable with numerical scores than with other types of test results that depend more upon examiner or teacher judgments. So, many communities and legislative bodies have continued to require formal test results to ensure educational accountability.

Consequently, teachers need to understand the characteristics, purposes, and features of formal tests.

Characteristics of Tests

When we select a tool to do a job, we typically know the nature of the job, the level of skill we possess, and the tools we have available. The same is true for selecting a formal measure of reading. When that selection is made, we, or those who did the selecting, should know what we want to do with the results, the level of skill or support we have in administering and interpreting the test, and the options that are available for selecting a test. Most districts have selected one test or a small group of tests that will be purchased and administered to students.

In the sections that follow, we briefly describe some fundamental concepts of testing and measurement that apply to all standardized tests, not just reading tests. These basic concepts are necessary to an understanding of such reading tests.

The quality of the tool that is selected to do a certain job directly affects the quality of the outcome. For formal tests, two qualities are critical to test performance: *reliability* and *validity*. Both are necessary for a good test, but of the two, validity is more important.

Reliability

Reliability is a measure of how stable test scores are. It refers to the results obtained from a test, not to the test itself. Every standardized reading test you consider for use should have reported reliability estimates and should identify the methods used to determine such estimates. Reliability is expressed in numerical terms by a reliability coefficient.

This decimal number between 0 and 1 shows how consistent the scores are likely to be. The closer to 1.0 the reliability coefficient is, the more reliable the scores will be.

Overall reliability can be profoundly affected by the consistency of individual subtests. Survey reading tests, generally given to large groups for screening purposes, usually have few subtests, and the reliability coefficients refer to the whole test. However, some reading achievement tests and most standardized diagnostic tests have many separate subtests, and the reliability of subtest scores can vary widely. These tests should report subtest reliabilities as well as a coefficient for the entire test, and scores on subtests of questionable reliability should be discounted. If a test that is under consideration has more than one or two subtests of low reliability, another test should be considered.

Another point about judging reliability concerns the standard error of measurement. This term does not mean there are mistakes in the test; it refers to the fact that no score is absolutely precise. The standard error of measurement is a number that indicates how much an individual's score might have varied depending on random chance factors. The standard error shows numerically how accurate any score is likely to be. A small standard error indicates high reliability.

There are three types of reliability: One is *stability*, or the consistency of test scores from one administration to another with the same group of subjects; the second is *internal consistency*, or the consistency of items within a test; and the third is *equivalence*, or consistency across different forms of the same test (Salvia & Ysseldyke, 2004).

Stability. If a group of students took a test several times, each individual's score would be somewhat different each time. If the test scores have good stability, the students' rank order would remain very similar from one testing to another. The student with the highest score the first time would have the highest, or nearly the highest, score the second time; the student with the lowest score would retain very low standing, and the order of students between highest and lowest would remain nearly unchanged. If stability is lacking, a score attained once is unrelated to the score attained another time. Obviously, such scores would have little meaning or usefulness because they would be influenced by random effects.

Stability is estimated using the *test-retest method.* The same test is given twice to the same group of subjects, and the rank order of their scores on each one is compared. Between administrations, subjects might remember a number of items and will be familiar with the format. This will tend to raise everyone's scores, but the rank order of the scores will remain much the same. The rank order of the scores, not the numerical value of the scores themselves, is what is important here.

Internal Consistency. This term refers to the degree to which items within a test are related. Internal consistency is determined by comparing subjects' performance on an entire test to their performance on two halves of the same test administered separately. However, since the more difficult items often come toward the end, it would not be a good practice to split a test at the middle. Instead, alternate items are selected: one-half with the odd-numbered items, the other half with the even-numbered items. If the scores on each half are closely related, good internal consistency has been demonstrated.

If scores on the two halves are not closely related, the total test score will not be reliable, and its usefulness is questionable.

Sometimes internal consistency is estimated by the *split-half method* in which students take the two halves of a test as separate tests. The scores on each half are correlated to each other and to the entire test. Other ways of estimating internal consistency involve giving the whole test once and applying one of several mathematical formulas to the total score. The computations are beyond the scope of this discussion, but you will find detailed information in any comprehensive text on measurement methods.

Equivalence. When alternate forms of a test are used, equivalence is important. Alternate forms that are used for pretesting and posttesting must be highly equivalent if the scores are to be useful.

The *equivalent forms method* is used to estimate this aspect of reliability. It requires the construction of two different tests, each one an equally good sampling of the content being tested. Each form must also be equivalent in difficulty and length. The two forms are administered to the same students in close succession, and the scores on the two forms are correlated. This method usually yields the most conservative estimate of reliability.

Validity

Reliability is necessary, but not sufficient, for a test to be a good one. A test can yield reliable scores but still not measure what it was intended to measure. This quality of actually measuring what was supposed to be measured is referred to as *test validity*.

There are three types of validity that are often referred to in test reviews and manuals. They are *content validity*, or the degree to which the test adequately samples the subject area or body of knowledge being tested; *criterion-related validity*, or the degree to which a test is related to other validated measures of the same ability or knowledge; and *construct validity*, or the degree to which a test measures observable behaviors that are related to traits or qualities, called *constructs*, that are not directly observable or measurable in themselves.

Content Validity. In assessing content validity, we ask if the test is an adequate sample of the content area or process being tested. Content validity is particularly important in achievement tests, which are designed to show subject mastery.

A spelling achievement test for elementary students that included only very difficult, unusual words from college textbooks would lack content validity because it did not represent what elementary children study in spelling. A reading test that was made up primarily of multiple-choice questions about reading passages only a few sentences long probably would not be considered a good test of reading ability by many teachers today.

Content validity is established when test makers study school curricula and submit their tests to the scrutiny of subject-area experts. The content validity of current reading tests is a major issue. Some critics claim that many reading achievement tests lack content validity because they measure only a narrow range of real reading behaviors, artificially partition the reading process into a host of separate skills, and ask trivial questions about meaningless passages.

Criterion-Related Validity. One way of establishing validity is to relate the test to other validated measures of the same ability or knowledge. The predetermined criterion may be other test scores, grades or subject-area performance, or other observable behaviors. A test has criterion-related validity if it calls for responses that relate closely to actual performance. *Concurrent validity* and *predictive validity* are both criterion-related.

When a new test is highly correlated to an existing test with established validity, it is said to have concurrent validity. Test makers frequently report coefficients of concurrent validity. But just because two tests are closely related does not necessarily mean that either one is valid, only that they measure the same attribute.

When scores are closely related to later performance on some criterion, the test is said to have predictive validity. This aspect is critically important in aptitude tests since they purport to determine whether someone has the potential to become skilled in a particular field at a later time. If students who do well on a test of mechanical aptitude later excel in woodshop and drafting, are admitted to college engineering and technical schools, or choose careers as engineers, architects, and machinists, that test is a good predictor of mechanical aptitude. The Scholastic Aptitude Test (SAT), used to predict high school students' potential for college success, is high in predictive validity because SAT scores and subsequent college grade-point averages are closely related.

Construct Validity. Traits or qualities that are not directly observable or measurable are called *constructs.* Attitudes, intelligence, or aptitudes are not directly measurable and must be inferred from observable behaviors. Thus intelligence, musical or mechanical aptitude, judgment, problem solving, attitudes, and interests are all constructs.

If a test has good construct validity, it allows the students to demonstrate behaviors directly related to the construct. In a test of attitudes toward reading, for example, students should be able to show how positively or negatively they would feel about getting a book for a gift, hearing a book discussed, going to the library or bookstore, or seeing someone vandalizing a book. Construct validity is important in all tests, but it is critical in psychological tests, personality tests, and attitude or interest inventories.

Interpreting Test Results

Once a valid and reliable test is selected, administered, and scored, the results are often presented in three ways:

- Distributions of test scores
- Measures of central tendency
- Measures of dispersion

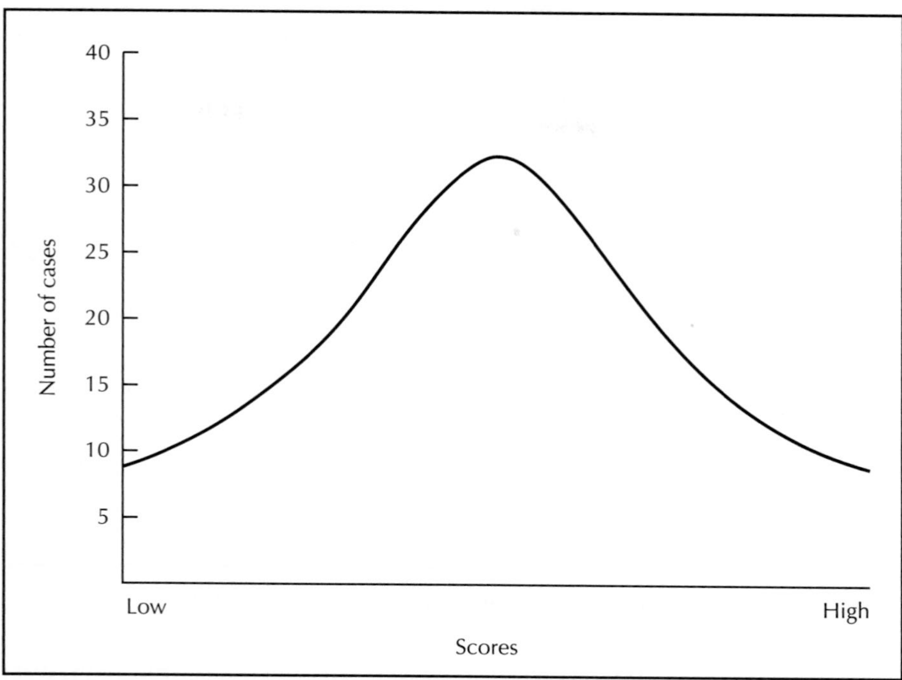

FIGURE 10.1 *Normal Distribution*

Distributions of Test Scores

A *distribution* of test scores is a visual representation of a group's performance on a given test. Two dimensions are typically used to describe the distribution of test scores. One is the score on the test itself, and the other is the number of students obtaining a particular score. You may be familiar with the *bell-shaped curve* or the *normal distribution* (see Figure 10.1). In this distribution, more students scored in the average range than at either extreme.

Not all distributions are normal. Instead of most of the scores clustering in the middle, a test might yield a distribution with many very high or very low scores. This is called a *skewed* or *asymmetrical distribution* (see Figure 10.2). The shape of the distribution of scores for a class, school, or district graphically represents the overall performance of a group or groups of students.

Compare the distribution of scores in Figure 10.1 to the two distributions in Figure 10.2. At least on the surface, the three sets of scores are distributed differently for different groups of students who completed the test. There are several possible explanations for this difference.

One is that for the asymmetrical distributions, the test might not have adequately measured the construct that was the object of instruction. The distribution that shows many high scores and few low scores is indicative of a test that was probably very easy

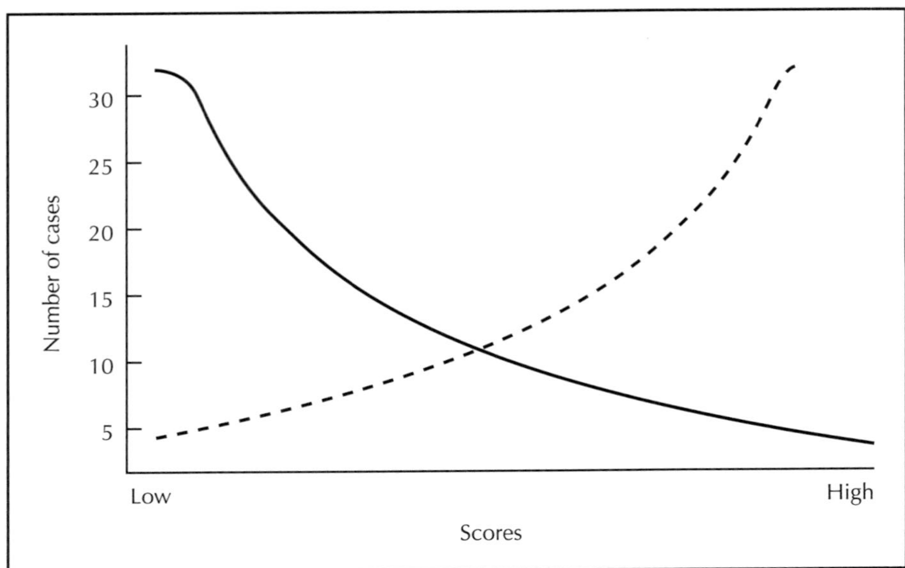

FIGURE 10.2 *Skewed or Asymmetrical Distribution*

for most of the test takers, while the opposite is true for the test illustrated by the distribution showing many low scores and few high scores.

In the latter case, the test might have been too hard for most of the test takers; in addition, variables such as disruptions during the testing, uncomfortable testing conditions, or test bias could have negatively influenced a large number of scores. For whatever the reasons, distributions that are highly skewed should be viewed with caution (Kubiszyn & Borich, 2006).

Measures of Central Tendency: Mean, Median, and Mode

Scores are most often thought of in relation to where they lie on some distribution. The most common measure of central tendency is the *mean*, or average. For example, many teachers use averages in assigning report card grades; a student who got math test scores of 67, 89, 73, 66, 92, and 80 had an average score of 78, which might be represented by a grade of C+. To get a mean score, add all the scores together and divide the sum by the number of scores.

Another measure of central tendency is the *median*, the point on a distribution at which there are equal numbers of scores above and below it. For example, if four students got scores of 14, 15, 16, and 17, the median would be 15.5, since there are two scores below 15.5 and two scores above it. In this case, the median is a point on the distribution but not an actual score, since no student obtained a score of 15.5.

The third measure of central tendency, the *mode*, represents the most frequently occurring score. If no score occurs more than once, there is no mode and the distribution

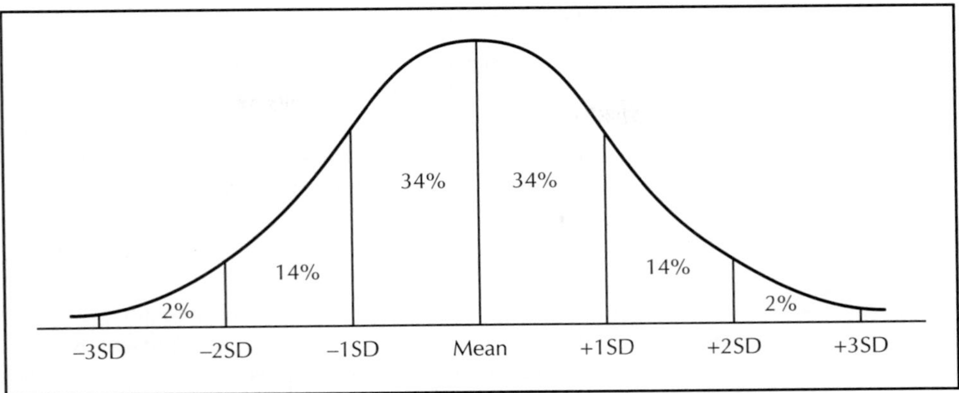

FIGURE 10.3 *Percentages of Scores within Standard Deviation (SD) Units*

is *amodal*. In general, the closer together the mean, median, and mode of a set of scores are, the more symmetrical their distribution will be. If the measures of central tendency are widely dissimilar, the distribution will be asymmetrical.

When the media report on test scores or school achievement, they most often refer to averages or mean test scores of a school or school district. It is fairly common to see mean scores for a particular school grade compared to other schools in the same division, divisions compared to each other, and divisions compared to state averages.

Measures of Dispersion: Range and Standard Deviation

Measures of dispersion of a set of scores can be expressed in two ways. The *range* of scores on a test represents the breadth of performance by a group of students. It is obtained when the lowest score is subtracted from the highest score and 1 is added to the result. A range of scores is only a gross indication of the dispersion of scores by a group of students. A more common measure of the dispersion of scores is the standard deviation (Lyman, 1998).

The *standard deviation* is an index of how scores are spread out around the mean, regardless of the shape of the distribution. In a normal distribution, most of the scores are grouped near the mean. But how many is "most"? How near is "near"? Statisticians have determined that 68 percent of the scores are arrayed around or at the mean, with smaller percentages near the extremes, as shown in Figure 10.3.

If a student's score were one standard deviation (1SD) below the mean, we would know where the score lay on the distribution; we would know that the student did as well or better than 16 percent of the norm group but that 84 percent did better. The range around the mean, from 21SD to +1SD, is considered the average range. A score of 21SD would be at the bottom of the average range.

The concepts of mean and standard deviation are fundamental to understanding how most scores such as those described below are reported.

Forms of Test Scores

Formal assessment scores are often reported in several different forms. While each of the forms of test scores is based on an individual student's performance, the final form of the score can vary depending upon the computations performed upon the raw score. The *raw score* shows simply how many items the student got right on the test or on each subtest. Raw scores are hard to interpret, so they are converted to more easily comparable forms. The most frequently encountered forms of test scores are grade equivalents, percentiles, stanines, Normal Curve Equivalents (NCEs), *T*-scores, and *z*-scores (Chase, 2000).

Grade-Equivalent Scores. *Grade-equivalent scores,* sometimes called *grade scores,* are frequently used in reporting reading test scores. They represent average achievement for a particular school grade. Grade scores are expressed in two-part numbers; the first number indicates the grade level, and the second number indicates the month within that grade. A grade score of 3.2, for example, means that the student correctly answered the same number of items as the average third grader in the second month of third grade.

Grade scores seem easy to understand, and many parents place great faith in them. They hope to hear that their children have achieved grade scores that are in line with the children's present grade placement; it is easy to understand scores that seem to say that your child is reading just as he "should be" for his grade. But is this what grade scores do?

Grade scores imply that there is some objective, generally accepted standard of achievement for every month of each school grade. But in reality, no such agreement exists. Such expectations are too heavily influenced by local standards, curricular goals, and learner characteristics for any one standard of achievement to exist. Grade scores imply that such objective standards exist, so they are often overinterpreted.

Percentile Scores. Percentiles are more easily understood than grade scores. Percentiles range from 1 to 99; where a score lies within this range indicates relative performance compared with the norm group. A score at the 10th percentile means the student did as well as or better than 10 percent but worse than 89 percent of the subjects in the norm group. A score at the 98th percentile means that the student did as well as or better than 98 percent of the norm group and that only 1 percent attained higher scores.

Sometimes parents misunderstand percentile scores, confusing them with the percentage of items correctly answered. Thus a parent whose child scored at the 50th percentile might think that the child had gotten only 50 percent of the items right, instead of correctly viewing the score as average.

Stanines, NCEs, T***-scores, and*** z***-scores.*** Other forms of scores take the distribution of scores of the norm group into account and provide comparable units across the range of scores. These standardized scores include stanines, NCEs, *T*-scores, and *z*-scores (Salvia & Ysseldyke, 2004).

Stanines are similar to percentiles. The term is derived from "standard nines," which means that the distribution has been divided into nine parts. Stanine scores range from 1 to 9; a score of 5 is the mean, and scores from just below 4 to just above 6 are considered average, with scores of 1 to 3 being below average and scores of 7 to 9 being above average.

Normal Curve Equivalents (NCEs) are derived from the average and standard deviation of a set of scores. Like percentiles, they range from 1 to 99, with a mean of 50. NCEs are widely used in the evaluation of federally funded reading and math programs. T-scores and z-scores, like NCEs and stanine scores, are based on the standard deviation. The T-scores range from 20 to 80, with a mean of 50. These values are computed from the standard deviations and indicate how close to the mean of the normal distribution a particular score lies. The z-score is based directly on the standard deviation, with a mean of 0 and a standard deviation of 1. Scores ranging from 21.0 through +1.0 are considered average. The range for z-scores is from 23.0 to +3.0.

Regardless of the type of test, the form of score, or the quality of the test, formal assessment of reading is only a single indication of a student's performance. Scores on norm-referenced standardized tests must be combined with other, more qualitative information to make the most valid instructional decisions.

Norm-Referenced Tests

Norm-referenced tests are developed by test publishers and administered to large numbers of students to develop *norms.* Norms represent average performances of many students in various age, grade, and demographic groups. They are used to compare the performance of students in schools to the performance of those in the norm group.

Test publishers create norm groups that include students from various geographic areas, urban and rural communities, different racial and ethnic groups, and economic groups. Many tests feature special sets of norms for local groups that may be unlike national averages—for example, urban schools, rural schools, high-achieving gifted populations, and highly affluent areas.

Norm-referenced tests serve two general purposes. Many are designed to measure achievement or past learning. These *achievement tests* vary in the scope of topics covered and the detail with which students' results are reported. Tests that assess specific knowledge and strategies associated with reading provide a range of difficulty that begins at a lower level. These tests, designed to show growth in these areas, are considered to be *diagnostic tests* (Chase, 2000).

Achievement Tests

Achievement tests are designed to measure the current level of learners' performance in a variety of areas. Many achievement tests are actually batteries of subtests representing different content or skill areas such as language arts, mathematics, science, and social studies. Tests that provide only a general performance score in each area are often called *survey tests.* Although survey tests can be helpful in pointing to areas in need of additional assessment, little detailed information can be obtained.

Achievement tests are designed to show the depth of students' knowledge and mastery of subject-area curricula. Because they are designed to assess mastery, or achievement, they are usually administered *after* the appropriate instruction has been given. Tests that are used for diagnostic purposes are often given before a program of instruction, or early on, to reveal strengths and so that instruction can be modified appropriately. The content of diagnostic and survey tests is sometimes very similar to that of achievement tests, but the purpose and timing of the testing differ.

Standardized achievement tests are probably the most common type of formal tests used in schools. Many students take a standardized achievement test of some kind yearly, often a battery covering the major curricular areas. Because subtests are usually given in separate sittings, completion of a battery can take several days or a week. Achievement tests must be given under strictly standard conditions for results to be compared across groups, so sometimes a team of school personnel administers all the tests, and sometimes the regular daily schedule is suspended so that all students can be tested simultaneously. The tests are machine-scored by the publishers, and results are sent back to the school.

Almost all achievement tests are group tests. They should be used to evaluate only groups of students, not individuals. For this reason, they are of very limited diagnostic use. They are useful only for evaluating the progress of large groups such as whole schools or all students in a grade.

To be valid, the content of achievement tests must represent typical school curricula. A math test, for example, will generally be made up of problems and calculations common to most school math programs for a particular grade. What is considered typical is decided by consulting subject-area experts, by studying widely used textbooks and materials and field-testing experimental test forms. Content validity, or how well a test represents the major aspects of the subject area, is of particular importance, but how closely the curriculum of an individual district, school, or classroom coincides with national trends is difficult to say. Achievement tests in any subject area should be carefully evaluated to see how well their content matches local curricula and materials.

Most of the widely used achievement batteries measure reading comprehension and vocabulary, English usage, science, math, and social studies. Most have forms for early elementary grades through high school, although some school districts do not begin using them until third or fourth grade. Some batteries have reading readiness tests for kindergarten and first grade.

Among the typical wide-ranging achievement batteries are the **Metropolitan Achievement Test,** the **Comprehensive Test of Basic Skills,** the **Stanford Achievement Test,** and the **California Achievement Test,** all designed for use in kindergarten through twelfth grade. The Metropolitan Achievement Test includes prereading, math, and language subtests for kindergarten; word recognition (first and second grades only), reading vocabulary, reading comprehension, language, science, math concepts and problem solving, math procedures, and social studies subtests, a norm-referenced writing test, and a diagnostic battery. The Comprehensive Test of Basic Skills includes readiness (kindergarten and first grade only), reading vocabulary, reading comprehension, spelling, language, math, social studies, science, and study skills subtests. The Stanford includes reading, language, study skills, spelling, math, science, social sciences, and listening subtests. The California Achievement Test includes reading, spelling, language, math, study skills, science, and social studies subtests.

There are also group tests of reading achievement that include only reading-related subtests. These are sometimes given at the end of each school year, usually beginning at the end of third grade. Fairly typical of this group of tests are the **Gates-MacGinitie Reading Tests,** with vocabulary and comprehension subtests and forms for kindergarten through twelfth grade, and the **Nelson-Denny Reading Test,** with vocabulary, comprehension, and reading rate subtests and forms for high school and college students and adults.

There are a few reading achievement tests for individual administration. Two examples are the **Peabody Individual Achievement Test (PIAT-R)** and the **Wide Range Achievement Test (WRAT-3).** These instruments are hybrids with characteristics of both group achievement tests and individual survey tests. Both tests are often given as diagnostic screening devices to students experiencing difficulty in either reading or math or to those with generally poor school achievement.

The PIAT-R contains reading recognition, reading comprehension, spelling, math, and general information subtests. Because it includes math as well as various reading skills and general information, the PIAT-R measures mastery of the largest part of typical elementary curricula.

The WRAT-3, often used in screening students for special education programs, is designed for ages 5 through senior adulthood. The WRAT-3 has reading, spelling, and arithmetic subtests. The reading portion of the WRAT-3 is made up entirely of lists of single words. Pronunciation within 10 seconds is the only criterion. It does not measure comprehension of either text or words, and no reading of connected text is included.

Diagnostic Tests

Diagnostic tests are norm referenced and standardized. They are administered to students who are showing signs of reading difficulties. Most diagnostic tests are individually administered. Diagnostic tests differ from achievement tests in three major ways:

1. They have a large number of subtest scores (sometimes called part scores) and a larger number of items.
2. The items are devised to measure specific skills.
3. Difficulty tends to be lower in order to provide adequate discrimination among students with reading problems.

Diagnostic tests, both the group and individual types, have numerous subtests and yield a profile of scores. Each subtest assesses a particular skill area. Developers of these tests maintain that analysis of a profile of subtest scores will reveal strengths and weaknesses in skill areas and that this analysis makes them more diagnostic than survey tests.

Diagnostic tests for group administration frequently include subtests assessing some or most of the following skills: reading comprehension, vocabulary, visual and auditory discrimination, structural analysis, numerous aspects of phonic analysis, sound blending, skimming and scanning, syllabication, sight-word recognition, and spelling. Because of the number of separate subtests, they usually have to be administered in several sittings.

An example of a group diagnostic test is the **Stanford Diagnostic Reading Test.** The Stanford, testing grades 1 through 12, includes subtests assessing auditory discrimination, auditory vocabulary, word meanings, phonic and structural analysis, and literal and inferential reading comprehension. Levels for grade 4 and beyond include reading rate, and for grade 8 and beyond include skimming/scanning/fast reading subtests. Scores are reported in grade scores, percentiles, and stanines. The test takes about two hours to administer.

There are many diagnostic reading tests for individual administration. They attempt a broad-based analysis of skills, with assessment of word recognition and decoding skills and comprehension of prose passages. An example is the **Diagnostic Assessments of Reading.** This test is composed of six individually administered subtests assessing word analysis, oral and silent reading fluency and comprehension, spelling, and word meanings.

Some standardized diagnostic tests focus on word recognition and word analysis skills. Among these are the **Diagnostic Screening Test—Reading,** the **Diagnostic Achievement Battery,** and the **Gates-McKillop-Horowitz Reading Diagnostic Test.** The latter is probably the best known of this type of test. Designed for students with reading problems in grades 1 through 6, the Gates-McKillop-Horowitz assesses oral reading fluency of story passages without comprehension assessment, flashed and untimed recognition of whole words, recognition of nonsense words, dividing words into syllables, producing letter sounds, letter naming, sound blending, auditory discrimination, spelling, and informal writing. The test yields grade-equivalent scores and overall reading ratings of average, above average, and below average. No estimate of reading comprehension is available, and all scores depend on the student's oral reading level.

Some specialized diagnostic tests focus on oral reading ability only. The **Slosson Oral Reading Test** is one of these. The student does not read connected text; the test is made up of lists of words in isolation. It purports to furnish an instructional reading level for the student on the basis of word pronunciation alone. Because this level is derived from reading words in lists, it is largely useless.

More typical of true oral reading tests are the **Gray Oral Reading Tests** and the **Gilmore Oral Reading Test.** In these tests, comprehension results are less important to the overall scoring than oral reading accuracy and speed. The Gray Oral Reading Test is not intended as a comprehension test, but it does include comprehension questions following passages and yields a comprehension score as well as an Oral Reading Quotient that combines the oral fluency and comprehension scores. The Gilmore Oral Reading Test yields separate oral fluency and comprehension scores. Testing is discontinued when a ceiling number of word recognition errors occur, even if comprehension continues to be adequate.

A number of individual diagnostic tests resemble Informal Reading Inventories, with silent and oral reading passages followed by comprehension questions. They differ from Informal Reading Inventories in that they are norm-referenced. The **Durrell Analysis of Reading Difficulty** and the **Diagnostic Reading Scales**—Revised are examples of these. As in a typical IRI, these tests assess sight vocabulary recognition, word analysis in isolation and in context, and silent and oral comprehension. They include graded word lists, graded story passages with comprehension questions, supplemental tests of phonics and decoding skills, and systems for determining reading levels by counting errors. Assessment of oral fluency includes counting the oral reading miscues, but no miscue analysis.

The Diagnostic Reading Scales assess comprehension with a preponderance of questions requiring short answers and literal recall; some questions are answered by yes or no. Rate of reading is measured, but does not take into account that good readers vary their rate for different reading purposes. In this test, the "instructional level" is the student's oral reading level, and the "independent level" is the student's silent reading level. This test also includes supplementary phonics subtests that assess initial and final consonant sounds, blends and digraph sounds, initial consonant substitution, auditory recognition of consonant sounds, long and short vowel sounds and variant vowels, recognition of syllables and phonograms, sound blending and auditory discrimination.

The Durrell Analysis of Reading Difficulty also assesses word recognition and word analysis, oral fluency, and silent and oral comprehension. It includes listening comprehension, identifying meanings of individual words, recognition of sounds of individual letters, blends, digraphs, phonograms and initial and final affixes, spelling, visual memory of words, and "prereading phonics abilities" including matching spoken with written sentences ("syntax matching"), identifying letter names in spoken names (such as *s* in *Esther*), and identifying and writing letters.

The **Woodcock Reading Mastery Test** is often used in special education. The Woodcock consists of six subtests: visual-auditory learning, letter identification, word identification, word attack, word comprehension, and passage comprehension. Designed for use in all grades from kindergarten through twelfth, it takes about 30 to 60 minutes to administer.

The letter identification subtest requires the student to identify letters shown in eight styles of type. The word identification subtest consists of 150 words in order of difficulty from preprimer (*the, and*) to twelfth grade (*facetious, picayune*). They are listed in isolation, and the student pronounces the words in an untimed presentation. The word attack subtest consists of 50 nonsense words to be decoded and pronounced. Items range in difficulty from *bim* to *wubfambif*. The word comprehension subtest contains 70 verbal analogies: bird—fly, fish—____. The subject reads the analogy silently and says a word to complete the set. The passage comprehension subtest consists of modified cloze items; a word is omitted from a sentence, and the subject reads the item silently, and then gives a word to complete it. Early items are single sentences with a picture clue; later items contain two or three sentences and have no picture.

The Woodcock yields percentiles, grade-equivalent scores, and age-equivalent scores for each subtest and a Total Reading score representing the combined subtest scores.

Criterion-Referenced Tests

Criterion-referenced tests enable teachers to compare a student's performance to a predetermined goal or outcome rather than to the performance of others. Criterion-referenced tests provide a way of determining whether a student has met instructional goals, or *criteria* (Kubiszyn & Borich, 2006).

An asset of criterion-referenced tests is their diagnostic potential. They can indicate with precision what a student can or cannot yet do. Appropriate instructional modifications can be made, which is the major goal of any diagnostic procedure. They have greater diagnostic power than norm-referenced tests because they yield information related to specific goals rather than information relating the performance of children to one another. Also, they tend to minimize damaging competition among students, since a student's achievement is not measured in terms of someone else's achievement but rather in terms of a preset criterion. Both parents and students can then concentrate on the goals to be attained rather than on invidious comparisons among individuals or groups.

However, criterion-referenced tests might be top-heavy with objectives that are easiest to measure, such as factual material. Higher-order learning processes, such as evaluation and application of knowledge, are naturally harder to assess and may be underrepresented. Also, since criteria of quality or accuracy are always arbitrary, they should be considered carefully. There is nothing magical about 80 percent, 90 percent or 100 percent accuracy. If skills are truly hierarchical, as with some math skills, then 100 percent might be necessary before the student goes on to more difficult skills. If there is no particular sequence of skills in one area, or no generally agreed-upon progression, then all quality criteria are arbitrary, and one may be just as good as another.

Goals and Objectives

Criterion-referenced testing is part of a three-part instructional model. First, the overall *instructional program goals* must be decided on and stated. These goals are usually broad statements of general educational outcomes. Examples of reading program goals might be to read different kinds of text with adequate comprehension, to appreciate different literary genres, or to recognize words fluently.

Program goals are often developed at the district or state level. Such goals rarely specify how such behaviors or attitudes will be conveyed or what specific levels of competency are required. They serve to define the general directions in which instruction will move.

Program objectives follow from instructional program goals. They define more narrowly the desired outcomes of the instruction, such as the following:

- Students will recognize and discriminate among basic speech sounds.
- Students will demonstrate effective listening skills.
- Students will identify characteristics that distinguish literary genres.

Program objectives are usually developed at the district or building level. They apply to specific educational programs, but they usually do not specify the level of proficiency desired or how such objectives will be implemented.

Instructional objectives are the specific statements of learner behavior or outcomes that are expected after a period of instruction. Instructional objectives define what specific content is taught, as in these examples:

- After completion of the Level 1 reader, students will recognize at sight all the basal words listed at the end of the book.
- After reading this story, students will formulate two inferences about the possible results of the main character's actions.
- By the end of November of kindergarten, students will name the months of the year, in order, from memory.

Instructional objectives are sometimes referred to as *behavioral objectives* because they describe the behaviors that learners are to demonstrate. Objectives that call for students to "appreciate" or "understand" are common, but they do not describe the behaviors to be shown. Because of this, instructional objectives often do not take into account attitudes or generally unmeasurable behaviors, instead focusing on discrete, measurable behaviors.

Good instructional objectives identify the *behavior* to be demonstrated, which is the observable learning outcome. They state the *conditions* under which the student will demonstrate the outcome: *from memory, by Friday, orally, in writing, given a list of 20 misspelled words*, and the like. These conditions are sometimes referred to as "the givens"; they are contained in objective statements such as the following:

- *Given* a list of 30 primer level basal words, the student will identify 25 words at sight.
- *Given* 20 two-digit addition problems, the student will compute all answers correctly.

Good instructional objectives also state the *criterion level* of mastery desired: the number of items correct, a percentage of accuracy, the number of consecutive times performed, the prescribed time limit (where speed of performance is required), or the essential features to be included (as in a composition or essay response).

From instructional objectives come the items that are used on criterion-referenced tests. To achieve its purpose of determining how closely a student has achieved mastery of a skill or objective, each test item must define the criterion or skill being assessed. Criterion-referenced test items are often taken directly from instructional objectives, when such tests are developed locally. When the instructional objectives have been written so that they are sufficiently clear, precise, and measurable, developing such test items is easy. For example, with an instructional objective like "After completing the Level 1 reader, students will recognize all of the basal words at sight," a criterion-referenced test item like "From the list provided, read these words with 90 percent accuracy" might follow.

As with any other kind of test, criterion-referenced test items must fairly and adequately sample the essential skills or knowledge desired. Test items must match the learning outcomes and conditions specified in the instructional objectives; this insures test validity. For example, if an instructional objective calls for students to discriminate between statements of fact and opinion in newspaper articles, then test items that require them to discriminate between statements of fact and opinion in a letter to the editor is a good match, but an item that requires them to state an opinion about the use of letters to the editor is not a good match.

When instructional programs and tests are developed locally, the tests usually match quite closely the instructional goals. So, too, do commercial skills programs that feature their own criterion-referenced tests. When tests are purchased separately from programs or when test programs are purchased but instructional programs are developed locally, a mismatch may occur between what is taught and what or how that content is tested.

When judging the objectives for a commercial criterion-referenced test or test program, keep these questions in mind:

1. Do these objectives call for appropriate learning outcomes for this subject area?
2. Do these objectives represent a balance of thinking and learning skills?
3. Are the desired outcomes realistically attainable?
4. Do these objectives fit the goals and philosophy of our schools?

Benchmarks and Rubrics

Many of today's criterion-referenced assessments refer to behavioral standards as *benchmarks.* Like behavioral objectives, benchmarks are statements of key tasks students are expected to perform or behaviors they are expected to demonstrate. Benchmarks are useful because they describe concretely what students are expected to do. Benchmarks are often used in elementary report cards and in documenting students' progress.

Some examples of benchmarks for emergent readers include the following:

- Can retell familiar stories such as "The Three Bears" after hearing them.
- Can accurately point to individual words in short memorized texts.
- Can accurately recognize at least 20 words at sight.
- Can sort pictures of common objects that have the same beginning consonant sound.

Some examples of writing benchmarks for upper elementary grades might include the following:

- The writing has a consistent central idea or topic throughout the piece.
- The writing has a clear lead and conclusion.
- Sentences are varied in length and structure throughout the piece.
- Vocabulary is precise, specific, and appropriate to the tone of the piece.
- Capitalization, punctuation, and spelling are largely correct and are appropriate to the standards of the writer's grade.

Another criterion-referenced measure is the rubric. A rubric specifies the expected performance or behavior and includes standards for demonstrating competence. Many rubrics feature a point scale that allows the performance to be rated. Rubrics are widely used to assess students' writing. For example, Figure 10.4 shows a writing assessment rubric that is based on the Virginia Standards of Learning for fifth grade.

State Standards and Assessment

To ensure school accountability and establish uniform academic standards, most states have instituted curricular goals for the core academic areas and have developed statewide testing programs for all public schools. These tests are criterion-referenced tests, in that scores necessary to pass each test are established in advance.

Domain	*Rating*			
COMPOSING	*4*	*3*	*2*	*1*
Central Idea	Throughout	Consistent	Inconsistent	Weak/absent
Elaboration	Fully detailed	Adequate detail	Inconsistent detail	Little or no detail
Organization	Intact, cohesive	Consistent, few lapses	Inconsistent organization	Little or no organization
WRITTEN EXPRESSION				
Vocabulary	Vivid, precise	Consistent, clear	Bland, imprecise	Repetitive, unclear
Information	Specific	Fairly specific	General	Lacking
Voice	Clear, memorable	Recognizable	Weak or inconsistent	Lacking or inappropriate
Sentence Variety	Consistent variety	Some variety	Little variety	Monotonous
USAGE/MECHANICS				
Sentence Formation	Consistently correct	Largely correct	Inconsistent	Largely incorrect
Usage	Consistently correct	Largely correct	Inconsistent	Largely incorrect
Mechanics	Consistently correct	Largely correct	Inconsistent	Largely incorrect

FIGURE 10.4 *Sample Rubric for Evaluating Writing*

Although each state's standards and assessments vary, most are similar. Curricular goals establish the basic knowledge and skills that teachers are to teach and students are to learn in each grade from kindergarten through twelfth grade. These goals are typically stated as instructional objectives—that is, they describe what the student is to do, with or without specifying the criterion.

Instructional objectives for all public school students statewide are generally developed over a period of several years by committees of parents, teachers, state and local education officials, business people, and subject-area experts (historians, mathematicians, etc.). Textbooks and curricula are studied to establish the content all students should be taught. Then criterion-referenced tests are developed to measure students' mastery of required content. Versions of the tests are field-tested in selected districts across a state to determine students' current status in mastering content, as well as problems in directions, time limits, item difficulty, response sheets, and other factors. The results of field-testing are used to fine-tune the tests that will eventually be given to all students in particular grades.

States also establish minimum criteria for passing each test and develop standardized testing procedures to ensure that all students take the same test at nearly the same time under the same conditions. Allowable adaptations for students with special needs are specified, and testing may be monitored in a variety of ways to make sure that the procedures are strictly followed. As mentioned previously, standardized conditions are necessary so that results can be compared.

Because states also determine the consequences of failing to achieve at a particular level, this kind of assessment is sometimes referred to as *high-stakes testing*. The stakes, in many cases, are indeed high. In some cases, students can be retained in grade or denied high school credits or diplomas. School divisions must achieve specified pass rates by a particular year, or show a certain amount of growth toward the pass rate, in order to maintain accreditation and funding. Administrators and teachers are under tremendous pressure in some areas to maintain or raise average scores and pass rates. In order to do so, many school divisions across the country have engaged in curriculum alignment, a process by which local curricula are analyzed and modified to match the state standards. Curriculum alignment helps schools make sure they are teaching the content their states require in enough detail and depth so that students can show mastery on the tests. However, it also tends to encourage schools to delete any subject matter that is not on the statewide tests. This in turn creates rigidity in curriculum development and a focus on teaching a narrow range of knowledge, skills, and operations that teachers know will appear on the assessments (Temple, Ogle, Crawford, & Freppon, 2011).

Summary

The basic test characteristics that teachers should be familiar with are *reliability* and *validity*. Reliability refers to the consistency of test scores. Aspects of reliability are *stability*, or consistency across repeated administrations; *internal consistency*, or consistency among test items; and *equivalence*, or consistency across alternate test forms. Validity refers to how well a test measures what it was intended to measure. *Content validity* is the quality of adequately sampling the subject area or process being assessed. *Criterion-related validity* is made up of *concurrent validity*, or how closely a test is related to another test of established validity, and *predictive validity*, the degree to which test performance is related to some other established criterion. *Construct validity* refers to how well the test measures traits or constructs that are not directly observable but must be inferred from observable behavior. Intelligence is an example of a construct.

Commonly used descriptive statistics include *distributions, indices of central tendency and dispersion*, and forms of *standard scores*. A distribution is an array of scores from highest to lowest. Many standardized tests assume a *normal distribution*, a symmetrical array with most scores falling near the mean and progressively fewer scores at the extreme high and low ends. Asymmetrical distributions are referred to as *skewed*. Indices of central tendency include the *mean*, an arithmetic average; the *median*, the point in a distribution at which there are equal numbers of higher and lower scores; and the *mode*, the most frequently occurring score. Indices of dispersion describe how far apart scores are from one another. They include the *range*, or the span from highest to lowest score, and the *standard deviation*, which shows how far from the mean each score is in standard or equal increments.

Standardized reading tests usually yield several forms of test scores. *Grade scores* are two-part numbers representing a grade and month. A grade score means that the student achieved the same score as the average student in that grade. *Percentiles* are standard scores that show what percentage of the norm population scored higher or lower than the individual tested. *Stanines* are scores in which the distribution has been divided into nine equal intervals; a stanine score indicates in which ninth a score fell. *T-scores* and *z-scores* use the concepts of mean and standard deviation to show where a score lies in relation to the mean of a normal distribution.

Norm-referenced tests are based on norms, or average performances across grades, ages, and demographic groups. Norms are used to compare the performance of local students and groups to these averages. *Achievement tests* are designed to measure past learning and to assess the effectiveness of instruction. *Diagnostic tests* are designed to reveal individuals' strengths and weaknesses in particular areas.

Criterion-referenced tests are used to compare a student's performance to a predetermined goal or criterion rather than to the performance of other students. They provide a way to document whether students have met instructional goals or criteria. In developing criterion-referenced tests, broad *instructional program goals* and specific *instructional objectives* are determined. Objectives describe what students are expected to do or demonstrate as well as the level of accuracy required for satisfactory performance.

Benchmarks are also behavioral statements of what students must be able to do or show. They are often incorporated into report cards and student progress documentation. *Rubrics* specify in detail what features comprise satisfactory performance and often feature point scales used to rate student performance. In recent years, many states have established statewide instructional goals that describe the knowledge and skills that teachers are to teach and students are to learn at each grade from kindergarten through twelfth grade. Criterion-referenced tests are used to determine whether students have met these instructional goals at an acceptable level of achievement. Such assessment is sometimes referred to as *high-stakes testing* because issues of retention, graduation, and funding are often associated with it. Many localities have conducted *curriculum alignment* in which local curricula are analyzed and modified to more closely fit state requirements. This can ensure that students are taught what they will be tested on, but can result in deleting curriculum that is not on the tests.

References

Board of Education. Commonwealth of Virginia. (1995/2002). *Standards of learning for Virginia public schools*. Richmond: Author.

Chase, C. I. (2000). *Contemporary assessment for educators*. New York: Longman.

Kubiszyn, T., & Borich, G. (2006). *Educational testing and measurement: Classroom application and practice* (7th ed.). New York: Wiley.

Lyman, H. B. (1998). *Test scores and what they mean* (6th ed.). Boston: Allyn & Bacon.

Salvia, J., & Ysseldyke, J. E. (2004). *Assessment* (8th ed.). Boston: Houghton Mifflin.

Temple, C., Ogle, D., Crawford, A. N., & Freppon, P. (2011). *All children read: Teaching for literacy in today's classrooms* (3rd ed.). Boston: Allyn & Bacon.

CHAPTER 11

Factors Related to Reading Problems

Chapter Outline

n this chapter we discuss intellectual, physical, linguistic, and learning factors that can be secondary or contributing causes of reading problems. Although these factors are often considered peripheral to reading, they can affect the entire enterprise of learning.

Most classroom teachers are more or less accustomed to assessing reading within their classrooms. The assessment of intelligence, vision and hearing, emotional and personality development, and special learning problems, however, usually takes place outside the regular classroom. The school nurse may provide vision and hearing screening, the school psychologist may administer intelligence tests, the guidance counselor may do personality and interest assessments, the speech-language pathologist may administer speech and language tests, and so forth.

Teachers might not be familiar with these special assessment devices and their results, which are typically used to determine whether students qualify for special programs and to plan instructional interventions. In the sections that follow, we discuss legislation related to students with special educational needs, the referral process, generic ways special learning problems are assessed, and some classroom-based interventions for students with special needs.

Philosophical and Legal Issues Related to Students with Special Needs

In the past, children with special intellectual, physical, or emotional needs were largely excluded from the regular curriculum. Changes in educational policy for students with special needs are the result of growing public awareness and legislative action. Public schools are required by law to provide "appropriate educational experiences" for all students, including those with emotional, physical, intellectual, and/or cognitive processing problems. The key issue is what is "appropriate" in each case.

Past Legislation Affecting Students with Special Needs

Initially, all students with emotional, physical, intellectual, and/or cognitive processing disabilities were afforded the right to free and appropriate public education in the least restrictive environment with the passage and signing of the Education for the Handicapped Act (EHA) in 1975 (P.L. 94-142).

Provision: *Free public education will be provided for all handicapped persons between the ages of 3 and 21 years of age.*

Implications: Schools must serve the needs of students who are both older and younger than those served in the past. The traditional concept of school-age children between ages 5 and 18 has been drastically modified. Since the law creates financial incentives for schools to identify preschoolers who have disabilities and to provide special services for them, kindergarten and primary-grade teachers are involved in early identification programs. In 1986, Public Law 99-457 amended special education law to apply to children from birth to age 5. This law guaranteed a Free and Appropriate Public Education (FAPE) to children aged 3 to 5 who have identified disabilities. It established Early Intervention Programs (EIP) for infants and toddlers between birth and two years of age who have identified disabilities, and it requires schools to develop Individualized Family Service Plans for families who have an infant or toddler with an identified disability.

At the other end of the age scale, teachers are affected by the inclusion of older students with disabilities into regular education classes. This is particularly important in high school, where students up to age 21 may be included in regular classes.

The legislation was reauthorized in 1990 and renamed the Individuals with Disabilities Education Act (IDEA) (P.L. 101-76). IDEA continued the major provisions of P.L. 94-142 while extending these rights to younger children with disabilities and to students with disabilities 16 years of age and older. IDEA emphasized the transition from school to the workplace and included postsecondary education, vocational training, rehabilitation services, and referral to adult service agencies.

Provision: *Students with disabilities will be placed in the least restrictive environment whenever and wherever possible.*

Implications: In 1997 IDEA was reauthorized as the Individuals with Disabilities Education Act Amendments of 1997 (P.L. 105-17), extending some of the existing components of the two earlier versions of the legislation. Most importantly, P.L. 105-17 clarified the rights of students with disabilities to spend much or all of their instructional time in general education settings and to have access to the general education curriculum. This means that special education is not a separate place or program, but rather a network of support services enabling students with special needs to reach the outcomes identified for all students in general education. The law also stipulates that students with disabilities participate in the same assessments expected of all students; if they are unable to do so, alternative assessment procedures with individualized criteria must be developed and implemented to ensure students progress toward their program goals.

Provision: *Every student with a disability receiving special education services will be provided with an individualized educational program, called an IEP, which spells out present abilities, short- and long-term goals, and the means by which goals will be achieved. Each student's IEP will be developed jointly by the special and general education teachers, the parents, and the student, where possible.*

Implications: The inclusion of students with disabilities in general education classrooms for part or all of the school day affects nearly every teacher. General education teachers are full members of the IEP team, along with the student's parents. All teachers working with students with special needs have direct responsibility for the planning, implementation, and evaluation of instructional programs. This means that teachers must understand students' special needs and how they affect learning, management techniques, and teaching strategies. In developing and updating IEPs, teachers join forces with the parents of students with disabilities for greater parental involvement and teacher accountability. In many cases, the students themselves are also included in the development of their IEPs, to the extent that they are able to participate.

Provision: *All tests and evaluative instruments used will be prepared and administered in order to eliminate racial and cultural discrimination.*

Implications: Because of the disproportionate representation of ethnic minority children in special education, IDEA of 1997 reflects decisions handed down by the courts over the years (see *Diana v. Board of Education*, 1970; *Larry P. v. Riles*, 1979). Tests and assessment devices must be closely scrutinized to eliminate bias. No single test, measure, or score can be used to classify a student. When necessary, tests must be modified so that students with disabilities can respond to them in ways that are best for them—for example, in Braille, sign language, or the student's first language. These modifications entail widespread changes in test construction, administration, and interpretation.

This provision has also been interpreted to mean that schools must provide a multidisciplinary team as an integral part of the identification process.

The provisions of the Individuals with Disabilities Education Act also establish certain basic rights for students with special needs:

- The right to due process protects the individual from erroneous classification, capricious labeling, and denial of equal education.
- The right of protection against discriminatory testing ensures against possible bias in tests used with ethnic and minority children.
- The right to placement in the least restrictive educational environment protects the individual from possible detrimental effects of segregated education for individuals with disabilities.
- The right to have individual program plans ensures accountability by those responsible for the education of individuals with disabilities.

The law also stipulates that a student's status and the special services being provided must be reviewed at least once every three years. The purpose of this triennial review is to determine whether the child is still eligible for special services. The review must include a complete reassessment of learning aptitude, speech, hearing, school achievement, adaptive behavior, and so forth.

More recently, and as we will see in the section entitled "Identifying Students with Special Needs," the law provides for a variety of experts to "reason together" to determine a student's special needs and to plan remediation. But parents may interpret their children's needs differently. In most cases, parents and educators in disagreement reach compromises, sometimes with the assistance of an appeal process. Sometimes, however, legal action is necessary. In some cases, parents have won the right to require that school districts pay for private schooling if the court is convinced that an "adequate" education is not possible within the local schools.

IDEA-2004 and NCLB

The revised Individuals with Disabilities Education Improvement Act of 2004 (IDEA-2004) provides several amendments to the earlier legislation. IDEA-2004 is carefully aligned with provisions of the No Child Left Behind (NCLB) initiative of the Department of Education (NEA, 2004). Special education teachers who teach a core subject, including English, reading, or language arts, are required to be "highly qualified," and students with disabilities are required to be assessed annually in NCLB-required assessments, with some reasonable accommodations, such as means of presentation and response, timing, and setting of the test. Alternative tests of grade-level knowledge are now allowed for as many as 2 percent of students with special needs in a district, and they may be applied to alternate achievement standards.

Students served under IDEA-2004 must meet the same state standards as all other students, including English language learners, with some exceptions for students with severe cognitive disabilities. Needless to say, these provisions in the law are the subject of much discussion in all school districts as they attempt to meet these new requirements.

In addition, the amendments are designed to reduce paperwork requirements for the IEP, even while ensuring that students continue to have access to a free, appropriate public education (FAPE).

Response to Intervention and Special Education

The revision of IDEA in 2004 had one more consequence of enormous significance. Previously, students were considered to have learning disabilities in reading if their performance in reading was well below their capacity. But procedures for identifying students for special education services were supposed to exclude students whose low performance was a result of inefficient teaching, or of socioeconomic factors such as belonging to a cultural minority group or coming from a family in poverty. The new regulations state,

> . . . a local educational agency shall not be required to take into consideration whether a child has a severe discrepancy between achievement and intellectual ability in oral expression, listening comprehension, written expression, basic reading skill, reading comprehension, mathematical calculation, or mathematical reasoning. (614,b,6,A).

The law goes on to say that a student may be selected to receive special education services if that student has not responded adequately to scientifically-based reading instruction delivered by highly qualified teachers (614 b, 2 & 3). This language gave rise to the Response to Intervention or RTI model.

In practice, as we saw in Chapter 2, the new law has resulted in frequent assessment of students, and the provision of different "tiers" of instruction—with the intention of better integrating the delivery of special education services with the full range of teaching available to students with varying degrees of need for specialized instruction in reading.

Student Participation in General Education

The concept of inclusion, or including students with disabilities into general education classes, has long been a topic of controversy. The amended IDEA of 1997 is more deliberate than earlier laws about students with disabilities participating in general education. Although it still considers the least restrictive environment when placing children, it indicates that these students are to be placed in settings where they have access to the same curriculum as all other students and receive this instruction in the same settings as these students, whenever possible. It also suggests that the general education teachers who are expected to teach inclusion students with disabilities develop partnerships with special educators when planning and implementing educational programs (Villa & Thousand, 2000).

Better ways of meeting the needs of students with special needs are being explored today. These include helping general education teachers to use methods that are effective with children with special needs, using special educators as co-teachers and consultants rather than providers of separate instruction, establishing teams to ensure that only those students who truly need special services are so identified, structuring classrooms to promote cooperative learning among students of various ability levels, and using materials and methods to improve students' attitudes toward peers with special needs (Friend & Bursuck, 2002).

Another result of the inclusion movement is to provide special services to identified students on a "push-in" basis, in contrast to a "pull-out" program in which identified students leave their regular classroom for special, separate instruction. The pull-out model allows students with special needs privacy and limits distractions during their instruction, but it can also isolate them from peers, disrupt their daily schedule, and inhibit general and special education teachers' efforts to collaborate.

In the push-in model, the special educator or reading specialist works with identified students as a co-teacher in the regular classroom. Students with special needs do not miss important learning or regular classroom events while they receive the extra support and attention they need. In addition, special educators and classroom teachers can share their areas of expertise and support each other's efforts. However, push-in programs require teachers to utilize very different skills and include expectations for teachers to work closely together in the same workspace. Administrative support and encouragement are essential for this cooperative effort to be successful.

Since general education teachers will continue to have greater responsibility for teaching children identified as having special needs, informal diagnostic methods take on even greater importance and utility.

Identifying Students with Special Needs

Individual school divisions differ in minor ways in the procedures they follow regarding referral and classification, but a sequence of events such as this is typical:

1. A request is made by teachers or parents to have a student considered for screening or diagnostic testing. Since each school must have a standing committee to handle identification procedures, this committee or evaluation team receives such requests.

2. Parental permission for testing is sought by the principal, special education supervisor, or screening committee. If parents or legal guardians refuse to give permission, no further action can be taken. The student's progress can be monitored and further requests made, but without parental permission no examination can take place.

3. After parental permission is given, the committee usually meets to discuss the child's progress and difficulties, determine what measures have already been taken to help the child, and decide what further assessment may be called for. If further assessment is recommended, arrangements are made for these assessments to be done. The committee must be multidisciplinary and typically includes a special education representative, a school psychologist, the school principal or principal's designee, one or more classroom teachers, and one or more parents. Other committee members may be a reading specialist, a speech-language pathologist, a visiting teacher or home-school liaison, or other specialists.

4. After assessments are completed, the team reconvenes to discuss the results and make recommendations. The student's parent(s) or guardian(s) and classroom teacher are included in this meeting. Parents may choose to bring their own advocate to help them understand the results and recommendations. Teachers working with the student are invited to share informal assessment data, observations about the child's performance, behavior, and so forth that might assist the committee.

5. The committee makes a joint recommendation about the student's eligibility for special services, including types of services that can be offered and the most appropriate placement for the student. Parental consent is needed for services to be provided. If parents do not give their permission, a mediator reviews the case and makes a determination that is binding on all parties.

6. After eligibility has been determined, an IEP must be developed. Included are the student's present achievement or performance levels, short-term and long-term goals, beginning and estimated termination dates for special services, evaluation procedures and criteria to determine if goals have been met, detailed descriptions of services to be provided, accommodations that the student will be permitted (e.g., taking tests orally or having an interpreter present), a statement of the student's involvement in general education classes, and how the student will be assessed. Again, parental agreement is required before an IEP can be implemented. If agreement cannot be reached with parents on aspects of the IEP, a hearing is held to ensure the family's right to due process.

7. Finally, the student is placed in the least restrictive educational environment and IEP implementation begins. All educators or agencies involved with the student's educational plan are required to make good faith efforts to help the student achieve the IEP goals. Parents can request program review and revision if they believe such good faith efforts have not been made. IEPs are reviewed and revised yearly to ensure that goals and procedures are appropriate. As mentioned previously, students are reassessed triennially to determine what changes have taken place and whether services are still required.

Assessment of Special Educational Needs

The IDEA requires that assessment for special services must include educational, psychological, medical, and sociological components. This ensures that the student's assessment is as comprehensive as possible. The use of a combination of standardized and informal assessments is common and in some states is required.

As you read in Chapter 10, formal assessment devices are usually standardized, norm-referenced tests. Administration, scoring, and interpretation procedures are clearly set forth. Formal tests yield many different types of scores and are given for many different purposes, but most compare a student's performance to that of other students.

Informal procedures yield results that are directly related to instruction. They often show what a student can do more directly and precisely than formal tests. Thus, both kinds of assessment provide useful information about students' abilities and achievement.

Screening assessments are mandated and reviewed by the school's identification or child study team, of which the general education classroom teacher and/or reading teacher are often a part. A team approach to assessment is a safeguard against potential bias. The IDEA contains two provisions to safeguard against test abuses:

1. Testing must be conducted in the language of the student, measures used must be nondiscriminatory and validated for the purpose for which they are used, and no single test score may be used as the sole basis for determining special education placement.

2. In determining mental or cognitive disability, concurrent deficits in both intelligence test performance and adaptive behavior must be demonstrated.

Assessment instruments have different purposes and evaluate different aspects of performance and potential. They fall into these general categories.

Tests of Learning Aptitude. *Learning aptitude* refers to the student's capacity for altering behavior when presented with new information or experiences. These often include intelligence tests, which measure scholastic aptitude, not general aptitude or intelligence, and also indirectly assess achievement in areas such as vocabulary and math computation. Intelligence tests are the primary means used to assess learning aptitude. Learning aptitude is also sometimes referred to as *cognitive ability, learning potential,* *cognitive factors*, and similar terms. Some school achievement batteries contain sections that assess learning aptitude, comparing it to present achievement levels.

Tests of Achievement. These are the primary means used to assess students' present levels of scholastic performance. These tests assess what has been learned, not what the child is capable of learning. Achievement test batteries include subtests dealing with reading, spelling, mathematics, written language, and the like. Tests that assess achievement in single areas only, such as separate reading, spelling, mathematics, and writing achievement tests, may be used instead of a battery.

Tests of Adaptive Behavior. *Adaptive behavior* refers to how effectively an individual meets standards of personal independence and social responsibility normally expected of her age and cultural group. These measures are used when mental or cognitive disability is suspected.

Tests of Specific Learning Processes. These tests assess various discrete learning processes such as auditory discrimination, short-term memory, visual perception, motor abilities, and the like. Some tests assess only one process; others are batteries with subtests evaluating different processes. Most intelligence tests also include measures of many of these abilities, such as short-term memory, visual perception, and visual-motor coordination.

Tests of Classroom Behavior and Adjustment. These tests include evaluation scales and rating scales for behavior, self-concept scales, and interest inventories. They are most often used in the identification of students with mental health conditions or those with behavior disorders, either as the primary or a secondary problem.

Intellectual Factors

When diagnosing a reading problem, one of the most frequently used instruments is an intelligence test. But research shows seemingly contradictory findings: that good readers tend to perform better on IQ tests than poor readers and that reading problems are not limited to students with lower IQs, but are found across the whole range of intellectual abilities.

General agreement has long existed that intelligence and reading achievement are fairly well correlated, particularly in the upper grades. This means that better performance on reading tests and intelligence tests tends to occur together; students generally do well on both or poorly on both. It does not imply causation; we cannot infer from positive correlations that one factor causes the other, only that they coincide.

It may be that above-average intelligence encourages above-average reading achievement. It may be equally true that good reading helps students do better on intelligence tests. Or it may be that both reading tests and IQ tests call upon the same kinds of abilities and knowledge. But poor readers may come from all ability levels.

What do IQ tests tell us? That depends very much on which test is used. Not all measure the same skills, and in order to evaluate results, we have to know something about their characteristics.

Tests of Intelligence and Learning Aptitude

Intelligence tests are essentially measures of verbal abilities and skills in dealing with abstract symbols. They are not intended to measure innate intelligence or potential but rather to predict future learning by sampling behavior already learned. The premise of these measures is that present performance is a predictor of future performance. They are appropriately viewed as predictors of academic success—and misinterpretation of their purpose and results leads to misunderstanding and inaccurate judgments about children.

Group Intelligence Tests. Some tests that yield an IQ or some kind of "ability quotient" are group tests. Group tests usually require students to read and mark answers; they consequently penalize poor readers, who generally score poorly on such measures, so they tend to underestimate poor readers' potential. Group intelligence tests or tests of learning aptitude are useful only as general screening devices; their results can be generalized only to large numbers of students, not to individuals.

Individual Intelligence Tests. An individually administered test that does not require a student to read or write will give a better estimate of real academic potential than a group test.

The **Wechsler Intelligence Scale for Children-IV (WISC-IV)** is the individual test most often used to assess intellectual performance of children between the ages of $6\frac{1}{2}$ and 16. It is one of several related tests that span all age levels. The **Wechsler Preschool and Primary Scale of Intelligence-Revised (WPPSI-R)** is appropriate for children between 4 and $6\frac{1}{2}$ years of age. The **Wechsler Adult Intelligence Scale-Revised (WAIS-R)** is used for persons between 16 and 74 years of age. These tests may be administered only by someone specially trained and certified to do so. Modified instructions for administering the WISC-IV to children who have hearing impairments are available (Sattler, 1992).

The WISC-IV assesses intellectual functioning by sampling performance on many different types of activities. The test attempts to assess verbal and nonverbal aspects of intelligence separately with 13 subtests—10 required and 3 optional or supplemental. The 13 subtests are organized into two scales, with those involving language operations directly in one, the Verbal Scale, and those involving the nonverbal or indirectly verbal operations in the other, the Performance Scale. Each scale yields a separate scale IQ, which can be compared to determine if both aspects of a child's intelligence seem to be equally well developed, and the scale IQs can be converted into a Full Scale IQ.

Raw scores from each subtest are converted to scaled scores, standard scores ranging from 1 to 19 with a mean of 10 and a standard deviation of 3. Transforming raw scores into standard units makes it possible to compare results of different subtests.

The Full Scale IQ represents a subject's overall intellectual functioning as measured by performance on the 10 subtests. The Verbal, Performance, and Full Scale IQs all have a mean of 100 and a standard deviation of 15. The test uses the following classification scheme for IQ scores:

130 and above	Very superior
120–129	Superior
110–119	High average
90–109	Average
80–89	Low average
70–79	Borderline
69 and below	Mentally deficient

To avoid overinterpreting IQ scores, keep in mind that they represent a sample of behavior taken at one point in time and consider IQ scores only in relation to the range in which they occur, rather than as single, fixed scores. The average standard error of measurement for the Full Scale IQ score is 3.2 IQ points. A Full Scale IQ could thus be expected to vary by three or four points in either direction. It is more accurate to speak of a student's IQ score as "within the high average range," for example, than to say that the student "has an IQ of 117."

Clinicians often look for differences between Verbal and Performance IQs and patterns of scores on individual subtests to recommend further psychological and academic testing (Sattler, 1992).

The **Kaufman Assessment Battery for Children (K-ABC and K-ABC II)** is another widely used individual measure. The original measure is appropriate for children between $2^1/_2$ and $12^1/_2$ years of age, and the revised version from 2004 expands the range to 18 year olds. The K-ABC battery contains mental processing and achievement subtests. A Mental Processing Composite, an index of intellectual functioning, is derived from the mental processing subtests. Two other global scores are derived from groups of subtests: Sequential Processing and Simultaneous Processing. Global scores have a mean of 100 and a standard deviation of 15.

A nonverbal scale is available that allows the examiner to conduct several of the subtests in mime with only motor response required. The scale is useful with students who have hearing impairments, mental health conditions, and speech or language impairments, as well as non-English speaking students.

The **Stanford-Binet Intelligence Scale** has recently been radically changed from its old format. Earlier versions of the Stanford-Binet were developed on the premise that as a child grows older, he develops knowledge and skills in a fairly steady, sequential way, resulting in a measurable mental age. For example, if a 7-year-old could correctly respond to items typically correctly answered by 9-year-olds, the student's mental age would be 9 years and some months. IQ scores were converted from mental ages. However, the concept of mental age has been convincingly challenged over the years; the development of the Wechsler Scales was a successful attempt to measure intelligence based on a scale other than age.

Items on the Stanford-Binet are arranged in ascending order of difficulty into 15 subsets that attempt to assess abilities other than strictly verbal. Scaled subtest scores can be combined into several global scores in Verbal Reasoning, Abstract-Visual Reasoning, Quantitative Reasoning, and Short-Term Memory, with an overall score similar to a global IQ score. These changes make the revised Stanford-Binet more like the Wechsler Scales.

The **Kaufman Brief Intelligence Test (K-BIT)** and the **Kaufman Brief Intelligence Test, Second Edition (K-BIT-2)** are brief assessments of verbal and nonverbal intelligence of children and adults from the ages of 4 to 90. They were developed to be used as screening devices, not as substitutes for more comprehensive individual IQ tests.

The K-BIT has two subtests: Vocabulary and Matrices. Designed to measure verbal and school-related skills, the Vocabulary subtest assesses a person's word knowledge and verbal concept formation. The Matrices subtests measure the ability to solve problems and other nonverbal skills. The KBIT-2 has subtests of verbal knowledge, matrices, and riddles (Kaufman & Kaufman, 2004).

The K-BIT and K-BIT-2 yield age-based standard scores having the same mean and standard deviation as the Wechsler and Kaufman scales. Scores are generated for each subtest and for an overall K-BIT IQ Composite or IQ standard score (Kaufman & Kaufman, 1990, 2004).

These individual intelligence tests assess both verbal and nonverbal intellectual abilities. Academic skills such as reading and writing are deemphasized. Although these tests yield results that can be used to predict academic success, no single test, used exclusively, can predict or evaluate a child's academic achievement. There are many factors that influence test results. One of these factors is the role of experience.

The **Leiter International Performance Scale-Revised (Leiter-R)** is a completely nonverbal individually administered measure of intelligence and cognitive abilities. Test items are game-like, maintain the student's interest, and require no language from the examiner or the student being tested. It is designed for use with subjects from infancy through adulthood. It is especially appropriate for non-English speaking students, students with ADHD, and students with autism spectrum disorders. Psychometric studies of the Leiter-R have demonstrated its appropriateness for subjects from all ethnic groups and cultures.

The Role of Experience

Standardized assessments are only part of the overall assessment and evaluation process when determining the educational abilities and needs of children. We cannot underestimate the importance of developmental experiences, both real and vicarious, in shaping standardized test performance and apparent educational ability.

What kind of experience are we talking about? Essentially, we learn in two ways: directly, by having real, concrete experience with objects and events, and vicariously, by observing and remembering the experiences of others. Students with disabilities, or those from other cultural backgrounds, use oral and other nontraditional communication forms to "engage in sophisticated acts of literacy and communication"—in both the informal and formal settings of schools, home, and communities where students spend their time (McIntyre, Rosebery, & Gonzalez, 2001, p. 5).

Real experiences in the formative years contribute to what most of us think of as an enriched environment. Enrichment means having plentiful opportunities to manipulate things; experiment with causes, effects, and consequences; talk and be talked to; and be encouraged to extend cognitive horizons and try new things. Learning is a process that involves both social and cognitive developments, and the essential experience for individual learning and development to occur is founded in people's interactions with others (Vygotsky, 1978).

These characteristics of an intellectually enriching environment know no economic, ethnic, social, or linguistic boundaries. They flourish where adults respect and nurture children's attempts to become competent and where those adults give conscious thought to providing opportunities for children to become independent and capable.

Direct, concrete experience with things and events is one critical aspect; experience with language is another. Verbal intelligence flourishes in the home, and later in the school, where children are talked to by adults, where adults really listen to their responses and encourage conversation, where events and behaviors are explained and verbal reasoning is demonstrated, and where adults model language use by expanding and elaborating on what children say.

In environments where children are rarely addressed except in commands, where their spontaneous utterances are rarely listened to or responded to, where their requests for explanations are routinely answered by "Because I said so, that's why!" and explanations are rarely given, verbal intelligence is stunted. These children enter the world of language poorly adapted to participate in it fully. Their learning opportunities are restricted by language, rather than expanded by it. Whatever their socioeconomic status, they are disadvantaged in school readiness.

The other important aspect of experience is vicarious experience. Fortunately for all of us, we can learn from observing others as well as by experiencing things ourselves. Learning from the experiences of others saves us from having to experience everything personally, and we can derive nearly as much from those experiences as from our own.

Perhaps the greatest benefit of literacy is that through reading we can vicariously experience events, emotions, and ideas completely outside our own environment. We can travel to places we will never go to, including places that exist only in the mind; visit the past and the future with as much ease as the present; meet the most famous people of history and share their innermost thoughts; and experience joy, rage, grief, amazement, and every other human emotion by reading. All this makes good reading a lifelong joy and avocation.

Reading and books, however, are more than a source of pleasure. In spite of the inroads of TV, videos, and cyberspace, print is still the largest source of information for many people.

These issues also arise in concerns about the overrepresentation of children from linguistic and ethnic minorities in special education. Historically, children were often assigned to special education classes on the basis of supposed language disorders and/or intellectual disabilities that may have been nothing more than limited English proficiency. Under provisions of *Diana v. State Board of Education* (1970) and subsequent special education legislation, such as P.L. 94-142, this is no longer permitted. Damico (1991) suggests that care be taken to ensure that referral to special education is not based on the following:

- Other factors that might explain the child's learning and language difficulties, including lack of opportunity to learn, cultural dissonance, and stressful life events, for example, among refugee children
- Language difficulties that the student has at school, but not at home or in the community
- Ordinary needs of children to acquire English as a second language or the Standard American English dialect
- Cross-cultural interference
- Bias in the assessment process, including data analysis that does not take into account the child's culture, language, and life experiences

There are many strategies that can be used very effectively in teaching children with these needs. According to Gersten and Baker (2000), teachers should do the following:

- Build children's vocabulary and use it as a curricular anchor.
- Use visual representations to reinforce major concepts and vocabulary.
- Use the children's mother tongue as a support system.
- Adapt cognitive and language demands of instruction to the children by using sheltered English strategies.

It is not only the physical needs of these students that should be addressed in inclusion efforts, but also the content of the curriculum. If students from ethnic minority groups or girls need to see themselves in the literature they read, then so should students with disabilities. According to Landrum (2001), this benefits not only those students, but also students without disabilities, who need to learn about and accept differences. Landrum has developed a set of criteria for the evaluation of novels that feature characters with disabilities. Among her criteria are the following:

- *Plot:* Story events are realistic, not contrived; characters with disabilities are active participants.
- *Character development:* Characters with disabilities are presented as strong and independent, not passive and dependent; the focus is on what they can do, not on what they cannot do.
- *Tone:* The text avoids using such terms as *retarded, handicapped,* and *crippled.*

Physical Factors

Many physical conditions and processes can be related to reading problems. The factors most commonly considered are visual and auditory. Each of these areas has been extensively studied in relation to reading difficulties, but the various conditions and processes themselves are complex and sometimes confusing. In this section, we consider vision and hearing.

Vision and Visual Problems

Reading is a visual act (for sighted persons) because we cannot read in the dark. It is, of course, much more than just a visual act because more goes on behind the reader's eyes than in front of them, but some visual competence is needed to activate the cognitive processes involved in reading. To make sense of print, the reader must be able to gain information from print through vision. For this reason, poor readers are often subjected to vision screening in diagnosis.

Teachers are often the first line of defense against vision problems. They are usually in an ideal position to spot potential problems and refer children for appropriate screening because they, more than parents, observe children in close contact with reading and writing materials. Also, children with vision problems often don't realize that others see differently, and they don't call adult attention to their difficulty. Therefore, it is important for teachers to understand vision problems and their symptoms. Figure 11.1 summarizes the nature and symptoms of some common visual difficulties.

When symptoms of vision problems are displayed frequently, are not common to the rest of the class, and are evidenced even when performing easy tasks, they signal a need for a parent conference and referral to an eye specialist. Referrals should be made through the principal, school nurse, supervisor, or other designated personnel.

Hearing and Auditory Problems

The relationship between auditory problems and reading difficulties has long been established. Hearing and language are as intimately related as language and reading. As teachers observe the oral and written language of their students, they can become aware of possible hearing problems.

When children learn to read, they employ their whole experience with oral language. Hearing problems can interfere with, delay, or even prevent the development of oral language fluency, and it is in this respect that hearing problems can affect reading.

Another factor is the interference of hearing problems with normal phonemic awareness. Across the entire spectrum of approaches, some features of every beginning reading program are standard: learning letter names and sounds, use of simple phonic analysis strategies to decode words, and frequent oral reading. These activities put a premium on clarity of hearing, and the youngster with auditory problems is at a distinct disadvantage.

Technical Name	*Common Name*	*Condition*	*Symptoms*
Myopia	Nearsightedness	Clear vision at near point; blurring of distant images	Squinting at the board; holding print close to face; inattention to board work
Hyperopia	Farsightedness	Clear vision at far point; blurring of close objects	Holding print well away from face; disinterest in close work; eye fatigue during reading
Astigmatism		Distortion and/or blurring of part (or all) of visual field, far and near	Eye fatigue; headache; squinting; tilting or turning head; nausea during reading
Amblyopia	Lazy eye	Suppression of vision in one eye; dimming of vision without structural cause	Tilting or turning head to read; eye fatigue on one side; headache
Strabismus	Crossed eyes	Difficulty converging and focusing both eyes on the same object	Squinting; closing or covering one eye to focus; eyes misaligned
Phoria or fusion problems; binocular coordination		Imbalance of ocular muscles; difficulty converging and focusing both eyes equally	Squinting; closing or covering one eye
Aniseikonia		Differences in size or shape of image in each eye	Blurring

FIGURE 11.1 *Vision Problems*

Thus, hearing problems that occur any time in the first eight to ten years of life may affect a child's reading by interfering with language development in the preschool years or with the development of phonemic awareness and phonics in beginning reading.

Testing of auditory acuity (keenness) involves assessment of the ability to hear speech sounds, music, and noises. In reading, the speech sounds are critical.

Hearing losses can affect the perception of pitch or volume or both. If the child can hear some sound frequencies but not others, it can be devastating in learning to read because it means that the child can hear some speech sounds accurately but not others. Hearing loss involving the high-frequency sounds is more common than loss of low-frequency sounds. Children with high-frequency hearing loss can accurately hear vowel sounds and maybe some consonant sounds, but not all of them.

Children with high-tone losses may hear spoken words in a garbled, indistinct fashion, depending on how many consonant sounds are affected. If only vowels can be heard, words are almost totally meaningless because consonant sounds are what make spoken words intelligible. (Read a line of print aloud to someone, pronouncing only the vowel sounds; repeat the line pronouncing only the consonant sounds. Which version could the listener more easily understand?)

Hearing losses are not always as severe as the previous example. Often only a few consonant and blend sounds are affected, but phonics instruction is made very difficult by this loss, and the student may be very poor at word analysis and word recognition. Also, the words that are most often taught in beginning reading frequently vary only in their consonant sounds, as in the word families and rhyming word patterns (*cat–hat–pat–mat–sat*). Learning word families can be very difficult for the child with high-tone hearing loss.

A topic related to auditory acuity is auditory discrimination, the ability to distinguish between highly similar sounds and to detect whether two (or more) sounds are alike or different. Being able to detect subtle differences in speech sounds helps students to master phonics; those with poor auditory discrimination may have persistent trouble with phonic analysis and may also have speech impairments.

Auditory discrimination can be assessed formally or informally. The student is required to distinguish between pairs of words or syllables that differ minimally (*rat–rap*, *ome–ote*). Teachers frequently make up and give such exercises themselves. Formal auditory discrimination tests are also common, and some standardized readiness tests include such a subtest.

In beginning reading it is common to combine phonics instruction with auditory discrimination practice. Beginning readers or prereaders who at first seem to have difficulty with auditory discrimination often need only to learn what to listen for and how to respond. In other words, they have no auditory disability, but they have to learn what the task is.

Auditory discrimination skill generally improves as children progress through the primary grades. It is as much a learned skill as an innate perceptual ability.

Language Factors

Print is a form of language, and to be a reader, one must be a language user. Serious language disorders can inhibit children's development as readers and writers. Those that occur in the early years, when language is being acquired, have the most serious effects on later literacy.

Language Acquisition and Difficulties in Infancy and Early Childhood

Children begin to use language, first to understand speech and then to produce it, in the first two years of life. Most children show that they can understand simple speech before they can produce any intelligible words and begin using one-, two-, and three-word utterances before age 3. First words are most often names of things (*ball, doggy, mama*) and social expressions (*bye-bye, no-no*) (Nelson, 1973). Words referring to animals and sounds, childhood games, and food and drink names occur very frequently among toddlers' first 50 words (Tomasello & Mervis, 1994).

Between $1^1/_2$ and 2 years, babies begin putting words together. Using just two words, they can express an amazing number of ideas, relationships, and needs; comment about objects and events; announce their own or others' actions; and even confess their own transgressions. Two-word, or telegraphic, utterances like "Allgone milk," "Doggie bye-bye," "Baby poopie," "Coat on," and "No nap!" convey a wealth of information with an economy of expression; indeed, as Trawick-Smith put it, "Babies speak as though they were paying for every word!" (1997, p. 202).

Longer utterances quickly follow, gaining in complexity. Young children seem to intuit and apply simple rules of their native language to determine the order of words in their two-word and longer utterances; rarely do they make word order errors like "On coat" instead of "Coat on." When they are unsure of word order, toddlers often produce the utterance with a rising, or questioning, inflection, as if to say, "Is this right?"

Although children acquire their language at somewhat different times and rates, most children have begun to babble expressively by the end of the first year, speak individual words by about $1\frac{1}{2}$, and combine words by $2\frac{1}{2}$. When these language features are absent, parents and caregivers often suspect a problem that may be interfering with normal language acquisition.

Language Development and Difficulties in Preschool and Primary Grades

For most children, language acquisition and development proceed rapidly in the years between 2 and 6. In the early childhood years children learn to recognize and use the most common sentence forms, including statements, questions, commands and exclamations. They acquire a working vocabulary of 5,000 to 8,000 words and can understand several thousand more (Reich, 1986).

In the preschool years, children's language develops along four equally important fronts:

- Their speech becomes clearer, articulation improves, and fluency develops. These areas of speech production are referred to as *phonology*.
- Their vocabularies grow as they acquire many new words and expressions, while they learn to understand even more words than they produce; thus, both expressive and receptive language grow. The system of word meanings is referred to as *semantics*.
- As they learn more words, their sentences become both longer and more complex. They begin to use embedded clauses, past and future tenses, plural forms, and the common sentence forms adults use most often. These aspects of language are referred to as *syntactic*.
- They develop greater skill in using language socially: to get things done, get their needs met, and direct the behavior of others in socially acceptable ways. The social uses of language are referred to as *pragmatics*.

Atypical phonology is fairly common in the preschool years, and most problems of pronunciation can be addressed with speech intervention. Many English phonemes, or phoneme clusters like *skw* or *sl*, are not typically mastered until 7 to 9 years of age. Children who make irregular or inconsistent sound substitutions such as saying *rabbit* as "babbit" one time and "dabbit" another time, who are highly disfluent after most children have developed fluency, or who generally cannot be understood are at risk for significant language delays and need identification and intervention.

Bilingual children often use the phonemes of their first, or more dominant, language when speaking their other language. A child bilingual in German and English, for example, might pronounce English words like *will* as "vill" or *valley* as "falley." These are language differences, not difficulties; they are caused by trying to learn and coordinate two different phonological systems.

Atypical semantic development is seen in children who suffer general language delay, as well as in children with Down syndrome and others with serious cognitive disabilities. These children often understand and produce words at a level similar to normal children who are much younger.

Some children show a somewhat different difficulty: They appear to have difficulty retrieving words and may use a variety of compensatory strategies to "fill in the blanks" in their communication. Children with word retrieval difficulties may stutter or pause for long periods as they try to recall the name of an object or a particular describing word; they may use very general terms like *that, things,* or *stuff* instead of labels for common objects; or they may describe objects by their function rather than by their names, as in "what you put your cereal in" for *bowl.*

Speech-language pathologists often use tests of receptive and expressive vocabulary to determine if a child has a language retrieval disability or a general linguistic delay. Two commonly used diagnostic tests for children up to the age of 7 are the Receptive One Word Picture Vocabulary Test and the Expressive One Word Picture Vocabulary Test-Revised. In the former, the child points to the correct picture that goes with a word pronounced by the examiner; the child does not need to speak. In the latter test, the child names pictures of objects shown by the examiner. For subjects from age 7 through adulthood, the Peabody Picture Vocabulary Test-Revised is often used. This test of receptive vocabulary also requires subjects to point to the correct picture and does not require speech.

Atypical syntactic development is evidenced when children do not construct sentences in age-appropriate ways. In this case children may fail to acquire, or acquire much more slowly, the basic sentence forms, questions, negatives, and word parts like *-ed, -s,* and *-ing* that most children use by about the age of 5. Children with atypical syntax usually use shorter utterances and fewer words than their peers. Their utterances tend to be grammatically confusing, and others often have trouble understanding what they mean.

Atypical syntax can be caused by intellectual deficits or cognitive disabilities, hearing impairments, and general language delays. A subtest of the Clinical Evaluation of Language Function called "Producing Model Sentences" may be used as a diagnostic tool. This assessment requires children to repeat sentences of increasing grammatical complexity. Long-term language intervention is required for these children.

Finally, children with quite profound disabilities often have atypical pragmatics development. The ability to use language socially, to get along with others, influence others and get one's needs met typically develops in the preschool years, as children learn how to use words, tone of voice, and body language to affect others' behavior. Most children quickly learn how to use language to get other children to give them a toy, share materials with them, or allow them to join in play.

But children with cognitive disabilities, mental health conditions, autism, hearing impairments, and other disabilities may have great difficulty learning how to use language effectively in social ways. Intervention for these children involves teaching them to speak so that the listener understands, take turns talking, show interest in others' talk, use appropriate position and body language, ask and answer questions, and so forth. When these children's social use of language becomes more effective, they are often better able to form relationships, become active members of a group, and experience enhanced feelings of self-worth.

Language Development and Difficulties in Later Childhood

Between the ages of about 5 and 12, children continue to develop as language users, primarily broadening their vocabularies and polishing their language use. They acquire the few sentence forms that are less common, including passive forms such as "A passing grade was earned by only three students" and produce longer, more grammatically complex sentences with embedded clauses. Their spoken vocabularies grow from around 5,000 to 20,000 or more words. By about 12, most children's language equals that of many adults.

The greatest part of language development, then, occurs in the early childhood years and around the age of school entry. The middle and later childhood years are periods in which language does not change substantially, but becomes broader, richer, and more precise. The pragmatic system develops fully, and by middle childhood most children have a variety of types of language they use in different social settings and for different purposes: The language of school, for example, may be somewhat more formal and more precise than the language of the playground or basketball court, and most children speak differently to a grandparent or teacher than they do to their best friends. Children learn more effective turn-taking and in general use language in a variety of ways to influence others.

Language intervention for older children often takes the form of direct teaching of language pragmatics, vocabulary development, and effective use of statements, questions, and other sentence forms. Children with disabilities or language delays can progress in language development when given appropriate special instruction.

Special Learning Problems

Learning disabilities and *dyslexia* are terms used for special learning problems. The issues involved in defining the terms, identifying students with these problems, and discovering methods of remediation have aroused considerable controversy for the past several decades, but educators appear to be moving toward a greater understanding of them.

Learning Disabilities

A *learning disability* is a severe problem in learning that qualifies a child for special education services. In 1977 the federal government adopted the following definition of *specific learning disability*, based on a 1969 definition proposed by the National Advisory Committee on Handicapped Children. This definition reappeared in the 1990 version of the Individuals with Disabilities Education Act (IDEA), P.L. 101-476, and its 1997 reauthorization:

> *Specific learning disability* means a disorder in one or more of the basic psychological processes involved in understanding or in using language, spoken or written, which may manifest itself in an imperfect ability to listen, think, speak, read, write, spell, or to do mathematical calculations. The term includes such conditions as perceptual handicaps, brain injury, minimal brain dysfunction, dyslexia, and developmental aphasia. The term does not include . . . learning problems that are primarily the result of visual, hearing, or motor handicaps, or mental retardation, or emotional disturbance, or of environmental, cultural, or economic disadvantage. (*Federal Register*, December 29, 1977, p. 65083)

According to the National Joint Committee on Learning Disabilities (NJCLD), *learning disabilities* refers to a group of disorders that include significant difficulties in the acquisition and use of listening, speaking, reading, writing, reasoning, or mathematical abilities. These disorders are intrinsic to the individual and are presumed to be due to central nervous system dysfunction. Problems in self-regulation, social perception, and social interaction may exist with learning disabilities but by themselves do not constitute a learning disability. Although learning disabilities may occur with other conditions such as sensory impairment, cognitive disabilities, mental health conditions, or with extrinsic influences such as cultural differences or insufficient or inappropriate instruction, learning disabilities are not the result of those conditions or influences.

Definitions of learning disability share these characteristics:

- Learning disabilities are thought to be caused by central nervous system dysfunction.
- Some degree of information processing difficulty interferes with academic or learning tasks.
- Children with learning disabilities show marked discrepancy between their potential and actual achievement.
- Other causes for the difficulty are ruled out.

Students with learning disabilities constitute a very diverse group, similar only in their unrealized academic potential. Many, but not all, children with learning disabilities have reading problems (Helveston, 1987; Merrell, 1990; Stanovich, 1988).

Many such students have basic sight recognition and decoding problems. Poor sight recognition of words and inefficient or inaccurate decoding skills can lead to poor comprehension, avoidance of reading and writing, and deficits in general knowledge.

Thus, poor readers with learning disabilities tend to share many of the same problems as other poor readers. They tend to have problems reading right from the start, especially with word recognition strategies taught in primary grades. They may experience a lag in the development of phonological sensitivity, the awareness and perception of speech sounds in words (Ackerman, Anhalt, & Dykman, 1986).

Because these students may not intuit how letters represent speech sounds in words by wide exposure to print, as more able learners do, they may need more systematic exposure to letter-sound patterns in words and more practice with decoding than their peers; many of the remedial techniques we have discussed for helping poor readers develop sight recognition and word analysis skills are effective with these students.

Although remedial instruction for these students often focuses on the teaching and practice of isolated reading skills, struggling readers with learning disabilities need the same emphasis on meaningful reading of connected text that other poor readers need. Practicing reading skills without using them in the context of real reading is ineffective for any student.

In the long run, teachers who specialize in learning disabilities work with many youngsters who are poor readers, and both regular classroom teachers and reading specialists will find that some of their poor readers may have learning disabilities. Regardless of whether they have been so identified, poor readers *all* need help in consolidating skills they have mastered, acquiring strategies they do not yet have, and closing the gap between their potential as readers and their present performance. They require instruction that is tailored to their individual strengths, needs, ages, interests, and prior experiences. They need to be placed in appropriate materials at their instructional levels; provided instruction that achieves a balance in word identification, comprehension, listening, speaking, and writing; and taught at a pace that is appropriately challenging without frustration. No single instructional method has been shown to be more effective than others in remediation.

Dyslexia

Dyslexia is a medical term for a profound inability to read or to learn to read. Dyslexia is a condition that everyone seems to agree exists, but about which there is little agreement otherwise. No single set of symptoms, means of diagnosis or identification, or method of remediation have been identified.

One of the first definitions was proposed by Samuel Orton (1937), who described children with dyslexia as delayed in reading compared to their peers, suffering from frequent letter and word reversals, and often being able to read only by holding the print up to a mirror. This led to widespread belief that dyslexia was primarily a neurological disorder involving visual perception and memory. Even today, many people believe that reading *was* as *saw* or writing letters backwards is a sure sign of a child with dyslexia. In many school districts until just a few years ago, well-meaning teachers were training young children to distinguish between nonsensical geometric shapes and pursuing other highly dubious instructional procedures that were intended to train children's visual perception.

By the 1970s, however, evidence was accumulating that suggested that dyslexia was a language processing problem rather than a problem of visual perception. Stanovich (1986) demonstrated that readers with dyslexia made no more reversal errors than did normally developing readers *at their same level of reading development.* Liberman et al. (1974) found that students with dyslexia were far more likely to have trouble processing sounds in words—specifically in recognizing that spoken words could be broken down into smaller bits of sound called *phonemes*. A number of researchers, including Bryant and Bradley (1985) and Ball and Blachman (1991), found that teaching children before first grade to be aware of speech sounds in words significantly reduced later reading failure. Today the central importance of language problems as causal factors in dyslexia is well established. The two factors that turn up most often in readers with severe disabilities is difficulty in segmenting words into phonemes and also rapidly naming objects ("serial rapid naming"). Of the two, however, phonemic segmentation is far more amenable to instruction, so it gets the lion's share of attention.

Is dyslexia a disease—analogous to tuberculosis—or is it a condition that occupies one end of a continuum that goes from healthy to unhealthy—analogous to high blood pressure? There is a growing agreement that it is the latter (Snow et al., 1998). Stanovich has demonstrated that what we might call *dyslexia* can develop over time, beginning as a relatively mild lack of ability that snowballs into a complex problem of disability. In his famous "Matthew Effects" article, Stanovich (1986) demonstrated that a first grader who has more difficulty than his classmates will be slower to learn to recognize words. (In alphabetic languages such as English, word recognition, after all, requires that a reader be able to make associations between written letters and phonemes. A child who doesn't have ready access to phonemes in speech may find word recognition difficult.) Depressed word recognition impairs reading fluency, and if after a certain point a student doesn't find it reasonably easy to read with fluency, he is not likely to practice reading. And if he doesn't practice reading . . ., the sequence continues until we find a child by fourth or fifth grade who appears to have dyslexia.

How many children have dyslexia? Estimates of the numbers of students with dyslexia in the school population range as high as 20 percent. But when Frank Vellutino and his associates (1996) identified a large number of struggling first graders and tutored them intensively for a year using conventional best practices, only 3 percent of them continued to have difficulty learning to read, and only 1.5 percent had severe difficulties. Vellutino and associates concluded that the difficulties in learning to read may well be caused by deficits in certain of the cognitive abilities underlying the ability to learn to read, especially phonological abilities such as phoneme analysis, letter-to-sound decoding, name encoding and retrieval, and verbal memory. However, they found that "the number of children impaired by basic cognitive deficits represents a relatively small percentage of beginning readers compared with the substantially larger percentage of those children whose reading difficulties are caused by experiential and instructional deficits" (Vellutino & Scanlon, 2001, p. 317).

No single set of symptoms exists that would clearly distinguish the characteristics of children with dyslexia from those who have other learning disabilities. In general, however, many people who have been assessed as having dyslexia share some or most of these characteristics:

- Measured intelligence at least in the average range, but often significantly above average
- Profound difficulty with phonemic awareness, phonemic segmentation, and decoding operations

- Frequent reversals of letters and words in both reading and writing
- Poor spelling, particularly when attempting to use phonetic strategies to spell unfamiliar words
- Both reading and writing far below their intellectual potential
- Persistent reading and writing failure in spite of personal motivation and appropriate special instruction

Individuals with dyslexia do not read up to their expected potential, in spite of having normal intelligence and having experienced adequate instruction. That seems to be the most persistent symptom of dyslexia. As we noted above, however, Vellutino et al. (1996) found that by providing intensive instruction to underperforming children, his team was able to get all but a small number of them to improve in reading. And Stanovich (1986) has shown that if even a single factor goes wrong in a child's reading development, that breakdown can lead to a lack of successful practice, which then affects the development of many other factors. It is no wonder that by fourth or fifth grade, readers with serious disabilities show a variety of symptoms. If they have found reading aversive and have not practiced reading, many things will be wrong with their reading ability.

Some researchers have been working on other explanations for the variety of symptoms of individuals with dyslexia. Max Coltheart (2005) has developed a model of word recognition that shows two routes between letters on the page and words in the mind. One of the routes connects letters to sounds directly in the mind. The other route relates groups of letters to words that are stored in memory. A disability that interrupts either route will result in a different kind of dyslexia.

Some readers seem to have limited access to stored words in memory, and tend to depend heavily on letter-to-sound correspondences and pronounce words as they are spelled. This phenomenon is called *surface dyslexia.* Evidence of surface dyslexia, according to Coltheart (2005), is found when readers pronounce phonetically regular words correctly, but mispronounce irregularly spelled words. Thus they would read *howl*, *growl*, and *fowl* correctly, but read *bowl* so that it rhymes with the first two. *Pretty* will be read to rhyme with *Betty* and *petty.*

Other readers appear to have a breakdown in the letter-to-sound route, but still have access to the storage or words in memory. These readers, who are rare, and most of whom have had trauma to the brain according to the reports, would see the word *goose* and say "duck" or "waterfowl." This condition is called *deep dyslexia.*

Still other researchers argue for the existence of a third kind of dyslexia in which the visual perceptual apparatus appears faulty. Readers with this condition are said to suffer from *visual dyslexia* (Smith, 1991).

There is room here for skepticism. Before we conclude that any reader who sees *goose* and says "duck" suffers from deep dyslexia, we should remember the normal readers who sometimes sample what a text is saying and pronounce the word they expect to be there without really looking at it. And before we conclude that a reader or writer who reverses letters suffers from visual dyslexia, we should compare that reader's tendency to reverse letters with other readers who function on that reader's same level.

Efforts to determine which remedial methods are most effective are similarly confusing. Those who have been referred to as having dyslexia are, like everyone else, more different from each other than alike. Most methods proposed have been successful with at least some people thought to have dyslexia. But none are reliably effective with everyone.

Most often, remediation centers around efforts to help individuals compensate for their difficulties by using recorded books and texts, teaching them to use special study skills and procedures to organize and learn aurally, and teaching them to use devices like digital dictionaries, spell-check, and grammar-check computer programs.

Some general approaches that have been somewhat successful for individuals with dyslexia are

- Teaching students how to break academic tasks into their component parts, adapt such tasks to their special academic needs, and tackle one part of a task at a time.
- Emphasizing whole-word or sight-word recognition and the use of context as a word recognition strategy, rather than overemphasizing phonic decoding. This is especially true if a reader tends to read by sounding out letters and produces nonsense words. (But we should remember the stages of word recognition we saw in Chapter 7. This could be an *alphabetic reader* who needs help to develop into an *orthographic reader*, to use Uta Frith's [1985] terminology.)
- Teaching phonics if a reader shows a lack of awareness of letter-to-sound correspondences. But the teacher should be mindful of the need to teach the child about whole words, too, and to develop fluency and comprehension at the same time phonics is stressed.
- Developing listening comprehension and general background knowledge by listening rather than relying on reading to convey information; using oral aids like taped texts and lectures, voice-activated microrecorders, and oral note taking.
- Teaching students how to break down writing assignments into manageable steps utilizing the steps in the writing process.
- Emphasizing specific thinking skills such as comparison-contrast and cause-effect using oral discourse, so that students with dyslexia can comprehend what they see and hear and not have to read everything.
- Teaching students to compose written work orally first, such as dictating onto audiotape, and then writing while listening to the tape; some students need to have their oral compositions typed for them.

Designing Individualized Interventions

The central purpose for creating curriculum or teaching accommodations is to provide equal access to learning for students with disabilities. As mentioned earlier, since the legal provision is for students with disabilities to participate more fully in general education curriculum and environments, both general and special education teachers are searching for innovative ways for these students to successfully participate in the same ways as all students. Changes in the environment, delivery, curricular content, and/or assessments may be required to benefit these students based on decisions about their individualized learning needs. By assessing individual strengths and needs and using this information to develop strategies to meet individual learning requirements, teachers will, in fact, develop effective interventions where all students, not only those with disabilities, will benefit.

The key to success in planning accommodations or curricular modifications is to match the student with the goals of the lesson. Begin planning effective accommodations and/or modification by identifying the general education curricular goals. Starting with general education outcomes helps to clarify the fundamental decisions that will guide your teaching while allowing for all students' participation in acquiring the essential knowledge and skills. Once the outcome learning is clarified and the tasks that demonstrate mastery of the essential learning are specified, design the individualized adaptations for students. Keep in mind that although the essential learning may be the same for all students, the content knowledge and/or skills may be adjusted for individual students who require adaptations while still meeting the objectives set out in the essential learning.

The following considerations will be useful when planning adaptations for students with disabilities:

- Will the student participate in the same curriculum as other students? If so, what environmental, delivery, or assessment accommodations will be required for her successful participation?
- Will the student participate in the same curriculum with modified objectives such as some of the same spelling words along with others more suited to a student's individualized requirements? If so, what environmental, delivery, curricular content, or assessment accommodations and modifications will be required for his successful participation?
- Will the student have the same objectives, but use a parallel curriculum on a more appropriate level? If so, what environmental, delivery, curricular content, or assessment accommodations and modifications will be required for her successful participation? As noted above, in this circumstance the student will still participate in the same essential learning objectives but will be using individualized content material that is matched to her or his particular needs (adapted from Giangreco, Cloninger, & Iverson, 1993).

Interventions for Phonological Awareness

One of the most consistent indicators of a child's potential for reading success is acquisition of phonological awareness. Phonemic awareness is a child's recognition that words and syllables can be broken into smaller units, individual speech sounds called *phonemes*.

Emergent readers must grasp that the sounds of speech are represented by letters and that these speech sounds can be purposely manipulated (Adams, 1990). Common deficiencies include an inability to identify and separate internal word sounds; an inability to understand that these word sounds are sequential; and difficulty with beginning, middle, or ending sounds (Simmons, Gunn, Smith, & Kameenui, 1994).

Phonological awareness can be improved for children with reading difficulties through direct, systematic instruction. Although this instruction can be taught separately or embedded into the curriculum, depending on the instructional style of the teacher's program, it is important that it be delivered individually or in small groups and taught on a consistent basis. Brief periods of about 20 minutes each day of explicit instruction in phonological awareness will improve student performance significantly (Blachman, 1997). The following guidelines will assist you when designing intervention strategies:

1. Begin with the auditory features of words; rather than focusing on alphabetic symbols, ask students to blend and identify sounds in a word.
2. Teach natural sound segments in language before moving to more complex sounds within words. Start segmenting sounds in sentences and then move to words into syllables, then syllables into phonemes.
3. Ensure student success by introducing words with fewer phonemes and where consonant and vowel patterns can be easily distinguished (e.g., *v-c* or *c-v-c* words).
4. Model blending and segmenting for practice and to ensure retention.
5. Once students are skilled with the auditory tasks, move to sound-letter correspondence. (Simmons et al., 1994, cited in Mercer, 1997)

This framework will be helpful when developing intervention strategies that are used with skill-building activities such as memory, flash cards, and rhyming activities.

Multisensory Language Experience. Integrating multisensory experiences with direct, systematic, and sequential instruction can be an effective means for students struggling to learn fundamental language skills. Multisensory Language Experience (MSLE) approaches expose learners through a variety of language concepts and associations while integrating vision, hearing, movement, and touch into the process (Birsch, 1999). In MSLE students trace letters with their fingers while seeing, saying, and hearing them; they can walk on letters written on the floor or touch textured letters and words to improve their understanding of how sounds are manipulated and sequenced in the written word. Writing with multiple crayons or markers; practicing using a paintbrush with watercolors or fingerpainting letters; writing with shaving cream; using raised or sunken letters, sandpaper letters, or sand trays for letters are all effective ways to increase sensory input into the language experience.

Whole-Word Recognition. Whole-word recognition strategies can be particularly effective with words that are not easily decoded using phonics. These strategies are also effective with older readers who can lose the literal comprehension of the text when struggling with decoding. Whole-word recognition is most successful when the student is exposed repeatedly to the words. The most effective way is to develop a running list of sight words and set aside time each day for students to practice the words with a partner. Write sentences or definitions on the back of the card. As the student learns words, these cards can be eliminated while new ones are added. The cards can be taken home for practice. Making up games similar to Concentration, matching words or words and their definitions, helps to motivate the student while using the flash cards. A variation that also helps build vocabulary skills along with word recognition is to pair the student with a partner. One student takes a turn writing the vocabulary word on the flash card while the partner must then write its definition on the back of the same card. Then, together, the students read each definition and then take turns identifying the word when its definition is read.

Another effective strategy for teaching whole-word recognition is variation on cloze procedures. Teachers can use a written selection with blanks that are to be filled in from a list of several choices for each omitted word, or from a word bank, to change traditional cloze activities to multiple-choice word recognition (Mercer, 1997).

Word Sounds and Word Categorization. One of the most helpful ways to teach students with reading difficulties to learn to organize words is by teaching word pattern similarities and highlighting the sound similarities in each word's phonemic components. Repetitive use of similar patterns in words that sound alike (*mat, bat, sat*) or similar sounds but different letter patterns (*site, right*) can assist children to see how the internal components of sounds are represented in written form. Using vocabulary or spelling words to demonstrate similar relationships can help students to reinforce these similarities. Teachers begin by associating spelling words with words the student already knows—the student's name, family or pet names, or other common words for children. Then, connect the spelling words with the familiar words to create simple sentences (Hammeken, 2000). For more advanced students, have students become word detectives—write the words on cards and do a code investigation, sorting them by sound or letter patterns.

Interventions for Improving Fluency

With students who are having trouble tracking the direction of the reading, use an index card with an arrow drawn on it pointing from left to right as a guide. Placing the card under the sentence while students are reading also helps to limit distractions or reduce instances of students' losing their place. Another strategy for students who tend to lose their place is to show them where to begin reading and then provide ongoing context clues to help them keep track of where they are when reading. A variation on this is to cut out a long rectangle in the card to place on the sentences and move along as the student reads.

Using highlighters to color-code reading selections can be very useful for students who respond well to visual organization during reading. Using different colors also assists students in picking out main ideas, recognizing important information they need to remember, and locating vocabulary or spelling words. When it isn't practical to highlight directly in the book, clear overlays can be taped into the book with the color-coded selections on them for easy removal later (Hammeken, 2000). Consider breaking a reading selection into more manageable segments or assigning only the essential portions of a chapter so students won't feel overwhelmed by too much reading. Smaller segments make it easier for a student to keep track of the content. These segments can be highlighted or bracketed prior to reading and previewed to ensure that students will be familiar with what to expect from the selection.

Audio cassettes are another effective way to facilitate fluency for all students, not just those with reading problems. Most textbooks and reading series are available on tape. Other resources to check for books on tape are the school librarian or the lending library for individuals with visual impairments. Book talks or literature circles where readers read to each other aloud in pairs can be recorded for use at a later time or put into the library for future use. Some of the recordings can be used with below-level readers for them to read along with for repetitive practice. The recordings of these below-level readers could also be used with younger readers from another class.

A variation on reading along with a recording is to have students read chorally while the teacher leads them. Choosing a text that provides repetitive response is the simplest way to begin, gradually progressing to assigning groups for different character and narrator responses. In choral reading each group is assigned a specific response selection, will read the responses of various characters, or will read a reading at the appropriate time.

Interventions for Improving Comprehension

Often students spend so much time and effort at reading a selection that they lose the meaning of the material they are reading. Comprehending what we read involves the complex process of matching information from our prior learning experiences with the content of the text. Following are several strategies that will assist students in understanding what they are reading if they are getting bogged down due to decoding or fluency problems or seem to be losing the meaning of the text due to language processing difficulties.

Previewing Texts. Read the text aloud to the class using a guided reading procedure. Provide a variety of cues as to where the teacher is with the reading and ask questions to probe for understanding. Sometimes it is more beneficial to divide the class into two or three groups when doing guided reading previews. A co-teacher or paraprofessional could take one of these groups, or students could be assigned independent work while the teacher works with the smaller group. Simple adjustments such as changing the pacing of the reading or dividing the text into more manageable segment sizes can go a long way in reducing the stress students feel.

Another way to preview a reading selection is to provide a student, in advance, an outline or brief overview of the upcoming material. Bold or color-code the important information and vocabulary in the overview for easy reference (Hammeken, 2000). Then have the student review the outline individually, with a partner, or with the paraprofessional prior to the guided reading. The overview enables students to link upcoming material with prior knowledge or experiences that activate her learning. Associating the new material with previous stories or with a personal experience or interest using questions at the end of the overview assists students in understanding the relevance of the material.

Keep in mind that students will need to be taught how to preview upcoming reading selections. Have them read and discuss the title and hypothesize what the reading selection may be about. Next, review the table of contents, read the chapter titles, and see if they offer clues about what the selection is about. Finally, have students examine the illustrations or any maps, tables, or graphs to see if they offer clues about possible subject matter. Ask them to make predictions and then encourage the use of questions as reading progresses to make sure they are correct. Previewing is an ongoing process that requires teachers to continually backtrack and review along with a continual search for context clues.

Teaching Abstract Concepts. Students with reading disabilities will often require concrete activities and examples to help them to grasp abstract concepts—for example, story sequences and the significance of a series of events. Creating illustration or word cards with a story element or event on each card is a way to teach the sequence of the story as well as how events will lead up to a climax and resolution.

The use of graphic organizers is also an effective way for teachers to demonstrate abstract concepts and new information by making them concrete. Graphic organizers are effective because they provide students with a concrete reference point for material when these reference points may not be solidly established in memory. Graphic organizers are an organizing representation of the new or abstract material. They provide visual representations of ideas, concepts, information, or facts. They also allow for visual comparisons, showing relationships and extending learning to other areas. Story maps range from simple relationships to hierarchal pyramids. These can be pictures or symbols that stand for concepts or ideas of objects, or they can show levels of details in a pyramid that can be used to examine the structure of a paragraph or longer selection. They can also be used to assist students in organizing details and to show evidence that supports main ideas. Character maps, a variation of story maps, expect students to complete simple illustrations that show how the character thinks, feels, sees, hears, smells, does, goes, says, and so on, or develop more complex comparisons between characters.

Summary

This chapter deals with special factors associated with reading. Among these factors are those that qualify learners for special education services under the Individuals with Disabilities Education Act (IDEA) and related legislation. Within this legislation are provisions that mandate serving these learners with appropriate educational programs that use the least restrictive environment. The identification of these learners and subsequent placement in special education programs must be conducted with assessment instruments and methods that protect against discrimination, erroneous classification, and undue labeling.

Identification of a student with special needs typically is initiated by the classroom teacher. Before additional assessment and screening can occur, permission must be obtained from the parents or legal guardians of the child. Once permission is granted, *assessment* and *screening* can take place. This assessment typically includes one or more of the following areas: intellectual, physical, special learning, or affective factors.

Initial assessment of *intellectual factors* typically includes the use of an initial screening instrument such as the Kaufman Brief Intelligence Test (K-BIT). If the initial screening instrument indicates a potential problem, additional testing is conducted using a more comprehensive assessment of intellectual factors such as the Weschler Intelligence Scale for Children–IV (WISC–IV). These tests typically provide scores for subtests, Verbal, Performance, and Full Scale IQ scores. When selecting assessment instruments, care should be taken to choose instruments that do not penalize a child with cultural differences. The Leiter International Performance Scale-Revised (Leiter-R) is a nonverbal measure that can be substituted for English language learners and others with language deficits.

Vision and *hearing problems* are also associated with reading difficulties. Again, a classroom teacher is often the first to notice potential problems during daily classroom activities. As with intellectual factors, the referral for additional screening begins with parental or guardian permission. Screening in the areas of vision and hearing is typically conducted by professionals or paraprofessionals in the allied health fields.

Language disabilities most often occur in late infancy and the preschool years, when normally oral language appears and develops fully. Most children are fluent language users, with extensive *receptive* and *expressive vocabularies* and well-developed grammatical capabilities, by the age of 5 or 6. In the early years, *hearing impairment or deafness, Down syndrome,* and *general language delay* can impair or inhibit language acquisition. In the later preschool and school years, difficulty with speech sound production (*atypical phonology*), acquisition of vocabulary and word meanings (*atypical semantics*), acquisition of grammatical forms and rules (*atypical syntax*), and use of language for social purposes (*atypical pragmatics*) can inhibit language learning and impact literacy.

Special learning problems include *learning disabilities* and *dyslexia.* While universally accepted and detailed definitions of these terms have yet to be identified, professionals do agree that they include a wide range of problems related to the acquisition, comprehension, and production of written language. Children who manifest these problems typically possess average or above-average intelligence, but exhibit serious, long-standing learning difficulties.

Reading is a complex process affected by a student's level of intellectual functioning, experiences, motivation, and physical and emotional well-being. By assessing the impact of these special factors on a student's literacy, appropriate changes in instructional strategies, referrals, and placements are more likely to be made.

Individualized interventions are designed to accommodate the specific needs of the learner and are best achieved by matching goals for learning with learner abilities. Principles for selecting adaptations include whether the learner will be participating in the same curriculum with or without modifications or whether she will require individualized learning goals and participate in a parallel curriculum.

Teachers must first determine whether a student requires interventions for deficiencies in phonological awareness, fluency, or comprehension and then apply appropriate instructional strategies to meet these need areas. Recent studies indicate that interventions are effective when applied consistently during brief daily activities. Interventions such as *multisensory language experiences, whole-word recognition, choral reading,* and *previewing texts* are all effective ways to improve reading skills while engaging the learner.

References

Ackerman, P. T., Anhalt, J. M., & Dykman, R. A. (1986). Inferential word-decoding weakness in reading disabled children. *Learning Disability Quarterly, 9*(4), 315–324.

Adams, M. J. (1990). *Beginning to read: Thinking and learning about print.* Cambridge, MA: MIT Press.

Ball, E. W., & Blachman, B. A. (1991). Does phoneme awareness training in kindergarten make a difference in early word recognition and developmental spelling? *Reading Research Quarterly, 26,* 49–66.

Birsch, J. R. (Ed.). (1999). *Multisensory teaching of basic language skills.* Baltimore: Brookes.

Blackman, B. (Ed.). (1997). *Foundations of reading acquisition and dyslexia: Implications for early instruction.* Mahwah, NJ: Erlbaum.

Bryant, P., & Bradley, L. (1985). *Children's reading problems.* Oxford: Blackwell.

Coltheart, M. (2005). Modeling reading: The dual route approach. In C. Hulme & M. Snowling (Eds.), *Science of reading: A handbook.* London: Blackwell.

Damico, J. S. (1991). Descriptive assessment of communicative ability in limited English proficient students. In E. Hamayan & J. S. Damico (Eds.), *Limiting bias in the assessment of bilingual students* (pp. 157–218). Austin, TX: PRO-ED.

Diana v. State Board of Education, No.C-70-37 (N.D. Cal. 1970).

Friend, M., & Bursuck, W. D. (2002). *Including students with special needs* (3rd ed.). Boston: Allyn & Bacon.

Frith, U. (1985). Beneath the surface of developmental dyslexia. In K. E. Patterson, J. C. Marshall, & M. Coltheart (Eds.), *Surface dyslexia* (pp. 301–330). London: Erlbaum.

García, E. E. (2005). *Teaching and learning in two languages: Bilingualism and schooling in the United States.* New York: Teachers College Press.

Gersten, R., & Baker, S. (2000). What we know about effective instructional practices for English-language learners. *Exceptional Children, 66*, 454–470.

Giangreco, M., Cloninger, C., & Iverson, V. (1993). *Choosing options and accommodations for children (COACH): A guide to planning inclusive education.* Baltimore: Brookes.

Hammeken, P. A. (2000). *Inclusion: 450 strategies for success: A practical guide for all educators who teach students with disabilities.* Minnetonka, MN: Peytral.

Helveston, E. M. (1987). Volume III Module I: Management of dyslexia and related learning disabilities. *Journal of Learning Disabilities, 20*(7), 415–421.

Hill, R., Carjuzaa, J., Aramburo, D., & Baca, L. (1993). Culturally and linguistically diverse teachers in special education: Repairing or redesigning the leaky pipeline. *Teacher Education and Special Education, 16*, 258–269.

Karger, J. (2005). *Access to the general curriculum for students with disabilities: A discussion of the interrelationship between IDEA '97 and NCLB.* Wakefield, MA: National Center on Accessing the General Curriculum.

Kaufman, A. S., & Kaufman, N. L. (1990). *Kaufman brief intelligence test manual.* Circle Pines, MN: American Guidance Services.

Kaufman, A. S., & Kaufman, N. L. (2004). *Kaufman brief intelligence test manual, Second Edition.* Circle Pines, MN: American Guidance Services.

Landrum, J. (2001). Selecting intermediate novels that feature characters with disabilities. *The Reading Teacher, 55*, 252–258.

Larry P. v. Riles, 343 F. Supp. 1306 (N.D. Cal. 1972), 502 F. 2d 963 (9th Cir. 1974), No. C-71-2270 RF (N.D. Cal., October 16, 1979), 793 F. 2d 969 (9th Cir. 1984).

Liberman, I. Y., Shankweiler, D., Fischer, F. W., & Carter, B. (1974). Explicit syllable and phoneme segmentation in the young child. *Journal of Experimental Child Psychology, 18*, 201–212.

McIntyre, E., Rosebery, A., & Gonzalez, N. (Eds.). (2001). *Classroom diversity: Connecting curriculum to students' lives.* Portsmouth, NH: Heinemann.

McLaughlin, J. A., & Lewis, R. B. (1990). *Assessing special students* (3rd ed.). Columbus, OH: Merrill.

Mercer, C. D. (1997). *Students with learning disabilities* (5th ed.). Upper Saddle River, NJ: Merrill.

Merrell, K. (1990). Differentiating low achievement students and students with learning disabilities: An examination of performances on the Woodcock-Johnson Psycho-Educational Battery. *Journal of Special Education, 24*(3), 296–305.

Moustafa, M. (1997). *Beyond traditional phonics: Research discoveries and reading instruction.* Portsmouth, NH: Heinemann.

National Education Association (NEA). (2004). *NCLB: The intersection of access and outcomes.* Washington, DC: National Education Association.

National Reading Panel. (2000, December). *Teaching children to read: An evidence-based assessment of the scientific research literature on reading and its implications for reading instruction.* (Reports of the Subgroups.) Washington, DC: National Institute of Child Health and Human Development, National Institutes of Health.

Nelson, K. (1973). *Structure and strategy in learning to talk.* Chicago: University of Chicago Press.

Orton, S. (1937). *Reading, writing, and speech problems in children.* New York: Norton.

Patton, J., Kauffman, J., Blackburn, J. M., & Brown, G. (1991). *Exceptional children in focus* (5th ed.). New York: Macmillan.

Reich, P. A. (1986). *Language development*. Upper Saddle River, NJ: Prentice-Hall.

Sattler, J. M. (1992). *Assessment of children* (3rd ed.). San Diego: Author.

Simmons, D. C., Gunn, B., Smith, S. B., & Kameenui, E. J. (1994). Phonological awareness: Applications of instructional design. *LD Forum, 19*, 7–10.

Smith, C. R. (1991). *Learning disabilities: The interaction of learner, task, and setting*. Boston: Allyn & Bacon.

Snow, C. E., Burns, M. S., & Griffin, P. (Eds.) (1998). *Preventing reading difficulties in young children*. Washington, DC: National Academy Press.

Stanovich, K. E. (1986). Matthew effects in reading: Some consequences of individual differences in the acquisition of literacy. *Reading Research Quarterly, 21*, 360–406.

Stanovich, K. E. (1988). Explaining the difference between the dyslexic and the garden-variety poor reader: The phonological-core-variable-difference model. *Journal of Learning Disabilities, 21*(10), 590–604, 612.

Tomasello, M., & Mervis, C. N. (1994). Commentary: The instrument is great, but measuring comprehension is still a problem. *Monographs of the Society for Research in Child Development, 59*, 242.

Trawick-Smith, J. (1997). *Early childhood development: A multicultural perspective*. Upper Saddle River, NJ: Merrill.

Vellutino, F. R. (1979). *Dyslexia: Theory and research*. Cambridge, MA: MIT Press.

Vellutino, F. R., & Denckla, M B. (1991). Cognitive and neuropsychological foundations of word identification in poor and normally developing readers. In R. Barr, M. L. Kamil, P. Mosenthal, & P. D. Pearson (Eds.), *Handbook of reading research: Vol. 2*. White Plains, NY: Longman.

Vellutino, F. R., & Scanlon, D. M. (2001). Emergent literacy skills, early instruction, and individual differences as determinants of difficulties in learning to read: The case for early intervention. In S. Neuman & D. Dickson (Eds.), *Handbook for research on early literacy*. New York: Guilford Press.

Vellutino, F. R., Scanlon, D. M., Sipay, S., Small, G., Pratt, A., Chen, R., & Denckla, M. B. (1996). Cognitive profiles of difficult-to-remediate and readily remediated poor readers: Early intervention as a vehicle for distinguishing between cognitive and experiential deficits as a basic cause of specific reading disability. *Journal of Educational Psychology, 88*, 601–638.

Villa, R. A., & Thousand, J. S. (2000). *Restructuring for caring and effective education: Piecing the puzzle together* (2nd ed.). Baltimore: Brookes.

Vygotsky, L. S. (1978). *Mind in society: The development of higher psychological processes*. Cambridge, MA: Harvard University Press.

http://www.reading.org/downloads/resources/IDEA_RTI_report.pdf

Name Index

Subject Index

S

T

Y

Z